NUMISMATIC STUDIES

No. 20

Fig. 1: A NEW AND CORRECT MAP OF THE UNITED STATES OF AMERICA BY ABEL BUELL (1783). This map, the first prepared following peace with England, is "one of the most important American cartographical documents." Its author was Abel Buell, the versatile silversmith, jeweler, and inventor, who engraved the dies for the Connecticut State coinages. The legend states: "A NEW and correct MAP of the UNITED STATES of NORTH AMERICA Layd down from the latest observations and best Authorities agreeable to the PEACE of 1783. Humbly Inscribed to his Excellency the GOVERNOR AND COMPANY of the STATE of CONNECTICUT by their Most Obedient and very humble servant, Abel Buell" (Stokes and Haskell, *Prints*, pp. 59-60). Courtesy The New York Public Library.

MONEY OF THE AMERICAN COLONIES AND CONFEDERATION

A NUMISMATIC, ECONOMIC AND HISTORICAL CORRELATION

BY

PHILIP L. MOSSMAN

NUMISMATIC STUDIES
No. 20

THE AMERICAN NUMISMATIC SOCIETY
NEW YORK
1993

ISSN 0517-404x
ISBN 0-89722-249-0

PRINTED IN BELGIUM AT CULTURA, WETTEREN

To MARY, my wife,
in appreciation of her encouragement and
forbearance during the countless
hours I devoted to this project
over the past decade.

"The whole story of the rebellious Colonies is a story which relates more
to monetary contentions and principles than to any other subject."
(Alexander Del Mar, *The History of Money in America* [New York, 1899], p. 74.)

TABLE OF CONTENTS

PREFACE

From the Declaration of Independence until the ratification of the Constitution of 1787, there extended that fascinating span of history which included the American Confederation. This was the era when the fledgling democracy strove to gain identity as a united country as it grew from the infancy of colonialism into the adolescence of a newly freed nation. During this period of self-discovery, several jurisdictions minted copper coins under the authority of the Articles of Confederation. This book is the result of my research into the circumstances surrounding those Confederation coinages of Connecticut, Vermont, New Jersey, New York, and Massachusetts. Minted for only a short period of time from 1785 to 1788, these series are, nevertheless, specific events within the unfolding numismatic history of British North America which extended from the earliest colonial times into the Federal period. To appreciate the proper position of these state coppers in this evolutionary sequence, they must be studied in the context of the entire colonial and pre-Federal tradition.

In 1980, I systematized my newly acquired knowledge concerning colonial coinages and Confederation coppers in a brief monograph which I shared with some colleagues who offered constructive criticisms. More material was subsequently gathered and the work rewritten and enlarged. The result was that in September 1986, "Money of the American Colonies and Confederation: A Numismatic, Economic and Historical Correlation" was published in *The Colonial Newsletter* as a preliminary review copy for patrons of that foundation dedicated to early American numismatics. The manuscript was reviewed by many members who extended helpful advice and data for inclusion. In February 1988, the corrections, additions and suggestions offered by the membership were printed as an emendation in *CNL*. Thus, this book owes its very being to James C. Spilman, the editor of *CNL*, whose guidance and encouragement steered me through the initial stages of this lengthy project. In its final form, this book is sponsored by the American Numismatic Society which has a long and distinguished tradition in supporting numismatic research and publications. It is to them I owe my final debt of gratitude for making my ambition a reality.

I have endeavored to describe and analyze the "small change" that jingled in the purses of the American colonists from the very beginnings up through 1789 and into the early Federal period. The major emphasis and the focal point of the book, of course, concerns the copper coinages of the Confederation, curiosity about which provided the initial stimulus for the entire research. I do not discuss paper currency in detail except in the overall context of the prevailing economy. This editorial decision should not infer that colonial paper money is not important, but rather that the author does not have a specialized knowledge. Information on this subject is available in the classic reference by Eric P. Newman, *The Early Paper Money of America*.[1] The role of small denominational paper should not be underestimated in the overall colonial monetary scene.

This book emphasizes the fact that numismatics is not limited to the study of the particular characteristics of a selected series of coins but rather requires an appreciation and interpretation of contemporary economic and political history during the era in which the coins were current as money. This reality is reflected in the selection of the title, *Money of the American Colonies and Confederation: A Numismatic, Economic and Historical Correlation*. The word "correlation" in its meaning "a relation of invariable accompaniment," keynotes this holistic approach to numismatics which is nicely expressed by Gabriel Calbeto de Grau.

[1] Newman, *Paper Money*.

> Numismatics enjoys world-wide popularity because its technical phase is a Science and its aesthetic phase an Art. It is closely related to History, Geography, and Economics (all of these being major influences on it), as well as such specialized areas as sculpture, Metallurgy, Chemical analysis, and Photography. Both the imaginative mind of the artist and the analytic and disciplined mind of the scholar may find relaxation and pleasure in studying the marvelous elements that make up modern Numismatics.[2]

De Grau omitted from his definition the technical aspects of minting which are central to the study of early American coinages. In regard to "early American coinages," Spilman notes, "we have the added attraction of a great deal of personal history of the coiners and promoters that can be integrated into the Science and Art aspects; and especially their futile attempts to make a profit from the coinage of copper!" [3]

Within the colonial and later Confederation periods, the circulation of currency was influenced by variable exchange rates and other economic pressures which varied from place to place and from time to time. It requires an appreciation and knowledge of these exchange rates and other monetary influences to answer many of the questions generated about the coins encountered in the period under study. In the preparation of this monograph, I received much help and encouragement from John J. McCusker, Professor of History at the University of Maryland. His work, *Money and Exchange in Europe and America, 1600-1775, A Handbook*, is an excellent resource for providing insights into the circulation of currency, the function of specie, exchange rates, bills of exchange, and monies of account, during these times.[4] In my interpretation of numismatic history, I have placed much emphasis on the economic issues surrounding the circulation of the currency under discussion. A more recent work by McCusker, in conjunction with Professor Russell R. Menard of the History Department at the University of Minnesota, *The Economy of British North America, 1607-1789*, fully interprets the early economic history of our country and provides a basis for an in depth numismatic survey.[5] We cannot lose sight of the fact that in this present study we are examining not only the humble coppers, the money of the poor which paid for their daily bread, beer, and ferry tolls, but also the gold and silver specie coin of international exchange and domestic commerce.

My research and analysis have not brought forth any startling revelations, but a few additions or "re-discoveries" to our knowledge have been made. A principal contribution may well be to foster further research into the most common copper of the period which has been ignored by all except a few writers. The counterfeit English halfpence, including those manufactured in America as well as those imported from England, formed the bulk of the small change medium, a fact confirmed repeatedly in contemporary newspaper accounts. Since Colonial America lacked a uniform coinage, it can be accurately stated that any world coin of the period could have shown up and circulated in the colonies and probably *did* at one time or another. The recovery of such pieces in old accumulations or hoards is to be anticipated, but unless found in sufficient numbers, does not imply that these issues formed a significant portion of the colonial currency, hence their appearance in America is inconsequential to our study. I have listed those coins which are properly included as an American currency when such a conclusion is supported by historical evidence.

Another area of great personal interest deals with overstruck coins. I have delved into this subject at great length and now understand quite clearly the purpose of such a seemingly irregular activity. Appendix 2 lists all recorded overstruck coins of which I am aware. Also I read all available newspapers from the summer of 1789 which provided me many new insights

[2] Calbeto de Grau, *Compendio*, vol. 1, p. 12.
[3] Personal communication, March 17, 1986.
[4] McCusker, *Money and Exchange*.
[5] McCusker, and Menard, *Economy*.

into the collapse of the copper medium which I have shared in Chapter 8. The major theme on which I have concentrated throughout this book is that the coins described were once money and as such circulated as the currency of the period. An understanding of their function as currency combines many otherwise loose and seemingly unrelated facts into a coherent perception of early American money.

There are many other people to whom I owe a debt of gratitude for their prior works and research which I used in my correlation and synopsis of this subject. While all of these individuals are cited in the footnotes and appear in the bibliography, there are three important works which deserve special mention. The first of these is, of course, Sylvester S. Crosby's classic, *The Early Coins of America*, first published in 1873 and made available to modern readers in reprint form by Quarterman Publications.[6] The next most important single reference is the 1976 American Numismatic Society publication, *Studies on Money in Early America*, featuring monographs by distinguished scholars on many aspects of colonial numismatics on which I have attempted to expand. Additionally every student of this period should be familiar with The Colonial Newsletter Foundation, Inc. of Huntsville, Alabama, a non-profit organization which sponsors research and education in early American numismatics. Its publication, *The Colonial Newsletter*, edited under the able direction of James C. Spilman, features many outstanding contributions on this subject and was widely consulted and quoted in the preparation of this book.[7]

In addition to those previously mentioned, I wish to acknowledge the help of others who assisted me at various stages of this manuscript. In particular, three individuals, Raymond H. Williamson, Eric P. Newman, and Michael Hodder, generously devoted large segments of their time and wisdom to this project and made available to me reference materials from their private collections. Mr. Newman shared with me illustrations of colonial paper currency for use in the text. Others who have contributed in various ways include Richard August, Edward R. Barnsley, Roy E. Bonjour, Charles E. Dixon, John A. Keefe, Joseph R. Lasser, Dan Lucas, John R. McGill, Alan Meghrig, Michael D. Packard, Donald Partrick, Sanborn Partridge, Jeffery Peck, John Ranlett, Rob Retz, Harry J. Rescigno, Charles W. Smith, David Sonderman, Anthony Terranova, Gary A. Trudgen, and Philip Zwick. I am indebted to Thea Hottentot and Anja Van Soest for the translation of the Dutch references. The American Antiquarian Society, through the courtesy of Georgia B. Barnhill, Andrew W. Mellon Curator of Graphic Arts, and Joyce Tracy, Curator of Newspapers, supplied materials from their collection. The I.N. Phelps Stokes Collection, Miriam D. Wallach Division of Art, Prints and Photographs, The New York Public Library (Astor, Lenox and Tilden Foundations) provided several of the early American prints which illustrate the text. This project could never have been accomplished without aid from the staff of the Library of the American Numismatic Association, the source of most of the literary materials. Other hard-to-find references were obtained for me by the Interlibrary Loan Department of the Bangor [Maine] Public Library and by Francis Campbell, Librarian of the American Numismatic Society. The Folger Library at the University of Maine, Orono, was the source of the eighteenth century newspapers. June Willing, Senior Librarian of the Glasgow City [Scotland] Libraries researched references from the Public Record Office. Miss M. M. Archibald and Philip Attwood of the Department of Coins and Medals of The British Museum offered helpful suggestions regarding counterfeit English coppers. My final expression of gratitude rests with the American Numismatic Society, Leslie A. Elam, Director, John M. Kleeberg, Associate Curator, Marie H. Martin, Editor and Frank Deak, Photographer, who were instrumental in transforming a raw manuscript into its published form. I would also like to acknowledge with thanks the financial support of the Donald Groves Fund.

[6] Crosby, *Early Coins*.
[7] P.O.Box 4411, Huntsville, AL 35802.

I hope this book will be of help to others who share my passion for this period of history and numismatics. There are many gaps in our knowledge and we may be seduced into speculation about what might have been and make unwarranted assertions. I have intended to remain conservative, but no doubt have been guilty of perpetuating traditional inaccuracies or inventing some of my own. I have always been impressed by the couplet first introduced to the numismatic community by Sylvester S. Crosby in 1875,

Whoever thinks a faultless piece to see,
Thinks what ne'er was, nor is, nor e'er shall be.[8]

This tells the story of my manuscript as well. I have made every attempt to summarize accurately existing facts, while at the same time identify those areas of speculation and hypothesis. Since the study of this period of history is hampered by incomplete or non-existent contemporary records, the challenge remains for students of this era, from multiple disciplines, to narrow these gaps in knowledge by continuing research into these mysteries. While writing this manuscript I remained mindful of the warning of the eminent historian Joseph A. Ernst; "To avoid a quagmire of unfounded generalities, the student of colonial currency must remain true to the facts, and prudent where there are none." [9] With this admonition in mind, the story begins.

[8] Pope, *Essay on Criticism*, part 2, lines 253-54.
[9] Ernst, *Money and Politics*, p. 6.

BIBLIOGRAPHY AND KEY TO ABBREVIATIONS

PUBLISHED MATERIALS

A

AnRep 1989 = *American Numismatic Society*, Annual Report, 1989.
AJN = *American Journal of Numismatics.*
ANSMN = *American Numismatic Society Museum Notes.*
ANSNNM = *American Numismatic Society Numismatic Notes and Monographs.*
A.S.P.C. = *American State Papers. Documents, Legislative and Executive, of the Congress of the United States* (Washington, 1832), Class 4, Commerce and Navigation, vol. 1.
A.S.P.F. = *American State Papers. Documents, Legislative and Executive, of the Congress of the United States* (Washington, 1832), Class 3, Finance, vols. 1, 2.
Adams, *Scholar's Arithmetic* = Daniel Adams, *The Scholar's Arithmetic; or, Federal Accountant:* (Keene, NH, 1828).
Adams, *CNL 1980* = John W. Adams, "Original Manuscript of 'The Earliest New York Token' for Historical Magazine," *CNL* 59 (1980), pp. 736-39.
Adler, *Money Units* = Simon L. Adler, "Money and Money Units in the American Colonies," *Rochester (N.Y.) Historical Society Publications* 8 (1929), pp. 143-73.
Anderson, *Liberty* = William G. Anderson, *The Price of Liberty, The Public Debt of the American Revolution* (Charlottesville, 1983).
Andrews, *Colonial Period* = Charles M. Andrews, *The Colonial Period of American History* (New Haven, 1938).
Anton, *CNL 1975* = William T. Anton, Jr., "A Modern Survey of the Copper Coinage of the State of New Jersey," *CNL* 44 (1975), pp. 487-513.
Anton, *CNL 1979* = —, "Vermont Ryder 3 Struck over 1785 Connecticut," *CNL* 56 (1979), p. 701.
Anton, *RCR 68* = —, "The Legendary 1785 Ryder-5 Vermont Coppers," *Rare Coin Review* 68 (1988), pp. 58-59.
Anton and Hodder, *CNL 1989* = — and Michael Hodder, "The Mark Newbie Home-Site," *CNL* 83 (1989), pp. 1111-17.
Askew, *Roman Britain* = Gilbert Askew, *The Coinage of Roman Britain* (London, 1951).
Atkins, *Tradesmen's Tokens* = James Atkins, *The Tradesman's Tokens of the Eighteenth Century* (London, 1892).
Atkins, *Coins and Tokens* = —, *The Coins and Tokens of the Possessions and Colonies of the British Empire* (London, 1889).

B

Bachtell, *World Dollars* = Lee M. Bachtell, *World Dollars 1477-1877, Pictorial Guide*, 2nd. ed. (Ludowici, GA, 1977).
Bank of N.Y., *CNL 1967* = Bank of New York, "The First American Cent," *CNL* 20 (1967), pp. 195-97.
Barnard, *NC 1926* = Francis P. Barnard, "Forgery of English Copper Money in the Eighteenth Century," *NC* 6 (1926), pp. 341-60.
Barnsley, *CNL 1962* = Edward R. Barnsley, "Humdingers and Buzzers," *CNL* 7 (1962), p. 50.
Barnsley, *CNL 1963* = —, "Foreign Undertypes of Overstruck Coppers," *CNL* 9 (1963), pp. 61-62.
Barnsley, *CNL 1964* = —, "Miller's Connecticut Listings Updated," *CNL* 11 (1964), pp. 76-108.
Barnsley, *CNL 1965* = —, "Reports, Letters etc.," *CNL* 14 (1965), p. 131.
Barnsley, *CNL 1968* = —, "Connecticut Coppers," *CNL* 22 (1968), pp. 206-12.
Barnsley, *CNL 1969* = —, "Henry Clay Miller," *CNL* 25 (1969), pp. 243-47.
Barnsley, *CNL 1972* = —, "The Bizarre Lettering of Connecticut Coppers," *CNL* 34 (1972), pp. 356-67.
Barnsley, *CNL 1973* = —, "Nicknamed Connecticuts," *CNL* 36 (1973), pp. 383-94.
Barnsley, *CNL 1976* = —, "The Problem of James F. Atlee," *CNL* 37 (1973), p. 400; 45 (1976), p. 536.
Barnsley, *CNL 1977* = —, "Importation of Halfpence & Farthings on the Unicorn," *CNL* 50 (1977), p. 609.

Batty, *Descriptive Catalogue* = D. T. Batty, *Batty's Descriptive Catalogue of the Copper Coinage of Great Britain, Ireland, British Isles, and Colonies, Local & Private Tokens, Jettons &c.* (Manchester, 1886), vol. 3, Regal Issues.

Baxter, *Hancock* = W. T. Baxter, *The House of Hancock: Business in Boston, 1724-1775* (Cambridge, 1965).

Beard, *Economic Interpretation* = Charles A. Beard, *An Economic Interpretation of the Constitution of the United States* (New York, 1935).

Behrens, *Maryland* = Kathryn L. Behrens, *Paper Money in Maryland 1727-1789*, Johns Hopkins University Studies in Historical and Political Science, Series 41, no. 1 (Baltimore, 1923).

Belknap, *New Hampshire* = Jeremy Belknap, *The History of New-Hampshire* (Boston, 1883).

Bell, *Foreign Protestants* = Winthrop Pickard Bell, *The "Foreign Protestants" and the Settlement of Nova Scotia* (Toronto, 1961).

Betts, *CNL 1981* = C. Wyllys Betts, "Counterfeit Half Pence Current in the American Colonies," repr. ed., *CNL* 60 (1981), pp. 747-65.

Bezanson, *Prices and Inflation* = Anne Bezanson et al., *Prices and Inflation During the American Revolution: Pennsylvania, 1770-1790* (Philadelphia, 1951).

Bezanson, *Prices in PA* = —, Robert D. Gray, and Miriam Hussy, *Prices in Colonial Pennsylvania* (Philadelphia, 1935).

Bilsland, *Letter* = Alexander Bilsland, Letter to Elias Boudinot, December 12, 1795. *Records of the Bureau of the Mint*. Record Group 104, *Correspondence of the Director of the U.S. Mint* (cited from ANS Microfilm Reel 63.)

Biography = *Dictionary of American Biography* (New York, 1957).

Boisvert, *CNL 1987* = Peter Boisvert, "Memoir of Jacob Perkins," *CNL* 77 (1987), pp. 1001-12.

Bonjour, *CNL 1985* = Roy E. Bonjour, "Vermont Coppers, From Landscape to Bust," *Num* 1987, pp. 292-97.

Bonjour, *Num 1987* = —, "Survey Update - Vermont Ryder 15 and Ryder 30," *CNL* 71 (1985), p. 920.

Bordley, *Monies* = John B. Bordley, *On Monies, Coins, Weights, and Measures, proposed for the United States of America* (Philadelphia, 1789), and *Supplement* (Philadelphia, 1790).

Bowers, *Coinage History* = Q. David Bowers, *The History of United States Coinage* (Los Angeles, 1979).

Bowers, *RCR 67* = —, "Re-evaluating a Famous American Token," *Rare Coin Review* 67 (1987), pp. 60-63.

Breen, *Num 1952* = Walter Breen, "Survey of American Coin Hoards," *Num* 1952, pp. 7-24.

Breen, *ANS Centennial* = —, "Brasher and Bailey: Pioneer New York Coiners, 1787-1792," *Centennial Publication of the American Numismatic Society*, ed. Harald Ingholt (New York, 1958), pp. 137-45.

Breen, *CNL 1963* = —, "Colonial Overstrikes," *CNL* 10 (1963), p. 72.

Breen, *CNL 1968A* = —, "Comments on St. Patrick Halfpence and Farthings," *CNL* 22 (1968), pp. 214-17.

Breen, *CNL 1968B* = —, "Additional Comment on St. Patrick Farthings," *CNL* 24 (1968), p. 233.

Breen, *CNL 1969* = —, (Assignment of New Jersey Mints), *CNL* 26 (1969), pp. 255-56.

Breen, *CNL 1970* = —, "Mintage Figures for the New Jersey Coinage," *CNL* 29 (1970), pp. 295-97.

Breen, *CNL 1973* = —, "Counterfeit 'peices [*sic*] of brass and Tin'," *CNL* 37 (1973), p. 398; 38 (1973), p. 417.

Breen, *CNL 1974A* = —, "Constellatio Nova," *CNL* 41 (1974), pp. 453-54.

Breen, *CNL 1974B* = —, "Six Connecticut Mints," *CNL* 41 (1974), p. 459.

Breen, *Dies* = —, *Dies and Coinage* (New York, 1962), repr. *Hewitt's Numismatic Information Series* (Chicago, 1975).

Breen, *Studies* = —, "Legal and Illegal Connecticut Mints, 1785-1789," *Studies on Money in Early America*, ed. Eric P. Newman and Richard G. Doty (New York, 1976), pp. 105-33.

Breen, *CNL 1977* = —, "More on the Importation of 1749 Halfpence and Farthings," *CNL* 48 (1977), p. 585.

Breen, *CNL 1979* = —, "The 'New York' IMMUNIS: A Mystery Unraveled," *CNL* 54 (1979), pp. 667-76.

Breen, *Encyclopedia* = —, *Walter Breen's Complete Encyclopedia of U.S. and Colonial Coins* (New York, 1988).

Bressett, *Studies* = Kenneth E. Bressett, "Vermont Copper Coinage," *Studies on Money in Early America*, ed. Eric P. Newman and Richard G. Doty (New York, 1976), pp. 173-98.

Brunk, *Countermarks* = Gregory G. Brunk, ed., *World Countermarks on Medieval and Modern Coins* (Lawrence, MA, 1976).

Bullock, *Douglass* = Charles J. Bullock, *Life and Writings of William Douglass*, in *Economic Studies*, American Economic Association, vol. 2, no. 5 (1897), pp. 259-90.

Bullock, *Essays* = —, *Essays on the Monetary History of the United States* (New York, 1900).

Burzio, *ANS 1973* = Humberto F. Burzio, "The Spanish Tradition," *Coinage of the Americas*, ed. Theodore V. Buttrey, Jr. (New York, 1973), pp. 7-29.

Buttrey, *ANS 1973* = Theodore V. Buttrey, Jr., "The Portuguese Tradition," *Coinage of the Americas*, ed. T.V. Buttrey, Jr. (New York, 1973), pp. 62-65.

C

CNL = *The Colonial Newsletter* (P.O.Box 4411, Huntsville, Alabama, 35802). All references for sequential pages.
CW = *Coin World* (Sidney, OH).
CW Almanac 1975 = *Coin World Almanac* (Sidney, OH, 1975).
Calbeto de Grau, *Compendio* = Gabriel Calbeto de Grau, *Compendio de las Piezas de Ocho Reales*, vols. 1, 2 (San Juan, 1970).
Cal. S.P. Dom. = *Calendar of State Papers, Domestic Series, Nov. 1667-Sept. 1668* (London, 1893).
Carothers, *Fractional Money* = Neil Carothers, *Fractional Money, A History of the Small Coins and Fractional Paper Currency of the United States* (New York, 1930; repr. Wolfeboro, NH, 1988).
Carver, *Travels* = Jonathan Carver, *Three Years Travels Throughout the Interior Parts of North America* (Boston, 1797).
Chalmers, *British Colonies* = Robert Chalmers, *History of Currency in the British Colonies* (London, 1893).
Chaplin, *Companion* = Joseph Chaplin, *The Trader's Best Companion* (Newburyport, MA, 1795).
Chard, *CNL 1990* = Jack Chard, "Late 18th Century Coinage Dies: The Metallurgical Processes Involved," *CNL* 84 (1990), pp. 1136-43.
Coffing, *CW 1976* = Courtney L. Coffing, "Colonies Had Friends Among British Foes," *Coin World* (June 30, 1976).
Cole, *Commodity Prices* = Arthur H. Cole, *Wholesale Commodity Prices in the United States, 1700-1861* (Cambridge, 1938).
Common Council = *Common Council of the City of New York 1784-1831, Minutes of*, vol. 1 (New York, 1917).
Cooper, *Coinmaking* = Denis R. Cooper, *The Art and Craft of Coinmaking: A History of Minting Technology (London, 1988).*
Coppers, Num 1928 = "When Coppers Were Light and Bad," *Num* 1928, p. 337.
Craig, *Newton* = John Craig, *Newton at the Mint* (Cambridge, 1946).
Craig, *Mint* = —, *The Mint* (Cambridge, 1953).
Craig, *World Coins* = William D. Craig, *Coins of the World*, 1st ed. (Racine, WI, 1966).
Crosby, *Early Coins* = Sylvester S. Crosby, *The Early Coins of America* (Boston, 1875; repr. Lawrence, MA, 1974).
Cross, *History* = Arthur L. Cross, *A History of England and Greater Britain* (New York, 1914).

D

Daniell, *Experiment* = Jere R. Daniell, *Experiment in Republicanism* (Cambridge, 1970).
Dasí, *Estudio* = Tomás Dasí, *Estudio de Los Reales De A Ocho, también llamados Pesos, Dólares, Piastras, Patacones O Duros Españoles* (Valencia, 1950).
Davenport, *Church Talers* = John S. Davenport, *German Church and City Talers 1600-1700*, 2nd. ed. (Galesburg, IL, 1976).
Davenport, *Crowns 1974* = —, *European Crowns 1600-1700* (Galesburg, IL, 1974).
Davenport, *Crowns 1977* = —, *European Crowns 1484-1600* (Frankfurt, 1977).
Davenport, *Secular Talers* = —, *German Secular Talers 1600-1700* (Frankfurt, 1976).
Davis, *Journal* = Samuel Davis, "Journal of a Tour to Connecticut - Autumn of 1789," *Massachusetts Historical Society, Proceedings* (1869-1870), pp. 9-32.
Davis, *Copper* = Watson Davis, *The Story of Copper* (New York, 1924).
DeLeonardis, *Num 1988* = William J. DeLeonardis, "A Date for All - Reasons," *Num* 1988, pp. 670-71.
DeLorey, *CW 1976A* = Tom DeLorey, "Enterprising New Yorkers Struck Own Tokens," *Coin World*, Aug. 18, 1976.
DeLorey, *CW 1976B* = —, "New York Jeweler Made Famous Rarity," *Coin World*, Aug. 18, 1976.
Del Mar, *History* = Alexander Del Mar, *The History of Money in America* (New York, 1899).
Delmonte, *Benelux* = A. Delmonte, *The Silver Benelux* (Amsterdam, 1967).
Dennis, *Metallurgy* = W.H. Dennis, *A Hundred Years of Metallurgy* (Chicago, 1963).
Dickens, *History* = Charles Dickens, *A Child's History of England* (Boston, 1875).
Dolley, *Ire. Num. 1978* = Michael Dolley, "'St. Patrick' Half-Groats and Pennies," *Irish Numismatics* 61 (1978), p. 39.
Doty, *Massachusetts* = Richard G. Doty, "Making Money in Early Massachusetts," *Money of Pre-Federal America*, ed. John M. Kleeberg, *Coinage of the Americas Conference Proceedings* 8 (1992), pp. 1-14.
Doty, *Coin* = —, "Coin Stand-Ins," *Coinage* (December, 1990), pp. 16-17, pp. 130-40.
Doty, *RCR 61* = —, "Matthew Boulton and the Coinage Revolution, 1787-1797," *Rare Coin Review* 61 (1986), pp. 34-36.

Douglas, *Fugio* = Damon G. Douglas, *James Jarvis and the Fugio Coppers*, original manuscript, ANS Library MS. Collection, New York.

Douglas, *CNL 1968* = —, "The Original Mint of the New Jersey Coppers," *CNL* 23 (1968), pp. 225-29.

Douglas, *CNL 1969* = —, "James Jarvis and the Fugio Coppers," repr. as excerpts from original manuscript, *CNL* 26 (1969), pp. 261-65; 27 (1969), pp. 273-78; 29 (1969), pp. 285-92; 48 (1977), pp. 578-82.

Douglass, *Discourse* = William Douglass, *A Discourse Concerning the Currencies of the British Plantations in America* (1740), repr. *Economic Studies*, American Economic Association, vol. 2, no. 5 (1897), pp. 291-375.

Draskovic and Rubenfeld, *Crowns* = Frank Draskovic and Stuart Rubenfeld, *Standard Price Guide to World Crowns and Talers 1484-1986* (Iola, WI, 1984).

Duffield, *Num 1919* = F.G. Duffield, "A Trial List of the Countermarked Modern Coins of the World," *Num* 1919 et seq., repr. 1962.

Duncan, *CNL 1975* = Charles V. Duncan, "The Auctori Plebis Token and Related Pieces," *CNL* 43 (1975), pp. 476-79.

E

East, *Enterprise* = Robert A. East, *Business Enterprise in the American Revolutionary Era* (New York, 1938).

Egnal and Ernst, *WMQ 1972* = Marc Egnal and Joseph A. Ernst, "An Economic Interpretation of the American Revolution," *The William and Mary Quarterly* (1972), pp. 3-32.

Ernst, *Money and Politics* = Joseph Albert Ernst, *Money and Politics in America, 1755-1775: A Study of the Currency Act of 1764 and the Political Economy of Revolution* (Chapel Hill, 1973).

Essex Inst., Hist. Colls. = *Historical Collections of the Essex Institute*, vols. 1, 2, 3 (Salem, MA, 1859-61).

Ewing, *Num 1987* = George E. Ewing, Jr., "The Transatlantic Link Between the Boultons and the U.S, Mint," *Num* 1987, pp. 1624-31.

F

FPL = Fixed Price List.

Feavearyear, *Pound Sterling* = Albert Feavearyear, *The Pound Sterling: A History of English Money*, 2nd ed. (Oxford, 1963).

Felt, *Massachusetts* = Joseph B. Felt, *An Historical Account of Massachusetts Currency* (Boston, 1839).

Ferguson, *WMQ 1953* = E. James Ferguson, "Currency Finance: An Interpretation of Colonial Monetary Practice," *The William and Mary Quarterly* (1953), pp. 153-80.

Ferguson, *Purse* = —. *The Power of the Purse* (Chapel Hill, 1961).

Fiske, *Critical Period* = John Fiske, *The Critical Period of American History 1783 to 1789* (Boston, 1888).

Fiske, *Dutch and Quaker* = —, *The Dutch and Quaker Colonies in America* (Cambridge, 1903).

Flannagan, *Trying Times* = John H. Flannagan, *Trying Times: Economic Depression in New Hampshire 1781-1789*, Ph.D. diss. Georgetown University, 1972.

Folklore = *Funk and Wagnalls Standard Dictionary of Folklore, Mythology and Legend* (New York, 1950).

Ford, *CW 1980* = "Long Lost American Half Cent Back Home, Ford Reassembles Set of First U.S. Coins," *Coin World*, Jan. 9, 1980.

Frey, *CW 1979* = Harold A. Frey, Jr., "New Jersey Cent Legend Steeped in History," *Coin World*, Dec. 19, 1979.

Frey et al., *CNL 1980* = —, S. A. Katz, Michael Pidatella, and Joseph Sowers, "'Fingerprinting' New Jersey Copper Coins by Energy Dispersive X-Ray Fluorescence Spectrometry," *CNL* 57 (1980), pp. 713-19.

Fuld, *CNL 1964* = George Fuld, "RF-9," *CNL* 12 (1964), pp. 112-17.

Funk, *CNL 1973* = Charles E. Funk, "More on RF-44," *CNL* 38 (1973), p. 418.

G

Gaine, *Register* = Hugh Gaine, *Gaine's Universal Register* (New York, 1787).

Gale and Gale, *Num 1985* = Charlotte Gale and David M. Gale, "Jonathan Swift and the Irish Coinage of William Wood," *Num* 1985, pp. 1328-43.

Gallagher, *Num. Soc. Ire.* = Colm Gallagher, "The Irish Copper Coinage 1660-1700; Notes Toward a History," *Numismatic Society of Ireland, Occasional Papers* 26 (1980).

Gaspar and Newman, *Hoards* = Peter P. Gaspar and Eric P. Newman, "An Eighteenth Century Hoard From Philadelphia," *Coin Hoards* 4 (1978), pp. 127-30.

Gladfelter, *TAMS 1974* = David D. Gladfelter, "Mark Newby: Quaker Pioneer," *TAMS Journal* 1974, pp. 167-76.

Glaser, *Counterfeiting* = Lynn Glaser, *Counterfeiting in America* (New York, 1968).

Gorelkin, *Num 1984* = Leo Gorelkin, "Currency and Its Counterfeiting in Colonial America," *Num* 1984, pp. 2273-85.

Gottfried, *NEQ 1936* = Marian H. Gottfried, "The First Depression in Massachusetts," *New England Quarterly* 9 (1936), pp. 655-78.

Greene, *America* = Evarts B. Greene, *Provincial America 1690-1740*, *The American Nation: A History*, ed. Albert B. Hart, vol. 6 (New York, 1905).

Greene, *Foundations* = —, *The Foundations of American Nationality* (New York, 1922).

Guizot, *England* = François P.G. Guizot, *A Popular History of England*, vol. 3 (Boston, 1876).

H

Harris, *Essay* = Joseph Harris, *An Essay upon Money and Coins* (London, 1757).

Hawke, *Experience* = David Hawke, *The Colonial Experience* (Indianapolis, 1966).

Hazlitt, *Coinage* = W. Caren Hazlitt, *Coinage of the European Continent* (London, 1893).

Henry, *Series* = J. Henry, *The Series of English Coins in Copper, Tin, and Bronze* (London, 1879).

Hickcox, *Account* = John H. Hickcox, *An Historical Account of American Coinage* (Albany, 1858; repr. Wofleboro, NH, 1988).

Hodder, *CNL 1987* = Michael Hodder, "The Saint Patrick Copper Token Coinage. A Re-evaluation of the Evidence," *CNL* 77 (1987), pp. 1016-18.

Hodder, *CNL 1989* = —, "Research in Progress; New Jersey Biennial Dies," *CNL* 82 (1989), pp. 1094-98.

Hodder, *CNL 1990* = —, "Did New Jersey Coppers Officially Circulate in 1792?" *CNL* 84 (1990), p. 1152.

Hodder, *CNL 1991* = —, "The 1787 'New York' Immunis Columbia; A Mystery Re-Ravelled," *CNL* 87 (1991), pp. 1203-35.

Hodder, *AJN 1989* = —, "The New Jersey Reverse J, A Biennial Die," *AJN* 1989, pp. 195-237.

Hodder, *RCR 74* = —, "The Life of a Die," *Rare Coin Review* 74 (1989), pp. 34-35.

Hodder, *ANA Centennial* = —, "The Continental Currency Coinage of 1776," *The American Numismatic Association Centennial Anthology*, ed. Carl W. A. Carlson and M. Hodder (Colorado Springs, CO, 1991), pp. 7-18.

Hodder, *NJ "U" Reverse* = —, "New Jersey Reverse 'U': A Biennial Die," *The American Numismatic Association Centennial Anthology*, ed. Carl W. A. Carlson and M. Hodder (Colorado Springs, CO, 1991), pp. 19-34.

Hoober, *Num 1953* = Richard T. Hoober, "Financial History of Colonial Virginia," *Num* 1953, pp. 1138-52, 1266-82.

Hoober, *Num 1962* = —, "Financial History of Colonial Maryland," *Num* 1962, pp. 1011-19, 1159-63.

Horace, *Ars Poetica*.

Horan, *CNL 1976* = John J. Horan, "Some Observations and Speculations on St. Patrick Halfpence and Farthings," *CNL* 47 (1976), p. 567.

Hull, *Diaries* = "The Diaries of John Hull," *Transactions and Collections of the American Antiquarian Society*, vol. 3 (1857), pp. 141-250.

Hull, *Family* = "Hull's Family," *Transactions and Collections of the American Antiquarian Society*, vol. 3 (1857), pp. 269-78.

Hume, *Caterpillers* = Ivor Noël Hume, "The Very Caterpillers of This Kingdome: or, Penny Problems in the Private Sector, 1600-1660," *The Scope of Historical Archaeology*, ed. David G. Orr and Daniel G. Crozier (Philadelphia, 1984), pp. 233-51.

Hutchinson, *Massachusetts* = Thomas Hutchinson, *The History of the Province of Massachusetts from 1749 to 1774* (London, 1828).

I

Irving, *Washington* = Washington Irving, *Life of Washington* (New York, 1882).

J

Jensen, *New Nation* = Merrill Jensen, *The New Nation. A History of the United States During the Confederation, 1781-1789* (New York, 1950).

Jour. Cong. = *Journals of Congress*.

Jour. Cont. Cong. = *Journals of the Continental Congress*, vol. 31.

Julian, *RCR 79* = R.W. Julian, "Copper for the Early Mint," *Rare Coin Review* 79 (1990), pp. 68-69; 80 (1990), pp. 68-69.

Julian, *Seaby 1977* = —, "British Copper and American Coinage," *Seaby Coin and Medal Bulletin* 702 (1977), pp. 50-54.

K

Kessler, *Fugio* = Alan Kessler, *The Fugio Cent* (Newtonville, MA, 1976).

Kleeberg, *New Yorke* = John M. Kleeberg, "The New Yorke in America Token," *Money of Pre-Federal America*, ed. J. M. Kleeberg, *Coinage of the Americas Conference Proceedings* 8 (1992), pp. 15-57.

Knight, Journal = Sarah Knight, *The Journal of Madam Knight* (New York, 1825).

Kurth, *NSM 1944* = Howard H. Kurth, "The Albany Church Penny," *The Numismatic Scrapbook Magazine* (1944), pp. 284-89.

L

LaMarre, *RCR 65* = Tom LaMarre, "Coins for a New Constellation," *Rare Coin Review* 65 (1987), pp. 48-49.

Larkin, "Account Book" = Jack Larkin, "The World of the Account Book: Some Perspectives on Economic Life in Rural New England in the Early 19th Century," *TARS Symposium*, (Keene, NH, Oct. 13, 1984).

Lasser, *Num 1989* = Joseph R. Lasser, "The Remarkable Feversham Hoard," *Num* 1989, pp. 234-37, 291-94.

Lecky, *England* = William E. H. Lecky, *A History of England in the Eighteenth Century*, 5th ed., vol. 2 (London, 1891).

Lefroy, *AJN 1877* = J.H. Lefroy, "The Hog Money of the Somers Islands," *AJN* 1877, p. 16, repr. *CNL* 14 (1965), pp. 137-41.

Lewis, *Stannaries* = George Randall Lewis, *The Stannaries: A Study of the English Tin Miner* (Cambridge, 1907).

Lindesmith, *CNL 1973* = Robert J. Lindesmith, "Striking Sequence of the Connecticut Obverse 4's and 5's of 1786," *CNL* 37 (1973), pp. 408-11.

Lindsay, *Ireland* = James Lindsay, *A View of the Coinage of Ireland* (Cork, 1839).

Lodge, *Federalist* = Henry C. Lodge, ed., *The Federalist; A Commentary of the Constitution of the United States* (New York, 1908).

Low, *Tokens* = Lyman Low, *Hard Times Tokens* (New York, 1899).

Lucy, *Revolution* = Dan Lucy, *The Meaning of the American Revolution* (New York, 1964).

M

Madaus, *Num 1983* = Howard M. Madaus, "Nova Constellatio, The Story of a Shared Heritage," *Num* 1983, pp. 238-46.

Maganzin, *Depression* = Louis Maganzin, *Economic Depression in Maryland and Virginia 1783-1787*, Ph.D. diss., Georgetown University, 1967.

Maris, *New Jersey* = Edward Maris, *A Historical Sketch of the Coins of New Jersey* (Philadelphia, 1881; repr. Lawrence, MA, 1974).

Mason, *Making Coins* = C.L. Mason, "Making Coins," *Seaby's Coin and Medal Bulletin* 358 (1948), pp. 101-2; 359 (1948), pp. 153-54; 360 (1948), pp. 197-201; 362 (1948), pp. 297-300.

Massachusetts Bay = *Records of Massachusetts Bay*, vol. 1 (Boston, 1853).

Massachusetts Coinage = "The Coinage of Massachusetts," *Transactions and Collections of the American Antiquarian Society*, vol. 3 (1857), pp. 281-306.

Massey, *Studies* = J. Earl Massey, "Early Money Substitutes," *Studies on Money in Early America*, ed. Eric P. Newman and Richard G. Doty (New York, 1976), pp. 15-24.

Massey, *Money* = —, *America's Money* (New York, 1968).

McCusker, *Studies* = John J. McCusker, "Colonial Paper Money," *Studies on Money in Early America*, ed. Eric P. Newman and Richard G. Doty (New York, 1976), pp. 94-104.

McCusker, *Money and Exchange* = —, *Money and Exchange in Europe and America, 1600-1775, A Handbook* (Chapel Hill, 1978).

McCusker and Menard, *Economy* = — and Russell R. Menard, *The Economy of British North America 1607-1789* (Chapel Hill, 1985).

McDonald, *Formation* = Forrest McDonald, *E Pluribus Unum: The Formation of the American Republic 1776-1790* (Boston, 1965).

McDonald, *Origins* = —, *We The People: The Economic Origins of the Constitution (Chicago, 1958).*

McKay, Currency = George L. McKay, *Early American Currency*, ANSNNM 104 (New York, 1944).

McLaughlin, *Confederation* = Andrew C. McLaughlin, *The Confederation and the Constitution, The American Nation: A History*, ed. Albert B. Hart, vol. 10 (New York, 1905).

Mease, "Coins" = James Mease, "Old American Coins," *Massachusetts Historical Society Proceedings*, vol. 7 (1838), pp. 282-83.

Miller, *Connecticut* = Henry C. Miller, *The State Coinage of Connecticut*, *AJN* 53 (1920; repr. New York, 1981).

Mintz, *Morris* = Max M. Mintz, *Gouverneur Morris and the American Revolution* (Norman, OK, 1970).

Montagu, *Coinage* = H. Montagu, *The Copper, Tin and Bronze Coinage and Patterns for Coins of England*, 2nd. ed. (London, 1893).

Morris, *Morris Diary* = Anne Cary Morris, *The Diary and Letters of Gouverneur Morris*, vol. 1 (New York, 1888).

Morrisson, *ANSMN 32* = Cécile Morrisson, Jean-Noël Barrandon and Claude Brenot, "Composition and Technology of Ancient and Medieval Coinages: A Reassessment of Analytical Results," *ANSMN* 32 (1987), pp. 188-99.

Mossman, *Connecticut Coppers* = Philip L. Mossman, "Weight Analysis of Abel Buell's Connecticut Coppers," *Money of Pre-Federal America*, ed. John M. Kleeberg, *Coinage of the Americas Conference Proceedings 8* (1992), pp. 103-26.

Mossman, *CNL 1990* = —, "Connecticut Revisited," *CNL* 84 (1990), pp. 1144-49.

Mulheim, *Rhymes* = Jennifer Mulheim, ed., *Popular Nursery Rhymes* (London, 1981).

Muñoz, *CW 1985* = Miguel Muñoz, "Mint of Mexico Celebrates 450 Years of Coins," *Coin World*, May 1, 1985.

Muñoz, *Num 1985* = —, "The Mexico Mint 450 Years of Tradition," *Num. 1985, pp. 882-92.*

Murray, *Num 1988* = Glenn S. Murray, "Exploring the Historic Lima Mint," *Num* 1988, pp. 1200-12.

N

NC = *Numismatic Chronicle.*

Nelson, *Wood* = Philip Nelson, *The Coinage of William Wood 1722-1733* (London, 1903; repr. 1959).

Nettels, *Money Supply* = Curtis P. Nettels, *The Money Supply of the American Colonies Before 1720*, University of Wisconsin Studies in Social Sciences and History, vol. 20 (Madison, 1934; repr. New York, 1964).

Nevins, *American States* = Allen Nevins, *The American States During and After the Revolution, 1775 to 1789* (New York, 1924).

New-Hampshire = *Documents and Records Relating to the State of New-Hampshire*, vol. 8 (Concord, 1874), 1776-1783.

New-Jersey = *Votes and Proceedings of the Fourteenth General Assembly of the State of New-Jersey* (New-Brunswick, 1790).

New York Directory = *The New York Directory, 1786.*

Newman, *CCJour 1952A* = Eric P. Newman, "The 1776 Continental Currency Coinage," *The Coin Collector's Journal*, (N.Y.), July-Aug. 1952, pp. 1-9.

Newman, *CCJour 1952B* = —, "Varieties of the Fugio Cent," *The Coin Collector's Journal*, (N.Y.), July-Aug. 1952, pp. 10-20.

Newman, *Num 1955* = —, "First Documentary Evidence on the American Colonial Pewter 1/24th Real," *Num* 1955, pp. 713-17.

Newman, *Colonial Virginia* = —, *Coinage for Colonial Virginia, ANSNNM* 135 (New York, 1956).

Newman, *Num 1957* = —, "Counterfeit Continental Currency Goes to War," *Num* 1957, pp. 5-16, 137-47.

Newman, *ANS Centennial* = —, "A Recently Discovered Coin Solves a Vermont Numismatic Enigma," *Centennial Publication of the American Numismatic Society*, ed. Harald Ingholt (New York, 1958), pp. 531-42.

Newman, *Samaritan* = —, *The Secret of the Good Samaritan Shilling*, ANSNNM 142 (New York, 1959).

Newman, *NSM 1960* = —, "The Source of the Nova Constellatio Copper Coinage," *The Numismatic Scrapbook Magazine* 1960, pp. 6-8.

Newman, *CNL 1968* = —, "Circulation of St. Patrick Farthings in America," *CNL* 23 (1968), p. 220.

Newman, *Franklin* = —, "Franklin Making Money More Plentiful," *Proceedings of the American Philosophical Society*, 1971, pp. 341-49.

Newman, *CNL 1973* = —, "RF-52," *CNL* 38 (1973), p. 422.

Newman, *Studies* = —, "American Circulation of English and Bungtown Halfpence," *Studies on Money in Early America*, ed. E.P. Newman and Richard G. Doty (New York, 1976), pp. 134-72.

Newman, *CNL 1979* = —, "The Face Value of English Copper Coins Sent to Massachusetts in 1749," *CNL* 55 (1979), pp. 681-84.

Newman, *Coppers* = —, "Circulation of Pre-U.S. Mint Coppers," *America's Copper Coinage 1783-1857*, *Coinage of the Americas Conference Proceedings 1* (New York, 1984), pp. 101-16.

Newman, *Num 1985* = —, "The Earliest Money Using the Dollar as an Official Unit of Value," *Num* 1985, pp. 2181-87.

Newman, *RCR 69* = —, "Did the Mott Firm Deal in Clocks in 1789?" *Rare Coin Review* 69 (1987), p. 57.

Newman, *ANSMN 33* = —, "Were Counterfeit British Style Halfpence Dated 1785 Made Specifically for American Use?" *ANSMN* 33 (1988), pp. 205-23.

Newman, *Paper Money* = —, *The Early Paper Money of America*, 3rd. ed. (Iola, WI, 1990).

Newman and Gaspar, *Num 1978* = — and Peter P. Gaspar. "The Philadelphia Highway Find," *Num* 1978, pp. 453-67.

Noe, *Castine Deposit* = Sydney P. Noe, *The Castine Deposit: An American Hoard*, ANSNNM 100 (New York, 1942).

Noe, *Willow Tree* = —, *The New England and Willow Tree Coinages*, ANSNNM 102 (New York, 1943).

Noe, *Oak Tree* = —, *The Oak Tree Coinage of Massachusetts*, ANSNNM 110 (New York, 1947).

Noe, *Pine Tree* = —, *The Pine Tree Coinage of Massachusetts*, ANSNNM 125 (New York, 1952).

Num = *The Numismatist.*

O

O.E.D. = *Oxford English Dictionary*, 2nd edition.

O.U.D. = *Oxford Universal Dictionary.*

Oechsner Bequest = "Oechsner Bequest of a Rare 1776 New Hampshire Copper to the ANS," *Seaby's Coin and Medal Bulletin* 831 (1988), pp. 134-35.

Osborne, *Num 1984* = Dale K. Osborne, "Approaches to the Definition of Money," *The Economic Review*, March, 1984; repr. *Num* 1984, pp. 1625-32, 1845-51, 2075-85.

Overholser, *Analysis* = Willis A. Overholser, *A Short Review and Analysis of the History of Money in the United States* (Libertyville, IL, 1936).

P

Packard, *CNL 1987* = Mike Packard, "Rarity Values of Massachusetts Coins," *CNL* 77 (1987), pp. 1013-15.

Packard, *CNL 1989* = —, "Auction Appearances of Massachusetts Coppers," *CNL* 82 (1989), pp. 1100-7.

Paper Money = "Paper Money Actually Served American Colonists Well," *Bank Note Reporter*, April 1990, p. 29.

Papers = *Papers of the Continental Congress*, vol. 139, folio 131.

Partridge, *RHSQ 1979* = Sanborn Partridge, "Currency and Coins from Vermont's Period of Independence," *Rutland Historical Society Quarterly* (Fall, 1979), pp. 29-67.

Peck, *British Museum* = C. Wilson Peck, *English Copper, Tin, and Bronze Coins in the British Museum 1558-1958*, 1st ed. (London, 1960).

Peters, *CNL 1975* = Norman G. Peters, "The 1784 Counterfeit English Halfpence," *CNL* 43 (1975), p.485.

Peters, *Num 1986* = —, "Machin's Mills Halfpence, America's Forgotten Early Coppers," *Num* 1986, pp. 1803-14.

Philadelphia Directory = *The Philadelphia Directory, 1785.*

Picker, *Studies* = Richard Picker, "Variations of the Die Varieties of the Massachusetts Oak Tree and Pine Tree Coinage," *Studies on Money in Early America*, ed. Eric P. Newman and Richard G. Doty (New York, 1976), pp. 75-93.

Picker, *CNL 1973* = —, "A Connecticut Double Overstrike," *CNL* 36 (1973), p. 395.

Pike, *Complete System* = Nicholas Pike, *A New and Complete System of Arithmetic*, 1st ed. (Newburyport, MA, 1788).

Pollock, *RCR 80* = Andrew W. Pollock, "A Fabricated NE Sixpence," *Rare Coin Review* 80 (1990), p. 50.

Pope, *Essay on Criticism* = *The Works of Alexander Pope*, ed. Joseph Warton, vol. 1 (London, 1822).

Posthumus, *Prices* = Nicholas W. Posthumus, *Inquiry into the History of Prices in Holland*, vol. 1 (Leyden, 1946).

Pridmore, *Commonwealth* = F. Pridmore, *The Coins of the British Commonwealth of Nations to the end of the reign of George VI, 1952*, vol. 3 (London, 1975).

Prime, *Coins* = William C. Prime, *Coins, Medals and Seals* (New York, 1861), Chapter VI, repr. *CNL* (1971).

Purvey, *Catalogue* = P. Frank Purvey, editor, *Standard Catalogue of British Coins: Volume I, Coins of England and the United Kingdom*, 20th ed. (London, 1984).

R

RF = "Research Forum," in *Colonial Newsletter.*

RF-24, *CNL 1969* = "RF-24," *CNL* 26 (1969), p. 254.

RF-48, *CNL 1973* = "RF-48," "Dies by Atlee," *CNL* 37 (1973), p. 400; 45 (1975), p. 536.

RF-52, *CNL 1973* = "Where were the Nova Constellatios coined—Birmingham or Greenwich?," *CNL* 37 (1973), pp. 401-2.

RF-59, *CNL 1977* = "RF-59," "John H. Hickcox's Observations on the Connecticut Mints," *CNL* 49 (1977), p. 591.

Radford, *Encyclopedia* = E. and M.A. Radford, *Encyclopedia of Superstitions* (New York, 1969).

Reit, *Collecting* = Seymour Reit, *Coins and Coin Collecting* (New York, 1965).
Richardson, *Num 1947* = John M. Richardson, "The Copper Coins of Vermont," *Num* 1947, pp. 331-54.
Risk, *CNL 1981* = James C. Risk, "The Yale University Brasher Doubloon," *CNL* 61 (1981), pp. 753-64.
Roberts, *Oliver Wiswell* = Kenneth Roberts, *Oliver Wiswell* (New York, 1940).
Rock, *CNL 1991* = Jeff Rock, "Corrigenda Millerensis Revisited; A Connecticut Coppers Update, 1785-1788," *CNL* 88 (1991), pp. 1242-57.
Rock, *Serpent* = —, "The Serpent in Copper," Rosa Americana FPL 1989," pp. 20-21.
Ruding, *Annals* = Rogers Ruding, *Annals of the Coinage of Great Britain and its Dependencies*, vols. 1, 2, 3rd ed. (London, 1840).
Ryder, *AJN 1919* = Hillyer Ryder, "The Colonial Coins of Vermont," *AJN* 53 (1919), pt. 1; repr. New York, 1981.
Ryder, *New England* = —, *The State Coinages of New England* (New York, 1920).

S

Sallay, *CNL 1975* = John M. Sallay, "The Depreciation of the Massachusetts Currency and the Effects of the Redemption in 1750," *CNL* 45 (1975), pp. 519-30.
Saunders, *Almanac* = R. Saunders, *A Pocket Almanack for 1751* (Philadelphia, 1751).
Schab, *Num 1984* = Henry W. Schab, "The Life and Coins of John Chalmers," *Num* 1984, pp. 2293-2312.
Schilke and Solomon, *Foreign Coins* = Oscar G. Schilke and Raphael E. Solomon, *America's Foreign Coins* (New York, 1964).
Scholten, *Dutch* = C. Scholten, *The Coins of the Dutch Overseas Territories 1601-1948* (Amsterdam, 1953).
Schuckers, *Finances* = J. W. Schuckers, *A Brief Account of the Finances and Paper Money of the Revolutionary War* (Philadelphia, 1874; repr. New York, 1978).
Scott, *New York* = Kenneth Scott, *Counterfeiting in Colonial New York*, ANSNNM 127 (New York, 1953).
Scott, *Pennsylvania* = —, *Counterfeiting in Colonial Pennsylvania*, ANSNNM 132 (New York, 1955).
Scott, *Connecticut* = —, *Counterfeiting in Colonial Connecticut*, ANSNNM 140 (New York, 1967).
Scott, *Swift* = Walter Scott, *The Works of Jonathan Swift, D.D.*, vol. 7 (Edinburgh, 1814).
Seaby, *English Coinage* = Peter Seaby, *The Story of English Coinage* (London, 1952).
Seaby and Bussell, *British Copper* = H. A. Seaby and Monica Bussell, ed., *British Copper Coins, Part 1, Regal Coins*, 2nd. ed. (London, 1963).
Sedwick, *Cobs* = Frank Sedwick, *The Practical Book of Cobs*, 1st ed. (Maitland, FL, 1987).
Sewall, *Diary* = "Diary of Samuel Sewall," *Collections Massachusetts Historical Society*, vol. 6 (1879).
Shaw, *Monetary History* = William A. Shaw, *Select Tracts and Documents Illustrative of English Monetary History 1626-1730* (London, 1935; repr. New York, 1967).
Simon, *Essay* = James Simon, *An Essay Toward an Historical Account of Irish Coins* (London, 1749; repr. 1975).
Sipsey, *CNL 1964* = Everett T. Sipsey, "New Facts and Ideas on the State Coinages," *CNL* 13 (1964), pp. 120-29.
Sipsey, *CNL 1965* = —, "Dies by Wyon," *CNL* 16 (1965), pp. 154-59; 17 (1966), pp. 168-72.
Slafter, *Vermont* = Edmund Slafter, *The Vermont Coinage* (Montpelier, VT, 1870; repr. New York, 1981).
Smyth, *Franklin* = Albert Henry Smyth, *The Writings of Benjamin Franklin* (New York, 1906).
Solomon, *Studies* = Raphael E. Solomon, "Foreign Specie Coins in the American Colonies," *Studies on Money in Early America*, ed. Eric P. Newman and Richard G. Doty (New York, 1976), pp. 25-42.
Sparks, *Morris* = Jared Sparks, *The Life of Gouverneur Morris*, vol. 1 (Boston, 1832).
Spilman, *CNL 1961* = James C. Spilman, "Some Comments on the Fugio Cents of 1787," *CNL* 4 (1961), pp. 24-32; 7 (1962), pp. 52-55; 18 (1967), pp. 179-83; 24 (1968), pp. 237-42; 31 (1971), pp. 320-27; 36 (1973), pp. 379-82; 71 (1985), pp. 922-25.
Spilman, *CNL 1972* = —, "Abel Buell-Our American Genius," *CNL* 34 (1972), pp. 352-55; 39 (1974), pp. 424-34.
Spilman, *CNL 1974* = —, "A Penny Saved Is A Penny Earned," *CNL* 42 (1974), p. 472.
Spilman, *CNL 1977* = —, "An Experimental Die Analysis Chart for the Connecticut Coppers," *CNL* 48 (1977), pp. 572-77; 49 (1977), pp. 594-602; 51 (1978), pp. 630-34.
Spilman, *CNL 1979* = —, "New CLUB RAY FUGIO 24-MM," *CNL* 55 (1979), p. 678.
Spilman, *CNL 1982* = —, "An Overview of Early American Coinage Technology," *CNL* 62 (1982), pp. 765-76; 63 (1982), pp. 780-98; 64 (1983), pp. 799-811; 65 (1983), pp. 812-30.
Spilman, *CNL 1984* = —, "Fugio Rarity Table, 1984 Statistics," *CNL* 69 (1984), pp. 887-95.
Spilman, *CNL 1987* = —, "A 'Quantity Analysis' of Massachusetts Cents & Half Cents," *CNL* 77 (1987), pp. 1014-15.
Spilman, *CNL 1988A* = —, "Preliminary Report. CNL Fugio Weight Survey," *CNL* 80 (1988), pp. 1053-68.
Spilman, *CNL 1988B* = —, "The Virginia Halfpence of 1773," *CNL* 80 (1988), pp. 1061-62.

Spilman, *CNL 1991* = —, "CNL Fugio Weight Survey Update," *CNL* 87 (1991), pp. 1236-40.
Starkey, *Devil* = Marion L. Starkey, *The Devil In Massachusetts* (New York, 1969).
Stephens, *Popular History* = Alexander H. Stephens, *A Comprehensive and Popular History of the United States* (Philadelphia, 1882).
Stickney, *Notes* = Matthew A. Stickney, "Notes on American Currency," *Historical Collections of the Essex Institute*, 1 (1859), pp. 154-56; 2 (1860), pp. 45-46, 99-100, 153-54, 205-6, 253-54, 292-96; 3 (1861), pp. 32-34, 140-142.
Stokes and Haskell, *Prints* = Isaac N. P. Stokes and Daniel C. Haskell, *American Historical Prints* (New York, 1932).
Stoutjesdyk and Hoge, *ANA 1989* = James R. Stoutjesdyk and Robert W. Hoge, *A.N.A. Museum Collection of Early American Coins* (Colorado Springs, 1989).
Sumner, *American Currency* = William Graham Sumner, *A History of American Currency* (New York, 1874).
Sumner, *Spanish Dollar* = —, "The Spanish Dollar and the Colonial Shilling," *American Historical Review* 3 (1897-98), pp. 607-19.
Sumner, *Yale Rev. 1898* = —, "The Coin Shilling of Massachusetts Bay," pt. 1, *Yale Review* 6 (1898), pp. 247-64; pt. 2; 7 (1899), pp. 405-20.
Swiggett, *Morris* = Howard Swiggett, *The Extraordinary Mr. Morris* (New York, 1952).

T

TN = "Technical Note" in *Colonial Newsletter*.
TN-81, *CNL 1979* = "TN-81: New CLUB RAY FUGIO 24-MM," *CNL* 55 (1979), p. 678.
Taxay, *Studies* = Don Taxay, "Thomas Jefferson and the Founding of the Mint," *Studies on Money in Early America*, ed. Eric P. Newman and Richard G. Doty (New York, 1976), pp. 209-16.
Taxay, *Catalogue* = —, *The Comprehensive Catalogue and Encyclopedia of United States Coins*, 2nd ed., ed. Joseph H. Rose and Howard Hazelcorn (New York, 1976).
Taxay, *U.S. Mint* = —, *The U.S. Mint and Coinage* (New York, 1966).
Thomas, *Reminiscences* = E.S. Thomas, *Reminiscences of the Last Sixty-Five Years* (Hartford, 1840).
Thomas, *Virginia Convention* = Robert E. Thomas, "Virginia Convention of 1788: A Criticism of Beard's *An Economic Interpretation of the Constitution*," *Journal of Southern History* 19 (1953), pp. 63-72.
Thompson, *Evasions* = J. D. A. Thompson, "Evasions," *Seaby's Coin and Medal Bulletin* 373 (1949), pp. 275-76.
Thompson, *Norweb* = R. H. Thompson, *Sylloge of Coins of the British Isles*, vol. 38, *The Norweb Collection; Tokens of the British Isles, 1575-1750*, pt. 2 (London, 1988).
Thompson, *Essay* = Samuel Thompson, *An Essay on Coining* (Dublin, 1783), ANS Library MS. Collection.
Treas. Papers, 1556 = *Calendar of Treasury Papers, 1556/7-1696* (London, 1868).
Treas. Papers, 1702 = *Calendar of Treasury Papers, 1702-1707* (London, 1874).
Trudgen, *CNL 1983* = Gary Trudgen, "Thomas Machin - Patriot," *CNL* 66 (1983), pp. 832-48.
Trudgen, *CNL 1984A* = —, "Machin's Mills," *CNL* 68 (1984), pp. 861-83.
Trudgen, *CNL 1984B* = —, "Machin's Mills Silver Coinage," *CNL* 69 (1984), pp. 896-99.
Trudgen, *CNL 1987A* = —, "James Atlee's Imitation British Halfpence," *CNL* 75 (1987), pp. 966-79.
Trudgen, *CNL 1987B* = —, "Gilfoil's Coppers," *CNL* 76 (1987), pp. 997-1000; TN-111, *CNL* 77 (1987), pp. 1019-21.
Trudgen, *CNL 1988* = —, "Mathias Ogden, New Jersey State Coiner," *CNL* 79 (1988) pp. 1032-51.
Trudgen, *CNL 1990A* = —, "John Bailey New York City Coiner," *CNL* 85 (1990), pp. 1154-85.
Trudgen, *CNL 1990B* = —, "New York City Mayor's Court and the State Coinages," *CNL* 86 (1990), pp. 1192-1202.
Trudgen, *RCR 63* = —, "The Mysterious Muttonhead," *Rare Coin Review* 63 (1986), pp. 74-75.
Trudgen, *RCR 73* = —, "The Illogical and Curious Vermont 'Britannia' Copper," *Rare Coin Review* 73 (1989), pp. 92-94.

U

Utberg, *Mexico* = Neil S. Utberg, *The Coins of Colonial Mexico 1636-1821* (Edinburg, TX, 1966).

V

VanGelder, *Munten* = H. Enno VanGelder, *De Nederlandse Munten* (Antwerp, 1965).
Vaughn, *Discourse* = Rice Vaughn, *A Discourse on Coins and Coinage* (London, 1675).
Verkade, *Muntboek* = P. Verkade, *Muntboek* (Schiedam, 1848).

Vice, *Wilkinson* = David Vice, "The Tokens of John Wilkinson," *Format 40* FPL (Mar. 1990), pp. 2-8.
Vlack, *Counterfeit* = Robert Vlack, "Early English Counterfeit Halfpence Struck in America" (1974). Photographic plates.
Vlack, *CNL 1967* = —, "Die Varieties of St. Patrick Halfpence," *CNL* 21 (1968), pp. 199-202.
Vlack, *CNL 1978* = —, "The Washington Coppers of 1783," *CNL* 52 (1978), pp. 635-52.

W

W.I.D. = *Webster's 3rd. International Dictionary.*
Waters, *Imitation Copper* = Arthur W. Waters, "Remarks on the Imitation Copper Regal Coins," *Seaby's Coin and Medal Bulletin* 425 (1953), pp. 404-5.
Weeden, *New England* = William B. Weeden, *Economic and Social History of New England 1620-1789*, vols 1, 2 (Boston, 1890).
Weiss, *Colonial Standard* = Roger W. Weiss, "The Colonial Monetary Standard of Massachusetts," *Economic History Review* 27 (1974), pp. 577-92.
Wescott, *Letter* = George Wescott, Letter to Elias Boudinot, December 15, 1795. *Records of the Bureau of the Mint.* Record Group 104. *Correspondence of the Director of the U.S. Mint.* (Cited from ANS Microfilm Reel 63).
Whiteman, *Hendricks* = Maxwell Whiteman, *Copper for America; The Hendricks Family and a National Industry 1755-1939* (New Brunswick, NJ, 1971).
Wild, *CNL 1969* = William J. Wild, "Six Over Twelve," *CNL* 26 (1969), pp. 257-60.
Wild, *CNL 1972* = —. "A Remarkable Product of Machin's Mill," *CNL* 35 (1972), pp. 370-71.
Williamson, *Castine* = Joseph Williamson, "Castine; and the Old Coins Found There," *Collections of the Maine Historical Society* 6 (1859), pp. 105-26.
Williamson, *CNL 1976* = Raymond H. Williamson, "On the Importation of 1749 Halfpence and Farthings," *CNL* 46 (1976), p. 545.
Williamson, *CNL 1980* = —. "Case Record ALBION COX vs. THOMAS GOADSBY in Manuscript Volume I of 'Chancery Court Register, 1781-1796' for the State of New Jersey," *CNL* 59 (1980), pp. 740-46.
Williamson, *Penny-Wise 1984* = —, "Copper For Early American Cents," *Penny-Wise* 1984, pp. 99-103.
Williamson, *CNL 1986* = —, "Virginia's Early Money of Account," *CNL* 72 (1986), pp. 926-48.
Willis, *Portland* = William Willis, "Remarks on Coins Found at Portland in 1849, and Richmond's Island in 1855 with a General Notice of Coins and Coinage," *Collections of the Maine Historical Society* 6 (1859), pp. 127-51.
Wilson, *Swift* = David F.R. Wilson, *Dean Swift* (Dublin, 1941).
Wish, *Sewall* = Harvey Wish, *The Diary of Samuel Sewall* (New York, 1967).
Wood, *AJN 1914* = Howland Wood, "Coinage of the West Indies," *AJN* 48 (1914), pp. 89-136; repr. in Brunk, *World Countermarks on Medieval and Modern Coins* (Lawrence, MA, 1976).

Y

Yeoman, *Guide Book* = R.S. Yeoman, *A Guide Book of United States Coins*, 44th ed. (Racine, 1991).

Z

Zelinka, *CNL 1976* = Jerry Zelinka, "The Enigmatic Voce Populi Halfpenny of 1760," *CNL* 47 (1976), pp. 555-65.

NUMISMATIC AUCTION CATALOGUES AND PRICE LISTS

Bangs, Mervin and Co. (New York)

Parmelee = *Lorin G.Parmelee Sale*, June 25, 1890.

Bowers and Merena (Wolfeboro, NH)

Taylor = *The Frederick B. Taylor Collection*, Mar. 26-28, 1987.
Norweb = *The Norweb Collection*, pt. 1, Oct. 12-13, 1987; pt. 2, Mar. 24-25, 1988; pt. 3, Nov. 14-15, 1989.
Saccone = *The Saccone Sale*, Nov. 6-8, 1989.
Boyd, Brand, & Ryder = *Selections from the Boyd, Brand, & Ryder Collections*, Mar. 28-31, 1990.
Schenkel = *The Chris Schenkel Collection*, Nov. 12-14, 1990.

Matlock = *The Marvin P. Matlock, M.D. Collection*, Mar. 21-22, 1991.
Frontenac = *The Frontenac Sale*, Nov. 20-22, 1991.
Quartette = *Spring Quartette Sale*, Mar. 26-27, 1992.

Bowers and Ruddy Galleries (Los Angeles)

Turoff = *Julius Turoff Collection*, Oct. 1-2, 1976.
Branigan = *Branigan Estate Sale*, Aug. 21-25, 1978.
Hall = *Hall Estate Sale*, Oct. 26-28, 1978.
MacFarland = *MacFarland Sale*, Jan. 14-16, 1981.
Garrett = *The Garrett Collection Sales*, pt. 1, Nov. 28-29, 1979; pt. 3, Oct. 1-2, 1980; pt. 4, Mar. 25-26, 1981.
B&R 34 = *Bowers and Ruddy Catalogue 34*, Winter/Spring 1980.

Christie's (New York)

Feversham = *Coins from the Wreck of H.M.S. Feversham*, Feb. 7, 1989.

Henry Christensen Inc. (Madison, NJ)

Santa Cruz = *The Santa Cruz Collection*, Dec. 9-10, 1983.

Coin Galleries (New York)

Mail Bid 1985A = *Ancient and Modern Coins of the World, Mail Bid Sale*, Aug. 7, 1985.
Mail Bid 1985B = *Ancient and Modern Coins of the World, Mail Bid Sale*, Nov. 13, 1985.
Mail Bid 1986 = *Ancient and Modern Coins of the World and the United States, Mail Bid Sale*, Feb. 12, 1986.

Herbert I. Melnick, Co. (Rockville Centre, NY)

N.Y. Collection = *New York Collection*, July 31, 1983.

N.A.S.C.A. (Rockville Centre, NY)

Bryan = *Bryan Collection*, Nov. 2, 1977.

New Netherlands (New York)

51st Sale = *51st Sale Catalogue*, June 19, 1958.

Pine Tree Auction Galleries (Albertson, NY)

EAC 1975 = *Early American Coppers Sale*, Feb. 15, 1975.
Morton = *Morton Collection*, Oct. 18, 1975.
Weimer and Hirt = *The William Weimer and David Hirt Collections*, Mar. 5, 1976.
Brown = *John Carter Brown Sale*, May 20-21, 1976.
Breen III = *Breen III*, June 19-20, 1978.
FUN 1977 = *F.U.N. '77*, Jan. 8, 1977.

Norman W. Pullen, Published Price Lists, (So. Casco, ME)

Mike Ringo, Fixed Price Lists (Albany, NY)

Rosa Americana, Fixed Price Lists, (San Diego, CA)

Spink and Son (Zurich)

Salvesen = *The Harald Salvesen Collection of Trade Dollars and Trade Coinage of the World*, Oct. 24, 1988.

Stack's (New York)

Park = *Laird V. Park Collection*, May 26, 1976.
ANA 1976 = *American Numismatic Association Sale*, Aug. 24-28, 1976.
Allen = *Allen Collection*, Feb. 4-5, 1977.
Roper = *The John L. Roper, 2nd, Collection of Colonial and Early American Coins*, Dec. 8-9, 1983.
Bareford = "The Bareford Collection of New Jersey Coppers" in *The Greater New York Numismatic Convention*, May 3-4, 1984.
Picker = *The Richard Picker Collection of Colonial & Early American Coins*, Oct. 24, 1984.
Romano = *The Estate of Corrado Romano*, June 16-18, 1987.
Oechsner = *The Herbert M. Oechsner Collection*, Sept. 8-9, 1988.
Gunlocke = *The Howard W. Gunlocke Collection*, Mar. 14-16, 1989.
Foreman = "The John M. Foreman, Sr. Collection" in *The Greater New York Numismatic Convention*, May 3-4, 1989.
Hessberg = *The Edward Hessberg Collection*, June 19-20, 1991.
Coins and Currency = FPL, *Coins and Currency of Early America*.
Colonial Coins = FPL, *Colonial Coins and Medals*.

NEWSPAPERS OF THE COLONIAL AND CONFEDERATION PERIOD

Am. Merc. = *The American Mercury* (Hartford, CT)
Bos. Gaz. = *The Boston Gazette and the Country Journal*
Bos. Post = *The Boston Evening-Post*
Carlisle Gaz. = *The Carlisle Gazette and the Western Repository of Knowledge* (PA)
Conn. Courant = *The Connecticut Courant and Weekly Intelligencer* (Hartford)
Conn. Jour. = *The Connecticut Journal* (New Haven)
Daily Adv. = *The Daily Advertiser* (New York)
Essex Gaz. = *Essex Gazette* (Salem, MA)
Fed. Gaz. = *The Federal Gazette and Philadelphia Evening Post*
Free. Jour. = *The Freeman's Journal or the North-American Intelligencer* (Philadelphia)
Gaz. of U.S. = *Gazette of the United States* (New York)
Her. Freedom = *The Herald of Freedom* (Boston)
Ind. Chron. = *Independent Chronicle and the Universal Advertiser* (Boston)
Ind. Gaz. = *The Independent Gazette or, the Chronicle of Freedom* (Philadelphia)
Loyal Merc. = *The Loyal and Impartial Mercury*
Mass. Cent. = *Massachusetts Centinel* (Boston)
Mass. Spy = *Massachusetts Spy: Or, The Worcester Gazette*
Md. Gaz. = *Maryland Gazette* (Annapolis)
Mid. Gaz. = *The Middlesex Gazette, or, Federal Adviser* (Middleton, CT)
Morn. Chron. = *The Morning Chronicle and London Advertiser* (London)
N.H. Gaz. = *The New Hampshire Gazette, and the General Advertiser* (Portsmouth)
N.H. Spy = *Osborne's New-Hampshire Spy* (Portsmouth)
N.J. Gaz. = *The New-Jersey Gazette*
N.Y. Adv. = *The New-York Daily Advertiser*
N.Y. Gaz. = *The New-York Gazette*
N.Y. Jour. = *New-York Journal or, the General Advertiser*
N.Y. Pack. = *The New-York Packet*
Newport Her. = *The Newport Herald* (RI)
Newport Merc. = *Newport Mercury* (RI)
Norwich Pack. = *The Norwich Packet and the Country Journal* (CT)
Penna. Merc. = *The Pennsylvania Mercury, and Universal Advertiser* (Philadelphia)
Penna. Pack. = *The Pennsylvania Packet and Daily Advertiser* (Philadelphia)
Prov. Gaz. = *The Providence Gazette and the Country Journal*
Salem Merc. = *The Salem Mercury* (MA)
U.S. Chron. = *The United States Chronicle* (Providence, RI)
Va. Gaz. = *Virginia Gazette and Weekly Advertiser* (Richmond)
Vt. Gaz. = *The Vermont Gazette* (Bennington)

LIST OF TABLES AND CHARTS

Tables

Charts

CHAPTER ONE

The Economic Relationship Between England and Her North American Colonies

Less than five years following the ratification of the Constitution of 1787, the first regular coinages of the United States were struck at the new Philadelphia mint. There had been much deliberation, with many discarded proposals, before the Federal coinage system assumed its final form. The architects of the new government had considered the experiences of the prior colonial and Confederation periods in the construction of their monetary plan. While in that first year, 1793, only copper cents and half cents were issued, these were soon followed by the silver and gold coins of the new republic.[1]

This book is the story of the early currency of British North America prior to the establishment of the Federal Mint. The pervasive theme of this study is that money, in whatever form—be it commodities, wampum, coin or paper—must be understood in the context of a circulating medium of exchange. This holistic approach to numismatics requires an appreciation of the prevailing economic, political, and historical factors which shaped the environment in which the money was current. Without such an awareness, the coinages of this fascinating era are reduced to interesting specimens in collectors' cabinets rather than active players in the living history of our national tradition.

The currency of pre-Federal America lacked uniformity with the majority of hard coin from Spanish American sources, while small copper coins were of English origin. Monetary exchange rates between the colonies themselves, and between the plantations and other world markets varied, a factor which complicated commerce. While the ready availability of hard coin fluctuated because of cyclical inflationary and recessionary periods, there was a chronic shortage of small denominational currency for daily business. The monetary history of this period is concerned with the various foreign coinages—gold, silver, and copper—which circulated in British North America and the several actions initiated by the colonists to supplement contracting money supplies during economic bad times. Despite these fiscal encumbrances, the local economy prospered and finally, for a variety of reasons, the rebellious colonies became their own master. After independence, foreign specie coins remained scarce while the copper money supply continued to expand by the proliferation of both domestic and imported issues, many of which were counterfeit. During the Confederation, the small change medium became so overburdened with both legal and counterfeit coins, that coppers ceased to circulate during the summer of 1789. The United States gradually emerged from the stranglehold of the post-Revolutionary War depression just as copper money began to circulate again and the new Federal Mint was becoming a reality. This is the point where our story ends.

ENGLAND AND HER COLONIES

Plus Ultra

An appropriate starting place for this narrative about the money of pre-Federal America is an account of the colonization of British North America and the developing relationship

[1] The Constitution became law on March 4, 1789, following ratification by the ninth state, New Hampshire on June 12, 1788. On March 1, 1793, the first copper cents were minted. (Breen, *Encyclopedia*, p. 177.)

between England and her plantations. It was in the sixteenth and seventeenth centuries that England had joined its maritime neighbors in a race to lay claim to the treasures of the New World. Although the impression is given that the early North American colonists were persecuted emigrants fleeing their homeland for religious and political reasons, this romantic view is not entirely accurate, since there were significant economic factors in the development of the new frontier. England viewed these colonies jealously, but not as a sanctuary for its restless, adventurers, or oppressed. On the contrary, the colonies were a valued economic asset to an island nation with limited natural wealth. Over the years they were cultivated as a source of raw materials for English manufacturing and later as an important marketplace for finished goods. As American exports to the mother country increased, any excess could then be sold in Europe to profit English merchants. The settlement and development of the North American colonies followed a series of restrictive covenants imposed by England which were designed to control all aspects of economic growth, trade, and development. Such strict regulation of the provincial and national economies is embodied in the theory of "mercantilism," a system designed to increase national wealth by decreasing reliance on foreign powers for raw materials and by securing a favorable balance of trade. The increased wealth and prosperity translated directly into bolstered national security and military power. The ultimate objective of all mercantilist powers was to manipulate their colonies in whatever ways necessary so that all possible wealth or advantage gleaned from their overseas territories would accrue to the benefit of the mother country.

Colonization of British North America proceeded under the principles of mercantilism whereby the colonies were expected to buy English goods for which they paid by selling raw products to England to supply her factories. "The trade should employ English merchants and vessels, thereby providing freights, profits and interest. These were the three pillars of colonial policy designed to support the mercantile edifice of state security and private profit." [2] Foreign competition was virtually eliminated while at the same time, colonial manufacturing was restricted. The colonial trade policy and England's mercantile system in general were governed by the English Board of Trade, a governmental department concerned with the promotion of domestic and foreign commerce and the administration of colonial departments particularly in matters relative to the development, expansion, and protection of trade.[3] This agency promulgated regulations and sponsored certain legislation in Parliament, the Acts of Trade and Navigation, a series of laws designed to exert a continued control over colonial commerce and raw materials by maintaining permanent colonial dependence on English manufactured goods and shipping.[4] Although these Acts were designed to strengthen English mercantilism, the colonists also prospered under their structure since competition from rival Dutch merchants was removed.[5] Prior to 1761, a total of 29 such laws was passed but many were difficult to enforce, virtually ignored, or effectively circumvented by experienced American smugglers. While in "theory and definition" these Acts of Trade and Navigation "appeared rigid and uncompromising, they were in practice elastic and adjustable and did not seriously interfere with the growth and prosperity of the colonies" until after the French and Indian Wars.[6] At that point England assumed a firmer stance toward her colonies as evidenced by the stricter Navigation Acts following 1763. These more stringent regulations have been cited as a cause of the American Revolution because of the growing resentment toward British restraint of colonial

[2] Nettels, *Money Supply*, quote p. 160; Greene, *Foundations*, pp. 179, 182; McCusker and Menard, *Economy*, chap. 2; Andrews, *Colonial Period*, chap. 10.

[3] Greene, *Foundations*, pp. 230-31.

[4] Nettels, *Money Supply*, p. 160; Ernst, *Money and Politics*, p. 19. The mission of the Board of Trade was succinctly described by Raymond H. Williamson (personal communication, Sept. 3, 1990), who stated, "they viewed the colonies as a farmer views a cow."

[5] McCusker and Menard, *Economy*, pp. 46-50.

[6] Andrews, *Colonial Period*, p. 179.

trade.[7] Even when all aspects of the Navigation Acts and the other impositions of mercantilism are considered, it becomes apparent that the balance of benefit swung in the favor of the colonies. Despite her attempt to exert full control, the mother country was unable to stifle the emergence of a colonial-based economy.[8] Moreover, England had failed to recognize "that the Colonies had changed from infants into adolescents, and would now have to be handled by their mother-country with supreme tact if harmony was to be maintained." [9] Lacking this insight, England witnessed a deterioration in her relationship with the colonies, culminating in the War of Independence.

Despite the controls engineered by the Board of Trade policies, a local prosperity emerged in the colonies. Initially the colonies were sparsely populated, lacked capital, but had an abundance of raw materials; a colonial economy evolved which corresponded closely to the "export-led," "vent for surplus," or "staples approach" model. This economic system was typified by "small domestic markets, limited supplies of labor and capital, and abundant natural resources" which were shipped to England in exchange for manufactured goods required by the colonists. Consequently, more labor and capital were attracted to North America which in turn stimulated further development within the colonial export market. Significant differences in the economic base and growth of the plantation-rich South and the developing frontier regions of the North were the natural consequences of the geographical, demographic, and climatic diversity of the regions. From its very inception, it is clear that British America was not a single economy but rather a series of "distinct regional economies, most of them tied more closely to Great Britain than to each other, and each distinguished from the rest by the goods it produced for export and by the ways it earned credits in the balance of payments." This economic regionalism was responsible for the unequal monetary exchange rates between the various colonial monies of account, a frustration which plagued intercolonial commerce throughout the entire period. This heterogeneity which emerged from the earliest days of settlement spawned a sectionalism which still characterizes the political, social, and economic life of this country.[10]

Inherent within the structure of mercantilism was the requirement that colonial manufacturing and foreign trade with nations other than England had to be discouraged, thus preventing the "American plantations" from economic competition with the parent country and ensuring continued subservience as a source of raw materials and a ready market for finished English goods. A natural consequence of this necessity to buy imported English merchandise was the rapid accumulation of a trade deficit since purchases by the colonies for needed manufactured goods exceeded credits derived from the sale of exported commodities. This imbalance affected the North more than the South whose exported agricultural products, tobacco and cotton, were a ready source of income.[11] In a very early attempt to keep hard money at home to circulate locally, the Massachusetts Bay Colony in 1636 imposed a 16.7% tax upon the purchase of certain nonessential imports such as fruit, spice, sugar, liquor, and tobacco. The logic of the Puritan fathers was that indulgence in such luxuries could lead to "disarrangement and detriment to the medium of exchange." [12] However, they moderated the harshness of this pronouncement by exempting from the imposition "such wine as the deacons of the Churches shall buy or procure bona fide for the Churches' publike use."

[7] The relationship between the "patriotic" and the "economic" causations of the American Revolution are discussed by Egnal and Ernst, *WMQ 1972*. This topic will be presented in Chapter Six.

[8] McCusker and Menard, *Economy*, p. 354.

[9] Baxter, *Hancock*, p. 225.

[10] McCusker and Menard, *Economy*, pp. 12, 17-34; quotes from pp. 12 and 26.

[11] Nettels, *Money Supply*, pp. 136-41, 149.

[12] Felt, *Massachusetts*, p. 21.

MONEY SUPPLY IN THE COLONIES

There are numerous contemporary reports throughout the colonial period lamenting the fact that the trade deficit with England constantly siphoned all available hard money across the Atlantic to pay for imported necessities and, in some instances, luxuries. Typical of such commentaries was the 1719 report from Massachusetts.

> All the silver money which formerly made payments in trade to be easy, is now sent into Great Britain to make returns for part of what is owing there. We have been so deficient in farming and managing our own manufacture, lived so much above our abilities, spent so much of our imported commodities, that our money is gone, there is scarce a penny of it passing for a twelvemonth.[13]

Estimation of the prevailing trade deficit has been attempted by a study of the existing custom houses' records such as Table 1 which relates New England's trade imbalance with England.

TABLE 1
Trade Deficit for New England with England; English Customs Records
(Data from Nettels, *Money Supply*, p. 139)

Periods	*Average yearly purchases from England (imports)*	*Average yearly sales to England (exports)*	*Average yearly deficit*
1698-1702	£ 92,200	£ 33,400	£ 58,800
1702-1706	62,750	26,750	36,000
1706-1712	121,000	33,000	88,000

Historical convention has perpetuated the supposition that such trade imbalances drained all ready cash from the colonies to pay for imported commodities. The fact is that customs ledgers only tell a portion of the story.[14] The accounts failed to give the current price for the goods which cleared the ports since values were quoted at levels current in the late 1690s and did not reflect price changes or the annual inflation rate.[15] Although customs house records do not correctly state the actual price of merchandise which passed their portals, such figures do record the volume of trade. Another serious flaw concerning these colonial ledgers is that data were only collected for transactions with England and Wales and trade with all other countries ignored. "Invisible" sources of income which would help offset the costs of imported purchases are not enumerated in customs tabulations. Such undocumented income would include monies earned through trade related activities including wages and the use or sale abroad of American ships. The profits derived from smuggling were considerable and, of course, these evaded official attention. While a negative balance of trade existed, it was not as severe as a first glance at existing customs house files would imply. A reevaluation of American colonial balance of payments from trade with Great Britain, Ireland, Europe, and the West Indies, including both "visible" and "invisible" trade related incomes, discards "the traditional notion of a severe, chronic deficit for the colonies" since the annual imbalance was only in the range of £40,000.[16]

[13] Felt, *Massachusetts*, p. 71.
[14] McCusker and Menard, *Economy*, pp. 73-78.
[15] The annual inflation rate from 1620 to 1730 was 0.09%, and from 1730 to 1770 was 0.75% (McCusker and Menard, *Economy*, p. 67).
[16] McCusker and Menard, *Economy*, pp. 80-84.

In their analysis of the colonial money supply, McCusker and Menard make the following assessment:

> A central question is whether the money supply of the colonists was "adequate." To be adequate for the purposes of an economy, money must be both available in sufficient quantities and of a recognized standard to facilitate rather than inhibit its use in the exchange of goods and services. The total quantity of money available to the colonists is unknown since contemporary or modern estimates are few and never include all forms of money. Some speak of the supply of coin, some of public paper, some of both; all omit commodity money and private paper.[17]

Hence, the "available money" supply for local and foreign transactions was more than just hard cash at hand, but also included paper currency, commodities and the credit extended by English merchants.[18] Calculations using the estimated per capita income from 1750 to 1775 suggest that within the colonies as a whole, there was an adequate quantity of money.[19] While there may have been sufficient gold for large transactions, there existed a shortage of smaller denominational currencies for the daily business transactions of the typical urban householder, or prosperous farmer who had limited access to specie. "We know very little about the real story of the money condition of the vast majority of the common people, because most of them were illiterate and hence left no 'paper trail'."[20] Many, especially those from rural areas, lived at a "subsistence" level without any actual need for money. For them daily commerce was conducted by barter or "work changing," which are other forms of "currency" to be discussed in the following chapter.

Writing in 1900, Bullock summarized his findings concerning the availability of specie during the colonial period.

> Nevertheless complaints of the scarcity of coin and the alleged impossibility of keeping it in circulation remained so common, and have been accepted so complacently by historians, that it will be necessary to present a little of the evidence that proves the presence of a moderate amount of specie in the colonies.[21]

Bullock supported his thesis by quoting sources which related that in Massachusetts in 1676 "there is a reasonable quantitie of silver money in the colony, but no gold." In 1671 in Maryland there was English, foreign, and Maryland silver. In the period around 1700 there was reported "a great quantity of Spanish money Plate and Bullion" available in Carolina, Philadelphia, the Tidewater districts of Virginia, New York, and New England; "but these evidences of coin are accompanied by many complaints of scarcity."[22]

In answer to this question regarding the adequacy of metallic currency during the colonial period, there is indication that specie, while rarely abundant, fluctuated in availability from place to place and from time to time, depending on the prevailing economic conditions. Modern economic research has satisfactorily solved the riddle of the cyclic availability and scarcity of hard currency. Definite times of economic expansion and stagnation within the colonial economy have been identified, particularly in postwar periods, which corresponded to similar activity within the English economy.[23] When hard money became scarce during a depression,

[17] McCusker and Menard, *Economy*, p. 338.

[18] Ernst, *Money and Politics*, p. 356.

[19] McCusker and Menard, *Economy*, pp. 338-40. Just prior to the Revolution, the money stock in America was calculated at £2.70 per person as compared to £3.50 in England and Wales for the same period.

[20] Raymond H. Williamson, personal communication, Sept. 3, 1990.

[21] Bullock, *Essays*, pp. 13-15, quote pp. 13-14.

[22] Nettels, *Money Supply*, pp. 204-7.

[23] McCusker and Menard, *Economy*, pp. 60-70.

Fig. 2: A VIEW OF NEW YORK FROM THE NORTH WEST (1773). This engraving appeared in the *Atlantic Neptune*, a collection of maps, plans, and views of America published by the British Admiralty from 1763 to 1784. Trinity Church is on the promontory to the far left and the fifth tower to its right with a flag is the cupola of City Hall. The second tallest steeple is on the Wall Street Presbyterian Church (Stokes and Haskell, *Prints*, pp. 42-43). Courtesy The New York Public Library.

there was clamor from contemporary observers who decried the shortage of specie and the burden this placed on the public. Perhaps complaints at such times reflected more a shortage of credit than of money. No doubt there was periodic scarcity of circulating hard coin for remittance to England for the purchase of imports, but the fact remains that colonial commerce generally flourished despite periods of cyclic economic decline. Several periods of sluggish economy were more significant than others and influenced the colonial monetary status in ways which will be detailed in subsequent chapters.

The earliest economic downturn occurred from 1638 to 1644 and has been termed the "first depression in American history." This event, to be described in Chapter Two, was an international rather than a local New England phenomenon. This period saw the start of a gradual "overvaluation" of silver currency, an inflationary measure which extended until the Proclamation of 1704. The subsequent depressions of 1650 to 1655 and 1662 to 1672 followed war with The Netherlands. The next three major periods of slump (1714 to 1716, 1751 to 1755, and 1764 to 1769) coincided with the end of Queen Anne's, King George's, and the French and Indian Wars, respectively.[24] Conflict with England over colonial paper money policies flared during 1751 and 1764 with wide-reaching paper currency reforms in America which are topics in Chapter Four. Many historians examined these hard times and attempted to blame the financial recessions on paper money practices in order to garner support for their own personal opposition to that medium. Typical of this attitude was the opinion advanced by Douglass, an avowed early eighteenth century foe of paper money, who claimed that silver coin was plentiful in Massachusetts until driven out by paper money first issued by the colony in 1690.[25] It was his interpretation that the availability of hard money was not a problem until the colony resorted to paper money whereupon this inflated medium drove specie out of circulation. This theory will

[24] See footnote 19, chap. 4.
[25] Bullock, *Essays*, p. 15.

be considered further in Chapter Four. Modern-day scholars have been more objective; in an analysis of contemporaneous commodity price indices, these currency fluctuations have been linked to worldwide business cycles rather than local currency mismanagement.

At the end of King George's War in 1748, Thomas Hancock, a prominent Boston merchant and uncle of the Revolutionary War patriot, wrote, "Peace hath put a stop to all our trade"; "money became 'monstrously scarce'."[26] The following year, a large amount of Spanish silver was awarded to Massachusetts by Parliament, creating a ready amount of available specie for the province right up until the Revolution. This story will be related in great detail in Chapter Three. An economic slowdown after the French and Indian War was the probable cause for the Massachusetts Council's petition to the House of Commons presented in December 1768 which described the circumstances present in the Bay Colony.

> The scarcity of money in the Colonies is owing to the balance of their trade with Great Britain being against them; which balance drains them of their money, to the great embarrassment of their trade, the only source of it. This embarrassment is much increased by the regulations of trade, and by the Tax Acts, which draw immediately from trade the money necessary to support it; on the support whereof the payment of the balance aforesaid depends. The exports of the Colonies, all their gold and silver, and their whole powers of remittance, fall short of all the charged value of what they import from Great Britain.[27]

The final depression to occur within the time frame of this book lasted from 1782 to 1789 and equaled in magnitude the Great Depression of 1929 to 1933 in terms of decline of the gross national product.[28] This period of economic stagnation during the post-Revolutionary War period, which had a notable impact on numismatic history and the hard money supply, is covered in the last four chapters. Rather than ascribe to a chronic, unrelenting shortage of hard money during the entire colonial period, it appears that specie supplies fluctuated depending upon the prevalent economic condition of the time. During war, when there was an increased demand for raw materials, colonial export trade flourished, there was local prosperity, and ample hard money was available to exchange for manufactured goods from England. When peace returned, the foreign markets for colonial exports softened and hard money became scarcer. In order to obtain specie to remit abroad during these recessionary times, the merchants had to pay dearly for it with other currencies to be described in Chapter Two. In such periods of economic decline, hard money for foreign remittance essentially traded as a commodity.[29] Undoubtedly, there was a maldistribution of hard money in favor of the merchant and business populations with most of it being sequestered in the counting houses awaiting shipment to England. When specie was thus unavailable for commerce, a relative shortage was induced. Since all foreign purchases did not require a specie transaction, hard money was not always essential for overseas trade. Nonetheless, the fact remains that there were numerous contemporary complaints recorded about inadequate stocks of silver and gold coin, but the accuracy of such lamentations may be difficult to assess because of the subjectivity of the speaker and the lack of complete records. McCusker summarizes this hard money "shortage" by suggesting that

> Complaints about the "dearth of available coin" in the colonies should always be read with the added phrase supplied by the reader: "at 'reasonable' price." [30]

[26] Baxter, *Hancock*, p. 111.
[27] Felt, *Massachusetts*, pp. 159-60.
[28] McCusker and Menard, *Economy*, pp. 373-74.
[29] Nettels, *Money Supply*, pp. 11-13; Ernst, *Money and Politics*, p. 20.
[30] McCusker, *Money and Exchange*, p. 124.

This is to state that hard coin could always be obtained but the question was whether the buyer was willing to afford the price. McCusker's position is well supported by the statement of Judge Samuel Sewall who spoke of the period when Massachusetts first issued paper currency.

> I was at making of the first Bills of Credit in the year 1690: They were not made for want of Money; but for want of Money in the Treasury.[31]

As previously noted, small denominational coins were scarce and at a premium during much of the colonial period. An inventory of hard money reported by Thomas Hancock was primarily in gold with only a scattering of small coins. "As a result, shopkeepers found great difficulty in providing their customers with small change." [32]

The same monetary situation was experienced outside the Thirteen Colonies; in Nova Scotia the government had to buy circulating medium, generally Spanish silver coins, on the open market to provide wages and payments.[33] Merchants who possessed hard money were reluctant to spend it locally. This is further indication that hard money was available if one had the means to buy it with other currencies, and when one owned it, there was a tendency to hoard it or use it for foreign purchases. Thus while the quantity of money "circulating" in the community was limited, hard coin was not impossible to obtain. Since those who held it, kept it, it was not so much an issue of quantity but of distribution. It was not an "absolute money shortage" but more of a "circulating money shortage," especially for small denominational coins where limited numbers impacted more severely on daily commerce rather than affecting overseas transactions.

How is this question to be resolved; was there an adequate supply of hard money for the colonists to conduct daily business? Writers of the past century certainly would have insisted there was a troublesome shortage of gold and silver. They would have added that such a deficiency was linked to many of the colonists' economic woes. Since it is human nature to complain about difficult times and take prosperity for granted, history is replete with subjective and anecdotal accounts of money shortages during a depressed economy. Modern historians have cited evidence for an adequate supply of specie whose immediate availability to those who could afford it was directly related to the prevailing economic cycle. During a period of expansion, hard money would have been more plentiful. In a recessionary period, colonists not having access to sufficient coin would have resorted to some non-specie monetary instruments such as commodity monies, paper currency, and other substitutes to be described in the following three chapters.

Any shortage in America of hard coin for daily use could not have been alleviated by England even if she wished since her own coinage was in such a desperate condition. As a result of this situation and her mercantilist policies, the exportation of specie out of England was outlawed, even to the colonies, except for the payment of its military forces.[34] In spite of this embargo, "there were countless subterfuges and devices for smuggling coin out of the kingdom ... and the state of the silver currency of England in the seventeenth and eighteenth centuries is ample proof of the failure of this prohibitive legislation."[35] English coins actively circulated in the colonies as evidenced by their inclusion in contemporary tables of exchange rates. England and her American colonies had no natural source of precious metals and depended on the wealth of the Spanish American mines from the profitable trade via the West Indies. Despite shortages of coin for daily commerce, the English government would never sanction the establishment of a

[31] Sewall, *Diary*, p. 366.
[32] Baxter, *Hancock*, p. 15.
[33] Bell, *Foreign Protestants*, p. 343.
[34] Nettels, *Money Supply*, pp. 163, 166; Bezanson, *Prices in PA*, pp. 316-17.
[35] Chalmers, *British Colonies*, pp. 4-5.

colonial mint, or develop a uniform coinage system, except for the feeble attempt of the Proclamation of 1704. For England to have inaugurated a colonial currency would have been contrary to the tenets of mercantilism since it would have encouraged specie to flow out of the realm if special coins had been minted for colonial use. England's monetary policy toward its plantations was simple: assure that the net drift of gold and silver was from the colonies to the mother country.[36] Thus the North American Plantations remained obliged to depend on foreign coin, especially Spanish American silver, as their source of circulating specie. The local money supply was not reliably stable since, during periods of recession, hard coin was tight and specie was in great demand for foreign purchases. Even during the best of times, low denominational coins were never abundant for daily use and this dearth of circulating hard currency became a chronic, continuing grievance of the American colonists and a theme central in the study of contemporary economic, political, and numismatic history.

[36] Andrews, *American History*, pp. 351-52.

CHAPTER TWO

Money In Early America: Wampum, Commodities, Foreign Coin

In the previous chapter it was concluded that throughout the colonial period there were adequate, although never excessive, hard money supplies except during the difficult periods of postwar economic slump or frank depression. The problem was that this coin money was expensive, traded as a commodity, commanded a premium, and so was not readily available for everyday commerce. While large denomination specie could be "bought," there was a shortage of lower denomination currency for everyday business transactions even in good times. Undoubtedly this monetary situation was an inconvenience to the colonists but certainly it came as no great surprise since most had emigrated from England where they were well accustomed to the vexations of a defective national currency as this chapter will reveal. In order to provide for daily money needs, it was necessary to create some additional monetary systems which could substitute for hard coin if domestic commerce were to proceed.

A DESCRIPTION OF "MONEY"

To begin, it is necessary to resolve what is encompassed by the term *money*. The definition of money, or currency, would be very restrictive if it only included "hard coin," or specie. Joseph B. Felt in the introduction to his classic work, *An Historical Account of Massachusetts Currency*, asserted that:

> Currency ... denotes whatever has been adopted, as a medium of exchange, by general consent and practice.... It is well known, that substances, adopted as a medium of circulation or standard value, have been essentially different in various ages and nations. In Italy, the ancient mode of estimating articles of property, was by cattle. Hence, the word, "pecunia," in their language, was from pecus, flock or herd; though it has long been translated, money.[1]

Felt offered other examples, through both the ancient and modern worlds, of how various materials, including those "of the animal, vegetable and mineral kingdoms," served as currency in different countries during different eras. Considering this broadened definition of "money" or "currency," one can easily understand how the colonists responded to this lack of "circulating" specie. Their initial reaction was to promote the use of readily available substitutes for coin by the adoption of indigenous Indian wampum, by the barter of goods, commodities and services, and by the use of commodity monies. The next expedient was to expand the pool of circulating hard money by prohibition of its export and by the systematic overvaluation of existing hard coin in terms of local currency. Also, a colonial mint was established in Massachusetts to provide a local source of hard money. The final stratagem to introduce a substitute for unavailable hard cash was the development of four systems of paper currency, (a) commodity notes, (b) bills of exchange, (c) land-office (land bank) notes, and (d) bills of credit. Some of these alternatives were more local in scope than others, and while they appeared more or less in

[1] Felt, *Massachusetts*, pp. 10-11; See also a recent scholarly study by Osborne, *Num 1984*.

succession, some existed simultaneously "and the adoption of a later, perhaps more sophisticated device did not necessarily mean the abandonment of an earlier one."[2]

Circulating media other than hard coin are referred to as "money substitutes."[3] If we accept the definition proposed by Felt that "money" can be anything upon which we agree, it is inconsistent to speak of "money substitutes" for such items as wampum and commodities for which specific values have been assigned by popular consent. While wampum, commodities, and the like may well be considered substitutes for "hard coin," they are, indeed, just another "species" of the genus "money," and are a currency in their own right.[4]

Money is either "real" or "imaginary." In the colonial era, "real" money invariably referred to metallic coin, while "imaginary" money was a bookkeeping contrivance also called "money of account." Money of account does not exist *per se* as a tangible item of value, but is rather a "notational device" where disparate coinage systems can be reconciled into a single monetary standard.[5] For example, in October 1672, the Spanish eight reales or piece-of-eight was valued at six New York shillings.[6] The eight reales was an actual "real" coin, whereas the New York shilling did not exist except on paper. It was the local "money of account" or "New York money" in which the current value of the eight reales could be reckoned in relationship to other coin money or other imaginary monies. Money of account was also a useful vehicle for reconciling underweight or clipped coins because their relative values, based on the actual weight of precious metals, could be established.[7] While the colonial monies of account were reckoned in the same denominations as England, namely pounds, shillings, pence, and farthings, there was no equality in the value of the currencies used in the mother country and her North American colonies; the only point they had in common was the name of the monetary units. Even among the various colonies themselves, there was no uniformity in the relative values of the several colonial monies of account which could be, and frequently were, different depending on the strength or weakness of the particular colony's local economy. The Spanish American eight reales, which was the monetary standard of the period, had four different value "zones" in colonial America. The rates noted below, or par of exchange, stabilized from about the mid-eighteenth century to the early Federal period (see Table 6 below):

4s. 6d. (54d.) in English sterling
4s. 8d. (56d.) in South Carolina and Georgia money
6s. 0d. (72d.) in New England and Virginia money
7s. 6d. (90d.) in New Jersey, Pennsylvania, Maryland, and Delaware money
8s. 0d. (96d.) in New York and North Carolina money

While there was no impediment in the financial calculation among colonies whose monies of account were at par, such as within the four New England colonies, this inconsistency in value of money from one colony to another, as expressed in the local monies of account, was an aggravation which added significant complexity to intercolonial commerce. (See Appendix 1 for calculations in the various monies of account.) The disparity between the rates of exchange from one colony to another, and later among the several states, was a frustration which existed into the Federal period.

Money is further defined as to its intrinsic worth.[8] "Fiduciary" coinage is money whose monetary value exceeds the value of the contained bullion. More specifically, a "subsidiary" coinage refers to fiduciary silver coins, whereas "minor" coins are base metal fiduciary coins. A

[2] McCusker, *Money and Exchange*, p. 117.
[3] Massey, *Studies*.
[4] Felt, *Massachusetts*, p. 8.
[5] McCusker, *Money and Exchange*, p. 6.
[6] McCusker, *Money and Exchange*, p. 157.
[7] McCusker, *Money and Exchange*, p. 8.
[8] Carothers, *Fractional Money*, pp. 2-5.

"token" coinage conveys the idea of a money substitute, and while there may be provisions for its exchange into specie, such tokens usually do not possess inherent legal tender status. "Fractional" coins are a currency in denominations less than the standard silver unit.

As part of our numismatic heritage and this historical survey, it is of interest to review the derivation of the monetary denominations used for both the real and imaginary systems.[9] Silver pennies date their origin to the beginning of the eighth century, the Middle Anglo-Saxon period, when they were introduced as a currency by King Offa of Mercia. By the ninth century, silver pennies were prevalent throughout England where they remained the sole denomination for about five centuries. They passed at 240 to a pound, money of account, but their weight was uncertain until defined by a statute of 1266 which stated that each silver penny should weigh "thirty-two wheat corns in the midst of the ear." Further legislation in 1280 redefined the penny's weight to equal 24 grains (of wheat); hence 24 grains came to comprise one pennyweight, abbreviated *dwt.* Although the penny was the only silver coin until 1279, these pence were struck with a deeply impressed cross such that they could be broken into two halfpence or into four parts called "fourthings" or farthings. The pound sterling of account (imaginary) was a unit which has been in existence since Anglo-Saxon times and it was the intent that the pound of money, divided into 240 pennies, equal a troy pound of silver. This pound of account was further divided into twelve shillings (also imaginary until the reign of Henry VII) of twenty silver pennies (real), or twenty shillings of twelve pennies.

The *d.* abbreviation for the silver penny (and later the copper and bronze) is from the Latin *denarius*, a Roman silver coin. The *s.*, as the abbreviation for shilling, is from the Latin *solidus*, a Roman gold coin but more importantly a medieval money of account equal to twelve denarii. The Roman unit of weight, *libra*, equal to 0.718 lbs., avoirdupois, is the source of the £ in reference to pounds. The term "sterling" refers to English currency in general, but specifically to the standard alloy of 925 parts silver and 75 parts copper. The purity of the silver is its "fineness"; the 92.5% silver content of sterling is otherwise expressed as 925.0 millesimal fineness or .925 fine. "Sterling" originally was the term for a pound weight of English silver pennies but the derivation of the word remains shrouded in mystery.[10] It has been conjectured that the word comes from the old English word for star, *steorra*, indicative of the small star on early silver pennies, or even from *staer*, a starling, suggestive of the four birds on pennies of Edward the Confessor. The theory that the word was derived from "Easterling money," silver coins from eastern Germany imported into England through continental trade, is no longer held.

INDIAN WAMPUM

When the early colonists were faced with an inadequate supply of coins to meet their currency needs, a natural response was to employ the indigenous currency of the natives, namely Indian wampum. Wampum was variously known as "sewan, seawan, and seawant," from the Algonquian for "loose beads," and as "roanoke" from the same language for "smoothed shells." In the Narraganset tongue, the name was "wampumpeag, peage, peag, peak and wampum." "Wampumpeag" specifically referred to the white polished shells which were less valuable than the dark purple or black "wampum."[11] The early American explorer, Jonathan Carver, provided a lucid description of these strings of hand-fashioned shell beads which were used as both ornamentation and money.

> These belts are made of shells found on the coasts of New-England and Virginia, which are sawed out into beads of an oblong form, about a quarter of an inch long, and

[9] Felt, *Massachusetts*, pp. 15, 249; Feavearyear, *Pound Sterling*, pp. 7-10; Seaby, *English Coinage*, pp. 13, 33-34; Peck, *British Museum*, pp. 2-3.
[10] *O.U.D.*
[11] *W.I.D*; Carothers, *Fractional Money*, p. 20.

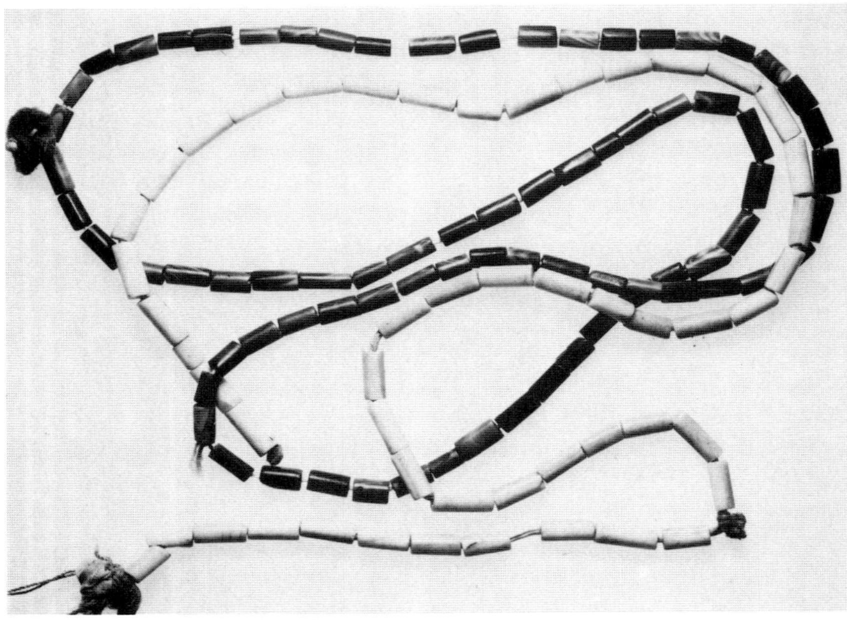

Fig. 3: Two strings of Indian wampum: the white beads passed at half the value of the darker ones which were variously described as black, violet or blue (blew).

> round like other beads. Being strung on leather strings, and several of them sewed neatly together with fine sinewy threads, they then compose what is termed a belt of Wampum.
>
> The shells are generally of two colors, some white and others violet; but the latter are more highly esteemed than the former. They are held in as much estimation by the Indians, as gold, silver, or precious stones, are by Europeans.
>
> The belts are composed of ten, twelve, or a greater number of strings, according to the importance of the affair in agitation, or the dignity of the person to whom it is presented. On more trifling occasions, strings of beads are presented by the chiefs to each other, and frequently worn by them about their necks, as a valuable ornament.[12]

Wampum, as a monetary medium, was introduced into the Plymouth Colony by the Dutch in 1627.[13] The schedule of value published the following year indicated that six beads of white wampum would pass for one English penny, three beads of black also for a penny, while "one fathom of this their stringed money is worth five shillings."[14] A notation of October 7, 1640 stated, "The want of coin enhances the rate of wampum. 'It is ordered, that white wampompeage shall passe at four a penny and blew at two a penny and not above 12d. at a time except the receiver desire more'."[15] "Wampum became a universal currency, exchangeable for merchantise, for labor, [and] for taxes" in New England, New Jersey, Pennsylvania and in New York by the Dutch, who had no other effective small change medium.[16] It was even inventoried in the estates of the deceased and passed on to their heirs.[17]

Wampum achieved and maintained its status as a coveted decoration and desirable currency since it was a highly labor-intensive article whose production costs could easily be translated

[12] Carver, *Travels*, pp. 207-8.
[13] Weeden, *New England*, p. 38.
[14] Felt, *Massachusetts*, pp. 12-13.
[15] Felt, *Massachusetts*, p. 24; Crosby, *Early Coins*, pp. 26-29.
[16] Weeden, *New England*, p. 41.
[17] Adler, *Money Units*, p. 167.

into other measures of value such as beaver pelts. For ages, the Indians had become very familiar with the amount of work involved in hunting and trapping and so these energies could be directly compared to the time requirements and skills necessary to craft sea shells into wampum. Thus a parity was established over the years between wampum and other local items of value.[18] The value of the wampum was maintained until counterfeit material appeared which was no longer fabricated by the ancient hand-made process; stone, bone, glass, mussel shells, horn, and wood were substituted for the traditional colored shells. The last record of wampum circulating as money was from New York in 1701.[19]

BARTER AND COMMODITY MONIES

The use of commodities as money was a practice common in the ancient world as well as in Elizabethan England whence the colonists had emigrated and so the introduction of this currency into the New World is not unexpected.[20] The simplest use of commodities in commerce would be in the nature of "barter," or trading agricultural products, staples or other necessities among two or more individuals. Hard money was not necessary within a rural subsistence economy. As the exchange of these goods became more complicated, involved parties "kept running accounts of the money value of the goods traded—in terms of money of account" through a system described as "bookkeeping barter." No money ever needed to change hands and the sales contract could even be expanded to accommodate a third party in a "triangular transfer of goods."[21] This account book procedure not only included bartered goods but also services, where physical work was also exchanged, "changing works" in common parlance, for other goods and services particularly within rural areas where cash was less frequently seen and less vital since people lived off the land.[22] Commodities were officially designated by colonial legislatures as legal tender for private debts and taxes according to an established price schedule. Thus, "commodity money" or "country pay," as it was also known, came into being as another system to compensate for the shortage of circulating coins.

Items which were legitimized at specific values as money included tobacco,[23] liquor, gunpowder, shot, furs, livestock, lumber, fish, and grain. Problems were encountered with commodity monies when non-marketable, inferior grade merchandise was misrepresented as high quality and passed as "money," while better goods were diverted into the export market where they brought hard coin, foreign credit, or imported products in exchange.[24] In one effort to control the quality of goods delivered as money, the Massachusetts General Court issued an order in 1658 that no man should attempt to pay his taxes in "lank cattle."[25] Tobacco, which was made the official currency of Virginia in 1619, was widely exported to England and Europe where its great demand created a favorable trade balance for the tobacco-producing colonies.[26] "Staple commodities formed the normal medium of exchange. Even when coined money was plentiful, it [coined money] was frequently used for external rather than internal payments."[27] Commodity monies in Massachusetts ceased for a time after 1690 following the introduction of paper currency,[28] but the system was resumed during the hard times of 1727 when rates were again published as to the value at which goods would be received for taxes.[29]

[18] Fiske, *Dutch and Quaker*, pp. 152-53.
[19] Bullock, *Essays*, pp. 8-9; Del Mar, *History*, pp. 86-90.
[20] Felt, *Massachusetts*, pp. 8-11, 13, 14.
[21] Baxter, *Hancock*, chap. 2.
[22] Larkin, *Account Book*, pp. 8-9.
[23] Williamson, *CNL 1986*, pp. 931-34.
[24] Nettels, *Money Supply*, pp. 208-28.
[25] Felt, *Massachusetts*, p. 38; Sumner, *American Currency*, p. 11.
[26] Massey, *Studies*, p. 17; Williamson, *CNL 1986*, pp. 931-34.
[27] Chalmers, *British Colonies*, p. 5.
[28] Sumner, *American Currency*, p. 15.
[29] Felt, *Massachusetts*, pp. 82-83.

TABLE 2

Scheduled Values of Commodity Monies as Established by the Massachusetts General Court in 1727
(From Felt, *Massachusetts*, pp. 82-83)

Item	£	s.	d.	*Measure*
Good merchantable beef	3			a barrel
Good merchantable pork	5	10		''
Winter wheat		8		a bushel
Summer wheat		7		''
Barley		6		''
Rye		6		''
Indian corn		4		''
Oats		2	6	''
Peas clear of bugs			9	''
Flax		1	4	a pound
Hemp			9	''
Bees' wax		2	6	''
Sweet firkin butter			12	''
Dry hides			6	''
Tanned leather		12		''
Merchantable dry cod-fish	1	10		a quintal
Mackerel	1	10		a barrel
Oil	2	10		''
Whale bone, six feet long and upwards		3	6	a pound
Bayberry wax		1	4	''
Turpentine full bound		13		a Cwt.
Merchantable bar iron		48		''
Cast iron pots and kettles		48		''
Well cured tobacco			4	a pound
Good tried tallow			8	''

Baxter, in his description of the business practices of Thomas Hancock imagines the following scenario as typical of the times:

> We can guess that the arrival of "country pay" must have put a severe test on a creditor's resourcefulness; on occasion, he might open his door to find a farmer there with rye, corn, wheat, poultry, and a couple of hogs, all of which had to be valued and disposed of as quickly as possible. A number of fates might befall such remittances. Presumedly they were sometimes eaten without further ado by Thomas and his wife. Often they were handed over to other Bostonians in payment for purchases made locally. But quite frequently they were exported to Newfoundland or the West Indies.... He thus looked upon the meat and fish, not as things to eat or sell, but as another kind of money.... Most of the staple commodities found in New England (pickled pork, corn, molasses, and so on) would serve as commodity money, since they were durable and had well-established markets.[30]

A further sophistication in the use of commodities as legal tender was the development of commodity notes called "storehouse notes" issued as receipts or in reality certificates of inspection when goods, particularly tobacco, were deposited in official government warehouses.[31]

[30] Baxter, *Hancock*, pp. 22-23.

[31] Massey, *Studies*, p. 20; McCusker, *Studies*, pp. 95-97; Ernst, *Money and Politics*, p. 21; and Hoober, *Num 1953*, pp. 1147, 1149.

Sumner, writing in 1874, was quite disparaging of commodity money or barter currency, as he called it, suggesting that its presence drove hard money out of circulation.[32] "The more barter currency was used because money [hard coin] was scarce, the scarcer money became! Prices rose to fit the worst form of payment which the seller might expect."[33] Even if barter currency were "inferior in status to specie" as Sumner wrote, and despite its acknowledged shortcomings, such as inconsistent quality and the requirement to provide storage space for bulky and perishable items, it was nonetheless a medium which was relatively stable in value and fulfilled currency needs in one form or another throughout the colonial period.[34] There were instances where commodity monies were more favorably received than certain colonial paper currencies, particularly those of Rhode Island.[35]

In his analysis of the business records of Thomas Hancock, Baxter summarizes his findings by stating...

> that the New Englanders, deprived alike of cash and satisfactory bank notes, ingeniously filled the gap by devising home-made means of exchange. They had no money; so they built up a barter system based on debits and credits. They had little precious metal; so they backed their notes with beef and pork. They had no banks; so every bookkeeper became a banker.
>
> Crude barter is an appallingly clumsy method of carrying on business. If goods had been exchanged only for goods, trade would have slowed down almost to a standstill. But when the New Englanders paid for goods with assignable titles to other goods (relying on money units for reckoning only), the situation improved immeasurably; as a result of this new lubricant, the machinery of commerce could run at a reasonable speed.[36]

The simultaneous circulation of commodity monies and hard coin necessitated the development of some equivalency rating among the several media and accordingly four different types of payment and price structures evolved.[37] The first monetary system to be described was "money" which was, of course, hard coin and wampum which was used for small change. The second called "pay" or "country pay" was actually the commodity monies legalized by the colonial legislatures for payment of taxes according to a specific schedule. Confusion is drawn into the discussion with the addition of the third interaction known by "Pay as money." This appeared to be commodity money, or "pay," at a one-third discount from the established rate. The relationship between "pay as money" and "pay" was at times unclear, but Weiss suggests that this ambiguity might have occurred when the official schedule for commodities differed from the actual market price.[38] The final system for the purchase of goods was

[32] When there are two currencies in circulation with equal debt paying power, but unequal intrinsic value, the better currency tends to be hoarded, or bad money drives good money out of circulation. This statement (known as Gresham's Law, after Thomas Gresham, [1519-1579], a financial advisor to Queen Elizabeth) is being applied in this instance to commodity money and specie. While this economic principle was attributed to Gresham by Macleod in 1892, it was first noted by Aristophanes (Feavearyear, *Pound Sterling*, p. 78n). "Under the mediaeval European currency system, bad money was allowed to buy up good money (Shaw, *Monetary History*, p. vi.)."

[33] Sumner, *American Currency*, p. 5.

[34] Weiss, *Colonial Standard*, pp. 580-85.

[35] Baxter, *Hancock*, pp. 23-24.

[36] Baxter, *Hancock*, p. 34.

[37] Knight, *Journal*, p. 42, as quoted in Weiss, *Colonial Standard*, p. 584; Crosby, *Early Coins*, p. 114; Felt, *Massachusetts*, p. 54; Del Mar, *History*, p. 78; Sumner, *American Currency*, pp. 15-16; *Essex Inst. Hist. Colls.*, vol. 1, p. 127.

[38] Weiss, *Colonial Standard*, p. 584.

aptly called "trusting," or a credit arrangement. Analysis of the price structure in New England in 1693 suggests a ratio of 1:1.33:2 between "money," "pay as money," and "pay." The distinction between "pay" and "money" was obvious, and hard coin, i.e. "money," was always received preferentially. In Massachusetts the taxpayer was entitled to a one-third discount when tax bills were settled in coin rather than "pay,"[39] while in Connecticut the reduction for specie payment could be as high as one-half.[40]

The desirability of coin over commodities was apparent since "pay" required storage and transportation, and was susceptible to spoilage and deterioration. Despite these problems, "pay," or commodity monies maintained relative stability over the years. As the eighteenth century progressed, commodity monies became less necessary and their popularity dwindled.

In a similar manner, the Dutch colonists regularly supplemented their hard currency with wampum, as a substitute for money, and with beaver pelts as a commodity money. The wampum and beaver "money" depreciated substantially over the years and by 1658 the quotation for the equivalent values of these three "currencies" was in the ratio of 10 guilders in silver coin equal to 15 guilders of beaver equal to 21 guilders of wampum.[41]

The "Crying Up" of Money

The Spanish American eight reales remained the coinage standard of reference from the earliest American settlements. During the first years, this standard was at par between America and England, passing at 4s. 6d.[42] Parity did not exist for long, since economic hard times soon hit the colonies, triggering a series of events which seriously affected the local economy and currency. By 1640 the population of the Plymouth Colony was about 2,500. Between 1630 and 1640 the population of the neighboring Massachusetts Bay Colony had grown to 22,000 persons representing about 4,000 families.[43] At the same time, the combined settlers in Virginia and the West Indies approached 52,000.[44] During these years, hard money had been plentiful, having been transported to America by the emigrating colonists apparently in spite of the specie exportation ban. Hard money did not remain in circulation long since it was soon returned to England to purchase needed imports. In post-1640 New England, there was a cessation of Puritan migration since there was no longer the motive for them to leave their homeland after the establishment of the Commonwealth under Cromwell. Of subsequent immigrants, more returned to England than remained in America since they found a very poor economic climate and low prosperity.[45] The situation was aggravated by a 1643 crop failure in New England during which prices fell, not to normalize again for five years.[46]

Felt quoted a contemporary description of this first American depression in New England.

> The scarcity of money made a great change in all commerce. Merchants would sell no ware, but for money. Men could not pay their debts, though they had enough. Prices of land and cattle fell soon to one half and less, yea to a third, and after to one fourth part.[47]

[39] Sumner, *Yale Review 1898*, p. 259.
[40] Weiss, *Colonial Standard*, p. 584.
[41] McCusker, *Money and Exchange*, p. 157.
[42] McCusker, *Money and Exchange*, p. 132.
[43] Gottfried, *NEQ 1936*, p. 656; Sumner, *American Currency*, p. 9.
[44] Nettels, *Money Supply*, p. 134.
[45] Sumner, *American Currency*, p. 9.
[46] Sumner, *American Currency*, pp. 9-10; Gottfried, *NEQ 1936*, p. 656.
[47] Felt, *Massachusetts*, p. 23, where Felt quoted Elder Winthrop.

Although this depression placed a significant burden on Massachusetts, one benefit accrued since the lack of money to buy imports from England obliged the colony to become more self-sufficient and hence a local textile industry was born. Although the product was crude and did not replace fine English cloth, it did transform the colony "from an agricultural to a diversified economy."[48] Such progress was of concern to English merchants.

Responses to the economic crisis in Massachusetts have already been noted when the General Court increased the rate of wampum by one-third in relationship to the money of account on October 7, 1640.[49] Commodity money became more prevalent and acts were passed to benefit debtors.[50]

A more successful expedient to increase the supply of hard coin was "the raising of the monies" by the Massachusetts General Court who increased the value of the monetary standard eight reales from a par of 4s. 6d. to 4s. 8d. and later, on September 8, 1642, to 5s.[51] The "crying-up of money," as it is also known, is merely currency overvaluation, a procedure commonly practiced in Europe. The theory is based on the premise that if coin is more highly valued in one country than another, there will be a natural flow of specie to that state where money has greater value and purchasing power, assuming that prices will not rise rapidly to reach a new equilibrium with the overvalued coin. "For say they, If we do observe these States which do soonest and most raise their Money, we shall find that they do most abound with Money; and that Trader and Manufacturer do most flourish there."[52] This is actually a currency devaluation of the money of account by an overvaluation of silver. As other colonies followed Massachusetts by local overvaluation of silver in terms of regional monies of account, the advantage of the inflated value was lost, and another spiral of overvaluation was triggered. The process of "crying up of money" is illustrated in Table 6 which shows the competitive increase in the rate for the eight reales among the colonies until the early 1700s, at which time all the possible advantage had been gained with this scheme for increasing the pool of local hard currency.

There is an interesting account of the "crying up of money" as it occurred in Virginia. As early as 1631 that colony had considered "raising" the value of coin but records are too fragmentary to ascertain the outcome of that early petition.[53] Definite action was taken in 1645, when the Spanish American eight reales was set at six shillings in local money of account. Ten years later the rate was reduced to five shillings because extensive clipping of Spanish silver coins had reduced the standard eight reales from 420 grains (17.5 dwt) to an average of 384 grains (16 dwt) for circulating specimens. This lowered value for specie in Virginia "tempted People to export the Coin to other Plantations, where it went for more than it did in Virginia."[54] Governor Culpeper rejected a 1679 proposal to "raise" the value of the Virginia currency until he managed to buy up all the lightweight silver he could at five shillings. Then by his own proclamation he "raised" its value to six shillings and thereby profited nicely from his personal speculation and subsequent manipulation of the exchange rates. However, the Governor's advantage was short-lived when he was required to receive his own stipend in inflated silver, at which point he reissued the proclamation restoring the five shilling rate.[55]

[48] Gottfried, *NEQ 1936*, pp. 665-66, 670, 678.
[49] Felt, *Massachusetts*, pp. 12-13, 24.
[50] Gottfried, *NEQ 1936*, pp. 657-59; Felt, *Massachusetts*, pp. 24-30; *Essex Inst. Hist. Colls.*, vol. 1, p. 126, 126n.
[51] Chalmers, *British Colonies*, p. 6; McCusker, *Money and Exchange*, pp 118, 118n, 132.
[52] Chalmers, *British Colonies*, p. 7, quotes Vaughn, *Discourse*.
[53] McCusker, *Money and Exchange*, p. 205.
[54] Crosby, *Early Coins*, pp. 22-24, quote p. 22.
[55] Hoober, *Num 1953*, p. 1145.

While some historians state that colonial legislatures prescribed overvaluation of silver to "attract" more specie into their jurisdiction, Ernst advances the theory that overvaluation or the "crying up of monies" was in fact a measure to control "the external drain of coin which resulted because of the chronically adverse balance of payments in the trade between the colonies and the mother country whenever the prices of colonial exports were depressed or English credits for colonial economic development fell short of the expanding needs in America."[56]

In addition to the local "crying-up of money," another measure enacted to assist in keeping hard coin within the colonies was the prohibition against the export of specie, an action identical to that taken in England. A law was passed in Massachusetts on May 12, 1654, which attempted to keep Massachusetts silver coins within the colony by imposing "forfeiture of the transgressor's whole estate" for anyone convicted of carrying over 20 Massachusetts Bay shillings out of the province.[57] A "searcher for money" was appointed for each port of entry. Other colonies shared the concern about the export of hard money from their borders. "An Act for the Advancement of Coin," enacted in Maryland on November 19, 1686, contained the provision that "persons exporting such Coins so advanced, to forfeit the same, Half to his Lordship, and Half to the Informer."[58] Similarly, there was a ban imposed by the New York Legislature on September 24, 1709, restricting the exportation of all foreign coin or bullion, both silver and gold, "under Penalty of forfeiting Double the Value of all Such."[59]

The Proclamation of 1704

The silver currency of British North America was in disorder by the end of the seventeenth century. Most of the silver was lightweight from severe clipping and an intact coin was a rarity. Spanish silver generally entered British colonial circulation via Jamaica, the military, naval, and piracy center during the troubled years of the seventeenth century, and from there hard coin was dispersed through the remainder of the West Indian and mainland colonies. In Jamaica, the Spanish real was roughly equivalent to the sixpence and hence the name "Spanish sixpence."[60] This amounted to a devaluation of the eight reales from 4s. 6d. to 4s. in that colony. There developed a rampant practice of clipping the eight reales down to an actual sterling value of 4s. and through this practice, the commerce of British North America became encumbered with lightweight coins. As commented by Chalmers, "... clipping by the subject was the counterpart of the debasement of coins by the sovereign."[61] To prevent economic loss, the various colonies stipulated that Spanish eight reales pass by weight and schedules of values were published. Not only was colonial commerce disturbed by light coins of varying weight, but the already mutilated money was also "cried up" by the competitive overvaluation of Spanish silver in terms of sterling.

This irregularity and inconvenience within the colonial currency system escaped official attention until it became the subject of concern presented to the Board of Trade in 1700.[62] At

[56] Ernst, *Money and Politics*, p. 14.

[57] Felt, *Massachusetts*, pp. 35-36; Hull, *Diaries*, p. 290. Crosby notes that while the May 12th proposal was defeated, it was later enacted on August 22, 1654, and reconfirmed both in 1669 and 1697 (*Early Coins*, pp. 104-5).

[58] Crosby, *Early Coins*, p. 132.

[59] Solomon, *Studies*, p. 30.

[60] Chalmers, *British Colonies*, p. 6.

[61] Chalmers, *British Colonies*, p. 8.

[62] Chalmers, *British Colonies*, pp. 10-13. See also McCusker, *Money and Exchange*, for a complete listing of exchange rates between all principal commercial centers from 1600 to 1775.

that time the following values for the unclipped eight reales were quoted in the respective colonial monies of account, although the value remained stable in England at 4s. 6d.:

Maryland 4s. 6d.
Virginia 4s. 6d.
Bahamas 5s.
Carolinas 5s.
New England 6s. 6d.
New York 6s. 6d.
Pennsylvania 7s.

This list notes that the Carolinas were not separated into North and South until 1712. From 1676 until 1702, New Jersey was split with East New Jersey economically tied to New York, while West New Jersey was identified with Pennsylvania. When the colony united in 1702, it officially adopted the monetary policies of New York although foreign currency in West New Jersey was exchanged at the Pennsylvania rate. Following 1750, all New Jersey currency shared a par with Pennsylvania.[63] Maryland and Virginia were in a unfavorable position since their hard money drained into Pennsylvania where the value of specie was significantly enhanced.[64]

Until 1704, the management of colonial currency had been pretty well left to the colonies themselves with the resultant complexity in exchange rates. An attempt was made to resolve these inconveniences by creating a single monetary standard for the colonies through the Royal Proclamation of 1704 (see Table 3). Since this regulation was initiated by the English Board of Trade the motive must be suspect. Rather than inspired by altruism toward the colonists, the authors were much more concerned that there be a stable currency to pay the English merchants. The document listed the comparative values of the most common current world silver coins based on an assay by Sir Isaac Newton, director of the Royal Mint.[65] This Proclamation dictated that the full weight Spanish American eight reales would pass at 6s. in all the colonies, the Massachusetts rate of 1697, but in no case at a value one-third greater than its sterling rate of 4s. 6d., effectively establishing an exchange rate of 133.33:100, colonial money of account to sterling. Fractional and other coins would pass proportionally to their intrinsic silver content and were not tabulated separately. The 133.33:100 ratio directed by the Proclamation of 1704 was not a new concept, having been enacted by France for its Canadian settlements in the seventeenth century.[66]

Only Barbados[67] and Maryland complied with the Proclamation, while the other colonies virtually ignored it. Massachusetts openly defied the order and refused to appropriate money for the support of local government which did not conform to the prevaling rate of 155.55:100.[68] This insubordination prompted the Crown to reissue the provisions of the Proclamation as an Act of Parliament in 1707 with the force of law.[69] Resistance to this legislation continued since the overvaluation of hard currency provided cheaper money for payment of debts and maintained a price level which would be reduced if the currency were standardized at a lower rate. The North feared that a reduction in the inflation rate for silver coin would give the South a competitive edge in their quest for hard money.[70]

[63] McCusker, *Money and Exchange*, pp. 168, 171; Nettels, *Money Supply*, p. 241n.

[64] Hoober, *Num 1953*, p. 1146.

[65] Chalmers, *British Colonies*, pp. 14-15; Nettels, *Money Supply*, pp. 231-48; McCusker, *Money and Exchange*, p. 126; Ruding, *Annals*, pp. 61-63.

[66] Chalmers, *British Colonies*, p. 14.

[67] Adler, *Money Units*, p. 170.

[68] Nettels, *Money Supply*, p. 243n.

[69] Nettels, *Money Supply*, p. 248; Chalmers, *British Colonies*, pp. 414-15.

[70] Nettels, *Money Supply*, pp. 233, 249.

TABLE 3

Coin Values as Documented in the Proclamation of 1704
Calculated at 5s. 2d. per Troy Ounce, Sterling
(Chalmers, *British Colonies*, pp. 67, 391, 414-15)

Current World Coins of 1704	*Weight in grains*	*Sterling Value in pence*
Sevill pieces of eight,[a] *old plate*[b]	420	54
Sevill pieces of eight, *new plate*[c]	336	43.25
Mexico pieces of eight	420	54
Pillar pieces of eight	420	54.75
Peru pieces of eight, *old plate*	420	53[d]
Cross dollars[e]	432	52.75
Ducatoons of Flanders[f]	501	66
Ecus of France, Silver Lewis	420	54
Crusadoes of Portugal[g]	268	34.25
Three Gilder Pieces of Holland[h]	487	62.25
Old Rix dollars of the Empire[i]	442	54

[a] The distinction between the four types of eight reales (pieces-of-eight) is not always precise or uniformly clear: *Sevill* [*Seville*] coins are from Spanish mainland mints; *Mexico pieces* are probably those New World coins without pillars on the design regardless of the actual mint of origin; *Pillar pieces* refer to all round coins struck in America with a pillar design but obviously not the machine-made Pillar dollars with the milled, protective edge which did not appear until 1732; *Peru*, or *Peruvians* refers to cobs from any mint, and not necessarily from that viceroyalty.

[b] *Old plate* refers to the 1497 to 1728 standard of 423.9 grains at .9305 fineness.

[c] *New plate* refers to a 20% reduction in value of the European Spanish real whereby Spanish American eight reales circulated in Spain at ten *new reales* according to the debasement of Philip IV of December 23, 1642 and of Charles II of October 14, 1686.

[d] Written in the Proclamation as 4s. 5d. or "thereabouts."

[e] Refers to the Patagon of the Spanish Netherlands with crossed cudgels on obverse design.

[f] Flanders was part of the Spanish Netherlands (modern Belgium).

[g] The crusado (cruzado) was named for the cross on the reverse design commemorating the struggle between the crusaders and the Muslims in Africa.

[h] These were three guilder pieces of 60 stuivers and not silver riders of 63 stuivers, also called *ducatoons*.

[i] *The Empire* refers to the German States. In his 1702 assay report, Newton examined thirteen such *rix dollars* and determined an average weight of 441.96 ± 2.53 grains and a sterling value of 54.65 ± 0.57d.

Fig. 4: Seventeenth Century world silver coins typical of those enumerated in the Proclamation of 1704 (Table 3).

(a) Spain: 1683 eight reales of Charles II, old plate, Segovia mint (408.6 grains).

(b) Spain: 1687 eight reales of Charles II, new plate, Segovia mint (327.7 grains).

(c) Mexico: 1655 eight reales of Philip IV.

(d) Mexico: eight reales of Charles II (1665-1700). This style of rough, irregular cob was probably what was called a "Peruvian," or "Peru piece of eight" without regard to the mint of origin.

(e) Brabant: 1625 "cross dollar" or patagon of Philip IV, Brussels mint. (ANS/HSA)

(f) Flanders: 1670 ducatoon of Charles II. (ANS/HSA)

(g) France: 1643 écu (silver Lewis) of Louis XIII, Paris mint.

(h) Portugal: 1690 cruzado of Peter II, Porto mint.

(i) United Provinces of the Netherlands: 1694 three guilders, Zeeland mint. (Joseph Lasser Collection)

(j) Lübeck: 1628 taler, typical "old rix dollar of the Empire."

Sumner called attention to some inconsistencies in the computations in the Proclamation of 1704 and further added that very few coins existed with these stated weights because of loose mint standards and the widespread practice of clipping.[71] Since coins passed according to weight, a reduction in value for lighter pieces could be calculated in local monies of account.

The complex history of the early money of the British North American colonies, or the currency prior to 1704, consisted of indigenous Indian wampum, commodity monies and their various ramifications and refinements, clipped, underweight and overvalued foreign coins, and Massachusetts silver. Chalmers summarized:

> the currency history of the period... is marked (a) by the rise of "denominational currency" systems as the result of competitive over-valuation of Spanish silver in terms of sterling, and (b) by the final predominance of the *clipped* piece of eight. But it was not till the close of this period that coin superseded commodities even in prosperous colonies; in the more backward settlements barter continued to dominate the currency.[72]

[71] Sumner, *Spanish Dollar*, pp. 614-15; and Sumner, *Yale Review 1898*, pp. 405-10. Sumner calculated that an eight reales of 17.5 dwt of sterling standard (.925 fine), should pass for 4s. 6d. 1f., not 4s. 6d., at the mint price for silver of 5s. 2d. per ounce.

[72] Chalmers, *British Colonies*, p. 15; McCusker, *Money and Exchange*, pp. 126, 257; Nettels, *Money Supply*, p. 249.

After the Proclamation of 1704 was enacted as law in 1707, there was no longer any advantage to be gained from the progressive overvaluation of silver. Following this Parliamentary restriction on silver coin, Bermuda[73] and the West Indies resorted to a gold standard since Spanish gold was so readily available and the Proclamation of 1704 carried no restrictions regarding gold. On the mainland, however, the colonies turned to paper money as the next and final expedient to increase currency supplies.[74]

FOREIGN COIN IN THE COLONIES

Up to this point there has only been passing reference to the silver and gold money of the period. It is important in our study to determine as accurately as possible the composition of the circulating currency in British North America. The most reliable evidence as to the actual coins which passed from hand to hand in commerce or were shipped abroad to settle large transactions would be from the examination of undisturbed hoards or access to contemporary inventories. The evidence from such tabulations would be "frozen in time," so to speak, and much more representative of the current monetary medium than data derived from coin accumulations whose origins are uncertain.

One early hoard indicates that English gold and silver, although scarce, were present in the colonies, either brought over by immigrants or otherwise smuggled out of the country. This is apparent from a cache of coins uncovered in 1855 at Richmond's Island, a coastal fishing settlement near Portland, Maine. This particular hoard contained some 50 English gold and silver coins dated no later than 1642, an indication of when the coins were hidden.[75]

Fig. 5: An old photograph of surviving specimens from the Castine Hoard.

An analysis of the Castine Deposit provides only limited clues as to the types of coins current in 1704, the date when this hoard was thought to have been hidden by the French near Castine, Maine, who were fleeing the English.[76] Unfortunately, only a fraction of this hoard was ever

[73] Pridmore, *Commonwealth*, p. 18.
[74] Chalmers, *British Colonies*, p. 10.
[75] Willis, *Portland*.
[76] Noe, *Castine Deposit*; Breen, *Num 1952*, pp. 7-9; Williamson, *Castine*.

inventoried, and then after the majority of the coins had been dispersed. The number of coins from the cache is uncertain with the count ranging from 400 to 2,000. As might be expected, French coins were the most numerous, Spanish American cobs the next most common, followed by Belgic and Portuguese issues. A large number of Pine Tree shillings and sixpence was recorded, perhaps as many as 75 of each. Only two English coins, shillings, were encountered in the whole lot. Other countries represented in the find were United Provinces of the Netherlands (lion dollars), Spain, and Brunswick-Luneberg. While interesting, this coin census cannot be considered representative of the British territories but is biased toward the French possessions.

A cross section of money current in New York is now available from the inventory of coins recently recovered from the wreck of the *H.M.S. Feversham* which sunk in a storm off Nova Scotia in 1711.[77] This ship withdrew £569 12s. 5d., sterling, from the New York Victualling Office of the British Treasury to outfit the fleet for an assault against Quebec City in an attempt to dislodge the French from Canada. Six hundred and thirty-six specimens have been reclaimed from the ocean amounting to £33 13s., which is considered the unspent sum remaining after the ship was provisioned. A census of the salvaged currency includes only 8 English coins, 22 Dutch lion dollars or their fractional parts, 5 Spanish pieces, 504 coins from Spanish American mints, and 92 examples of Massachusetts silver. The recovery gives only a qualitative notion of the content of the original allotment since the actual distribution of the coin varieties received by the purser prior to disbursement is unrecorded. In this sample, small denominational issues were well represented.

On the contrary, an inventory of £1626 10s. 11d. in hard coin conducted by Thomas Hancock in 1762 revealed that the total value was 80% in large Portuguese gold coins and 18% in English guineas.[78] The remainder was in 15 other smaller gold coins and 33 sundry pieces, most being cut Spanish silver. A single copper halfpenny was found. Such large denominational sums were better suited for overseas remittances rather than for the daily market place.

Much information about the current world coinage of the period is revealed from assays conducted at the Tower Mint by Sir Isaac Newton in 1702 and 1717, and that of the Royal Mint in 1740 (see Appendix 3).[79] It was the analysis of world currencies by Newton in 1702 which provided the basis for the monetary reform as promulgated in the Proclamation of 1704. His 1702 assays tabulated the weight, fineness, and value in sterling currency of some 47 silver and 21 gold major specie coins. Information from this and other sources is listed in Tables 5, 7, 8, and 9 which describe world silver and gold coins, commonly encountered in colonial commerce. Any change from the prescribed alloy should be considered a deliberate manipulation on the part of the mint. Refining techniques for precious metals had been perfected since the Roman days when any variation greater than 1% was significant.[80]

Spanish and Spanish American Silver

Despite the English heritage of the American colonies, the most important and preponderant coin of the period was, of course, the Spanish American eight reales which had become the world's silver standard. This coin, first minted in Mexico City in 1535, eventually appeared from many other mints in Central and South America. The earlier coinages were circular but without a protective edge. Beginning in 1556, the style was changed to the so-called "cob," a crude and irregular coin cut from a bar of silver and imperfectly stamped with a design and designation of value on a planchet usually too small to receive the impression from the entire die. The finished specimen was a most primitive product, not for lack of an existing technology to mint more attractive coins, but because the primary purpose of the cob was to provide a convenient means

[77] *Feversham*; Lasser, *Num 1989*.
[78] Baxter, *Hancock*, p. 15.
[79] Shaw, *Monetary History*, pp. 133-79.
[80] Morrisson, *ANSMN 32*, pp. 188-89.

Fig. 6:
(a) Mexico: 1766 "pillar" eight reales, or "Spanish milled dollar" of Charles III. This famous design, minted from 1732 to 1772, was also issued in fractional denominations of four, two, one, and half reales.

(b) Mexico: 1753 fractional half real, medio, half bit, or picayune of Ferdinand VI.

(c) Mexico: 1773 "portrait" eight reales of Charles III, the new motif adopted after 1772.

for shipping bullion to the melting pots of Spain rather than to furnish money for general circulation. Although cobs were minted in certain locations up through 1773, the famous pillar dollar, or Spanish milled dollar of eight reales, and its fractional parts, were introduced in 1732. This series was replaced in 1772 by portrait coins bearing the bust of the reigning monarch.[81]

For the period 1497 until 1728 the eight reales was authorized at all mints to weigh 423.9 grains at .9305 fine. There were local exceptions to this provision made in 1642 and 1686 which were applicable to Spain only. According to assays conducted at the Tower Mint in 1626, eight reales weighed 420 grains (17.5 dwt) and were .9166 fine with a pure silver content of 385 grains. The sterling equivalent (i.e. English currency value calculated at 62d. per troy ounce for the .925 fine standard) in this circumstance was 53.76d., a value which held quite constant as recorded by other assays through the first quarter of the next century. In 1728, the weight of the eight reales was further reduced to 417.6 grains and the fineness lowered to .9166. For a coin adhering to this standard, the value in English currency was essentially unchanged at 53.45d. The eight reales was reduced for the last time in 1772, to .90277 fineness, with a sterling value of 52.64d.[82] For the entire 351 year period from 1497 until 1848, Spanish eight reales minted according to authorized standards, depreciated a meager 4.4%, and for those pieces examined by actual assay, the reduction was only 5.9%.[83] This level of constancy is why Spanish American silver was the revered standard for world currency. Calbeto de Grau describes the Spanish American coinage and particularly the eight reales piece "as a principal symbol of the world's monetary economy during almost three centuries."[84] These relationships are recorded in Table 5. This uniform value for the Spanish eight reales was also due in part to the stability of the price of sterling silver throughout the period. From 1601 the Tower Mint price for .925 fine standard per

[81] Burzio, *ANS 1973*, pp. 8-10; Sedwick, *Cobs*, pp. 5, 15.
[82] Chalmers, *British Colonies*, pp. 390-94, 402.
[83] Sumner, *Spanish Dollar*, p. 617.
[84] Calbeto de Grau, *Compendio*, vol. 1, p. 8.

troy ounce remained at 62d. and was the rate used by Newton during his tenure of office. On the open market where silver varied 1.5d. to 3d. above the Mint price,[85] the price of sterling averaged 64.8d. during the first half of the eighteenth century, and from that point to the America Revolution advanced only by an additional 1.1d.[86]

Fig. 7:
(a) Potosí: 1645 eight reales of Philip IV with the Hapsburg coat of arms, the style minted prior to discovery of the "debasement."

(b) Potosí: 1660 eight reales of Philip IV, with the "crowned columns of Hercules." A recoinage of the debased Potosí silver was ordered in 1651; the new coins were struck with this different design as a guarantee that all currency with this emblem had the proper silver content (ANS/HSA).

Spanish American silver was not always held in high esteem as evidenced by an uncommon event during the reign of Philip IV when there "occurred a scandalous falsification in the fineness of silver monies coined in our Peruvian mints."[87] Under the framework of the Spanish colonial system, the mint was essentially a proprietary enterprise purchased by the mintmaster for life and operated under royal license. A fraudulent scheme of coinage debasement, which had been operating for eight years, was uncovered in 1648 involving a silver merchant and an assayer at the Potosí mint who were apprehended and two years later condemned to death.[88] Silver coins from that mint depreciated up to 50% in 1649. An October 1650 decree ordered that all Potosí cobs either be turned in for melting or be counterstamped as an indication of their officially devalued status.[89] Another royal decree of February 17, 1651, ordered a recoinage of the depreciated currency and a change in design to distinguish new issues from the mint of proper weight and standard from the inferior money of the previous decade. Therefore, in 1652 the familiar insignia of the Hapsburg coat of arms was replaced by the "crowned columns of Hercules floating over the waves of the sea." This new emblem on an eight reales became a guarantee that such coins bearing it had returned to the authorized standard. Adulteration of the Peruvian coinage almost caused the demonetization of Potosí silver in England and its colonies during the last half of the seventeenth century. An "exact assay" of "base Peru-pieces" performed in Ireland in 1652 revealed an almost 37% deficiency from the standard.[90] By the end of the century, eight reales examined at the English mint had returned to an English currency equivalence of 53.86d. and there was renewed faith in the standard.

85 Feavearyear, *Pound Sterling*, pp. 151, 158, 435.
86 McCusker, *Money and Exchange*, pp. 13-17.
87 Chalmers, *British Colonies*, p. 391.
88 Calbeto de Grau, *Compendio*, vol. 1, p. 288; vol. 2, pp. 580-81; Dasí, *Estudio*, vol. 2, nos. 793, 796, 798, 800, 806, 811, 817, 860, CXL-CLV; Murray, *Num 1988*, p. 1204.
89 Sedwick, *Cobs*, p. 29.
90 Simon, *Essay*, p. 49.

The scarcity of hard money was further complicated by the fact that Spanish American silver arriving in the colonies was severely clipped, sweated, filed, shaved, "whirled, slung," or otherwise reduced from its mint weight of 420 grains or 17.5 dwt.[91] In New England the money of account eight reales was calculated at 15 dwt, in Philadelphia at 12 dwt,[92] while in Virginia, the 16 dwt coin was usual.[93] A full weight coin was a rarity and traded as a commodity rather than used as money. One remedy for receiving coins of varying weight adopted in the Leeward Islands was the use of a sliding scale whereby a "cried up" 17 dwt eight reales passed for 7s., a 15 to 17 dwt coin at 6s. 6d., and any piece below 15 dwt at 6s.[94] A similar system in South Carolina provided values for eight reales weighing from 13 to 17 pennyweight.[95]

Spanish silver eight reales were also cut into fractional pieces to accommodate the need for small change. These eighth parts were called "cut money, sharp change," or "bits" with "two bits" being one-fourth of the Spanish milled dollar, a term which still endures in our language in reference to a quarter of a dollar.[96] A small Spanish American coin of the period, the picayune or half real, was useful as small change both in the colonial and early Federal times. The expression "picayune" was adopted into the English language to denote something of trivial worth. Table 4 lists the common terms for the fractional Spanish silver coins used as small change from colonial times until passage of the Act of February 21, 1857, which demonetized all foreign specie coins. For generations in Pennsylvania, where the real had passed for eleven pence in money of account, the U.S. dime was called a "levy" and a half dime a "fip," a contraction for five pence.[97] In the early Federal period, when the worn real or bit was roughly equivalent to the dime, it was christened a "short-bit" and the picayune became the common name for the half dime.

TABLE 4

Common Terms For Fractional or Cut Spanish Silver Coins Used as Small Change
(See below, p. 157 and n. 64 there)

Spanish Coin	*Four reales, four bits*	*Two reales, two bits*	*One real, one bit*	*Half real, medio, half bit, picayune*
Value of eight reales in local money of account				
at 96d.				
Area: New York, North Carolina				
Local Value	48d.	24d.	12d.	6d.
Local Name	4 shillings	2 shillings	shilling	sixpence
at 90d.				
Area: Maryland, Pennsylvania, Delaware, New Jersey				
Local Value	3s. 9d.	22.5d.	11.25d.	5.6d.
Local Name			eleven pence or levy	fippenny bit, fip, five penny bit or fippence
at 72d.				
Area: New England, Virginia				
Local Value	36d.	1s. 6d.	9d.	4.5d.
Local Name	3 shillings	one and six	ninepence nine penny bit	four pence ha'-penny

91 *Sweating* was a process of removing particles of metal from a coin by abrasion. *Slinging* or *whirling* was a method of obtaining metal from coins by placing them in a canvas bag which was violently "slung" or "whirled" for hours. The bag was then burned and the chips of metal recovered from the ash (Sedwick, *Cobs*, p. 15; Utberg, *Mexico*, p. 35).

92 Sumner, *Spanish Dollar*, p. 614.

93 McCusker, *Money and Exchange*, pp. 205-6, 206n.

94 Chalmers, *British Colonies*, p. 67.

95 Adler, *Money Units*, pp. 160-61.

96 Carothers, *Fractional Money*, p. 27.

97 Carothers, *Fractional Money*, pp. 34-35; see also Adler, *Money Units*, pp. 143-73, and Williamson, *CNL 1986*, pp. 937-939.

Fig. 8:
(a) Spain: 1719 two reales or "cross" pistareen of Philip V, Madrid mint

(b) 1776 "head" pistareen of Charles III, Seville mint.

Another small but important coin of the period was the debased silver pistareen (little piastre) or provincial peseta of two reales which was minted in mainland Spain after 1707.[98] This series was officially .8333 fine, or "new plate," as compared to .9305 for the standard eight reales and its fractional parts. Pistareens and their fractional one-half and one-quarter parts were inscribed with the arms of Castile and León within their familiar cross on the reverse and the Hapsburg crest on the obverse. This motif was responsible for the name, "cross pistareen." In 1772 the fineness was reduced to .8125 and the design changed to include the head of the monarch on the obverse and the Castile and León crest on the reverse, giving rise to the name, "head pistareen." Although intended solely for use in the Iberian peninsula, these two reales coins traveled rapidly across the Atlantic to the British Colonies, including Nova Scotia,[99] Bermuda,[100] and particularly the West Indies where they became an important "colonial currency for more than a century" passing at five to the Spanish milled dollar. The 20% debasement of this Spanish "new plate" currency as compared to the Spanish American silver coins, protected it from the melting pot which was the frequent fate of coins of lesser alloy, including Massachusetts silver. Because of lower intrinsic value, pistareens circulated as a subsidiary coinage while higher quality specie from Spanish America was treated as bullion. Lest there be confusion between these two issues, the pistareen was a debased Spanish two reales valued at five to the Spanish milled dollar whereas the Central or South American two reales passed at one-fourth of the standard eight reales or dollar.

Because of a ready supply of Spanish gold, the West Indies adopted a gold standard following the Proclamation of 1704. Since Spanish American silver was traded more as a commodity than used as money, it was not generally available as a currency. For this reason the debased "new plate" pistareens became important in the West Indian economy since no threat existed that they would be either exported or melted. Hence this humble coin became the small change in an area where it "served for internal and subsidiary circulation under cover of a gold standard."[101] Counterstamped cross and head pistareens are attributed to several West Indian locations.[102]

In 1750, Massachusetts paper currency was redeemed by a quantity of Spanish silver which had arrived from England on the ship *Mermaid* the previous year. The inventory of this shipment contained some debased Spanish "new plate" coins, including pistareens.

[98] Chalmers, *British Colonies*, pp. 15-16, 395, 403; Solomon, *Studies*, pp. 32, 35, 41.
[99] Bell, *Foreign Protestants*, pp. 267, 343.
[100] Pridmore, *Commonwealth*, p. 18.
[101] Chalmers, *British Colonies*, p. 395.
[102] Wood, *AJN 1914*; Duffield, *Num 1919*, pp. 47-64.

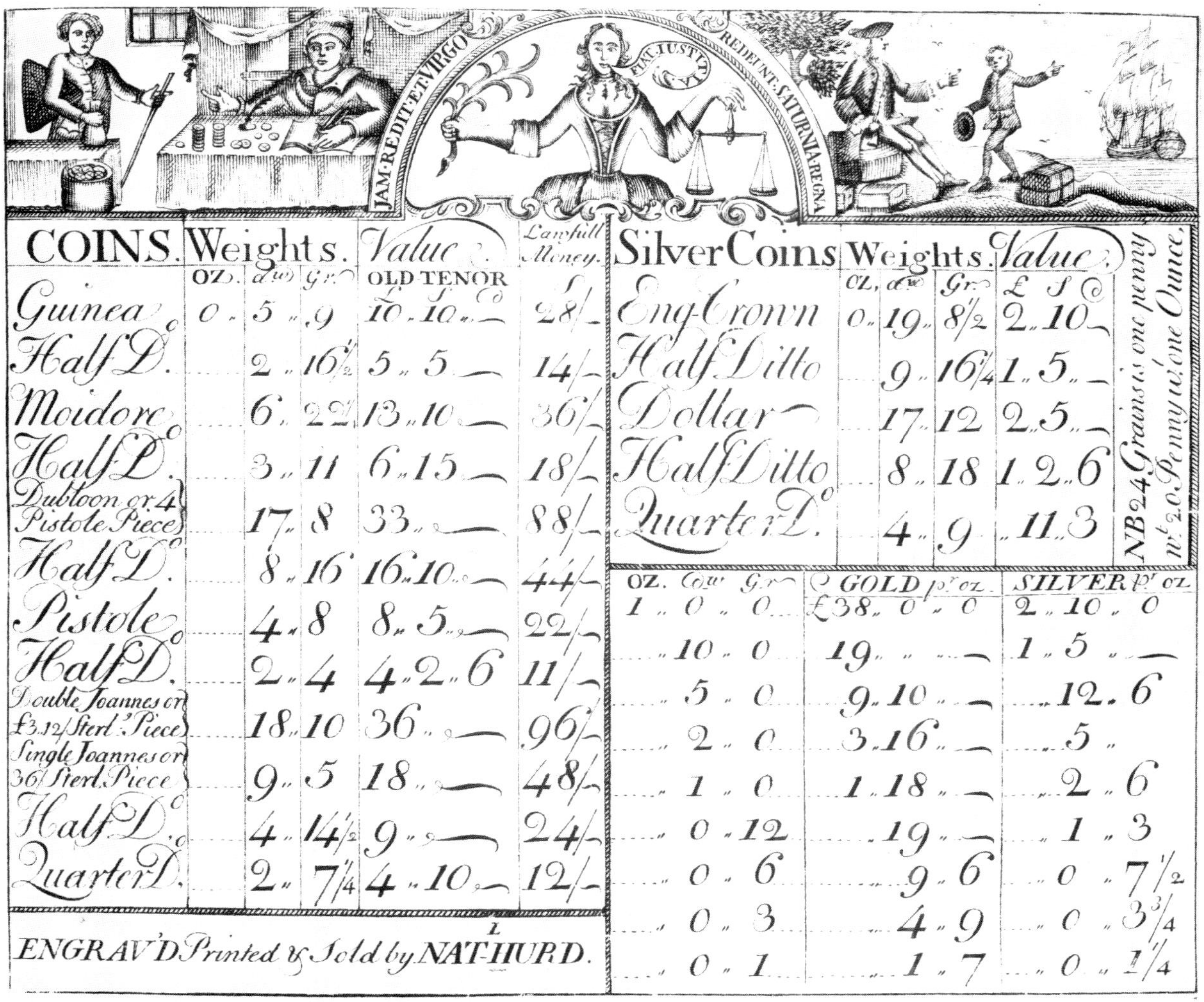

COINS	Weights. oz. dwt. gr.	Value OLD TENOR £ s d	Lawfull Money.
Guinea	0 . 5 . 9	10 . 10 . —	28/-
Half D°	2 . 16½	5 . 5 —	14/-
Moidore	6 . 22	13 . 10 —	36/-
Half D°	3 . 11	6 . 15 —	18/-
Dubloon or 4 Pistole Piece	17 . 8	33 . . —	88/-
Half D°	8 . 16	16 . 10 —	44/-
Pistole	4 . 8	8 . 5 —	22/-
Half D°	2 . 4	4 . 2 . 6	11/-
Double Joannes or £3.12/ Sterl. Piece	18 . 10	36 . . —	96/-
Single Joannes or 36/ Sterl. Piece	9 . 5	18 . . —	48/-
Half D°	4 . 14½	9 . . —	24/-
Quarter D°	2 . 7¼	4 . 10 —	12/-

ENGRAV'D Printed & Sold by NAT HURD.

Silver Coins	Weights. oz. dwt. gr.	Value £ s d
Eng Crown	0 . 19 . 8½	2 . 10 . —
Half Ditto	9 . 16¼	1 . 5 . —
Dollar	17 . 12	2 . 5 . —
Half Ditto	8 . 18	1 . 2 . 6
Quarter D°	4 . 9	. 11 . 3

NB 24 Grains is one penny wt 20 Penny wt one Ounce.

oz. dwt. gr.	GOLD pr oz.	SILVER pr oz.
1 . 0 . 0	£38 . 0 . 0	2 . 10 . 0
10 . 0	19 . . —	1 . 5 . —
5 . 0	9 . 10 . —	12 . 6
2 . 0	3 . 16 . —	5 . .
1 . 0	1 . 18 . —	2 . 6
0 . 12	19 . —	1 . 3
0 . 6	9 . 6	0 . 7½
0 . 3	4 . 9	0 . 3¾
0 . 1	1 . 7	0 . ¼

Fig. 9: A TABLE OF COIN WEIGHTS AND VALUES (ca. 1750). This table, engraved and printed by the silversmith Nathaniel Hurd, listed the common gold and silver coins and their fractional parts which were current in Massachusetts. This table was to aid in the redemption of depreciated "Old Tenor" bills, issued prior to 1737, into Proclamation, or "lawfull" money, at the rate of 7½ to 1. This redemption was completed by 1751 after the colony had received sufficient specie from England in 1749 on the *Mermaid* to retire its inflated paper currency and placed the colony in a "hard money" status (Newman, *Paper Money*, p. 13). Courtesy American Antiquarian Society.

> It having been discovered that pistareens and larger and smaller pieces of the same stamp [new plate], had been imported among the specie from London, and paid out of the treasury for Province notes, an order is issued, that all such money considered of greater alloy than others, shall be retained until further action of the Court. Here we are introduced to coins, which became current and are familiar to the memory of many.[103]

The description of this occasion by Felt also indicates that the "new plate" coinage within the shipment was apparently withheld from circulation until an equitable exchange rate could be calculated. On April 6, 1753, the exchange rate for pistareens in Massachusetts was established

[103] Felt, *Massachusetts*, pp. 128-29. A "greater alloy" means a larger amount of base metal in the mixture.

at 14.5d., at which time the quantity of base Spanish silver from the *Mermaid* consignment was released.[104] These newly arrived coins were apparently popular since the colonists chose to receive "the Spanish pistorines at 20 percent over the intrinsic value" in preference to the lesser denominational paper money printed to provide small change at the time of the 1750 redemption of the bills of credit.[105]

The American Negotiator of 1765 printed the following commentary regarding pistareens:

> All Spanish monies, great or small, either gold or silver, if full Spanish standard weight, are fit to remit to Europe, except a particular sort which circulates in great quantities in the British Sugar Islands which are called Pistareens, whose current value is two ryals. Those pieces of money, if full weight, are not fit to remit to Europe, as they are coarse silver at least 6d. sterling the ounce under standard silver. The blackness of their color is a sufficient mark to distinguish them by.[106]

The value of the pistareen was not always constant because the weight varied from 84 to 96 grains and the fineness from .8125 to .842.[107] In 1759, a Spanish pistareen passed at 17.8% and 18.75% (instead of 20%) of a Spanish milled dollar in Philadelphia and New York, respectively, while a Spanish American two reales, as a fractional coin, would have passed at 25% of the dollar in both cities.[108] In New York in 1775 the pistareen passed for 1s. 7d., New York money, while in 1793 its value was reduced to 1s. 4.5d., despite the fact that the value of the Spanish milled dollar and its fractional parts remained constant.[109]

The pistareen was so well received in Virginia by the outbreak of the Revolutionary War, when it passed for 15d., money of account, that the 1s. 3d. Virginia paper money note of 1775 carried the additional designations of "A Pistereen [*sic*]" and "fifteen pence."[110] At a rate of 72d. Virginia money to the Spanish milled dollar, the other fractional paper denominations of 30d., 60d., and 90d. coincided to two, four, and six pistareens, respectively, all passing at a rate 20% lower than the Spanish American dollar standard. The status of the pistareen during the late Confederation period in 1786 is outlined in Table 17. Thomas Jefferson, in his early writings on monetary units, noted:

> The tenth (of a dollar) will be precisely the Spanish bit or half pistareen in some of the States, and in others will differ from it but by a very small fraction.... Perhaps it would not be amiss to coin three more pieces of silver, one of the value of five-tenths or half a dollar, one of the value of two-tenths, which would be equal to the Spanish pistareen, and one of the value of five coppers, which would be equal to the Spanish half bit.[111]

Despite the approval and popularity of the pistareen, the coinage never attained legal tender status in the United States after 1792 although the Spanish milled dollar and its fractional parts remained legal tender until 1857.[112] In an interesting Supreme Court decision in 1836, *The United States vs. Joseph Gardner*, the defendant was found innocent of the charge of counter-

[104] Felt, *Massachusetts*, p. 136.

[105] Hutchinson, *Massachusetts*, p. 9, as quoted in Sallay, *CNL 1975*, p. 528. Felt (*Massachusetts*, p. 127) listed the denomination of these small bills as 1d., 2d., 3d., 4½d., 6d., 9d., and 18d., which are documented by Newman (*Paper Money*, p. 180). Newman writes that due to the preference for the small coins, most of this emission of small change notes remained unissued (Newman, *Num 1985*, p. 2186).

[106] Adler, *Money Units*, p. 159. There would be no reason to expect a color change at this reduced fineness, but indeed an ounce of pistareens of authorized weight (5.07 coins) would be 6.2d. under an ounce of standard.

[107] Chalmers, *British Colonies*, p. 403.

[108] Solomon, *Studies*, pp. 32, 35, 41.

[109] Adler, *Money Units*, p. 158.

[110] Williamson, *CNL 1986*, pp. 937-38, 946; Newman, *Paper Money*, p. 480.

[111] *A.S.P.F.*, vol. 1, p. 106.

[112] Schilke and Solomon, *Foreign Coins*, pp. 73-79. This book catalogues foreign coins which had legal tender status from 1793 to 1857. There is an excellent chapter dealing with pistareens.

Fig. 10: A Virginia 15d. "pistareen" note of July 17, 1775.

feiting legal currency, since the 100 "head pistareens" he forged were not considered legal coins of the United States and thus no crime was committed. Only the Spanish milled dollar and its fractional parts enjoyed legal tender status pursuant to the presidential proclamation of October 15, 1797. Whereas the role in numismatic history of the eight reales and its fractional parts, including the various sized bits and the picayune, is familiar to modern day collectors, the Spanish pistareen remains an unsung hero among other contemporary Spanish American coinages which circulated widely in the colonies. The pistareen's low silver content afforded it protection from bullion speculators and the export market. Since there was no external competition for the pistareen, it was free to circulate as an important coin within the small change segment of the colonial economy.

Table 5

Spanish and Spanish American Silver Coins Which Circulated in the American Colonies and their Equivalent Value in English Money Calculated at 62d. per Ounce Sterling
(from Chalmers, *British Colonies*, pp. 392, 395, 402-3;
Shaw, *Monetary History*, pp. 85-89, 126, 140-42)

Denomination[a]	*Weight in grains*	*Fineness*	*Pure silver content, grains*	*Sterling Value d.*
eight reales, 1497-1728				
authorized	423.9	.9305	394.4	55.1
1626 assay	420.0	.9166	385.0	53.8
1651 value				54.25
1696 value				52.5
1704 assay	420.0	.921-.933	386.8-391.9	54.0-54.7
1717 assay	417-420	.921-.925	384.1-388.5	53.6-54.25
eight reales, Seville "old plate"				
1702 assay	420.0	.9187	385.9	53.9

[a] The fractional silver coins of four, two, one, and half real are in proportion.

Denomination	*Weight in grains*	*Fineness*	*Pure silver content, grains*	*Sterling Value d.*
eight reales, Seville "new plate," raised to 10 reales[b]				
1702 assay	336.0	.9188	308.7	43.1
eight reales, 1728-1772				
authorized	417.6	.9166	382.8	53.5
1765 assay	416.5	.9060	377.3	52.7
eight reales, 1772 to 1848				
authorized	417.6	.9028	377.0	52.6
Cross pistareen, 1707-1772				
authorized	94.6	.8333	78.8	11.0
1712 assay	96.25	.8417	81.0	11.3
1721 assay	88.5	.8125	71.9	10.0
Head pistareen, from 1772				
authorized	92.0	.8125	74.8	10.4
1775 assay	90.0	.8020	72.2	10.1

[b] The "new plate" was a devaluation of the Spanish real which occurred in 1642 and 1686 where the Spanish American eight reales was ordered to pass in Spain at 10 "new" reales.

It has already been mentioned that the Spanish American eight reales became established as the world's silver standard, a measure that applied not only to England but her colonies as well. In England the basis was 54d. but among the colonies this rate was variable which proved vexatious to commerce. The colonial value of the standard was fixed by market forces according to the strength of the local economy and also, as previously described, by legislative edict designed to sustain the currency by "crying-up the money" in a competitive race with neighbors to attract or preserve circulating silver. The Proclamation of 1704 was an unsuccessful attempt to stabilize the currency and control the inflationary spiral precipitated by the "crying up of monies." Following the Proclamation, many colonies resorted to paper money and the rate for silver was unstable and inflated in several others, especially Massachusetts where constancy was not achieved until 1750 after the colony received a large shipment of specie and returned to a silver standard. By about 1750 the exchange rate or par of exchange, for the standard in the colonies settled down and remained constant until the Federal period. A summary of the fluctuating standard for the several colonies is given in Table 6.

TABLE 6

The Value, Expressed in Pence of Local Money of Account, for the Standard Spanish American Eight Reales in the Various Colonies as Compared to the English Rate of 54d.[a]

(Data from McCusker, *Money and Exchange* and Newman, *Paper Money* pp. 467-73)

Year	*New England*	*New York*	*Penna. & Del.*	*New Jersey*[b]	*Maryland*	*Virginia*	*Carolinas*[c]	*Georgia*[d]
1620	54							
1640		66						
1642	56/60							
1645						72	60	
1655						60		
1671					72			
1672	72	72						
1676				92	54			
1683			72				72	
1684		81						

Year	*New England*	*New York*	*Penna. & Del.*	*New[b] Jersey*	*Maryland*	*Virginia*	*Carolinas[c]*	*Georgia[d]*
1685				90 East				
1686					72			
1688					54			
1691							81	
1692	74				72			
1693			74	97.7 West				
1694					54			
1700			94	81				
1705	83.6							
1708		96	72					
1709				96	72			
1710						65.5		
1712							81 North	
1714							108 South	
1723			72				324 South	
1726			78					
1728						70		
1735								54
1740		96		96				
1742			90				372 South	
1748				100			96 North	
1750	72			90		72[e]		54
1752					90		382 South	
1755								54
1761				88 West				
				94 East				
1764						86		60
1771							390 South	
1775	72	96	86	90	90	67	390 South	59
1783[e]	72	96	90	90	90	72	56 South	56
							96 North	

[a] The last value listed under each colony is the rate which applied into the Federal period. The advantage of "cried up money" was lost after the early 1700s and the Proclamation of 1704. From 1708 to the late 1740s there was significant inflation in many colonies.

[b] New Jersey was divided into East and West from 1676 to 1702. After reunion, the official rate followed New York until 1750 when the exchange rates of Pennsylvania were adopted. For a few years prior to 1761, New Jersey paper money circulating near Philadelphia (West) "curiously" acquired a 6% premium over the same currency circulating near New York City (East).

[c] In 1712 Carolina split into North and South. The paper money of both colonies inflated enormously from 1712 until 1748; North Carolina depreciated its currency whereas the paper of South Carolina remained stable.

[d] Georgia was a corporate colony until 1754 whose currency was at par with England at 54d.

[e] These are local values for the eight reales according to contemporary trade schedules.

Dutch Money in America

Although it has been estimated that up to one-half of the circulating coins in the colonies was eight reales,[113] mention is made of other specific foreign coins, especially from the United Provinces of the Netherlands and the Spanish Netherlands. As has been described, the Spanish

[113] McCusker, *Money and Exchange*, p. 7; Chalmers, *British Colonies*, p. 394. While this estimate is speculative, it is based on the prodigious output of the Spanish American mints. From 1537 to 1821, the Mexican mint produced over $2,082,000,000 in silver, while in the decade 1766 to 1776, over 20,000,000 eight reales were minted annually.

influence extended into the New World with their acquisition of Mexico, Central and South America. The Dutch also became a great commercial nation and had the largest merchant fleet during the seventeenth century, and supplied about half the world's shipping. The histories of Spain and the Low Countries (The Netherlands, Belgium, and Luxembourg) are significantly intertwined and deserve some brief comment.

The Low Countries were successively under the domination of the Dukes of Burgundy beginning in the 1300s and the Austrian Hapsburgs after 1477. When in 1516, Charles of Burgundy fell heir to the Spanish throne, all the territories of Austria, Burgundy, including the Low Countries, and Spain, including the New World, were united under the same monarch, Charles V, Emperor of the Holy Roman Empire. Upon his abdication in 1555, the empire was divided with the Spanish possessions and the Low Countries coming under the rule of his son, Philip II. The Low Countries, which had always enjoyed a fair degree of autonomy, soon revolted and in 1581 the northern provinces declared themselves independent as the Republic of the Seven United Provinces of The Netherlands. The southern provinces, including South Brabant, Luxembourg, and Flanders remained under Spanish authority as the Spanish Netherlands until 1795 when they fell to France. The United Provinces became a powerful mercantile nation and as such founded the Dutch colony of New Netherland which included parts of Connecticut, New York, New Jersey, and Delaware.

Much silver from the mines of the New World found its way to the Netherlands via Spanish American and Dutch merchants. The Dutch mints were actively producing coins for the profitable export trade and "some issues never circulated at all within the borders of the country itself."[114] Frequently, there was not enough coined money for use at home and thus many foreign coins were employed in the Netherlands to meet local needs.[115] In the early years, there was active trading between the English of Massachusetts and the Dutch of New Netherland. Commerce was so advantageous to the New Englanders that they were "indisposed to the war with their Dutch neighbors, the other colonies being otherwise disposed."[116] As might be anticipated since "currency followed the flag,"[117] the Dutch settlers also brought their current silver coins with them to the New World, which circulated freely in Massachusetts, along with English and Spanish money, bullion, wampum, and commodities. Specifically the ducatoon of three guilders and the rix-dollar (rijksdaalder) of two and one-half guilders were cited by the Massachusetts General Court on September 8, 1642, when that body established the value of those coins at six and five shillings, respectively, a law which placed the rijksdaalder and the eight reales at par.

> This Cort [Court] considering the oft occasions wee have of trading wth hollanders at the Dutch Plantation and otherwise; do therefore order that the holland ducatoon being worth 3 gilders shalbee current at 6s. in all paymts [payments] within or [our] jurisdiction & the rix doller being two & a half gilders shalbee likewise currant at 5s., & the ryall of 8: shalbee also currant at 5s.[118]

Perhaps as a reaction to the Massachusetts provision, the Dutch in New Netherland reciprocated by raising the value of the eight reales in their territory to three guilders, a rate 20% higher than at home.[119] In 1686 in Maryland, "An Act for the Advancement of Coins," a provision which "cried up of money" by 25%, placed the rix dollar, French écu, and eight reales at 6s. each, while the ducatoon was made current at 7s. 6d., local money of account.[120]

[114] Delmonte, *Benelux*, p. 186.
[115] Van Gelder, *Munten*, pp. 108-10.
[116] *Essex Inst. Hist. Colls.*, vol. 1, pp. 79, 124.
[117] Chalmers, *British Colonies*, p. 4.
[118] Chalmers, *British Colonies*, p. 6.
[119] McCusker, *Money and Exchange*, pp. 156-57.
[120] Crosby, *Early Coins*, p. 132.

The ducatoon (ducatone) was originally a silver coin of three guilders first minted in the Spanish Netherlands in 1618, successively displaying the portraits of the monarchs, Albert and Isabelle, Philip IV, and Charles II.[121] This quality coin was .944 fine, weighed 501.23 grains, and passed at 60 sols (stuivers), or three guilders. Beginning in 1659, all seven independent northern United Provinces minted the so-called silver rider, named because of the mounted knight on its obverse. The coin, authorized at 505.86 grains at .941 fine, passed at 63 stuivers. Because of the similarity in size and value with its southern counterpart, the silver rider also became known as a ducatoon. From 1726, ducatoons or silver riders were also minted for the United East India Company as a trade coin with the company's insignia.[122] In addition to the silver rider, alias ducatoon, another important large silver coin was the three guilder piece which passed at 60 stuivers. The silver guilder was an actual coin only from 1544 to 1558 and after 1681. In the intervening years, it was a money of account. From 1578, the value of the guilder continually fluctuated, adjusting itself to the value of other silver coins. The value of the guilder was stabilized in 1681 at 148.30 grains, or 200 azen, of pure silver, and its twentieth part, the stuiver, in proportion.[123]

The rijksdaalder was another common Dutch silver piece which by 1581 was minted by most cities and provinces of the Republic. Although attempts were made to standardize this coin, many variations were encountered. The usual weight of the rijksdaalder was 448 grains at .885 fine which passed at 50 stuivers, or two and one-half guilders. Another Dutch coin of similar size to the rijksdaalder was the silver ducat, or "leg dollar" (since the right leg of the standing knight is evident), which after 1659, also passed at two and one-half guilders. There were many other German and Scandinavian versions of the rix-dollar, rijksdaalder, reisedaler, or reichstaler rendering the definition of this coin very imprecise. The average value of 13 different "rixdollars" of "the Empire," i.e. the German states, assayed at the Tower mint by Sir Isaac Newton in 1702 revealed a weight 441.96 grains at .886 fine which was comparable to the Dutch issue.[124]

The lion dollar (leeuwendaalder) was probably the most important Dutch coin to circulate in the New World.[125] It was the first coin struck by the United Provinces during their war of independence against Spain. First issued in 1575 in the province of Holland, it was soon minted by all seven provinces and five cities, and was last struck in 1713. It is among the crudest of all the crown-sized coins ever minted to the extent that the lion was mistaken for a dog and, hence, the sobriquet, "dog dollar."[126] This coin had the lowest silver content of all large Dutch silver at .750 fine and a weight of 427.16 grains. It passed initially at a low of 36 stuivers from 1586 to 1606, to a high of 42 in 1659. During the seventeenth century, the lion dollar was primarily a trade coin minted for use in the eastern Mediterranean countries or the Levant. The coin was so popular and successful that it was even copied by several other states, particularly in Germany and Italy.[127] Together with rijksdaalders and silver ducats, lion dollars circulated widely in the Dutch East Indies before the ducatoon became the prevailing currency of the region.[128] In the

[121] General information regarding Dutch coinages from Van Gelder, *Munten*; Delmonte, *Benelux*; Bachtell, *World Dollars*. Data regarding weights and fineness are from Van Gelder, pp. 124-25, 221, 230-31, 265, passim.

[122] Scholten, *Dutch*, pp. 23, 38.

[123] Posthumus, *Prices*, pp. liv-lvii.

[124] "Sir Isaac Newton's Mint Reports," p. 142, in Shaw, *Monetary History*.

[125] Verkade, *Muntboek*, pp. 33-34; Delmonte, *Benelux*, pp. 193-204.

[126] Draskovic and Rubenfeld, *Crowns*, p. 281.

[127] Imitation lion dollars are known from the German states of Emden, Jever, and Rietberg; the Italian states of Bozzolo, Corregio, Ferrara, Genoa, Massa Di Lunigiana, Maccagno, Messerano, Mirandola, Rovegno, and Tassarolo; Norway; and Bouillon and Sedan, in present day Luxembourg and northern France. See Davenport, *Crowns 1977*; *Crowns 1974*; *Church Talers*; *Secular Talers*.

[128] Scholten, *Dutch*, pp. 33-38.

Fig. 11:
(a) United Provinces of the Netherlands: 1674 over 73 double ducatoon, Holland mint.

(b) United Provinces of the Netherlands: 1583 rijksdaalder, Holland mint.

(c) United Provinces of the Netherlands: 1641 leeuwendaalder or lion dollar, Overijssel mint. From the Aitub hoard.

(d) Utrecht (United Provinces): 1625 copper duit.

next century, the lion dollar was displaced as the prominent trade coin of the Levant by the famous and still popular Austrian Maria Theresa taler which first appeared in 1780.[129]

As might be expected with any trade coin, the lion dollar made its way to the New World where it was reported to be the "chief metallic currency of Maryland in 1701." It was mentioned again in 1708 as "the only generall coyne among us," with its value set at 4s. 6d.[130] In New York in the same year, the rate for the lion dollar was established at 5s. 6d. and the half lion dollar was proportionally set at 2s. 9d.[131] Since the same regulation pegged the eight reales standard at 6s., the lion dollar was significantly overvalued and should only have passed at 4s. 10d. as determined from Tables 5 and 7; the Maryland rate was far more equitable. There is an interesting New York paper money emission dated November 1, 1709, issued in denominations

[129] Van Gelder, *Munten*, pp. 79, 109, 149, 221-22, 230-31, 263; *Salvesen* pp. 34-36.
[130] Chalmers, *British Colonies*, p. 12n.
[131] Solomon, *Studies*, pp. 29-30.

of 20, 16, 8 and 4 "Lyon Dollars" expressed in terms of sterling silver equivalency. The largest bill of this series is for 13.75 ounces of sterling (plate) or 20 Lyon Dollars with all others in proportion.[132] This calculates to 6600 grains of sterling for the 20 pieces which is about 2.5% below the expected sterling content of 6767 grains based on Newton's assay as recorded in Table 7 and Appendix 3. This reduction in value would be anticipated since the average lion dollar was probably clipped by that amount or otherwise reduced in weight from ordinary wear.

The presence of the lion dollar, or "dog dollar," along the Eastern Shore of Virginia as late as 1696 was due in part to the ineffectiveness of the Navigation Laws to prevent active smuggling by Dutch merchants.[133] The lion dollar also saw significant service in Pennsylvania and New Jersey. The several lion dollars salvaged from the wreck of the *H.M.S. Feversham* indicate that the currency was readily available in New York in 1711 when the ship was provisioned. Two lion dollars were recovered in the Castine, Maine, hoard hidden in the early 1700s, giving further evidence of their wide circulation.[134] Additional indication of their popularity is suggested by the report that lion dollars were counterfeited in Massachusetts in 1701/2.[135] The acceptance of the lion dollar was not a universal phenomenon. In Ireland in 1677, lion dollars passed at 57d. (Irish) but in proportion to the standard Spanish dollar, were worth only 45d. As a result of this inflated value, no one was required to take these "New lyon Dollars."[136]

The "Cross Dollar of Flanders," or the patagon of the Spanish Netherlands, first minted in 1612 as a "Burgundian rijksdaalder," also received contemporary attention as it was specifically mentioned in the Proclamation of 1704. This interesting coinage, valued at 48 stuivers and bearing the inscriptions of the Spanish king, was so named because of the crossed staves of its design. Its lower silver content, 433.64 grains at .875 fine, tended to drive better coins into the export market. The name *patacón* or *patagon* was applied to coins of both the Portuguese and Brabantine series, the word having the same derivation as *piedfort*, or "large foot," the term commonly applied to heavy pattern or multiple denomination coins.[137] In the Leeward Islands, the "Cross and Lyon dollars, and all Peru Pieces of Eight [i.e. cobs], without weighing" passed at five shillings, a schedule which substantially overvalued the lion dollar.[138] From 1680 to 1712 in Ireland, the eight reales from Spain and Spanish America (exclusive of the "old Peruvians" [i.e. cobs]), all rix-dollars, cross dollars, and French crowns circulated by proclamation at the same rate which varied between 57 and 64d., Irish. According to Newton, and as it is apparent from the accompanying Tables 5, 6, and 8, this edict overvalued the cross and rix-dollars in terms of the Spanish and French currencies.[139]

Another interesting minor Dutch coin was the copper duit, doit, or dite, worth one-half farthing. Eight duits made one stuiver, and 20 stuivers equaled one guilder. The word *dite* remains in our local language, much like *picayune*, to characterize a trifle or something small.[140] *Dite* is not to be confused with *mite* (pl. *myten* or *miten*), a contemporary copper or billon coin of very little value current in Brabant and the Netherlands. *Mite* also has other meanings including 1/20th of a grain as well as being the monetary standard unit of the Spanish Netherlands where 1440 mites equaled a gold real.[141]

[132] Newman, *Paper Money*, p. 246.
[133] Hoober, *Num 1953*, p. 1146.
[134] Noe, *Castine Deposit*, p. 27.
[135] Felt, *Massachusetts*, p. 250.
[136] Simon, *Essay*, pp. 53, 137-38.
[137] Hazlitt, *Coinage*, p. 221. A *piedfort* is a heavy coin struck on a planchet of double or more thickness.
[138] Chalmers, *British Colonies*, p. 67.
[139] Simon, *Essay*, pp. 50, 55, 57, 65-66, 67, 68-69; Shaw, *Monetary History*, p. 159. Irish to English during this period averaged 108.00:100.00.
[140] "When they will not give a doit to relieve a lame beggar, they will lay out ten to see a dead Indian." *The Tempest*, II, scene 2, 34-36.
[141] Hazlitt, *Coinage*, pp. 216, 400. A *mite* is also a New Testament half-farthing; "And there came a certain widow, and she threw in two mites, which make a farthing." (Mark xii, 42.)

The role of Dutch coinage in the American colonies, while certainly not as prominent as the Spanish, is not usually appreciated. New Netherland was a sizeable colony, and although it did not survive under Dutch authority, its money remained an important medium especially in Maryland and along the shores of the Chesapeake where there was continued contact with Dutch merchants. The inclusion of Dutch money in the Proclamation of 1704 together with Spanish, French, and Portuguese silver, suggests that it was considered significant in the colonial economy.

TABLE 7

Silver Coins of the United Provinces of the Netherlands and the Spanish Netherlands which Circulated in British North America
(Shaw, *Monetary History*, pp. 85-89, 126, 140-42; Van Gelder, *Munten*)

Denomination	*Weight in grains*	*Fineness*	*Pure silver content, grains*	*Sterling Value*[a] *d.*
UNITED PROVINCES				
Lion dollar of 40 stuivers, 1575-1713				
Authorized	427.16	.750	320.37	44.7
1696 value				40.5
1702 assay	422.0	.7416	312.95	43.7
Rijksdaalder of 50 stuivers, 1591-1700[b]				
authorized	448.0	.885	396.48[c]	55.36
1651 value				55.125
1696 value				52.0
1702 assay	432.0	.8667	374.39	52.28
Three guilder piece of 60 stuivers, 1694-1800				
authorized	491.0	.920	451.72	63.08
1702 assay	488.0	.91666	447.33	62.46
Silver rider or ducatoon of 63 stuivers, 1659-1798				
authorized	505.86	.941	476.01	66.47
1702 assay	501.0	.93746	469.67	65.58
SPANISH NETHERLANDS				
Cross dollar or patagon of 48 sols,[d] from 1612				
authorized	433.64	.875	379.44	52.98
1651 value				52.75
1696 value				50.5
1702 assay	433.0	.87512	378.93	52.91
Ducatoon of 60 sols				
authorized	501.23	.944	473.16	66.07
1651 value				66.25[e]
1696 value				66.0
1702 assay	502.0	.94361	473.69	66.15

[a] Values for 1702 assay and authorized weight based on 62d. per troy ounce of sterling, .925 fine, silver.
[b] The silver ducat, 1659-1808, had the same value as the rijksdaalder.
[c] The Leicesterrijksdaalder was finer at .888 and weighed 451.23 grains.
[d] The Spanish Netherlands *sol* was equivalent to the *stuiver*.
[e] Value given from 66.125 to 66.25d.

Other Foreign Coins in America

Other important coins, both gold and silver, were prominent in the New World. As far back as 1655, the Virginia legislature regulated the value of several other foreign coins in current circulation.[142]

	£.	s.	d.
The Spanish Double Doublon	03	00	00
The Doublon, consequently,	01	15	00
The Pistole,	00	17	06
Arabian Chequins,	00	10	00
Pieces of Eight, (except of *Peru*,) weighing 16 penny Weight,	00	05	00
French Crowns,	00	05	00
Peru Pieces of Eight, and Dutch Dollars,	00	04	00
And all English Coin as it goes in *England*.			

From the above schedule, it is evident that the "crying-up of money" had not yet occurred but the weight of the eight reales in common circulation was reduced from 17.5 to 16 dwt indicative of the extensive clipping of the coinage which did not have a protective milled edge until 1732. Silver from the Peruvian mints was depreciated by an additional 20% because of the discovery of debasement at the Potosí mint extending from 1640 to 1648. The Dutch dollars, which were at par with the debased Peruvian coinage, were probably lion dollars. Although the export of English specie was prohibited, there were sufficient quantities of crowns and shillings in circulation to warrant their inclusion in published rates of exchange.[143]

This tabulation introduces the smallest Spanish gold unit, the *escudo*, or *shield*, which was equivalent to sixteen reales in silver. Two escudos equaled one *pistole*. Originally the double pistole was the Spanish *doubloon* of four escudos, but in later usage the doubloon became the quadruple pistole of eight escudos. Another coin mentioned in this early document was the *chequin* or *sequin*, a gold ducat-sized piece common to the Arabic countries bordering on the Mediterranean and introduced into the American colonial trade as the Barbary ducat.[144] Comparable coins to this piece were the Venetian *zecchino* and the Turkish *altun*.[145] These small gold coins which essentially passed for two eight reales circulated in the West Indies and the American Colonies in the first half of the eighteenth century but were soon discarded because of their low gold content.

Gold coins were relatively unimportant in the American colonies until after the Proclamation of 1704, when gold became the monetary standard in the West Indies. At that point, Spanish doubloons, pistoles, escudos, and Portuguese gold assumed great importance. The *moidore* series of Portuguese gold (1640 to 1732) was primarily a European currency where it was the principal gold for Ireland and Western England during the early eighteenth century. Containing 22 carat gold, the basic unit was the *moeda de ouro* (money of gold) of 83 grains. The largest coin in the series was the *dobrão* of 830 grains, whereas the most familiar coin was its fifth part called the *moidore*, double *moeda de ouro*, or *Lisbonine*. This popular coin, originally worth 4,000 réis, was inflated to 4,800 réis in 1688. The *moidore* system was later replaced by the "Johannes" series (1722 to 1835), so named for the monarch of Portugal whose effigy was on the obverse of the

[142] Crosby, *Early Coins*, p. 23.
[143] Nettels, *Money Supply*, p. 162; Ernst, *Money and Politics*, p. 20n; Solomon, *Studies*, p. 35.
[144] Chalmers, *British Colonies*, pp. 67, 397.
[145] Craig, *World Coins*, p. 742. The sequin was also known as the sultani, checken, checkeen, and chequeen (Solomon, *Studies*, p. 38). *Sequin* is French for the Italian *zecchino*, a Venetian ducat first minted around 1280. *Zecchino* is derived from the Spanish word, *zeca*, a mint, and the Arabic, *sikka*, a die for stamping coins.

coin. The advantage of these new denominations was their easy conversion to Spanish currency since the *Johannes, dobra, joe* or eight Portugese *escudos* of 12,800 réis was roughly equivalent to the Spanish doubloon or quadruple pistole, although the Portuguese gold was about 5.5% stronger than the corresponding Spanish. The Johannes series, and particularly the "half joe" of 6,400 réis, became an important colonial currency. Portuguese gold was highly prized because of its uniform consistency in both alloy and weight. Such a good reputation "led to the wholesale manufacture of counterfeit joes in North America and Birmingham."[146]

French money was also an important New World currency not only in Canada and Louisiana but also in British North America as evidenced by the inclusion of its various denominations on conversion tables.[147] French silver écus, or crowns, were inconsistent in composition until 1726 when they remained stable into the Federal period, falling between the Spanish eight reales and the English crown in value.[148] These relationships are documented in Tables 5 and 8.

Fig. 12: France: contemporary counterfeit of 1787 écu of Louis XVI with Orleans (R) mint mark. This contains only 24.5% silver; note ancient test clip upper left obverse (Private Collection).

Many aspects concerning the circulation and exchange rates in colonial America of world monies can be gleaned from the study of the tables in this chapter. The inflated value of the lion dollar in New York in 1708, and the overrating of the rix and cross dollars in Ireland are two examples already mentioned. French currencies are noted to have been very unstable in terms of weight and alloy, whereas Portuguese money, especially gold, was of constant value and highly esteemed. Table 5 demonstrates the stability of the Spanish eight reales and the minor depreciation which occurred over the years accounted for its popularity as a standard. Although it was of a lesser alloy than English coins, its current value was easily calculated by converting its silver content into sterling of .925 fine. The details of this conversion are presented in Appendix 1. The price relationship between silver to gold, as evidenced by the sterling values of the eight reales and the doubloon (Tables 5 and 9), remained about 15.6 to 1 but this ratio varied according to the market forces of supply and demand. Despite the massive imports of silver from South American mines, the great supply was offset by the constant demands for silver by eastern markets which managed to keep the price up.[149] Tables 8 and 9 note that in England, gold was overpriced as compared to silver as demonstrated by the nominal gold guinea of 21s. which would actually command 21s. 6.8d. in silver. Since gold guineas could be converted to silver at a profit, such transactions placed a bounty on full weight English silver coins which were diverted into the bullion market. They virtually disappeared from circulation since they were constantly drained to India where the ratio of value of silver to gold was as high as 9 to 1.

[146] Chalmers, *British Colonies*, pp. 396, 408; Buttrey, *ANS 1973*, pp. 62-64. *Réis* is the Portuguese equivalent of the Spanish *reales* (royals). *Moidore* is a contraction of *moeda de ouro*, money of gold, and as a coin specifically refers to the double *moeda de ouro*. The Johannes or Joannes series derives its name from the monarch, King John. Theoretically the "joe" or "joannese" was the half-dobra of 6,400 réis, but in the New World this coin was known as the "half-joe" while the dobra of 12,800 réis became the "joe."

[147] See Breen, *Encyclopedia*, pp. 43-58, for a complete description of coinage of the French régime in North America from 1640 to 1763.

[148] Chalmers, *British Colonies*, p. 404; Schilke and Solomon, *Foreign Coins*, p. 144.

[149] Feavearyear, *Pound Sterling*, p. 151.

Fig. 13: England: 1695 crown of William III.

The reactive legislation to prevent export of minted specie coins from England was ineffective and the flux of silver to the east continued. These uncurbed market forces were damaging to a mercantilist economy and accounted for the scarcity of full weight domestic hard money in England and the relative absence of English money from its American colonies. Even after the Revolution, English silver was not abundant in North America as Alexander Hamilton explained in his famous memorial, "On The Establishment Of A Mint."

> In Spain and England, where gold is rated higher than in other parts of Europe, there is a scarcity of silver; while it [silver] is found to abound in France and Holland, where it is rated higher, in proportion to gold, than in neighboring nations. And it [silver] is continually flowing from Europe to China and the East Indies, owing to the comparative cheapness of it in the former, and the dearness of it in the latter.[150]

Newton called attention to the fact that the guinea in England was priced up to 1s. above comparable currencies in most of Europe except for Spain and Portugal where the vast imports of silver arriving from America made gold relatively more expensive. If bimetallism were to be successful in England so that silver and gold could circulate together, either the official price of silver had to increase or that of gold decrease to maintain the ratio which had been dictated by the law of supply and demand on the world market. In order to preserve the English silver medium from the melting pot and subsequent exportation as bullion, Newton proposed a devaluation of gold by whatever amount was necessary to correspond with the price of gold in neighboring countries on the Continent. This and other suggestions to preserve and improve English money went ignored and the currency situation in England languished in morbidity until 1816 when the country adopted a gold standard and silver became a subsidiary coinage. Some improvement did result following a proclamation of December 1717 which pegged the guinea at 21s. 0d. and other gold coins proportionately. Although still overrated, the mint price for gold was thereby reduced from £4 to £3 17s. 10.5d. per troy ounce.[151]

Thus in the period of British North America colonialism, English currency remained in a lamentable state and the colonists relied on Spanish American, and to a lesser extent Dutch and other European currencies for their commercial needs, since English specie was not available to them. Earlier English monetary history is replete with many accounts of shortages, debasements and recoinages so this was nothing new. Silver had virtually disappeared from England but the available gold, because of its high value in relation to the income of the common people, was not a satisfactory medium for ordinary commerce. When small change was in particularly tight supply, local businessmen resorted to the issue of merchants' tokens redeemable in legal tender. A regal copper coinage was created to fill this need during the reign of Charles II, but the inherent profit from minting and circulating coppers was so great that counterfeiting

[150] *A.S.P.F.*, vol. 1, pp. 91-100, quote p. 93.

[151] Feavearyear, *Pound Sterling*, pp. 150-58; "Report of the Officers of the Mint About the Preservation of the Coyne," in Shaw, *Monetary History*, pp. 136-39; Sumner, *Yale Rev. 1898*, pp. 405-6.

became a very lucrative activity for the unscrupulous. Although English specie coins were forbidden to the colonists, counterfeit copper coinage was imported in great quantities to become the most common small change in America.

Fig. 14: Common Gold Coins Which Circulated in Colonial America (See Table 9).

(a) France: 1641 louis d'or (French guinea) of Louis XIII, Paris mint.

(b) Mexico: 1762 eight escudos or doubloon of Charles III.

(c) Mexico: 1779 two escudos or pistole of Charles III.

(d) Brazil: 1699 moeda de ouro of 2,000 reis of Peter I.

(e) Brazil: 1767 four escudos, half dobra or "half-joe" of 6,400 reis of Joseph I, Río mint.

(f) England: 1688 guinea of James II.

(g) Venice: zecchino or sequin of Francisco Loredano (1752-1767).

TABLE 8

Representative Seventeenth and Eighteenth Century World Silver Coins Which Circulated in the American Colonies.[a]

Denomination	Weight in grains	Fineness	Pure silver content, grains	Sterling Value[b] d.
		FRANCE[c]		
Louis d'argent of 60 sols, 1641-1709*				
authorized	423.3	.9166	388.0	54.18
1702 assay	421.0	.9208	387.66	54.13
Ecu aux trois Couronnes, 1709-1718				
authorized	472.2	.9166	432.8	60.44
Navarra taler, 1718-1724				
authorized	374.9	.910	341.16	47.64
Ecu aux deux L., 1724-1726				
authorized	364.0	.9166	333.64	46.59
Ecu, 1726-1773				
authorized	440.0	.912	401.28	56.03
Ecu, 1774-1792				
authorized	444.0	.912	404.93	56.54
		PORTUGAL[d]		
Cruzado "of 400 Réis now raised to 480"*				
1702 assay	268.0	.91689	245.73	34.31
		ENGLAND[e]		
Shilling, 1601-1816				
authorized	92.9	.925	85.9	12.0
Crown, 1601-1816				
authorized	464.5	.925	429.6	60.0

[a] Coins marked [*] are also listed in Table 3, having been included in the Proclamation of 1704.
[b] Based on 62d. per Troy ounce of sterling, .925 fine, silver.
[c] Chalmers, *British Colonies*, pp. 397-98, 404; Shaw, *Monetary History*, p. 140.
[d] Shaw, *Monetary History*, p. 140. This 20% inflation applied also to silver currency.
[e] Chalmers, *British Colonies*, p. 405.

TABLE 9

Representative Seventeenth and Eighteenth Century World Gold Coins Which Circulated in the American Colonies with Relative Values Expressed in Sterling Currency Calculated at £4 per Troy Ounce of .9166 Fine (22 Carat) Gold, the rate prior to 1717. (See Appendix 3)

Denomination	Weight in grains	Fineness	Pure gold content, grains	Sterling s.	Value d.
		FRANCE[a]			
Louis d'Or (French guinea) 1640-1709					
authorized	104.2	.9166	95.5	17	4.4
1702 assay	104.0	.9113	94.8	17	2.8
Louis au Soleil 1709-1715					
authorized	125.9	.9166	115.4	20	11.8

[a] Chalmers, *British Colonies*, pp. 397-98, 409-10. A U.S. Mint assay noted the gold content of the 1726 to 1792 Louis d'or to be considerably lower than those stated (Schilke and Solomon, *Foreign Coins*, p. 103).

Denomination	*Weight in grains*	*Fineness*	*Pure gold content, grains*	*Sterling s.*	*Value d.*
Louis a la Croix de Malte 1718-1723					
authorized	151.1	.9166	138.5	25	2.2
Louis d'Or (Mirliton) 1723-1726					
authorized	100.7	.9166	92.3	16	9.4
1740 assay	100.0	.901	90.1	16	4.6
Louis d'Or 1726-1785					
authorized	125.9	.9166	115.4	20	11.8
1740 assay	126.0	.8985	113.2	20	7.0
New Louis d'Or 1785-1794					
authorized	118.0	.9166	108.2	19	8.0
		SPAIN and SPANISH AMERICA[b]			
Escudo 1537-1772					
authorized	52.2	.9166	47.85	8	8.4
Escudo 1772-1786					
authorized	52.2	.901	47.0	8	6.6
Pistole 1537-1772					
authorized	104.4	.9166	95.7	17	4.8
1702 assay	104.0	.9115	94.8	17	2.8
Double pistole 1537-1772					
authorized	208.8	.9166	191.4	34	9.6
Quadruple pistole or doubloon 1537-1772					
authorized	417.6	.9166	382.8	69	7.2
1717 assay	416.0	.9115	379.2	68	11.4
Quadruple pistole or doubloon 1772-1786					
authorized	417.6	.901	376.3	68	5.0
Quadruple pistole or doubloon 1786-1848					
authorized	417.6	.875	365.4	66	5.3
		PORTUGAL[c]			
		Moidore series 1640-1732			
Moeda de ouro of 2,000 réis					
authorized	83.0	.9166	76.1	13	10.0
Double moeda de ouro, doppia moeda, moidore or Lisbonine of 4,000 réis					
authorized	166.0	.9166	152.16	27	8.0
1702 assay	165.0	.914	150.8	27	5.1
Dobrão of 20,000 réis					
authorized	830.0	.9166	760.8	138	4.0
		Johannes series 1722-1835			
Half-escudo (800 réis)					
authorized	27.6	.9166	25.3	4	7.2
Escudo (1600 réis)					
authorized	55.3	.9166	50.7	9	2.6
Quarter-dobra (3200 réis, ¼ joe)					
authorized	110.6	.9166	101.4	18	5.2
Half-dobra (6400 réis, ½ joe)					
authorized	221.1	.9166	202.6	36	10.2
Dobra or Johannes (12,800 réis, joe)					
authorized	442.6	.9166	405.7	73	9.2

[b] Chalmers, *British Colonies*, pp. 395-96, 407.

[c] Chalmers, *British Colonies*, pp. 396, 408. Portuguese gold closely followed the legal standard. The moidore series was raised 20% in 1688.

Denomination	Weight in grains	Fineness	Pure gold content, grains	Sterling s.	Value d.
		ENGLAND[d]			
Guinea 1660-1816					
authorized	129.4	.9166	118.6	21	6.8
		MISCELLANEOUS[e]			
Barbary ducat, Arabian chequin					
1717 assay	61.25	.818	50.1	9	1.3
1740 standard	53.75	.875	47.0	8	6.6
Sequin, chequin, zecchino or zacksen of Venice					
1702 assay	53.75	.9985	53.7	9	9.1

[d] Chalmers, *British Colonies*, p. 412. During the early 1700s, the guinea actually passed for 21s. 6d. (Feavearyear, *Pound Sterling*, pp. 154-55.)
[e] Chalmers, *British Colonies*, pp. 67, 397.

Many schedules of exchange rates were printed in the colonies for the convenience of the merchants as a quick reference to the value of the foreign monies. A typical one for 1759 appeared as follows:[152]

A Table of COINS, as they now pass in the following Places.

	England			Philadelphia			New York		
	£.	s.	d.	£.	s.	d.	£.	s.	d.
English Sixpence,	0	0	6	0	0	9	0	0	9
English Crown,	0	5	0	0	7	6	0	8	0
French Crown,	0	5	0	0	7	6	0	8	0
Guinea,	1	1	0	1	14	0	1	16	0
Spanish Pistole,	0	16	6	1	7	0	1	9	0
French Pistole,	0	16	0	1	6	6	1	8	0
Moydore,	1	7	0	2	3	6	2	6	0
Johannes,	3	12	0	5	15	0	6	6	0
Half Johannes,	1	16	0	2	17	6	3	3	0
Doubloon,	3	6	0	5	8	0	5	16	0
Spanish Dollar,				0	7	6	0	8	0
Pistareen,				0	1	4	0	1	6

N.B. Most sorts of Spanish Silver are sold in London, by the Ounce, and often varies, but seldom or ever exceeds 5s. 5d.

The par of exchange values for the monies listed in this 1759 table are identical to those from a previous 1751 almanac printed for use in Pennsylvania by Benjamin Franklin.[153] This is because the rate for the Spanish milled dollar between England and Pennsylvania had stabilized at 100.00:166.67 and between England and New York at 100.00:177.78 as indicated in Table 6. The values for the Spanish dollar are represented as 90d. and 96d., in those respective monies of account. Although the weaker pistareen was undervalued here, it can be assumed that fractional Spanish coins passed proportionately. The only new coin appearing in this tabulation is the

[152] From *Father Abraham's Almanack*, Philadelphia, 1759 (Solomon, *Studies*, p. 35).
[153] *Pocket Almanack for 1751*, by R. Saunders, printed by B. Franklin, Philadelphia, 1751 (Solomon, *Studies*, p. 39).

"French Pistole," the name applied to the Louis d'Or, or Mirliton, of 1723 to 1726 that was slightly lighter than its Spanish counterpart.

The 1751 edition of the exchange rate table indicated the minimum permissible weight required for each coin to pass at the determined amount. This allowable reduction from mint weight, made for circulated and lightly clipped specimens, was about 0.5% to 2.6% below the authorized weights for the gold coins listed in Table 9. In addition to this accommodation made for wear and clipping, the gold pieces enumerated in both the 1751 and 1759 almanacs are slightly lower in value than recorded in Table 9 due to the stabilization of the guinea in 1717 at 21s. 0d., when the 22 carat standard was reduced by 2.6% from £4 to £3 17s. 10.5d. an ounce, as previously related. For French crowns, the "least weight" from the 1751 almanac was 414 grains to pass at 7s. 6d., Pennsylvania money, a tolerance of 5.9% below the 1726 standard of 440 grains listed in Table 8. Except as noted, all other foreign coins in the 1751 and 1759 almanacs were rated within two to three percent of their theoretical values from the preceeding tables.[154] Notable exceptions were the French and English crowns; French crowns in England were overvalued by about 4d. but correctly rated in Philadelphia and New York, whereas English crowns were undervalued in the colonies by 10d. in Philadelphia and 10.6d. in New York in their local monies of account. This inequitable differential between French and English crowns became an issue of public concern to be further discussed in Chapter Nine. Of course, there was always the option for any underweight coin to pass by weight rather than tale. In 1751 Pennsylvania money, these rates were 8s. 6d. an ounce for sterling quality silver and £6 5s. per ounce for gold.

A distinction must be made between the exchange rates for foreign coins in the colonies based on the Spanish standard as noted in Table 6, and the commercial rate charged for bills of exchange with which the colonists could make foreign remittances to pay for imported goods. While the rates which evolved in the exchange of hard money, the par of exchange, were relatively stable and frequently fixed by law, the commercial rates for the purchase of bills of exchange fluctuated more widely according to current business cycles. These variations were determined by many factors such as the availability of foreign credit, the balance of payments, and the relative supply and demand for such fiscal instruments. For example, in 1751, when specie, based on the Spanish standard, passed at a ratio of 100:166.67 between London and Philadelphia, the average prevailing price for a bill of exchange for £100 sterling was set at £169.86 in Pennsylvania money of account, or expressed as the ratio, 100:169.86.[155] In this instance, it was more expensive to obtain sterling credits by buying a bill of exchange with local money of account than it was to send specie by the next ship to England to cover the indebtedness. In 1759, when market forces had reduced the commercial exchange rate to 100:153.32, it would have been less expensive to have made payments to England using bills of exchange purchased with Pennsylvania money than to have sent hard money. At any time when it became more profitable to export specie for foreign purchases than to buy bills of exchange, it was said that the "specie export point" had been reached.[156] This subject will be covered in greater depth in Chapter Four where bills of exchange and other paper currencies are described more fully.

This chapter has discussed the important emphasis on the intrinsic value of the circulating currencies and their relative exchange rates one with another. If one asks why this is essential to

[154] The differential between England and Philadelphia for the gold coins in the 1759 table averaged 100:161.69, rather than the expected 100:166.67. This 2.98% deficiency is not significant considering allowances made for variations in weight. For New York, the average for the seven gold pieces was 100:174.45, or only a 1.9% deviation from the established rate of 100:177.78.

[155] McCusker, *Money and Exchange*, pp. 18, 185; McCuster, *Studies*, p. 103.

[156] McCusker, *Money and Exchange*, pp. 18-24. There were other expenses associated with remitting specie abroad such as the costs of freight and insurance.

the study of numismatics, the truth becomes immediately apparent. What we cherish in our coin cabinets today as numismatic specimens were the monies of our forebears. As money, these coins had intrinsic value as metal and monetary value as currency; if these two amounts approached parity, then the currency was successful and circulated in commerce. The Spanish milled dollar is the paramount example of such a success. When a coin became more valuable as metal than as money, as was the case for full weight English silver, then the melting pot was its certain fate. The foreign coins which circulated in the colonies did so only because they were supported by their own intrinsic worth and it is vital to the study of numismatics to have an appreciation of that value and how it was derived.

CHAPTER THREE

Massachusetts and Maryland Silver Coinages

MASSACHUSETTS SILVER

From a numismatic viewpoint, the most famous solution for increasing the pool of circulating currency in the New England area was the founding of the Massachusetts Bay mint. Its most well known product, the "Pine Tree Shilling," is familiar to many who have had no more than a passing exposure to colonial history or numismatics. The mint came into existence as a reaction to the lightweight, counterfeit and debased silver coins which appeared in New England very quickly after the initial settlements. The unreliable currency prevalent in the colonies was generally cut, clipped or otherwise underweight Spanish silver that had penetrated mainland commerce via Jamaica, which was the hotbed of piracy and military and naval operations against the Spanish. As described by Chalmers:

> It is at any rate certain that by the close of the first half of the 17th century light Spanish coins were being circulated from the West Indies through the Plantations of the New World. And the predominance of these light coins (and counterfeit money), coupled with the inconvenience of barter and of an inadequate medium of circulation, led the colony of New England on 31st May 1652, boldly to set about minting money for itself "of good silver of the just allay of new sterling English mony ...."[1]

Initially the General Court had responded to this uncertain Spanish money by passing a bill on May 26, 1652, designed to counterstamp all silver coins with a mark of value. It would be a safe speculation that some of this questionable money was from the Potosí scandal of 1648. No evidence exists that the cumbersome scheme to label each legitimate coin was ever initiated. Instead, more definitive legislation a few weeks later authorized a mint for the recoining of Spanish silver, received from the profitable West Indian trade, into a local currency.[2] John Hull, a skillful silversmith, was appointed mintmaster with Robert Sanderson as his partner. In Hull's own words:

> Upon occasion of much counterfeit coin brought into the country, ... (and that did occasion a stoppage of trade), the General Court ordered a mint to be set up, and coin it, bringing it to the sterling standard for fineness; and, for weight, every shilling to be three pennyweight.[3]

The proposed coinage conformed to the newly established colonial standard of 72 grains of .925 fine silver to the shilling. An assay of Pine Tree money done at a later date at the United States Mint indicated a fineness of .926 and an average weight between 65 and 67 grains.[4] Since the standard English shilling of that period was 92.6 grains, this represented a 22.25% overvaluation of the Massachusetts shilling in terms of sterling currency.

[1] Chalmers, *British Colonies*, pp. 8-9.

[2] Crosby, *Early Coins*, pp. 29-43; Nettels, *Money Supply*, p. 171; Hull, *Diaries*, pp. 145, 383; Felt, *Massachusetts*, pp. 29-35; see also *Massachusetts Coinage*, an early general reference on Massachusetts silver.

[3] Hull, *Diaries*, pp. 118-19, 145.

[4] *Essex Inst. Hist. Colls.*, vol. 1 (1859), p. 125; An assay from 1660 in Massachusetts recorded that the shilling, sixpence, and threepence were equal in "allay" "to his majesty's silver coin of England" (i.e. .925 fine) but 22½% lighter (*Massachusetts Coinage*, p. 303).

The rationale for this inflated rating was to encourage Massachusetts money to circulate only at home and escape exportation. The operation was conducted by patrons bringing "Bullian, Plate, or Spanish Coyne" to the mint where the silver was melted and "brought to the Allay of Starling mony" for which they were given a receipt.[5] Spanish silver was authorized at a standard of .9305 fine and if it became necessary to increase the alloy to .925 fine prior to reminting, there was then a potential for gain. The mint was a profitable venture for Hull and Sanderson. Under their first contract with the colony, which ran from 1652 to 1667, they received 15 pence for each 20 shillings minted plus an additional allowance of three pence to cover wastage. The commission of 6.25% paid to the mintmaster and his associate was formidable, and when the expense for wastage was included, the mint fee totaled 7.5%. The amount was charged to all those who brought silver to the mint to be recoined. The effective price paid for a shilling included the cost of the intrinsic 72 grains of silver plus the mint charges which equaled another 5.4 grains, bringing the effective total value for every recoined shilling to 12.9d.[6]

The expense incurred in recoining silver at the mint created a significant operational problem since it became more profitable for people to export their silver than to patronize the mint. To complicate further this predicament, newly minted New England, Boston, or Bay Colony shillings[7], as this Massachusetts silver was contemporaneously known, were exported as bullion to Europe where they were melted down.[8] In fact, so much coin left the colony that the General Court enacted prohibitions on August 22, 1654, and May 19, 1669, which were reconfirmed on December 21, 1697, allowing for the removal of no more than 20 shillings personal expense money for any departing traveler. "Searchers" were appointed to examine persons, ships, and cargoes at the various ports and "impowered & required to search for and seize all moneys of the Coyne of this Jurisdiction" and were authorized "to breake open any chest, Trunck, Box, Cabbin, Cask, Truss, or any other suspected place or thing where they ... conceiue [conceive] money may be Concealld, & seize the same." Conviction under this new law would result in the forfeiture of the transgressor's entire estate.[9]

Despite the determination of the colonial fathers to confine these new coins within the bounds of their own territory, there are records that Massachusetts silver circulated widely in the mainland colonies as far south as Virginia.[10] Some of the Spanish silver recoined into Bay Colony shillings returned to the West Indies where it circulated as legal tender in Barbados;[11] in the Leeward Islands, legislation of September 1670 rated "all New England money at its full value in New England," and in Antigua and Nevis two years later, "pine-tree" coins were to pass at the same valuation as in New England.[12] A Massachusetts shilling was officially regulated in New York in 1672 to pass for one local shilling,[13] while in West New Jersey, in 1682, the value of the Boston shilling was legalized at 14d., New Jersey money of account.[14] An act in Maryland in 1694 pegged New England shillings and sixpence at the same rate for sterling currency, or 15d. per Boston shilling in local money of account.[15] Pine tree shillings "found their way to

[5] Crosby, *Early Coins*, pp. 88-89.

[6] Sumner, *Coin Shilling*, pp. 249-57. This calculation does not take into account that when .9305 fine Spanish American silver was brought to sterling alloy, there was some further potential for profit.

[7] Felt, *Massachusetts*, p. 54.

[8] Del Mar, *History*, p. 78.

[9] Crosby, *Early Coins*, pp. 70-71, 79, 101-2; Hull, *Diaries*, p. 290.

[10] Hoober, *Num 1953*, p. 1145.

[11] Carothers, *Fractional Money*, p. 30.

[12] Chalmers, *British Colonies*, p. 64. A Leeward Islands Act of September 24, 1670, legalized " ... all New England money at its full vallue [*sic*] in New England."

[13] Crosby, *Early Coins*, p. 289.

[14] Spilman, *CNL 1974*, p. 472; Gladfelter, *TAMS 1974*, p. 173.

[15] Crosby, *Early Coins*, p. 132.

Canada, where they apparently passed as 12 Sols pieces."[16] Based on 60 sous tournois to the écu at a sterling value of 54d., the Massachusetts money in French Canadian *monnaie du pays*, would be equivalent to 14.4d., Massachusetts currency.[17]

Until 1642, the Spanish eight reales was at par between Massachusetts and England, passing at 4s. 6d. in both locations. As the depression of 1638 began to engulf New England and specie became scarcer, a balance-of-payments crisis emerged as less hard money became available to pay for imported goods. The Massachusetts General Court responded to this financial emergency by overvaluing, i.e. "crying up," the Spanish eight reales to 5s., the rate which was current when the Massachusetts mint was established. Since most of the Spanish silver which arrived in New England had already been generously clipped, or otherwise relieved of a portion of its metal, full weight coins were exceptional. Typical eight reales circulating in New England were clipped down to about 15 dwt (360 grains), and in Philadelphia to about 12 dwt (288 grains).[18] Sumner calculated, based on the actual cost of a Boston shilling at 77.4 grains of silver, a full weight Spanish eight reales of 420 grains could be minted into 5s. 4d. 3f. of Massachusetts money.[19] The sum would be further modified depending on the assay of the Spanish silver presented to the mint. By this formula, an enterprising colonist could turn a profit of 4d. 3f. on every full weight Spanish eight reales delivered to the mint for recoinage, and even more for coins of greater purity than sterling alloy. The profit margin, of course, was proportionally reduced for the lighter, clipped Spanish silver. All potential financial advantage for sending an eight reales to the mint for recoinage was lost whenever such a coin weighed under 389.18 grains, the break-even point for the scheme. When under that weight, it would be more advantageous to pass the coin as five shillings if anyone would accept a clipped coin at full value.[20]

In 1672 the value of the eight reales piece in Massachusetts was "cryed-up" to 6s., a ratio of 100.00:133.33 when compared to sterling equivalence since the same coin still passed at 54d. in England. Massachusetts silver was not advanced beyond face value by this regulation although it had been proposed to increase the shilling to 14d., the sixpence to 7d., the threepence to 4d., and the twopence to 3d.[21] This overvaluation of Spanish coin still did not keep silver within the colony since it was more profitable to export it than to present it to the mint for recoinage because of additional fees incident to Hull's commission. This situation is evidenced by an action of the Massachusetts General Court on October 8, 1672, which begins, "Whereas peeces-of-eight are of more value to carry out of the country then [than] they will yeild [sic] to mint into our coyne, by reason whereof peeces-of-eight which might else come to coyning are carried

[16] Breen, *Encyclopedia*, p. 17.

[17] McCusker, *Money and Exchange*, p. 282. From the 1640s to 1727, the par exchange between France and her American colonies was 100 livres tournois (*monnaie de France*) to 133.33 livres colonial currency (*monnaie du pays*).

[18] Sumner, *Spanish Dollar*, p. 614.

[19] Sumner's calculations (*Yale Rev. 1898*, pp. 254-55) are as follows:
420/72 = 5.833 or number of shillings per eight reales
5.833 × 5.4 gr. mint fee per coin = 31.5 grains mint fee per eight reales
31.5/72 = 0.4375 of a shilling expense × 12d. value of a shilling = 5.25d. expense
5.833 shillings per eight reales = 5s. 10d. less expense of 5.25d. = 5s. 4d. 3f. per eight reales when reminted as Massachusetts silver.

Sumner stated that an eight reales "fresh from the mint was 420 grains [and] assumed to be of sterling alloy." His calculations disregarded that the legal Spanish-American silver standard until 1728 was .9305 fine and not sterling quality of .925 fine. Since the Spanish silver would have been assayed and then adjusted prior to minting, either the colonist, taking his money to the mint for reissuance as Massachusetts silver, or the mintmaster could have gained a little in the process. If the Spanish silver were of greater alloy than sterling, then there could have been a loss.

[20] Sumner calculated that for 5 shillings at 72 gr. = 360 gr. plus a 7.5% mint fee (for the total weight) = 389.18 gr. It could be reasoned that each Pine Tree shilling actually cost 77.4 gr. × 5 = 387 grains. This 387 grains was the break even point for the eight reales to be recoined.

[21] Crosby, *Early Coins*, p. 106.

out of the country....''[22] This Act, acknowledging that few, if any, Spanish eight reales were of full weight, contained a provision whereby all circulating Spanish silver be stamped according to its value, as determined by size, at a fee of four pence per 20 shillings. The notion to label all circulating coins with a mark of value is reminiscent of the May 26, 1652 legislation, but in neither case does evidence exist that counterstamping was ever conducted and all coins with such counterstamps are forgeries.[23]

Fig. 15: A genuine 1663 eight reales from the Potosí mint with a fake "NE" counterstamp.

Crosby noted that because these schemes to keep money at home, namely recoinage into Massachusetts silver, stamping with indication of weight and just value, and export prohibition, did not succeed, the final act of desperation for the General Court was to regulate the value of circulating silver. This was done on May 24, 1682, by approval of a provision which pegged the value of Spanish coins of sterling alloy at 6s. 8d. per troy ounce. Thus one ounce, 480 grains, of Spanish silver, worth 80d., was now accurately priced according to the same ratio of a Massachusetts shilling of 72 grains passing for 12d.[24] Spanish silver was no longer overvalued in terms of Massachusetts money to which it was now fixed according to a weight relationship.[25] Subsequent legislation in 1692 and 1697 returned the value of the seventeen pennyweight eight reales again to six shillings and also reaffirmed "that the coyn of the late Massachusetts Colony shall pass currant at the rate it was stampt for."[26] However, if a Spanish eight reales of seventeen dwt (408 grains) were to pass at 6s. (72d.), then to maintain the proper ratio, the rate for all coins of sterling silver should have been proportionately advanced to 84.7d. per ounce. An interesting inconsistency is that such a proposal to increase the value of silver money to 7s. per ounce was defeated in 1696.[27]

The Boston mint was obviously becoming unpopular due to the relatively high fixed costs paid as commissions to Hull and Sanderson and by the fact that Spanish silver could be more

[22] Felt, *Massachusetts*, pp. 41-42; Sumner, *Yale Rev. 1898*, p. 258; Crosby, *Early Coins*, pp. 80-81, quote p. 80.

[23] Wild, *CNL*, p. 257; Newman, *Samaritan*, pp. 62-63.

[24] Crosby, *Early Coins*, pp. 84-85. In these instances, the value is given for silver calculated at sterling fineness so the actual purity, or fineness, was inconsequential. Examples of such computations are in Appendix 3. This rate of 12d. per Massachusetts Bay shilling, does not accomodate for the mint charges of 0.9d.

[25] By establishment of the weight criterion, the problem of underweight eight reales, which typically varied anywhere from 12 to 15 dwt, was satisfactorily circumvented. This legislation failed to recognize that individual coins could be of unequal fineness, either greater or lesser than sterling alloy, and also disregarded the fact that the additional fees imposed by the Boston mint effectively increased the value of Massachusetts money. Sumner commented (*Yale Rev. 1898*, p. 261) that this law was not very effective.

[26] Crosby, *Early Coins*, pp. 99-100. The net effect of this change either suggests that accommodation was now provided for the mint charges for the Massachusetts money, or that Spanish silver was again overvalued. The reference is made to the "late Massachusetts Colony" since the royal charter was revoked in 1684.

[27] Crosby, *Early Coins*, p. 99.

profitably disposed of elsewhere. Suggestions, made from 1677 to 1680, were intended to encourage citizens to patronize the mint. These included a reduction in weight of the shilling by nine to twelve grains and a plan to abolish the mint fee entirely as was the practice at the English mint.[28] None of these proposals for revitalization prevailed and the mint was closed in 1682. In addition to fiscal difficulties, the Massachusetts Bay mint was clearly illegal since minting coins was a royal prerogative denied by charter to all colonies except Virginia. Acting under whatever self-justifications they chose, the enterprising colonists took advantage of the interregnum from 1649 to 1660, when England had no monarch during the Commonwealth under Cromwell, and opened the Boston mint. An ingenuous passage written in 1684 on the subject of the establishment of the mint claimed innocence from any wrongful actions on the part of Massachusetts authorities who were unaware until 1662 that the mint was "against any Law of England, or against His Majesties Will or pleasure, till of late; but rather that there was tacit allowance & approbation of it."[29] Agitation was recorded in 1665 for the abolition of the mint which was clearly an infringement on the royal privilege once the monarchy had been restored. Rather than disband the mint as the king's commissioners had demanded, the General Court, instead, hoped to appease Charles II with a gift of masts for his navy with the hope of retaining royal favor.[30] At any rate, the mint continued and the second contract between Hull and the colony was negotiated in 1667. The General Court looked for some concessions from Hull and Sanderson under the second contract. Sumner speculated that the bargaining position of the partners had eroded because of the recent termination of mint charges in England which encouraged the exportation of silver to England leaving less available to the Boston mint. The second agreement left the fee arrangements unchanged, but provided that the minters pay the colony £40 within six months and £10 annually thereafter for the next seven years.[31] Even in 1675 when the third contract between the Colony and Hull reduced his fee to one shilling per 20 shillings minted and the wastage allowance was set at 3d.,[32] the effective value of a 72 grain shilling was 76.5 grains for anyone bringing silver to the mint to be recoined into "Boston money" including the mint fees.[33] The actual value of the shilling now was 12.75d, down from 12.9d.

Even though the General Court disregarded the criticism of the king's commissioners in 1665, there remained agitation in England against the Boston mint, not so much concerning its legality, but rather the standards of weight, since the Board of the London Mint was adamant that all regal coinage conform to the same standards.[34] If the Boston shilling had been made equal to the English standard, then there would have been economic chaos produced in the colonies where the parity between the two currencies would have enriched "the Landlord and Creditor, but it would ruyne the Tenant and Debtor, destroy the Trade of that Country, and bring no advantage, but loss to the King...."[35] Sumner suggested that if the King's bust had been placed on the Boston coins instead of a Pine Tree, and if the coinage had conformed to the English standard, then little objection would have been directed toward the mint. Nevertheless, in 1684 when the Massachusetts Bay Colony charter was annulled, the issue of the mint was

[28] Crosby, *Early Coins*, p. 108; Sumner, *Yale Rev. 1898*, pp. 259-60. Sumner calculated that if the Massachusetts shillings had been reduced from 72 to 62 grains, and the mint fees proportionally decreased to 3.875 grains, then a Boston shilling would effectively be worth 65.875 grains. At this new theoretical weight, a full weight eight reales would be convertible to 6s. 4.5d. when reminted as Bay shillings, but otherwise as the original Spanish coin it would pass for only 6s.

[29] Crosby, *Early Coins*, p. 76.

[30] Crosby, *Early Coins*, pp. 76-78, 82.

[31] Sumner, *Yale Rev. 1898*, p. 257; Crosby, *Early Coins*, p. 78.

[32] Crosby, *Early Coins*, pp. 81-82.

[33] This includes the commission of 3.6 grains and the 0.9 grains allowance for wastage.

[34] Nettels, *Money Supply*, p. 172; Sumner, *Yale Rev. 1898*, p. 254.

[35] Crosby, *Early Coins*, pp. 91-94, quote p. 92.

another charge leveled against the colony, citing that it had defied royal authority, that the silver was from pirate plunder, that the inflated value of the Boston money lowered the royal standard, and that the seigniorage was excessive.[36]

Four distinct periods of Boston shillings are generally recognized: the New England coinage from the inception of the mint on June 11, 1652 until October 19, 1652; the Willow Tree variety struck intermittently until 1660; the Oak Tree variety from 1660 to 1667; and lastly the Pine Tree design from 1667 until 1682 when all mint operations ceased.[37] Although the mint operated from 1652 to 1682, all of the coins are dated 1652, with the single exception of the Oak Tree twopence which bears the date 1662. Traditionally it was thought that the repetitious use of the date 1652 was a ruse to obscure the fact that the mintage was continuous over a long period, and that the twopence was dated, perhaps by error, in the year it was first struck. A more accurate explanation is that all the dies for Massachusetts silver were engraved with the year in which the particular coin was authorized—the shilling, sixpence, and threepence in 1652 and the twopence ten years later.[38]

The initial reference to the Massachusetts silver was as "New England," "Boston" or "Bay Colony money" ; the term "Pine Tree" was not recorded until the second proposal in 1680 to abolish the mint fee, just two years before the mint was closed.[39] From that time to the early nineteenth century, the phrase "Pine Tree" was a generic reference to all products of the mint. Felt in 1839 illustrated "Pine Tree Money" in which he included an Oak Tree twopence, without any distinction between the Pine Tree and Oak Tree varieties.[40] Prime in 1861 described the New England coinage and its successor, the "Pine-tree Coinage," with its variants "the *Shrub* or *Scrub Oak* shillings." [41] Further distinction between the Oak Tree and Willow Tree varieties did not come into usage before 1867. Until that time, the Willow Tree coinage may have been considered a contemporary counterfeit due to its crude appearance. There is also an earlier reference to Willow tree money as a *Palmetto shilling* because of the tangled appearance of the branches.[42] When Crosby published his work in 1873, the designation between the four major divisions of Massachusetts silver appears to have become firmly established.[43] The die varieties were well described by Crosby and further amplified and defined by Noe from 1943 to 1952, with new discoveries still being reported.[44]

The initial design for the Massachusetts silver was detailed in the enabling legislation which required that the recoined Spanish money be stamped with NE on the one side and the mark of value, be it XII, VI or III on the other.[45] These initials and Roman numerals were transferred to the planchets by punches rather than by dies with three different obverse and reverse punches identified for the shilling for a total of six combinations.[46] The "New England" motif was

[36] Del Mar, *History*, pp. 76-77; Sumner, *Yale Rev. 1898*, p. 261, 261n. The seigniorage (the excess between the monetary and bullion value of a silver coin which becomes revenue to the government) for the royal mint was 3.5%, whereas Hull and Sanderson received a 6.25% commission under the 1652 contract and 5% under the 1675 agreement.

[37] Taxay, *Catalogue*, pp. 4-6. The precise date of 1660 separating the Willow Tree and Oak Tree coinages must be viewed with caution, since this date is derived by calculating backwards from 1682 (Michael Hodder, personal communication, Dec. 2, 1986). See Wild, *CNL 1969*, p. 259.

[38] DeLeonardis, *Num 1988*, pp. 670-71; Michael Hodder, personal communication, Dec. 2, 1986.

[39] Felt, *Massachusetts*, p. 54; Crosby, *Early Coins*, pp. 108-9.

[40] Felt, *Massachusetts*, illustration facing p. 38.

[41] Prime, *Coins*, pp. 3-4.

[42] Noe, *Willow Tree*, pp. 15-16.

[43] Noe, *Willow Tree*, p. 46.

[44] Crosby, *Early Coins*, pp. 43-65; Noe, *Willow Tree*; Noe, *Oak Tree*; Noe, *Pine Tree*; Bowers, *Coinage History*, pp. 105-11; Picker, *Studies*.

[45] Felt, *Massachusetts*, p. 31.

[46] Noe, *Willow Tree*, pp. 7, 28. There now have been described six die combinations for the shilling (Michael Hodder, personal communication, Dec. 2, 1986).

Fig. 16:
(a) Commonwealth of England: 1652 shilling which was contemporaneous with the early output of the Massachusetts mint.

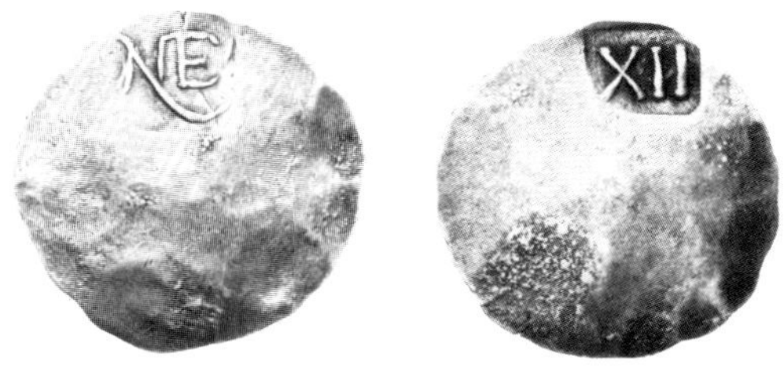

(b) New England (NE) shilling, dies 3-C.

changed by the General Court of October 19, 1652, when the coinage was redesigned with a single ring at the margin and another toward the center to discourage and detect clipping. The new style depicted "a tree in the center of the one side—and New England, and the yeere of our Lord, on the other side."[47]

The New England coinage is excessively rare but Noe was able to study 20 specimens of shillings in 1942.[48] He noted that those pieces were of good weight and that the coinage was very uniform. None of those examined signaled any indication that the change to the ringed margin was necessary because of clipping, but Noe postulated that damaged pieces may not have survived or been retained as collectors' items.

Fig. 17:
(a) Willow tree shilling, dies 3-E.

(b) Willow tree sixpence.

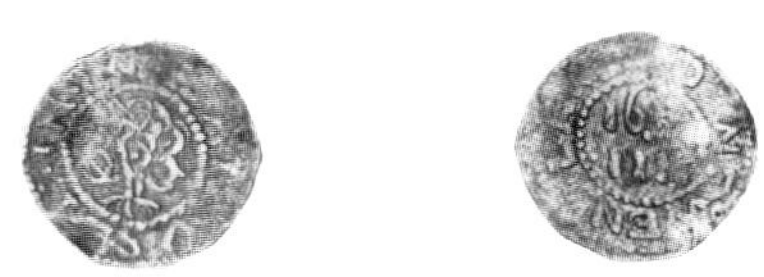

(c) Willow tree threepence.

The pattern of the new Willow Tree coinage allowed for the detection of clipping because of the double inner and outer rings. In contrast to the rather neat "New England" style, the

[47] Felt, *Massachusetts*, p. 35; Hull, *Diaries*, p. 119. The suggestion was also raised that the device on the Pine Tree money actually represented the Scriptural Cedar Tree from the prophet Ezekiel and the double ring meant Independence and Growth (*Essex Inst. Hist. Colls.*, vol. 1 [1859], p. 126).
[48] Noe, *Willow Tree*, p. 6.

Willow Tree coinage was hand struck from poorly prepared dies that were free to rotate and chatter (i.e. bounce) during the process producing double or even triple impressions such that the "tree" became "a mass of confusing lines." [49] The double and triple striking created jumbled legends but analysis by Noe revealed that there were only three obverse and five reverse dies (Crosby thought there were seven reverse dies) for the 36 specimens he examined. There is a total of six die combinations for the shilling [50] and a single pair of dies each for both the sixpence and threepence. Both Crosby and Noe were disparaging of the Willow Tree coinage.

> The coins bearing this tree [willow] are so rude in conception and bungling in execution, ... as to deserve none other than a position among the experimental attempts of novices in the art of coining; unless, as has been suggested, they are to be considered as counterfeits, which to us does not appear probable. So rude, indeed, are they, that it is difficult to believe them to have been accepted by any people except under urgent necessity for coin of some kind, however imperfect.[51]
>
> On the other hand, if these Willow Tree pieces were all as badly made as the ones which have been examined herein, it would not be surprising to learn that they were melted down at the first opportunity.[52]

Fig. 18:
(a) Oak tree shilling, Noe 14.

(b) Oak tree sixpence, Noe 22.

(c) Oak tree threepence, Noe 24.

(d) Oak tree 1662 twopence, Noe 29.

The change from the Willow Tree to the Oak Tree varieties was more than an alteration in design, since it also marked a distinct advance in minting technology as evidenced by the employment of some fashion of fixed dies and even striking. The improved manufacturing technique prompted Noe to theorize the introduction of a screw press by the Massachusetts mint since the quality of the Oak Tree series suggested to him that mechanization was now

[49] Noe, *Willow Tree*, p. 17.
[50] There have been described to date six die combinations (Michael Hodder, personal communication, Dec. 2, 1986).
[51] Crosby, *Early Coins*, p. 46.
[52] Noe, *Willow Tree*, pp. 19-20.

employed.[53] Further research by Doty confirms that a simple rocker press was used for all Oak Tree pieces and the early Pine Tree series, the screw press being employed at a later date for the small planchet Pine Tree money.[54] The surfaces of well preserved coins, minted by a rocker press, may show a characteristic sinusoidal warping. Parallel bends in some specimens, previously attributed as so-called witch pieces, are actually artifacts caused by the passage of the silver planchet between the opposing dies.

Within the Oak Tree series appeared the only Massachusetts silver coin dated other than 1652, namely the 1662 Oak Tree twopence, whose production probably began in that actual year.[55] The enabling legislation stipulated that during the first year of production, £50 worth of the new twopence were to be minted for every £100 of silver coined, and for the next six years, £20 for every £100.[56] This rather ambitious minting schedule was accomplished with a single pair of dies which survived six recuttings without any significant breaks.[57] The added longevity for the twopence dies resulted from the fact that less internal stress occurs within dies which impress smaller, thinner planchets than within those used with larger planchets. The working life of dies is also extended whenever planchets are annealed, or softened by heating, prior to striking, since the metal is rendered more malleable. In the case of the Massachusetts mint, it remains unknown whether the annealing process was ever used.[58]

Fig. 19:
(a) Pine tree shilling, large planchet, Noe 1.

(b) Pine tree shilling, small planchet, Noe 16.

(c) Pine tree sixpence, Noe 33.

(d) Pine tree threepence, Noe 36.

[53] Noe, *Willow Tree*, pp. 24-29.
[54] Doty, *Massachusetts*; See also *Schenkel*, lot 5505 for the commentary by Michael Hodder (personal communication, Dec. 2, 1986).
[55] Noe, *Oak Tree*, pp. 10-12, 22-23.
[56] Sumner, *Yale Rev. 1898*, p. 256; Crosby, *Early Coins*, pp. 73-74.
[57] Newman, *Samaritan*, pp. 29-34, 68; Michael Hodder, personal communication, Dec. 12, 1986.
[58] Noe, *Willow Tree*, p. 28.

The transition in design from the Oak Tree to the Pine Tree emblem was gradual. Spiney branches appeared on the Oak Tree shilling now designated Noe 14 (see fig. 18a), and a common reverse was shared by three Oak Tree sixpence, Noe 20 to 22, and one Pine Tree sixpence, Noe 32.[59] The change from the Oak Tree to the Pine Tree motif is thought to have occurred in 1667 when Hull's second agreement with the Colony was ratified.[60] The early Pine Tree shillings were struck on large planchets in a rocker press, but the later small planchet issues were minted by a screw press with occasional evidence of double striking. It has been surmised that the small planchet Pine Tree shillings were introduced in 1675, the year when Hull's third and last contract was signed.[61] The final agreement ran until 1682 when the mint was closed; Hull died the following year and Sanderson survived another ten.

There is little information on the quantity of "Boston" coins minted over the 30 year span of the mint, except that it was a formidable output. Felt noted that "the products of its [the mint's] operation were long current in our country. Down to the Revolution of our Independence, they were often seen, and passed readily in business transactions, with other coin."[62]

An interesting collection of Massachusetts silver was salvaged from the 1711 wreck of the *H.M.S. Feversham*. Of the 92 specimens recovered, all but 2 were shillings and the census was as follows: 1 New England shilling, 4 Willow Tree shillings, 27 Oak Tree shillings, and 54 Pine Tree shillings, 2 sixpence, and several cut pieces. It is tempting to speculate that this was the appoximate ratio in which these four styles of shillings circulated as a currency in the early eighteenth century. Certainly in the twentieth century, these proportions are in the order of magnitude in which they appear in auction catalogues. Of particular interest were the few Pine Tree shillings which had been cut into fractional pieces, a practice very common with Spanish silver.

Contemporary records speak of counterfeit Boston money and those people who attempted to defraud the public by debasing the currency.[63] The earliest documented account was the 1674 conviction of John du Plisse who fabricated Massachusetts silver from pewter. A 1683 report from Pennsylvania and New York described counterfeit Boston, Spanish, and other coins in circulation. Current evidence suggests that the Noe 4 New England sixpence,[64] and the Oak Tree sixpence coins, Noe 15, 18,[65] and 19,[66] are forgeries, as are the Pine Tree shillings designated as Noe 13, 14, 31, and possibly 12. These pieces are about 65% normal weight and were intentionally made to appear heavily worn and severely clipped and as such masqueraded as widely circulated coins to obscure their true origins.[67] There are numerous other contemporary counterfeits and later day fabrications of Pine Tree money illustrated by Noe and other more recent writers.[68] It is clear that these questionable pieces are not the work of Hull and Sanderson since the crude design of the tree and the amateurish style of the lettering differ substantially from the genuine products. Two recent discoveries have reported fabricated Massachusetts silver coins struck over Spanish American one real pieces. One is a counterfeit Pine Tree shilling struck over a 1781 Mexican one real,[69] and the second is a New England sixpence over a similar

[59] Noe, *Oak Tree*, pp. 8-9, 20, Plate V; Noe, *Pine Tree*, p. 40.
[60] Noe, *Pine Tree*, pp. 6-8.
[61] Noe, *Pine Tree*, pp. 7-8.
[62] Felt, *Massachusetts*, p. 49; Hull, *Diaries*, p. 306.
[63] Glaser, *Counterfeiting*, p. 12; Scott, *Pennsylvania*, p. 1; Scott, *New York*, pp. 2-3.
[64] Pollock, *RCR 80*, p. 50.
[65] Taxay, *Catalogue*, p. 5.
[66] Newman, *Samaritan*, pp. 45-50, plate V.
[67] Picker, *Studies*, pp. 86-87; Taxay, *Catalogue*, p. 6.
[68] Noe, *Pine Tree*, pp. 423-47, plates VII, VIII; Noe, *Willow Tree*, pp. 50-55, plate II; *Picker*, pp. 21-22.
[69] Trudgen, CNL 1984B, pp. 896-99. Trudgen speculates that this coin, discovered by Robert Vlack, was the product of Machin's Mills in the late 1780s.

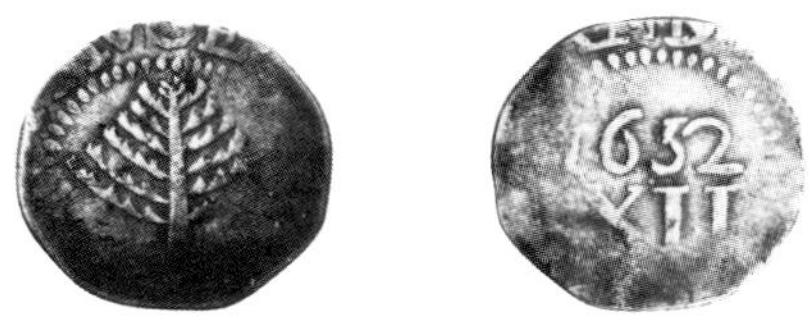

Fig. 20: Contemporary counterfeit pine tree shilling, Noe 13 (34.0 grains)

host coin, dated 1772 or later.[70] The sixpence is a Noe 4 variety, a combination whose authenticity has been the subject of controversy. Now that these dies have been implicated in an obviously contrived situation, Noe 4 is confirmed as a forgery, a conclusion first reached by Newman in 1959 based on other evidence. The problem is to determine which of these coins were contemporary counterfeits made during the last half of the seventeenth century to masquerade as legitimate specimens and which are modern forgeries produced to deceive unwary collectors.

It is not surprising that money as famous as the Massachusetts Pine Tree coinage, used in an inclusive sense, has developed its own lore and legends. One famous tale is that John Hull became so rich from his minting operation that when his daughter, Hannah, married Judge Samuel Sewall in 1675,[71] her dowry was her weight in Massachusetts silver, some 10,000 coins.[72] Such a sum would place the young bride's weight at almost 103 pounds, avoirdupois, or £500 in Massachusetts currency, a tidy sum in its day. This would be equivalent to Hull's commission for the manufacture of 160,000 shillings. Another account of this event states that the dowry was some £30,000, obviously not calculated from Hannah's weight![73]

Another popular story is told of the visit of Sir Thomas Temple, the Royal Governor of Nova Scotia, to Charles II in 1662. The anecdote continues that as the two were discussing the affairs of New England, including the illegal mint, the Governor presented the monarch some Massachusetts silver. "Seeing a tree on one of the pieces, Charles inquired what sort of a tree that was. The immediate reply, it was the royal oak, which preserved his majesty's life.[74] Such an answer brought the king to good humor, and induced him to hear the pleas which the governor made in favor of our colony."[75] Although quoted by some as a "ridiculous story,"[76] it does emphasize the fact that the Massachusetts mint, although illegal, operated for many years with royal knowledge and indifference.

It has been popularly promoted that New Englanders, during the latter half of the seventeenth century, carried bent silver coins to protect themselves from the evils of witchcraft, a frenzy which had engulfed Massachusetts. Such bent and restraightened coins are called "witch pieces" and it is reported that some still show the teeth marks as an indication of how they were doubled. It is now known that these bends were the result of the rocker press in which the Oak Tree and large planchet Pine Tree shillings were minted. While silver, usually a symbol of purity, has been used in various cultures as a protection from evil and witchcraft,[77] the first recorded

[70] Pollock, *RCR 80*, p. 50.
[71] Wish, *Sewall*, p. 10.
[72] Reit, *Collecting*, p. 39; Crosby, *Early Coins*, p. 98; Prime, *Coins*, p. 4; Hull, *Family*, p. 275.
[73] Crosby, *Early Coins*, p. 33.
[74] The "royal oak" makes reference to an event in September 1651, when the royalist forces in support of Charles II were defeated by Oliver Cromwell at the Battle of Worcester, and the king fled for his life. The newly-crowned sovereign took refuge in the branches of the large oak of Boscobel while soldiers searched in vain for him in the woods below (Dickens, *History*, pp. 267-68; Guizot, *England*, vol. 3, p. 147).
[75] Felt, *Massachusetts*, pp. 38-39; Crosby, *Early Coins*, p. 75.
[76] Ruding, *Annals*, vol. 1, p. 416.
[77] *Folklore*, p. 1012. One English superstition held that witches could change themselves into hares which could only be shot with a silver bullet or a crooked silver sixpence (Radford, *Encyclopedia*, p. 261).

mention of the bent silver coin superstition in American numismatic literature is credited to Noe in his 1952 monograph.[78] While the story of the bent silver "witch pieces" needs authentication from contemporary sources, it is ironic that the presiding judge at the Salem witch trials of 1692 which condemned 20 persons to death, was none other than Samuel Sewall (1653-1730), Hull's son-in-law. The Judge, a very prominent citizen, was a diarist whose commentaries on contemporary Massachusetts are a valuable resource.[79]

Noe suggested that the "crooked sixpence" mentioned in the nursery rhyme, "There was a crooked man ..." could have been a witch piece.[80] While the point is suggestive, another interpretation proposes that Charles I was the "crooked sixpence" and the rhyme refers to granting religious and political freedoms to Scotland.[81]

When first organized in 1652, the purpose of the Massachusetts mint was to supply silver coins of sterling fineness for local commerce since even at that early time "uncertain" money was finding its way into the colony. The new silver pieces were reminted from Spanish coins obtained from the West Indian trade. To ensure that this "Pine Tree" money, generically speaking, remain truly local and not be exported, it was undervalued at 72 grains of sterling to the shilling which did not include an additional mint cost equivalent to another 5.4 grains. Neither this reduced value nor stiff penalties imposed for exporting the money out of the area prevented the Massachusetts silver from circulating widely. Although the mint costs were eventually reduced, the population were still not persuaded to take their money there to be reissued as "Boston" money. Despite some vague suggestions to revitalize the mint, it was closed in 1682 for what appears to be a combination of economic and political reasons.

MARYLAND SILVER COINAGE

Encouraged by the example of his northern neighbors, Cecil Calvert, Lord Baltimore, had a silver coinage of shillings, sixpence, and groats, minted in England for use in Maryland some time before October 1659.[82] This money bore the bust of Lord Baltimore on the obverse facing left and on the reverse a crowned lozenged shield with the Latin legends, "Cecil Lord of Maryland," and "Increase and be Multiplied." Although the weight of Maryland silver was 75% of the English, or 69.82 grains for the shilling, it was of sterling alloy.

The Maryland charter of 1632 did not specifically permit the coinage of money, but the second Lord Baltimore assumed this right. An action was initiated against his lordship by Richard Pight, Clerk of the Irons of the Tower Mint, which caused Calvert to be arrested as a "false coiner" by an order of October 4, 1659, and summoned to appear before the Privy Council. The indictment charged "that Cecill Lord Baltimore and diverse others with him, and for him, have made and transported great Sums of mony and doe still goe on to make more." The warrant commanded the seizure of Lord Baltimore and his colleagues together with their coins, coining "stamps, tooles, & Instruments." The following day, Lord Baltimore appeared before the Council where it was learned "that a great quantity of Silver is coyned into peeces of diverse rates & values, and sent into Maryland by the Lo. Baltimore or his Order." His lordship was ordered to attend a meeting of the Committee of the Council for the Plantations who were given the responsibility to investigate and report "the whole business."[83]

There are several reasons why Lord Baltimore's coinage provoked official displeasure. As noted in the Privy Council minutes, his lordship was exporting specie out of the realm which was

78 Noe, *Pine Tree*, p. 19. Noe gives no source other than the statement, "We are told ...."

79 Wish, *Sewall*, passim; Starkey, *Devil*, passim.

80 Noe, *Pine Tree*, p. 19n.

81 Mulheim, *Rhymes*, p. 78.

82 Crosby, *Early Coins*, pp. 123-32; Taxay, *Catalogue*, p. 7; Craig, *Mint*, p. 376; Hoober, *Num 1962*; Breen, *Encyclopedia*, pp. 18-19; *Norweb*, pp. 232-38.

83 Crosby, *Early Coins*, pp. 129-30.

Fig. 21: Maryland Silver
(a) Lord Baltimore shilling, Breen 64 (64.2 grains).

(b) Lord Baltimore fourpence or groat, Breen 74 (21.7 grains).

against the law. In 1658 and 1659, England was approaching insolvency which would have prompted authorities to plug any drain of hard money from the country.[84] Secondly, the coined money "of diverse rates & values" did not conform to the standards of the Tower Mint. While Maryland silver was sterling in quality, the weight fell short of Tower Mint issues. The fact that Lord Baltimore assumed the royal prerogative of coinage and even dared place his bust on the money would have been less offensive to the Privy Council, since these events occurred during the interregnum of the Commonwealth when there was no reigning monarch. Apparently a compromise must have been reached between Calvert and the Privy Council since there is no record of any disciplinary action and his coinage continued to circulate.

The total coinage placed in circulation was in the vicinity of £2,500. This is implied from a Maryland law of April 12, 1662, requiring every "Householder and Freeman in the Province" to exchange 60 pounds of tobacco for ten shillings of the new silver money.[85] Although colonial records indicate that a mint was authorized in 1661, there is little doubt that all this coinage is of English origin. The few copper pennies known to exist were probably patterns, never produced in significant numbers.

* * *

Massachusetts and Maryland silver coinages share some common features. Both were currencies created for the want of a domestic, circulating medium, having originated without any precise legal authority during the period of the Commonwealth. A major difference was that Boston money was locally minted over the span of many years from clipped, worn Spanish silver, while Maryland money was minted by contract for a few months in England.

England had "refused to allow separate colonial mints on the grounds that all the money of the Empire should conform to one single standard,"[86] but such conformity was an unacceptable alternative for the colonists since it would devastate creditor-debtor relationships. In both colonies, their respective monies were of sterling alloy but significantly lighter than their Tower Mint counterparts. The reduced weights of the colonial monies were necessary because of the inherent inequities between colonial and metropolitan exchange rates and monies of account. Had the colonial and Tower shillings been of equal weight, then the bullion price for the Massachusetts and Maryland issues would have far exceeded their commercial value of 12d., thus ensuring a immediate trip to the melting pot and subsequent export.

Unlike Massachusetts money, there are no existing records to indicate that Maryland silver ever circulated outside the province. In a manner similar to Massachusetts, Maryland also

[84] Andrews, *Colonial Period*, p. 53.
[85] Crosby, *Early Coins*, p. 128.
[86] Nettels, *Money Supply*, pp. 278-83, quote p. 280.

forbade the export of foreign specie coins, including Massachusetts silver, outside their colony, except for the payment of "protested Bills of Exchange."[87] These currency regulations, designed to keep circulating gold and silver at home and to "cry up" its value, together with the issuance of domestic coinages, were similar actions by both Massachusetts and Maryland to provide and maintain an adequate store of money for local use.

[87] Crosby, *Early Coins*, p. 132.

CHAPTER FOUR

Colonial Paper Currency

In spite of England's mercantilist policies and the repressive actions of the Board of Trade, the North American economy grew and prospered. Even though the colonists complained loudly and frequently that they did not possess all the specie they thought necessary, and small denominational coins were subject to cyclical shortages at best, domestic and foreign commerce did proceed through the use of alternatives to hard coin or by the manipulation of exchange rates. The final method to be described for the expansion of the domestic money supply was the employment of four varieties of paper currencies: (a) commodity notes against warehoused goods; (b) bills of exchange; (c) bills of credit based on anticipated tax revenues; and (d) bills of credit, or land bank notes, issued by public loan offices. The first alternative was quasi-public in scope, the second was a more private or individual contract, whereas the latter two options were public in that the notes were issued by governmental authorities or private institutions. As previously stated, all of these schemes to augment the currency supply were not mutually exclusive, but while they were introduced successively, several operated simultaneously since one plan was not abandoned before another system was initiated. This chapter will summarize the introduction, use, and refinement of these several genera of paper currency.[1] The large emissions of paper currency by the Continental Congress and colonies during the Revolutionary period is a subject to be covered in Chapter Six.

COMMODITY NOTES

"Store house" or "commodity notes," were issued as receipts when marketable goods were consigned to official warehouses. Tobacco notes of Virginia, Maryland, and the Carolinas typify these warehouse receipts which circulated as money among the merchant class and were more convenient to handle than the commodities themselves. These notes were secured by the market value of the goods against which they were issued, but because of the potential for deterioration of tobacco, such notes had an eighteen months' restriction as a circulating medium.[2] Newman makes the interesting observation that the Virginia currency issue of July 11, 1771, was actually emitted to fund the colony's obligation for some of its tobacco warehouse receipts given for stored tobacco which was subsequently destroyed when a public warehouse was flooded.[3] This use of warehouse receipts was described by Benjamin Franklin as follows:

> The Usages [i.e. customary transactions agreeable to all parties] in Buying and Selling Merchandises, are much the same as in Europe, except that in Virginia the Planter carries his Tobacco to Magazines, where it is inspected by Officers, who ascertain its Quality and give Receipts expressing the Quantity. The Merchants receive these Receipts in Payments for Goods, and afterwards draw the Tobacco out of the Magazines for Exportation.[4]

[1] For a complete treatment of public paper money, namely bills of credit and land bank notes, the reader is referred to Newman, *Paper Money*. This work is the standard reference for paper money of the colonial period.

[2] Hoober, *Num 1953*, p. 1151; McDonald, *Origins*, p. 389.

[3] Newman, *Paper Money*, p. 435.

[4] Smyth, *Franklin*, vol. 9, pp. 235-36.

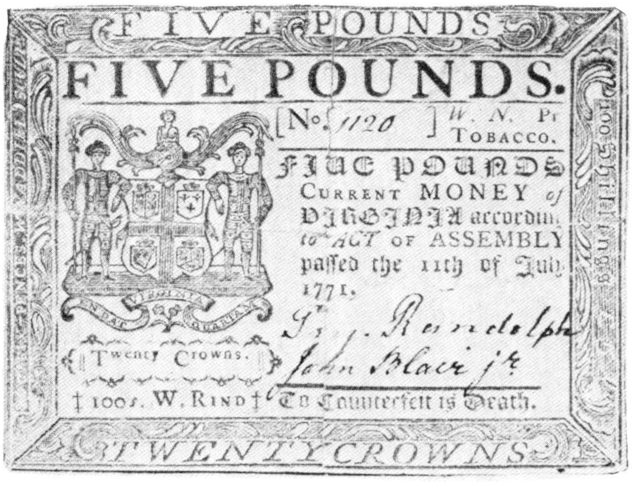

Fig. 22: A £5 VIRGINIA TOBACCO NOTE OF JULY 11, 1771. This non-legal tender "Tobacco" note was issued by the colony to pay for tobacco destroyed by floods. Since 1730 Virginia had provided public warehouse receipts for stored tobacco and these certificates circulated as currency. When the stored tobacco was lost in floods, the colony was obliged to raise money to compensate the holders of receipts for the damaged commodity. The note pictured is a counterfeit (Newman, *Paper Money*, p. 435). Courtesy Eric P. Newman Numismatic Education Society.

Warehouse receipts, or tobacco notes, were usually issued for a minimum of 950 lbs. of tobacco making the payment of a small debt very inconvenient with this medium. In earlier days, small parcels of tobacco were carried about making it "incredible that such bulky material was actually lugged into the courthouse to pay taxes and fees ...." Later there developed "transfer" tobacco notes to accomodate these smaller consignments of tobacco deposited with officials, and as such, the receipts for these smaller portions became a kind of circulating medium. "To date, no specimens of 'transfer' tobacco notes have been located."[5]

Initially, tobacco was all important for large domestic payments and overseas transactions as described in Maryland in 1708:

> Tobacco is their Meat, Drink, Cloathing, and Money: Not but that they have both Spanish and English Money pretty plenty, which serves only for Pocket-Expences, and not for Trade, Tobacco being the Standard of that, as well as with the Planters and others, as with the Merchants.[6]

As other commodities gained in economic importance and the tobacco market became more volatile, this money, based on commodity receipts, became less important, particularly in Virginia, where paper bills of credit appeared after 1755.[7]

BILLS OF EXCHANGE

The negotiable "bill of exchange" was another form of individual, or private, paper currency which saw limited circulation among colonial merchants and was the chief payment method of foreign debts for imported goods.[8] "The bill of exchange, basically a negotiable instrument for the transfer of money, became a form of money itself when it circulated for a while before being presented for payment."[9] Such a bill was created when a colonial merchant purchased a draft from a second party who had foreign credit and through this vehicle the merchant could pay for his goods in the foreign market. In its simplest form, a Boston merchant contracts to buy cloth from a London dealer. The merchant has the option of remitting the agreed price to his supplier in specie via the next sailing ship. The more common practice is for him to negotiate with another Boston firm who regularly exports dried cod fish to England and through the sale of this

[5] Williamson, *CNL 1986*, pp. 932-33.
[6] Chalmers, *British Colonies*, p. 5.
[7] Ernst, *Money and Politics*, p. 45.
[8] Ferguson, *WMQ 1953*, p. 158.
[9] McCusker, *Studies*, p. 102.

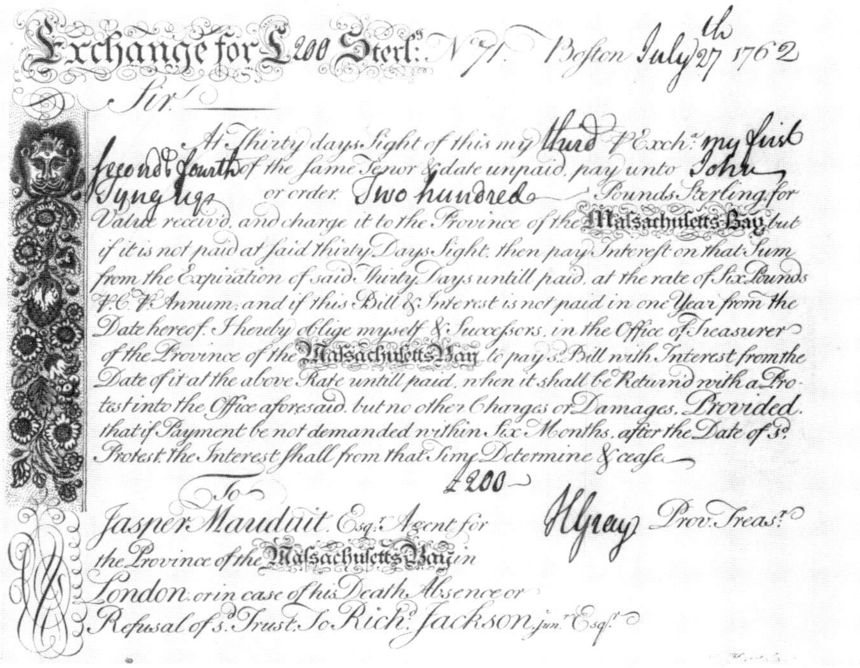

Exchange for £200 Sterl.: No 71. Boston July 27th 1762

Sir

At Thirty days Sight of this my third Exch.a my first second & fourth of the same Tenor & date unpaid, pay unto John Tyng Esqr or order Two hundred Pounds Sterling for Value receiv'd, and charge it to the Province of the Massachusetts Bay but if it is not paid at said thirty Days Sight, then pay Interest on that Sum from the Expiration of said Thirty Days untill paid, at the rate of Six Pounds P.C. P. Annum; and if this Bill & Interest is not paid in one Year from the Date hereof, I hereby oblige myself & Successors, in the Office of Treasurer of the Province of the Massachusetts Bay to pay sd Bill with Interest from the Date of it at the above Rate untill paid, when it shall be Return'd with a Protest into the Office aforesaid, but no other Charges or Damages. Provided that if Payment be not demanded within Six Months, after the Date of sd Protest the Interest shall from that Time Determine & cease.

£200

To Jasper Mauduit Esqr Agent for the Province of the Massachusetts Bay in London, or in case of his Death, Absence or Refusal of sd Trust To Richd Jackson jun. Esqr

H Gray Prov. Treasr

Fig. 23: BILL OF EXCHANGE. This is an ornately printed bill of exchange engraved by Nathaniel Hurd of Boston in 1762. Most bills of exchange were handwritten and less decorative, although the elaborate design on this issue would have discouraged counterfeiters. This particular bill was drawn for £200, sterling, by H. Gray, Treasurer of the Province of Massachusetts, on the London account of the government of Massachusetts Bay under the control of their London agent, Jasper Mauduit, Esq., and made payable to John Tyng, Esq. Courtesy The American Antiquarian Society.

commodity has a sterling credit balance with its London agent. Our Boston cloth merchant can arrange with his Boston colleague to buy some of his London sterling assets by purchasing a "bill of exchange." In summary, the Boston cloth merchant buys pound sterling credit from the Boston cod fish exporter who has earned money which is deposited in London, and for this transaction, the Boston merchant pays the fish exporter in Massachusetts money of account at the prevailing commercial exchange rate of Massachusetts on London (see above, p. 76).

An appreciation of the problems colonial merchants encountered in paying for imported merchandise helps in understanding the intricacies of colonial finance and commerce and the maneuvers undertaken to increase the pool of domestic currency. The colonial merchant, without a personal source of credit but desiring English imports, had to buy English pounds sterling to pay for such goods and those pounds were purchased with colonial monies of account. The price he had to pay for the real English money, in terms of his local money of account or imaginary money, was determined by the prevailing commercial exchange rate. The financial instrument, through which such transactions were usually conducted, was the bill of exchange or draft, bought in America, payable in England, and drawn on an account which had sterling credit. Such instruments were "commonly drawn at 30 Days' Sight," meaning that they were payable 30 days after presentation.[10] The rate of exchange, which determined the price of the English credit purchased in America, was a reflection of local short run economic factors, the trade deficit, the strength of the local currency, and conditions of war, to name a few.[11]

To return to the example of the Boston merchant and his consignment of English cloth, if he had ordered this material in August 1695, he would have had to pay his cod fish exporter friend

[10] Smyth, *Franklin*, vol. 9, p. 235. Complications developed when bills of exhange were refused payment and returned to the buyer with "protest." Legal actions for damages and interest usually ensued.

[11] Ernst, *Money and Politics*, p. 8.

for the bill of exchange £130 in Massachusetts money for every £100 of English sterling credit he required, not including any additional amounts for fees and expenses. Examples of the actual calculations involved in figuring the cost of such transactions are presented in Appendix 1. If the Boston merchant bought the same bolts of cloth 30 years later, the price in Massachusetts money of account would have risen to £300! This was the time that commodity monies were reintroduced into Massachusetts due to an economic downturn and shortage of available specie.[12] The worst was yet to come when in July 1747, during the depression following King George's War, the rate had advanced to £1050![13] Thomas Hancock wrote of the postwar deflation in 1748, "Peace has put a stop to all our trade."[14] Indeed, international commerce cooled for New England after hostilities ceased and earned foreign credits were very scarce since the export trade was sluggish and anyone who wanted to buy a bill of exchange on London had to be prepared to pay handsomely for it. Hard money supplies dried up, or better stated, the purchase of foreign credits for needed imports became exorbitantly expensive and people were reluctant to part with their coin. As the depression deepened, few New England merchants would risk spending scarce money on foreign purchases which they would have had little likelihood of selling now that imported goods, more expensive than ever, piled up on their shelves as domestic money supplies became tighter. During this period, commerce was lethargic in New England, but for the other colonies the cost of foreign credit remained stable although inflated in the Carolinas. Relief was in sight for New England, when in 1749, Massachusetts received a large shipment of specie from England. Such an account, as this hypothetical example of our Boston cloth merchant, demonstrates the interaction between the prevaling local, or worldwide, economic climate, the health of the import-export trade, the availability or scarcity of specie, the expense of foreign credits, the requirements for other hard money substitutes, and, of course, the inevitable complaints about all of the above.

The diverse economic conditions prevailing within the thirteen colonies created varying strengths of the local monies of account. For that reason different exchange rates existed between the various colonies and England, and among the colonies themselves. This inequality within the colonial monies was a frustration which made intercolonial commerce confusing and complicated. If exports were low and foreign credits, therefore, scarce, then the price for the bills of exchange increased to meet the demand.[15] Not all colonies had a flourishing export trade from which to derive sterling credit. This factor was a frustration to Thomas Hancock who noted that New England, unlike the tobacco producing south, produced few commodities for which there was any great demand in England. As he wrote, "our Country Produce being so Low in London makes it Difficult to get money there."[16] As a resourceful merchant, Hancock soon turned to whale oil and related products for which there was an active overseas market and a ready supply of sterling credit.

At such a time when the commercial exchange rate was unfavorable, the merchant might find it economically more advantageous to ship hard coin to England to meet his obligations rather than to pay the premium for the scarce sterling credits earned by sluggish colonial exports. The level at which it was cheaper to pay by sending coin rather than buying expensive credits was called the "specie export point."[17] The colonial merchant was assisted in this decision whether to ship coin

[12] Felt, *Massachusetts*, pp. 82-83.

[13] McCusker, *Money and Exchange*, pp. 138-42. Newman, *Paper Money*, pp. 467-75, lists the prevailing exchange rates among the paper monies of the various issuing colonies, expressed in their local monies of account, and £100 sterling. For the Massachusetts example, the gradual inflation of bills of credit can be followed through the emission of the "old, middle, and new tenor" notes.

[14] Baxter, *Hancock*, p. 111.

[15] Ernst, *Money and Politics*, p. 10.

[16] Baxter, *Hancock*, pp. 45-49.

[17] McCusker, *Money and Exchange*, pp. 22-23, 116-17; Ernst, *Money and Politics*, pp. 15-16n; Ferguson, *WMQ 1953*, p. 158.

or buy bills of exchange by consulting published reference tables. When colonial exports were low and earned credit became expensive, more specie was drained away to England where it was remitted for imported goods as the "specie export point" was exceeded; thus the supply of circulating coin dwindled in the colonies. The adequacy of the local hard money supply was, therefore, related to the strength of the colonial export market. This is one explanation for the variable reports concerning the availability of coin in different areas at different times, and why exchange rates, or the price of credit, differed among the colonies.

BILLS OF CREDIT

Previous chapters have described colonial monetary practices to augment domestic circulating currencies. These actions occurred against the background of English mercantilism whose stated objectives were to keep the colonies dependent, yet wealthy enough to buy English goods but not so prosperous as to develop competitive local industry. Initially the individual colonies became competitive in attracting specie into their own territories, or discouraging drain, so that the local "crying up" of money or overvaluation of silver became a popular option. The advantage of this currency manipulation was lost after the early 1700s when such practices became the target of the Proclamation of 1704. Massachusetts minted its own overvalued local coinage (in terms of sterling) and unsuccessfully forbade its export in order to maintain enough circulating medium for domestic commerce. Maryland imported a silver currency. By the early eighteenth century, the American colonies were still faced with the situation of insufficient available specie to conduct commerce, to underwrite military campaigns and to finance domestic projects. More inflationary programs were envisioned, the most significant of which was the emergence of colonial paper currency or bills of credit.

"If coin shortage was the underlying cause, war provided the immediate occasion for paper money."[18] A series of wars was fought in North America between the French and English from 1689 to 1763, which, with the exception of the French and Indian War, were local extensions of European conflicts.[19] In 1690 an ill-fated military expedition to French Canada failed to return the anticipated booty to the Massachusetts treasury so that the colony was unable to raise funds to pay troops and other war incurred obligations. The colonial government could not afford to borrow to meet these expenses and their only recourse was to issue "bills of credit," backed only by the good faith of the colony in the expectation of redemption funded by taxes. The fact was that hard money was available, but at what price? The statement of Judge Samuel Sewall quoted in Chapter One is to be recalled again. "I was at making of the first Bills of Credit in the year 1690: They were not made for want of Money; but for want of Money in the Treasury."

The system under which these bills of credit were authorized is described as "currency finance." This is a stratagem whereby "the heavy burden of military expenses and other public demands" is underwritten by "short-term lending by issuing notes in anticipation of future tax-

[18] Nettels, *Money Supply*, pp. 255-56.

[19] The Colonial Wars from 1689 to 1763 are collectively known as the French and Indian Wars, while the last conflict of the series is specifically the French and Indian War (1754-1763).

Dates	*Colonial War*	*European War*	*Colonial Involvement*
1689-1697	King William's	League of Augsburg	N.Y., N.E.
1702-1713	Queen Anne's	Spanish Succession	N.E., Florida, S.C.
1744-1748	King George's	Austrian Succession	Northern colonies
1754-1763	French and Indian	Seven Years'	Began in America as a territorial dispute

returns."[20] While this first emission of money solved the immediate problem of quelling mutinous soldiers who demanded their wages, it launched the colonies on a hundred years' career of paper currency. A similar campaign in 1702 was responsible for additional paper money in Massachusetts, and within the next year South Carolina followed suit to support its military objectives in Florida. By 1710, further armed excursions into French Canada and the immediate need for ready cash lured the other New England colonies, New York, and New Jersey to solve their financial deficits with a printing press.[21] In 1712, North Carolina authorized paper money to defray the expense of war against the Tuscarora Indians. Typically the bills of credit issued by these eight colonies in anticipation of tax revenues were interest bearing, had legal tender status, were receivable for taxes, and contained specific provisions for their redemption.[22]

LAND-BANK NOTES

In addition to the bills of credit issued as fiat money and secured by future tax assessments for immediate government expenses such as war, a second system of "currency finance" depended on paper money emitted by authorized colonial "land banks" or public "loan-offices."[23] In this format, a public loan office chartered by the colonial legislature provided low interest loans by issuing bills of credit to qualified individuals who mortgaged their property as security. The land bank system has been described as:

> the primary social legislation of colonial America. It was a method of putting currency into circulation and at the same time affording loans to farmers which they could scarcely obtain from other sources.... As the annual installments due on the principal came back into the loan office, the bills were cancelled and retired, though they were often reissued, or successive banks established to maintain a continuous flow of loans. The colonies thus developed a medium of exchange out of "solid or real property ... melted down and made to circulate in paper money or bills of credit."[24]

The land bank system, introduced in Barbados in 1706,[25] functioned on the assumption that mortgaged real estate and silver plate would maintain the value of the paper currency and that the additional available money would stimulate the economy. In 1712, South Carolina was the first mainland colony to set up a public loan office, and by 1755, all colonies except Virginia participated in this type of currency venture.[26] The land banks established in the middle colonies of Pennsylvania, New Jersey, Delaware, New York, and Maryland, were particularly successful since their money achieved stability and depreciated little.[27] The well-managed Maryland paper currency would have been redeemable at face value had it not been for the

[20] Ernst, *Money and Politics*, quote p. 22; Ferguson, *WMQ 1953*, pp. 171-72; Ferguson, *Purse*, chap. 1.

[21] McKay, *Currency*, pp. 13-25. The order of emission of paper money was as follows: Massachusetts 1690; the Carolinas (South) 1703; New York, New Hampshire, Connecticut, and New Jersey 1709; Rhode Island 1710; North Carolina 1712; Pennsylvania 1723; Delaware and Maryland 1733; Georgia 1754; Virginia 1755 (from Newman, *Paper Money*).

[22] Newman, *Paper Money*, pp. 12-13, 22, 248. For example, the February 3, 1690/91 Massachusetts emission, receivable at a 5% premium for tax payments, was redeemed within three years. The July 1, 1714 New York issue for £27,680 matured in 25 years and was thus nicknamed the "First Long Bills."

[23] McCusker and Menard, *Economy*, pp. 334-37; Ferguson, *WMQ 1953*, pp. 168-77; Ferguson, *Purse*, chap. 1.

[24] Ferguson, *WMQ 1953*, pp. 168-69.

[25] McCusker, *Studies*, p. 100.

[26] Newman, *Paper Money*, p. 13.

[27] Ferguson, *Purse*, chap. 1.

Revolution.[28] In New England and the south, land banks did not fare as well. Paper currency had depreciated in Massachusetts prior to 1750, the year when it was redeemed for specie. North Carolina continued with inflated paper money, whereas South Carolina managed its currency well from 1731 until the Revolution. Rhode Island had nine land bank emissions[29] and flooded the New England area with large quantities of depreciated paper which "undermined the currency of her neighbors."[30] The abuses within her land bank system precipitated the Currency Act of 1751.

Virginia did not issue paper money until 1755 when forced into that position by expenses of the French and Indian War. Prior to that time, hard coin had been supplemented with tobacco notes. "The expansion of population, the conversion of a barter economy into a rapidly growing market economy," periodic fluctuations in the tobacco market,[31] and the shortage of circulating specie,[32] together with military expenses, pressed the colony to create a paper currency. The new money, secured by anticipated tax revenues rather than a land bank,[33] fared well until 1760 when falling tobacco prices in the export market created a depression. Specie and bills of exchange then became so expensive that Virginia currency was depreciated up to 60% for the purchase of expensive sterling credits.[34]

A unique paper currency circulated in the corporate Colony of Georgia from 1735 to 1750. These "sola" bills were printed, endorsed, bills of exchange, denominated in pounds sterling, and drawn in England on behalf of the trustees of the Colony. The money circulated at par in the Colony until returned to England for redemption.[35] Hard money was very scarce in Georgia since the colony had no provision for inflating silver as did the other twelve (see Table 6). The typical practice for anyone in Georgia possessing silver coin was to buy inflated, yet stable South Carolina paper money at an exchange of £600 or £700, South Carolina currency, to £100, Georgia currency. It was wiser to spend South Carolina paper money in Georgia rather than to part with a silver eight reales for a mere 54d.[36] In 1754, Georgia became a royal colony and issued its own land bank secured bills of credit one year later.[37]

* * *

The study of colonial paper currency has been punctuated with much controversy. Ernst and Ferguson point out to modern day readers that some historians of the past century allowed their personal views on "sound money" (paper backed by bullion) to bias their interpretation and commentaries on the colonial period especially in regard to the stability of colonial currency and the purported conflict between the creditor and debtor classes.[38] Historians of the last century retrospectively blamed the depreciation of colonial paper money on low public confidence in fiat money unsecured in bullion, issued in excess, and printed at the instigation of debtors to lessen the burden of their obligations. They further supported their position by quoting such contemporary observers as William Douglass, an avowed foe of paper money, who was described by his biographer as "a man of strong prejudices, always inclined to espouse one side of any question and unable to see the other ...."[39] Douglass, a Boston physician, leveled many tirades against

[28] Behrens, *Maryland*, p. 58.
[29] Newman, *Paper Money*, p. 13.
[30] Ferguson, *WMQ 1953*, p. 162.
[31] Ernst, *Money and Politics*, p. 45.
[32] Hoober, *Num 1953*, p. 12 and passim.
[33] Newman, *Paper Money*, p. 13.
[34] Ferguson, *WMQ 1953*, p. 160.
[35] Newman, *Paper Money*, pp. 13, 108-9.
[36] McCusker, *Money and Exchange*, pp. 227-28.
[37] Newman, *Paper Money*, p. 13.
[38] Ernst, *Money and Politics*, pp. 1-17, 354; Ferguson, *WMQ 1953*, pp. 153-55, passim.
[39] Bullock, *Douglass*, pp. 259-90, quote p. 277.

the paper money practices of the 1700s with the typical denunciation that "paper money-making assemblies have been legislatures of debtors"[40] which encouraged its issue to reduce their own personal indebtedness "for [their] private iniquitous ends."[41] He further claimed that the overabundance of paper money caused its own depreciation, did not successfully augment the "medium of trade" but on the contrary was responsible for an increased price of silver. Modern historians have refuted such arguments and have emphasized that the conditions responsible for the depreciation of colonial currency, such as occurred in Virginia in the 1760s, were normal market forces and currency fluctuations, simple price inflation, and short-run economic factors rather than the depreciation of large quantities of unsecured paper money which lacked public confidence.

The assertion is made that it was the unrestricted profusion of colonial paper money that was responsible for its own depreciation. While the "quantity theory" may be argued for the decline of paper money in Rhode Island and other colonies during certain periods, it would be an untrue generalization for all regions, despite the opinions of earlier writers. These earlier historians also generalized that class conflicts existed between creditors and debtors, and merchants and farmers, where the creditors and merchants stood for secure currency, such as hard coin, while the debtors and farmers lobbied for paper currency since they sought a depreciating medium with which to satisfy their obligations.[42] In fact, this inaccurate concept that opposing fiscal policies continued to excite class-oriented animosity "is so widely and uncritically made ... that it is almost a cliche."[43] This alleged creditor-debtor and merchant-farmer class struggle was not broadly representative of conditions in all the colonies and this concept is an inexact portrayal of colonial life, except in specific locations such as Rhode Island. In general, colonial paper money was a stable medium throughout its history.

Financing colonial participation in the French and Indian Wars was largely a local responsibility. Massachusetts successfully persuaded the English Parliament to redeem the colonial bills of credit issued to offset the expense of the Cape Breton offensive of 1745. A large shipment of 650,000 ounces of Spanish silver coins and ten tons of English coppers arrived in Boston on the ship *Mermaid* on September 18, 1749.[44] These coppers are of numismatic importance since 801,376 halfpence and 424,032 farthings, mostly dated 1749, continued to circulate for years and should be considered an important and legitimate colonial coinage.[45]

The supply of specie stabilized Massachusetts paper money, which had previously undergone significant depreciation. This strong, provincial currency lasted until the Revolutionary War, earning for the area the epithet, the "hard money Colony."[46] Another stipend of £115,000 was distributed to New England, New York, and New Jersey in 1756 " 'as a free gift and reward for past services', against the French."[47] Further reimbursements were offered to North Carolina, South Carolina, and Virginia in 1757, to Massachusetts and Connecticut the following year, and to New Hampshire in 1770, all for the campaigns of 1756. Despite these and other specific grants made in 1759 and 1762, the colonies recovered only about one-fourth of their expenses incurred in the French and Indian Wars.[48]

[40] Bullock, *Essays*, pp. 47-48.
[41] Douglass, *Discourse*, p. 295n.
[42] Ferguson, *WMQ 1953*, pp. 155, 161, 163, 165.
[43] McDonald, *Formation*, p. 265n.
[44] Sallay, *CNL 1975*, pp. 525-26; Crosby, *Early Coins*, pp. 226-29.
[45] Williamson, *CNL 1976*, p. 545; Breen, *CNL 1977*, p. 585; Prime, *Coins*, p. 5; Newman, *CNL 1979*, pp. 681-84.
[46] Felt, *Massachusetts*, pp. 124-39.
[47] Felt, *Massachusetts*, p. 140. This stipend was allotted as follows: Massachusetts £54,000; New Hampshire £8,000; Connecticut £26,000; Rhode Island £7,000; New York £15,000; New Jersey £5,000.
[48] Coffing, *CW 1976*; Felt (*Massachusetts*, p. 150) quotes the 1762 grant at £200,000.

The paper money policies of the mainland colonies came under the scrutiny and attack of English merchants and the Board of Trade which proposed corrective legislation. Parliament was finally goaded into action when the Rhode Island Assembly issued £50,000 loan office notes in a popular request for more depreciated currency. The reaction from London was the passage of the Currency Act of 1751 which regulated paper money in the New England colonies by outlawing land banks, forcing existing paper to be retired strictly according to the terms of its issue, and stating that any new paper could only be used to pay the current expenses of government and must be redeemable by taxes. The final provision of this restrictive act was to deny the legal tender status of paper currency for private debts.[49]

Fig. 24: MARYLAND $2 BILL OF APRIL 10, 1774. This note, issued at the sterling rate of exchange of 4s. 6d. to the Spanish milled dollar (not Maryland money of account), lacked legal tender status and was receivable for Bills of Exchange, payable in London. This provision avoided the constraints of the Currency Act of 1764, the loan office having been closed in 1765. This and similar issues of January 1, 1767, and March 1, 1770, were secured by Bank of England stock. The tiny Spanish milled dollars on the $1 and $2 notes of these three series are the first instance that coins illustrated American paper money. Also the word "dollar" was used for the first time as an official monetary unit on the 1767 emissions (Newman, *Paper Money*, pp. 145-47; Newman, *Num 1985*). Private Collection.

As events in Rhode Island had precipitated currency reform in 1751, the economic depression of 1760 in Virginia caused by a slump in the tobacco market, prompted Parliament to pass the Currency Act of 1764. This legislation extended parliamentary control over paper money practices within all the colonies for the self-serving purpose of protecting English mercantile interests. This action denied legal tender status to all other colonial paper currency and required that all existing issues be retired according to the provisions of the enabling legislation.[50] These

[49] Ernst, *Money and Politics*, pp. 37-42; Ferguson, *WMQ 1953*, p. 177; Chalmers, *British Colonies*, pp. 16-18.
[50] Ernst, *Money and Politics*, pp. 76-88; Ferguson, *WMQ 1953*, p. 177; McCusker, *Money and Exchange*, p. 131; Chalmers, *British Colonies*, p. 18.

Fig. 25: A PENNSYLVANIA BILL PRINTED BY BENJAMIN FRANKLIN. Franklin printed paper currency for New Jersey, Delaware, and Pennsylvania. This issue of August 10, 1739, used a deliberate misspelling, Pensilvania, on its four highest notes to detect fraudulent alteration of lower denominational bills. The complex reverse leaf or nature print was another counterfeiting deterrent introduced by Franklin on this emission (Newman, *Paper Money*, pp. 27, 328). Courtesy Eric P. Newman Numismatic Education Society.

currency regulations were subsequently relaxed when specific colonies were again permitted to establish land banks, but still Parliament refused to permit legal tender status for paper in private debts, responding to the apprehensive English merchants who wished for a guarantee that sterling debts be satisfied in hard money.[51] In the final analysis, "the Currency Act of 1764 appears as a move to safeguard British investments in America, a move dictated by metropolitan, not colonial, needs."[52] "Although the Board of Trade and later Parliament never offered any help, they were quite ready to regulate and restrict."[53] Compromise monetary proposals were forwarded by leaders such as Benjamin Franklin, a staunch advocate of paper money, to develop a single colonial land bank system with offices in each colony.[54] This innovation never survived the planning phase and the rift between mercantilistic England and its maturing American colonies widened. Franklin's advocacy for well managed paper currency, was not only in theory but in practice, since he, himself, printed 3 issues of paper money for New Jersey, 9 for

[51] Ernst, *Money and Politics*, pp. 43-44, 76, 87.
[52] Ernst, *Money and Politics*, p. 359.
[53] McCusker, *Money and Exchange*, p. 131.
[54] Ferguson, *WMQ 1953*, p. 179; Ferguson, *Purse*, p. 23. Franklin summarized his position regarding paper money in his tract, "A Modest Enquiry into the Nature and Necessity of a Paper Currency (1729)," in Smyth, *Franklin*, vol. 2, pp. 133-55. Smyth observed that "All Franklin's economical works had their origins in the social circumstances and public exigencies of the times when they were written. They were intended to subserve a definite political purpose, and might be called campaign documents. They contain, therefore, no system of economic thought, no carefully reasoned scheme of philosophy, no congeries of laws underlying and interpreting the complicated fabric of society. Their author is often inconsistent, he frequently contradicts himself, and is obviously pursuing what he regards as political expediency (vol. 1, p. 139)."

Delaware, and 15 for Pennsylvania from 1728 to 1764, with over 2,500,000 notes from his presses.[55]

There is substantial reason to conclude that the parliamentary restraints on colonial paper money which directly influenced commerce was a significant factor in precipitating the Revolutionary War.[56] Now that the French and Indian Wars had come to an end, England could direct closer attention to its colonies and its protective policies became more restrictive. This increased scrutiny occurred at the time of a postwar depression when the wartime economy cooled after the termination of hostilities. The regulation of colonial currency by the English at this time of economic upheaval only added to the local burden. Bankruptcies were commonplace but a positive outcome was the stimulation and encouragement of local manufacturing. "Increasingly after the French and Indian War, the colonial importer looked upon the development of domestic industry as an integral part of a program to achieve economic sovereignty to counter the restrictions imposed by membership in the British Empire."[57] As the years passed, the colonists became increasingly vexed with English authority, and the antagonisms which arose eventually culminated in the War of Independence.

[55] Newman, *Franklin*, pp. 341-49; Smyth speculated (*Franklin*, vol. 1, p. 139) that while Franklin's essay, "'A Modest Enquiry into the Nature and Necessity of a Paper Currency (1729)' was intended primarily to increase 'the trade, employment, and number of inhabitants in the province,' ... the hope of securing the printing of the money was not absent from the author's thrifty mind."

[56] Bullock, *Essays*, p. 59; Felt, *Massachusetts*, p. 132; McCusker, *Money and Exchange*, pp. 119, 131; Greene, *America*, p. 180; Ernst, *Money and Politics*, chap. 11. Franklin, himself, supported the position that currency restrictions were leading causes of the Revolution (see Ferguson, *WMQ 1953*, p. 164). These provocative economic restraints are in addition to the more popularized and familiar encroachments on political freedom such as "taxation without representation."

[57] Egnal and Ernst, *WMQ 1972*, passim, quote p. 20.

CHAPTER FIVE

The Emergence of Copper Coinage

The role of foreign specie in the currency of British North America has been explored in previous chapters. Large denominational gold and silver coins, while never plentiful, could be obtained at a price for overseas transactions. In contrast, lower denominational foreign and domestic silver coins, the money of daily, domestic commerce, were usually scarce in the colonies. English farthings and halfpence, however, which formed the small change medium, were imported in great abundance. Since the history of copper money in the American colonial and Confederation periods is inextricably linked to the emergence of English and Irish base metal coinages, it is important to examine the development of the small change currency in England and Ireland, the subject of this chapter.

SMALL CHANGE IN ENGLAND

England continued to experience significant domestic monetary problems during the colonial period and ignored the coinage requirements of her New World colonies except perhaps for the impotent expression of concern presented in the Proclamation of 1704. Her own specie was being drained to India and the Continent where it fetched higher prices. She was in no position to rescue her American possessions from their monetary predicaments even if it had been her intent to do so. Laws were passed forbidding the exportation of English silver and gold coin except when British currency was required to pay armed forces on foreign duty. This general export prohibition did not apply to bullion, foreign coins, and English copper.[1] The sorry state of England's disordered currency was further intensified by the abundance of worn, clipped, lightweight coins, which, with few exceptions, were hammer-struck until 1663. In February of that year, the mint finally adopted the technology of the screw press and milled, or reeded, edges which, although developed fully a century earlier, had been blocked from introduction by the opposition of the organized moneyers.[2] To remedy the inequities in weight of the antiquated, clipped, hammered coins, a recoinage was ordered in 1696. All old money was thereby demonetized and recalled to the mint where, under the supervision of Sir Isaac Newton, new coins were reissued with a milled, i.e. reeded, or lettered edge.[3] The newly designed rim discouraged clipping since any alteration was easily detected. However, this innovation in manufacture did not protect newly minted coins from the melting pot and subsequent exportation as bullion since the mint price of silver was frequently lower than the market price. The net result was a continued shortage of English coined silver money.[4]

While the precious metals obviously had greater importance in trade and commerce, copper filled the need for small change and was the money of the poor. In this chapter, the origins of the various copper token and regal coinages are traced from their beginnings in England to their subsequent use in British North America. Of great significance in the study of these series is the

[1] Nettels, *Money Supply*, pp. 162-66.

[2] Feavearyear, *Pound Sterling*, pp. 93-94.

[3] Ruding, *Annals*, vol. 2, pp. 48-49. The larger gold and silver coins had a lettered edge frequently with the date and the inscription DECUS ET TUTAMEN, "A Decoration and a Safeguard." Lesser coins had a reeded (milled) edge to detect clipping (Seaby, *English Coinage*, p. 78).

[4] Feavearyear, *Pound Sterling*, pp. 122-23.

parallel circulation of both legitimate and counterfeit issues. It is important to understand the history of this money, both legal and spurious, because of the direct relationship to the American copper coinages of the Confederation period.

In England from 780 until 1279, the only silver coinage had been the penny. At that time, the currency was expanded under Edward I with the introduction of the silver farthing and halfpenny for small change and the larger four penny groat. There existed the need for smaller coins but these could not be produced in sufficient numbers to satisfy the needs of commerce since lower denominational coins were uneconomical to make because of their diminutive size; one farthing required sixteen times the labor and time to mint as that expended on a silver penny. Another reason for their scarcity was that they were so tiny "they were liable to slip between the stitching of purses, and when dropped, were only slightly easier to find than contact lenses." [5] Over the years the buying power of these tiny coins declined as inflation developed and the silver coinage underwent periodic debasement. By the reign of Elizabeth I, if a farthing were minted at .925 fine, the piece would have weighed a mere two grains! The queen rejected proposals to make the lower denominational coins larger by using debased silver. Instead, the halfpenny became the smallest silver coin and the monarch introduced a three-farthing piece so that one could make a farthing purchase with this new coin and receive a halfpenny in change from the shopkeeper.[6]

Still there was not ample small change for commerce. "The Crown seems to have considered it beneath the royal dignity to issue coins struck in base metal," and to supplement the short supply of silver small denominational currency, merchants resorted to local tradesmen's tokens.[7] Accordingly, English merchants, as early as 1404, introduced their own halfpenny or farthing tokens, or "pledges," made of "lead, tin, latten, and even of leather." The inconvenience was that these "pledges" were only redeemable by the issuing tradesman. Private lead tokens were very common through the reign of Elizabeth I. These tokens, later made of copper and pewter, were an unofficial fiduciary coinage in that their metal content was worth far less than their denominational monetary value.[8] James I, who ascended to the throne in 1603, outlawed these private tokens, having a different scheme to address the small change crisis.

By King James's plan, the Royal Mint in 1613 began to strike copper farthings authorized by a royal patent granted to Lord Harington with whom the king shared tremendous profits. These coppers "were ordered to pass equally current in England and Ireland."[9] The tiny farthings were required only to weigh six grains at a minimum, the early ones weighing only five grains, but later issues averaging nine. Initially they were tinned to present the more valuable appearance of silver, but this veneer of respectability soon wore off. These issues were easily counterfeited at great profit. The patent passed to the Duke of Lennox, and successively to the Duchess of Richmond in 1624 and ten years later to Lord Maltravers. The farthing tokens were not well received because of their lightweight and very low intrinsic value. To make matters worse, Lord Maltravers refused to honor token farthings of the previous patentees, thus swindling the public, especially the poor, out of vast sums. His outward excuse was to discredit the volume of counterfeit tokens that had appeared over the years. One denunciation against the patentees for their profiteering at popular expense referred to them as "the very Caterpillers

[5] Hume, *Caterpillers*, p. 234.

[6] Peck, *British Museum*, pp. 2, 7; Purvey, *Catalogue*, p. 151; Hume, *Caterpillers*, p. 234. Hume, pp. 236-39, suggests that "copper-alloy jettons or casting counters ... originally intended as mathematical aids," may also have served as low denominational currency since these pieces frequently turn up in archeological sites. Several of these jettons dating from the mid-16th century have been found in Virginia. See also Peck, *British Museum*, pp. 3-4.

[7] Seaby, *English Coinage*, p. 63, quote from p. 60.

[8] Peck, *British Museum*, pp. 5-6; Feavearyear, *Pound Sterling*, pp. 169-70.

[9] Lindsay, *Ireland*, pp. 54-55.

Fig. 26:
(a) England: contemporary counterfeit farthing of Charles I, in the style of Peck 156 (Richmond patent). Private Collection.

(b) England: genuine farthing of Charles I, Peck 156 (Richmond patent).

of this Kingdome." Popular dissatisfaction with the tokens became intense; in 1642 the Puritan Parliament, which on principle denounced both monopolies and base coinage, ordered production of the Maltravers farthings stopped.[10]

There is a colonial connection with the token farthings. The coinage was familiar to the Puritan colonists of Massachusetts Bay who similarly disapproved and rejected them in favor of commodity money for small change. The General Court was quicker to condemn this lightweight money than Parliament since the first legislation ever enacted in Boston in reference to small currency was the demonetization of these tiny coins on March 4, 1635. "It is ordered that hereafter farthings shall not passe for currant pay. It is likewise ordered, that muskett bulletts of a full boare shall passe currantly for a farthing a peece, provided that noe man be compelled to take above 12d att a tyme of them."[11] In Virginia, farthing tokens apparently circulated as evidenced by the numbers found at archeological sites. In fact, in 1636, the governor of Virginia, Sir John Harvey, petitioned James I for a supply of farthing tokens to be sent to his colony for want of money to pay laborers. As discussed in the previous chapter, it was difficult for tobacco to act as currency for small sums and hence the desire by the governor for small change tokens to fill this gap. The request was never filled, but in 1639 Lord Maltravers was granted a 21 year patent to mint copper farthing tokens for all British plantations except Maryland. This plan was interrupted by the English Civil War and was never revived.[12]

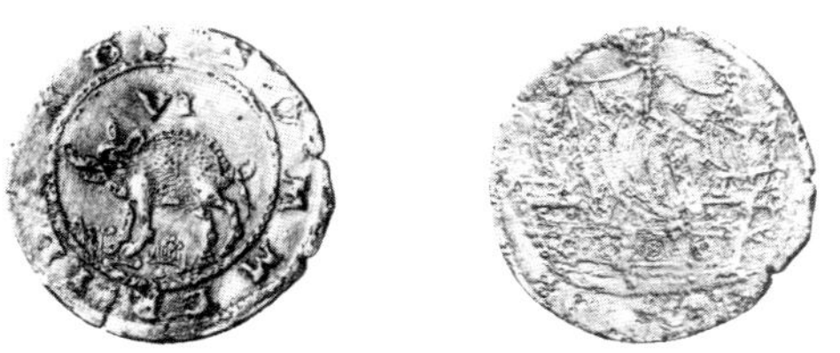

Fig. 27: Sommer Islands (Bermuda Hogge money) sixpence, 1615 (36.5 grains). These brass tokens were originally washed with silver, a condition that facilitated surface corrosion when exposed to salt. The humid Bermuda sea air explains why these coins commonly have such deteriorated surfaces (Breen, *Encyclopedia*, pp. 9-10).

[10] Craig, *Mint*, pp. 141-42; Hume, *Caterpillers*, pp. 239-45, quote p. 243.

[11] *Massachusetts Bay*, p. 137, item 187 for 4 March 1634/5; Felt, *Massachusetts*, p. 20; Crosby, *Early Coins*, p. 26; Breen, *Encyclopedia*, p. 11. Matthew A. Stickney, a prominent numismatist of the last century, reported a Charles I farthing found with a group of Pine Tree pieces in Boston. This occurrence made him conclude that "it is probable that the last [Charles I farthings] found a currency here to some extent." (Stickney, *Notes*, vol. 1 [1859], p. 155).

[12] Hume, *Caterpillers*, pp. 233, 247-49.

The first coinage actually designed for a British North American colony was the Bermuda Hogge Money. These shilling, sixpence, threepence, and twopence brass tokens were authorized by James I on June 29, 1615, "to pass Currant in their said Somer Islands, betweene the Inhabitants there for the more easey [*sic*] of comerce and bargaining between then." These tokens represented a certain weight of tobacco which was the legal tender commodity money in the islands. The hog money experiment proved unsuccessful since the currency was abandoned by 1624 possibly because it lacked intrinsic value.[13]

After the cessation of patent farthings, the continued need for small change again prompted merchants to strike another round of copper halfpenny and farthing tokens, this time in very large numbers with some 3,500 different varieties originating from London alone.[14] At long last on August 5, 1672, during the reign of Charles II, the English government finally took some official, definitive action to relieve the shortage of small change and replace the vast number of disparate tradesmen's tokens then in circulation by the introduction of a royal copper coinage. While all the English small change coppers were demonetized with the appearance of regal coppers, some of these seventeenth century trade tokens saw some limited circulation in the plantations since several have been uncovered in New York and New Jersey.[15]

Fig. 28:
(a) England: 1673 halfpence of Charles II.

(b) Sestertius of Antoninus Pius, A.D. ca. 140, which was the pattern for the regal English copper coinages first minted in 1672. In 1785 the State of Connecticut chose a similar motif, thus perpetuating 1,645 year old Roman numismatic art in America.

(c) 1670 halfpenny token issued by Robert Book of Maidstone, Kent (Boyne-Williamson Kent 381). Examples of this variety have been unearthed in Long Island indicative of at least a limited colonial circulation of some seventeenth century English tradesmen's tokens.

The reverse design for the new regal farthings and halfpence was adapted from a bronze sestertius of the Roman Emperor Antoninus Pius commemorating triumph over the Britons with the familiar seated reverse figure facing left holding a spear with a shield to the right and the legend, *BRITAN*.[16] It becomes of particular interest within the scope of this current book that the Connecticut and Vermont coppers of the late 1780s will adopt this motif first used in A.D. 140!

[13] Pridmore, *Commonwealth*, pp. 18-19; Breen, *Encyclopedia*, pp. 9-11; Lefroy, *AJN 1877*, pp. 137-41; Crosby, *Early Coins*, pp. 11-18; McCusker, *Money and Exchange*, p. 276.

[14] Seaby, *English Coinage*, pp. 63, 66-67, 73-74; Peck, *British Museum*, pp. 19-82.

[15] John M. Kleeberg, personal communication, May 29, 1991.

[16] Seaby, *English Coinage*, p. 79; Craig, *Mint*, p. 174; Peck, *British Museum*, p. 110; Askew, *Roman Britain*, p. 12.

There were several important differences between copper coins and those of precious metals. First of all, copper was calculated in avoirdupois at 7,000 grains to the pound, while gold and silver were measured by the troy system at 5,760 grains to the pound. A second important distinction to be emphasized was that there was no export restriction for copper thus explaining how English halfpence and farthings could be included in the Spanish specie shipment to Massachusetts in 1749. The final and most significant point was that base metal coins, i.e. copper, tin or brass, were never considered money *per se* but only as a token substitute for money. English officialdom looked upon copper coinage in a rather condescending manner while at the same time acknowledging its utility. Its manufacture was not a regular duty of the mint but rather was a special arrangement between the king and the mintmaster.[17] Although copper coins were made legal tender by a Proclamation of August 16, 1672, their minting costs were included in the overall value of the coin and could not be waived because of "the disproportionately high cost of manufacturing copper coin, as compared with gold and silver."[18] The new coppers, therefore, passed at a rate greater than the intrinsic value of the metal. To make matters more complicated, the mint actually produced the halfpence and farthings at a substantial profit to the Crown. This potential for gain in the minting of coppers encouraged counterfeiting, "and so laid the seeds of much trouble for the future."[19] The status of the small change medium is well described in an account written in 1757 by the king's assaymaster, Joseph Harris.

> Copper coin with us are properly not money, but a kind of tokens passing by way of exchange instead of parts of the smallest pieces of silver coin; and as such, very useful in small home traffic.... A silver penny is too small for common use; and yet pence, and their halfs, and quarters enter daily into accounts. To supply the want of very small silver coins, a kind of TOKENS or substitutes have been instituted; these are now with us, all made of copper, and of two species only, called half-pence, and farthings; and these are a legal tender in all sums below sixpence .... But these base coins should never be thrust upon the public in too great abundance; or be made to pass for more than the value of the copper, and the necessary expense of workmanship; otherwise they will be counterfeited, notwithstanding any laws to the contrary.[20]

From 1672 until 1679, finished copper planchets for the farthings and halfpence of Charles II were imported from Sweden where an export duty of 2½d. per pound had been imposed. To circumvent this situation and to assist a failing domestic industry, substitution of tin for copper was an alternative which had been proposed for years. An expanded market for tin would bolster sagging tin prices, curry political favor from the Western England parliamentary delegations, and increase royal revenues. The tin mines of Cornwall, the property of the Crown, were leased out to operators or "tin farmers." As far back as 1651, plans were discussed to exploit the stannaries for the royal advantage. In 1667, the tin farmers petitioned the king for a tin coinage in the hope that an increased demand would support prices and protect them from financial ruin.[21] The price for tin continued to decline and by 1676 would have fallen even further had not the Crown arranged to buy the output of the mines at 8d. per pound.[22]

To promote Devonian, Cornish, and regal interests, the proposal was enacted that several Tower Mint commissioners would be granted a patent to mint tin farthings during the last two years of the reign of Charles II in 1684 and 1685. During the times of James II and through 1692

[17] Craig, *Mint*, pp. xiii, 174-75.

[18] Peck, *British Museum*, p. 106n, relates, "the present-day farthing (1960) costs about a halfpenny to produce."

[19] Peck, *British Museum*, p. 106.

[20] Harris, *Essay*, p. 45, as quoted in Peck, *British Museum*, p. 204; Barnard, *NC 1926*, pp. 343-44.

[21] *Cal. S.P. Dom.*, vol. CCXXX, 75; Lewis, *Stannaries*, p. 140n.

[22] Craig, *Mint*, pp. 178-79; Seaby, *English Coinage*, p. 79; Peck, *British Museum*, pp. 105-7, 118; Feavearyear, *Pound Sterling*, p. 170.

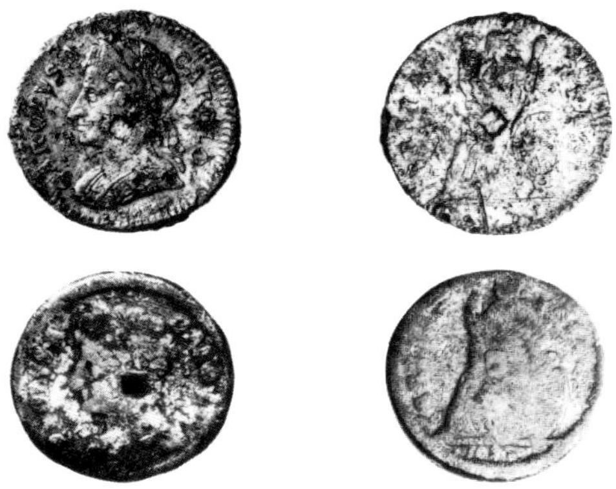

Fig. 29:
(a) England: genuine 1684 tin farthing of Charles II with copper plug (84.8 grains, sp.g. = 7.28). Private Collection.

(b) England: contemporary cast counterfeit tin farthing with copper plug of Charles II (90.3 grains, sp.g. = 8.36). This coin was cast in an alloy heavier than tin (sp.g. = 7.28) using a genuine copper farthing as the mold. This is easily discerned since the date is on the reverse and not on the edge as is the case for genuine tin issues. Private Collection.

under William and Mary, both farthings and halfpence were exclusively of tin. The edge inscription on these pieces, *NVMMORVM FAMVLVS*, "The Servant of Coinage," emphasized their token and fiduciary status. The entire tin coinage from March 1684 until January 1692 amounted to some 344 tons. At a cost for finished tin of only 8d. per pound as compared to 14½d. for copper, the profit margin for the crown was substantial as revealed in Table 10.[23] The substitution of tin for copper was so lucrative that it encouraged large scale counterfeiting. This illegal activity was thwarted to a degree since all genuine tin coins had a square plug of copper through their centers, but in spite of this device to deter counterfeiting, a large quantity of cast lead forgeries was produced.[24]

Despite large sales of tin to the Mint, the Crown was unable to maintain prices at a level sufficient to prevent depreciation of the coinage. The tin experiment proved unpopular and was discontinued on April 17, 1694, based on the coins' low intrinsic value, the ease of counterfeiting, and that they became "an obstruction to trade and a grievance to the subject[s]."[25] The tin money, by terms of the contract to the patentees, could be exchanged by tale for copper coins. By May 16, 1694, some £40,000 of the £65,000 minted tin coinage had been turned in for copper[26] imposing substantial losses on the patentees.[27]

Other schemes to dispose of unwanted tin involved sending large shipments to the army in Ireland, whence £2,500 was consigned on March 24, 1689/90.[28] "When that means proved insufficient to exhaust the output, it was urged that they [tin farthings and halfpence] be dumped upon the American plantations."[29] There is no evidence that this suggestion was ever implemented except for the hint contained in an account from Philadelphia in 1698 when local business men petitioned the Crown against " 'leaden and pewter farthings' that were about to be sent over."[30] It remains unclear to which "farthings" this reference was made, but more likely than not, the subject was the rejected regal tin. The probable reason, in retrospect, which kept surplus tin money out of British North America was the fact that it was redeemable in copper and so much was exchanged that it disappeared from circulation and was not a problem. As another proposition to utilize more tin, Thomas Neale, one of the patentees, suggested on

[23] Henry, *Series*, p. 12. This reference further notes that tin at £65 a ton cost nearly 7d. a pound or 1d. less than other quotations. In total £65,929 15s. 9d. of tin money was minted. Craig (*Mint*, p. 178) states the 8d. was the delivered price.

[24] Seaby and Bussell, *British Copper*, p. 9; Craig, *Mint*, pp. 179, 182. See Mason, *Making Coins*, pp. 101-2, for a description of the casting technique.

[25] Craig, *Mint*, p. 182.

[26] *Treas. Papers, 1556*, vol. XXVIII, 1.

[27] *Treas. Papers, 1702*, vol. LXXXIV, 138.

[28] *Treas. Papers, 1556*, vol. VII, 73.

[29] Lewis, *Stannaries*, p. 140n.

[30] Taxay, *Catalogue*, p. 8.

January 19, 1691/2 that New England might "be Supplyed with Pence, Halfe Pence, & farthing, of Tinn, from England, to their Majesties Advantage."[31] Nothing is known to have materialized from this proposal.

Fig. 30: American Plantation tin 1/24 real (1688) of Richard Holt (148.4 grains).

A colonial tin coinage did result when Richard Holt petitioned the Crown for authorization to mint a 1/24th real tin emission for the American plantations.[32] While the petition survives, the patent granting permission remains to be discovered. It is supposed that the Spanish denomination was selected because of colonial familiarity with Spanish money which would facilitate acceptance in commerce. Holt's 1688 patent tin coinage lacked the copper plug incorporated into the regal tin coins to thwart would-be counterfeiters. The American issues appear to have been lighter than the English and hence the profit to the patentee was greater since production costs were otherwise equal. Not much is known of Holt's coinage except that Newman has identified six pairs of dies. Restrikes made in 1828 from original dies were struck in a pewter-like metal whereas the original 1688 issues were pure tin.[33] Prime, writing in 1861, rejected these 1/24th real pieces as belonging to the American colonial series since there was no evidence of local circulation.[34] Crosby likewise excluded this tin coinage from consideration,[35] although Atkins in his 1889 work included them.[36] The exact role these interesting coins played in America has not been defined.

Production of copper farthings and halfpence was resumed at the royal mint in 1694 for just one year. After the death of Queen Mary, the manufacture of copper coinages under William III was granted to patentees who resorted to the economy of casting the planchets rather than by rolling the copper and then cutting the blanks. Although this process was more profitable, it resulted in inferior coins with pitted surfaces and poor definition since pure "copper does not ... cast with any degree of sharpness, unless there is a slight admixture of some other metal, such as tin or zinc." The contractors not only produced their planchets by a cheaper method, but they also employed less skilled engravers, who, while working for lower wages, committed numerous blunders in the legends. An inverted "V" was frequently substituted for an "A." Complaints were received that some of these coppers were light in weight, sometimes as low as 52 to 56 per pound rather than the required 42. Protests about the quality of this coinage were so frequently received that Parliament almost enacted legislation to ban the further minting of all copper money.[37]

After 1701, no more coppers were minted because supplies were adequate, any shortages being attributable to unequal distribution.[38] Only patterns were produced under the next

[31] Chalmers, *British Colonies*, p. 10n.
[32] Newman, *Num 1955*, pp. 713-17; Breen, *Encyclopedia*, pp. 21-22. There is no evidence existing today that Holt's petition was ever granted by James II (Michael Hodder, personal communication, Jan. 21, 1988).
[33] Newman, *Colonial Virginia*, p. 1n.
[34] Prime, *Coins*, p. 7.
[35] Crosby, *Early Coins*, p. 348.
[36] Atkins, *Coins and Tokens*, pp. 249-65.
[37] Henry, *Series*, pp. 13-14, quote p. 14n; Peck, *British Museum*, pp. 167-68.
[38] *Treas. Papers, 1702*, vol. LXXXXVI, 102.

TABLE 10

Mint Costs and Profits for Tower Mint Tin and Copper Halfpence

Year period	*1672*[a,b,c,d]	*1672-1675*[a,b,c,d]	*1685-1692*[a,c,e,f,h]	*1694-1701*[a,c,g,h,i,j,k]	*1717-1724*[a,c,h,l,m,n,s]	*1729-1754*[a,c,h,k,o,p,q,s]	*1770-1775*[a,c,h,r,s]
Price copper/lb.	12d.	12d.	n.a.	12d.	13d.	values included below	
Processing/lb.	nil	nil	n.a.	3d.	4.25d.		
Swedish Tax/lb.	nil	2.5d.	n.a.	nil	n.a.		
Total cost/lb.	12d.	14.5d.	n.a.	15d.	17.25d.	15.75d.	15.75d.
Price tin/lb.	n.a.	n.a.	8d.	n.a.	n.a.	n.a.	n.a.
Mint fees/lb.	4d.	4d.	4d.	2.8d.	4.64d.	4.61d.	4.11d.
TOTAL COSTS/lb.	16d.	18.5d.	12d.	17.8d.	21.89d.	20.36d.	19.86d.
Halfpence/lb.	40	44	a) 40 b) 42	42	46	46	46
Authorized weight (grains)	175.0	159.1	a) 175.0 b) 166.7	166.7	152.2	152.2	152.2
Average observed weight (grains)	169.5	169.5	a) 170.9 b) 176.2 to 169.7	156.9 to 161.9	150.0	153.3 to 153.7	153.4
Monetary value per lb. avdp.	20d.	22d.	a) 20d. b) 21d.	21d.	23d.	23d.	23d.
Profit to Crown or contractor per lb. avdp.	4d. crown	3.5d. crown	a) 8d. b) 9d. crown	3.2d. contractor	1.11d. contractor 1.31d. crown	2.64d. crown	0.14d. discount 2.16d. crown
Profit/total costs % profit	25%	18.9%	a) 66.6% b) 75%	18.0%	11% total	13%	10.9%

[a] Data from Craig, *Mint*, pp. xv, 175, 178, 221, 416, 427-28.
[b] Data from Peck, *British Museum*, pp. 106, 140.
[c] Data of observed weights from Peck, *British Museum*, pp. 620-21.
[d] These imported planchets were ready to strike. Later in 1672 a 2½d. Swedish export tax was imposed thus raising the production costs. The weight of the coin was appropriately adjusted with a greater yield per pound of copper. The profit to the crown was decreased by ½d.
[e] Data from Peck, *British Museum*, pp. 107, 147, 151.
[f] No tin halfpence of Charles II were made, only tin farthings.
The 8d. for the tin included delivery costs.
The 4d. mint costs included distribution of finished coins.
[a] Halfpence were minted under James II from 1685 to 1687 at 20d. to the pound, or a 66.6% profit to the Crown.
[b] Under William and Mary from 1689 to 1692 the tin halfpence were coined at 21d. to the lb. or a profit margin of 75%.
[g] Peck, *British Museum*, pp. 151-53, 167-69.
[h] The range in average weights is obtained since Peck calculated averages for each type of coin of the period.
[i] William and Mary halfpence (1694) were made of English copper on rolled and cast blanks, whereas those of William III were from cast blanks generally of inferior quality to the Swedish copper of Charles II.
[j] The profit for William and Mary and William III coinages went to the contractors who coined for the Mint. The cheaper production methods for the William III coins are held responsible for the poorer quality of the series (Peck, *British Museum*, p. 168).
[k] The processing costs included the preparation of copper fillets (strips) to the proper dimensions ready for cutting (Ruding, *Annals*, vol. 2, p. 74).
[l] Data from Peck, *British Museum*, p. 198.
[m] The price of copper and Mint charges had increased reflecting a change in the issues of George I when more small copper coins were needed in 1717.
[n] Craig (*Mint*, p. 427) notes a Crown profit of 1.31d. and an actual face value of 23.2d. per lb., whereas a face value of 23d. would reduce the king's profit to 1.11d. or 5%.
[o] Data from Peck, *British Museum*, p. 204; Craig, *Mint*, p. 250; and Ruding, *Annals*, vol. 2, p. 74.
[p] Under the reign of George II, the cost of prepared fillets dropped to 15.75d. per lb.
[q] Mint costs include the mintmaster's fee of 4.5d. per lb. and fee to the king's clerk of 20s. per [long] ton.
[r] There was a 0.14d. per lb. allowance for the purchase of halfpence from the Mint. Considering this discount as a cost, the Crown's profit was 10.8%.
[s] Contracts after 1717 provided that the scissel (the metal remaining after the blanks had been cut) was to be taken back by the supplier at the same price. In effect, only the metal actually coined was paid for.

monarch, Queen Anne.[39] By this time, counterfeit copper coins were starting to become a problem, a situation that the Mint commonly regarded as a symptom of shortage;[40] Newton disagreed, contending that the small change supply was still ample. In 1713 he estimated that the copper change requirement for all England would not exceed 600 long tons of which there were about 500 "already current."[41] The regular minting of coppers did not resume again at the Royal Mint until 1717 during the reign of George I.[42]

From this point, all copper coinage was to be manufactured at the Tower Mint when previously the planchets had either been purchased from Sweden or provided by private contractors. Since Newton insisted on pure copper, it was no longer permissible to add minute quantities of tin, even under 0.25%, to facilitate casting or rolling. To develop a practical method for the determination of pure copper, Newton adopted an assay based on the physical characteristics of the metal. When heated to a red hot glow, only pure copper resisted cracking when beaten with a sledge hammer. If copper were cheapened by adulteration with any tin or zinc, it would become brittle and break or crack when subjected to this test.[43] Newton further advised that annual coinages not exceed 40 long tons lest his demand for the copper affect the market price.[44]

Copper coinage was relatively continuous from 1717 until 1754 when there was a hiatus until 1770. It is of interest to examine the cost of production of English coppers at the Royal Mint. As previously noted, not only the cost of the copper, but all labor, fees, and planchet preparation expenses were figured into the value of the copper coins (see Table 10), whereas such costs for silver and gold were absorbed by the government as a legitimate charge.[45] In that these coppers were a token coinage which represented money rather than being of full money value themselves, any manipulation that either decreased production costs or increased yield per pound of metal, augmented the profit margin to the Crown or the patentee. The windfall experienced upon changing to tin from 1684 to 1692 has already been cited. A similar maneuver occurred in 1718 when the Royal Mint, faced with higher costs, increased the yield of halfpence from 21d. to 23d. per pound of copper, and farthings proportionately.[46] Conversely, no coppers were minted during the early reign of George III until 1770 because of the high price of copper.[47]

English Coppers in America, Genuine and Counterfeit

English copper was not restricted from colonial use and was the principal minor coinage in Britain's American possessions. It was estimated that about £69,000 in English farthings and halfpence were exported to America from 1695 to 1775 which approximated 17.5% of the total copper minted.[48] The first large shipment of £300 was sent to Philadelphia in 1682.[49] "In 1734

[39] The 1714 Queen Anne farthing may have been a currency issue (Montagu, *Coinage*, p. xix).

[40] Craig, *Newton*, pp. 86, 96.

[41] "Sir Isaac Newton's Mint Reports (27 January 1713/14)," in Shaw, *Monetary History*, pp. 164-65. Newton estimated the needs for circulation would fall between £120,000 and £130,000 with an annual loss by attrition of £2,500 to £3,000 (Craig, *Newton, p. 96*).

[42] Henry, *Series*, pp. 15-16.

[43] Craig, *Newton*, p. 97.

[44] Craig, *Newton*, p. 99.

[45] In England, the charges for individuals bringing bullion to the mint to be coined were abolished in 1666 as a measure "for the encouraging of coinage" (Feavearyear, *Pound Sterling*, pp. 95-96). This arrangement differed from the Massachusetts Bay Mint where minting costs for "Boston Money" were the responsibility of the individual who brought specie to the mint for recoining and were not assumed by the Province.

[46] Craig, *Mint*, p. 221.

[47] Seaby, *English Coinage*, p. 92. See Table 24 for copper prices.

[48] Craig, *Mint*, pp. 251-52, 416-18. The total copper mintage from 1672 to 1775 was £448,466, and for the 80 year span in question, 1695 to 1775, was £393,466. This is an interesting comparison to Wood's Hibernia patent which was £100,800 over only 14 years indeed, an "absurd" and exaggerated estimation of Irish needs for small change.

and 1735, shipments of English halfpence and farthings by the ton" were dispatched to Georgia, where money circulated at sterling rates such as it would in England.[50] Ten long tons of coppers were consigned to Massachusetts in 1749 as part of the settlement from Parliament for the colony's participation in the Cape Breton offensive. This amounted to £2,111 4s. 8d. which was divided among 801,376 halfpence and 424,032 farthings. The majority were dated 1749 and comprised about 23% of the Royal Mint's copper production for that year. By 1770, most colonies had published exchange rates for the regal English halfpence which were the prevalent small change of the plantations. These rates are enumerated in Table 11 but there is no differential for the heavier copper coins of 1672 to 1701. The exchange ratios for English halfpence (Table 11) held well for royal coppers of consistent weight until 1787. Circumstances were significantly altered when debased, lightweight, and counterfeit coins were introduced into commerce and public confidence in the circulating token copper coinage weakened. As it was, the intrinsic metallic value of English coppers was approximately 50% of monetary value, therefore, public acceptance was delicate at best for this token coinage.

Since token regal coinage was minted at a substantial profit above the legitimately incurred costs and fees as described in Table 10, counterfeiting of copper and tin was invited and became

TABLE 11

Exchange Rates for Regal English Halfpence in the Various Colonial Monies of Account.

Colony[b,c]	*Reference Year*	*Number of English Halfpence per Colonial Shilling*
New Hampshire	1765[e]	18
Massachusetts	1750[e,f]	18
Rhode Island	1763[e]	18
New York	1750[e]	12
	1753[e]	14
New Jersey	1750[d,e]	15
Pennsylvania	1698[g]	12
	1741[h]	15
	1750[e]	15
Maryland	1754[e]	18
Virginia	1770[e,i]	19
North Carolina	1768[c,e]	12
Georgia	1735[a,c,e]	24

[a] Georgia, a corporate colony until 1752, remained at par with England.

[b] Connecticut never assigned an official value to the English halfpence but 18 to the shilling was the rate noted in a legislative report for state coppers (Crosby, *Early Coins*, p. 223).

[c] Less is known about the circulation of coppers in the south where they were not as commonly used (Newman, *Coppers*, p. 108).

[d] The New Jersey rate of 15 per shilling is based on "West" New Jersey exchange since it is quite probable that "East" New Jersey continued to remain under the economic influence of New York (Williamson, *CNL 1986*, p. 941; Nettels, *Money Supply*, p. 241n).

[e] Newman, *Studies*, pp. 143-54.

[f] Felt, *Massachusetts*, p. 128.

[g] Scott, *Pennsylvania*, pp. 9-10.

[h] Crosby, *Early Coins*, p. 170.

[i] Newman, *Colonial Virginia*, p. 10.

---

[49] *Loyal Merc.*, Oct. 2-6, 1682, from *CNL* 49 (1977), p. 589; Barnsley, *CNL 1977*, p. 609. £300 would contain 144,000 halfpence. For those dated 1672, at 40 to the pound, this would translate into 1.61 long tons. The lighter sort from the remainder of the coinage at 44 to the pound, would come to 1.46 long tons.

[50] Newman, *Studies*, pp. 148-49.

a prevalent social evil just as Harris predicted. The extensive Batty collection catalogued many contemporary counterfeit issues which were coined in England and it is obvious that this false money rapidly found its way into the New World. As early as 1698, reports circulated from Philadelphia of "large numbers of lead and pewter farthings and halfpence" with the warning "that they should be 'wholly suppressed' because of the damage they can do ... 'only those of Copper which are the King's Coyn may pass the farthings for two a penny the half pence for a penny'."[51] In Massachusetts, in 1700, counterfeit money of "brass and Tin" was the subject of a legislative action which punished any persons who "shall presume to make or Stamp any such peices [*sic*] ... and to Emit, utter, or put off the same for pence ...."[52]

These counterfeit pieces cannot be identified with certainty. Considering that counterfeit copper halfpence with the bust of Charles II are decidedly rare, although two are listed by Batty,[53] a reasonable conclusion is that some of these counterfeits represented cast tin farthings of Charles II (fig. 29) and cast brass William III halfpence (fig. 31).[54]

Fig. 31:
(a) England: 1699 Type 2 cast contemporary counterfeit halfpenny of William III from the Philadelphia Highway Find (106.1 grains).

(b) England: 1700 Type 3 cast contemporary counterfeit halfpenny of William III (131.8 grains, sp.g. = 8.34). Private Collection.

(c) England: 1699 genuine halfpenny of Type 3 William III (183.7 grains). The specific gravity of this copper series averages 8.84 ± 0.05.

[51] Scott, *Pennsylvania*, pp. 9-10. This exchange rate would be twelve halfpence to the Pennsylvania shilling.
[52] Crosby, *Early Coins*, pp. 114-15.
[53] Batty, *Descriptive Catalogue*, pp. 742, 508 and 509.
[54] Breen, *CNL 1973*, pp. 398, 417. Batty, *Descriptive Catalogue*, pp. 821-22, lists a 1699 William III cast counterfeit in lead or tin and then bronzed (1605) and a rough cast 1700 (1633). Counterfeit tin farthings are noted by Seaby and Bussell (*British Copper*, p. 9) but these pieces are very crude compared to the 1685 cast tin farthing pictured by Peck, (*British Museum*, p. 146, plate 50q), which may have been a forgery of an exceedingly rare date made to deceive collectors.

A great cache of cast counterfeit William III halfpence, dated 1699, was uncovered during a highway excavation in Philadelphia in 1975.[55] Such sand cast counterfeit halfpence of William III began to appear in England around 1725 when genuine coins were melted down and cast into lightweight counterfeits. The apparent motive here, in order to avoid suspicion, was to manufacture coins of a prior monarch since it would be anticipated that a 25 year old coin would appear worn and imperfect. People expected coppers of that period to be flawed anyway since so many were struck on roughly cast planchets.[56] This is doubtless the origin of the coins in the Philadelphia highway find. It has been postulated that this hoard of William III counterfeits was imported prior to 1735 at a time when the exchange rate in Pennsylvania was legally set at 12 halfpence to the local shilling although considering strict adherence to the exchange rates it should have been 14.4d. This was a 2.4d. overvaluation per Pennsylvania shilling for coppers, thereby securing a 20% profit for anyone who imported halfpence. The overvaluation of halfpence enticed both genuine and counterfeit coppers into the region, creating an over-abundance. The surplus of small money led in turn to public unrest when merchants objected to the established rate of twelve to the shilling. Some minor riots ensued in 1741 when certain tradesmen insisted on taking 15 halfpence to a Pennsylvania shilling. "The bakers refused to bake bread and the mob broke windows in many shops." The halfpence were subsequently revalued to 15 to the Pennsylvania shilling, more in keeping with the exchange rate as recorded in Table 11.[57] Newman and Gaspar suggested that the owner of these counterfeit William III coppers dumped them during this period of agitation when there was even a problem passing genuine coins, let alone spurious pieces.

Fig. 32:
(a) England: struck contemporary counterfeit farthing of George II, obverse brockage (15.4 grains). Private Collection.

(b) England: struck contemporary counterfeit halfpenny of George II (94.3 grains). This dateless, barbarous coin would have deceived only the most unsophisticated individual. Private Collection.

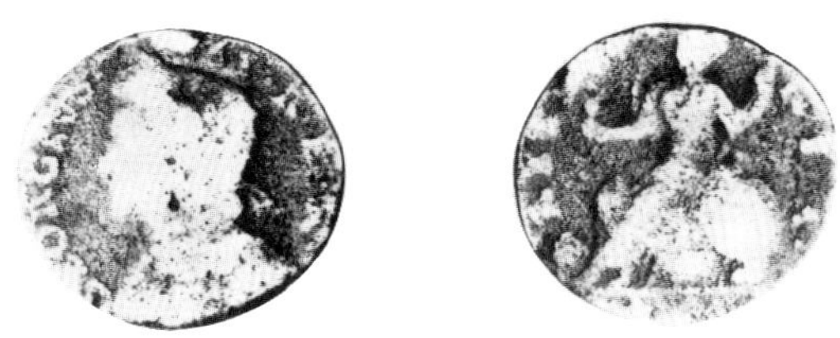

(c) England: struck contemporary counterfeit halfpenny of George II (98.6 grains). Private Collection.

(d) England: 1737 genuine halfpenny of George II (152.1 grains).

[55] Newman and Gaspar, *Num 1978*, pp. 453-67; Gaspar and Newman, *Hoards*, pp. 127-30.
[56] Peck, *British Museum*, pp. 204-5.
[57] Crosby, *Early Coins*, pp. 169-70; Newman, *Studies*, pp. 149-50, quote p. 150.

Counterfeit coppers with the bust of George I are infrequently encountered but cast forgeries do exist.[58] Spurious coppers made during this reign commonly bore the image of a prior monarch, William III, as a deceptive measure. In England, by the reign of George II, counterfeits were rife and now their authors were becoming more brazen as they actually struck current bogus halfpence from dies in a coining press rather than casting them in sand.[59] Struck counterfeits bearing the bust of George II are usually very crude and easily identified as such and would only deceive the most unsophisticated. It was observed in 1751 that "every town and village had its mint."[60] These illegal issues, added to the £173,000 coined since 1717, exceeded the £130,000 limit suggested by Newton as the maximum requirement for small change needs. The combined regal and counterfeit coins created an absolute overabundance of copper currency which was accumulating with merchants who could not pass it along. The halfpence were so numerous that they had practically displaced gold and silver in commerce. Some claimed, in a 1754 petition to the king, that they were saddled with £50 to £500 of unnegotiable halfpence which were not legal tender for taxes, would not be received in purchase of a bill of exchange, and could only be spent for small purchases. Many employers used this money to pay their workers. The Mint rejected as impractical the suggestions either to withdraw all coppers and start over, or to devalue existing ones to remove the profit motive for counterfeiters.[61] England was in a sorry state in regard to their small change, but still there was no collapse of the copper medium which continued to circulate. By 1753 it was estimated that about one-half of the circulating copper money was counterfeit[62] which could be purchased at seven pence a pound.[63]

The false money easily found its way to America where it caused problems. The *Pennsylvania Gazette* of November 15, 1753, observed:

> Our Readers are cautioned to beware of counterfeit English Halfpence, great Quantities of which we understand are lately imported. They are of all Kings and Years from King William downwards; but besides being of base Metal, they are much lighter than the true Ones. They may be known by their Colour, Thinness, and Roughness, occasioned by their being cast in Sand. 'Tis said that above Forty Thousand Pounds Sterling in such Halfpence, have been lately made in England; but their Currency being now stopt at home, some evil-minded Persons are buying them up to send to the Plantations. The other Provinces are already on their Guard, and 'tis hoped our People will likewise be too prudent to give them a Currency; since if they can be passed here, our Silver and Gold, to an equal Value, will be carried off in Exchange for them, to the Ruin of the poorer Sort, in whose Hands they must at last sink; since all the Merchants and knowing Dealers, will absolutely refuse them.[64]

Simultaneous stories in *The Boston Weekly News-Letter* of November 2, 1753, and *The Boston Gazette* of October 30, 1753, reported the seizure of several bags "of counterfeit Pieces in Imitation of the Copper English half Pence" in the possession of a passenger recently arrived from London. In the same year, a report from New York indicated that the inspection of a bag containing 2,880 halfpence revealed no less than 884 sand cast coins of various dates.[65] The unremitting increase of false coppers within the Massachusetts Bay Colony came to the official

[58] Montagu, *Coinage*, p. xix. Cast halfpence of George I are listed by Batty, *Descriptive Catalogue*, 1898, 1899. The cast specimen in the author's collection has a specific gravity of 8.23 at 120.2 grains. Since the only Queen Anne coppers, 1714 farthings, were very rare, it is unlikely that any counterfeits were made for the purpose of circulation but rather as forgeries to defraud collectors.

[59] A George II cast halfpenny in the author's collection weighing 102.7 grains has a specific gravity of 8.09 indicating significant dilution of the copper with a lighter metal or much trapped air.

[60] Craig, *Mint*, p. 253.

[61] Craig, *Mint*, pp. 251, 253.

[62] Ruding, *Annals*, vol. 2, p. 80.

[63] Scott, *New York*, p. 102.

[64] As quoted by Scott, *Pennsylvania*, p. 86.

[65] Scott, *New York*, p. 102.

attention of the General Court which noted on March 27, 1755, "as large quantities of counterfeit half pence, of base metal, had been imported, and, with French and other small copper coin continually increase, a committee are ordered to report measures to prevent such practices."[66]

This continued influx of base metal coppers into America resulted in grievances among the merchants, economic losses in commerce, and eroded public trust in the medium. Responding to this situation, the New York legislature on December 12, 1753, imposed a £100 fine on anyone convicted of importing counterfeit coppers and a penalty of ten times the value of any false coins passed. Because of market pressures, New York merchants had generally agreed to accept only 14 coppers to the New York shilling, in stead of 12. Based on the established value of the Spanish American eight reales, the genuine regal halfpenny was overvalued in New York in 1750 at 12 to the colonial shilling. This differential, unfavorable to New York, had created a flow of coppers into that colony from adjacent Massachusetts and Pennsylvania where the rate of exchange for halfpence, in comparison to the Spanish standard, was more accurately reflected.[67] To curb this stream of coppers into the colony where they were overvalued and had more purchasing power, New York in 1753 devalued the halfpence and established an equilibrium in the movement of English halfpence from its neighboring plantations. This was accomplished by increasing the exchange ratio to 14 coppers per colonial shilling, without discrimination as to the weight of the copper, a rate already set by the local merchants and now confirmed by law.[68] The rate is summarized in Table 12. (See also Appendix 1.)

The readjustment of the value of coppers in New York was not without conflict; an incident was reported where three arrests resulted when individuals encouraged a mob to riot by throwing coppers among them. In Philadelphia, the abundance of false coppers had so diluted and debased the circulating currency that there was some discussion of a further increase of the exchange rate from 15 to 18 coppers per colonial shilling, the prior adjustment having been made in 1741. There was an orderly depreciation of the copper medium first in Philadelphia and 12 years later in New York.[69] Despite expansion of the copper currency with a plethora of English counterfeits, the medium continued to sustain public confidence. Apparently the 1753 New York rate increase to 14 coppers per shilling, the crackdown on imports of illegal coppers, and the heightened general awareness of spurious coins, restored public confidence in coppers so that the exchange relationships outlined in Table 11 remained quite stable up through the Confederation period until 1787 when significant troubles developed. The equilibrium in the intra and intercolonial circulation of currency, in this case copper, was driven by local market pressures fired by exchange rates and the size of the money supply.

TABLE 12

Relative Ratings of English Halfpence in England, Massachusetts, Pennsylvania and New York in Local Monies as Determined by the Eight Reales Standard
(Newman, *Studies*, pp. 143-44)

Locality	*1750 Rate for Eight reales, in local money*	*Number of Halfpence per Local Shilling*	
		Theoretical	*Actual*
England	54d.	24.0	24.0
Massachusetts	72d.	18.0	18.0
Pennsylvania	90d.	14.4	15.0
New York[a]	96d.	13.5	12.0

[a] In 1750, the halfpenny was overvalued in New York by 1½d., and undervalued in Pennsylvania by 0.6d., or a 2.1d. differential. The flow of coppers into N. Y. was stemmed when the exchange rate was advanced to 14 per N. Y. shilling in 1753, causing a slight undervaluation based on the sterling rate.

[66] Felt, *Massachusetts*, p. 138.

[67] Newman, *Studies*, pp. 143-44.

[68] Crosby, *Early Coins*, p. 291. "Without discrimination" makes no distinction regarding genuine or counterfeit, or whether full or under weight.

[69] Scott, *New York*, pp. 102-9; Newman, *Studies*, p. 144.

The people were not completely indifferent to the nature of counterfeit coppers. An interesting description of Newton's assay technique appeared in 1754.[70] "Pennies [*sic*] of bad Coppers are easily detected, by making them red hot, and striking them with a Hammer, which will make them fly to Pieces; while good Copper will bear forging in a red hot State, and in a lower Degree of Heat, like Iron."

In England, petitions to the king in complaint against this avalanche of false money were responsible for the cessation of copper coinage until 1770. It was evident "that the forgeries were due to the great difference between their nominal and intrinsic values."[71] Feavearyear described the situation:

> Thus by the last quarter of the eighteenth century the copper money was getting into as bad a condition as the silver, and no one seems to have been able to make satisfactory proposals for dealing with either. There was a shortage of silver coins because the Mint made them too heavy. There was an excess of copper ones because the Mint made them too light. So long as it lay beyond the administrative capacity of government to put down counterfeiting, the remedy for the position clearly lay in making copper coins much heavier and the silver ones a trifle lighter.... Public opinion was strongly in favour of raising the weight of the copper coins so that they should contain their full value of metal, but there was no willingness as yet to see the silver coins degraded to mere tokens.[72]

Fig. 33:
(a) England: 1771 contemporary counterfeit farthing of George III (48.6 grains). Private Collection.

(b) England: 1773 contemporary counterfeit farthing of George III (49.5 grains). Private Collection.

(c) England: 1773 contemporary counterfeit halfpenny of George III (119.8 grains). Private Collection (Table 21, no. 23).

(d) England: 1774 contemporary counterfeit halfpenny of George III. The king's bulbous nose suggests that the engraver sported a sense of humor. (89.1 grains). Private Collection (Table 21, no. 23).

70 Scott, *New York*, p. 106.
71 Montagu, *Coinage*, p. 91.
72 Feavearyear, *Pound Sterling*, pp. 171-72.

(e) England: 1775 contemporary counterfeit halfpenny of George III (121.1 grains). Private Collection (Table 21, no. 23).

(f) England: 1775 contemporary counterfeit halfpenny of George III (139.3 grains). Note massive obverse die break (Table 21, no. 23).

(g) England: 1775 genuine halfpenny of George III (154.9 grains) (Table 21, no. 23).

When regal copper coinage was resumed under George III from 1770 to 1775, counterfeiters were again off and running to claim some of the profit available from the manufacture of illegal farthings and halfpence. By now, underworld technology had become more sophisticated and engraved dies and coining presses were the norm, the casting method being rarely used. Counterfeiters even melted down regal halfpence to obtain copper for their products.[73] Batty catalogued in his collection some 567 different British halfpence specimens dated from 1770 to 1775, of which 515 were contemporary counterfeits while the remaining 52 were genuine issues from the Tower Mint.[74] Although only four pairs of genuine die varieties for 1775 are recorded from the Tower Mint, Batty identified a total of 248 different counterfeits for that year. For 1773 and 1774, when there were but ten and seven legitimate die pairs, the Batty Collection catalogued 93 and 87 different coppers with those dates, respectively, the difference being due to the large number of spurious issues. Earlier counterfeit halfpence dated 1770, 1771, and 1772 are much less frequently seen although the Batty Collection contained some 18, 44, and 42 varieties, respectively for those years. All counterfeit farthings of George III are quite rare, whereas even today, counterfeit halfpence with his effigy are still encountered in old accumulations and dealers' "junk boxes." As with the Batty experience, 1775-dated counterfeit halfpence are found to be about three times more common than each of the 1774 and 1773 issues, the earlier years being definitely scarcer in comparison. These counterfeit George III coppers, especially the halfpence, were exported to the colonies in vast numbers where they comprised the bulk of the small change medium into the early Federal period.

Considering that counterfeit coppers were so commonplace within the fabric of the English monetary system where they circulated, both at home and abroad, without significant challenge, it is not at all surprising to learn that ambitious colonists also began to engage in counterfeiting practices. The most famous domestic manufacturer of the so-called imitation English halfpence is believed to have been Captain Thomas Machin from Newburgh, New York. Specimens attrib-

[73] Peck, *British Museum*, p. 214.

[74] Batty, *Descriptive Catalogue*, pp. 928-73. Newman, *Studies*, p. 169; Newman, *ANSMN 33*, pp. 205-23. This article also summarizes the Batty catalogue data.

uted to this source share some dates with legal issues (1747, 1771, 1772, 1774, and 1775) but there are many positively fictitious varieties dated 1776, 1777, 1778, 1787, and 1788, since no legal issues exist for those dates. The imitation halfpence from Machin's Mills are easily identified by their characteristic figures and lettering, and when punch linked to other colonial coppers thought to be from that mint, their source is easily traced. The details of this Newburgh mint are contained in a subsequent chapter.

Another counterfeiting operation has been placed in the village of Barneyville in the township of Swansea, Massachusetts. The community, also known as Bungtown, was the site of the Barney family shipbuilders who "are said to have cast, in sand-moulds, fac-similes of the English Halfpennies of that period and circulated them as Cents; to these clumsy products the name of Bungtowns was given, from the popular name of the village where the Barneys lived."[75] This location has been proposed as the origin of a 1784-dated copper designated Vlack 14-84A, but those specimens are not sand cast from a contemporary issue but rather struck from crude dies on inferior planchets.[76] If the statement is accurate that the "Barneyville mint" sand casted copies of current English coppers, then one would expect their product to have been rough cast copies of legal halfpence. This hypothesis is supported by a 1786 account which details the conviction of a local resident for passing "mixed metal" counterfeit British halfpence in Boston. Since the sand casting technique would leave no identifying features as to manufacturer, such coins would be difficult to trace. While the unrefined appearance of the 1784 halfpence points to an American source rather than English, its mint of origin remains a mystery. Another domestic counterfeit English halfpenny dated 1786, listed by Vlack, has no characteristics in common with the above mentioned 1784 or other Newburgh issues and is obviously from another clandestine mint. The American provenance of this copper is irrefutable since it shares a common reverse with a counterfeit Connecticut copper, Miller 1786 2.4-U.[77]

Batty catalogued other copper halfpence of George III with purely imaginative dates which included two varieties for 1766, eight for 1776, four varieties each for 1777 and 1781, and one variety for 1794. Also in his collection of fictitious dates were a 1787 Machin's Mills copper (Vlack 17-87B) and the 1784 (Vlack 14-84A) just described. It is anyone's guess how these colonial counterfeits found their way to England. Additionally, four die combinations of 1785 counterfeit George III halfpence have been researched by Newman.[78] The paradox is that these coppers are typically English in their style of manufacture but this 1785 series was unknown to Batty since it was not represented in his collection of over 35,000 coppers. None bearing this date has ever been located in England, a fact which has prompted Newman to conclude that these 1785 varieties were made in England solely for export to British North America. Whereas this whole raft of English manufactured copper counterfeits listed above circulated widely in England and the New World, the spurious 1785-dated issues enjoy a special place as a distinctly colonial coinage.

Another source of domestic counterfeit English halfpence has recently been introduced to the numismatic literature by Trudgen.[79] Prior to 1774 in Fort Crown Point, New York, William Gilfoil, a private in the 26th Regiment of the British Army, who served as a blacksmith, was known to have "beat out" coppers which passed locally as halfpence at the current rate of 14 to the shilling. Nothing is known regarding the design on these early American "blacksmith tokens," or their method of manufacture, whether cast or hammered.

Counterfeit coppers were ubiquitous. In England, a 1787 examination of false halfpence conducted by the Tower Mint stated that " '8 percent had tolerable resemblance to the king's

[75] Newman, *Studies*, pp. 164-65; Breen, *Encyclopedia*, pp. 89-90; Low, *Tokens*, p. 40.
[76] Newman, *Studies*, pp. 171-72; Peters, *CNL 1975*, p. 485.
[77] Breen, *Encyclopedia*, pp. 68, 90; Vlack, *Counterfeit*.
[78] Newman, *ANSMN 33*, pp. 212-13.
[79] Trudgen, *CNL 1987B*, pp. 997-1000, 1019-21.

coin; 43 per cent were blatantly inferior; 12 per cent were blanks; and the balance [37%] was trash which would disgrace common sense to suppose it accepted for coins'."[80] In 1789, Matthew Boulton wrote, "in the course of my journeys I observe that I receive upon the average two-thirds counterfeit halfpence for change at toll-gates ...."[81] Of local interest, all the George III halfpence excavated at Colonial Williamsburg were counterfeit.[82] In the Stepney, Connecticut hoard of colonial coppers buried in 1788, 56 of the 72 inventoried counterfeit halfpence were of English manufacture while the remainder have been attributed to Machin's Mills.[83]

The counterfeit English halfpence of this era earned the generic name "Birmingham coppers" or "Brummagens" after the city of origin while in America the invective "Bungtown" was applied to any counterfeit copper, irrespective of source.[84] The prime reasons for the propagation of "Birmingham coppers" was that the enterprise was profitable, as Harris had noted, and the risks minimal since in England counterfeiting copper coinage was pretty well ignored by authorities and treated only as a misdemeanor although after 1742, conviction drew a two year prison sentence. The falsification of gold or silver, however, had always been a felony punishable by death. Barnard concluded that this obvious inequity within the legal system for counterfeiting precious versus base metals identified the prejudicial attitude of the wealthy, ruling elite toward the poorer working classes who would stand to suffer more economic damage from illegal, lightweight coppers. It was not unusual for common laborers to receive their wages in counterfeit coppers which merchants might only accept at a discount, if at all.[85] In the colonies, the laws against counterfeiting were inconsistent, with punishments varying from the pillory to the gallows. As the eighteenth century progressed, more severe sentences were pronounced not only for the falsification of coins but for the alteration and printing of paper money.[86]

"EVASIVE" ISSUES

A loophole existed in English statutes. There was only a restriction against the manufacture of coppers which "resembled" regal halfpence but no restraint existed if the bogus copper were not an exact copy.[87] Because of this legal ambiguity, a thriving business developed in the production of "evasive halfpence" which had only a similarity to the real coins with legends of a non-regal nature such as GEORGIUS III RUX, GOERGIUV III PAX, and on the reverse, BRITAIN RULES, BONNY GIRL, and BRITISH TARS. While these coins were not counterfeits under a legal definition, they were foisted upon the poor and illiterate and inflicted as much economic damage on these classes had they been outlawed. Birmingham was the business center for this activity of "evasive" money as it was also for counterfeits,[88] but other evasives were minted in London, Bilston, and Wolverhampton. Substantial profits were made by the manufacturers and "smashers" (utterers or passers) of these evasive issues which were produced in great numbers and sold "at the rate of 28/- to 30/- worth for a good guinea."[89] These coins circulated in areas where royal coppers were in short supply and did fill a need. Atkins catalogued some 491 different varieties of evasives with many more recently discovered.[90]

[80] Craig, *Mint*, p. 253.
[81] Henry, *Series*, p. 18.
[82] Newman, *Colonial Virginia*, p. 33.
[83] Breen, *Num 1952*, pp. 7-24.
[84] Peck, *British Museum*, p. 206; Newman, *Studies*, pp. 159, 168.
[85] Barnard, *NC 1926*, pp. 342-46.
[86] Counterfeiting in the colonies is well described by Scott in his three monographs, *New York*, *Pennsylvania*, and *Connecticut*, and by Glaser, *Counterfeiting*.
[87] Peck, *British Museum*, pp. 205-6; Barnard, *NC 1926*, passim.
[88] Ruding, *Annals*, vol. 2, p. 80; Peck, *British Museum*, pp. 206-7.
[89] Waters, *Imitation Copper*, pp. 404-5.
[90] Atkins, *Tradesmen's Tokens*, pp. 385-95.

Fig. 34:
(a) Evasive English farthing: GEORGE RULES.

(b) Evasive English halfpenny, 1791.

Crosby listed several evasive halfpence in his book which he mistakenly identified with the American series as contemporary English counterfeits.[91] However, there is no evidence that evasive halfpence ever circulated in America nor is there any report of such pieces being recovered in accumulations or hoards of the colonial period. There is some indication that the evasives were introduced into America as collectors' items between 1877 and 1883.[92] Further research has shown that the legends on these evasive pieces parodied historical events from 1776 through the French Revolution and into the early years of the Napoleonic Wars, and thus belong to an era substantially beyond the American colonial period.[93] No reliance can be placed on the dates or monarch appearing on the evasives as an indication of their time of manufacture.

* * *

The study of small change has thus extended from a brief description of early silver pieces, through the various cycles of merchant tokens, and finally into the period of regal patent and official copper and tin coinages. Of equal interest to the legally minted coins is the parallel appearance of counterfeit coppers whose manufacture was promoted because of the potential for a quick profit against which there was little personal risk. Legitimate and false English coppers together saw extensive service in British North America as the small change of the colonists, and their presence is well documented in contemporary accounts. From such supporting evidence it is appropriate to include the genuine and counterfeit farthings and halfpence from their beginnings with Charles II through the first coinage of George III as part of the American Colonial series. Without argument, the 1749 English farthings and halfpence exported for use in Massachusetts are as distinctly "American" as the Spanish milled dollar.

Thus, the English series of coppers, both the legal and spurious, and their North American connections, have been examined up through the time of the Revolution. The story is far from over since English coppers take on a new complexion in our numismatic history during the period of the Confederation. The successful counterfeiting experience for regal coppers in England no doubt encouraged establishment of the practice in America where it is believed to have flourished under the hands of Captain Thomas Machin and others yet to be identified. The continuing saga of English copper coinages, genuine and false, will be resumed in subsequent chapters.

[91] Crosby, *Early Coins*, pp. 172-73.
[92] Newman, *Studies*, pp. 151-53; Breen, *Num 1952*, p. 23.
[93] Thompson, *Evasions*, pp. 275-76; Barnard, *NC 1926*, p. 356.

IRISH COPPER CURRENCY; THE ST. PATRICK COPPERS

Our attention now shifts to Ireland where the shortage of small coinage was as acute as it was in England during the seventeenth century. The royal patent farthings of 1613 to 1644 were also intended to pass current in Ireland, but these very lightweight pieces proved unpopular and production ceased in 1642. To facilitate trade, a number of merchant tokens and other divers coppers appeared in Ireland, generally with the promise of redemption by the specific issuing individual. These promissory notes were about the size of a standard farthing, although thinner, and most of them passed for one penny.[94] Lindsay catalogued 195 such "Town pieces and Tradesmen's tokens" from the time of the Commonwealth until the end of the reign of George II. The tokens were dated in three clusters; the first primarily included the years 1654 to 1673, the next span was 1677 to 1679, while the last sequence appeared from 1728 to 1735.[95] The hiatus between 1673 and 1677 was due to the decree of October 17, 1673, stipulating that no tokens could be produced without a royal license. The effectiveness of this proclamation in stemming the production of tokens is evidenced by Lindsay who found none dated between 1673 and 1676. The problem of the small change shortage was satisfactorily addressed on May 18, 1680, when letters patent were granted to Sir Thomas Armstrong and Colonel George Legg to mint legal tender copper halfpence for Ireland for a term of 21 years. These halfpence were of good weight, 110 grains each, and the monopoly was secured by the decree of July 19, 1680, which outlawed all other copper tokens. These royal patent halfpence, minted from 1680 to 1684, were described by Simon as "certainly the best and handsomest copper money yet struck in, or for Ireland."[96]

Fig. 35:
(a) St. Patrick "halfpenny", Vlack 4-C (134.1 grains).

(b) St. Patrick "farthing" (96.1 grains).

During the second half of the seventeenth century and within the context of the small change shortage, there appeared two different St. Patrick copper tokens which figured prominently in the American colonial period. Nothing suggests that the St. Patrick coppers were promissory merchants' notes, but instead were a true token coinage. The origin of this series still remains shrouded in mystery but recent research has expanded our knowledge. The obverse of the elusive series portrays a King David-like figure playing his harp with the crown of England above. To provide the illusion of gold, the crown is accentuated by a brass splasher which is also an anti-counterfeiting measure; the legend, FLOREAT REX (May the King Prosper), indicates support of the monarchy. The reverse of the larger coin, or so-called halfpenny, shows the mitred St. Patrick as the central figure holding his cross out to the people. To his left is a shield with three castles, the arms of the City of Dublin, and the inscription, ECCE GREX (Behold the

[94] Simon, *Essay*, pp. 48-49.
[95] Lindsay, *Ireland*, pp. 56-57, 108-25.
[96] Simon, *Essay*, pp. 52-55, quote p. 54.

flock), surrounds the design. The reverse of the smaller coin, or alleged farthing, again shows St. Patrick as the central figure but in this instance he holds a double, or metropolitan cross, in his left hand. His right arm extends over a "parcel of serpents ... as if driving them out of the church" which is to St. Patrick's left side. QVIESCAT PLEBS (May the people be at ease), is the accompanying legend. Several theories have been proposed as to the provenance of these coppers which are interesting to recount.

Early numismatists considered the St. Patrick series to have been struck pursuant to an act of the Kilkenny Assembly of 1642 by the Catholic confederacy in defiance of the "Malignant" Puritanical Parliamentary forces. A passage in this act relating to "an institution and order of knighthood, concerning the honour of Saint Patrick, and the glory of this kingdom" was so suggestive of the allusion conveyed by themes on these tokens, that Simon was convinced of the relationship of this series to the "rebel" Irish forces. He even postulated that the snakes St. Patrick was chasing out of the church were a direct reference to "the malignant party," or "protestants."[97] A second theory also ascribes the coinage to the reign of Charles I, around 1645. Instead of being of Irish manufacture, the St. Patrick coppers are attributed to the Tower Mint from dies engraved by Nicholas Briot and punch-linked to his Scottish pieces.[98] It was further postulated that the Roman Catholic symbolism explained why this coinage was not circulated during the anti-royal and anti-papist sentiment of the Commonwealth era. Other sources place the coinage still around 1645 but on the order of the Earl of Glamorgan who attempted to raise an Irish army against Cromwell's forces in the siege of Chester.[99]

More recent work compiled by Hodder dates the St. Patrick tokens after the Restoration of the monarchy to the period 1672 to 1675.[100] The dates coincide with the era of the proliferation of merchants' promissory tokens just described. The arms of Dublin on the larger coin and the 1681 observation of a contemporary writer that the piece passed as a halfpenny are strong evidence of an Irish origin from Dublin. The fact that a St. Patrick "farthing" was recovered from a ship wrecked on March 25, 1675, helps establish the early limit of its manufacture. The reverse design of the "farthing" is very similar to that of the penny token issued by the merchant, Richard Greenwood, of High Street, Dublin. Simon ascribes Greenwood's token and six others to the period of the Commonwealth. A generic description of these seven issues indicates they "are made of brass, or copper, not broader, but thinner than our present farthings, and like so many promissory notes passed for one penny each, in the neighbourhood, and amongst the customers of those who issued them, whose names, together with the value 1d. and their coat of arms, sign, or cypher, are printed on their respective pieces ...." [101]

There has long been the tradition that the obverse figure of King David is an allegorical reference to Charles I. Hodder points out in his study that this biblical theme appeared on several earlier European pieces and clearly was not original with the St. Patrick series. He further describes the imagery as "one of non-specific royalist sentiments clothed in quasi-religious symbolism redolent of Caroline divine right theory." Hodder summarizes the available information to support the belief that the St. Patrick tokens were a semi-official coinage struck in Dublin around 1672 to 1675, perhaps with the sanction of the Lord Lieutenant of Ireland, the Earl of Essex, who was the author of the decree of October 17, 1673, regulating all token coinage. The occurrence of this series in silver and gold, the inclusion of a brass splasher, and a reeded edge similarly suggest sophistication in their manufacture and sponsorship.

Although the current evidence provides a logical explanation about the origin of the series, there are still unanswered questions about the nature and value of the coins themselves. Simon felt they were halfpence and farthings whereas Batty, Lindsay, and "other distinguished

[97] Lindsay, *Ireland*, p. 56; Simon, *Essay*, pp. 47-48, quote p. 118; Ruding, *Annals*, vol. 1, p. 398, vol. 2, p. 388.

[98] Breen, *CNL 1968A*; Crosby, *Early Coins*, pp. 135-38; Vlack, *CNL 1967*.

[99] Taxay, *Catalogue*, p. 39.

[100] Hodder, *CNL 1987*. See also *Norweb*, pt. 2, pp. 221-31.

[101] Simon, *Essay*, pp. 48-49, 7 plate 2 Supplement; Lindsay, *Ireland*, 118, p. 112.

Numismatists" considered them halfpence and pennies.[102] Simon calculated the larger coin at 130 to 135 grains, and the smaller at 90 to 106 grains.[103] Lindsay's specimens were 133 and from 86 to 89 grains, respectively.[104] Analysis of specimens from recent auctions and private collections reveal an average weight of 135.7 ± 9.5 for 21 larger coins or "halfpence," and an average of 92.3 ± 9.2 for 46 "farthings."[105] From this 1:1.47 weight ratio, it is evident that the two coins are not related to each other as a typical farthing to halfpenny with a 1:2 relationship.

TABLE 13

Description of Actual Irish Regal and Patent Halfpence Compared to English Halfpence and Theoretical Irish Equivalent as Determined by the Prevalent Exchange Rate

Period of Exchange Rate[a] Irish to English	*Official Standard[b] English ½d.*	*Comparable Theoretical[c] Irish ½d.*	*Actual Irish Halfpence*
1660-1689 105.56:100	1672 175 grains	165.8 grains	1680-1684 Charles II ½d.[d] patent weight 110 grains observed wgt. 105-119 gr.[e]
	1672-1675 159.1 grains	150.7 grains	1685-1688 James II ½d.[f] patent weight 110 grains observed wgt. 101-130 gr.
1689-1695 108.33:100	1694 166.7 grains	153.9 grains	1692-1694 Wm. & Mary ½d.[g] patent weight ?110 grains observed wgt. 85, 106-116 gr.
1695-1701 116.67:100	1695-1701 166.7 grains	142.9 grains	1696 William III ½d.[h] patent weight? 110 gr. observed wgt. 106-116 grs.
1701-1826 108.33:100	1717-1775 152.2 grains	140.5 grains	1722-1724 George I ½d.[i] patent weight 116.7 grains observed wgt. See Table 15
			1736-1760 George II ½d.[j] legal weight 134.6 gr. observed wgt. 95-110, 134-135 gr.
			1766-1782 George III ½d.[k] legal weight 134.6 gr. observed wgt. 81-125 gr.

[a] From McCusker, *Money and Exchange*, p. 34.
[b] From Table 10.
[c] Values calculated from English standard based on current exchange rate; if the English halfpenny of 1694 weighed 166.7 grains, then at the exchange rate of 108.33:100, Irish currency to English, the comparable Irish halfpenny should weigh 153.9 grains. The actual weight observed was 106-116 grains indicating an excessive token value (overvaluation) for the Irish copper.
[d] Under the patent of Armstrong/Legg (Simon, *Essay*, pp. 54-55).
[e] All observed weights from Lindsay, *Ireland*, pp. 100-6, or Simon, *Essay*, pp. 54-56, 64-65.
[f] The patent passed to Sir John Knox (Simon, *Essay*, p. 56).
[g] The patent next passed to Roger Moore (Simon, *Essay*, pp. 64-65).
[h] Also produced under Moore's patent.
[i] New patent awarded to William Wood.
[j] Minted at Tower Mint for years 1736-1738, 1741-1744, 1746-1753, 1755, 1760 (Simon, *Essay*, p. 73).
[k] Minted at Tower Mint for years 1766, 1769, 1774-1776, 1781-1782.

---

[102] Lindsay, *Ireland*, p. 56; Batty, *Catalogue*, 1605, p. 821; Horan, *CNL 1976*.
[103] Simon, *Essay*, p. 48.
[104] Lindsay, *Ireland*, p. 99.
[105] Auction specimens are from the following sales: *Roper*; *Garrett*, pt. 3; *Norweb*, pt. 2.

In order to study the relationship between the two St. Patrick tokens, it is important to recall the weights of other Irish coppers of the period (see Table 13). One should bear in mind that for any coin to circulate, it must be acceptable in commerce based on either its intrinsic or acceptable token value. Typically such tokens were minted at a considerable profit to the authors. Numismatic history is replete with examples of rejected coinages which the citizenry considered lightweight and overvalued. The unpopular copper farthings of the Harington, Lennox, Richmond and Maltravers patents are good examples. In comparing the St. Patrick coinages with other coppers of the period, some insight may be gathered as they are examined within the context of other circulating coinages thus better defining their contemporary value.

The official coinage closest in time to the St. Patrick token are those Charles II Irish halfpence minted from 1680 to 1684 under the Armstrong and Legg patent which required a halfpenny to weigh 110 grains. Simon observed that this requirement was consistently met if not exceeded.[106] The issue also carried the approval of Dean Jonathan Swift who, in his third Drapier's letter, considered the 1680 halfpence superior in weight and metal composition to Wood's halfpence.[107] From these data it is evident that the Irish coinage had less intrinsic and more token value than the corresponding English coppers, thus providing a greater profit margin for the Irish patentees. Another contemporary token was the 1679 Dublin halfpenny, probably a semi-official issue, which Simon remarked was "very fair ... of the bigness of our present half-penny" which in 1749, when he wrote, would have weighed 134.6 grains.[108]

The problem remains that the St. Patrick halfpenny is heavier than the official patent halfpenny coinage of the period, although it compares favorably to the Dublin halfpenny which also bears the arms of the city. Therefore, all three issues, the larger St. Patrick coin, the Dublin halfpenny, and the regal halfpenny starting with George II weigh in the same order of magnitude. If the heaviness of the halfpenny presents a problem, then the smaller St. Patrick coin of 92 grains is a greater enigma since one might reasonably expect that it is far too heavy to have been minted as a token farthing, which in the time of Charles II weighed from 22.5 to 28 grains.[109]

In considering all the available evidence, it is difficult to conceive that the two St. Patrick coins are related to each other as farthing and halfpenny. Not only are their relative weights incorrect, but the St. Patrick "farthing" would even be heavier than the corresponding regal English farthing of Charles II. In a period of tokens and lightweight coins, it would be unlikely for its sponsors to have minted a heavier St. Patrick farthing for Ireland. The near 1:1.5 weight ratio is more consistent with a halfpenny and three-farthing. In regard to sheer numbers, there are considerably more farthings than halfpence—while the estimated number of farthing die varieties is in the vicinity of 120,[110] only 10 varieties for the halfpence have thus far been identified.[111] Typically, six-sevenths of the coppers minted were halfpence, but here the situation is reversed by a considerable ratio, since the St. Patrick "farthing" is significantly more common than the "halfpenny."[112] Writing in 1839, Lindsay proposed that the larger coin was a Rarity 6 out of 8, while the smaller was a Rarity 2 out of 8, and as numismatic items, the halfpenny was worth about 5 times more than the farthing.[113] Only the smaller coin comes in

[106] Simon, *Essay*, pp. 54-55.
[107] Scott, *Swift*, vol. 7, p. 143.
[108] Simon, *Essay*, pp. 53-54.
[109] Lindsay, *Ireland*, p. 100.
[110] Breen, *Encyclopedia*, p. 34.
[111] Vlack, *CNL 1967*, pp. 199-202.
[112] Craig, *Mint*, pp. 220, 428.
[113] Lindsay, *Ireland*, p. 127. The specifics of the scale are not given except that Rarity 8 out of 8 means about 3-4 pieces known.

silver perhaps as a presentation piece. One puzzling fact is that in all contemporary references, only the halfpenny is mentioned. Where was the "farthing" and why was it omitted from these discussions? There are two considerations; the first is, what were the intended denominations when the two coins were originally issued, and next, for what rate did they pass subsequently?

There is an explanation that can reconcile these seeming disparities; both coins were originally struck as halfpenny tokens although the later rating may have changed by custom. Such an answer is just as reasonable as the attempt to designate them farthings and halfpence. Consider the possibility that the larger halfpence varieties were minted first in small numbers; because of the added expense for the larger coins and the increased die wear, it became more profitable to mint smaller coins of lesser weight. The style and technique improved and presentation issues were produced. A clue in support of this hypothesis comes from Swift's "Drapier's Letter III" as he wrote in 1724 of "the small St. Patrick's coin, which passes *now* [emphasis added] for a farthing" suggesting that it may not always have done so.[114] He next spoke of "the great St. Patrick's halfpence" implying the existence of both small and great halfpence and that *now* the small St. Patrick coin passed as farthings. However apocryphal this deviation from traditional wisdom may appear, the fact remains that while the larger St. Patrick coin may well be a halfpenny, the smaller issue cannot have been a farthing when measured by the same criteria.

More is known about the circulation of the coinage but still there are unanswered questions in this area. The St. Patrick's tokens were introduced into the Isle of Mann where they were current during the minority of its hereditary lord, the Earl of Derby. When he came of age in 1679, the St. Patrick money was demonetized in favor of a local token currency.[115] Following the Manx rejection, these unwanted tokens somehow came into the possession of Mark Newby, an English Quaker who was established as a merchant in Dublin where he suffered religious persecution. In 1681, at age 43, Newby and his family emigrated from Dublin to West New Jersey to settle in a Quaker community established by William Penn.[116] Newby brought an unknown quantity of the larger St. Patrick tokens with him, probably acquired in bulk and at a considerable discount. Newby was elected to the West Jersey Assembly which, in May 1682, authorized the tokens to pass as legal tender. Prior to that time, only wampum was available as small change currency.[117] Mention is made only of the halfpence which were to "pass for half-pence Current pay of this Province." The exchange rate for Newby's coppers was not specified in the enabling legislation except by the vague phrase "for pay Equivalent." It has not been proven that any of the smaller tokens ever circulated in America, but had they, they would have been rated as halfpence since no other schedule was published. In 1682, the exchange rate for West New Jersey, as determined by Philadelphia, was 133.33:100, money of account to sterling. "Pay Equivalent" would therefore have been 18 coppers to the New Jersey shilling.[118] It is to be recalled that New Jersey was split into West and East from 1676 until 1702, with the eastern section following the monetary practices of New York while the western part adhered to those of Pennsylvania. Newby was required to post surety for the token coinage and after his death within the following year, his estate redeemed £30 of the coppers which would have totaled 10,800 coins at the current exchange rate. There is no mention of the smaller farthing denomination in any of these records or deliberations. Only the larger ones have been found in the

[114] Scott, *Swift*, vol. 7, p. 143. The early American numismatist, Matthew A. Stickney, also read this as "the small St. Patrick and the great St. Patrick half-penny" (*Notes*, vol. 2 [1860], p. 46).

[115] Gallagher, *Num. Soc. Ire.*, pp. 26, 37n.

[116] Gladfelter, *TAMS 1974*, pp. 167-76; Anton and Hodder, *CNL 1989*, pp. 1111-17.

[117] Stickney, *Notes*, vol. 2 (1860), p. 46.

[118] McCusker, *Money and Exchange*, pp. 157, 175.

ground,[119] but "farthings" have been reported in uncontrolled accumlations.[120] Stickney observed in 1859 that St. Patrick pieces were rarely found in New Jersey and that he had to send to England to obtain good specimens for his personal collection.[121]

Following the speculation that Newby acquired the St. Patrick tokens at a significant discount when they were demonetized on the Isle of Mann, there was potential for considerable gain when he brought them to New Jersey. The level of profit is difficult to calculate since so many unknowns shroud this series. Assuming mint costs similar to the Tower Mint and the weight of the halfpenny at 135.7 grains, or 51.6 coins per pound, figures similar to those in Table 10 can be constructed to show the profit for the unknown sponsor of the series. Table 14 also demonstrates the profit for the smaller St. Patrick coin if it were to pass either as a farthing or halfpenny. The table expresses these values in Irish currency whose exchange rate to English during the 1672 to 1675 period was 105.56:100.00. The presumed costs of minting the coppers are from Table 10 for 1672, assuming there was no Swedish export tax for the metal. Since the discount, if any, at which Newby acquired this hoard of coppers is unknown, his profit realized in New Jersey cannot be estimated.

TABLE 14
Relative Weights, Presumed Mint Costs, and Profits for the Large and Small St. Patrick Tokens[a]

	Large St. Patrick Coin	*Small St. Patrick Coin*	
	Halfpenny	*As farthing*	*As halfpenny*
Observed weight	135.7	92.3	92.3
Coins/lb.	51.6	75.8	75.8
Mint costs/lb.	17.3d.	17.3d.	17.3d.
Monetary value/lb.	25.8d.	19.0d.	37.9d.
TOTAL COSTS[b]	17.3d.	17.3d.	17.3d.
Profit	8.5d.	1.7d.	20.6d.
Profit/total cost	49.1%	9.8%	119.1%

[a] The assumption is that the coins were made in Ireland for Irish use.
[b] The assumed mint costs of 17.3d., Irish, (16d., English) are extrapolated from the known costs at the Tower Mint in 1672 as expressed in Table 10. Of course, this sum cannot estimate the added expense for placement of the brass splasher on the planchet.

Inspection of Table 14 shows that the profit margin for the smaller St. Patrick coin to pass as a farthing is a scant 9.8%, while that for the larger St. Patrick halfpenny is almost 50%. If the smaller coin were to pass as a halfpenny, then the profit would be more compatible with the patent halfpenny of the period from Table 13, which, at 110 grains, would accrue an 84% gain to the patentee. This aspect of potential profit is a further reason to suspect that the smaller St. Patrick was originally intended to be a halfpenny, although it may have later passed as a farthing as the weight of Irish coins increased. Whatever facts may eventually be uncovered, it remains unsatisfactory to consider the two St. Patrick coppers as companion coinages in a farthing-halfpenny relationship. The "farthing" is too heavy to be a farthing and the profit margin of 9.8% is too meager for a token coinage, considering the profit potential for the larger coin at 49.1%. If the farthing were never intended to exist, it would explain the lack of correspondence in weight between a so-called farthing and halfpenny, the relative rarity of an earlier minted larger coin, and the lack of contemporary discussion about the farthing. This would

[119] Crosby, *Early Coins*, p. 135.
[120] Breen, *CNL 1968A*, pp. 214-15; Breen, *CNL 1968B*, p. 233. Eric P. Newman questions whether the St. Patrick farthings ever circulated in America. (See Newman, *CNL 1968*, p. 220).
[121] Stickney, *Notes*, vol. 2 (1860), p. 46n.

assume that the smaller planchet token was easier to mint than the larger, whose manufacture was abandoned after ten or so die combinations. This novel proposal that the St. Patrick tokens were originally intended as two sizes of halfpence may be a leap into fantasy, but it is no less plausible than to call them farthing and halfpenny. This hypothesis is substantiated by calculation of the potential profit of the coinages, a very important factor to examine when considering the economic determinants of minting and the dynamics of circulation. In later years, by custom, they could have passed as farthing and halfpenny. If judged by weight alone, the halfpence and three-farthings demoninations are the most logical.[122] Dolley also stresses the distinction between the value of the tokens "at the time of their first utterance" and any subsequently adopted monetary value. In this regard, he is inclined "to accept the larger of the 'St. Patrick' pieces as halfgroats which quite soon may have been retariffed as halfpence."[123] It is clear from the cited observations about weights and potential profits that the two St. Patrick pieces were not originally minted in the 1:2 ratio expected for the farthing and halfpenny. While we can say what they were not, we can only speculate as to the original intention of their authors.

THE COINAGES OF WILLIAM WOOD

In Ireland, the implacable resistance to the Hibernia coinages of William Wood mounted by a determined surge of Irish nationalism, adds another interesting dimension to the study of numismatics. The severe lack of minor coins persisted in Ireland well into the eighteenth century. The poorer classes were victimized by a flood of unregulated and frequently worthless tokens. Circumstances were described to the king's Privy Council in 1724 in which employers "have been obliged to give tallies or tokens in cards, to their workmen for want of small money, signed upon the back, to be afterwards exchanged for larger money.... a premium was often given to obtain small money for necessary occasions." The report continued:

> The great want of small money was further proved by the common use of *raps*,[124] a counterfeit coin, of such base metal, that what passes for a halfpenny is not worth half a farthing, which raps appeared to have obtained a currency out of necessity, and for want of better small money to make change with; and, by the best accounts,... there can be no doubt, that there is a real want of small money in Ireland ...."[125]

In the dual purpose of relieving this shortage of small coin as well as securing personal gain for the king and patentee, an issue of farthings and halfpence was authorized by George I for Ireland. This favor was granted to the king's mistress, the Duchess of Kendal, which she subsequently transferred to Wood for £10,000 on June 16, 1722. This patent entitled its owner to produce 360 tons of coins at 30 pence, Irish money,[126] to the pound of copper over a period of 14 years.[127] Of this amount, 100 tons were to be coined the first year and 20 tons annually for the remaining life of the contract. The total value of the patent in Irish money amounted to

[122] Peck, *British Museum*, pp. 10-12, describes a similar confusion regarding the assignment of denomination for some of the pattern pieces of Elizabeth I; thus the question raised regarding the designation of the St. Patrick coinages is not without precedent and is an area for further numismatic research.

[123] Dolley, *Ire. Num. 1978*, p. 39.

[124] This passage refers to a "rap," a counterfeit Irish halfpenny of the period or a coin of trifling value, giving rise to the expression, "I don't give a rap."

[125] "The Report of the Committee of the Lords of his Majesty's most honourable Privy Council, in relation to Mr. Wood's Halfpence and Farthings, ... 24 July 1724," from Scott, *Swift*, vol. 7, pp. 125-34, quotes p. 132.

[126] At that time the exchange rate between England and Ireland was 100:108.33, so that 30d., Irish money, was worth 27.75d., English sterling (McCusker, *Money and Exchange*, p. 34).

[127] Nelson, *Wood*, pp. 9-14; Craig, *Mint*, pp. 370-71; Craig, *Newton*, p. 115; Cross, *History*, p. 691; Simon, *Essay*, pp. 69-71.

Fig. 36: Ireland: 1723 William Wood halfpenny of George I.

£100,800. Considering Newton's estimate that 600 tons of coppers would be a sufficient quantity for all England, 360 tons for Ireland alone was "an absurd amount, almost one-fourth the total value of all the Irish currency."[128] Although the Irish economy needed an infusion of money, it was not copper it lacked. "We have more halfpence than we need already. It is true we want change, but it is sixpences, shillings, halfcrowns, and crowns."[129] Since the proportion of copper in the money supply was to be so great with this new proposal for 360 tons,

> the question of intrinsic value [became] vitally important, for the new coins would necessarily enter into all large payments, would gradually displace gold and silver, and would place the country at a ruinous disadvantage in commerce .... Rightly or wrongly, all classes believed that under these circumstances the small amount of precious metals in the country would all or nearly all pass to England in the shape of rent, leaving nothing but a debased copper coinage at home.[130]

At that time in history, Ireland was economically destitute and living conditions were deplorable. Jonathan Swift, the Dean of Dublin's Protestant Episcopal St. Patrick Cathedral, had become a local hero striking out with "indignation against English tyranny in Ireland." "Burn everything that comes from England except the coal" was one of his injunctions to his countrymen.[131] When Wood's coinage was prepared for the Irish without their knowledge, consultation or consent, Swift attacked the action in a series of four letters purportedly penned by a Dublin dry goods merchant, signed anonymously "M.B."[132] This savage diatribe published in "The Drapier's Letters" against Wood's profiteering at the expense of "an impoverished voiceless people," whipped the Irish people into a frenzy. "He set the country ablaze from Derry to Cork. Swift did far more than to scourge the Government, he gave to Ireland a spirit she never knew she had. He created a public opinion in a nation of slaves."[133] In their interesting review of Swift and the Hibernia coinages, Gale and Gale ask the rhetorical question whether the drapier's rancor was taken literally by his countrymen. "There's no way to tell for certain. One recent critic, David Ward, suggests that 'the sophisticated would enjoy the joke; the unsophisticated would be scared out of their wits'."[134] Regardless of how one may view Swift's motives or style, the impact of his activities remains indisputable, many feared having any identification with Wood's project and trembled at the accusation of having any of his coppers in their possession. Even newsboys (flying-stationers) were entreated neither to accept nor give change for Wood's coppers.

[128] Gale and Gale, *Num 1985*, p. 1333. See note 41.

[129] Lecky, *England*, p. 422n. The quote is attributed to Archbishop King who agreed with others that no additional copper was needed.

[130] Lecky, *England*, p. 423.

[131] Wilson, *Swift*, pp. 20-21.

[132] "Letter I," 1724; "Letter II," Aug. 4, 1724; "Letter III," Aug. 25, 1724; "Letter IV," Oct. 23, 1724, from Scott, *Swift*, vol. 7.

[133] Wilson, *Swift*, p. 21.

[134] Gale and Gale, *Num 1985*, p. 1336.

> Let Wood and his accomplices travel about the country with cart-loads of their ware, and see who will take it off their hands: there will be no fear of his being robbed, for a highwayman would scorn to touch it.[135]

Wood countered these attacks and distortions of his motives with the injudicious retort "that he would cram his brass down their throats in spite of them."[136] This threat and the documented need for small change notwithstanding, his money was completely rejected. Swift's position prevailed. The terms of the patent were initially reduced from 360 to 142.75 long tons, or £40,000 (English); subsequently the contract was completely voided and in compensation for his losses, Wood received a grant of £24,000. Simon estimated that "About £17,000 value of these Halfpence and Farthings were sent over and uttered in this kingdom in the years 1722 and 1723."[137]

Although it is frequently repeated that Wood conspired to benefit at the expense of the Irish people, less has been publicized in his defense. When the financial statements regarding his patent are scrutinized, it can be seen that Wood would have lost money over the course of the 14 years had the full terms of the patent been met, a circumstance hardly deserving of the term "profiteering." In the analysis of the patent by Swift and Simon, many hard facts were either ignored or conveniently distorted in order to support their nationalist position. The Privy Council report cited above attempted to correct the misconceptions espoused by Swift. The document quoted the assay report prepared at the Tower Mint by Sir Isaac Newton conducted on Wood's coppers. This "trial of the pix" demonstrated that this patent coinage surpassed the required weight and, when compared to the regal coppers since Charles II, "considerably exceeds them all in weight, very far exceeds them all in goodness, fineness, and value of the copper." Wood's Hibernia coppers "were heavier and intrinsically more valuable than any issued before in Ireland."[138] Newton judged that the refined copper in Wood's coins was worth about 13d. per pound while the prepared copper fillets ready for coinage were worth 18d. Simon, in his interpretation of these statements, asserted that the copper in Wood's money "was not worth in the market above twelve or thirteen pence the pound," completely discounting the price of planchet preparation and minting, expenses that are traditionally absorbed in the nominal value of minor coins. Calculating another 4d. for the actual coining, Nelson arrived at a total minting cost for Wood at 22d. per pound.[139] Other fixed expenses included the £10,000 paid by Wood to the Duchess of Kendall for the patent, and the annual "rent" of £800 to the king, £200 for the king's clerk comptroller, and from his profits, Wood had to pay charges for transportation, distribution, and Irish customs on his coins. These data are recorded in Table 15 where it is noted that at 60 halfpence to the pound, or at a weight of 116.7 grains per halfpenny, Wood would have incurred a net loss of about £4,871 over the 14 year term of the agreement. Nelson made similar calculations but disregarded the exchange rate differential between England and Ireland. Simon claimed, on the basis of the average weight of four randomly selected lots of halfpence, that Wood reduced the average weight of the halfpenny to 107.5 grains to increase his profits. Although the samples which Simon and Swift quoted will never be available for our inspection, an analysis of 164 Wood's halfpence in Table 16 from current auction sales shows an absolute conformity to the requirements of the patent. These data do not support Simon's allegation that Wood's coinage was lightweight; it may be that this accusation of malfeasance was just another scheme to vilify and discredit the patentee by his Irish enemies.

[135] "Letter III," from Scott, *Swift*, vol. 7, pp. 161, 161n, 162n, 166n, 167n.

[136] Nelson, *Wood*, p. 13. "Brass" in this sense is "a generic term for copper money, as a well as a slang term for money in general." Into the seventeenth century, "brass" was a synonym for "copper." (Funk, *CNL 1973*).

[137] Simon, *Essay*, p. 71. This calculates to 60.7 long tons of coppers.

[138] Scott, *Swift*, vol. 7, quote pp. 128-129; Craig, *Newton*, p. 115.

[139] Nelson, *Wood*, p. 10.

TABLE 15

A: Production Costs of Wood's Hibernia Coinage; Full Weight (60 halfpence/lb. or 116.7 grains each); and Reduced Weight (a) (65.12 halfpence/lb. at an Average of 107.5 grains each)[a]
B: Net Profit (Loss) Figured over the Terms of the Patent of 14 Years and 360 [Long] Tons of Copper[b]

A: Production Costs	*Authorized Weight*	*Reduced Weight*
Mint costs/lb. copper		
English[c]	22d.	22d.
Number halfpenny/lb.	60.0	65.12
Weight halfpenny	116.7 grains	107.5 grains
Monetary value/lb.[d]		
English	27.69d.	30.06d.
Irish	30.0d.	32.56d.
Profit, English	5.69d.	8.05d.
Profit/cost, English	25.86%	36.59%
B: Profit (Loss) for Term of Patent Over 14 Years		
Monetary Value[d]		
English	£93,049	£100,989.2
Irish	100,800	109,401.6
Mint costs, English[d]	73,920	73,920
Cost of Patent	10,000	10,000
Fees to King/Clerk	14,000	14,000
Total costs, English	97,920	97,920
Profit (Loss), English	(4,871)	3,069.2

[a] The alleged weight of 107.5 grains is from the analysis of Simon, *Essay*, p. 70, who averaged four samples of halfpence sent to Ireland to arrive at this value.
[b] Since the coins were minted in Bristol, England, all calculations are in English currency.
[c] The mint costs of 22d./lb. are from Nelson, *Wood*, p. 10, and closely agree with Table 10 for mint costs of the period. Costs for minting one pound of copper: metal 13d., planchet preparation 5d., and coining 4d.
[d] The monetary values, English and Irish, are based on the exchange rates of the period 100:108.33 (McCusker, *Money and Exchange*, p. 34). Nelson omitted this important factor in his calculations.
360 long tons = 806,400 lbs; at 30d./lb = £100,800 (Irish)
£100,800/108.33 (exchange rate) = £93,049 (English).

TABLE 16

Weight of 164 Wood's Hibernia Halfpence from Current Auction Sales and Private Collections[a]

Year	*Number*	*Weight*
1722	40	117.1 ± 7.3 grains
1723	108	116.0 ± 6.1 grains
1724	16	113.5 ± 6.8 grains
all years	164	116.0 ± 6.5 grains

[a] The authorized weight was 116.7 grains.

The Irish, in denouncing the alleged fraud perpetrated upon them by Wood's coinage, considered only the intrinsic value of the copper at 12d., Irish, per pound, and ignored the costs of planchet preparation and the various mint fees and royalties. Swift would have been entirely correct in his condemnation of Wood if the preceding expenses could have been legitimately omitted. If labor and manufacturing costs for 360 tons of copper coins passing at £100,800

(Irish) could indeed have been ignored, then a £60,480 loss would have been sustained by the Irish public as Swift asserted; if the halfpenny had been reduced in weight to 107.5 grains, as claimed, then the loss would have been increased to £69,064 16s. The mint costs could not be waived, and when these were borne by Wood, he suffered an economic loss. When Wood's coinage was rejected by the Irish and did not circulate, the Crown indemnified him for his efforts with a pension of £3,000 annually for eight years.

There is possibly more to this story of Irish nationalism then just patriotism. Craig notes that Swift "distorted" Wood's project at a time when he suffered personal disappointment at having been denied a bishopric.[140] He further elaborates that some of those who created such ferment about Wood's Hibernia coinage were members of the Irish Parliament, who themselves, were profiteering from the issue of token coppers. In their review, Gale and Gale quote some biographers who incorrectly asserted that the malice with which Swift attacked his adversaries was symptomatic of an "incipient insanity." Others "recognized the savage vituperation as typical political invective of the time, not to be taken too seriously."[141] In 1729, Swift proposed a token scheme to which he, himself, would be a party, but nothing ever materialized from that venture.[142]

It has been maintained that large numbers of unwanted Hibernia coppers, following their rejection in Ireland, found their way to America and have appeared in accumulations of various and sundry other coins of the period.[143] There is no evidence of any substantial colonial circulation for these coppers, numismatic catalogues and trade publications notwithstanding, although it can be reasonably concluded that any current European coins could have ended up in North America, either brought over by the steady stream of immigrants or in the merchant trade. The New York legislature report, quoted by Crosby, contains a generic reference to Irish halfpence "with a bust on one side, and a harp on the other." While no specific dates or monarchs are mentioned, the description matches the later regal varieties of George II and George III.[144] The history of Wood's Irish coinage was recalled both in a debate in the Philadelphia Common Council during the "coppers panic" of 1789 and in a news release datelined New York City, without any hint given that his money had been current in America.[145] Indeed, three Wood's halfpence were reported by Newman in company with the counterfeit 1699 William III halfpence in "The Philadelphia Highway Find," but this deposit was located in the vicinity of a former seafarers' haunt. These coppers could have been dropped there by any sailor patronizing the local tavern without any inference as to a general circulation. In Stickney's essay of 1859, he discussed in detail the St. Patrick coinages and the failure of local circulation for the Rosa Americana series without any acknowledgment of Wood's Irish coins. It would have been unlikely that Wood or any other businessman would have invested in sending Hibernia coppers to America right on the heels on the Rosa Americana failure. Crosby only mentions the Hibernia series in relationship to the better known Rosa Americana products of Wood. Prime stated in 1861 that Wood's Hibernia coppers could still be found in circulation in America but this is no testimony as to when they arrived here.[146] Breen has associated the widespread importation of several styles of Washington "cent" tokens from Birmingham with the coin shortage of 1815 to 1817.[147] Doty reported that late eighteenth century English trade tokens, once they were no

[140] Craig, *Mint*, pp. 370-71.
[141] Gale and Gale, *Num 1985*, p. 1329.
[142] Ruding, *Annals*, vol. 2, p. 73.
[143] Breen, *CNL 1968B*; Breen, *Encyclopedia*, p. 27.
[144] Crosby, *Early Coins*, p. 291.
[145] *Ind. Gaz.*, July 27, 1789, and Aug. 1, 1789.
[146] Prime, *Coins*, p. 7. Prime's accuracy in all his observations about the circulation of colonial currency is suspect. He stated without authority that Massachusetts silver never circulated outside New England, and that the *Washington and Independence* tokens appeared in 1783, two assertions now known to be erroneous.
[147] Breen, *Encyclopedia*, p. 134.

longer required for the small change medium in Great Britain, were imported into the United States where they circulated as substitute cents in such places as Savannah, Georgia, right up until the Civil War.[148] Why could this not have been the same occasion for the appearance of Wood's Irish coppers? In support of this interpretation, it is recalled that evasive halfpence had once been considered a colonial currency until demonstrated that they were an import of the last quarter of the nineteenth century. In the later state coinages when it was commonplace to overstrike other lightweight coppers, no Hibernia halfpence have ever been identified as host coins. The nagging question as to the widespread currency of Wood's Hibernia coinages in America cannot be satisfactorily resolved until there is some further positive literary or hoard evidence.

Fig. 37:
(a) 1722 Rosa Americana halfpenny (52.8 grains). Although the Rosa Americana series were very handsome coins, there was very poor colonial acceptance of these lightweight tokens.

(b) 1723 Rosa Americana (crowned rose) penny (126.0 grains).

(c) 1722 Rosa Americana twopence (238.7 grains).

On July 12, 1722, William Wood was also granted a patent to mint 300 tons of coppers for the North American Colonies over a span of 14 years for an annual fee to the Crown of £300.[149] The resultant Rosa Americana coinage was handsomely engraved and struck in Bath metal, an alloy of 75% brass, 20% tutanaigne,[150] and 5% silver. Since the planchets had to be impressed while the metal was hot, these coins frequently display a bubbly surface. The twopence, penny, and halfpenny denominations of this emission are dated 1722, 1723, and 1724. One pound of alloy was to produce 120 halfpence, thus securing a substantial profit for the patentee.[151] The obverse depicted the laureated head of George I, while a Tudor rose with the inscription ROSA AMERICANA, UTILE DULCI was on the reverse.[152]

[148] Doty, *Coin*, p. 134.

[149] Nelson, *Wood*, pp. 15-18, 25-32; Crosby, *Early Coins*, pp. 145-68; Taxay, *Catalogue*, pp. 9-13; Craig, *Mint*, p. 378.

[150] Tutanaigne is an alloy of zinc, tin, and bismuth.

[151] The alloy cost about 16d. per pound, considering that it contained about 2.4d. of silver. All other manufacturing expenses would be no more than 9d. At 120 halfpence to the pound, there was a potential profit of 35d. per pound of alloy or 140%!

[152] The UTILE DULCI inscription is from Horace, *Ars Poetica*, 343, "Omne tulit punctum qui misquit utile dulci" ("He has won universal approval who has combined the useful with the agreeable"). It is intriguing to speculate why Wood chose this passage. Did he think that because his coinage was so handsome that it would be well received? The complete quotation appeared on the masthead of the *Essex Gazette* (Salem, MA) from 1768 to 1771 and on the higher denominations of the Massachusetts "Cod Fish" bills of October 18, 1776 (Newman, *Paper Money*, pp. 185-86).

Fig. 38: MASSACHUSETTS SMALL CHANGE BILLS OF JUNE 1722. These geometrically shaped parchment notes were authorized in Massachusetts as small change to frustrate the introduction of William Wood's Rosa Americana coinages into New England (Newman, *Paper Money*, p. 169). Courtesy Eric P. Newman Numismatic Education Society.

Wood was no more successful in his Rosa Americana venture than he was with the Hibernia series since his lightweight, overvalued coins needed more than an "agreeable" appearance to be acceptable as money by the colonists. There is evidence that some Rosa Americana coins did circulate, although with disapproval, due to numbers found in accumulations and excavated in Colonial Williamsburg.[153] The rejection of Wood's underweight coinage even came at a time when the small change shortage was so intense in Massachusetts that the General Court had authorized issuance of £500 in parchment notes of penny, twopence, and threepence denominations.[154] The failure of the Rosa Americana series to win the confidence of the colonists explains why so many uncirculated specimens have survived until present times.[155] Shortly before his death in 1730, Wood proposed to the Board of Trade that he mint coins in gold and silver for the colonies at 75% of the sterling rate, a scheme which did not survive the planning phase.[156]

After the repudiation of Wood's Hibernia coppers, there was still no acceptable solution to the Irish small money shortage. History repeated itself as numerous copper and, now for the first time in Ireland, silver tokens and promissory notes were issued by merchants in the late 1720s and into the 1730s to satisfy the demands of commerce.[157] Finally in response to a desperate need, there appeared in 1736, under George II, regal farthings and halfpence minted at the rate of 104 and 52 to the pound, respectively.[158] Any profits derived from production of these coins after deduction for mint costs and transportation, would be deposited in the Irish public treasury, a conciliatory gesture to assuage anti-English sentiment after the Wood affair.

In 1760, after a 13 years' lapse in the minting of regal Irish coppers, there appeared from Dublin a lightweight token coinage of uncertain provenance, the Voce Populi farthings and halfpence.[159] Without any convincing reason, these primarily Irish coppers are included in the American colonial series. Doubtless, this money along with many other European coins of the

[153] Breen, *CNL 1968B*; Newman, *Colonial Virginia*, p. 33.
[154] Crosby, *Early Coins*, pp. 148-50; Felt, *Massachusetts*, p. 78.
[155] One of Wood's partners was said to have had great quantities of Rosa Americana coins in his cellar since there was as much trouble passing them as the Hibernia series (Crosby, *Early Coins*, p. 160; Nelson, *Wood*, p. 15).
[156] Chalmers, *British Colonies*, p. 17.
[157] Lindsay, *Ireland*, pp. 108-15.
[158] Ruding, *Annals*, vol. 2, pp. 75-76; Simon, *Essay*, pp. 72-73.
[159] Craig, *Mint*, p. 372.

Fig. 39: Ireland: 1760 Voce Populi token.

period, could have serendipitously arrived in the New World and, therefore, be located by chance in old accumulations.[160]

As in England, counterfeit Irish coppers began to appear in great numbers. There were even counterfeits of Wood's coppers which Swift actually accused Wood "or his accomplices" of making and scattering about. Some of these false Wood's pieces were so poorly executed that Swift, in a moment of concession, was obliged to recognize that they were "so ill performed, that in my conscience I believe it is not of his [Wood's] coining."[161] Many counterfeit Irish coppers were represented in Batty's holdings. He catalogued numerous cast counterfeits of George II dated 1737, 1738, 1742, 1744, and 1760.[162] Particularly common were cast lightweight counterfeit halfpence of George III dated 1781, 1782, and 1783. Along with their regal counterparts, this series of Irish counterfeits was destined to play a distinct role in the numismatic history of Confederation coppers.

Fig. 40:
(a) Ireland: 1782 genuine halfpenny of George III (141.0 grains).

(b) Ireland: 1782 contemporary counterfeit halfpenny of George III (92.1 grains). This was the typical host coin for several varieties of Vermont coppers minted at Machin's Mills (Table 21, no. 24).

(c) Ireland: 1769 contemporary counterfeit halfpenny of George III (95.9 grains) (Table 21, no. 24).

[160] No mention is made of Voce Populi coppers by Crosby, Atkins or Prime. The question is asked (RF-24, *CNL 1969*), why are these Irish pieces included in the colonial series? Zelinka, *CNL 1976*, presents an excellent review of this series replete with descriptive plates. His historical search concludes that late nineteenth century numismatists and dealers must have associated them with Bungtown evasive halfpence and the like, which is not sufficient proof of a colonial connection.

[161] "Letter III," from Scott, *Swift*, vol. 7, pp. 142, 164.

[162] Batty, *Descriptive Catalogue*, vol. 3, pp. 915-21, 1036-46.

(d) Ireland: 1744 contemporary counterfeit farthing of George II (51.6 grains). Note "S" counterstamp on obverse of uncertain significance.

Other Coinage Proposals for the American Plantations

In addition to the efforts of William Wood, numerous other proposals for colonial coinage were submitted throughout the seventeenth and eighteenth centuries, in that "nearly every important colony asked to be allowed to set up a Mint."[163] Many of these petitions originated in England but none of them was ever granted. Sumner opined, "It was one of the greatest mistakes in the colonial policy of England that a colonial mint was not allowed."[164] The only proposal for a legal colonial coinage which ever materialized was the 1773 copper halfpenny for Virginia, an action which was permitted by charter. A summary of eight recorded propositions for colonial coinage includes:

1) 1638: a license was granted to Lord Maltravers to produce farthing tokens for America which was never accomplished because of the outbreak of the English Civil War (Newman, *Colonial Virginia*, pp. 3-4; Hoober, *Num 1953*, pp. 2-3; Hume, *Caterpillers*, pp. 233, 247).
2) July 5,1700: a proposal by John Fysack to the Board of Trade to establish a colonial mint (Crosby, *Early Coins*, p. 139; Chalmers, *British Colonies*, p. 13; Ruding, *Annals*, vol. 2, p. 59).
3) May 21, 1701: a proposal by Samuel Davis to mint small copper coins for the colonies which was apparently seconded by J. Stanley, Isaac Newton, and John Ellis on July 9, 1701 (Crosby, *Early Coins*, pp. 139-41).
4) March 17, 1702/3: a proposal from William Chalkhill to produce coppers for Massachusetts (Crosby, *Early Coins*, pp. 224-25; Chalmers, *British Colonies*, p. 19).
5) April 5, 1715: Jeremiah Dummer reported a proposed billon coinage of one-third copper and two-thirds silver for New England (Crosby, *Early Coins*, pp. 141-42; Felt, *Massachusetts*, p. 69).
6) 1739: John Reed of Boston petitioned the Connecticut Legislature for a patent to mint a Connecticut coinage from local copper (Crosby, *Early Coins*, pp. 203-7). (See Higley coinage.)
7) July 14, 1748: Sir Alexander Cuming proposed the establishment of a provincial bank for all British colonies in America and a sterling coinage from the Tower Mint (Ruding, *Annals*, vol. 2, p. 79; Crosby, *Early Coins*, pp. 142-43).
8) 1754: Arthur Dobbs proposed a copper twopence, penny, and halfpenny for the Carolinas with 61 halfpence per pound. This would have been similar to the 1773 Virginia halfpenny (Crosby, *Early Coins*, pp. 143-44; Chalmers, *British Colonies*, p. 19; Ruding, *Annals*, vol. 2, p. 80).

OTHER NORTH AMERICAN COPPERS

There are other tokens of the late seventeenth century minted in England which pertain to the American Colonies. Included in this group of very rare tokens are the 1694 Carolina and New

[163] Chalmers, *British Colonies*, p. 12n.
[164] Sumner, *Yale Rev. 1898*, pp. 253-54. England would give her colonies no economic advantage which might threaten the established mercantile system. (See Nettels, *Money Supply*, p. 283.)

Fig. 41:
(a) 1694 Carolina Elephant token (140.0 grains).

(b) New Yorke in America token (ca. 1668-1673).

England Elephant pieces which may have been intended as medals to promote interest in the new colonies.[165] Another equally rare issue is the New Yorke Token whose origin has been the subject of much speculation.[166] Recent research by Kleeberg places this token as a product of the Bristol, England, mint where it was manufactured upon the order of Francis Lovelace, the Governor of New York from 1668 to 1673.[167] The sylvan scene on the reverse is a dramatization of the "lovelace" theme depicting the frolics of cupid, while the obverse displays the Lovelace crest. This piece has features in common with the Bristol farthings, abundant trade tokens of the period.[168]

Fig. 42:
(a) Higley threepence, Breen 242.

(b) 1773 Virginia halfpenny, Newman 25-M (118.4 grains) (Table 21, no. 19; Chart 7).

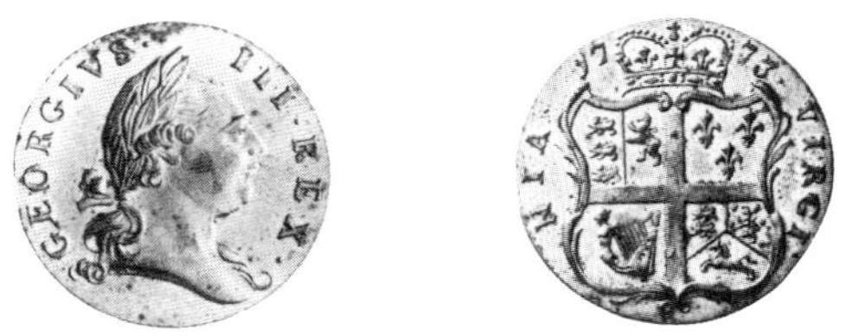

The first domestic copper coinage in the colonies is attributed to Dr. Samuel Higley of Granby, Connecticut, a physician, metallurgist, and local mine operator who, in 1737, minted three pence tokens of pure copper.[169] Seven die varieties of this excessively rare money have been identified with varying legends. It would appear that the earlier inscription, THE VALUE OF THREE PENCE, gave way to the revision, VALUE ME AS YOU PLEASE, since it was unlikely that a New Englander who rejected Wood's coinage would accept any other copper

[165] Crosby, *Early Coins*, pp. 337-38; Taxay, *Catalogue*, pp. 8, 39; Atkins, *Coins and Tokens*, pp. 259-60; Peck, *British Museum*, pp. 137-38; Breen, *Encyclopedia*, pp. 32-33.

[166] Atkins, *Coins and Tokens*, p. 258; Adams, *CNL 1980*; Breen, *Encyclopedia*, pp. 40-41; Crosby, *Early Coins*, pp. 114, 345-46; Taxay, *Catalogue*, pp. 37-38.

[167] Kleeberg, *New Yorke*.

[168] Thompson, *Norweb*, pt. 2, pp. ix-xxxiii.

[169] Crosby, *Early Coins*, pp. 324-27; Taxay, *Catalogue*, pp. 13-14.

which passed for about ten times intrinsic value![170] Crosby suggested that the Higley coppers are so rare today because they were of high quality copper and were in great demand by goldsmiths for use in alloys.

The final authorization for the Virginia copper halfpence, the only legally sanctioned colonial coinage, was signed on May 20, 1773 after several months of negotiations with English authorities.[171] This coinage struck at the Tower Mint was to weigh 60 to the pound and at a production cost of 20.86d. sterling, a profit of 16% accrued to the colony before transportation and insurance costs were deducted. These well-made coins bearing the bust of George III on the obverse and the Virginia crest on the reverse with the legend, VIRGINIA, were to pass at 24 to the Virginia shilling. The shipment arrived in America on February 14, 1774, but distribution was delayed until royal permission was received one year later, or only 50 days prior to the start of the Revolutionary War. Consequently, the Virginia halfpence were hoarded and saw little circulation until after hostilities had ceased. Virginia halfpence obviously did circulate since many have been recovered in the excavations and restorations at Colonial Williamsburg.[172] The availability of brilliant, uncirculated specimens today is because of the cache of uncirculated coins that came into the possession of Colonel Mendes I. Cohen of Baltimore sometime around 1870.[173]

The Virginia halfpence were well made coins that attracted the attention of Benjamin Franklin.[174] Writing about them from his post in London on January 5, 1774, he commented, "Virginia has lately had a Quantity of Copper Halfpence struck at the Mint here for their Province. Inclos'd I send you a Specimen of theirs. They may serve to keep out the worthless counterfeit Trash of late so common." While such a statement is complimentary of the quality of the Virginia coinage, it also is an indication about the status of the small change in America just before the Revolution.

*
* *

At this point, our survey of colonial coinage approaches the brink of the American Revolution, a conflict which arose as the Plantations looked for more economic self-determination while an equally resolute mother country strove to protect her markets and raw material supply; it became a losing battle for England to maintain her possessions in America both prosperous but dependent. Paper currency, a necessity to increase the visible money supply, had, generally speaking, achieved moderate stability despite Parliamentary restrictions that were regarded as more protective of British investments than nurturing of colonial commerce.[175] Foreign silver, as recorded in the Proclamation of 1704, and gold coins were the primary hard money of the period. The copper currency had undergone dilution with counterfeit English halfpence creating an absolute excess of small change. A readjustment of exchange rates in the

[170] The average weight of the ten Higley specimens from the combined Garrett Collection (lots 1304, 1305 and 1307) and the Roper Collection (lots 148 to 154) is 142.06 grains, less than the weight of the current British halfpenny. A pound of copper would, therefore, produce 49 threepence tokens at a market value of 12s. 3d. At a maximum production cost of 26d. per lb. in Connecticut money, Dr. Higley would realize about 465% profit. Little wonder the legend was changed!

[171] Newman, *Colonial Virginia*, passim. This excellent monograph describes the 22 die varieties. Taxay, *Catalogue*, p. 14; Crosby, *Early Coins*, pp. 338-40; Breen, *Encyclopedia, pp. 30-31.*

[172] Newman, *Colonial Virginia*, p. 33; Spilman, *CNL 1988B*, p. 1061. Thomas Jefferson, a Virginian himself, stated in 1791, "In Virginia, coppers have never been in use" (*A.S.P.F.*, vol. 1, p. 106). His comment is not supported by the archeological evidence.

[173] See also Breen, *Num 1952*, pp. 16-17.

[174] Smythe, *Franklin*, vol. 6, pp. 175-76.

[175] Ernst, *Money and Politics*, pp. 359-60.

mid-century kept the medium in circulation. Commodity monies were gradually being phased out of former positions of importance as paper money gained in popularity. Bills of exchange continued to be the most important instruments of foreign credit. This was the visible money supply, as indicated by Ernst, which played an important and vital role in daily commerce.[176] A total picture of colonial economics requires an evaluation of other factors such as capital flow, and domestic and foreign debt and credit. For whatever reasons, political, economic or social, the Revolution was here. This summary, although incomplete and abbreviated, has attempted to present the pertinent monetary and numismatic history leading up to this revolt as well as lay the background for further events to be related during the Confederation period.

[176] Ernst, *Money and Politics*, pp. 355-56.

CHAPTER SIX

The New Constellation

Colonial America, at this point in numismatic history, was on the verge of achieving freedom from England. Previous chapters have described the economic conditions within the colonies, emphasizing the cycles of recession and expansion which influenced the ready availability of circulating hard money. The colonies had no natural mineral wealth in gold and silver and relied on specie earned in the West Indies trade with Spanish possessions. The mercantile theory of colonization favored English interests over American and discouraged colonial economic self-sufficiency. The scarcity of hard money for conducting commerce stimulated the development and use of alternative currency forms - wampum, bookkeeping barter, commodity monies, domestic silver coinages, and several options in a paper medium. In 1763, following cessation of the French and Indian Wars, England directed more attention and energies toward America. The increasing regulations placed on colonial trade and paper currency became chronic irritants and were factors in leading to the eventual independence of the colonies. The new liberty will introduce some changes in the domestic currency but many old traditions will continue as in the past.

Fig. 43: A VIEW OF THE TOWN OF BOSTON WITH SEVERAL SHIPS OF WAR IN THE HARBOUR (1773). This historic line engraving by Paul Revere appeared as the frontispiece in the January 1774 issue (vol. 1, no. 1) of the *Royal American Magazine*. Long Wharf (A) is prominent in the foreground and the beacon (G) of Beacon Hill is at the center left. The British fleet had arrived in Boston on September 30, 1768, to land troops "to compel obedience" (Stokes and Haskell, *Prints*, p. 44). Courtesy American Antiquarian Society.

THE AMERICAN REVOLUTION

Multiple factors have been identified in an effort to establish the causes of the American Revolution. Prominent among these were the economic restraints which were imposed by England especially after 1763, a time that coincided with a period of postwar slowdown. The stage for confrontation was being set.

> After 1760 colonists faced policymakers in Great Britain who were determined to change the loose and unrestrictive commercial empire within which the colonial economy had prospered, by increasing and enforcing regulations and by tightening connections between business and politics. At the same time, American ability to influence policy was in sharp decline.[1]

Fig. 44:
(a) A TRIO OF TWO SHILLING SIX PENCE TAX STAMPS. The Stamp Act of 1765 was passed by Parliament on March 22, 1765, to raise money to support the British troops stationed in America. Such tax stamps were required on all legal documents, licenses, and even newspapers within the colonies. Organized opposition to this "taxation without representation" was intense. The colonial position against this tax was championed in Parliament by Sir William Pitt whose intervention resulted in repeal of this unpopular provision on March 18, 1766. Courtesy American Antiquarian Society.

(b) 1766 Pitt medalet or "farthing" struck in recognition of Sir William Pitt who successfully advocated in Parliament for repeal of the onerous Stamp Tax. This piece is reputed to have been minted in Philadelphia but its overall quality is more reminiscent of English manufacture (Atkins, *Coins and Tokens*, p. 264; Breen, *Encyclopedia*, pp. 41-42).

Besides these commercial and economic factors, there was the developing influence of a class of wealthy and powerful "elite" who sought autonomy from the crown. At the other end of the social ladder were the "lower orders" or "poorer sort," who, while never in control, voiced their individual grievances and demands. Of this relationship it has been said, "the wealthier patriots in the cities ... used the colonial 'mob' to their own ends, directing its furies against stamp distributors and customs officials." Lest we become too persuaded by the romantic imagery of a war fought by oppressed citizens striking out for freedom, the further caution must be added that while "lower-class movements and social upheaval may in part characterize the Revolutionary movement; they do not explain it."[2]

Whereas the relative contributions of the economic, social, and political influences remain incalculable, their composite effect was that conflict became inevitable and at last occurred on April 19, 1775, at the Battles of Lexington and Concord. "... the great war for independence was

[1] McCusker and Menard, *Economy*, p. 355.
[2] Egnal and Ernst, *WMQ 1972*, pp. 28, 32, passim.

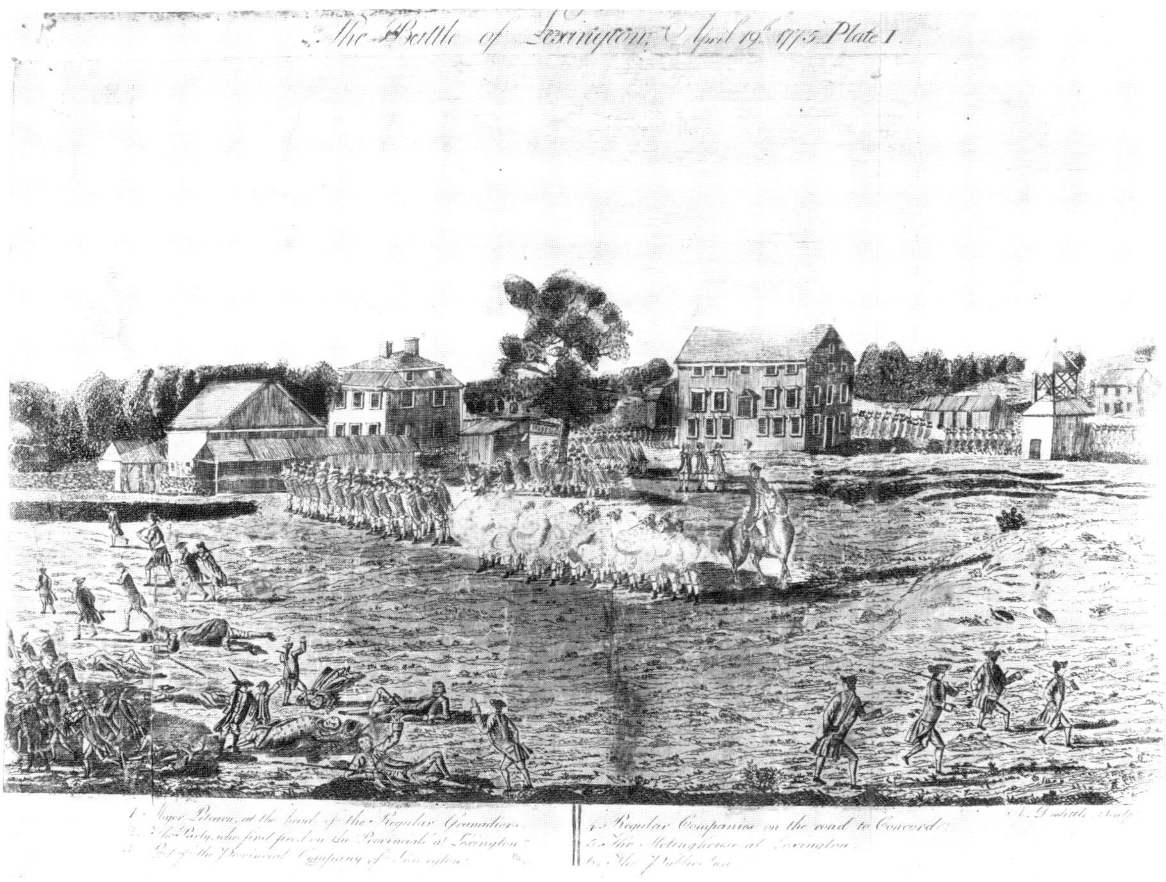

Fig. 45: THE BATTLE OF LEXINGTON, APRIL 19TH, 1775. This engraving by Amos Doolittle was one of a series of four views of the Battles of Lexington and Concord published in December 1775. This scene on Lexington Common shows the Minute Men being dispersed by the British under the command of Major Pitcairn, shown on horseback. The British were marching to Concord to seize military stores but the countryside was warned of their approach by the famous riders, Paul Revere and William Dawes, who spread the alarm (Stokes and Haskell, *Prints*, pp. 45-46). Courtesy The New York Public Library.

not simply a conflict between the imperial government and a group of revolting colonies, but almost as truly a civil war between two American parties, one standing for an old allegiance and an old patriotism, the other looking forward hopefully to the establishment of a new order."[3] Kenneth Roberts' classic, *Oliver Wiswell*, is a fascinating account of the civil strife between the so-called patriots and the old order Tories, who in many instances were economically distinct groups. It was estimated that between one-third to one-half of the American colonists remained loyal to the Crown with at least 20,000 serving in the English forces.[4] In New York alone, at least half the population of 180,000 were loyalists of whom some 35,000 emigrated to Canada, the British West Indies, and Bermuda at the end of the war.[5]

The Continental Congress, which first assembled in August 1774, was meeting in the summer of 1776. Thomas Jefferson was appointed to prepare the Declaration of Independence which was signed on July 4, only two days after its completion. To have declared independence was easy, but to decide on the form of self government was another matter.

[3] Greene, *Foundations*, pp. 456-57.
[4] Schuckers, *Finances*, p. 103.
[5] Nevins, *American States*, p. 646, 646n.

Fig. 46: TWO SHILLING "SWORD IN HAND" BILL OF AUGUST 18, 1775. Paul Revere, an accomplished silversmith, engraved and printed the famous Massachusetts "Sword in Hand" legal tender bills of 1775 and 1776. He also completed engraving the plates for the 1776 "Codfish" bills which had been started by Nathaniel Hurd (Newman, *Paper Money*, pp. 182-88). Courtesy Eric P. Newman Numismatic Education Society.

Another committee selected by that Second Continental Congress in July of 1776 was assigned the task of composing a constitution by which these new states would launch themselves as a free nation. These Articles of Confederation were the subject of heated debate for 16 months before approval by Congress. Those six colonies with fixed boundaries were unwilling to accept this document until some provision was made for those western lands claimed by the other seven, which by compromise became part of the national domain. The new constitution was forwarded to the state legislatures for ratification but did not come into effect until March 1, 1781, when Maryland became the last of the required nine states to mark its approval.[6]

The Articles of Confederation were a very weak instrument providing only for a "firm league of friendship" between the several states, primarily to ensure mutual defense and security of liberties, but did not establish a single nation. "The thirteen states approved a document that in effect gave no more power to Congress than the colonies had been willing to give to Parliament."[7] The states maintained all those powers not explicitly delegated to the Continental Congress. Only the state legislatures could levy taxes and when the national government required funds, requests for money would be forwarded to the states according to a specific formula. In an area of parallel authority, the states and the national government could each establish mints and print paper money. Within the Congress, each state had a single vote and only a simple majority was necessary for most legislation. However, nine votes were required in Congress to coin money, to regulate the alloy thereof, to emit paper money, to borrow and appropriate money, to declare war, to enter into treaties and alliances, and to regulate the size

[6] Hawke, *Experience*, pp. 647-51; Jensen, *New Nation*, pp. 8-10, 18-27.
[7] Hawke, *Experience*, p. 648.

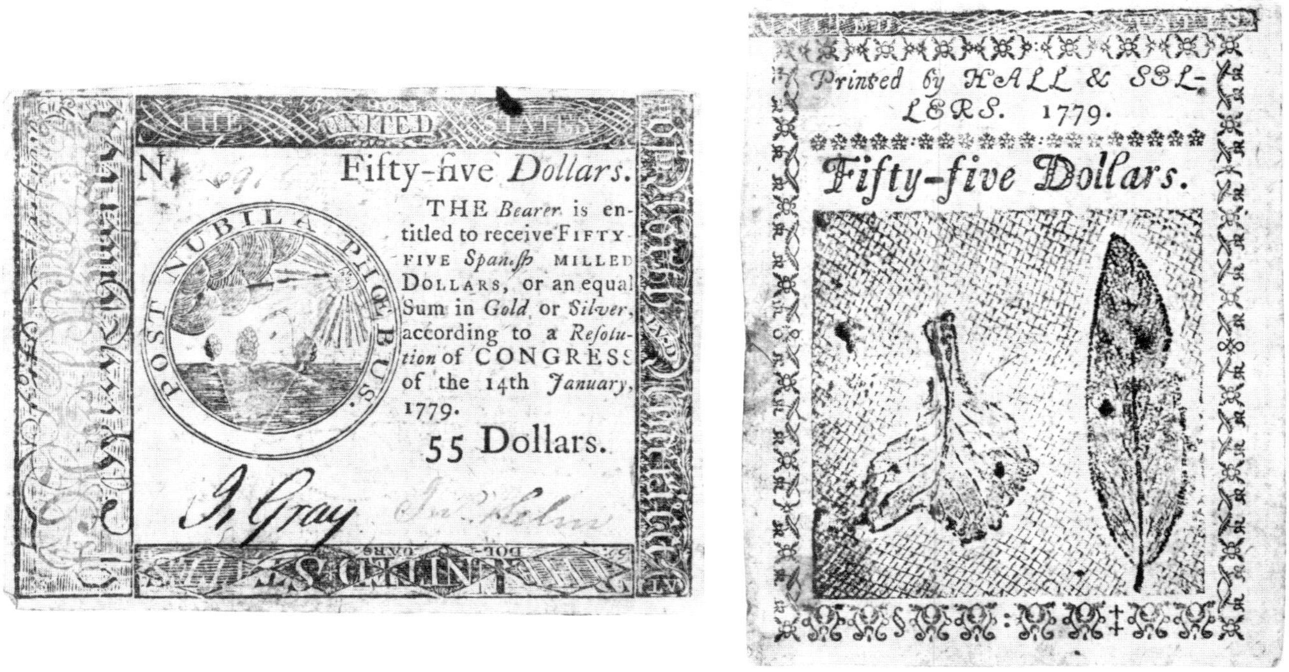

Fig. 47: A "KITE-FACED" BILL OF CREDIT. This Continental Currency $55 note of January 14, 1779, is printed in red and black such that the diamond on the emblem appears as a kite. This is the allusion in the poem, "The Coppers Done Over," in Chapter Eight (Newman, *Paper Money*, pp. 48-49, 311).

and composition of the armed forces. It was evident that the states exercised extreme caution before abdicating to the new Congress of the Confederation their individual interests in areas of finance, foreign policy, and war powers.

To meet wartime expenses, Congress authorized $2,000,000 in paper currency soon after the Battle of Lexington and Concord and by the end of 1779, a total of $241,552,780 had been issued.[8] The Continental currency was fiat money, backed only by the credit of Congress. The states were reluctant to exercise their prerogative under the Articles of Confederation and levy taxes to assist with the war effort, but were not at all timid about printing their own bills of credit as an alternative to taxation, and so an additional $200,000,000 in state currencies was placed in circulation through 1779.[9] Although this paper money was secured only by the good faith of the issuing authority, the currency maintained its value during the first year or two of the Revolution because the public had had good experience and faith in the recent prewar colonial paper money.[10] This confidence was soon shattered by wartime inflation and all Revolutionary paper money depreciated rapidly. Franklin ascribed the failure of this paper money to overissue. He argued that Congress, unable to borrow enough funds because of its inability to meet interest payments, was "forced to print more Bills, and the Depreciation proceeded."[11] By 1781 this paper was essentially worthless, giving rise to the aphorism, "not worth a Continental." Tables published the schedule of depreciation of Continental currency "to provide for

[8] Newman, *Paper Money*, p. 17.

[9] Massey, *Money*, p. 57; Hawke, *Experience*, pp. 608-9; Bullock, *Essays*, pp. 64-65. In 1776, Congress discarded the English money of account denominations of £, s., and d. in favor of dollars and 90ths. See Newman, *Paper Money* as the definitive reference listing all state and Congressional paper currencies.

[10] Ferguson, *WMQ 1953*, p. 167; Ferguson, *Purse*, pp. 18-19.

[11] Smyth, *Franklin*, vol. 1, p. 140, vol. 9, pp. 231-33.

the more equitable Payment of Debts."[12] One hundred dollars in paper fell from a par of $100 in specie on September 1, 1777 to $ 60/90 or $0.66⅔ by May 1, 1781.[13] Depreciation was accelerated by wholesale counterfeiting of paper currency which even resulted in the recall of entire issues because of the great number of false bills. Many of these counterfeits were produced in Europe - Germany, Holland, and Ireland. England blatantly waged an economic war by printing large quantities of counterfeit American notes which were smuggled into the country to discredit an already failing currency.[14]

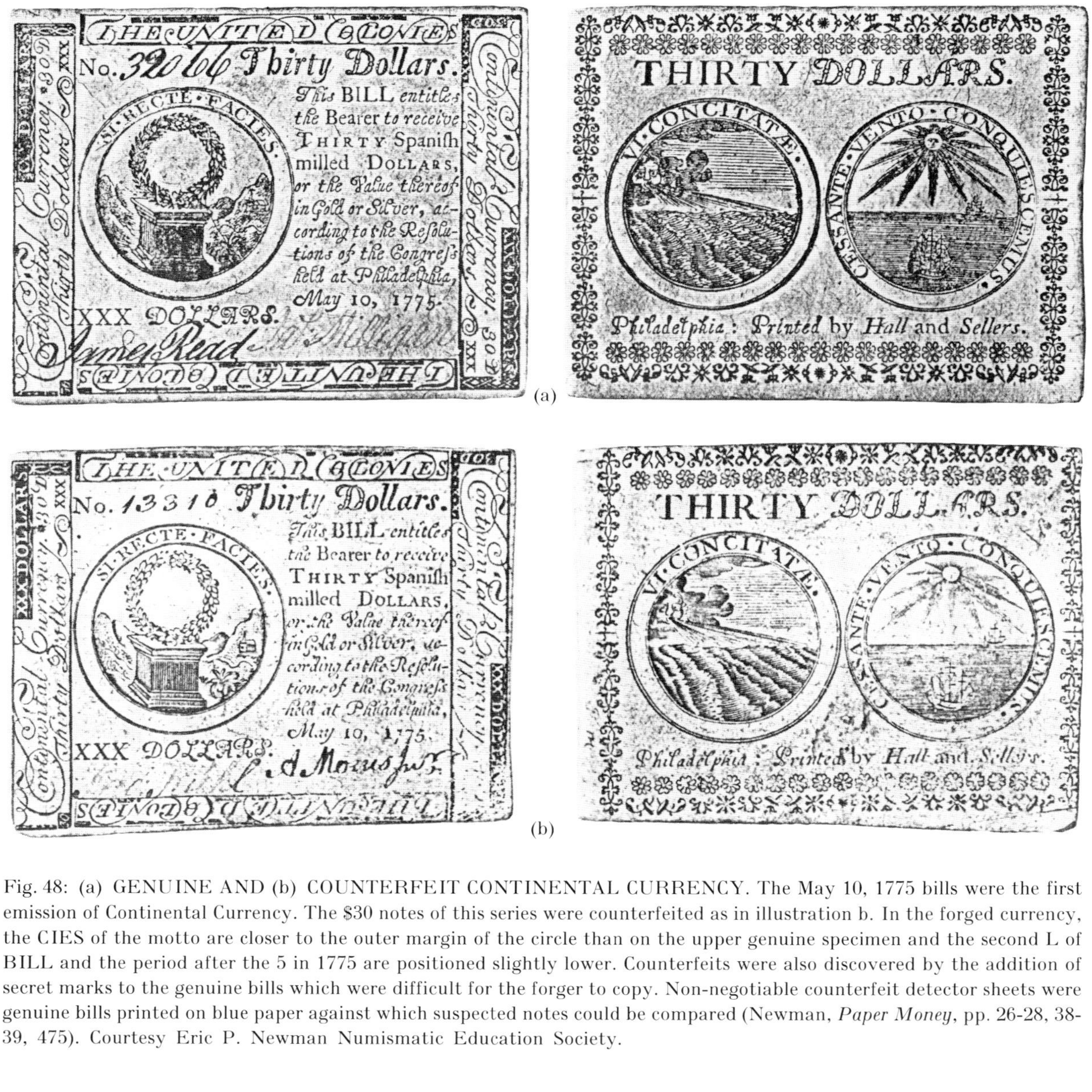

Fig. 48: (a) GENUINE AND (b) COUNTERFEIT CONTINENTAL CURRENCY. The May 10, 1775 bills were the first emission of Continental Currency. The $30 notes of this series were counterfeited as in illustration b. In the forged currency, the CIES of the motto are closer to the outer margin of the circle than on the upper genuine specimen and the second L of BILL and the period after the 5 in 1775 are positioned slightly lower. Counterfeits were also discovered by the addition of secret marks to the genuine bills which were difficult for the forger to copy. Non-negotiable counterfeit detector sheets were genuine bills printed on blue paper against which suspected notes could be compared (Newman, *Paper Money*, pp. 26-28, 38-39, 475). Courtesy Eric P. Newman Numismatic Education Society.

[12] *N.J. Gaz.*, Jan. 9, 1782. See also Felt, *Massachusetts*, p. 196.

[13] The notation $ 60/90 will be described subsequently.

[14] Newman, *Num 1957*, pp. 5-16, 137-47; Gorelkin, *Num 1984*, pp. 2273-85; Felt, *Massachusetts*, p. 174; Overholser, *Analysis*, pp. 31-32; Glaser, *Counterfeiting*, p. 39. In the Newman monograph, an incident is recounted where counterfeit Continental paper money was smuggled through the American lines in a British convoy under a flag of truce carrying humanitarian relief. This historical vignette describes the level to which the English stooped to place this forged money into circulation to discredit and weaken the currency.

Schuckers estimated the cost of the Revolution from $170,000,000 to $180,000,000 of which no more than $30,000,000 had been paid by 1784.[15] A recent study by Anderson describes and illustrates other fiscal paper of the period.[16] These certificates of public debt issued by the states and Continental Congress, in addition to paper money, were another means by which the War was financed. Whereas bills of credit were intended as a circulating paper currency and payable to the bearer, these usually interest-bearing debt certificates for private loans to the government were issued to specified individuals. Although these notes were transferable, they were not intended for general circulation, and while not legal tender, they were generally receivable for taxes.

Another Revolutionary War expense which remains incalculable was the value for goods and services impressed from the general public for military consumption.[17] As early as December 1776, General Washington was authorized by Congress to commandeer any necessary supplies for the war effort in exchange for which the owners, willingly or not, were recompensed with Quartermaster or Commissary certificates as "reasonable" payment. This "mass expropriation" of civilian commodities prompted popular unrest and amounted to "legal robbery."[18] The total of these certificates is unknown, but those issued by the Federal government alone may have approached the entire sum of the Continental currency, both instruments depreciating tremendously in real value as inflation mounted. This massive certificate debt proved a significant financial burden; some states received them for taxes while others were sorely tempted to emit paper money to cover this indebtedness. The Continental currency and Quartermaster certificates, considered the "common debt" of the war, were redeemed at depreciated values, whereas the private loan certificates mentioned above, were "preferred securities" and received more favorable consideration from Congress in their liquidation.

Following the Declaration of Independence another element of complexity was added to the monetary system. The Continental dollar became the money of account for the Federal government and was made equivalent to the Spanish milled dollar. Since the Spanish standard did not have a uniform value among the states' monies of account, neither could the Continental dollar.[19] Because the Continental Congress had a permanent base in Philadelphia, the finances of the Revolution were typically expressed in Pennsylvania funds where the Spanish milled dollar (and now the Continental dollar) passed at 7s. 6d., or 90d., Pennsylvania currency. Fractions of the Continental dollar were, therefore, expressed on the basis of 90 parts to the dollar. The unit of 90 supported the issuance of fractional paper money in denominations of 1/6, 1/3, 1/2, and 2/3 of a Spanish milled dollar which were equivalent respectively to 15d., 30d., 45d., and 60d., Pennsylvania money of account. An example of this notational system is the expression that French gold coin was valued at $16 68/90 per ounce, etc. In other states, the fractional basis for the Continental dollar would be similarly determined according to the current value of the Spanish milled dollar in the local money of account; New York and North Carolina calculated fractional dollar values in ninety-sixths, South Carolina and Georgia in fifty-sixths, the New England states and Virginia in seventy-seconds, and all others in ninetieths. In areas where the the Spanish eight reales was valued at 6s., the currency was called "Proclamation money," "proc." or "Lawful money," since the rate corresponded to the official par, 100:133.33 ratio, sterling to colonial money of account, which was required by the Proclamation of 1704.[20] In colonies where the rate was 7s. 6d., terms used to describe commercial money included "common money," "common currency," "running money," "current money," "currency," and "Pennsyl-

[15] Schuckers, *Finances*, p. 109; Fiske, *Critical Period*, p. 166.
[16] Anderson, *Liberty*, pp. 67-69, passim.
[17] Ferguson, *Purse*, pp. 57-69; Anderson, *Liberty*, pp. 11-12, 93-95.
[18] Nevins, *American States*, p. 506.
[19] Schilke and Solomon, *Foreign Coins*, pp. 12-17.
[20] Williamson, *CNL 1986*, pp. 935, 936.

vania money."[21] Certainly, independence brought no improvements toward a manageable money system which was further complicated by the authority given to each state under the Articles of Confederation to issue its own currency, even though the decimal basis of 100 was adopted by Congress on July 6, 1785.

THE ELUSIVE CONTINENTAL DOLLAR

The Revolutionary War had hardly started before problems with the circulation of counterfeit coppers were brought to public attention. New York newspapers alluded to the potential devaluation of copper and the introduction of a Continental copper currency.

> We hear it proposed that after 3 months the currency of all copper coin made of base metal or wanting in weight is to be totally suppressed and that the rest is past at the rate of 15 for an eighth part of a dollar. And if it shall appear that there is not a sufficiency for common use, that it will be all called in, and a new impression struck of Continental Copper coin, of a larger size, twelve of which is to pass for an eighth of a dollar, after which no other coppers are to pass current.[22]

Fig. 49: Continental dollar in pewter, Newman 3-D (271.6 grains).

The passage detailed, without attribution of source, a scheme both to "suppress" lightweight counterfeit coppers and to devalue "the rest" to fifteen to the New York shilling. Failing satisfactory accomplishment of these goals, then all current coppers would be "called in" for replacement with a new issue. The rumored "Continental Copper coin" described above was to pass at twelve to the New York shilling, or one penny each. This newspaper commentary has been interpreted to imply a connection between the "proposed" Continental copper coin and the well-known Continental Currency which has been considered to be denominated as a dollar. These Continental "dollars" belong to an assemblage of enigmatic early American coinages about which little is known. To date, there have been no clues yet discovered as to the origin of these dollar-sized pieces, the value at which they passed in commerce, and no secure linkage established with the "rumored" penny copper denomination.[23]

As if this New York report were not perplexing enough by itself, a letter published in the *London Gazette* of December 2, 1776, adds more to the confusion.[24] Here it was reported that Congress already was minting copper and silver coins about the size of a half crown; the silver

[21] Newman, *Num 1985*, pp. 2181-87; McCusker, *Money and Exchange*, pp. 121n, 126; Bordley, *Monies*. Pennsylvania fictitiously adopted the term "Proclamation Money," although their Spanish eight reales was rated at 7s. 6d. in their money of account (Willaimson, *CNL 1986*, p. 933).

[22] *N.Y. Jour.*, June 27, 1776; *N.Y. Gaz.*, July 1, 1776.

[23] Newman, *CCJour. 1952A*; *Garrett*, pt. 3, pp. 109-11; Bowers, *Coinage History*, pp. 159-60; Taxay, *Catalogue*, pp. 197, 201-2; Breen, *Encyclopedia*, pp. 110-12; Taxay, *U.S. Mint*, chap. 1; *Romano*, pp. 14-17; Norweb, pt. 2, pp. 245-47; Hodder, *ANA Centennial*.

[24] *AJN*, Oct. 1891, p. 45.

pieces purportedly passed for 12 shillings each and the copper for 14 pence. Little confidence can be placed in the accuracy of this account since neither of these values corresponded to the current exchange rates for copper or silver coins of that size. These two newspaper bulletins provide no assistance in unraveling the mystery of the illusive Continental copper coin or the actual Continental Currency and so numismatic research has had to rely on the examination of the coins themselves and reference to other historical evidence.

Fig. 50: FRANKLIN'S SUNDIAL. The common theme of the sundial motif, first engraved by Elisha Gallaudet for these fractional currency issues of February 17, 1776, was repeated on the 1776 Continental Dollars and the 1787 Fugio coppers (Newman, *Paper Money*, p. 40).

The design on these Continental dollars was highly influenced by the themes of Benjamin Franklin. The dies, some of which bear the initials E.G., were the work of Elisha Gallaudet, who also engraved the plates for the fractional Continental paper emissions of February 17, 1776, using the same motif of the sundial and linked circles.[25] A similar representation was later repeated on the Fugio cents. These dollar-sized coinages are known in seven die combinations and were struck in three different metals. Those in pewter, typically ranging in weight from 244 to 285 grains,[26] are the most common survivors with many hundred known today from an estimated original mintage of 6,000 or more.[27] The motive for the selection of pewter is arcane since this material had no significant intrinsic value although many surviving specimens show obvious signs of circulation. Pewter may have been used to give the allusion of silver or perhaps it was the most available material, not unlike the gun money of James II or certain European seige or "necessity" monies.

Fifteen or more brass specimens exist in a wide range of weight from 199 to 314 grains with an average weight of 241. These pieces would roughly correspond to the coins referenced in the June 1776, New York notice concerning the new copper penny-sized denomination.[28] The four known silver copies, which may properly be called Continental dollars, average 374 grains.[29] It

[25] Newman, *Paper Money*, pp. 40-41.
[26] Hodder, *ANA Centennial*, p. 17.
[27] This is based on the three pewter varieties, Newman 1-C, 2-C, and 3-D each being low rarity 3, which census ranges from 201 to 500 specimens (*Romano*, pp. 15-16).
[28] Hodder, *ANA Centennial*, pp. 8-9; *Norweb*, pt. 2, p. 246.
[29] Hodder, *ANA Centennial*, p. 17.

has been suggested that these planchets were shaved down Spanish American silver.[30] One specimen, examined for silver content by the specific gravity method, was determined to be .880 fine, an alloy greater than would be expected for Spanish American coins, but not out of the limits of error considering the poor reliabilty of this analytical technique.

The emission sequence of the Continental Currency has been studied by Hodder who demonstrated that all three metals were minted interchangeably indicating that the silver and brass specimens were not preliminary strikes such as trial pieces or patterns would be. Although the brass and silver coins were manufactured randomly during the pewter mintage, there remains the possibility that these rarer issues were presentation pieces or souvenirs. It becomes apparent from these die emission studies, that the Continental dollars were minted in two distinct groups without any connecting die or punch linkages.[31]

The previously cited letter published from the *London Gazette* suggested that the copper and silver coins, while of the same size but of different metals, would circulate at different values. If these issues had been struck from the same or similar dies, such an arrangement would have been unsatisfactory because of the potential for tampering. It would not have been long before the unscrupulous would have disguised the copper pieces with a silver or tin wash to pass for silver, particularly with the wartime shortage of specie.

There is some historical evidence which offers clues as to the origins of the Continental dollars. When the Continental Congress authorized paper currency, the one dollar denomination was included only in the first four issues through May 6, 1776. Thereafter, the dollar note was omitted from the next six emissions to be resumed in the final series of January 14, 1779. The New York bills of credit authorized August 13, 1776, similarly omitted the dollar unit but included four lower fractional denominations from $1/16 to $1/2 and then continued from $2 to $10.[32] In his pioneering study of this coinage, Newman concludes that this exclusion of the dollar note in these several paper currency emissions was purposeful since it was Congress's intent that this slot be filled with a minted coinage. "The $1 note would be most convenient for circulation and would be one of the last denominations to be eliminated unless a substitute [e.g. Continental dollar] was intended." Inflation had not progressed to the point that the dollar denomination would have been unprofitable to print.[33] It can be speculated that the pewter Continental dollar was a fiat metallic currency intended to circulate in conjunction with the higher denominational Continental paper money, the intent of the brass and silver issues being yet undiscovered. It is highly improbable that the "Continental Copper coin" described in the newspaper account relates to the Continental dollar. In the middle of a war with so many more vital matters to consider, the Continental Congress would not have expended so much energy on a large copper coin "to circulate as basic small change," but it would have been appropriate to help strengthen the paper currency with a specie coinage. If this money had been intended as a copper coinage, why are there no specimens in that metal and why are there pieces in silver? The floreated edges found on some of these varieties would be an unreasonable garnish for a copper coinage but appropriate to protect silver currency.[34] Numismatists can hope that some documentary evidence will be uncovered which finally will solve the riddle of the Continental Currency, one of America's noblest coinages.

The Problems of Peace

On October 19, 1781, Cornwallis surrendered to Washington at Yorktown, Virginia, ending the war. The question was whether these "thirteen commonwealths bound in a league of friendship" would emerge as one nation or thirteen. A preliminary peace treaty was signed on

[30] *Romano*, p. 14.
[31] Hodder, *ANA Centennial*, pp. 7-18.
[32] Newman, *Paper Money*, pp. 37-49, 264.
[33] Newman, *CCJour. 1952A*, p. 1.
[34] Eric P. Newman, personal communication, Sept. 4, 1990.

January 20, 1783, in Paris. Provisions of this treaty dealt with boundaries, fishing rights, and the more difficult issues of confiscated Tory holdings and the satisfaction of private debts incurred with England prior to the hostilities. Congress claimed it had no jurisdiction over the Loyalist properties and that the issue should be settled at the state level. The treaty confirmed that the private debts were still binding and should be discharged at full value although the states did not enforce this arrangement.[35]

The war debt became an overwhelming issue. Congress was saddled with $200,000,000 in bills of credit. Since only the states could levy taxes, Congress was at their mercy for funds to retire this Continental currency and the state legislatures showed no enthusiasm to raise money for this purpose. Large accounts were still outstanding for war supplies and food requisitioned from civilian merchants; the armed forces had gone unpaid. In 1776, at a time when the American cause looked bleakest, the military officers had demanded from Congress half pay for life after the war was over, and common soldiers were granted an $80 bounty if they agreed to serve until the peace.[36] The army had been paid in depreciated money and "... four month's pay of a private soldier would not procure for his family a single bushel of wheat; the pay of a colonel would not purchase oats for his horse ...." Some states demonstrated a genuine concern for the physical comfort and welfare of their militias and "undertook to make good to their troops the loss in pay caused by the depreciation of the currency," whereas others "left theirs troops almost destitute."[37] Now, in 1781, the hostilities were over and the chief legacy from the war was hard-won freedom, a large war debt, unpaid and disquieted troops, and much worthless paper money.

It was evident that the Articles of Confederation were powerless to cope with such a situation. Congress needed to raise money independently of the several state legislatures. Leaders of the day recognized the need for a strong central government to contend with this economic crisis. In 1780, even before the war was over, when the army had become so desperate and discontented, it was proposed in Congress that General Washington be given dictatorial powers to deal with the dilemma.[38] One historian suggested that in the early 1780s the United States was on the brink of anarchy;[39] others point out that the national responsibility and concern for the war debt was the "cement" which was holding the Union together.[40]

Immediately following the war, hard money became plentiful from the specie which had been spent in the occupied territories by the now departed foreign troops.[41] It has been calculated that the French armies placed about 35,000,000 livres (about £1,500,000) into colonial circulation while English forces, stationed in the colonies, exclusive of the Royal Navy, were paid in excess of £10,000,000. These enormous sums of hard money caused an unprecedented, yet short-lived, prosperity in the postwar era. More wealth entered circulation from confiscated Loyalist holdings and from proceeds recovered from privateering against English shipping. This abundance was only temporary since the hard currency was soon exported to England and Europe in exchange for manufactured goods and luxuries which had been in short supply during the Revolution. The country had gone on a buying spree and now, with all its money spent, merchants were burdened with shelves overstocked with "an amazing Superfluity of all kinds of European goods."[42] A serious postwar depression was at hand.[43] Between 1784 and 1786, a

[35] Fiske, *Critical Period*, pp. 28-33, 131, 154-55.
[36] Jensen, *New Nation*, pp. 31-32, 37-43, 72.
[37] Irving, *Washington*, vol. 4, p. 31.
[38] Jensen, *New Nation*, pp. 46-47.
[39] Fiske, *Critical Period*, pp. 134-86.
[40] Jensen, *New Nation*, p. 73.
[41] Maganzin, *Depression*, pp. 22-24.
[42] Weeden, *New England*, p. 819. The glut of imported merchandise was more severe in New England. In the fall of 1784, the Boston firm of J. & J. Amory was offering goods at 2 to 3% over cost.
[43] Jensen, *New Nation*, pp. 185-93, 303. See also Maganzin, *Depression*, passim, and Flannagan, *Trying Times*, pp. 10-15; McCusker and Menard, *Economy*, passim. Maganzin describes the depression in Maryland

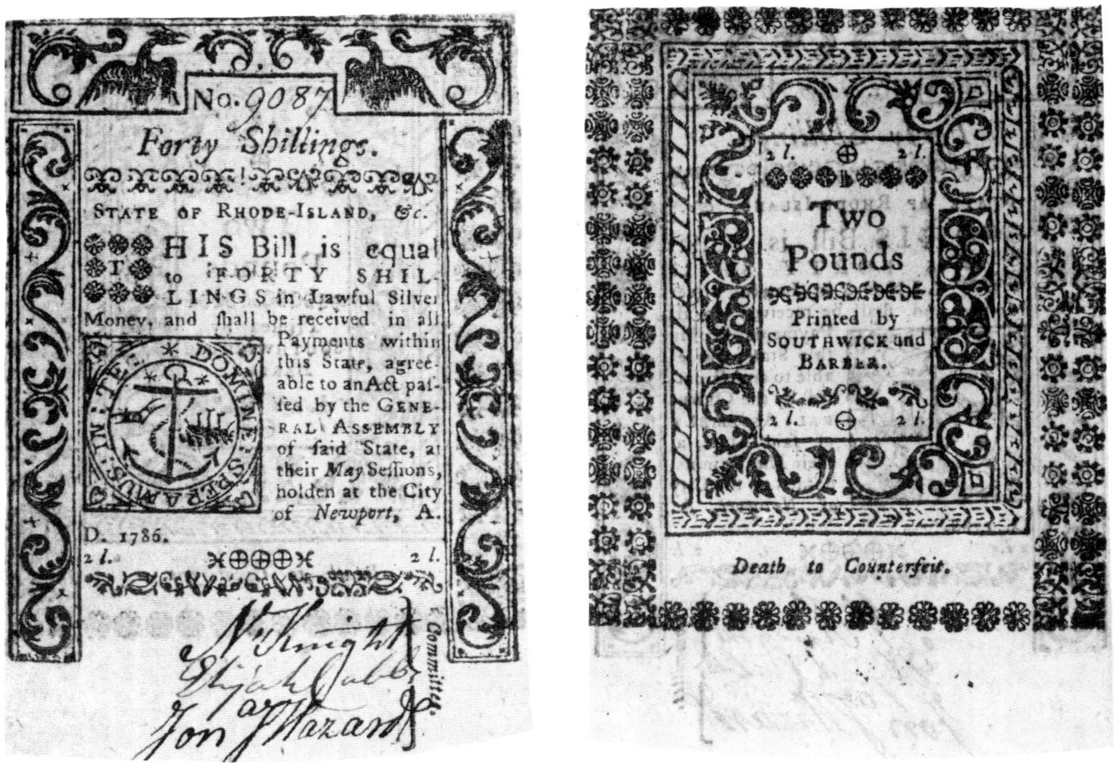

Fig. 51: 1786 Rhode Island £2 Bill of Credit, an example of postwar "rag" money which depreciated widely.

£5,000,000 trade deficit with Great Britain shattered all hope for a stabilized currency, caused bankruptcies, depressed prices, and deepened the commercial depression.[44] Credit was overextended. Many Americans were annoyed that although they had just gained their political independence from England, British capital still controlled their trade.[45] Farm prices had held until 1785 at which time they gradually began falling.[46] The absence of circulating medium revived the practice of barter, for example, whiskey in North Carolina, and tobacco in Virginia. The editor of the Worcester, Massachusetts, *Spy* advertised that he would receive subscriptions in salt pork.[47] Early in 1782, the United States Treasury contained not a single dollar, and only from loans through the Bank of North America, engineered by the financial genius of the Revolution, Robert Morris, was a total economic disaster averted.[48] The American economy, while seriously affected, continued to expand as exports gradually increased through 1788.[49]

Debtors were particularly hurt by the lack of available circulating currency with which to meet obligations. State legislatures became battle grounds as the demand for cheap money swept the country. By 1786, nine states had resorted to "rag money," a currency that did not

---

and Virginia even as it affected George Washington, a very wealthy man of the period. Flannagan takes issue with those historians who minimize this depression as "temporary" or insignificant as he documents commercial and economic collapse in New Hampshire.

[44] Hawke, *Experience*, p. 662.
[45] Weeden, *New England*, p. 819.
[46] East, *Enterprise*, pp. 239-62.
[47] Fiske, *Critical Period*, p. 165; Jensen, *New Nation*, p. 192.
[48] Fiske, *Critical Period*, p. 167; Hawke, *Experience*, p. 609.
[49] East, *Enterprise*, p. 248.

enjoy the stability of the pre-Revolutionary colonial bills of credit.[50] A particularly desperate situation existed in Rhode Island where a larger percentage of citizens was in debt. "Noisily complaining about hard times was the Rhode Islanders' most apparent trait."[51] The debtors and farmers favored paper money because they had nothing, whereas the commercial interests were opposed since they "knew the difference between hard money and promissory notes of a bankrupt government."[52] A Rhode Island dollar which passed at full value in May 1786 had depreciated to 16 cents by November even though secured through real estate by a land bank.[53] Commerce essentially ceased when the pro-paper Rhode Island legislature decreed that their currency must be received at full value, a condition which merchants refused to honor.[54]

Typical of the paper money controversy was New Hampshire, a state which itself was bankrupt during the year 1781 to 1782. The state was mired in a terrible postwar depression, and while the economy was based on specie, none was available. Most farmers lived at a subsistence level but had no hard money for taxes and so personal bankruptcies and foreclosures were rampant. The state had nothing to sell abroad since ship building was at a standstill and, therefore, it had no way to earn hard money. Other parts of the country fared better, such as Pennsylvania, where "silver and gold is plenty" because of earned foreign credits from the export of flour. To alleviate the money shortage and provide means for retiring public and private debts, it was advocated in New Hampshire in 1786 to issue paper currency by a land bank. Some critics of the proposal "were opposed to a paper currency backed by land because their debts to English merchants had to be paid in specie and consequently little use could be made of forfeited land."[55] The New Hampshire legislature resisted the paper money plan, perhaps apprehensive because of the riotous behavior of some paper money supporters who demonstrated violently during September 1786, in Exeter, New Hampshire, and "raised a cry for paper-money, and equal distribution of property, and a release from debts."[56] Riots also occurred in neighboring Vermont at Windsor and Rutland.[57]

The Massachusetts legislature also withstood the excitation for paper money despite the fact that there was an average debt of $50 per person, arising from private debts, the war debt, back pay for soldiers, and the current expense for running the government. The situation was further compounded by the requirement that taxes be paid in hard money, which particularly injured the farmers who protested the fact that they fought in the Revolution, were either unpaid or paid in valueless money, and now were forced to produce hard currency for taxes or face foreclosure or debtors' prison. Their resistance to authority led to a confrontation with the state militia in an encounter called "Shays's Rebellion."[58]

Significant problems existed as well with hard currency during the Confederation period. While paper money was subjected to devaluation and counterfeiting, hard coin currency itself could fall victim to tampering, debasement, and devaluation. Such mutilated and debased coins also tended to drive sound, full-valued coins out of circulation, making unclipped silver and gold pieces rarities. In his reminiscences of the Revolutionary period, E.S. Thomas recalled that as his family fled their home in the face of advancing English troops, his mother risked running back into the building to fetch a small bag of coins since money was so scarce at that time.[59]

[50] Bullock, *Essays*, p. 73; Newman, *Paper Money*, p. 18. The states were Pennsylvania, Vermont, New York, New Jersey, Maryland, North Carolina, Rhode Island, South Carolina, and Georgia.

[51] McDonald, *Formation*, p. 119.

[52] Fiske, *Critical Period*, pp. 174, 176.

[53] Flannagan, *Trying Times*, p. 162.

[54] Fiske, *Critical Period*, pp. 173-77; Ferguson, *Purse*, p. 243.

[55] Flannagan, *Trying Times*, p. 163.

[56] Flannagan, *Trying Times*, pp. 160, 162, 163, 174, 177, 191, 225, 245, 298-315, quote from 177. See also Daniell, *Experiment*.

[57] Fiske, *Critical Period*, p. 183.

[58] Fiske, *Critical Period*, pp. 177-83; Hawke, *Experience*, p. 667; Ferguson, *Purse*, pp. 245-50.

[59] Thomas, *Reminiscences*, vol. 1, p. 11, April 18, 1775. The author was the nephew of Isaiah Thomas, the publisher of *The Massachusetts Spy*.

> During the period of the Confederation the chaotic state of the currency was a serious obstacle to trade, and it offered endless opportunities for fraud and extortion. Clipping and counterfeiting were carried to such lengths that every moderately cautious person, in taking payment in hard cash, felt it necessary to keep a small pair of scales beside him and carefully weigh each coin after narrowly scrutinizing its stamp and deciphering its legend.[60]

Clipping of coins was not limited to the private sector. In 1782, when the United States government had received a quantity of French guineas as part of a loan, the coins were clipped by treasury officials before being placed into circulation with the rationalization that if the government did not clip them, the first people who received the intact coin would certainly do so, therefore any derived profit should accrue to the public benefit.[61]

Following the war, lightweight counterfeit English halfpence again flowed into America with large numbers arriving with every ship from England, imported as consignments of "hardware." A 1781 proclamation from the Pennsylvania legislature declared that the effect of such counterfeits was to raise prices, cause "injury to the community in general: and the poor in particular" and "introduce new confusion in the currency of the country."[62] Specific allegations against the counterfeit halfpence are stated in the following memorandum:

> The coinage of copper is a subject that claims our immediate attention. From the small value of the several pieces of copper coin, this medium of exchange has been too much neglected. The more valuable metals are daily giving place to base British half-pence, and no means are used to prevent the fraud. This disease, which is neglected in the beginning because it appears trifling, may finally prove very destructive to commerce. It is admitted that copper may, at this instant be purchased in America at one-eighth of a dollar the pound.
>
> British half-pence, made at the tower, are forty-eight to the pound. Those manufactured at Birmingham, and shipped in thousands for our use, are much lighter, and they are of base metal. It can hardly be said that seventy-two of them are worth a pound of copper; hence it will follow, that we give for British half-pence about six times their value. There are no materials from which we can estimate the weight of half-pence, that have been imported from Britain since the late war, but we have heard of sundry shipments being ordered, to the nominal amount of one thousand guineas; and we are told that no packet arrives from England without some hundred weight of base half-pence. It is a very moderate computation which states our loss, on the last twelve months, at 30,000 dollars, by the commerce of vile coin.[63]

The preceeding statement, by an unknown author, was not only descriptive of the troubled copper medium, but also prophetic. It asserted that the invasion of the small change currency by counterfeit English coppers, while seemingly non-threatening in the beginning, was not only

[60] Fiske, *Critical Period*, p. 166.

[61] Nevins, *American States*, p. 569.

[62] Crosby, *Early Coins*, p. 172.

[63] *A.S.P.F.*, vol. 1, pp. 100-101, quote p. 101. Neither the author nor the date of this passage, "Propositions Respecting the Coinage of Gold, Silver, and Copper," is identified, except that it is not by Alexander Hamilton. The editors of the *American State Papers* placed these remarks together with a 1782 tract by Robert Morris. The context implies that it was written prior to any of the state coinages. To estimate the volume of counterfeit halfpence imported, 1000 English guineas amount to 504,000 regal halfpence. In America, one pound, containing 72 coppers, sold for 1/8 dollar and thus a 100 lb. consignment of 7200 coppers would cost $12.50. At the Pennsylvania exchange rate of 90d. per dollar, the cost basis for 100 lbs. of coppers would be 1125d. or £4 13s. 9d. (93.75s.) local money. At the exchange rate of 15 coppers per local shilling, the market value for 7200 halfpence would be 480s. or 5760d., for a profit margin of 412% [(5760-1125) ÷ 1125 = 412%].

Table 17

Table of the Value of Several Pieces of Coin, in the Federal Coin, and the Several Currencies of the United States
(From Pike, *Complete System*, p. 378)

			Federal Coin.	*N. Hampshire, Massachusetts, Rh. Island, Connecticut, Virginia.*			*New-York and North-Carolina.*			*N. Jersey, Pennsylvania, Delaware and Maryland*			*S. Carolina & Georgia*		
	pw.	*gr.*	*Cents*	*£*	*s.*	*d.*	*£*	*s.*	*d.*	*£*	*s.*	*d.*	*£*	*s.*	*d.*
1/16 Dollar			0.06 1/4			4 1/2			6			5 5/8			3 1/2
1/2 Pistareen			0.10			7 1/5			9 3/5			9			5 3/5
				Vir.		8									
1/9 Dollar			0.11 1/9			8			10 2/3			10			6 2/9
1/8 ditto			0.12 1/2			9		1	0			11 1/5			7
A Pistareen			0.20		1	2 2/5		1	4 1/2		1	6			11 1/5
				Vir.	1	4									
An Eng. Shill.			0.22 2/9		1	4		1	7 1/3		1	8		1	0 4/9
1/4 Dollar			0.25		1	6		2	0		1	10 1/2		1	2
Half ditto			0.50		3	0		4	0		3	9		2	4
A Dollar			1.00		6	0		8	0		7	6		4	8
En. or Fr. Crown			1.11 1/9		6	8	N. York	9	0		8	4		5	2 2/9
							N. Caro.	8	9						
	pw.	*gr.*													
Fr. Guin.	5	5	4.62 26/27	1	7	6	1	16	0	1	14	6	1	1	5
In Mass.	5	6	4.55 1/9	1	7	4									
En. Guin.	5	6	4.66 2/3	1	8	0	1	17	0	1	15	0	1	1	9
In S. Caro.	5	7											1	1	10
1/2 Johann.	9	0	4.00	2	8	0	3	4	0	3	0	0	1	17	4
Pistole	4	5	3.66 2/3	1	2	0	1	8	0	1	7	0		17	6
In Mass.	4	3	3.66 2/3												
Moidore	6	18	6.00	1	16	0	2	6	0	2	5	0	1	8	0
Doubloon	17	0	14.66 2/3	4	8	0	5	16	0	5	12	0	3	10	0

The Standard weight of an Eagle 11 pwt. 4 2/3 gr. - Half ditto 5 pwt. 14 1/3 gr. - A Dollar 17 pwt. 1 3/4 gr. - Half ditto 8 pwt. 12 7/8 gr. - A Double Dime 3 pwt. 9 4/5 gr. - A Dime 1 pwt. 16 9/10 gr.

driving small silver denominations out of circulation, but also had the potential to inflict injury on commerce itself. By 1789 these predictions all came true.

Such was the turbulent scene of the 1780s: a severe depression with struggling commerce, a practically worthless paper money, a shortage of hard money, counterfeit and clipped coins, and a young nation staggering under a burdensome war debt. Fiske provides an excellent insight into the hard money situation of the Confederation.

> English, French, Spanish, and German coins of various and uncertain value, passed from hand to hand. Besides the ninepences and fourpence-ha'-pennies there were bits, and half bits, pistareens, picayunes, and fips. Of gold pieces there were johannes, or joe, the dubloon [doubloon], the moidore, and pistole, with English and French guineas, Carolins, ducats, and chequins [sequins]. Of copper there were English pence and half-

pence and French sou: and pennies were issued at local mints in Vermont, Massachusetts, Connecticut, New Jersey, and Pennsylvania.[64]

On July 6, 1785, Congress passed a resolution regarding the money units of the United States and the content thereof.[65] The proposed coins were to be in a decimal ratio starting with the half cent and cent of copper, a dime, double-dime, half dollar, and dollar in silver, and in gold, a half eagle of five dollars and eagle of ten dollars. Despite this effort to achieve some conformity in the monetary system, the states still calculated in their old monies of account. An attempt to reconcile these several schemes is exemplified in the chart written by Nicholas Pike in 1786 and published in 1788 which is reproduced as Table 17.[66]

In the above table, in the far left column, was the Spanish American milled dollar. It is represented here as a whole unit and also in its fractional parts, all of which actually existed as circulating coins. Of these, the 1/16th dollar was the half-real or picayune, the 1/8th the real, the quarter dollar the two reales, and the half dollar the four reales. The 1/9th of a dollar was only an imaginary money of account, but it was a very convenient denomination in which to calculate in view of the fact that the value of the Spanish milled dollar in local monies for the New England and Middle Atlantic states was 72d. and 90d., respectively. The two Spanish coins tabulated were the half pistareen, conforming quite well to the newly proposed dime, and the full pistareen which was nearly identical in assay to the "double" dime. The content of .925 fine standard in the "head" pistareen minted in Spain after 1772 was 80.9 grains (see Table 5) whereas the "double" dime was proposed at 81.8 grains. Nothing ever came of the "double" dime proposition until many years later when for four years, 1875 to 1878, a twenty cent piece was minted.[67]

If we assume that the other monies enumerated in Pike's table were the common coins of 1786, then the other silver coins of the period were generally English and French, and the gold coins were French and English guineas, the Portuguese moidore and "half-joes," and Spanish pistoles and doubloons.

It was soon apparent that the Articles of Confederation were ill-equipped to meet the problems and challenges of the new nation. The final solution for these dilemmas was the establishment of the Constitution of 1787.

From a numismatic perspective we must pause and describe some very significant events which occurred from 1785 to 1789. While the country was still in the grips of a severe postwar depression and hard money shortage, the circulating copper currency, the money of the poor, was also in motley disarray and chaos. The prevalent copper money of the period, English halfpence and farthings, was diluted with large quantities of lightweight counterfeits of impure

[64] Fiske, *Critical Period*, p. 165. Fiske is in error about copper English pence since these would not appear until the second coinage of George III in 1797. The term local "pennies" is also a misnomer in reference to the state coppers, especially from Pennsylvania where counterfeit coppers were erroneously attributed (see Newman, *Studies*, pp. 149-54). Of the other coins described here, the "ninepence" and "fourpence-ha'-pennies" refer to the Spanish real and half-real when the eight reales passed at 72d. A "fip" or fivepenny bit is another accounting for the half real. Hence, the medio, half real, half bit, picayune, fip, fippenny, fippence, and fourpence ha'-penny, were all terms for the same coin. See Table 4. The Carolin, an 18th century German gold coin of .770 fineness and 149 grains, was named after Prince Charles Albert of Bavaria (See Solomon, *Studies*, p. 38). The "sou" was the smallest French copper coin. All other denominations are defined in Tables 5 and 9.

[65] *Jour. Cong.*, August 1786, pp. 503-4.

[66] Pike, *Complete System*, p. 378.

[67] Breen, *Encyclopedia*, p. 334.

copper.[68] The legal coppers at best were themselves a token coinage passing at about double their intrinsic value. The introduction of lightweight and false coppers undermined public confidence in this medium. In an attempt to rid commerce of these illegal coppers which eroded the economy and caused financial damage especially to the poor who could afford it least, various states authorized projects under the authority of the Articles of Confederation to mint domestic copper coinage which would provide a stable currency. The next chapter, "Coinage of the Confederation Period," details this experience.

[68] When analyzed by specific gravity measurements, many struck counterfeits are found to be pure copper. Cast specimens, however, tend to have a lower specific gravity, either due to adulteration with zinc or tin to facilitate casting or as the result of trapped air bubbles, or both.

CHAPTER SEVEN

Coinage of the Confederation Period

The scarcity of silver and gold coins during the serious post war depression of the 1780s has been discussed in prior chapters. In contrast, the small change copper medium of the colonies was polluted by an abundance of lightweight counterfeit English halfpence. Several state legislatures attempted to curb the economic injury caused by this unrestricted volume of counterfeit coppers, since it was perceived that these false coins were inflicting financial damage especially on the poorer, working classes. In 1781, the Pennsylvania legislature issued a decree recommending "all faithfull [sic] inhabitants of this State to refuse it [counterfeit British halfpence] in payment, and by all other lawful ways and means discourage the currency thereof ...."[1] A more definitive course was adopted by Vermont and Connecticut in 1785, New Jersey in 1786, and Massachusetts in 1787, when these four jurisdictions authorized mints for the purpose of replacing these spurious coppers with high grade, pure copper coinages on the theory that these new coppers would be received preferentially and thus drive the lightweight imports out of circulation. New York adopted a different strategem in 1787. Rather than to mint its own copper currency, it strove to regulate the circulation of existing coins by demonetizing all coppers less than 145.8 grains and devaluing all others from 14 to 20 per local shilling. The coinages of these Confederation mints is the subject of this present chapter.

COINING TECHNOLOGY DURING THE CONFEDERATION

The state coinages of the Confederation period are a fascinating series. While much is known about them and the circumstances of their manufacture, significantly more remains undiscovered. Many of the actual coins themselves reside today in the cabinets of individual numismatists and in museum collections, but none of the punches, dies, presses or other hardware used in the minting process is reported to have survived.[2] The information we have is derived from examination of the coins themselves and existing historical records such as legal proceedings, contracts, legislative debate and enactments, newspaper accounts, and sundry other contemporary documents. A large number of coppers from this period are "orphans" in that nothing is recorded about their provenance.

A great deal of information has been preserved regarding eighteenth century English mints,[3] but it is unwise and inaccurate to apply these facts uncritically to America. Spilman has studied the technology of coining used in America during this period.[4] He qualifies his conclusions about colonial minting practices since they were based on visual observations and recognizes the need for firmer laboratory evidence. The major technical problem confronting the Confederation mintmaster was the inability to produce and roll planchet stock to uniform dimension. Many inherent technical problems can be envisioned in this rudimentary rolling process, including the ambient temperature, and the alignment, compliance, and resiliance of the iron rollers. For example, a decrease in roller spacing from 1.71 to 1.61 millimeters could reduce the final weight of a Connecticut copper, 28 millimeters in diameter, from the authorized 144.0 to 135.3 grains.[5]

[1] Crosby, *Early Coins*, p. 172.
[2] Spilman, *CNL 1982*, p. 766.
[3] Excellent summaries of English and European minting practices are offered by Cooper, *Coinmaking*, Mason, *Making Coins*, and Breen, *Dies*.
[4] Spilman, *CNL 1982*.
[5] Mossman, *Connecticut Coppers*.

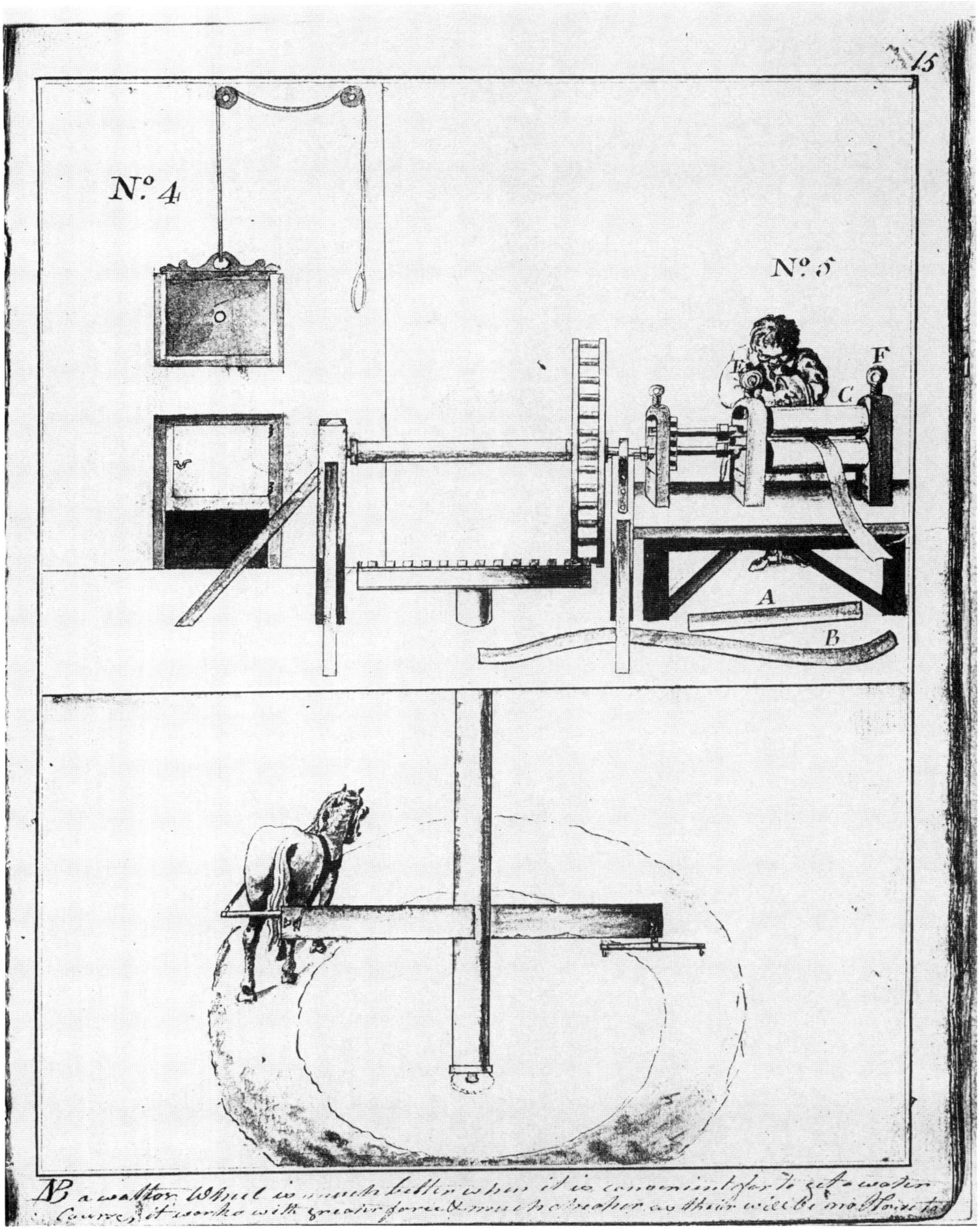

Fig. 52: SAMUEL THOMPSON'S ROLLING MILL (1783). This illustration is from the Thompson manuscript in the ANS Library showing the process for rolling metal fillets from which to cut planchets. The power source could be either from a horse or water wheel. The thickness of the strip could be controlled by the space between the rollers adjusted by the set screws "E" and "F". Thompson, working in Ireland, equipped his machine with "polished steel rollers" whereas those in America were probably rough cast iron with surface irregularities which flawed the planchets. These roller marks are visible on certain finished coins.

Residual striations impressed on the surfaces of copper fillets by the rough surfaces of the cast iron rollers are commonly seen on finished Connecticut coins when the planchets were insufficiently annealed, or softened, prior to striking.[6] Crosby relates how planchets for Massachusetts coppers were cast into ingots at the Boston mint and then carted to nearby Dedham where the copper "was drawn under a trip-hammer, and rolled into sheets, when it was returned to the mint, where the blanks were prepared and the coin stamped."[7] The rolling procedure practiced in England was more complex where the fillets were initially prepared in a horse or water powered "roughing mill," and then passed through a power driven "finishing mill" prior to being brought to exact dimensions by passage through a set of polished, hardened, steel rollers on a hand operated "drag-bench."[8]

Given this imperfect techology in rolling copper fillets to the proper thickness, there is little wonder that the coppers of the late eighteenth century were so variable in weight. In Chapter Eight there is an extensive gravimetric analysis of the Confederation coinages. While most of these issues conform reasonably to a bell curve, indicating a normal distribution above and below the average, the question is raised as to what allowable tolerances in coin weights should be permitted these early American mintmasters in view of their imprecise machinery. Since the Tower Mint, with its more sophisticated equipment, sanctioned tolerances per pound of 2.5% for George II halfpence[9] and 3.33% for the Virginia halfpence,[10] a 5% remedy for Confederation mints appears to be a reasonable expectation.[11] Any value within these limits of error should not raise the suspicion of impropriety on part of the mintmaster, but only confirms his frustration with his primitive equipment.

The source of the copper used in the Confederation mints is uncertain except in some specific instances. This subject will be covered more fully in the following chapter where the costs of coining are examined fully. All planchets of American manufacture appear to have been fashioned from the same style of planchet cutter. Spilman describes this device as "two telescoping cookie cutters," not unlike a pair of circular scissors which could be resharpened. The cleavage plane around the circumference of planchets cut by this technique formed a rounded edge. Contemporary English planchets were punched from strips in a screw press forced through a single cutting surface which resulted in a straight, sharp rim. These planchets were bent by this process and required passage through a second machine which then flattened them.[12] The rolling and cutting of the planchets caused the metal to become work-hardened by the applied stress. The metal then required softening, or annealing, by heating in furnaces prior to coining in order to restore its former malleability.[13] If flans were not annealed and remained hard, the impression was not as clear and the dies wore rapidly, showing signs of early failure. It is unknown if American mints consistently annealed their planchets except from circumstantial evidence which will be cited in specific instances.

Because there are no known dies of Confederation coppers, most information is inferred from examination of the actual coins. The process of die manufacture in the late eighteenth century has been summarized by Chard with particular emphasis on the metallurgical aspects.[14] Working, or embossing dies for these coppers were constructed from cylindrical shaped bars of steel with one end milled to the circumference of the desired coin. This end was then annealed to a softened state and the design for the intended coin was impressed into the smooth face of the

[6] Spilman, *CNL 1982*, pp. 808-9.
[7] Crosby, *Early Coins*, p. 274.
[8] Mason, *Making Coins*, p. 197.
[9] Craig, *Mint*, p. 250.
[10] Newman, *Colonial Virginia*, p. 52.
[11] Hodder, *AJN 1989*, p. 224.
[12] Craig, *Newton*, p. 6; Craig, *Mint*, p. 162.
[13] Cooper, *Coinmaking*, pp. 106-7, 183, 190-91.
[14] Chard, *CNL 1990*, pp. 1140-41.

die with a series of punches or hubs. After each step of the process, the die would become work-hardened requiring further softening lest it become brittle and fracture producing premature die failure.

The completed die and the embossing punches and hubs were mirror images of the final design on the struck coin, the die being a negative and the finished coin a positive representation. The central effigies frequently were sunk into the face of the die by a hub on whose surface the desired design previously had been engraved, or impressed from a master matrix, and the hub then hardened. This transfer was usually accomplished by a screw press due to the required force.[15] This central hub, or puncheon, then could be used again thus imparting identical patterns on several embossing dies. The other alternative was for the central figures to be engraved directly onto a single die. The legends, dates, and other ornamentation were added to the die with individual punches, or tools. There are instances in the 1785 and 1786 Connecticut series where the entire detail of the coin was raised on complex hubs so the complete obverse and reverse features could be sunk into the working die, with all subsequent dies from the same complex hub being exact copies. In this process, to be described later, some of the completed features required hand strengthening with punches.

Fig. 53(a-b): 1787 "Horned Bust": This contemporary counterfeit from dies attributed to Walter Mould, may be the most common Connecticut copper. 1787 Miller 4-L. (a) The first specimen (139.4 grains) is from an earlier die state just as a break appeared in the obverse field under the figure's chin. As the break enlarged, the engraver attempted to repair the damage by grinding down, or lapping, the obverse field. As the height of the field was reduced, the more shallowly engraved curls behind the neck lost relief and became indistinct. (b) The second specimen (105.1 grains) demonstrates the poorer detail of the lower hairline and the well-developed break which appears to project as a horn from the figure's armor (Table 21, no. 13a; Chart 24).

The letter and number punches were in the form of miniature, wedge-shaped chisels with sharpened edges such that their imprint could be hammered into the face of the die. The deeper the punch was sunk into the surface of the die, the deeper the resulting impression, and due to the wedge-shaped characteristic of the punch, the wider the positive shape of the letter appeared on the struck coin. If the punches were unevenly cut into the die, then the final positive image on the struck coin would be uneven. As the die wore from use or the field was purposely ground, or lapped, the less deeply sunk portion of the letter might become less clear or even disappear.

[15] Breen, *Dies*, pp. 10-11.

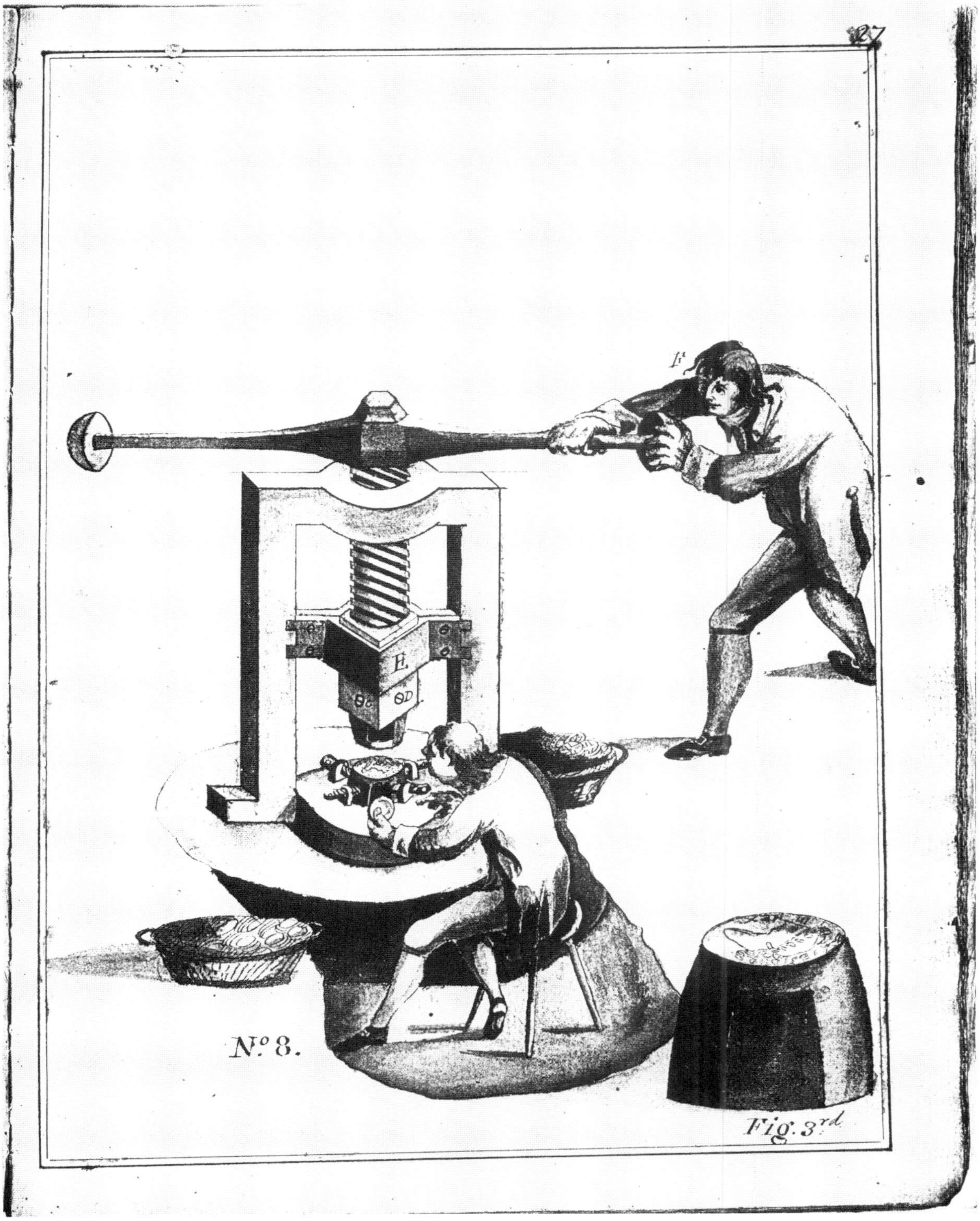

Fig. 54: SAMUEL THOMPSON'S COINAGE PRESS (1783). This screw press, or "fly" from Thompson's manuscript, is probably the style of press that was in general operation during the Confederation period. Thompson noted that this screw press was well suited to strike copper coins.

This phenomenon is well illustrated on the 1787 Connecticut Muttonhead where the reworked die had so much metal ground from the surface of the field that several letters became indistinct while others, which were not as deeply impressed in the original die, were completely obliterated.[16] Due to flaws originating around included impurities in the steel, cracks could appear on the surface of the die usually connecting with some element of the engraved design producing the familiar die break. By grinding down the face of the die, such acquired defects could be eradicated but they were usually ignored. In the engraver's attempt to repair the die break which originated in the left obverse field on the famous 1787 Connecticut Horned Bust, Miller 4-L, variety, so much of the surface was ground away that the more shallow curl detail down the back of the neck was eliminated as the height of the field was reduced (see fig. 53).[17] If a die were improperly case hardened, after repeated use its weakened center might start to sink in a concave fashion, imparting as a mirror image on the struck coin a convex contour within the central field. This central bulging is particularly obvious on some large planchet New Jersey varieties.

It is universally held that a screw press operated by two opposing fly weights on the end of a long arm was used in all instances for minting Confederation coppers. From the location of edge pinch defects on coins when the machine malfunctioned, it appears that the press used for the Connecticut and Fugio series by Abel Buell even possessed an automatic planchet feeder. A typical coining press at the Tower Mint was described as:

> two horizontal arms, each loaded with a hundredweight of lead at its tip ... As a Moneyer inserted a blank between the two dies through an aperture in the foot of the press, four laborers pulled the arms violently; the capstan spun, ... and ... as it crashed down [it] drove the die in its base against the blank and the latter against the nether die. These great machines could strike nearly a coin every two seconds—according to Newton; the Moneyers put the average stroke at three a minute—but the strain was so great that the labourers could only keep up work for fifteen minutes at a time. And few Moneyers were nimble enough to save their fingers indefinitely.[18]

All of the American coppers were struck without collars resulting in some radial expansion of the planchet during the procedure. This is particularly evident on multiply struck coins which have significantly greater diameters by one to two millimeters.[19]

History has remained silent on another important aspect of the Confederation coinages concerning the mechanism for the distribution of newly minted coppers. There must have been some scheme by which the mintmaster placed this money into circulation considering there were no banks or other financial institutions which could assume this role. For the legal operations, a percentage of the coppers was paid into the treasury as the required royalty and the disposal of these coins became the problem of the state. It is probable that other coins were sold in bulk at discount rates to middlemen who acted as "utterers" who then entered them into commerce. It is unlikely that merchants would have welcomed any large quantity of coppers, at any price, unless they had means to pass them on in order that they not be encumbered with large numbers of unwanted coins. The requirement to dispose of coppers at wholesale prices would have diminished any potential profits to the minters. The only published reference regarding the dispersion of any actual coppers is contained in the account of Royal Flint and the Fugios.

Many individuals were connected with the Confederation coinages as investors, mintmasters, engravers, and die sinkers. For some, their connection with a particular mint is clear and definite, whereas for others, due to lack of records, their precise involvement still remains shroud-

[16] Barnsley, *CNL 1973*, pp. 383-89, 392-94.

[17] Barnsley, *CNL 1973*, p. 385; Spilman, *CNL 1982*, pp. 824-25; James C. Spilman, personal communication, June 15, 1991.

[18] Craig, *Newton*, pp. 6-7. See also Crosby, *Early Coins*, p. 191, for a similar description of the coining procedure at Machin's Mills.

[19] Douglas, *Fugio*, pp. 63-64.

ed in conjecture. There have been attempts to identify the artisans who engraved particular dies through study of the letter and number punches, style, and hubs. Whenever it is believed that the product of a certain engraver is recognized, it has become appealing to assign all similar work to the same individual through this punch-link evidence. Using this approach, a large number of Confederation coppers have been attributed to particular men, James F. Atlee being noteworthy in this regard. While existing contracts confirm that Atlee played an important role in certain coinages, his precise function is undocumented, except in the latter day recollection of Thomas N. Machin, son of the famous mintmaster, who referred to him as "Atlee, the engraver ...."[20]

If the sharp cutting edge of a punch were broken, the damage could be so characteristic that the so-called "broken letter punch" could be followed through all the dies on which it was used. Broken "A," "N," and "P" letter punches were identified by Crosby and subsequently attributed to Atlee who is assumed to have been the responsible engraver.[21] Whenever these and other telltale marks and stylistic similarities appear, the die and related coinages have been attributed to Atlee through this punch-link evidence. Hodder has demonstrated, by photographic enlargement rather than reliance on naked eye examination, that several "broken A" punches can be identified and so the trail of this defective letter does not necessarily lead to Atlee.[22] Crosby remarked on what he assumed to be the recurrence of identical letter punches and considered "it certain that many of the dies of New Jersey and Vermont, and some of the AUCTORI CONNEC were the work of the same artist; but whether the dies for the different mints were made at one place, or whether the artist followed an itinerant practice, and visited the mints as occasion required, which probably would be the more convenient method of conducting his business ... must be left to conjecture."[23] The imitation British halfpence from Machin's Mills have also been attributed to Atlee on the strength of the same type of evidence.[24] While the use of identical punches on many coinages may be fact, nothing tells us whose hand used the punches. Could more than one punch, made from a common letter punch matrix, have been used by several engravers in their own individual work? There is no proof that each engraver fabricated his own tools and did not procure them from some common source. It is reasonable to speculate that with the volume of minting activity centered in Birmingham, there would have been some commercial supply of punches available to American artisans. While it is certain that many dies are related by punch-link evidence, it remains speculative to link all similar work to one particular artisan without supporting documentary evidence. The material in this chapter covers the whole spectrum of hypothesis ranging from fact to opinion. But until the Rosetta Stone is uncovered which can unravel the unsolved mysteries relative to the minting and circulation of these coppers, research continues in the hope that our current concepts about Confederation coppers will be expanded, supported and/or refuted. In the meanwhile, it is vital to remain objective in our interpretation of the available information and not look for facts where there are none.

CONNECTICUT COPPERS

Since Vermont was outside the Confederation, Connecticut was actually the first state to introduce a legitimate, full weight, copper currency designed to suppress circulation and acceptance of these counterfeit English coppers. This coinage was launched in response to the petition by the business association of Samuel Bishop, James Hillhouse, John Goodrich, and Joseph Hopkins to the Connecticut legislature on October 18, 1785, for a franchise to mint state

[20] Spilman, *CNL 1982*, p. 806.
[21] Barnsley, *CNL 1976*, p. 536; *RF-48*, *CNL 1973*, p. 400; Crosby, *Early Coins*, pp. 287-88.
[22] Hodder, *CNL 1991*.
[23] Crosby, *Early Coins*, pp. 287-88.
[24] Crosby, *Early Coins*, pp. 191, 288; Trudgen, *CNL 1987A*, pp. 967, 971.

coppers under the authority of the Confederation, which permitted both federal and state mints. Two days later, the legislature granted this partnership, the Company for Coining Coppers, approval to mint coppers for a period not exceeding five years. It further stipulated that the coins weigh 144 grains each, or 46 to the pound, that a five percent royalty be paid to the State Treasury, and that the coppers were not legal tender.[25] Besides the legally sanctioned organization, at least six or possibly seven other mints participated in manufacturing Connecticut coppers over a span of four or five years, although in some instances these different "mints" were just a business reorganization or realignment of previous shareholders.[26] The classification method by Henry C. Miller, first published in 1920 and subsequently enlarged by others, is the accepted designation with some 355 different die varieties or combinations currently identified.[27] Miller's system has its inadequacies since it considers only the punctuation and devices in the legends rather than the more obvious bust styles that better identify coins of similar mint and engraver. It is thought that the legend ornamentation contains some as yet undeciphered code indicating the circumstances of manufacture or the identity of the diesinker.[28]

All Connecticut coppers have the same basic motif, with an obverse bust either draped in a toga or clad in mail, facing left or right in the pose of George II or George III, respectively, and the abbreviated legends, AUCTORI CONNEC, "By the Authority of the State of Connecticut," or some variation thereof. The reverse design is a Britannia-like figure with the peripheral inscription, INDE ET LIB, "Independence and Liberty," rarely ET LIB INDE, or a modified abbreviation of INDE as IND. This new coinage was purposely modeled after the already familiar British halfpenny on the assumption that the population would be more inclined to accept in commerce a coin similar to those well known to them for years.

Among the 355 different die combinations, there are 145 varietal types listed in Breen's *Complete Encyclopedia of U.S. and Colonial Coins*, and about 26 distinct bust styles. An attempt has been made to identify these coppers as to engraver and mint. During the first year, the engraver and diesinker for those pieces from the Company for Coining Coppers was Abel Buell, a man of many skills and accomplishments, about whom much documentary evidence exists.[29] Buell produced the 1785 bust right copper by using a common obverse head puncheon and a common reverse seated figure puncheon to impress the dies and then strengthened the impressions by hand and then added the legends using individual letter punches.[30] A few of the 1785 Mailed Bust Right coins vary from Buell's style, notably the "African Heads" and those related by common letter punches, suggesting either a different engraver with his own set of tools, or the possibility of a second mint entirely. Buell, described by his biographer as "an uncommonly ingenious mechanic," next began to make dies for the 1786 Connecticut series by impressing them from a common hub, employing a technology fully 50 years before its time in America. The Mailed Bust Left coins dated 1785 and 1786 were manufactured by this method.

Fig. 55: The Different Obverse Bust Types of Connecticut Coppers.

(a) 1785 Mailed Bust Right: Much variation of this obverse figure exists in these issues struck from hand-engraved dies by Abel Buell at the Company for Coining Coppers. 1785 Miller 3.1-L (129.7 grains) (Table 21, no. 10a; Chart 17).

[25] Crosby, *Early Coins*, pp. 207-10.
[26] See Breen, *CNL 1974B*, for a brief summary of the six known Connecticut mints.
[27] Miller, *Connecticut*. An interesting biographical sketch, "Henry Clay Miller," appears in Barnsley, *CNL 1969*. Miller's list was updated by Barnsley with the addition of newly discovered die varieties and combinations (Barnsley, *CNL 1964*.) The most recent revision (1991) of the Miller attributions is by Rock, *CNL 1991*.
[28] Breen, *Studies*, pp. 127-28.
[29] Spilman, *CNL 1972*.
[30] Breen, *Dies*, p. 12.

(b) 1785 "African Head": This copper is from an uncertain source but probably not the work of Buell. 1785 Miller 4.1-F.4 (140.1 grains).

(c) 1785 Mailed Bust Left: Buell's dies, from which these 1785 and 1786 Mailed Bust Left issues were struck, were impressed from a common hub with the details later strengthened by hand. Some have considered the Vermont 1786 and 1787 Bust Left to have been copied from this design. 1785 Miller 7.2-D (128.7 grains) (Table 21, no. 10a; Chart 18).

(d) 1786 Mailed Bust Left: 1786 Miller 5.2-H.1 (106.2 grains) (Table 21, no. 10a; Chart 18).

(e) "Hercules Head" of 1786 and 1787: This is a drastically recut Mailed Bust Left die from the Company for Coining Coppers. 1786 Miller 5.3-N (130.6 grains). The obverse was used again in 1787 as Miller obverse 7. When the same obverse die was employed in a subsequent year in combination with a different reverse die containing a new date, this occurrence is described as "biennial pairing," a circumstance which has been observed eleven times in the Connecticut series (see Barnsley, *CNL 1968*).

(f) 1786 Draped Bust Left: This is the first use of Buell's new design from the Company for Coining Coppers to be continued in 1787 and 1788. Note the large letters in the legends which are typical for this mint. 1786 Miller 6-K (133.9 grains) (Table 21, 10b).

(g) 1786 "Small Round Head": This is a contemporary counterfeit attributed to James F. Atlee, a connection which needs verification. 1786 Miller 2.1-D.3 (149.5 grains) (Table 21, no. 12).

(h) 1786 "Larger Round Head with Double Chin": This a second contemporary counterfeit also attributed to Atlee. The double chin appearance is the result of a die break. 1786 Miller 1-A (138.3 grains) (Table 21, no. 12).

(i) 1786 "Very Large Head": This is the third 1786 counterfeit speculated to be the work of Atlee. It has been assumed that Vermont RR-9, the Baby Head, was copied from this piece. 1786 Miller 3-D.1 (175.6 grains) (Table 21, no. 12).

(j) 1787 Draped Bust Left; large letters: This is a continuation of the Draped Bust Left design from the Company for Coining Coppers with large letters and cross-like punctuations in the legends (see fig. 55f). These issues were of full weight. 1787 Miller 20-a.2 (142.9 grains) (Table 21, no. 10c; Chart 19).

(k) 1787 Draped Bust Left; crosses: These several small letter varieties with crosses in their legends are of full weight and probably are from Jarvis and Company. 1787 Miller 19-g.4 (154.3 grains) (Table 21, no. 11b; Chart 20).

(l) 1787 Draped Bust Left; transitional: This is a transitional variety with crosses on the obverse and fleurons on the reverse. This coin typifies a "blundered legend" where a missing letter is substituted with an available one; in this instance lack of a T letter punch is compensated by use of an I in AUCIORI. 1787 Miller 38-l.2 (153.2 grains).

(m) 1787 Draped Bust Left; fleurons: These full weight varieties with small letters have fleurons, or ornamental flowers, in both legends. They are probably from Jarvis and Company. 1787 Miller 37.13-HH (139.2 grains) (Table 21, no. 11c; Chart 21).

(n) 1787 Draped Bust Left; cinquefoils: This underweight, small lettered coin is easily identified as a product of Jarvis and Company, the mint for the Fugio cents which also shared cinquefoils as punctuation marks. This style is the most commonly encountered Connecticut copper. 1787 Miller 33.17-gg.2 (122.7 grains) (Table 21, no. 11a; Chart 22).

(o) 1787 "Tallest Head": This 1787 Mailed Bust Left variety, the Miller 8 obverse, has the tallest figure of all Connecticut coppers and was struck from a hand cut die prepared by Buell. 1787 Miller 8-O (166.0 grains).

(p) 1787 Triple Leaves: This copper is representative of Abel Buell's Triple Leaves varieties, so named because of the headband on the obverse figure. The provenance of these coppers is uncertain; the 1787-dated issues are divided into two planchet populations according to weight, the lighter ones being similar to the 1788-dated varieties. 1787 Miller 11.1-E (158.8 grains) (Table 21, 16a; Chart 25).

(q) 1787 "Muttonhead" or "Bradford Head": This contemporary counterfeit is from an unknown source. 1787 Miller 1.2-C (149.8 grains) (Table 21, no. 14).

(r) 1787 "Laughing Head": This and the three other 1787 combinations, 6.2-M, 1.3-L, and 4-L are contemporary counterfeits attributed to dies by Walter Mould (see fig. 53 for 4-L). 1787 Miller 6.1-M (119.8 grains) (Table 21, no. 13b; Chart 24).

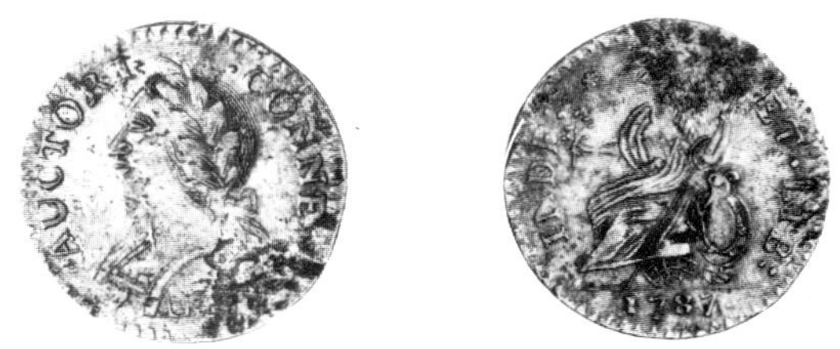

(s) 1787 "Simple Head" or "Outlined Head": This die is a recut version of the preceding obverse by Mould. 1787 Miller 6.2-M (101.2 grains) (Table 21, no. 13b; Chart 24).

(t) 1787 Medium Bust Right: This is the rarest within this group of four coppers attributed to Mould. 1787 Miller 1.3-L (104.6 grains) (Table 21, no. 13b; Chart 24).

(u) 1787 Small Head Right: This and the four following specimens are contemporary counterfeits believed to be products of Machin's Mills. This obverse die appears again in 1788 Miller 1-I, another example of biennial pairing. The 1788 Connecticut I reverse is likewise used in four other Vermont die combinations. 1787 Miller 1.1-A (113.3 grains) (Table 21, no. 15).

(v) 1787 Large Head Left with Broad Shoulders: 1787 Miller 3-G.1 (100.8 grains) (Table 21, no. 15).

(w) 1787 "Romanesque" Large Head Right: This is the rarest of the 1787-dated Machin's Mills contemporary counterfeits. 1787 Miller 52-G (107.7 grains) (Table 21, no. 15).

(x) 1787 "Childish Face": The features on this obverse figure are similar to 1788 Miller 9-E, both from the same source. 1787 Miller 13-D (129.0 grains) (Table 21, no. 15).

(y) 1788 Medium Head Right: All the Connecticut 1788-dated coppers are attributed to Machin's Mills. On average, they fall significantly below the authorized standard of 144 grains. The 1788 Connecticut D reverse is muled with Machin's Mills imitation halfpenny, Vlack 13-88CT. 1788 Miller 2-D (114.0 grains) (Table 21, no. 18a).

(z) 1788 "Pouting Boyish Head Right": 1788 Miller 6-H (114.5 grains) (Table 21, no. 18a).

(aa) 1788 Mailed Bust Right: This specimen is representative of the Mailed Bust Right series whose busts share a familial resemblance with other Connecticut and Vermont coppers and many imitation halfpence, also from the Machin's Mills mint. This occurence has been taken as evidence for a common engraver (see fig. 56a). 1788 Miller 3.2-B.2 (96.1 grains) (Table 21, no. 18a).

(bb) 1788 Draped Bust Left: This is a usage of Abel Buell's hubs and punches to make dies for 1788-dated coppers which were minted well below the authorized weight standard. 1788 Miller 16.5-H (128.1 grains). Four of his 1787-dated obverse Draped Bust Left dies were muled, or biennially paired, with new 1788 reverses. (Barnsley, *CNL* 1968, pp. 210-12) (Table 21, no. 17; Chart 23).

(cc) 1788 Bust Left with Hair Bow: This copper has similar features to 1787 Miller 13-D except for the prominent hairbow. The 9-E dies were severely clashed, the mirror image of the date being evident over the obverse figure's head. 1788 Miller 9-E (146.1 grains) (Table 21, no. 16d; Chart 26).

At the same time there was a distinct departure in obverse design on Connecticut coppers. On most 1785 issues, the bust faced to the right, similar to the motif for George III coppers. Starting with Buell's 1785 and 1786 dies impressed from a common hub, the style changed and the obverse mailed bust now faced to the left, reminiscent of George II halfpence since on English coins the bust orientation alternates with each succeeding monarch. The reason for this variation is unclear but it has been suggested that the shift in bust presentation was Buell's attempt to enable the public to distinguish between his legitimate Connecticut coppers and a flood of contemporaneous, counterfeit, 1786-dated, Mailed Bust Right coppers, of an entirely different style, recently placed in circulation from a yet unidentified source.[31] It is just as reasonable to speculate that Buell made this change in bust direction, now to the left, to assist a largely illiterate population to discriminate between Connecticut coppers as a group, and the very large number of bust right counterfeit George III British coppers which was the predominate small change currency. Of interest, the bust left orientation continued on all of Buell's subsequent dies. The obverse bust faced right again only on some other rare contemporary counterfeits, on the Muttonheads, and on those issues dated 1787 and 1788, thought to be from Machin's Mills since they possess characteristics linking them to imitation George III halfpence.

The appearance of these six 1786-dated Mailed Bust Right counterfeit varieties may have been the stimulus for subsequent legislative action in October 1785, prohibiting the manufacture of "Copper Coin" without permission of the General Assembly. In May of the following year, an act was proposed forbidding the importation into Connecticut of more than 50 coppers except those "coined & put forth by the Authority of Congress or some of the united [*sic*] States and of equal Value with the Copper coined in this State by lawful authority." This reference also has been interpreted as a recommended action against the introduction and circulation of spurious 1786-dated Connecticut coppers into the state.[32]

There has been an attempt to attribute the above discussed counterfeit 1786-dated Connecticut coppers by punch link evidence to James F. Atlee as previously narrated. Little is recorded about James F. Atlee except that he was known to have been a foreign born resident of New York City.[33] He and another individual, Samuel Atlee, whose relationship has not yet been established, had in their possession "certain implements for carrying on said trade [minting]" which they agreed to lend to the Machin's Mills partnership, of which they were both members.[34] In the contract of April 18, 1787, and in a subsequent agreement with the Rupert, Vermont, mint, dated June 7 of the same year, definite duties and responsibilities were delegated to the several partners. James F. Atlee and Thomas Machin were assigned the technical aspects of "Coinage of Money & Manufacturing Hard Ware" ("hard-ware" traditionally interpreted as the partners' euphonism for imitation British halfpence).[35] The other partners were allowed the freedom of the establishment "... to have liberty, ingress, egress and regress into, out of, and from the compting [counting] house, store house or room where the same Thomas Machin and James F. Atlee may be employed in the manufactory aforesaid."[36] From this description, it appears that James F. Atlee could likewise have been a metallurgist or mintmaster; if he worked as an engraver in the described "room" he could have encountered problems engraving dies amid the clamor and vibration of a nearby screw press and rollers. The "certain implements," brought to the partnership by the Atlees were not defined but always have been presumed to be die punching tools, whereas they just as reasonably could have been large pieces

[31] Breen, *Studies*, p. 120.
[32] Crosby, *Early Coins*, pp. 219-21, quote p. 220; Breen, *Studies*, p. 120.
[33] Trudgen, *CNL 1990B*, pp. 1193-94.
[34] Crosby, *Early Coins*, pp. 192-96, quote p. 193.
[35] Crosby, *Early Coins*, pp. 194, 199; Trudgen, *CNL 1984A*.
[36] Crosby, *Early Coins*, pp. 194-95.

of equipment such as a press or rollers.[37] Of the ten partners, Samuel Atlee was identified in the Vermont contract as a "Porter Brewer," Daniel Van Voorhis as a "Goldsmith," James Giles as an "Atty at Law," but no trade or profession is listed for James F. Atlee which is a curious omission if he were an accomplished engraver, the position traditionally assigned to him.[38] Further research into James F. Atlee's career may settle this nagging historical question.

Several punches, notable for their identifiable flaws and characteristics, have been traced through the dies for several different series of Confederation coppers as previously described, but there is nothing to confirm where or by whom the engraving was actually done. Crosby thought that the die cutter responsible for these common punches was "itinerant," going from place to place as work was requested.[39] Based on his association with Machin's Mills and the Rupert mint, in the evidence just cited, James F. Atlee is considered by many to be the artisan responsible for the group of spurious 1786-dated Connecticuts and related coinages. The belief is expanded further, also on the basis of punch-link evidence, to suggest that he was also employed for about eight months as the engraver at the Rahway, New Jersey, mint of Goadsby and Cox.[40] Although the hypothesis is possible, all that is certain is that the group of 1786 Connecticuts shares common punches with selected New Jersey and other coppers, there being no evidence to verify where or by whom the dies were cut or under whose auspices they were struck. In any case, this group of spurious 1786 Connecticuts could be minted at a greater profit than available to Buell, since a counterfeiting operation owed no royalties to any authority and was not bound to any weight specifications. The Birmingham experience was now being reenacted in America since there was considerable profit to be made at little risk.

In addition to the six unauthorized varieties, three other very primitive and rare 1786 Connecticut varieties are known. These Connecticut coppers are so crude in execution that it is doubtful that they would have inspired much credibility as a legitimate coin except with the illiterate and unsophisticated.[41]

Although first inspection of the "Hercules Head" of 1786 and 1787, probably minted by the Company for Coining Coppers, suggests a totally different style, it is actually a standard Mailed Bust Left design of 1785 and 1786 which had been significantly recut to produce the scowling face, thick neck, and rectangular chin of this familiar piece.[42]

A new Draped Bust Left copper appeared in 1786 from dies also prepared by Buell. Breen surmised that this new design was introduced when business arrangements for the Company for Coining Coppers were modified and their equipment was leased for seven weeks beginning September 10, 1786, to Mark Leavenworth, Isaac Baldwin, and William Leavenworth.[43] This was the first use of the Draped Bust Left motif; the varieties dated 1786 are rare, whereas the later 1787 Draped Left issues are by far the most common of all Connecticut coppers. Following

[37] This imprecise reference to "implements" has been the source of much confusion regarding the roles of James and Samuel Atlee in the Machin's Mills partnership. The vague language could have been a purposeful ruse to obfuscate the activities of the operation. "Implements" is defined as "the apparatus, or set of utensils, instruments, etc. employed in any trade or in executing any piece of work" (*O.E.D.*). A "tool" is "an instrument or apparatus necessary to a person in the practice of his vocation." Swift wrote in 1724, (*The Drapier's Letters*, III) "Wood hath ... his tools and implements prepared to coin six times as much more." (Swift, *Scott*, p. 149). In this usage "tools" appear to refer to die sinking equipment and "implements" to presses and rollers. In the context of the Machin's Mills contract, "implements" could have been heavier minting equipment rather than the finer tools for die preparation as traditionally assumed.

[38] Crosby, *Early Coins*, p. 196.

[39] Crosby, *Early Coins*, p. 288.

[40] Trudgen, *CNL 1987A*, pp. 967, 971.

[41] Two of these, Miller 1786 2.3-T and 2.4-U are plated in Breen's *Encyclopedia*, p. 68, 761 and 762. See Barnsley, *CNL 1964*, pp. 85-86. The 2.4-U is die linked with the counterfeit English halfpenny, Vlack 16-86A. A third primitive 1786 Connecticut counterfeit is 2.5-V (Trudgen, *CNL 1987A*, p. 973).

[42] Miller, *Connecticut*, p. 15; Barnsley, *CNL 1973*, p. 390.

[43] See also Hickcox, *Account*, in *RF-59*, *CNL 1977*, p. 591.

introduction of the Draped Bust Left design, this type was then minted by the Company for Coining Coppers for the remainder of 1786 and until June 1, 1787. On this date the business dissolved and the operation passed into the hands of Jarvis and Company, which included some of the previous partners, who reorganized the firm to mint Fugio coppers under a Federal contract. The principal in this organization, James Jarvis, was a well known figure and much is known about his career.[44] This new enterprise continued to mint Connecticut coppers from 1787 Draped Bust Left dies although there is no existing record that the state granted this new business specific authority to do so except as provided in the original franchise designed to run for a period "not exceeding five years." There must have been some tacit approval for the continuation of a mint after June 1, 1787, since on June 20, 1789, the legislature suspended the further production of copper coinage. More 1787 Connecticut coppers were emitted by far from Jarvis and Company, whatever their legal position, than came from the authorized Company for Coining Coppers. Of further interest is that the copper used by Jarvis for his Connecticut coins was fraudulently diverted from Federal stocks intended for the Fugio series.

Individual characteristics of this abundant 1787 Draped Bust Left coinage, described by Breen, help identify the mint of origin, whether the Company for Coining Coppers prior to June 1, 1787, or Jarvis and Company which operated until the Fall of 1788. Those earlier 1787 Draped Bust Left coppers attributed to the Company for Coining Coppers have large letters in their legends, whereas those later issues from Jarvis and Company have small letters. The abundant 1787 Draped Bust Left Connecticut series with small letters from the Jarvis Mint is not a homogeneous group since significant weight differences exist between certain varieties. Specifically those 1787 coppers characterized by small crosses in both obverse and reverse legends (Miller obverses 17, 18, 19, 21, 22, 24, 38, 45, 46, and 48 and reverses g, BB, CC, DD, FF, and GG) and those with both obverse and reverse fleurons (Miller 34, 36, 37, 39, and 56 with e, h, i, k, l, cc, ee, ff, HH, and RR) are significantly heavier than the remaining Draped Bust Left population. The remainder of the small lettered Jarvis coppers, which are lighter in weight, possess cinquefoils in the legends, an ornament also found on the Fugio cents. In earlier research, Breen ascertained that the order of emission within the small lettered 1787 Draped Bust Left issues began with the varieties with crosses, followed by those with fleurons, and was concluded by the very large population with cinquefoils, a sequence characterized by decreasing planchet weight.[45] This suggests that as the 1787 Draped Bust Left coinages progressed, the average coin weight lessened with diminished regard for the authorized 144 grain requirement. A number of these 1787 Draped Bust Left hubs were used again in 1788 with new reverses, but these, and all other 1788-dated Connecticut coppers, weighed substantially below the required 144 grains. The significance of these weight differences will be discussed at length in Chapter Eight.[46]

Breen has further calculated the total output of the Company for Coining Coppers at 1,407,000 for the years 1785 to 1787, while Jarvis and Company produced about 3,500,000 Connecticut coppers from 1787 to 1788.[47] With about five million coins thus accounted for, a conservative estimate of Connecticut coppers minted from all sources would exceed seven million. While there are 355 die combinations, many of these dies probably fractured very early in use since some of these varieties are very rare today.

At least three other illegal mints produced Connecticut coppers bearing the date 1787, although the date inscribed carries no guarantee as to the actual year of manufacture. The first

[44] Douglas, *CNL, 1969*.
[45] Breen, *Studies*, p. 128.
[46] Mossman, *CNL 1990*, pp. 1144-47, and *Connecticut Coppers*.
[47] Breen, *Studies*, pp. 125, 127; *E.A.C. 1975*, p. 25. Reviewing recent auction experience, it appears that 1787 Connecticut coppers from the Company for Coining Coppers, characterized by larger letters in the legends, are about one-eighth as common as those from the Jarvis mint bearing the smaller letters.

of these obviously contemporary counterfeit pieces is nicknamed the "Bull Head," "Muttonhead," or "Bradford Head," after a seeming likeness to the second governor of the Plymouth Colony, William Bradford. The "Muttonhead" is found in three obverse die states representing significant reworkings of the original with varying degrees of boldness in the legends. A clue as to the location of the clandestine operation responsible for this issue is provided by examination of the number punches for the date and the artistic style of the central devices. These bear striking similarity to those used by the New York City mint of John Bailey on his NOVA EBORAC and EXCELSIOR coppers.[48] However, caution must be exercised in the interpretation of punch-link evidence derived only from naked-eye examination unless corroborated by more precise photographic techniques.[49]

There are four distinct 1787 dated Connecticut die combinations from a different source than those already discussed. This group is punch-linked with coppers believed to have come from the Morristown, New Jersey, mint of Walter Mould. These four Connecticut and the Morristown varieties all demonstrate by naked-eye examination a characteristic horseshoe shaped "U." However, using the superposition technique of enlarged transparent films, it becomes the "N," "C," and "A" punches which are actually identical, and not the "U" punch as has been traditionally asserted.[50] An interesting and very common member of this Connecticut series is Miller 4-L, the so-called "Horned Bust," which exhibits the gradual emergence of a die break in the central left field in front of the obverse figure's armor. As this die flaw enlarges, it runs into the figure's mail so that subsequent impressions look like a horn emanating from the chest (see fig. 53).[51]

The last illegal location responsible for 1787-dated Connecticut coppers is considered to have been the mint of Captain Thomas Machin. The attribution of some 1787-dated Connecticut coppers to this mint is based on the fact these coppers possess common punches and a bust style typical of the the legal Vermont bust right coppers and the imitation English halfpence, both possibly the work of James F. Atlee. While there is nothing that documents who actually engraved these similar appearing figures, from naked-eye observation there is certainly a common theme to various dies suggesting the same author. Machin's Mills was particularly active in minting Connecticut coppers dated 1788 despite the fact that no legal authority existed for manufacturing coins of that date. It is speculated that this operation bought out, or otherwise acquired, the existing equipment of Walter Mould, Jarvis and Company, and the remaining dies by Abel Buell, including the mailed bust left Triple Leaves hubs which are described below. The procurement of the discarded equipment by Machin is the most logical explanation for the existence of so many muled 1788-dated coins struck from combined dies from so many different sources.

The greatest mystery surrounds the provenance of the mailed bust left Triple Leaves design of 1787 and 1788. The hubs from which these dies were prepared were the work of Abel Buell who apparently did not pass them along to Jarvis and Company when the Company for Coining Coppers dissolved. When Buell departed for England in early 1789, it is supposed that he gave these Triple Leaves hubs to his son, Benjamin, who minted some 1787-dated varieties from a presently unknown location early in 1789, despite their 1787 date. After minting a few coppers from his father's Triple Leaves hubs, Benjamin seemingly retired from minting activies and relinquished his residual gear, including the hubs, to Captain Machin. The Machin organization muled some of Buell's Triple Leaves obverse dies with new reverses, attributed to James F. Atlee, to produce several die varieties of 1788-dated Connecticut coppers.

[48] Barnsley, *CNL 1973*, pp. 388-89, 392-94; Trudgen, *RCR 63*.

[49] Naked-eye evidence is in "the eye of the beholder." Newer methods, such as enlarged photographic film overlay and computer imaged digital, or background subtraction techniques will no doubt become future tools for analytic numismatics to facilitate punch-link verification.

[50] Footnote to lot 1648, *Saccone*, by Michael Hodder.

[51] Barnsley, *CNL 1973*, p. 385.

The practice of overstriking new coins on existing coppers occurred in the 1788 Connecticut series, when Constellatio Nova coppers and, rarely, counterfeit Massachusetts cents, were used as host coins for Connecticut coppers, instead of using new planchets. This was an economy measure whereby the minter avoided the cost of planchet preparation by feeding preexisting coins of the correct size into the presses where they received a new stamp. It was particularly advantageous when the host coins were less valuable than the newly stamped coppers, since the profit margin derived from the manufacture of the new money could be substantially increased. The stratagem of overstriking a copper coin of higher commercial value on a lighter, cheaper coin was not an original one in the colonies. Batty described a 1773 counterfeit English halfpenny struck over a genuine Irish halfpenny as a host coin.[52] The differential in exchange rates between England and Ireland would have allowed an immediate 9.25% profit for the entrepreneur.[53]

A perusal of the Connecticut series not only reveals an impressive number of bust styles but also what appears to be at first glance misspelled legends such as AUCIORI, AUCTOBI, AUCTOPI, CONNFC, CONNLC, FNDE, INDL, IIB, and LIR. These so-called blundered legends have been scrutinized by Edward R. Barnsley who presents convincing evidence that these "misspellings" are not orthographic errors committed by some untutored diesinker, but rather the substitution of similar letters when the proper letter punch required to complete the inscription was unavailable and presumably broken.[54] "B" appears to be the most frequently missing letter. The die maker would fashion missing letters out of resources at hand, such as developing an "E" from an "F" or a "B" from a "P". Barnsley concluded that some blunders may actually have been unfinished improvisations where, for example, the "L" was not hand finished into an "E" as in INDL and CONNLC. The one blunder which Barnsley postulates as a true error is FNDE for INDE, for which no attempted correction is evident. Other errors were corrected by overpunching, the most notable being the dates 1787 over 1877, and 1787 over 1788. Since numbers in the dates were punched into the die one at a time, the first error occurred when the middle two digits were reversed and then rectified. The second error resulted from a perseveration with the "8" number punch, which was then corrected when the appropriate "7" was punched over the erroneous final "8," "or perhaps the calendar year was inadvertently entered, rather than the fictitious 1787."[55] In Chapter Eight there is an extensive evaluation of the average weights of the Confederation issues to determine if the various mints fulfilled their obligation to produce full weight coppers designed to improve the quality of the circulating small change medium. Within the Connecticut series, it will be demonstrated that the Company for Coining Coppers was conscientious in its duty, but after the operation was assumed by Jarvis and Company, the coins generally became lighter. The 1786 and 1787 coppers from illegal mints and any coppers dated 1788 were below the authorized 144 grains, with many of the latter overstruck on light host coins. The promise of good Connecticut coppers to replace the counterfeit halfpence was lost as clandestine mints just added to the glut of inferior coins.

NEW JERSEY COPPERS

The year following the award of the Connecticut mint franchise, a similar proposal reached the New Jersey legislature. The declaration to the enabling act, which was passed on June 1, 1786, summarized the problem succinctly.

[52] Batty, *Descriptive Catalogue*, vol. 3, p. 945, 3340.
[53] McCusker, *Money and Exchange*, p. 34.
[54] Barnsley, *CNL 1972*.
[55] Michael Hodder, personal communication.

Fig. 56: 1788 Connecticut Coppers Overstruck on Host Coins.
(a) 1788 Miller 5-B.2 (119.0 grains) overstruck on a Constellatio Nova copper, the stars of the host coin being apparent on the obverse figure and the wreath of the host coin encircling the seated Connecticut reverse figure. The 1788 Mailed Bust Right varieties, Miller 3, 4, and 5, are usually overstruck on Constellatio Nova coppers, invariably dated 1785 (see fig. 55aa and Appendix 2) (Table 21, no. 18b; Table 28).

(b) 1788 Miller 16.3-N (109.7 grains) overstruck on a counterfeit Massachusetts cent, probably 1787 Crosby 1-B, a coin also attributed to the Machin's Mills mint. This rare overstrike clearly shows the wings of the Massachusetts eagle above and beneath the obverse figure, while the feet of the Massachusetts Indian extend to the right of the shield of the seated reverse effigy (Table 21, no. 17, and n. h; Table 28).

(c) 1788 Miller 10-C (119.9 grains), this Triple Leaves variety is typically found struck on a Constellatio Nova copper. On this specimen, the CONST of CONSTELLATIO is visible at the reverse date (Table 21, no. 16e; Table 28).

> Whereas Copper Coin now current and passing in this State consists mostly of base Metal, and of copper so small and light as to be of very little real value, whereby the Citizens of the State are subject to manifest loss and inconvenience, and are liable to be greatly defrauded: for remedy whereof ....[56]

The act empowered Walter Mould, Thomas Goadsby and Albion Cox to mint three million copper coins of 150 grains pure copper over the next two years.[57] A 10% royalty was payable to the state for the privilege of minting these coppers which were to pass at 15 to the New Jersey shilling. The motif selected for most New Jersey coppers depicts a horse's head facing right above a plow on the obverse, surrounded by the legend NOVA CAESAREA and the date below. The legend NOVA CAESAREA for New Jersey, refers to the fact that the Island of Jersey in the English Channel, for which the state was named, was once called Caesar's Island, the name *Jersey* being a corruption of Caesarea.[58] The reverse design has an American shield with the peripheral inscription E PLURIBUS UNUM, the first use of our national motto on coins, later adopted for use on Federal coinage starting with the gold issues of 1796.

The New Jersey mint was established in a Rahway mill leased from Daniel Marsh; the rent guaranteed by Matthias Ogden, who acted as bondsman. From the beginning, the partnership fared poorly because Mould failed to post his one third share of the surety bond. The other two partners petitioned the Legislature to allow them to pursue their own two-thirds interest in the franchise independently of Mould. The request was approved on November 22, 1786, authorizing Goadsby and Cox to mint two million coppers, who then continued their project at Rahway. Mould was allowed to mint his one-third portion of the coinage and he established his solo operation at Morristown but could not proceed until January 19, 1787, when he

[56] Crosby, *Early Coins*, p. 278.

[57] The principle references used for New Jersey coinage are as follows: Anton, *CNL 1975*; *Weimer and Hirt*; Sipsey, *CNL 1964*; Douglas, *CNL 1968*; Maris, *New Jersey*; Crosby, *Early Coins*, pp. 275-88; Breen, *CNL 1969*; Breen, *Encyclopedia*; Trudgen, *CNL 1988*; and *Taylor*.

[58] Frey, *CW 1979*.

finally secured his own bond. The Rahway mint had a series of legal problems when its principals became entangled in a number of law suits.[59] There is no clear record of the engravers responsible for the Rahway mint dies, although there has been an attempt to link this work to James F. Atlee, but the claim is refuted by evidence advanced by both Sipsey and Hodder.[60] In fact, Sipsey suggests it would have been more likely that the New York City gold and silversmiths, Daniel Van Voorhis and William Coley, were the artists who cut the New Jersey dies for Albion Cox, and not Atlee. The horse "head left" varieties have been attributed also to the Rahway mint but again the engraver has not been identified. Thomas Goadsby has been mentioned but there is no evidence that he was an engraver or possessed the technical skills necessary for the task. Problems continued at the Rahway mint and on June 7, 1788, the equipment was placed by court order in the custody of the bondsman, Matthias Ogden, who in June 1789, relocated the equipment to Elizabethtown and continued production there in association with Gilbert Rindell. Despite the unsettled business environment, "Goadsby and Cox," first by the partnership and next under the auspices of Ogden and Rindell, either completed the franchise for two million coppers by July 3, 1788, or paid the required 300,000 coppers by that date.[61] It is evident that Ogden illegally exceeded the franchise by producing more New Jersey coins at his Elizabethtown location well into 1790. Many of his coppers were overstruck on existing lighter weight coins using leftover Rahway dies. He must have had a supply of original planchets as well, since not all coppers were impressed on existing host coins.

Mould continued his work at Morristown and by August 1788, fulfilled his authorized allotment of one million coppers.[62] The Morristown mint produced the large planchet New Jersey coppers; although the die sinkers are undocumented, it could have been Mould, himself, since he was reputed to have worked in Birmingham, possibly as an engraver, prior to his arrival in America. The 1788-dated Morristown coppers are generally inferior in quality and workmanship to the 1787 varieties. There is a series of 1787 Connecticut coppers punch linked to the Morristown output but the circumstances concerning these issues are unknown. Again by tracing dies and punches, it has been proposed that some of Mould's engraving tools came into the possession of Machin's Mills where they were later used.

Other New Jersey coppers of 1788 appear to be the work of John Bailey of New York City, the partner of Ephraim Brasher, well known for his famous Brasher gold doubloon. Recent research by Trudgen reveals that Bailey was a subcontractor for New Jersey coppers working most probably on the behalf of Walter Mould.[63] On two occasions, Bailey acted as surety for Mould in law suits. The New Jersey coppers attributed to Bailey bear a characteristic "running horse" mint mark in the reverse legend.[64] These 1788 New Jersey coins are said to be punch linked to the Nova Eborac and Excelsior coppers and to the famous Brasher gold doubloon. Of less certain origin is the contemporary counterfeit nicknamed the "Serpent Head" (Maris 54-k) which has been attributed to a Mr. Hatfield of Elizabethtown.

Considerable controversy attends the role of Machin's Mills in the manufacture of New Jersey coppers and at least two lines of speculation have been advanced, each supported by documentary evidence. A book published in 1891, *Newburgh: Her Institutions, Industries, and Leading Citizens*, stated that Captain Machin's mint was the source of the first coins bearing the motto E PLURIBUS UNUM.[65] Crosby quoted Charles I. Bushnell who wrote that some coppers from the mint bore the figure of a plough, a possible reference to either Vermont or New Jersey

[59] Hodder, *CNL 1991*, pp. 1223-31; Williamson, *CNL 1980*; Trudgen, *CNL 1990B*.
[60] Hodder, *CNL 1991*, pp. 1223-31; Sipsey, *CNL 1964*, pp. 122-23.
[61] Breen, *CNL 1970*, pp. 296-97.
[62] Breen, *CNL 1970*, pp. 295-96.
[63] Trudgen, *CNL 1990A*, pp. 1160-65.
[64] Breen, *ANS Centennial*.
[65] Trudgen, *CNL 1984A*, pp. 881, 883.

coppers.[66] Some letters on the New Jersey "Camel Heads" (Maris 56 to 58-n) were punched by tools, originally the property of Jarvis and Company, which, when discarded, eventually came into Machin's possession. These same letter punches were used on some 1788 Connecticut coppers considered the work of Atlee and struck at Machin's Mills. For these several reasons it is held that Atlee engraved and minted the New Jersey "Camel Heads" at Machin's Mills using some of the same ex-Jarvis punches, the same ones with which it is supposed Atlee prepared some 1788 Connecticut dies.[67] The other explanation is that Atlee made the "camel head" dies for the Elizabethtown mint of Matthias Ogden.[68] Atlee, or whoever was the die sinker for the "camel heads" series, could have traveled widely selling his services to various mints without requiring any permanent residence at a specific location, hence the artist and the mint do not have to coincide geographically. There are other reasons, based on the overstriking characteristics of the "camel heads," which make Machin's Mills a less likely place of origin for this very sizable group of New Jersey coppers.

Fig. 57: New Jersey Coppers.
(a) Typical 1786 and 1787-dated copper from the Rahway mint, Maris 14-J (147.8 grains) (Table 21, no. 4; Chart 11).

(b) One of the three varieties of "Horse Head Left" coppers from the Rahway mint; note the greater detail on the ploughshare, Maris 50-f (141.7 grains) (Table 21, no. 4b; Chart 12).

(c) Large planchet copper typical of 1787 varieties from the Morristown mint, Maris 63-q (141.5 grains) (Table 21, no. 5c; Chart 15).

(d) 1788 coppers attributed to the Morristown mint were typically lighter and inferior to the 1787 issues, except for the Maris 67-v variety which approached full weight, Maris 65-u (124.1 grains) (Table 21, no. 5d; Chart 16).

[66] Crosby, *Early Coins*, p. 191.
[67] Breen, *CNL 1969*, p. 256.
[68] Anton, *CNL 1975*, pp. 499-501.

(e) Copper attributed to the Elizabethtown mint overstruck on a counterfeit George III halfpenny; note the NNIA of BRITANNIA visible on the obverse, and the II RE of III REX on the reverse (the host bust is facing right so this must be George III). This specimen has an "X" cancellation graffito, Maris 73-aa (120.5 grains) (Table 21, no. 6b; Table 29).

(f) 1788 New Jersey copper attributed to Bailey's mint with the horse/fox mint mark visible in the lower left reverse legend, Maris 78-dd (150.6 grains) (Table 21, no. 7; Chart 14).

(g) Contemporary 1787 New Jersey counterfeit "Serpent Head" attributed to Mr. Hatfield's mint: Maris 54-k (92.4 grains) (Table 21, no. 8).

(h) Maris 56-n is the most common of all Confederation coppers and was overstruck on many types of lighter host coins (see Appendix 2). This specimen was struck over a 1787 Connecticut Miller 30-hh.1 whose residual legends, including the ETLIR reverse, are clearly evident (129.6 grains) (Table 21, no. 9; Table 29).

The standard reference for the attribution of New Jersey coppers was published by Dr. Edward Maris in 1880. Considering the number of engravers who produced New Jersey dies, there is a surprising level of consistency in design among the coins except for the head left obverses and the two rare obverse patterns, Maris 7 and 8. Maris described the more complex plough on Head Left coppers by drawing attention to the detail of the coulter which "after widening, is joined to the share, which is made out of a sword beaten into proper shape," the engraver obviously yielding to the entreaties of the Old Testament prophets.[69] There are a number of rare contemporary counterfeits (Maris-79, 80, 81, 83, and 84) from unknown sources but the common "serpent head," supposedly by Hatfield, was manufactured in fairly large numbers. The total number of New Jersey coppers includes the three million authorized coins in addition to those minted independently by Ogden at Rahway and Elizabethtown, the prolific Maris 56 to 58-n group, plus those attributed to Bailey and Hatfield sources. A conservative estimate of New Jersey coppers from all mints would be, therefore, in the range of four million or more pieces.

The same irony attended the last issues of New Jersey coppers as was observed in the Connecticut series. The enabling legislation for both mints decried the abundance of counterfeits in circulation and the fraud inflicted on the people, especially the poor, "honest & unsuspicious

[69] Maris, *New Jersey*, p. 13; Isaiah 2:4 and Micah 4:3, "... and they shall beat their swords into ploughshares and their spears into pruning hooks ...."

Citizens."[70] Following the expiration of the legal franchises in both states, coining fell into the hands of other entrepreneurs who flooded commerce with their own lightweight products, notwithstanding the fact that coppers had the appropriate designs and labels. In New Jersey, Matthias Ogden, a celebrated Revolutionary War hero, after his less than satisfactory business experience with the authorized mints, concluded his coining career in Elizabethtown after taking over the Rahway mint franchise. Here, Ogden followed the popular practice of overstriking New Jersey emblems on existing coins which were significantly lighter than the prescribed 150 grains although he did use some original planchets which were likewise underweight. The Connecticut coinage had also been adulterated with lightweight money from other still unidentified clandestine operations. Lightweight coppers, rather than being suppressed by these state mints, were paradoxically encouraged.

Recent work by Hodder on New Jersey die emission sequences of the Maris J, U, f, and g families of reverse dies has exploded some of the traditional concepts about the minting practices of these early coiners.[71] The J reverse for the Rahway mint was a very durable die since it survived long enough to be married to ten different obverses. In the course of its life, progressive breaks, clash marks, or other signs of die failure occurred resulting in the possible identification of five distinct J reverse die states. These physical markers provide the means for the relative chronological dating of when the J die was combined with the various observes. This study was expanded to include the U reverse and the 15 and 33 obverses, all of which have inherent deformities from progressive die injury.

One might intuitively think that the colonial mintmaster placed a pair of dies in the press and stamped them until one or both of the dies failed. A spent die would then be retired or discarded, and any surviving die partner, if still serviceable, would then be combined with a new mate, and so on. Sometimes two completely new dies would be employed and removed simultaneously. The assumption would be that the use of dies followed a relatively orderly and logical paradigm. On the contrary, Hodder's investigations demonstrate that nine of the ten obverse dies were used intermittently throughout the entire life of the J reverse; one obverse die was not spent before another was placed into service, and then the former one was called out of retirement in a haphazard sequence for yet another session in the press. In only one instance, Maris 15-J, was the obverse used with only one stage of the reverse, never to be called upon again. Maris 34-J, in contrast, was found married to all five J reverse conditions, meaning that 34-J coppers were periodically minted from the earliest days of the Rahway mint in 1787 into 1790 by which time the equipment had been relinquished to Ogden in Elizabethtown.

Obverse dates on these coppers are inconsequential and provide no indication as to when the coin was actually struck. A few of the 1786-dated coppers studied by Hodder could have been minted in that year, but the majority were made from 1787 into 1790. Conversely, a few 1787-dated coins, Maris 33-U for example, could possibly have been minted in 1786. At best, the date may only be a useful guide to when the die was prepared. Examination of the J die states also reveals that coins were being simultaneously overstruck on host coins and struck on original planchets after mid-1789 when the operation moved from Rahway to Elizabethtown. Ogden obviously had a source for new copper. With a few notable exceptions which are still being studied, a gradual decrease in weight from the authorized standard of 150 grains has been observed within these families over the passage of time. When the Rahway mint first opened in November 1786, until the spring of 1787, the average weight of J family coppers was 147.4 ± 7.9 grains, but by the closing bell in 1790, the weight decreased to a final low of 134.9 ± 15.3 grains. These data exclude any overstruck coins. Not only did the average weight decrease during that period, but the standard deviation increased. This increase in the standard deviation, a measure of dispersion more sensitive than the range, indicates a wider weight range

[70] Crosby, *Early Coins*, p. 207.
[71] Hodder, *AJN 1989*; Hodder, *CNL 1989*; Hodder, *N.J. Reverse "U"* .

or lack of conformity in weight within the planchet population, another clue as to the relaxation of quality standards at the mint operation with the passage of time.

New research on New Jersey coppers supports the notion that it is hazardous to assign with certainty the facility where the coins were actually minted. Further work with other traceable dies may confirm this mosaic pattern of emission sequence for other Rahway coppers. What does become evident is that many more coppers, once considered the products of the Rahway mint, were actually minted by Ogden after he took control of the operation and moved to Elizabethtown in mid-1789. This bench mark is based on the occurrence of overstruck coppers midway in the useful life of the J reverse as determined by the physical configuration of the die. This subject is far more complex than once considered and requires further research for elucidation.

VERMONT COPPERS

Although by an Act of June 15, 1785, Vermont was actually the first American jurisdiction to authorize a local mint for the production of coppers, the territory was not part of the Confederation but rather a self-proclaimed, independent republic. Vermont was not one of the original colonies; its lands were claimed both by New Hampshire and New York; the Crown recognized the ownership by the latter. Ethan Allen and his Green Mountain Boys were organized to defend land titles granted by New Hampshire against the intrusion of New York. The dispute became of secondary importance during the Revolution when all forces were united against the English. Ignoring the authority of both its neighbors, Vermont declared itself a republic on January 15, 1777, and remained so until admission into the Union on March 4, 1791. It was under the independent regime that copper coins were minted dated 1785 to 1788.[72]

Fig. 58: Vermont landscape copper representative of the six varieties minted at Rupert and dated for 1785 and 1786. The state legend varied from VERMONTS, VERMONTIS and VERMONTENSIUM, RR-4 (116.5 grains) (Table 21, no. 20a; Chart 27).

The franchise to produce Vermont coppers was awarded to Reuben Harmon, Jr., of Rupert, who engaged a New York engraver, presumably the goldsmith, William Coley, to prepare the dies. The first issues were the handsome landscape types of 1785 and 1786, featuring the sun rising to the right above a wooded hill with a plow facing left in the foreground, the inscription "Republic of Vermont," in various Latin forms, and the date surround the design. The reverse simulates the Constellatio Nova coppers as it depicts a central eye of Providence with rays radiating to the periphery.[73] The legend, STELLA QUARTA DECIMA, "The Fourteenth Star," alluded to the Republic's ambition to become the fourteenth state. The originally prescribed

[72] The major references for the history of Vermont coinage are as follows: Crosby, *Early Coins*, pp. 177-202; Bressett, *Studies*; Richardson, *Num 1947*; Partridge, *RHSQ 1979*.

[73] There has been an attempt to link the 1785 and 1786 Vermont landscapes by Coley to the Constellatio Nova coppers from Birmingham and prove a common source. Although very similar, the reverses on these two series are not identical. See Sipsey, *CNL 1965*, pp. 155, 170-71. One possible explanation is that Coley was influenced in the Vermont reverse design by Mould, since both Coley and Mould were thought to be in New York City at the same time.

weight of 160 grains was unrealistically heavy and soon was reduced to 111 grains. Two successive five year franchises were contracted. During the first five years no royalties were required, but over the second, a 2.5% fee was payable to the Republic.

In 1786 an obverse bust design was adopted with new legends, AUCTORI VERMON, "By the Authority of Vermont." The seated reverse figure was a likeness of the contemporary English halfpenny with the inscription, INDE ET LIB, very much like the Connecticut coinage. There has been discussion of the motivation that prompted the abrupt change in the appearance from the landscape to the bust motif. The traditional reasoning was that figures like the current English halfpence would be familiar and, therefore, more acceptable to the population. The argument is weak since the average person showed no reluctance to accept Massachusetts or New Jersey coppers, both of which displayed originality in their designs. Additionally, since people had felt cheated by so many counterfeit English coppers, they might have had more faith in something distinct and obviously genuine. Bonjour postulates that the prime reason for the change was an expedient to obtain dies from the experienced Connecticut die cutter, Abel Buell.[74] No formal connection with Buell ever materialized, perhaps because his energies were consumed by the Fugio project, and so the Rupert mint sought assistance elsewhere.

One of the new 1786 designs was the famous bust right "Baby Head" which has a striking similarity to the counterfeit 1786 Connecticut "Large Head" (1786 Miller 3-D), speculatively attributed to Atlee while he was still in New York City inferring that Coley copied his work. The Vermont bust left coppers of 1786 and early 1787 closely resemble the standard Connecticut Mailed Bust Left series prepared by Abel Buell and debate continues as to the identity of the actual engravers and die sinkers for these early Vermont issues.[75] Some of this mystery has been unraveled in unpublished studies by Spilman who demonstrates that these Vermont coppers were produced from Buell's genuine 1786 Connecticut

> ... "complex" hubs from which the legend letters and border details were ground away and the hair on the head of the obverse bust also "cut" or shortened by grinding. The date element on the reverse was retained ... note the shape of the 6 in the date element. The dies were sunk from these altered hubs and the Vermont legends were added on the individual dies .... The reverse figure on Ryder-Richardson 11 [Bressett 9-H] is badly double hubbed (the legend letters are not) indicating inexperienced die sinking.[76]

Fig. 59:
(a) "Baby Head" whose design is thought by some to have been influenced by the 1786 Connecticut Miller 3-D.1. Planchet flaws due to impurities in the locally mined copper are very common on all these early Vermont coppers, RR-9 (117.6 grains) (Table 21, no. 20b).

(b) There are three Bust Left issues, the single 1787 variety, RR-15, being very rare due to early fracture of the reverse die through the date. This series is similar in design to the 1785 and 1786 Connecticut Mailed Bust Left series, RR-11 (114.2 grains) (Table 21, no. 20b).

[74] Bonjour, *Num 1987*.
[75] Crosby, *Early Coins*, pp. 188-89; Bressett, *Studies*, pp. 175-76; Breen, *Studies*, p. 113.
[76] Personal communication, March 25, 1986.

(c) The standard Bust Right issues were minted at the Rupert facility in both 1787 and 1788. Appendix 2 lists those which were commonly overstruck on 1785 Constellatio Nova coppers. The remainder, dated 1788, were from Machin's Mills where many, including the following RR-18, were overstruck on counterfeit Irish halfpence. The obverse busts on this series have an unmistakable familial resemblance to many imitation English halfpence and certain Connecticut coppers from the same mint, RR-21 (122.1 grains) (Table 21, no. 20c; Chart 28).

(d) GEORGIUS III REX Vermont copper, RR-31 (110.0 grains) has obverse legends in keeping with the Machin's Mills imitation halfpence series while it shares a reverse with several other Vermont issues (RR-25, 28, and 29) and the 1788 Connecticut Miller 1-I (Table 21, no. 21a; Chart 29).

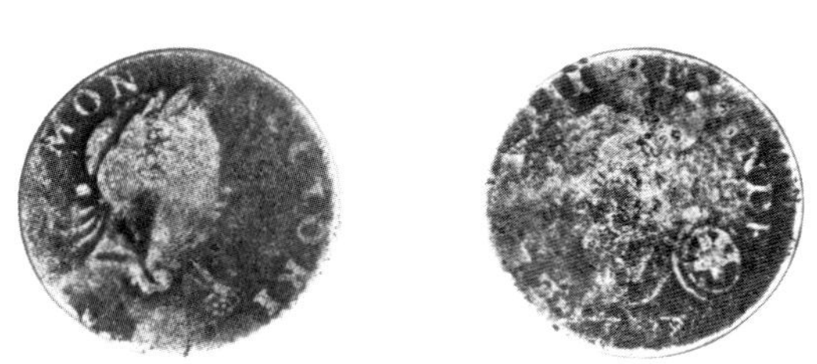

(e) This 1788 Vermont RR-18 (106.2 grains) from Machin's Mills was overstruck on a counterfeit Irish halfpenny (usually dated 1781 or 1782) remarkable for its deficient weight (genuine Irish halfpence weigh 134.6 grains). The III REX is visible over the reverse seated figure's head (Table 21, no. 21c; Table 27).

The reverse of Ryder-Richardson 15 (Bressett 9-I) was very poorly executed and a die break immediately occurred which obliterated the date causing its early abandonment and, hence, its extreme rarity. The extensive recutting used to create these Vermont dies is reminiscent of the Connecticut "Hercules Head" which was also altered from the Mailed Bust Left complex hub.

In 1787, the Rupert enterprise was expanded by Harmon to include Coley, who had moved from New York. This occurred at the same time that Captain Thomas Machin was developing his operation in Newburgh, and an agreement was reached between the Rupert and Newburgh mints providing for profit sharing arrangements and the authority to produce Vermont coppers legally at Machin's Mills. Daniel Van Voorhis, the New York goldsmith, was also a party to this contract. The 1787 and 1788 Vermont Bust Right dies, the illegal 1786 Connecticut coppers, and the imitation English halfpence from Newburgh all have a "familial" resemblance and are punch linked together. One 1788 Vermont copper, Ryder-Richardson 27 or Bressett 18-W, in particular, has both obverse and reverse "device punch identity" with certain imitation British halfpence and the 1788 Connecticut Miller 2-D reverse, confirming a common origin to this sundry group of coppers.[77] The reverse shields of 1787 and 1788 Vermont Bust Right coppers, in common with the imitation halfpence, display the crosses of St. Andrew and St. George whereas previous Vermont bust coppers and the entire Connecticut series either have a plain shield or a local emblem. The association between the later Vermont coinages and the Machin's Mills partnership is confirmed both by documentary and numismatic evidence.

Both Rupert and, later, Newburgh used a ready made source of planchets by overstriking other coppers with their Vermont designs. From the Rupert facility, 1785-dated Constellatio Nova coppers, which were heavier than the required 111 grains, are frequently encountered as undertypes for 1787 Bust Right issues.[78] A New York Act of April 20, 1787, designed to curb the

[77] Newman, *ANS Centennial*.

[78] There is no "authorized" weight for Constellatio Nova coppers but the average weight of 74 high grade specimens is 118.1 ± 11.4 grains. See Table 21.

circulation of coppers under 145.8 grains, effective August 1, 1787, was likely responsible for the ready availability of these otherwise unwanted Constellatio Nova pieces.[79] As the commercial value for these unauthorized coppers dropped because of regulation, such coins assumed a greater role as ready-made planchets than as inflated token money. When the Rupert mint closed early in 1789, the serviceable equipment was removed to Newburgh where some still workable Rupert dies were used to overstrike counterfeit Irish halfpence dated 1781 and 1782, substantial numbers of which were catalogued in the Batty collection.[80] The assumption is made that these spurious coppers arrived here from Ireland and were bought up in bulk by the Machin's facility, which used them solely for Vermont host coins.

The classification of Vermont coppers follows three schemes. The oldest one is by Hillyer Ryder, published in 1919,[81] and later expanded by John M. Richardson; the second was "issued about 1957 by Kenneth E. Bressett, using a numbering system devised by Walter Breen";[82] the last system of attribution, also by Bressett, arranges the obverse and reverse combinations in order of use.

While there is no available census as to the number of Vermont coppers minted, Bressett has estimated that there are no more than 5000 specimens of all the 40 die combinations in existence today. A rare counterfeit, designated as Ryder-Richardson 5, is known struck from dies and a second, more common variety, is cast from the first. The origin and source of these pieces is unknown.[83]

MACHIN'S MILLS COINAGE

Much has been said previously about Captain Thomas Machin. His mills seem to have been the graveyard for other defunct coining operations since leftover minting equipment apparently wound up in his possession. This interesting figure in early American numismatics was born in England in 1744 where he trained as an artillery cadet and civil engineer.[84] He emigrated to New York in 1772 and eventually moved to Boston where his sympathies supported the patriot cause. His combined talents were used in the fortification of Bunker Hill and later in the defense of the Hudson River where he engineered the successful installation of a chain over the river at West Point to impede the advance of the English fleet. He was wounded in the War where he served as an engineer, artilleryman, and recruiter. Following discharge after eight years of service, he entered civilian life and built a number of water-powered mills. In March 1787, Machin unsuccessfully petitioned to mint coins for the State of New York. On April 18, 1787, he formed a partnership with a number of individuals, including James F. Atlee, to mint coins in a mill he had previously erected in Newburgh, New York. The mint may have been erected in the confident expectation of providing a New York coinage, a proposal which was defeated. While no New York coinage was ever authorized, the Machin's Mills group did negotiate an arrangement with the legal Rupert, Vermont, mint on June 7, 1787, to assist them with their contract.

[79] See Crosby, *Early Coins*, pp. 294-96, for text of this legislation.

[80] More Vermont coppers overstruck on Irish halfpence must be examined to determine whether any regal Irish host coins were ever used. Eleven lower grade Vermont overstruck coppers, Ryder-Richardson 18 and 25, averaged 103.7 ± 15.9 grains, whereas regal Irish halfpence were minted at 134.6 grains. Twenty-one Irish counterfeits of various dates, averaging 106.7 ± 12.6 grains, are recorded in Table 21. Batty counted 64 varieties of 1781 Irish halfpence, at least 8 of which were cast counterfeits. For the following year, his collection contained 50 varieties, 5 of which were spurious, 4 being cast and 1 die struck. As with the English series of counterfeits, there were three purely fictitious dates, 1772, 1773, and 1783 (Batty, *Descriptive Catalogue*, vol. 3, pp. 1036-46).

[81] Ryder, *AJN 1919*, and Ryder, *New England*.

[82] *E.A.C. 1975*, p. 88.

[83] Anton, *RCR 68*.

[84] Trudgen, *CNL 1983* and *CNL 1984A* provide an excellent description of Captain Machin and his mint. Peters, *Num 1986*, has good illustrations of this interesting series.

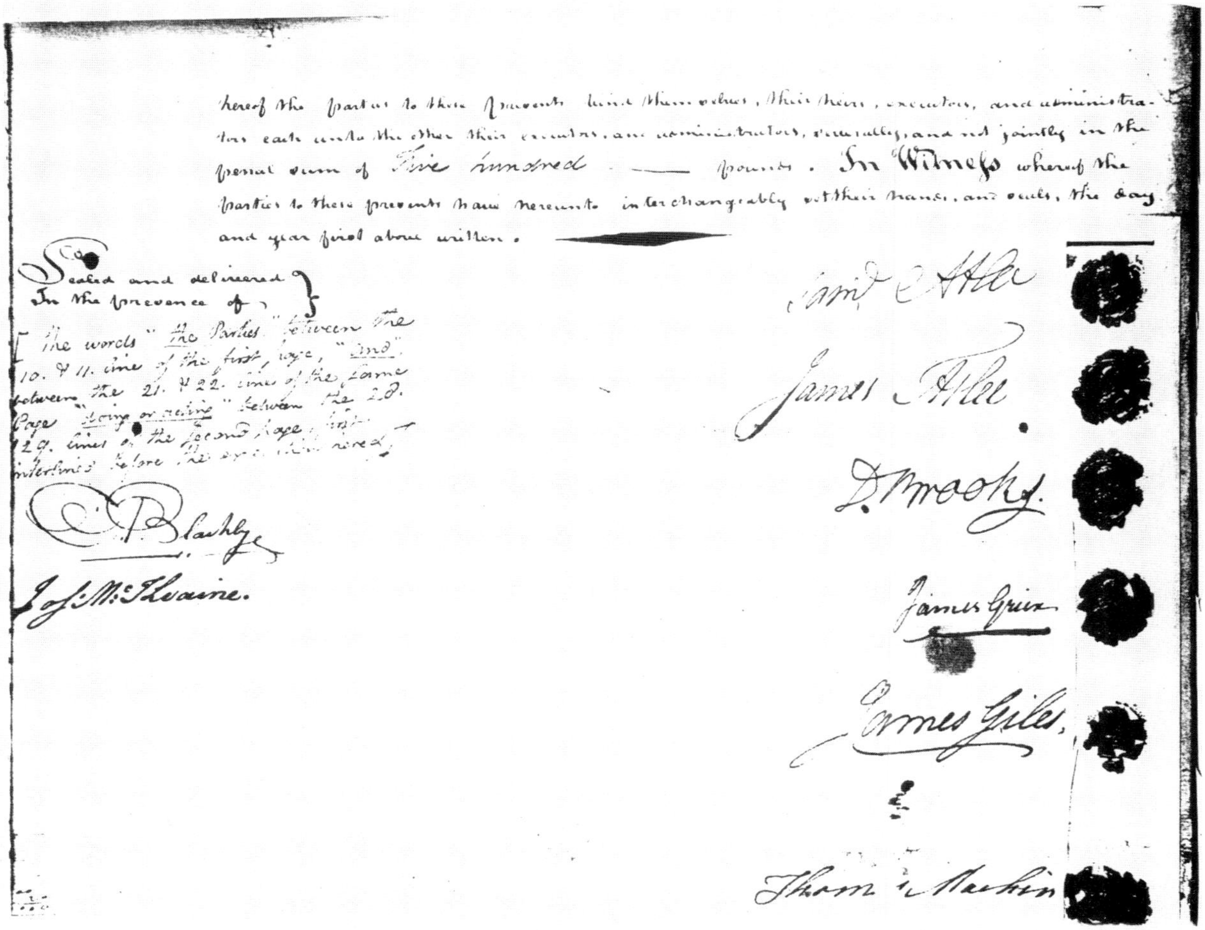
hereof the parties to these presents bind themselves, their heirs, executors, and administrators each unto the other their executors, and administrators, severally, and not jointly in the penal sum of Five hundred —— pounds. In Witness whereof the parties to these presents have hereunto interchangeably set their hands, and seals, the day and year first above written.

Sealed and delivered In the presence of

C. P. Blackley

Jos. McIlvaine.

Saml Atlee

James Atlee

D. Brooks.

James Grier

James Giles.

Thom. Machin

Fig. 60: SIGNATORIES OF THE MACHIN'S MILLS INDENTURE OF April 18, 1787: Samuel Atlee; James Atlee; David Brooks; James Grier; James Giles; and Thomas Machin.

The output of Machin's Mills, described as a "manufactory of hardware," was varied.[85] It has been speculated that a number of patterns was prepared in anticipation that the New York legislature would authorize a state coinage. Such trial pieces with a New York connection include the 1786 NON VI VIRTUTE VICI/NEO-EBORACENSIS,[86] the 1787 GEORGE CLINTON, and perhaps the various EXCELSIOR coppers.[87] The low mintage of these patterns accounts for their extreme rarity today.

Machin's Mills participation in a number of 1787 and 1788 Connecticut coppers has been previously described. Many of the 1788-dated Connecticut Mailed Bust Right issues and coppers

[85] Trudgen, *CNL 1983*, p. 842, and Trudgen, *CNL 1984A*, pp. 876-81.

[86] This legend translates, "I Conquered by Virtue, Not by Force/of New York." *Eboracus* is Latin for the Roman settlement of York, England.

[87] EXCELSIOR translates "Higher." Another pattern in this series has the motto, LIBER NATUS LIBERTATEM DEFENDO, "Being Born Free, I Defend Liberty." (See DeLorey, *CW 1976A*.) There is not full agreement as to the author of the EXCELSIOR coppers, be it Atlee alone, or Ephraim Brasher and John Bailey. See Taxay, *Catalogue*, p. 32, Trudgen, *CNL 1984A*, pp. 876-77, and Sipsey, *CNL 1965*, p. 155.

Fig. 61:
(a) New York: 1787 Excelsior copper (134.7 grains).

(b) "1747" Machin's Mills imitation English halfpenny with bust of George II, Vlack 1-47A (117.5 grains). Private Collection (Table 21, no. 22; Chart 30).

(c) The Brasher Doubloon, the only gold coin minted in pre-Federal America.

struck from Buell's Triple Leaves hubs, which came into Machin's possession, are encountered overstruck on 1785 Constellatio Novas. The procedure of striking over existing coins obviously produced more profit for Captain Machin and was more expedient than original planchet preparation.

A major product from Machin's Mills was a large number of English halfpence dated 1747, 1771, 1772, 1774 to 1778, 1787, and 1788.[88] Since regal halfpence of George II were minted in 1747, and legitimate George III halfpence were made only from 1770 to 1775, the other dates selected were imaginary. The halfpence which carried the same dates as legal issues are technically counterfeits, whereas the other fanciful ones are only "in imitation" of the real coins. This series of American made, counterfeit English coppers can be identified and attributed from die punch evidence from which Trudgen has identified three chronologically distinct groups and a fourth miscellaneous group.[89] Trudgen attributes the first group to Atlee while he was still in New York City and the important aspect is that these are punch linked with 1786-dated counterfeit Bust Right Connecticuts, also attributed to Atlee, suggesting that all these dies were prepared contemporaneously in 1786.

The second group of imitation halfpence have letters and numbers in common with John Bailey's coppers and Ephraim Brasher's doubloon, whereas the central figures are characteristic of a bust style typical of that attributed to Atlee. These findings must suppose a close working relationship between Atlee and the other coiners. The third cluster, thought to be the work of Atlee, was minted at Machin's Mills after his connection with that organization. The last miscellaneous group comprises several illogical die combinations including the rare IMMUNE COLUMBIA die.

[88] Vlack, *Counterfeit.*
[89] Trudgen, *CNL 1987A.*

The counterfeit halfpence from Newburgh are distinct and must not be confused with the immense number of English forgeries, generally of finer quality, which were imported during that time. Both the imported and domestic counterfeit halfpence circulated together as evidenced by the Stepney, Connecticut hoard where about one-quarter of the 72 counterfeit British halfpence inventoried were of Machin's Mills origin, the rest being from England.[90] It cannot be determined from the sample uncovered in this hoard if these numbers are representative of the coppers in circulation during that period. There are other counterfeit English halfpence of American manufacture but these crude pieces have nothing in common with the Machin's Mills output.

The only "legal" coinage from the Newburgh mint was the Vermont series that was produced under agreement and in cooperation with the Rupert mint. The busts on these Vermont pieces bear a distinct familial appearance with the likeness of George III on the imitation halfpence attesting to a common engraver. Those overstruck on 1785 Constellatio Nova coppers were from the Rupert, Vermont, mint, while those impressed on counterfeit Irish halfpence were from the New York facility toward the end of its minting operation and must have been the work of unskilled individuals. This is evidenced by the fact that the last Vermont coppers from Machin's Mills were carelessly executed from old, broken, and rejected dies. Moreover, some dies were not sufficiently hardened or the Irish host coins not properly annealed prior to striking with new Vermont labels. Consequently the dies fractured very early in their lives and thus we have few survivors today. The later Vermont issues, many of which are on Irish host coins, are among the rarest of all state coppers. This slipshod workmanship probably occurred as the mint was about to close.

A number of mules were minted by Captain Machin, employing obverse and reverse dies from different sources. The unusual 1788 Connecticut Miller 1-I combines an Atlee small head from Machin's Mills, also used in 1787 as Miller 1.1-A and 1.1-VV, which is now married with Vermont reverse, Bressett-U. This same Vermont reverse is in turn combined with an imitation English halfpenny, Vlack 22-88 Vt. This one coin, 1788 Miller 1-I, therefore, is claimed by three series of coppers, Connecticut, Vermont, and the imitation English halfpence.

Fig. 62:
(a) "1787" Machin's Mills imitation English halfpenny with bust of George III, Vlack 18-87C (117.1 grains). In its later life, this reverse die was severely lapped with obliteration of the more shallowly engraved details and used for the Vermont RR-13 (Table 21, no. 22; Chart 30).

(b) 1787 BRITANNIA reverse, RR-13 (113.7 grains): This obverse Vermont die was muled with the Machin's Mills Britannia reverse, Vlack 87C, after it had been severely lapped and the details obscured. Private Collection (Table 21, no. 21a; Chart 29).

[90] Breen, *Num 1952*, pp. 22-24; Newman, *ANS Centennial*, pp. 540-42. Even today among accumulations of old English halfpence in dealers' "junk boxes," the author has found several Machin's pieces and many counterfeit "Birmingham" copper halfpence.

The Vermont copper, Ryder-Richardson 13 (fig. 62), is another interesting piece. The coin, made in Newburgh, is a mule displaying a new, typical bust with Vermont legends while the reverse, Vlack 87C, had been used in several previous varieties in the imitation English halfpence series. The old reverse is very weak on the Ryder-Richardson 13 combination since there is selective disappearance of less deeply sunk details of the letters and central figure on this very shallow die due to a grinding down of the surface.[91] The traditional reason offered for this characteristic is that the die had been lapped intentionally to obscure the legend, BRITANNIA. In a recent article, Trudgen disagrees with this explanation and supports the observation, first made by Wyllys Betts in 1886, that the indistinct reverse results from previous, honest wear and not a deliberate attempt to obliterate the legends.[92] This piece also belongs to two separate series. The Vermont 1785 IMMUNE COLUMBIA (Ryder-Richardson 1), marries a severely damaged or perhaps rejected Vermont obverse with an equally inferior IMMUNE COLUMBIA reverse die. This IMMUNE COLUMBIA reverse also saw service with an imitation halfpenny obverse as Vlack 15-85NY. It can be speculated that this illogical muling of dies occurred in the final months of Machin's Mills activity, indicative that the operation had become desperate, amateurish, and deteriorated.

Speculation links the New Jersey camel heads (Maris 56 to 58-n) to Machin's Mills, or at least attributes the die preparation to Atlee. The very common Maris 56-n (fig. 57h) is found struck over the largest variety of host coins (see Appendix 2). The long life of the Maris 56 obverse can be attributed to the fact that the die was well prepared and that there must have been annealing capability to soften the host coins. If the Maris 56 clone were minted at Machin's Mills, it had to have been accomplished either before or separate from the last Vermont coppers, since these demonstrate such technical inferiority in workmanship. These two emissions could not have been coeval. Since the Maris 56 group appears over all descriptions of host coins, it is equally difficult to think that they were minted contemporaneously with the 1788 Connecticut issues from Machin's Mills which were only overstruck over Constellatio Novas and nothing else. These distinct host coin personalities must mean that these two emissions, the Maris 56 issues and the 1788 Connecticuts, had to have been separated in time, but which came first? The finding of a Maris 56-n overstruck on a 1788 Connecticut, Miller 3-B.1, indicates that the "camel heads" were minted after the time that particular Connecticut copper was made.[93]

Activity at Machin's Mills ceased although the termination date is unconfirmed. Bushnell,[94] quoted by Crosby, said that operations ceased in 1791 which appears illogical since Connecticut coppers and British halfpence, assumed to be the major products of the mint, had all but ceased to circulate by August 1789. New Jersey coppers would have been the only reasonable coins for anyone to have continued minting after the summer of 1789 since these still circulated preferentially due to legal tender status. There is no firm evidence linking New Jersey issues to Machin's Mills and certainly the Maris 56 to 58-n group, characterized by the superior, long-lived Maris 56 obverse and host coin attributes, has nothing in common with the deteriorated Vermont coppers thought to be the agonal output of the mint. It is not known how much impact the Machin's Mills operation had on the Confederation coinage, but certain Connecticut coppers attributed to that mint, the 1788 Miller 2-D in particular, remain fairly common coins. A report, cited by Crosby, was less optimistic as it quoted the mint's 1789 production at about 1000 pounds of coppers, or about 63,000 coins, with little more accomplished in preceding years. From these data the source concluded that the mint was not a profitable business.[95]

[91] James C. Spilman, personal communication, June 6, 1991.
[92] Trudgen, *RCR 73*; Betts, *CNL 1981*.
[93] *Romano*, lot 59.
[94] Crosby, *Early Coins*, p. 191.
[95] Crosby, *Early Coins*, p. 202, from Simms, *History of Scoharie County*.

NOVA EBORAC SERIES

The Nova Eborac coinage, punch linked to Brasher's famous gold doubloon (fig. 61c) and the 1788 New Jersey "running horse" mint marked coppers (fig. 57f), are attributed to the partnership of Ephraim Brasher and John Bailey.[96] Crosby did not recognize the domestic origin of any in the Nova Eborac series which he considered to be of English manufacture.[97] Stylistic similarities on the small head 1787 Nova Eborac, the "Muttonhead," (fig. 55q) and the EXCELSIOR coppers (fig. 61a) also suggest a common source with Bailey as the author.[98] As noted in Table 21, the coppers with the reverse figure seated to the left (Crosby 1-B) appear significantly heavier ($p = <0.0001$) than those with the figure oriented to the right (Crosby 1-A). Breen assigns the small head Nova Eborac, which is different from others with that legend, to the Elizabethtown mint.[99]

Fig. 63: New York: 1787 Nova Eborac, reverse figure left (137.5 grains) (Table 21, no. 26a).

This partnership had petitioned the State Assembly for permission to mint coppers, as had Captain Thomas Machin.[100] Both requests were denied and the legislature responded not with a copper coinage but rather with the Act of April 20, 1787, which restricted the circulation of light weight coppers within the State after August 1, 1787.

> ... no copper shall pass current in this State except such as are of the Standard and weight of one third part of an Ounce averdupois [*sic*], of pure copper, which coppers shall pass current at the rate of twenty to a Shilling of the lawful current money of this State and not otherwise.[101]

The enactment specified that coppers, to be lawful, must weigh at least 145.8 grains each or 48 to the pound. The condition was exceeded by regal English halfpence, and New Jersey, Massachusetts, and Fugio issues. All others, including the Constellatio Nova and Vermont coppers, were categorically excluded for acceptance within New York by this legislation. This weight requirement of 145.8 grains was very close to the Connecticut standard of 144 grains, and as will be described, the coppers of this neighboring state were not well received in New York.

THE SECOND MASSACHUSETTS MINT

The legal state coppers so far described were minted by private enterprise on contracts awarded by the various legislatures. Similarly, petitions for a contract coinage were addressed to the Massachusetts General Court early in 1786 by Seth Reed and James Swan, independently of

[96] Sipsey, *CNL 1965*, pp. 155-57; Breen, *ANS Centennial*; Risk, *CNL 1981*; Bowers, *Coinage History*, pp. 156-59.
[97] Crosby, *Early Coins*, pp. 296, 340-41.
[98] Trudgen, *RCR 63*.
[99] Breen, *Encyclopedia*, p. 94.
[100] Crosby, *Early Coins*, pp. 290, 294-96.
[101] Crosby, *Early Coins*, p. 294.

each other.[102] Both applications were denied in favor of a state run mint which was authorized by legislative action on October 17, 1786. Joshua Wetherle was appointed mintmaster for this project which lasted for about two years. The Massachusetts coinage of 1787 and 1788 conformed to the Federal resolution adopted July 6, 1785, which established the decimal ratio dollar as the money of account where each dollar of 100 cents equaled one Spanish milled dollar. The coppers, in half cent and cent denominations, were to contain 78.75 and 157.5 grains pure copper, respectively. The new Federal system and the established New England money of account, at six shillings to the Spanish milled dollar, were not exactly reconciled with each other. Coppers in Massachusetts, including the new decimal based cents, still passed at 18 to the shilling, or 108 to the Spanish dollar, on the old money of account, rather than the 100 dictated by the Federal decimal requirement.[103] By settling a debt using coppers at 18 to the shilling, one would pay 8% more than under the Federal stipulations. The disparity in value between the two systems further complicated financial transactions of the period.

Felt, in 1839, described the Massachusetts decimal copper coinage with nostalgia as "familiar with the earliest remembrances and enjoyments of many, who yet survive," and further recollected that they entered circulation in about January 1788, having been unexpectedly delayed in their release.[104] Prior to this coinage, Felt noted that the prevalent copper medium current in the Bay State was the 1783 Constellatio Nova series.

Fig. 64:
(a) 1788 Massachusetts cent: Closed "S" dies of Jacob Perkins, Ryder 11-F (157.9 grains) (Table 21, no. 2; Chart 5).

(b) 1787 Massachusetts half cent: Open "S" dies of Joseph Callender, Ryder 4-B (68.5 grains) (Table 21, no. 3; Chart 6).

The Massachusetts cents and half cents were well made pieces of uniform weight and quality. An Indian was depicted on the obverse and a heraldic eagle on the reverse. It was the only copper of the period with all legends in English. The state-run mint proved unprofitable with expenses 55% greater than the value of the struck coins.[105] Aware of the provision in the new Constitution which would forbid states the right to coin money and also refusing to resort to private contractors, the Massachusetts legislature ordered the mint closed on November 17, 1788, after the existing supply of copper had been exhausted. Despite financial and production difficulties, there was no deterioration in the quality of Massachusetts coppers during the last months of the mint. Four lightweight counterfeit Massachusetts cents dated for both years were produced from some unidentified location. One variety of these, the 1787 1-B, was used as a host coin for a few 1788 Machin's Mills Connecticut (Miller 16.3-N) coppers (fig. 56b). Legitimate Massachusetts cents would have proven unprofitable as a ready source of planchets for overstruck coinage due to their heavy weight. There are no instances recorded where authorized Massachusetts cents were overstruck, only the counterfeits.

[102] Crosby, *Early Coins*, pp. 229-74. An excellent summary of Massachusetts copper is found in Bowers, *Coinage History*, pp. 147-55.
[103] Newman, *Coppers*, pp. 106-8.
[104] Felt, *Massachusetts*, pp. 205-7.
[105] Crosby, *Early Coins*, pp. 262-63.

Because the mint was under legislative scrutiny, records were kept but unfortunately there are still vacant areas in our knowledge about the operation. As the available information is pieced together it has been established that all the legal dies dated 1787 were engraved by Joseph Callender. His services were then replaced by Jacob Perkins, whose work can be distinguished from his colleague by the "S" punch which closely resembles an "8".[106] It is known that $3,500 was the total production of which about 300,000 were cents and 100,000 half cents. Recent research suggests the following tabulations presented in Table 18:

TABLE 18

Estimated Massachusetts Copper Mintage from Data Developed by Spilman and Packard (Spilman, *CNL* 1987; Packard, *CNL* 1987, *CNL* 1989)

( ) = number of dies attributed to each engraver[107]	*Callender*	*Perkins*	*Totals*	*Packard's Estimates*[108]
1787 half cents	61,538 (9)	0	61,538	79,500
1787 cents	90,909 (11)	0	90,909	93,000
1788 half cents	0	38,462 (2)	38,462	35,500
1788 cents	109,524 (15)	99,567 (10)	209,091	199,000
Total Coins	261,971	138,029	400,000	407,000
Dollar Value	$2,312.02	$1,187.98	$3500.00	$3495.00
Coinage %	65.492%	34.507%		

NEW HAMPSHIRE PATTERNS

The cast coppers of New Hampshire, dated 1776, require mention for the sake of completeness.[109] The original coinage was established by the New Hampshire Legislature on June 28, 1776. Each copper was to weigh 130 grains and pass at 108 to the Spanish American milled dollar, the usual rate of 18 to the local shilling. Nothing is documented regarding their manufacture and genuine specimens are exceedingly rare; many present day specimens are of doubtful origin with authentication mandatory to identify modern forgeries.

Fig. 65: 1776 New Hampshire copper.

THE CONSTELLATIO NOVA COPPERS

There has been frequent reference made to the Constellatio Nova coppers which have been attributed as a speculative venture of Gouverneur Morris who ordered the coins from Birmingham.[110] There have been some attempts to establish a domestic origin for the Constel-

[106] A biographical sketch of Jacob Perkins and his accomplishments is found in Boisvert, *CNL 1987*.

[107] Spilman, *CNL 1987*.

[108] Packard, *CNL 1987*, p. 1013, and *CNL 1989*.

[109] Taxay, *Catalogue*, p. 19; Bowers, *Coinage History*, p. 133; Breen, *Encyclopedia*, pp. 60-61; Crosby, *Early Coins*, pp. 175-76; *Oechsner Bequest*, pp. 134-5.

[110] Wild, *CNL 1972*; see also *RF-52*, *CNL 1973*, and Newman, *CNL 1973*; LaMarre, *RCR 65*, pp. 48-49. Persuasive evidence is given that the correct name of this interesting coinage is *Constellatio Nova* and not *Nova Constellatio* as frequently stated (Breen, *CNL 1974A*).

latio Nova coppers, linking them to the Nova Eborac coppers of Brasher and Bailey with which they appear to share some common letter punches. The reverse designs on the Vermont landscape issues of 1785 and 1786 by William Coley are similar to, but not identical with the Constellatio Nova series[111]. The mutual resemblance of these dies does suggest some common, yet unidentified, bias. Despite any temptation, however strong, to suggest an American source for the Constellatio Nova coppers, contemporaneous newspaper accounts state that the Constellatio Novas are an English product "coined at Birmingham by the order of a merchant in New York" who tradition identifies as Gouverneur Morris."[112]

There are three 1783 and six 1785 die pairs and three instances where a die is used in a second combination. This results in nine combinations but excludes the very rare 1785 and 1786 contemporary counterfeits, which bear no relation to others in the series.[113] A statement, quoted by Crosby from *The Massachusetts Centinel*, alleged that 40 tons of copper were coined from one die pair alone, a most unlikely event.[114] A sample of Constellatio Nova coppers suggests that they were intended to weigh about 58 to the pound or 120 grains each. Forty [long] tons would have amounted to over 5,000,000 pieces which indeed is an exaggeration for one set of dies, let alone the entire coinage! The actual quantity of Constellatio Nova coppers can only be estimated from the fact that there were only nine die pairs, two of which are rare. One could expect from 18,000 to 50,000 impressions per die under the best of circumstances and these data would imply that the size of the coinage ranged from 162,000 to 450,000 pieces, or a maximum of 3.44 long tons of copper.[115]

In 1788 and perhaps into 1789, several mints, including Machin's Mills, Rupert, Vermont, and Elizabethtown, New Jersey, struck their own dies over preexisting coins at a time when it was less expensive or more convenient to do so. The Elizabethtown mint may not always have had the necessary equipment to roll and cut copper stock into planchets. The circulation of lightweight coppers was restricted in New York after August 1, 1787. Thereafter, such pieces, including the Constellatio Novas, became fair game for the coining presses of other operators who sought to legitimize underweight coins by impressing on them an acceptable design and to send them off again into circulation with a new identity. Examination shows that 1785 Constellatio Nova coppers were used as host coins for many 1787 Vermont coppers from Rupert (Ryder-Richardson 14, 12, and 32; Bressett 10-K, 11-K, and 12-K) and for 1788 Connecticut coppers from Machin's Mills. An occasional 1783 Constellatio Nova is found as the host for New Jersey coins from the Elizabethtown mint. The most common 1785 Constellatio Nova host coin which can be attributed is the Crosby 5-E, followed next by the 4-C and 4-D.[116]

From these data, some speculation can be made about the circulation of Constellatio Nova coppers. Research by Newman suggests that, although dated 1783 and 1785, the coins were not common before May 1786.[117] In fact it would have been unexpected, despite the 1783 date, to have found this series in America prior to the signing of the peace treaty. Felt noted that in

[111] Sipsey, *CNL 1965*.

[112] *RF-52*, *CNL 1973*, p. 402; Newman, *CNL 1973* (quote from *Morn. Chron.*, March 16, 1786); Newman, *NSM 1960*, pp. 6-8; Breen, *Encyclopedia*, pp. 117-19.

[113] Taxay, *Catalogue*, pp. 16-17; Breen, *Encyclopedia*, p. 119.

[114] Crosby, *Early Coins*, p. 331.

[115] Spilman, *CNL 1961*, p. 24; Hodder (*RCR 74*) estimated the life of the dies used for the 1796 cents from the Federal Mint. Extrapolating from his calculations and considering the rarity of some 1785 die varieties, it is doubtful that the entire Constellatio Nova coinage exceeded 200,000 because, as a group, these coins are certainly less plentiful today than Massachusetts coppers for which there were a certain 400,000 minted.

[116] The census of 20 identifiable Constellatio Nova host coins is as follows: 1783: 1-A [1], 3-C [2]; 1785: 2-A [2], 4-C [5], 4-D [4], 5-E [6]. These numbers are too few for statistical analysis but suggest a trend; the most common 1785 copper, 3-B, is not represented at all, whereas 4-D, the rarest of all, is frequently encountered overstruck. See also Breen, *Encyclopedia*, p. 119, 1114.

[117] Newman, *NSM 1960*, p. 7.

Fig. 66:
(a) 1783 Constellatio Nova token, Crosby 2-B (121.6 grains) (Table 21, no. 25a).

(b) 1785 Constellatio Nova token, Crosby 3-B (115.1 grains) (Table 21, no. 25b).

1788 the most common copper in Massachusetts was the 1783 Constellatio Nova.[118] Further inspection of the 1785 Constellatio Nova die varieties shows stylistic differences on the obverse changing from 30 to 29 and later to 26 paired leaves in the wreath. The 1785 Crosby 1-B, 2-A, and 3-B have 30 pairs as do all the three 1783 varieties. The 1785 1-B shares a common obverse with the 1783 3-C, both displaying a misspelled CONSTELATIO. The six varieties mentioned with 30 paired leaves are less commonly seen as host coins than are the other three issues, 5-E, 4-C , and 4-D, which in and of themselves are much rarer coins. This suggests that as the first group arrived in America they directly entered into commerce, but when the second group, i.e. 4-C (30 pairs), 4-D (29 pairs), and 5-E (26 pairs), arrived at a later date the circulation of coppers was becoming more sluggish and many were sold in bulk to minters. The last three varieties of the 1785 Constellatio Nova coppers must have appeared on the scene by July 1787, for them to have been used in the Rupert mint.[119] Felt, writing in 1839, apparently was not familiar with the 1785 Constellatio Nova coppers anytime before January 1788, an observation which further indicates that those varieties were uncommonly seen in the Bay State by the time of the Massachusetts mint.

Crosby's scale of rarity adds further evidence that the 4-C, 4-D, and 5-E varieties were not as commonly circulated as the others but bought up in quantity.[120] He observed that the 1785 1-B is rarity 3, the 2-A is rarity 4, and the 3-B is common, whereas the 4-C is rarity 5, the 4-D is rarity 6, and the 5-E is rarity 4. While the last three coins are much rarer as unaltered coins, they are more common as host coins than the preceding three or any of the 1783 varieties. When these 1785 Constellatio Nova coppers reached Machin's Mills and the Rupert mint they became host coins for 1788 Connecticut coppers and 1787 Vermont coppers, respectively. For the Connecticut coinage, the lighter weight Constellatio Nova coppers defrauded the public, but for Vermont, these ready-made host coins were heavier than the authorized weight.

The following observations can be made about the Constellatio Nova coppers: [1] those predated 1783 were introduced in about May 1786; [2] the first three varieties of 1785 arrived in close succession, either late 1786 or early 1787; [3] the last three 1785 varieties arrived before July 1787; [4] the rarity census noted by Crosby for the 4-C, 4-D, and 5-E does take into account that many of these coins were overstruck and, therefore, fewer exist as originals; [5] the total coinage cannot exceed 450,000 and is probably closer to 200,000; [6] the average weight for 28

[118] Felt, *Massachusetts*, p. 206.

[119] Bressett notes that "nearly the entire 1787 Bust Right group of Vermont coins was produced by over-striking" on Constellatio Novas but no others were produced by that method through 1788 or into 1789 when the Rupert mint closed (Bressett, *Studies*, p. 177).

[120] The Crosby scale of rarity extends only to R-6, whereas current scales go to R-8 (2 to 3 specimens) and R-9 (unique). See *E.A.C. 1975*, p. 9; Anton, *CNL 1975*, p. 502.

circulated 1783 specimens is 120.8 ± 15.8, and for 46 1785 varieties, 116.5 ± 7.2; the combined average is 118.1 ± 11.4, or about 59 to the pound (see Table 21). The higher standard deviation of ± 15.8 grains for the 1783 issues indicates less consistency in planchet weight than for the 1785-dated tokens.

FUGIO CENTS

By the late 1780s, several states had taken action against the deluge of counterfeit coppers which saturated the small change medium. Within the Confederation, Connecticut, New Jersey, and Massachusetts had established mints or arranged for contract coinages as had the autonomous Republic of Vermont. The New York Legislature responded to this raft of lightweight coins on April 20, 1787, by imposing restrictions on their currency which prohibited those under 145.8 grains from circulation and devaluated all others from 14 to 20 coppers per local shilling.[121] New Jersey, in "AN ACT to prevent the circulation of bad and light Coppers in this State," decreed that after July 20, 1787, only its own coppers, or any produced by Congress, could pass.[122]

Congress, also, resolved to provide a solution for removing undesirable coppers from circulation and proposed a full weight coin of 157.5 grains, the same Federal standard to which Massachusetts adhered.[123] These new coppers were heavier than the New Jersey standard of 150 grains, the Connecticut standard at 144 grains, and significantly greater than the Vermont standard of 111 grains. Since 100 of the new coins were to pass for the Spanish milled dollar, they could technically be called "cents." Petitions were received early in 1787 by Congress from both Matthias Ogden, who was involved in the Rahway mint, and James Jarvis, who had a controlling interest in the Connecticut Company for Coining Coppers, to obtain the contract to mint this proposed copper coinage. However, by devious means, Jarvis had already secured the privilege for his newly organized company by offering a $10,000 bribe to Colonel William Duer. In the meanwhile, Jarvis had received 12,809 pounds of federally owned copper from Duer and later an additional 35 tons even prior to Congressional authorization for his project. The Federal contract coinage manufactured by Jarvis was the Fugio cent, the first official coin of the United States government. Of the 300 tons of Fugio coinage Jarvis agreed to produce, only 400,000 pieces, or about four long tons, were delivered by May 1788.[124] Jarvis was unsuccessful in arranging acceptable financing and as the project faltered, he departed for England to enlist the assistance in the project of Matthew Boulton, owner of the Soho mint in Birmingham. In the end, much of the copper intended for the Fugio coinage was fraudulently diverted into the production of an unauthorized 3,500,000 1787 Connecticut coppers, since the mint was simultaneously striking both types.

It is speculated that the Fugio cents may have been produced at sites other than New Haven, but this is disputed. The suggestion that "Club Rays Fugios" came from Machin's Mills after the regular Fugio coinage ceased is not feasible.[125] Spilman suggests that the Club Ray varieties were manufactured later than the more common and better executed Fine Rays issues, but by a different party who possessed less technical skills.[126] The "round" Club Rays

[121] Crosby, *Early Coins*, pp. 294-95.

[122] Crosby, *Early Coins*, pp. 281-82.

[123] References on the Fugio coinage include: Newman, *CCJ 1952B*, an expansion of his original 1949 classification; Kessler, *Fugio*, a later enlargement with plates of 55 die combinations; Spilman, *CNL 1961*; Douglas, *CNL 1969*, an historical account of James Jarvis and the saga of the Fugio cents, relating the entire episode.

[124] Spilman concludes "that the maximum possible Fugio coinage was in the order of 1.5 million (*CNL 1961*, p. 24)."

[125] *Mail Bid 1985B*, 1611; *TN-81*, *CNL 1979*.

[126] Spilman, *CNL 1961*, pp. 922-25.

Fig. 67:
(a) 1787 Fine Rays Fugio: Significant clash marks are noted on this uncirculated specimen from the Bank of New York hoard. As a group, these coppers were below the required 157.5 grains, this example being an exception, Newman 11-B (165.3 grains) (Table 21, no. 1a; Chart 8).

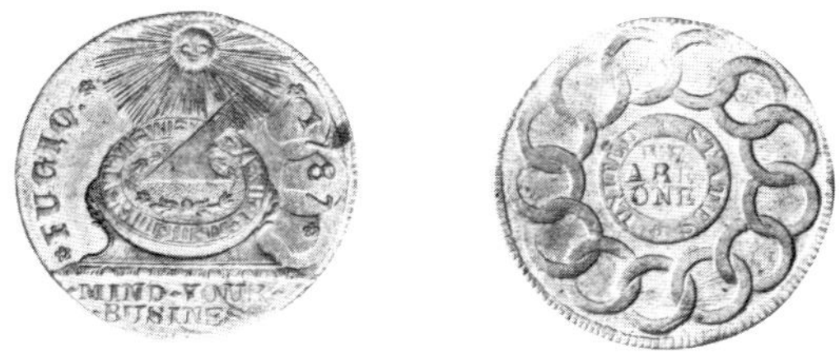

(b) 1787 Club Rays Fugio with round "Convex ends": These issues are not as neatly executed as the previous type. There is reason to believe that these three groups of Fugio cents were minted under different circumstances, Newman 3-D (154.0 grains) (Table 21, no. 1b; Chart 9).

(c) 1787 Club Rays Fugio with "Concave ends": As a group, those club rays issues with concave ends are significantly heavier than the preceding two types, Newman 5-HH (168.0 grains). Courtesy James C. Spilman (Table 21, no. 1c; Chart 10).

and the rarer "concave" Club Rays fall into two distinct weight groups, the latter being distinctly heavier (see Table 21). Since it was the practice of the Machin's Mills organization to produce coppers which were lighter in weight than the genuine article, it would be inconsistent to ascribe the Club Rays to that mint since as a group, they are heavier or equal to the Fine Rays varieties.[127] Spilman postulates that Benjamin Buell produced the Club Rays, having damaged the obverse working hub from which subsequent defective dies were produced. Abel Buell, the engraver for both the Connecticut and Fugio series, was apprehensive about the mint's illegal activities, and therefore, departed for England. His anxiety was well founded since he had earlier suffered one ear to be cropped due to a forgery conviction.[128]

The Fugio experiment was a failure because of bribery and corruption; it was unsuccessful in its stated purpose as recorded in the newspapers of the time.

> ... these [Fugio cents] will free us from the impositions to which we are now exposed from the floods of light half-coined British halfpence, introduced among us - and as, from the excellent monitorial caution, "MIND YOUR BUSINESS," impressed on each of these, they may prove an antidote to insurgency, they will doubtless be held in high estimation.[129]

[127] A weight analysis of 84 Club Rays Fugios in Table 21, reveals an average of 150.3 ± 10.5 grains for the "round" Club Rays and 162.0 ± 10.4 for the "concave" varieties. (Personal communication, James C. Spilman.)

[128] Spilman, *CNL 1972*, p. 354.

[129] Crosby, *Early Coins*, p. 302. The MIND YOUR BUSINESS motto shows Benjamin Franklin's influence. In a letter of October 2, 1779, when discussing small change copper coin, Franklin wrote, "Instead of repeating continually upon every halfpenny the dull story that everybody knows, (and what it would have been no loss to mankind if nobody had ever known) that Geo. III is King of Great Britain, France, and Ireland, ... to put on one side, some important Proverb of Solomon, some pious moral, prudential or economical Precept, the frequent Inculcation of which, by seeing it every time one receives a piece of Money, might make an impression upon the mind, especially of young Persons, and tend to regulate the Conduct; such as, on some ... Keep thy Shop, and thy Shop will keep thee; on others, A penny saved is a penny got ...." (Smythe, *Franklin*, vol. 7, pp. 381-82.)

To make a bad situation worse, the Federal government was unable to place their 400,000 new cents into circulation and sold them in bulk to a speculator. Although the legislation of October 16, 1786, which provided for copper coinage, gave it legal tender status, this provision must have been rescinded or else the Fugios would never have been dumped in such an unorthodox manner by the government.[130] If they had been receivable for taxes, they would have enjoyed the same popularity as the legal tender New Jersey coppers. The man who purchased the Fugio consignment was Royal Flint of New York City, who received them in June 1789, just prior to the Coppers Panic. Flint was unable to dispose of his newly acquired coppers and landed in debtors' prison when he couldn't meet his obligations. Fortunately for present day numismatists, a keg of new Fugio cents was uncovered in the Bank of New York in 1856 and again rediscovered in 1926. One hypothesis is that the Bank of New York, aware of some implicit legal tender status, obtained the unwanted Fugios for investment purposes in anticipation of a quick profit which never materialized.[131] Over 5,000 of these uncirculated pieces have come into the hands collectors from this hoard.[132]

WASHINGTON AND MISCELLANEOUS PIECES

The numismatic literature lists another series of coppers generally referred to as "Washington Pieces." Although dated 1783, coinciding with the formal end of the Revolutionary War, the only piece which was actually minted and circulated during the Confederation period is the Georgius Triumpho copper.[133] This coin is either of English or French manufacture and is said to have circulated in Georgia, Virginia, and Jamaica. It is usually seen in circulated condition and falls in a weight range similar to the Constellatio Nova coppers.[134] In that a Georgius Triumpho has been identified as a host coin for an Elizabethtown copper, this series would have been in circulation in the period between June 1788 and June 1789 when that mint was operational.[135]

Fig. 68:
(a) 1783 Georgius Triumpho copper (111.1 grains).

(b) 1787 Immunis Columbia copper (170.7 grains).

(c) "1789" Mott trade token (122.2 grains).

[130] Douglas, *Fugio*, original manuscript, p. 182n.
[131] Donald G. Partrick, personal communication, Sept. 22, 1990.
[132] *Bank of N.Y.*, *CNL 1967*; Kessler, *Fugio*, pp. 6-7.
[133] Fuld, *RF-9*, *CNL 1964*; Taxay, *Catalogue*, p. 16; Vlack, *CNL 1978*, p. 651.
[134] *Roper*, lot 368, and *Garrett*, lot 1699, weighed 125.8 and 135.5 grains, respectively. Crosby (*Early Coins*, p. 341) lists his coin at 117 grains.
[135] *Weimer and Hirt*, pp. 98, 106; Anton, *CNL 1975*, p. 511.

The 1787 IMMUNIS COLUMBIA coppers have stimulated recent research about their origin. Originally they were thought to have been the patterns presented to Congress in 1787 by Matthias Ogden in his petition for the federal contract coinage ultimately awarded to the Fugio contractors.[136] Hodder studied the die emission sequence and found that the series was minted over a period of time from late in 1788 to mid-1789, therefore, the coinage was too late to have participated in negotiations for the Federal contract.[137]

Other miscellaneous copper tokens circulated during the Confederation period, including the Bar "cent," the Albany, New York Church penny, the 1787 Auctori Plebis token, The IMMUNE COLUMBIA patterns, and the CONFEDERATIO coppers.[138] There has been controversy whether the famous Mott token, although dated 1789, belongs to this or a later period.[139] It is of particular interest that this storecard comes in two weights, a heavy version from 164 to 233 grains, and a thin planchet at 108 grains. This distinction will be discussed in the following chapter. For the most part, these miscellaneous coppers are primarily of numismatic and historical interest with little contemporary economic impact.

SILVER COINAGES

Two silver coinages were current during the Confederation period, both issued privately by Maryland silversmiths. Cut Spanish eight reales were the usual small change silver currency of the period but this money was unreliable in weight. The eight reales piece may not have been divided evenly to start, and then the individual sections, of whatever size, could have been honestly worn or fraudulently clipped. John Chalmers of Annapolis received this lightweight and cut Spanish silver which he recoined into threepence, sixpence, and shilling denominations dated 1783.[140] There is little documentation about the conduct of this operation. In 1783, the Spanish milled dollar weighed 417.6 grains but the fineness was now .9028, the reduction having occurred in 1772. This standard still passed in England for 54d., sterling, or in Maryland for seven and one-half local shillings (90d.). The Maryland money of account shilling would then be equivalent to 55.68 grains of .9028 fine silver. While the average weight of the Chalmers shilling is 54.0 ± 2.9 grains,[141] the metal was alloyed with more copper since analysis of the silver content is in the 81 to 86% range, thereby providing Chalmers with about an 8% gross profit on the transaction.[142] It would appear that Chalmers provided a community service by removing

[136] Breen, *CNL 1979*, pp. 670-72.

[137] Hodder, *CNL 1991*, pp. 1233-35; Taxay, *Catalogue*, pp. 16, 34, 35; Breen, *Encyclopedia*, passim. This list excludes pieces appearing after April 2, 1792, when the act was passed to establish the Federal Mint since they fall outside the scope of this book. It is important to distinguish the blundered Latin die, IMMUNE COLUMBIA, from the correct version, IMMUNIS COLUMBIA.

[138] Evidence is presented that the Auctori Plebis token is of American origin (Duncan, *CNL 1975*). Felt (*Massachusetts*, p. 252) was in error attributing the "1783" Washington Unity States (Baker 1) as a coin current in this period, since it was probably made after 1820, the reverse imitating early large cents (Taxay, *Catalogue*, pp. 44-45; Vlack, *CNL 1978*, p. 650). The ranges of weights are from the following sources: *Garrett*; *Roper*; Crosby, *Early Coins*, passim; and Duncan, *CNL 1975*, p. 476: Bar cent, 85 to 87 grains; Albany Church penny, 93 to 122 grains; and Auctori Plebis, 110 to 120 grains.

[139] Bowers, *RCR 67*; Newman, *RCR 69*.

[140] Crosby, *Early Coins*, pp. 328-30; Bowers, *Coinage History*, p. 118; Taxay, *Catalogue*, p. 15. A biographical sketch of John Chalmers and a description of his coinage appears by Schab, *Num 1984*.

[141] The average weight of better grade Chalmers' coinage is as follows: 22 shillings, average very fine, 54.0 ± 2.9 grains (expected 55.7); 8 sixpence, average very fine, 26.6 ± 1.2 grains (expected 27.8); 4 threepence, average about uncirculated, 11.4 ± 0.7 (expected 13.9). The low 1st standard deviation indicates excellent consistency in planchet preparation. Data from Crosby, *Early Coins*, pp. 328-30; *Roper*; *Garrett*; Stack's FPL *Colonial Coins*.

[142] A preliminary analysis by Dispersive X-ray Fluorescence Spectrometry reveals from 81 to 86% silver with the residual metal being copper. This procedure has a ±6% error and the analysis is influenced by the surface history of the coins and any possible contamination. Data from more specimens of this rare issue will need to be averaged to establish significance. Personal communication, Charles W. Smith.

Fig. 69:
(a) 1783 Chalmers' "Short Worm" shilling: the most common variety of this private silver issued by the Annapolis silversmith, John Chalmers. The dies were prepared by Thomas Sparrow, the engraver of Maryland paper money from 1767 to 1775. The clasped hands on the obverse are from the state seal, the allegorical message on the reverse is explained in the text. (Newman, *Paper Money*, pp. 145-49; Breen, *Encyclopedia*, pp. 100-101), Breen 1011 (57.9 grains).

(b) 1783 Chalmers' sixpence, Breen 1017 (27.9 grains).

(c) 1783 Chalmers' threepence, Breen 1018 (10.9 grains).

(d) 1790 Standish Barry threepence, Breen 1019 (12.0 grains).

cut and worn Spanish silver from circulation and providing a current substitute, although at "a considerable advantage to himself."[143] The reverse design on this coin evokes much interest depicting two birds fighting over a worm while a serpent is behind the hedge waiting his chance to devour the pair of them. The allegory was an admonition to the citizens not to squabble over trifles lest the Federal government, the snake, absorb them all. The series was obviously well received as evidenced by the number of well-worn survivors and the fact that lightweight counterfeits have been reported.[144] The shilling dies failed early with many specimens showing a weak obverse center despite a bold periphery and good weight. Chalmers obviously gained indirectly from the advertising of his establishment on the coins' labels.

The Standish Barry 1790 threepence from Baltimore is more obscure in its origin and is a great rarity.[145] This coinage is of proper weight according to Maryland money of account.[146] Its scarcity today is attributed to the very early fracture of the reverse die.

The 1783 Constellatio Nova silver patterns for a United States coinage were engraved by Benjamin Dudley, an "experienced mechanic and metallurgist."[147] This proposed coinage, supported by Robert Morris (no relation to Gouverneur Morris who may have commissioned the Constellatio Nova coppers) was designed to utilize a 1000 unit decimal system but never progressed beyond the trial stage.

* * *

[143] Crosby, *Early Coins*, p. 330.
[144] Breen, *Encyclopedia*, pp. 100-101.
[145] Crosby, *Early Coins*, p. 330; Taxay, *Catalogue*, p. 34.
[146] *Roper*, lot 339, in extremely fine condition weighed 13.0 grams. Full weight for 3d. according to Maryland money of account would be 13.9 grains.
[147] Madaus, *Num 1983*, quote p. 239; Bowers, *Coinage History*, pp. 134-35; Ford, *CW 1980*, Jan. 9, 1980; LaMarre, *RCR 65*.

CHART 1

A Diagrammatic Representation Speculating the Possible Interrelationships Between the Various Mints Operating from 1785 to 1790

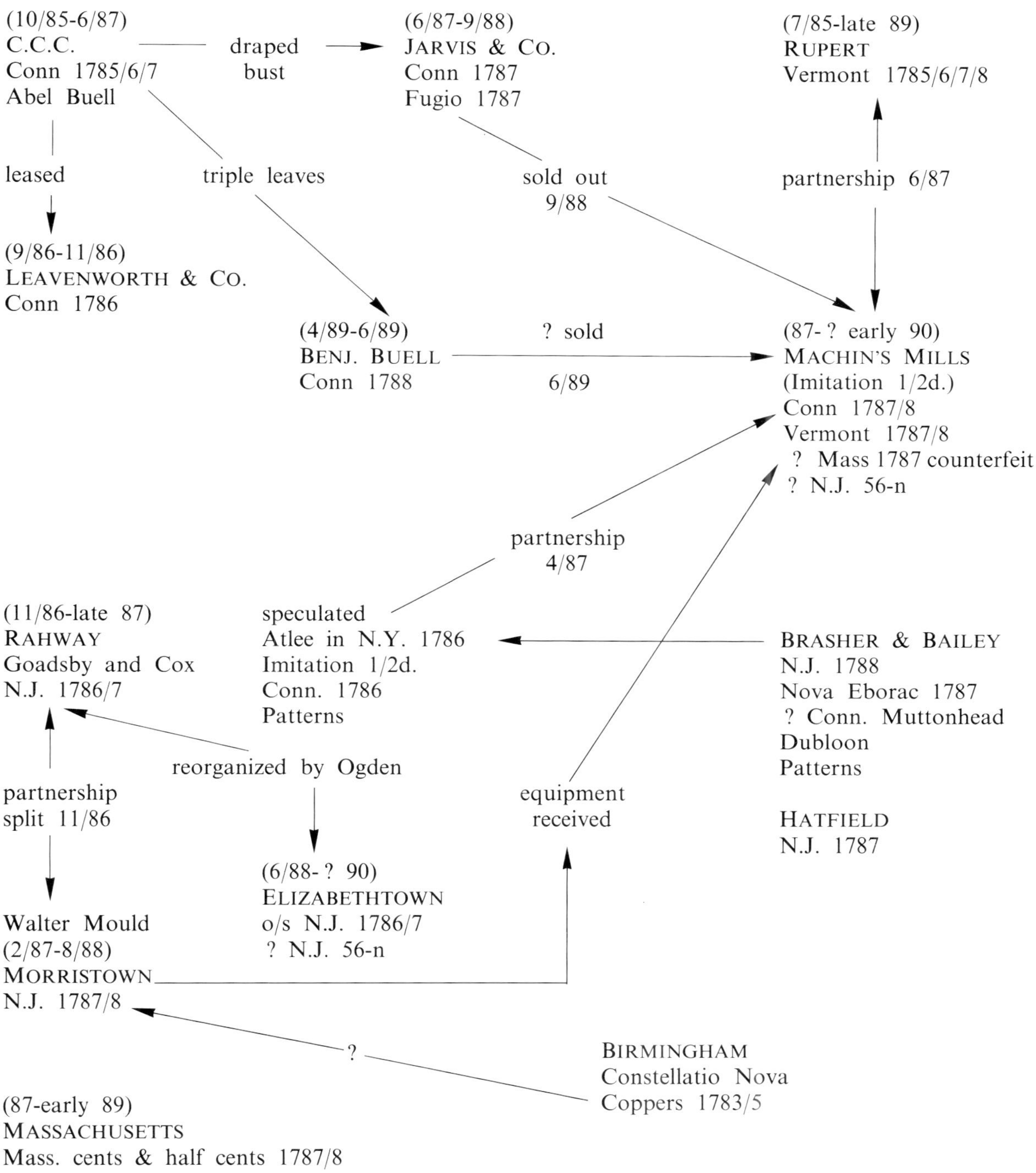

Legends: (10/85-6/87) = date of operation
C.C.C. = name of mint (Company for Coining Coppers)
Conn 1785/6/7 = date and type of coin issued
Abel Buell = name of principal operator/engraver

CHAPTER EIGHT

The Coppers Panic of 1789

CHANGING PUBLIC ATTITUDES

The summary of the specific copper coins minted in America during the Confederation period is now complete. The list includes some 693 die varieties or combinations of coppers produced from 1785 to 1789 or into 1790.[1] Some of the questions raised in the Preface of this book can now be examined. Why was the copper coinage short-lived and why did it fail?

Earlier chapters have described how hard money in the Colonies and Confederation, although available at a price, was never abundant except for a short time after the Revolution. Reasons for periodic shortages of specie coin have been proposed and the response of the American colonists with hard money substitutes narrated. Whereas the majority of silver and gold coins was Spanish, Portuguese, and French, the prevalent copper medium was English since it could be exported without restrictions. The monetary value of such English coppers was about double the worth of the intrinsic metal content, a margin which extended an open invitation to counterfeiters. The risks of serious legal consequences if convicted for duplicating regal coppers were insignificant when compared to the potential gain. The need for circulating coppers as small change and money for the common people in both England and America invited unscrupulous individuals to fabricate lightweight counterfeit halfpence, a practice rampant since the institution of regal copper coinage and one that reached its peak in the reign of George III. During this one hundred or more years, countless English coppers, both genuine and fake, were exported to the colonies where there was certainly no shortage. In fact, this plethora of counterfeit coppers damaged commerce both in Great Britain and the Colonies, cheated the public, and undermined confidence in the copper medium. In 1754 appeals were directed to the English government by distressed butchers, bakers, and grocers of London complaining they were burdened with large numbers of essentially unnegotiable and unwanted coppers they could not spend since coppers were unacceptable for taxes and could not be used except for small transac-

[1] This probably incomplete list includes the following die varieties and combinations, both authorized and contemporary counterfeits, of coppers minted in America:

Connecticut	355	
New Jersey	139	
Massachusetts	50	
Vermont	40	
Imitation English Halfpence	36	(excludes those counted elsewhere)
Fugio	57	
New York	4	
Domestic Patterns	10	
Domestic counterfeits of Constellatio Nova	2	
	693	

This list excludes British patterns and coins minted in England or Europe for use in America, such as Constellatio Nova coppers. The most important omission of imported coins are the regal and counterfeit English halfpence which were the prime coppers of the period.

tions.[2] Domestic violence was provoked in Philadelphia in 1741, and in New York in 1753, when the public reacted to large volumes of false coppers in circulation since the excess of small change depressed the exchange rate at which merchants would received them.[3] Nonetheless, the current coppers of that period, genuine and counterfeit English halfpence, continued to pass in America according to the rates listed in Table 11 for the next 34 years.

Further protests against the counterfeit halfpence were recorded in the Proclamation of July 14, 1781, from the Supreme Executive Council of Pennsylvania "prohibiting public officials from accepting base metal counterfeit British halfpence and recommending that the populace refuse them."[4] In 1786, Massachusetts residents were warned of the counterfeit lightweight coppers arriving with each ship from England and the damaging effect on commerce "yet shameful as it certainly is, this inundation of base metal is passed with impunity and indifference."[5] Another newspaper account that year estimated that "nearly one half of the copper coin in this country for twenty or thirty years" were Birmingham counterfeits which passed "for the same value as those which are genuine."[6] Coins recovered from hoards contain generous portions of counterfeit English halfpence.[7]

The public indifference toward counterfeit coppers began to give way to indignation and concern when from 1785 to 1787, several state legislatures authorized coinages of specific weight to replace the sundry English counterfeits, tokens, and other lightweight issues. While the intent was noble, the plan did not work. The quality of the Connecticut coppers declined over the years as clandestine mints flourished. Although the authorized three million coppers from New Jersey were frequently up to the 150 grain standard, later issues were light, particularly when New Jersey designs were struck over existing underweight coins. Vermont, although outside the Confederation as an independent republic, produced coppers considerably lighter at a 111 grain standard which doubtlessly circulated outside its boundaries. Many Vermont coppers were overstruck on heavier Constellatio Nova coppers, so no fraud was perpetrated. The Massachusetts mint essentially went bankrupt since it could not afford to produce quality coinage without incurring losses. In summary, all the coinage schemes to eradicate spurious halfpence and thereby revitalize the circulating copper medium eventually failed. In several instances counterfeit state issues were manufactured which were equally inferior in quality to the glut of lightweight coppers the legal mints were created to replace.

Despite occasional protests about lightweight coppers, the public remained relatively unconcerned about the composition of this token money until early 1787. In that summer, merchants in New Jersey received copper halfpence from 24 to 30 to the shilling, depending on locality.[8] After July 20, 1787, only New Jersey and United States coppers would be current in that state which would continue to pass at the official rate of 15 per local shilling. Effective August 1, 1787, the New York legislature outlawed all coppers less than 145.8 grains, and

[2] Craig, *Mint*, p. 251.

[3] Newman, *Studies*, pp. 144, 149-50.

[4] Newman, *Studies*, pp. 150-51. Crosby (*Early Coins*, pp. 172-74) thought this edict referred to "bungtowns" or "evasive halfpence," a theory which has been refuted. Throughout this book, the term "base" halfpence is quoted from contemporaneous sources. Although copper and tin are "base" metals themselves, in this context "base" refers to "inferior" or "vile," other censorious adjectives used for the counterfeit money of inadequate weight and impure metal.

[5] Newman, *Studies*, p. 148, quote from *Mass. Cent.*, Jan. 11, 1786.

[6] Newman, *Studies*, p. 148, quote from *Mass. Spy*, March 16, 1786, and *Newport Merc.*, March 27, 1786. In New York, halfpence were to pass "without discrimination" and so genuine and counterfeit coins circulated together.

[7] Newman and Gaspar, *Num 1978*, pp. 466-67; Newman, *Colonial Virginia*, p. 33; Breen, *Num 1952*, pp. 22-24.

[8] Newman, *Studies*, pp. 153-54.

devalued all others from a rate of 14 to 20 per New York shilling. A Newport, Rhode Island, report of August 13, 1787, confirmed that all coppers, except *Bungtowns*, were fixed to pass by law in New York at 160 to the dollar, that is 20 to the New York shilling of account. In New Jersey the accepted rate was 180 to the dollar for non-local coppers, or 24 to the local shilling, while in Rhode Island the par remained at 18 to the New England shilling, or 108 for a dollar.[9] Public confidence in copper as a token coinage, which had allowed it to pass at about twice intrinsic value for all these years, had started to erode. The downward spiral, once begun, was destined to demonetize practically all coppers in the Coppers Panic of 1789, even during the time of a significant postwar depression and extreme hard money shortage. The emotional sentiment against coppers must have been extreme to have caused people practically to have abandoned this medium at a time when all other money was so scarce.

An understanding of the Coppers Panic of 1789, when coppers declined in value and ceased to circulate, requires a detailed analysis of the copper medium of the period. The various coinages have been described in the preceding chapters. These were token or fiduciary coinages in that their metallic content was worth about half the monetary value. This was never the case with gold and silver where intrinsic and monetary values were equal. Copper coin was so expensive to mint in comparison to its pecuniary value that the practice developed in the English mint whereby the cost of manufacture was included in the monetary value of the copper coinage.[10] Even at that, the minter had a substantial profit margin which encouraged counterfeiting. The acceptance of such token coinage was regulated by law and succeeded only because of public confidence in the monetary system. At times in history when there was a shortage of small change, "ordinary folk ... cared nothing about either intrinsic value, high quality of copper, pattern [design] or limits of legal tender."[11] But when commerce was flooded with coppers of inferior quality and intrinsic worth well below the regulated standard, public approval in this token system had to have faltered for this money to fall into disrepute.

The questions can be appropriately asked, how and why did this lack of faith in circulating tokens take place? Who suffered the most from this excessive copper medium which was primarily composed of underweight counterfeit British halfpence with an assortment of new state issues, many of which fell below the authorized standard? Was it the farmer or laborer who cared about the deficiencies in the intrinsic weight or purity of copper coins? It is unlikely that such aesthetic considerations ever bothered the common people; their only interest was whether they could spend their hard-earned coppers at the established rate and not be forced to accept less. Merchants, on the other hand, had much more reason to worry about the condition of the copper currency since large numbers of lightweight coins could accumulate very quickly in their coffers such that their profits could become tied up in unspendable, undesirable money. The potential in America was similar to the situation described in London in 1754 when merchants complained about the quantities of virtually unnegotiable counterfeit coppers with which they were burdened. It was the merchant class that was most prone to be inconvenienced from an excess of copper and it was this class that had the greater influence with the state assemblies and newspapers, and thereby could mold public opinion and public approval. The urban poor, however, just wanted fair exchange for their token coppers, while rural farmers, as a group, lived at more of a subsistance level so that money was of less importance. At the height of the Coppers Panic, some editorialists hastened to spread the word to the "farmers and industrious

[9] Newman, *Studies*, p. 157. Newman states that this account in the *Newport Mercury* contained the first written use of the word *Bungtown*. The calculation is that 160 coppers to the Federal dollar in N.Y. would be the same as 160 to 96d., or 8 shillings, N.Y. money of account, or 20 to the shilling.

[10] Peck, *British Museum*, p. 106; Craig, *Mint*, p. 220.

[11] Craig, *Mint*, p. 253.

poor" that coppers were devaluated and warned them of the situation lest they be victimized by unscrupulous "vermin."[12] Other reports specifically stated that "many of the merchants and shop-keepers ... have large sums by them of this coin, by which they will be great sufferers." Thus it appears that from a generic viewpoint, business interests stood the most to lose on account of the accumulation of a defective copper medium and the most to gain from its regulation and improvement. But on a more personal level, the "poorer class of citizens" were most affected by the devaluation of coppers since "many ... had their little all invested in this most uncertain of all human possessions ... a fluctuating medium."[13]

WEIGHT ANALYSIS OF CONFEDERATION COPPERS

Table 21 enumerates the various coppers known to have circulated during the Confederation period and their theoretical and observed weights. This table was constructed from almost 4,300 specimens listed in several auction sales, fixed price lists, and from institutional and private collections.[14] The assignment of the manufacturing mint follows the conventions accepted by several authorities, although these designations are not universally recognized and are subject to change based on newer research.[15] The first standard deviation, a sensitive measurement of the dispersion of values around the mean, was calculated for all averages to determine whether the observed weights of the coins approached, within limits of error, the authorized standard. Comparisons in the observed weights and the standards were made between the various coinages in Charts 2 to 4.

In this gravimetric analysis of Confederation coppers, a wide weight range exists even within the same variety of coin. This lack of uniformity reflects imperfect quality control in planchet manufacture, particularly with regard to the thickness to which the planchet stock was rolled; coins cut from a thicker fillet would obviously be heavier. Planchet diameters could vary naturally since all these coins were struck without collars. Overstruck and double struck coppers are characteristically greater in diameter since they have been subjected to the deforming pressure of the press more than once. As a general statement, the more rudimentary the conditions of planchet preparation the greater the weight range and the less uniformity. In Table 21, the disparity in coin weights is expressed by the value of the first standard deviation; the lesser consistency in weight of the coppers in a particular series, the greater the first standard deviation. From Table 21, the Virginia halfpence, group 19a, have the smallest first standard deviation, and the most obvious explanation for this consistency was the better manufacturing technology available at the Tower Mint. Despite these improved conditions at the Royal Mint, there was still quite a variation in uniformity; Peck listed a range of 140.9 to 167.9 grains for regal copper halfpence minted between the years 1770 and 1775.[16] While overweight silver and gold planchets of the period were individually reconciled prior to striking as evidenced by file adjustment marks, it would have been ridiculous to have expended such efforts on the copper medium. The question appropriately arises about acceptable tolerances in the manufacture of these coppers. Referring again to the Virginia halfpence, the royal warrant addressed the "small errors as may happen in and by the unequal sizing of the Bars which errors you shall endeavour

[12] *Conn. Jour.*, July 29, 1789.
[13] *Ind. Gaz.*, July 23, 1789.
[14] *Garrett, Roper, Bareford, Picker, Mail Bid 1985A, Norweb, Gunlocke, Oechsner, Taylor*, Stoutjesdyk and Hoge, ANA 1989, *Saccone, Boyd, Brand*, & Ryder, *Schenkel, Rosa Americana* FPL, *Frontenac, Hessberg, Matlock*, American Numismatic Society collection, and other private holdings.
[15] Assignment for New Jersey mints follows Breen, *CNL 1969*; see also *Weimer and Hirt*, pp. 97-98. The Maris 56 to 58-n series, the "camel heads," are considered separately due to controversy regarding their origin (see Anton, *CNL 1975*, pp. 499-501). The Connecticut attributions are from Breen, *Studies*, and the Vermont attributions from Bressett, *Studies*.
[16] Peck, *British Museum*, pp. 620-21.

that they be not in Excess & Defect above the 30th Part of a Pound Weight (i.e. 3.33%) and this not by Design but only by accident...."[17] Acceptable variations for George II coppers were "up to one-fortieth in the pound avoirdupois" or 2½%.[18] While the royal authority recognized the potential for some discrepency in the weight of individual coppers, it was clearly expected that the average weight of the entire series would adhere to the warrant specifications. Although minting procedures have advanced over the years, the process is not yet perfect, since as late as the most recent halfpence of Elizabeth II with an authorized standard of 87.5 grains, the average weight was 87.38 grains and the range varied from 84.7 to 89.2 grains.[19] Coppers from the Confederation mints would be expected to show a greater tolerance in weight than those contemporaneous coins from England since quality control would have been less well developed in the late eighteenth century America. In the previous chapter it was proposed that a 5% deviation from the standard would be acceptable for Confederation coppers considering the problems inherent in rolling the planchet stock to the exact thickness. The best American pieces, as a group, were from the Massachusetts mint, although some individual New Jersey issues showed good consistency.

CONDITION GRADE VERSUS WEIGHT

At first thought, one might query how coins in varying conditions of wear can be considered and averaged in the same group. The fact is that the ravages of usual circulation do not appreciably reduce the coin's weight. Spilman reported a loss of 6.84% for Virginia halfpence recovered from archaeological digs at Colonial Williamsburg when compared to a standard derived from uncirculated specimens.[20] Frequently the state or grade of a coin is a reflection of its manufacture rather than wear per se. This circumstance is well illustrated by Machin's Mills imitation halfpence where the dies were shallowly engraved on purpose to simulate wear, although the specimens may have seen little actual circulation. Uncirculated Vermont coppers may show significant weakness in the design because of die preparation whereas mint condition Massachusetts coppers may show exquisite detail because of high quality dies and planchets, and uniform striking. "The grading of early copper state coins is very subjective, for there is no way to differentiate light wear from light striking in many instances."[21]

The most accurate weight analysis would require uncirculated specimens. Except for certain series where hoards have been recovered, namely the Fugio cents and the Virginia halfpence, such data are not available. Since we must work with the circulated specimens available to us, the logical question arises, by how much does normal wear reduce a coin's mint weight? This complex problem was addressed in regard to Machin's Mills imitation halfpence where three lots of coppers, grouped according state of preservation, were compared as to weight, range of weight, and the first standard deviation (Table 19). The data derived from the Machin's Mills imitation halfpence suggest that at least for this series, coppers of different grades, as long as there are no obvious planchet flaws or corrosion, can be included together in weight analysis since there is not enough metal lost in average wear to create any substantial difference. The average values in Table 19 are all in statistically significant agreement with each other, even if the "Fine" category of only 12 specimens is omitted.

[17] Newman, *Colonial Virginia*, p. 52.

[18] Craig, *Mint*, p. 250. The warrants specified the number of coppers per pound and not the weight per individual coin.

[19] Peck, *British Museum*, p. 621.

[20] Spilman, *CNL 1988B*, p. 1061.

[21] *Garrett*, lot 1416. "The grading of state coppers is as close to being a 'black art' as any grading discipline in the American series. Time and time again, we have seen one specialist designate an issue as Very Good, for example, and another call it Very Fine, the differences being attributable to interpretations of original striking sharpness and die detail." (*Taylor*, lot 2162.)

TABLE 19

Comparison of Weight Data of 46 Machin's Mills Imitation Halfpence of Varying Condition Grades; Weights in Grains

Number of Specimens: Good 10, Very Good 9, Fine 12, Very Fine 12, and Extra Fine 3.
Weights Expressed in Range, Mean with 1st Standard Deviation (SD), and Median.

Grade	*Good and Very Good*	*Fine*	*Very Fine and Extra Fine*	*Entire Group*
Number	19	12	15	46
Range	89.8 to 137.6	96.2 to 135.5	89.7 to 128.4	89.7 to 137.6
Mean	108.9	114.0	112.8	111.5
1st SD	± 10.1	± 9.7	± 10.3	± 10.4
Median	108.6	112.7	114.4	112.6

A similar weight analysis was done for 113 Massachusetts cents separated according to lesser and excellent grades. Again no significant differences were noted.

TABLE 20

Comparison of Weight Data of 113 Massachusetts Cents of Varying Condition Grades; Weights in Grains

Number of Specimens: Very Good 6, Fine 12, Very Fine 36, Extra Fine 30, Almost Uncirculated 18, and Uncirculated 11.
Weights Expressed in Range, Mean with 1st Standard Deviation (SD), and Median.

Grade	*Very Good, Fine and Very Fine*	*Extra Fine, Almost Unc., and Uncirculated*	*Entire Group*
Number	54	59	113
Range	134.7 to 185.0	136.8 to 171.4	134.7 to 185.0
Mean	153.5	153.5	153.5
1st SD	± 10.2	± 7.8	± 9.0
Median	152.2	154.5	153.4

Observed vs. Authorized Weights

TABLE 21

Comparison Between Observed and Authorized Weights of Copper Coins Current during the Confederation Period

Column A: Authorized weight in grains.
Column B: Observed weight in grains with first standard deviation.[a]
Column C: Number of specimens examined.
Data on less than 15 specimens included only for interest.
Column D: Comparison between observed and authorized weights; see text.
W = Weights within range of error of authorized standard in Column A; see text.
EX = Exceeds standard.

B = Below standard.
NA = Standard weight Not Applicable.
Column E: % variation from standard in Column A.

Description of Coinage	*A*	*B*	*C*	*D*	*E*
1.1787 Fugio Cent (CNL data)[b]	157.5				
1a Fine Rays		150.0 ± 12.6	675	W	−4.8
1b "Round" Club rays		150.3 ± 10.5	65	W	−4.6
1c "Concave" Club Rays		162.0 ± 10.4	19	EX	+2.9
2.Massachusetts Cent	157.5	153.9 ± 9.1	156	W	−2.3
3.Massachusetts Half Cent	78.75	76.5 ± 6.3	68	W	−2.9
4.New Jersey: Rahway mint	150.0	147.4 ± 8.7	471	W	−1.7
4a "Post-replevin"[c]		149.8 ± 9.8	78	W	−0.1
4b Obverse horse head left		148.5 ± 9.4	26	W	−1.0
4c Coulterless		143.0 ± 12.5	48	W	−4.7
5.New Jersey: Morristown mint	150.0				
5a Patterns		137.9 ± 19.4	6	NA	−8.1
5b Maris 3-6 C, D.		139.9 ± 9.0	35	B	−6.7
5c 1787 Morristown mint		148.0 ± 10.4	132	W	−1.3
5d 1788 Morristown mint, entire sample		143.3 ± 11.2	39	W	−4.5
22 Maris 67-v		148.8 ± 6.4	22	W	−0.8
remaining 17 specimens		136.6 ± 13.3	17	B	−8.9
6.New Jersey: Elizabethtown mint 150.0					
6a not overstruck		138.3 ± 18.1	31	W	−7.8
6b overstruck on other coppers		125.1 ± 20.3	43	B	−16.6
7.N.J.: Brasher and Bailey mint	150.0	143.8 ± 8.5	53	W	−4.1
8.N.J.: counterfeits, Maris 54-k	150.0	117.9 ± 14.7	25	B	−21.4
9.New Jersey: Maris 56 to 58-n[d]	150.0	127.2 ± 16.8	70	B	−15.2
10.Connecticut: C.C.C.[e]	144.0				
10a 1785 MBR, 1785/6 MBL		135.3 ± 11.2	294	W	−6.0
10b 1786 DBL		148.3 ± 15.1	18	EX	+3.0
10c 1787 DBL		143.5 ± 11.6	109	W	−0.3
10d 1787 MBL		143.8 ± 11.8	27	W	−0.1
11.Connecticut: Jarvis mint	144.0				
11a 1787 DBL "cinquefoils"		134.6 ± 12.0	610	W	−6.5
11b 1787 "crosses"[f]		145.0 ± 12.7	73	EX	+0.7
11c 1787 "fleurons"[g]		142.0 ± 11.6	134	W	−1.4
12.Connecticut: 1786 MBR	144.0	116.8 ± 19.4	34	B	−18.9

[a] This is the first standard deviation which on the bell-shaped normal distribution curve includes 68.26% of the specimens. See Chart 5, Appendix 4.

[b] The Fugio weights are provided through the courtesy of James C. Spilman and are reported in *CNL* 87 (1991), pp. 1236-40.

[c] See footnote #27.

[d] No weight difference was noted for the sample of nine 56-n to 58-n specimens which were not overstruck. The host coins in these instances may not have been detected by usual visual examination. All non-overstruck coppers of this series should undergo more precise scrutiny with planchet analysis and diameter measurement before it is concluded that they were struck on virgin planchets.

[e] C.C.C. is the Company for Coining Coppers; MBR is Mailed Bust Right, MBL is Mailed Bust Left, and DBL is Draped Bust Left, all descriptive terms for the obverse effigy.

[f] 1787 17-g.3, 18-g.1, 19-g.4, 21-DD, 22-g.2, 24-g.3, 24-g.5, 24-FF, 38-GG, 45-CC, and 46-BB. The copper, 48-g.5 has fleurons on the obverse and crosses on the reverse and may be a transitional piece.

[g] 1787 reverses e, h, i, k, l, cc, ee, ff, HH, and RR with obverses 34, 36, 37, 39, and 56.

Description of Coinage	*A*	*B*	*C*	*D*	*E*
13. Connecticut: 1787 "Morristown" related, entire sample	144.0	122.5 ± 12.0	64	B	−14.9
13a Miller 4-L		126.9 ± 11.3	35	B	−11.9
13b Miller 1.3-L, 6.1-M, 6.2-M		117.0 ± 10.4	29	B	−18.8
14. Connecticut: 1787 Muttonhead	144.0	131.0 ± 12.1	19	B	−9.0
15. Connecticut: 1787 Machin's Mills	144.0	115.9 ± 13.6	49	B	−19.5
16. Connecticut: Triple Leaves	144.0				
16a 1787 entire sample		130.1 ± 21.2	145	W	−9.7
16b 1787 Miller 11-E,K, 10-E, 9-E, 2-B, heavy		142.1 ± 17.5	74	W	−1.3
16c 1787 all others, light		117.6 ± 17.1	71	B	−18.3
16d 1788 not overstruck		121.0 ± 16.3	57	B	−16.0
16e 1788 overstruck (o/s) on CONSTELLATIO NOVAS		115.8 ± 5.4	15	B	−19.6
17. Connecticut: 1788 DBL (Machin's Mills)[h]	144.0	118.7 ± 14.7	79	B	−17.6
18. Connecticut: 1788 MBR (Machin's Mills)					
18a Not overstruck	144.0	112.8 ± 13.2	40	B	−21.7
18b 1788 MBR overstruck on CONSTELLATIO NOVAS		112.3 ± 7.9	27	B	−22.0
19. Virginia 1773 halfpence	116.7				
19a current data		117.2 ± 4.5	47	EX	+0.4
19b CNL data mint state specimens[i]		115.74 ± 5.49	32	W	−0.8
19c CNL data worn specimens		107.82 ± 5.47	33	B	−7.6
20. Vermont: Rupert mint	111.0				
20a 1785/6 landscapes		121.3 ± 10.4	58	EX	+9.7
20b 1786 busts		120.1 ± 8.1	31	EX	+8.2
20c 1787/8 busts right		115.4 ± 10.4	79	EX	+4.0
21. Vermont: Machin's Mills mint	111.0				
21a not overstruck		113.8 ± 12.4	57	EX	+2.5
21b o/s on CONSTELLATIO NOVAS		123.1 ± 3.9	8	EX	+10.9
21c o/s on counterfeit Irish halfpence		103.7 ± 15.9	11	W	−6.6
22. Machin's imitation halfpence	152.2	111.5 ± 10.4	46	B	−26.7
23. English counterfeit halfpence	152.2	110.4 ± 17.7	68	B	−27.5
24. Irish counterfeit halfpence	134.6	106.7 ± 12.6	21	B	−20.7
25. CONSTELLATIO NOVA	NA			NA	
25a 1783		120.8 ± 15.8	28		
25b 1785		116.4 ± 7.2	46		
25c all 1783 and 1785		118.1 ± 11.4	74		
25d 1786 counterfeits		107.9 ± 16.8	5		
26. NOVA EBORAC[j]	NA			NA	
26a reverse figure left		135.7 ± 12.1	16		
26b reverse figure right		109.1 ± 6.6	13		
26c small head		132.0 ± 17.3	4		

[h] Excludes three 1788 Miller 16.3-N coppers overstruck on counterfeit Massachusetts coppers which average 116.8 grains.

[i] Spilman, *CNL 1988A*, reported the weights of 32 mint state specimens which are listed in 19b but there may be duplication with some of those in 19a. Those in 19c recovered from excavations in Colonial Williamsburg just exhibited normal wear and were not corroded from being buried. Group 19a contains 36 uncirculated coins of the total 47.

[j] The greater weight of the reverse figure seated left was reported in *Frontenac*, lot 365. The difference is significant at $p = <0.0001$.

Analysis of Table 21

Table 21 is important since it is descriptive of the surviving Confederation coppers which at one point in our history circulated as the small change medium of our forebears. Whatever theoretical errors may exist between these samples and the "true" average mint weight, a value which can never be known for certain but only inferred, the coins being measured today *are* the circulating coppers of the period which were rejected for the most part by the public during the Coppers Panic. Even at their best, these coppers were only a token coinage minted at a profit to someone. To add insult to injury, counterfeiters of even lighter weight coppers made further gains at public expense. Because of inequities in exchange rates, there were periods in our history when importers of both regal and illegal money could turn a quick profit when such coppers were transported to the colonies in bulk. Eventually, the state legislatures responded to this situation and endeavored to provide a reliable, fit copper coinage, the currency of the poor and disadvantaged classes. The degree to which these state issues achieved their authorized weights was in some part an index of reliability and public trust in these new coppers which were projected to correct all the past evils which had plagued the medium. Some of the coppers were more successful than others in fulfilling this goal, but ultimately all failed the test of public confidence in July 1789, when the Coppers Panic occurred. The following three bar graphs summarize the weight analyses of Table 21 by indicating how well the Confederation coinages, both legal and spurious, conformed to their respective legal standards. Considering the imperfect technology available for planchet preparation, a five percent error was probably within the limits of acceptable tolerance.

CHART 2

Weight of Coppers Minted at 157.5 Grain Standard
(Massachusetts and Fugio Cents from Table 21)

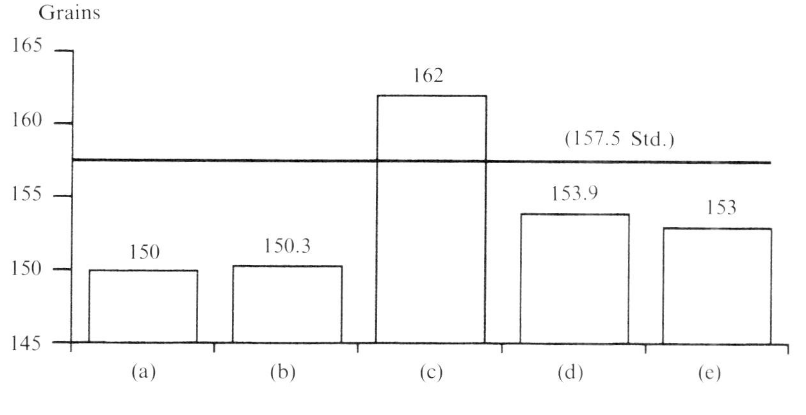

a. Group 1a: Fine Rays Fugio Cent: 150.0 grains.
b. Group 1b: Round End Club Rays Fugio Cent: 150.3 grains.
c. Group 1c: Concave End Club Rays Fugio Cent: 162.0 grains.
d. Group 2: Massachusetts Cent: 153.9 grains.
e. Group 3: Massachusetts Half Cent (×2): 76.5 × 2 = 153.0 grains.

CHART 3

Weight of New Jersey Coppers Minted at the 150.0 Grain Standard
(From Table 21)

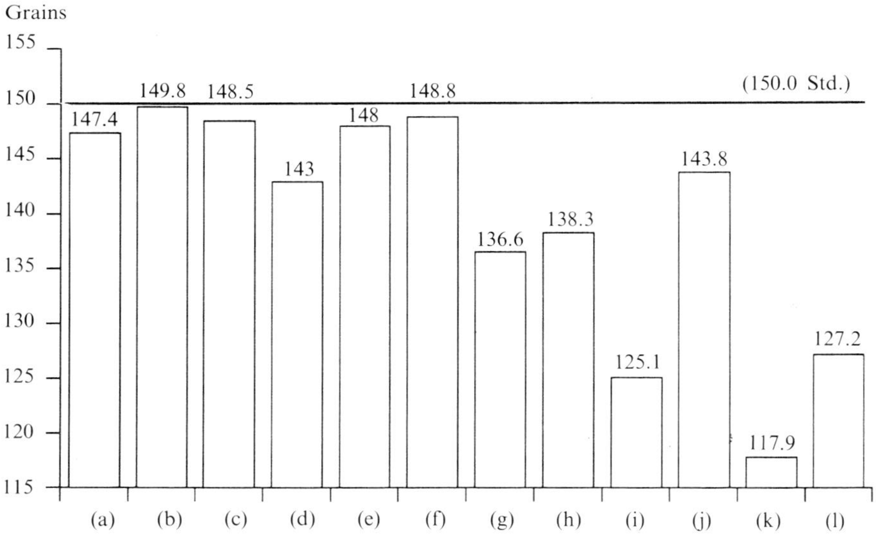

a. Group 4: Rahway Mint: 147.4 grains.
b. Group 4a: Ogden "Post-Replevin" : 149.8 grains.
c. Group 4b: Horse head left: 148.5 grains.
d. Group 4c: Coulterless: 143.0 grains.
e. Group 5c: 1787 Morristown: 148.0 grains.
f. Group 5d: 1788 Morristown, Maris 67-v: 148.8 grains
g. Group 5d: 1788 Morristown, others: 136.6 grains.
h. Group 6a: Elizabethtown, not overstruck: 138.3 grains.
i. Group 6b: Elizabethtown, overstruck: 125.1 grains.
j. Group 7: Brasher and Bailey: 143.8 grains.
k. Group 8: Counterfeits, Maris 54-k: 117.9 grains.
l. Group 9: Maris 56 to 58-n series: 127.2 grains.

CHART 4A

Weights of Connecticut Coppers Minted at the 144 Grain Standard: Part 1, Company for Coining Coppers and Jarvis Mint (See Table 21)

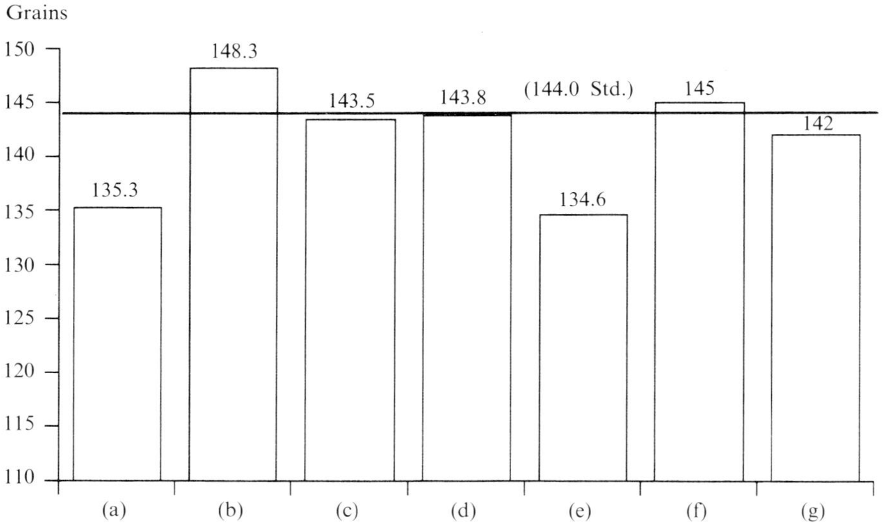

a. Group 10a: 1785 MBR and 1785/6 MBL; C.C.C.: 135.3 grains.
b. Group 10b: 1786 DBL; C.C.C.: 148.3 grains.
c. Group 10c: 1787 DBL; C.C.C.: 143.5 grains.
d. Group 10d: 1787 MBL; C.C.C.: 143.8 grains.
e. Group 11a: 1787 DBL; Jarvis: 134.6 grains.
f. Group 11b: 1787 DBL; "crosses": 145.0 grains.
g. Group 11c: 1787 DBL; "fleurons": 142.0 grains.

CHART 4B

Weights of Connecticut Coppers Minted at the 144 Grain Standard:
Part 2, Illegal Mints: (See Table 21)

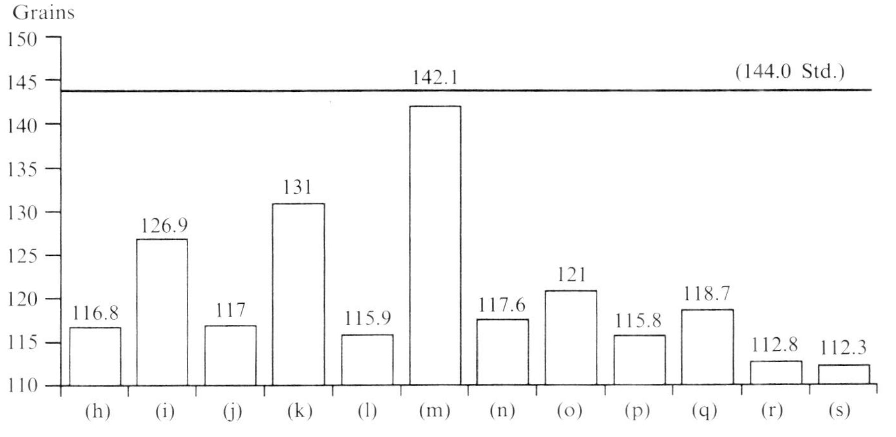

h. Group 12: 1786 MBR; "? Atlee-related" : 116.8 grains.
i. Group 13a: 1787 "Morristown-related," 4-L: 126.9 grains.
j. Group 13b: 1787 "Morristown-related," 1.3-L, 6-M: 117.0 grains.
k. Group 14: 1787 Muttonheads: 131.0 grains.
l. Group 15: 1787 Machin's Mills: 115.9 grains.
m. Group 16b: 1787 heavy Triple Leaves: 142.1 grains.
n. Group 16c. 1787 light Triple Leaves: 117.6 grains.
o. Group 16d. 1788 Triple Leaves, not overstruck: 121.0 grains.
p. Group 16e: 1788 Triple Leaves, overstruck: 115.8 grains.
q. Group 17: 1788 DBL: 118.7 grains.
r. Group 18a: 1788 MBR, not overstruck: 112.8 grains.
s. Group 18b: 1788 MBR, overstruck: 112.3 grains.

Besides the contemporary economic implications of proper weight coins as indicated in Table 21, there are also some interesting numismatic considerations. Weight comparisons of specific coppers provide morphological evidence that certain mintmasters strove to maintain legal weight requirements whereas others, whose coppers fell well below legal requirements, were motivated "to milk the system" for personal advantage. The other consideration is that fillet rolling and planchet preparation in these early mints were quite primitive and the finished products were inconsistent in weight. It could well be that the occurrence of heavy coppers was not always an indication of altruism on part of the mintmaster to give full measure, but rather his inability to roll the copper stock to the desired dimension. The greater the value of the first standard deviation, the greater the inconsistency in planchet weight and, by inference, the less sophisticated the technology of flan production. The weight distributions of the Confederation coppers from Table 21, with a sufficient number of specimens in the sample for meaningful analysis, are shown in Appendix 4. These curves give a visual representation of the mintmasters' ability to cut uniform planchets as an overall indication of their fillet rolling expertise. In several instances, coppers, which otherwise have been considered related varieties, are now seen to differ in average planchet weight suggesting that they were not struck on flans of the same fabric. Without a complete planchet composition analysis, such a finding is difficult to interpret except to state that a difference has been identified.

Table 21 was constructed having recorded the weights of each individual copper variety available from the numismatic literature. When similar varieties or types were identified, they were combined as groups, or subgroups, such that 60 final categories emerged within 26 major groupings. Column A lists the authorized standard for the particular issue under consideration. Column B gives the average weight and the first standard deviation which accounts for 68.26% of the specimens within each sample. Column C lists the number of specimens examined but those with 15 or less are included for interest only. Those coinages are marked in Column D with an "EX" when their average weights exceeded the standard listed in Column A, with a "W" when the standard falls within the first standard deviation of the average, and a "B" when the first standard deviation of the average falls below the standard. Using these criteria, eight American coinages exceed the limits of the authorized standard (EX), 21 are within range of the standard by their first standard deviation (W), and 18 are clearly below the standard (B). Column E notes the percentage and direction of variance of the average in Column B from the standard in Column A. The 21 groups which fall within range of their standard (W) are collectively an average of 3.4% below their authorized weights, while those 18 categories which are below their respective standards (B), as a group are deficient in weight by an average of 16.5%. These calculations indicate that the proposed 5% tolerance suggested as a remedy for the Confederation mintmasters is a reasonable figure since 16 of the 21 groups within the range of the standard fall within this estimate.

The first standard deviation values reported in Table 21 indicate the consistency in planchet weights within the respective coinages. The lower the value, the less variation in flan manufacture which infers a more technologically sophisticated operation. The potential flaw in this analysis is that certain varieties, New Jersey coppers in particular, may have been struck over an extended period of time and by one or more mints.

The most uniform coinage, as determined by the lowest value for the first standard deviation, is the Virginia halfpence from the Tower Mint. The other copper of English manufacture with good consistency in planchet weight is the 1785 Constellatio Nova token. When this issue was the host coin for several Connecticut and Vermont varieties, groups 16e, 18b, and 21b, the low first standard deviation is again reflected. The 1783 Constellatio Nova, group 25a, showed much greater weight variation suggesting less quality control for that particular year. The 1783 issues are rarely seen overstruck. Those coppers with a first standard deviation ranging from six to ten grains include the Massachusetts cents and half-cents, many Rahway issues, the Bailey New Jersey coppers, and the Vermont 1786 bust issues. The Maris 67-v variety, a coin attributed to the 1788 Morristown mint, has one of the most consistent planchet weights.

Coppers with a first standard deviation from 10 to 14 grains include most of the other legal Confederation issues, the Machin's Mills counterfeit halfpence, and several issues from New Jersey and Connecticut which fall below the standard. The first standard deviation for most lightweight counterfeits is above 14 grains showing little regard for the statutory standard, poor technique for planchet manufacture, or both.

Group 1 contains data for the Fugio series from the *Colonial Newsletter* database. All three subgroups are within the range of the 157.5 grain standard but there is a much heavier subgroup of 19 specimens, the "concave end" Club Rays, the average of which exceeds the standard at 162.0 grains. The Fugio Fine Rays and the residual "round end" Club Rays varieties are statistically lighter than the "concave end" group. From a numismatic perspective, the "concave end" Club Rays may have been heavier because the minter was unable to obtain sheet copper of the proper thickness to match the planchet cutter.[22] The other possibility is that these varieties were minted in a facility which had a regard for the legal standard and exceeded it. The suggestion that the Club Rays, particularly the "concave end" varieties, are a Machin's Mills product is untenable, since the output from that facility was always lighter than the coppers they imitated. This is well demonstrated by the various known Machin's issues examined elsewhere in this table. It is possible that these three styles of Fugios, the Fine Rays and both Club Rays varieties are all from separate sources or at least minted under different circumstances.

[22] James C. Spilman, personal communication, March 14, 1990.

Fugio coppers were also studied extensively by Douglas who measured their weights as individual groups for each of the varieties available to him.[23] The average weight of the complete sample of 1,810 specimens was 149.4 grains, while that for the 1,639 uncirculated specimens from the Bank of New York hoard, which included only eight varieties, was 149.2 grains, values which are in excellent agreement with Table 21. The average weight for each group of these eight uncirculated varieties showed a spread of only three grains from 148 to 151 grains, or a variation of ± 1%, demonstrating excellent quality control in manufacture. However, the average weight of 149.2 grains for the entire lot of uncirculated coins fell 8.3 grains, or 5.3%, short of the 157.5 grain standard, perhaps outside any existing remedy. The fact that the Fugio coinage was lightweight may have provided another cause of anxiety for Jarvis and an additional reason for Buell to have retreated to England. The weight distribution curve constructed by Douglas shows a single peak at about 147.5 grains with the first standard deviation (68.26% of all the specimens) falling approximately between 137 and 159 grains as roughly extrapolated from his chart. These points on Douglas's distribution curve agree exactly with the *CNL* data which is reproduced in Chart 8, Appendix 4.

Douglas made further interesting observations about the variation in the size of the Fugio cents. He concluded that the weight discrepancies were due to the uneven thickness of the copper sheets from which the planchets were cut. The variable diameters were a function of unequal pressures applied by the coining press with those for double struck coins significantly greater by one to two millimeters.[24]

Massachusetts coppers, as a group, consistently have the finest planchets within the state series, an observation familiar to numismatists. This large sample of coins in Group 2 from a state-run mint strayed 2.3% below the established standard of 157.5 grains but their average meets the standard within range of error.

New Jersey coppers are more complicated than previously imagined. The recent work by Hodder has demonstrated that specific die combinations were emitted sporadically over the useful life of the dies and that the dates give no accurate indication as to when the coppers were actually minted.[25] Since coppers of the same die variety made a scattered appearance over the period from late 1786, or early 1787, into 1790, it becomes evident that workable die combinations which were initiated at Rahway under Goadsby and Cox, continued to be employed by Ogden in Elizabethtown after he assumed operation of the defunct Rahway venture following June 7, 1788. Certain Rahway dies, whose temporal careers can be traced by diagnostic surface injuries, were obviously used by Ogden in Elizabethtown after the practice of overstriking coppers began in late 1788. Hodder demonstrates a gradual weight reduction in the non-overstruck, traceable J reverses over the life of the dies from 1786 into 1790. This decrease was accompanied by a simultaneous increase in the first standard deviation indicative of gradual relaxation of quality control in planchet production as the average weight was diminished.[26] Within the Head Left coppers (group 4b), certain of the so-called "post-replevin" issues (group 4a), and the Maris obverse 15 family, a gradual progression toward heavier planchets after June 1788, is observed which Hodder interprets as an improvement in quality as Ogden made a concerted effort to return to the statutory requirement of 150 grains.[27]

[23] Douglas, *Fugio*, pp. 55-65.

[24] Other reasons were responsible for diameter variation in early coinages. In the Federal Mint, it was technically very difficult to control the thickness of cold-rolled copper fillets. To compensate for this inequity in thickness and yet provide planchets of proper weight, the diameters of the 1794 cents were regulated since "several sizes of cutting-out punches were used to produce copper blanks near legal weight, even though the thickness [of the planchets] had not been properly controlled. This diameter variation is greater than the expected variance due to striking without a collar." (Williamson, *Penny-Wise 1984*, p. 104.)

[25] Hodder, *AJN 1989*.

[26] Hodder, *AJN 1989*, pp. 228-29. A possible exception is Maris 37-J.

[27] Hodder, *CNL 1989*. The "post replevin" label has been applied to certain Rahway coppers in an attempt to identify those coined by Matthias Ogden after the minting equipment was placed in his care

The 1787-dated coppers attributed to Morristown (group 5c) compare favorably with the standard of 150 grains but differ significantly in weight from their 1788-dated (group 5d) counterparts ($p = 0.024$). The deterioration in quality of the 1788 Morristown output is evident not only from the data in Table 21 but also from casual inspection of the coins themselves. However, the 1788 varieties are not a homogeneous group since the Maris 67-v variety is heavier than the remaining 1788 coppers ($p = 0.0029$), and its lower first standard deviation suggests an improved quality planchet preparation in contrast to the others of that year. These differences are sufficient to suggest that there may have been a different source for the Maris 67-v issue. The double peak in the 1788 Morristown distribution curve clearly indicates the heavier 67-v variety (Chart 16, Appendix 4). Newer research by Hodder emphasizes that many coppers traditionally attributed to Rahway were actually minted by Ogden in Rahway or Elizabethtown after June 1788, as indicated by the evolution of die flaws which establish a sort of "genetic marker." As a result there is a continuum of coppers from Rahway into Elizabethtown with the passage of time and it may be inaccurate to assign particular die combinations exclusively to the Rahway mint. Group 6a comprises those "traditional" Elizabethtown coppers for which there are no visually detectable host coins, but in such cases the clue to an otherwise obscure overstrike will be an increase in the usual diameter. In Hodder's study of the J reverse, coppers in the latest die state V, which were probably minted in Elizabethtown late in 1789 into 1790, weighed 134.9 ± 15.3 grains, a value quite compatible with the Elizabethtown coppers on original planchets, group 6a in Table 21.

As described in great detail in Appendix 2, the only commonly encountered overstruck coins are the 1788 Vermont and Connecticut coppers on Constellatio Novas (groups 16e, 18b, and 21b), the 1788 Vermont coppers on counterfeit Irish halfpence (group 21c), the Maris 56 to 58-n triad (group 9), and those attributed to Elizabethtown (group 6b). Of practical significance is the fact that the weight of the overstruck coin will be that of the host coin. All these specimens, except for Vermont group 21b, fall well below their respective standards at an average weight deficiency of 16%.

The motivation for a coiner to overstrike existing coppers could include any or all of the following three reasons: the coiner had no access to virgin planchet material and was obliged to use whatever copper was available; the coiner bought up lightweight coppers to overstamp with labels of a heavier authorized coinage to increase his profit margin; or, that unacceptable, or less acceptable, coppers were transformed into a more negotiable currency by an identity change in a coining press. An opportunity developed after August 1, 1787, for minters to procure a cheap, ready supply of potential host coins to overstrike, while increasing their profits and cheating the public, when New York demonetized all coppers under 145.8 grains. Thus, many non-negotiable coppers became available, probably in bulk discounts, including the Constellatio Nova coppers and counterfeit Irish halfpence, so popular at Machin's Mills. Heavier coins, such as legal Massachusetts cents and Fugio coppers are not found as undertypes whereas lighter coppers from other sources would prove more profitable.[28] As a result, New Jersey overstruck coins appear on practically every conceivable copper of the period lighter than 150 grains, although exceptions exist. It has been surmised that at the Elizabethtown Mint after the summer of 1789, Ogden did not have sufficient sheet copper stock from which to cut blanks and so supplemented his supply of planchets with unwanted cheap coppers which also allowed him the additional advantage of increasing his profit by the use of ready-made host coins. Certainly after the summer of 1789, the time when Connecticut coppers were no longer acceptable in New York, and New Jersey

---

pursuant to a June 7, 1788 court order (Breen, *CNL 1969*, p. 256). Because coppers were emitted in a spectrum from Rahway and Elizabethtown, this distinction is probably inconsequential but it does identify specific varieties. See also Williamson, *CNL 1980*.

[28] A 1788 Connecticut, Miller 16.3-N, is found over a 1787 Massachusetts cent, Crosby 1-B, but this host coin, itself, is a lightweight counterfeit from an unknown mint.

coins were the only negotiable copper medium, there would have been a great incentive to convert all Connecticut coppers into New Jersey currency. Although no statement can be made as to the date of manufacture, two-thirds of the overstruck coppers attributed to Elizabethtown represented in group 6b, and one-half of the Maris 56 to 58-n varieties in group 9, are over Connecticut coppers.

This alchemy, whereby minters transformed lesser coppers into the more desirable New Jersey medium, was no doubt the stimulus for the New Jersey legislative report of June 7, 1790, which advised that such overstruck coins were so light that they should have passed at 45 to the shilling rather than the 15 to the shilling as established by law for full weight, pure copper, New Jersey coins.[29] It is evident that the large number of lightweight, overstruck New Jersey issues undermined the credibility of legitimate coins.

The 1788 Connecticut overstruck coppers (group 18b) appear on Constellatio Nova host coins except for the rare occurrence of the counterfeit Massachusetts cent undertype as previously acknowledged in group 17. The Vermont overstruck issues from Rupert (group 21b) were also on Constellatio Nova coppers but in doing so, their weight standard was not violated since the average Constellatio Nova coin exceeded the authorized 111 grain standard for the Republic of Vermont. The Irish undertypes used at Machin's Mills for certain 1788 Vermont coppers (group 21c) were apparently counterfeit since their average weight is almost identical with the Irish counterfeits listed in group 24. Regal Irish halfpence of the period were minted in 1766, 1769, 1774 to 1776, 1781, and 1782 at an established weight of 134.6 grains.[30] Batty described a large number of Irish counterfeit halfpence of that era including 1772, 1773, and 1783, years for which there were no legitimate Irish coppers.[31] With such an abundance of contemporary Irish counterfeit halfpence, some found their way into American minting presses.

This discussion must include the Maris 56 to 58-n clone, since by itself, 56-n is the most common coin among the sample of 4,300 American coppers in Table 21, being represented 55 times.[32] The fact that this particular variety appears so frequently in the auction experience

[29] Newman, *Studies*, p. 154.

[30] The variation for regal Irish halfpence was not to exceed 3.3% (Ruding, *Annals*, vol. 2, p. 75).

[31] Batty, *Descriptive Catalogue*, vol. 3, pp. 1023-47.

[32] Table 21 is compiled from auction experience and collections where coin weights are listed. In many of these auctions, there was a heavy representation of New Jersey coppers and so the frequency rate for these Confederation coppers may be subject to significant sampling errors. This following list is only an approximation of the frequency for the three most common coppers followed by groups of five for those issues with 15 or more representatives in Table 21. No Massachusetts coppers appear on this list but the closest ones for this distinction are the 1788 half cent, Ryder 1-B, with 14 specimens, and the 1787 "horned eagle" cent, Ryder 2b-A with 12. Reference is made to the article by Packard, *CNL 1989*, which addresses this issue. All Vermont coppers are decidedly rarer but the presence of the Nova Eborac was unexpected.

Census	*Copper*
55	New Jersey 56-n, "camel head"
35	Connecticut 4-L, "horned bust"
30	Connecticut (1787) 33.7-r2, Draped Bust Left
25-29	New Jersey 64-t, 46-e, 48-g, 17-b (R-4).
20-24	New Jersey 67-v, 43-d, 14-J, 18-M, 63-S.
	Connecticut (1788) 2-D.
15-19	Connecticut (1787) 31.1-r4, 6.1-M, 33.15-r1 (R-2), 13-D (R-4), 1.2-C (R-3), 33.2-Z5.
	(1788) 16.3-N (R-2).
	New Jersey 54-k (R-3), 77-dd (R-2), 21-N, 6-D.
	Nova Eborac, figure left.

The coins on this census are rarity 1, except where indicated. The frequent occurrence of New Jersey 17-b and 54-k, and Connecticut 1.2-C and 13-D suggests that the rarity estimated for these issues is exaggerated and needs reappraisal.

from which this table is derived, may be due to its popularity among numismatists who are attracted by the prospect of collecting the various host coins. Nonetheless, the number of survivors today supposes a prodigious output of a single die combination, to say nothing of the fact that the n reverse saw further use with two other obverses.

There is debate as to whether the "camel heads" were from Machin's Mills or Elizabethtown. The arguments will not be repeated here except to state that the host coin utilization for the Maris 56 clone is far more characteristic of the Elizabethtown practices where all available lighter weight coppers were fed into the presses. Since the Maris 56-n dies lasted so long, it is also evident that whoever struck them had the capability to anneal the host coins since if they were not softened, the dies would have long since shattered. Also when a host coin was not annealed, the new dies would make very poor impressions with the old design showing through very plainly as often seen in the 1788 Connecticuts struck over Constellatio Nova coppers.[33]

The 56-n specimens in Table 21 alone comprise 5.2% of all the New Jersey coppers examined. This does not even address the fact that the Maris n reverse was even more durable than its obverse partners and accounts for over 6.6% of all the New Jersey samples in the table. Although the number of "camel heads" consigned to auction is inordinately large and does not represent their original proportion within the total New Jersey coinage, it is still a significant number. If we consider that there were about four million or more New Jersey coppers of all varieties, then at a maximum of 5.2% of the total, the original census for 56-n would be 208,000, while the n reverse would have endured almost 265,000 impressions! Even half of this maximal estimate for 56-n would be 104,000, still too large an emission to have been the progeny of a single die pair.

Spilman suggested that 50,000 impressions was an excessive expectation for the Fugio die pairs.[34] Hodder in a recent article, calculated that in 1796, less than 20,000 large cents were minted per die pair.[35] Even postulating that the finest current technology was available to the authors of the "camel heads," it is intriguing to postulate the existence of a complex hub from which several identical Maris-56 dies were made and used over the life of the coinage. Since coin detail can be difficult to interpret because of overstriking (only 5 of the 55 specimens did not include reference to a host coin) the existence of several 56-n die pairs could be hard to prove by naked-eye examination. If this notion of several completely hubbed dies is plausible, then who could have provided Buell's hubbing technology?[36] It is safe to say that whatever facility produced this series, it possessed the capacity to case-harden dies and anneal the host coins prior to overstriking or else the obverse 56 die would have long since shattered as did the obverse Maris 58. This is in contrast to the later days at Machin's Mills where the Vermont dies fractured quickly while overstriking the counterfeit Irish halfpence, group 21c.

Whatever time may reveal, the facts suggest that the 56-n variety was produced by a highly skilled artisan. The clones of 56-n, namely 57 and 58-n, were far fewer in number to suggest more than one obverse die but since the obverse devices on these varieties are so similar, could these have been partially hubbed obverse dies which fractured earlier than Maris 56? So the question remains, is the currently observed census of the Maris 56-n New Jersey copper due to an original prolific output, perhaps employing more than one die pair, or is its frequency more apparent than real because of a significant modern-day sampling error? This is the challenge for future research using photographic overlay techniques.

The coppers attributed to Brasher and Bailey approach the 150.0 grain standard within error (group 7). The obvious counterfeits, 54-k, 80-ff, 81, 83-ii, and 84-kk (group 8) make no effort to achieve full weight.

[33] James C. Spilman, personal communication, March 14, 1990.
[34] Spilman, *CNL 1961*, p. 24.
[35] Hodder, *RCR* 74.
[36] Spilman, *CNL* 1972, pp. 424-34.

The weight analyses of Connecticut coppers reveal some interesting results. Since the average weight for each of the first three types from the Company for Coining Coppers (1785 Mailed Bust Right, 1785 Mailed Bust Left, and 1786 Mailed Bust Left) fall within 1.9 grains of each other, these types are combined. As a composite group (10a) of 294 specimens, their average is 135.3 ± 11.2 grains which falls barely within the range of error of the 144.0 standard. It is unlikely that these underweight coppers were a contrived deception by the newly franchised mint to increase their profit margins, but rather represented a technical problem due to the inability to roll the copper fillets to the required dimensions. A decrease of only 0.10 millimeter in the thickness of the copper sheets, the thickness of a single sheet of paper, could account for this weight reduction. When the new style Draped Bust Left coppers was introduced in 1786 (group 10b), the average weight exceeded the standard. This increase could have represented an improvement in rolling technology, since from this point on, the Company for Coining Coppers produced standard weight coins. The historical event which coincides with this appearance of typically full weight coppers, was the six week period starting September 10, 1786, when the Company for Coining Coppers had exhausted their supply of copper and leased their equipment to the group of Mark Leavenworth, Isaac Baldwin, and William Leavenworth who are considered responsible for the 1786 Draped Bust Left issues.[37]

The 1787 Draped Bust Left (large letters) in group 10c, and the 1787 Mailed Bust Left in group 10d, both from the Company for Coining Coppers, cannot be distinguished from each other by weight and compare favorably with the legal requirement. The remaining 1787 Draped Bust Left issues, identified by their smaller letters in the legends, are attributed by Breen to their successors in business, Jarvis and Company (group 11). The 1787 Draped Bust Left coppers of group 11 are not a homogeneous population; the first of these exceptions, group 11b, are those with the g, BB, CC, FF, and GG reverses, comprising Miller 17-g.3, 18-g.1, 19-g.4, 21-DD, 22-g.2, 24-g.3, 24-g.5, 24-FF, 38-GG, 45-CC, 46-BB, and 48-g.5.[38] These varieties all have crosses on both the obverse and reverse except for 48 which has obverse fleurons. When the average weight of this group 11b is compared statistically with the larger group 11a, the "cross" group 11b differs significantly from the remainder of its Draped Bust Left colleagues of group 11a ($p = < 0.0001$). The "cross" group exceeds the 144.0 grain standard whereas group 11a is deficient by 6.5%.

There is a second subset represented in group 11c consisting of Miller 34, 36, 37, 39, and 56 with "fleurons" on the reverse (e, h, i, k, l, cc, ee, ff, HH, and RR). Many of these varieties also have an R substituted for a missing B in LIB in the reverse legend. When isolated and examined separately from the 1787 Draped Bust Left coppers of group 11a, this group, 11c, tips the scale at 142.0 ± 11.6 grains, which is a highly significant increase over group 11a ($p = < 0.0001$). The remaining Draped Bust Left issues represented in group 11a are by far the most common Connecticut coppers. These issues are characterized by the presence of cinquefoils in the legends, a design shared with the Fugio coppers which were minted by the same organization. The weight analysis of these 1787 Draped Bust Left Connecticut issues is displayed in Charts 19 to 22, Appendix 4.

It is entirely possible that the punctuation of Connecticut legends is a code which indicates some circumstance within the minting process. Breen has suggested that the different ornamentation identifies the "workmen who completed the dies from Buell's hubs."[39] The emission sequence of the 1787 Draped Bust Left series has four separate cycles, beginning with the large lettered issues from the Company for Coining Coppers. These are next followed by those coppers with small letters from Jarvis and Company with crosses in the legends, then fleurons, and lastly

[37] Breen, *Studies*, p. 122; Crosby, *Early Coins*, p. 222.
[38] The 1787 Miller 38-GG appears to be the heaviest of all Connecticut varieties with six specimens averaging 156.1 grains.
[39] *EAC 1975*, p. 26.

by those with cinquefoils, a design shared with the Fugios.[40] The first three emissions are of good weight, whereas the last and largest is deficient. It is not as though Jarvis and Company lacked the technology to set the proper roller spacing, since they minted Fugio coppers at 150 grains. It would appear that this weight reduction for the last Draped Bust Left issues was quite purposeful. The final Draped Bust Left production in 1788 using Buell's hubs (group 17), probably from Machin's Mills, is very much lighter on average than any of their earlier counterparts.

Groups 12 to 14 represent contemporary counterfeits illegally minted and the lower weight values are anticipated. Group 12 contains the 1786 Mailed Bust Right coppers traditionally attributed to Atlee. Group 13 has been considered a product of Walter Mould due to punch link evidence previously described. When the planchet weights of these four varieties are plotted, the curve has a definite double peak, the heavier issues being the 4-L or "horned bust." These gravimetric data indicate that the planchets of the so-called Mould Connecticut counterfeits are dissimilar and all were not cut under the same circumstances (see Chart 24, Appendix 4). The Machin's Mills output of 1787 (group 15) and 1788 (group 18) are only about three grains apart in average weight; the 1788 Machin's Mills coppers on original planchets (group 18a) are similar in weight to their overstruck varieties represented in group 18b.

Within the 1787 Triple Leaves varieties included in group 16, there is a wide variation in planchet weight as indicated by the elevation in the first standard deviation. There is a heavier sub-population which has been found to consist of 11-E, 11-K, 10-E, 9-E and 2-B (16b) which approach the authorized standard, whereas the remainder are significantly lighter (group 16c) and are similar to those dated 1788 (group 16d). See Chart 26, Appendix 4. This is very suggestive that the Triple Leaves are not a homogeneous group with certain members very near the standard while others are quite deficient. The logical explanation is that they were minted under different auspices although both display a wide range of planchet weights indicating difficulty in rolling the copper stock to a consistent thickness. The heavier 1787 Triple Leaves of 16b have been identified by Breen as a specific group.[41] These heavier varieties may have been struck independently from the lighter 1787 (group 16c) and 1788 (group 16d) varieties which are similar in weight. An explanation for this observation is that Benjamin Buell struck coppers from his father's dies before relinquishing his equipment to Machin's Mills. Possibly this weight profile is due to the fact that the full weight 1787 Triple Leaves coppers were minted by Buell and the lighter 1787 and 1788-dated coins later came from Machin's Mills.

Crosby stated that the 1785 Connecticut coppers showed the greatest "degree of regularity" in weight when compared with the other three years.[42] In writing of the 1786 varieties, he added that "few are found ... which do not reach the legal requirement of 144 grains." A sample of 28 coins from the Company for Coining Coppers of 1785 and 1786 reported by Lindesmith showed that only nine coins met or exceeded 144 grains and the average of all examined was 133.2 grains.[43] Considering the 1787 issues Crosby observed that "most of the mailed busts exceed the legal weight, though some fall much below it; the draped busts show less variation, few of them much exceeding that required, and many of them, when slightly worn, falling a little short of it."[44]

The Tower Mint Virginia halfpence (group 19a) were the most consistent of all these coinages but, of course, were not an American product.

All the Vermont issues in Table 21 surpassed the established standard, an observation also recorded by Crosby.[45]

[40] *EAC 1975*, pp. 25-26.
[41] *EAC 1975*, pp. 21-22; Breen, *Encyclopedia*, 775, 776; see below, p. 292, n. 1.
[42] Crosby, *Early Coins*, pp. 214, 215.
[43] Lindesmith, *CNL 1973*, p. 411. The condition of all coins was not specified here or by Crosby.
[44] Crosby, *Early Coins*, p. 217.
[45] Crosby, *Early Coins*, p. 186.

The report of the New York legislative committee of March 5, 1787, cited "Birmingham coppers," the contemporary name for counterfeit English halfpence, at 60 to the pound.[46] From Table 21, the 68 counterfeit British halfpence in group 23 are 63.4 to the pound, at an average weight of 110.4 grains, and the Machin's Mills imitation halfpence of group 22 are at 62.8 to the pound at an average of 111.5 grains. These low weights support the committee's contention of public fraud when these lightweight counterfeits passed in commerce. The Constellatio Nova coppers (group 25) were also viewed with disfavor and mint state specimens would have weighed in the vicinity of 59 per pound, again, well below the standard for New York effective August 1, 1787, of 48 coppers to the pound.[47] The two varieties of Nova Eborac coppers do not appear to be homogeneous in planchet weight. The emission with the reverse figure seated to the left seems significantly heavier than the variety with its figure oriented to the right. More specimens must be examined to substantiate this preliminary observation.

How can these variations in observed coin weights from the standard be interpreted and placed in perspective? First of all, the original purpose of the state coinages was to provide a reliable, true, copper medium which for many years had been adulterated with lightweight counterfeits of reduced intrinsic worth. Thus the challenge of the Confederation mints was to correct the fraud which, according to contemporaneous reports, had bilked the public for so many years. The official expectation was that if high quality coppers of a weight that people had come to expect as reasonable were made available, the public would accept only them and effectively the lightweight trash would be rejected and disappear from circulation.[48] To guarantee some criterion of value to the proposed coinages, the various states established weight standards for coppers minted within their jurisdictions; for Connecticut it was 144 grains of pure copper. Any deviation below this standard would mean increased profit to the contract minter at public expense. Into 1788, most coppers, with the notable exceptions of Massachusetts and Vermont, fell well below the authorized weights when much coining was conducted without legal franchise and overstriking became common practice. Counterfeit English halfpence and Constellatio Nova coppers were never up to legal measure except in Vermont. Even though mints were authorized for the express purpose of improving the quality of the small copper change, a paradoxical effect was encountered as the condition of this coinage continued to deteriorate and matters worsened. The net effect was that many Confederation copper coinages deteriorated in quality over time and failed to bolster public confidence in this medium. The underweight state coppers just added to the existing surplus of other essentially valueless coins whose circulation came to an abrupt halt in the summer of 1789, despite the fact that the country was in a deep depression and specie was in very short supply.

The important point to make is not whether a citizen of the times was satisfied with the weight or quality of a particular copper coin in his pocket, but rather the entire medium was on trial. All coppers were "being painted with the same brush" and unless there was the guarantee of legal redemption status, as was the case for New Jersey coppers, to bolster the falling intrinsic metallic worth, trust in coppers as a medium of exchange wavered. The determination of average coin weights, rather than the weight of any individual copper, serves as an index of the minters' reliability and success in meeting assigned standard requirements; since obviously some variation was to be expected among coppers manufactured by relatively primitive methods, the

[46] Crosby, *Early Coins*, p. 291.

[47] Crosby, *Early Coins*, p. 294.

[48] Since the copper medium was only a token coinage, it is difficult to conceptualize why the weight or purity of the metal made any difference to the average person. As long as the money could be spent at a constant rate per shilling, any shape or description of copper should have proved acceptable; therefore, for many years coppers passed "without discrimination." There had to have been some compelling force which made coppers unpopular. Perhaps it originated with the merchants who could not dispose of their accumulations of small change as a currency and also came to realize that these coppers even lacked value as scrap metal.

occurence of some low weight coppers is not evidence of dishonesty on the part of the minter. On the other hand, when the average weight of a large sample falls below the standard, minting practices are suspect and the coinage failed to meet its objective of correcting the perceived evil of underweight coppers. It is evident from contemporaneous records that public officials were sensitive when this weight obligation was not realized and responded as though the public were being cheated. From a numismatic viewpoint, the achievement of the weight requisite for a particular style or type of copper may also assist in identifying the mint of origin assuming that the quality of workmanship and fulfillment of the weight requirement is a reflection of a particular minter's standard of practice. Similarly, an alteration in weight may indicate different production methods in planchet preparation.

PROFIT POTENTIAL FOR COPPERS

If the coppers listed in Table 21 were prescribed to pass "by consent without discrimination" in New York at 14 to the shilling, it is evident that the intrinsic value of the coins received in commerce would depend on the varieties of coins offered and accepted, although the "token" values would be equal. Since the heaviest of the coins in Table 21 contains about 50% more copper than the lightest, only public confidence in this token medium allowed such disparate coins to circulate side by side.

However, the legislative report of March 5, 1787, already cited, suggests that this "public confidence" was beginning to fray. This document listed the

> ... various sorts of copper coin circulating in this State, the principal whereof are, *First.* A few genuine British half-pence of George the Second, and some of an earlier date, the impressions of which are generally defaced. *Second.* A number of Irish half-pence, with a bust on one side, and a harp on the other. *Thirdly.* A very great number of pieces in imitation of British half-pence, but much lighter, of inferior copper, and badly executed. — These are generally called by the name Birmingham Coppers, as it is pretty well known that they are made there, and imported in casks, under the name of Hard Ware, or wrought copper. *Fourthly.* There has lately been introduced into circulation, a very considerable number of coppers of the kind that are made in the State of New-Jersey. Many of these are below the proper weight of the Jersey coppers, and seem as if designed as a catch-penny for this market.[49]

The report is of interest in that no mention is made of genuine George III halfpence but only the counterfeits which obviously outnumbered the former, a fact to be explained later. Thus, these Birmingham coppers are described as the chief small money of the period. The lightweight New Jersey coppers censured by the committee were probably the so-called Hatfield's counterfeits (group 8) since none of the other underweight New Jersey coppers had appeared by the spring of 1787 and this Maris 54-k is a fairly common coin.[50]

The committee report continues by making a public exposure of the excessive profits allegedly turned by those who produced the regal and counterfeit English halfpence and the New Jersey coppers. It was estimated that a pound of suitable copper for cutting into blanks would cost no more than 20d., New York money, and that the additional expense for minting would not exceed 6d., for a total cost of 26d. per pound of token copper coins. A summary of the financial disclosures presented by the committee is found in Table 22 together with some corrections made for errors in their calculations. The committee acknowledged that they "have not been able to

[49] Crosby, *Early Coins*, pp. 290-96, quote pp. 290-91.

[50] The subject of Maris 54-k is reviewed in depth by Rock, *Serpent*, who concludes that this variety was the probable counterfeit copper referred to in the New York Legislature report. See also *Weimer and Hirt*, p. 107. Eighteen 54-k coppers were represented among the 25 counterfeits in group 8 of Table 21, making it a common coin which is popular with collectors as a single type issue.

ascertain with any degree of accuracy" the "real expense of coinage." While the committee correctly quoted the cost of copper, it completely overlooked the value of the reworked scissel, i.e. the remains of the copper fillet after the planchets had been cut or stamped from it. For the early Federal Mint in 1791, it was reported that:

> Copper of the best quality, in plates, may be purchased in Europe at 10½d. sterling. In cutting blanks, there will be a waste of twenty-two percent. These clippings are worth 7½d. per pound; thence the blanks will cost 11½d. nearly—it may be stated at 1s. 9d. [21d.] New York money, per pound, exclusive of cutting them, which is not great, as one man can readily cut one hundred weight in a day.[51]

By these figures, it would appear that the 20d., New York money, estimated by the committee as the total cost for copper was sufficient to accomodate for the loss incurred from the wastage. In the Tower Mint, about half the copper was returned to the supplier for reprocessing but at the same price.[52] Therefore, the final cost at the Royal Mint was only for the copper actually used. At the Federal Mint in 1794, only 60% of the copper plate was consumed in manufacturing acceptable planchets, the remaining scissel and imperfect or "defaced" blanks being recast into ingots to be rolled again.[53] In 1795, the quote to the Federal Mint per pound for copper plate of appropriate thickness was 30d. (Pennsylvania money) with the offer to take back "clean copper clippings" at 14d. per pound, or a recovery of 47%.[54] In a coinage proposal to the Massachusetts General Court in 1786, a contractor, James Swan, estimated that if the scissel were reworked into sheets, about 50% of its original cost could be returned, but the clippings would have to be sent to England for reprocessing "for it can't be done in America."[55]

Production costs were significantly understated by the New York Legislature. The cost of striking coppers at Matthew Boulton's private Birmingham mint during the period 1789 to 1792 was only 5d. per pound.[56] Published accounts from the Tower Mint indicated the charges for planchet preparation, moneyers, engravers, and smiths was 7d. sterling (12.4d. New York money), or double the committee's estimate of 6d. The actual profit for Tower Mint halfpence was stated at 10.9%, while that for the 1773 Virginia halfpence was 16%, excluding any shipping and insurance fees to America.[57] This is a far cry from the 57% calculated by the committee. Minting costs for clandestine operations producing counterfeit halfpence must have been lower than those from well regulated mints with coins of standard weight and composition. Profits would have been substantially higher for a counterfeiting venture but defy accurate computation. The profits for the New Jersey coppers were grossly misstated, with no provision made for the 10% franchise royalty owed to the state from the legal mints, all of which were known to have had serious financial difficulties. One additional cost to the state mints which cannot be ascertained was the expense associated with placing the newly minted coins in circulation. In England those who wanted a supply of new coppers applied at the Mint where they were available in packets of five and ten shilings since there was no official provision for the dissemination of freshly minted farthings and halfpence.[58] The distribution network for the Confederation mints has never been studied but logic dictates that in the absence of banks and subtreasuries there must have been a system of jobbers or middlemen who might have received the new coppers at wholesale.[59]

[51] *A.S.P.F.*, vol. 1, p. 101.
[52] Craig, *Mint*, pp. 162, 427.
[53] *A.S.P.F.*, vol. 1, p. 273. Rittenhouse opined that some copper plates, "if cut to the best advantage," could yield at least 70% in finished planchets.
[54] Wescott, *Letter*, p. 36.
[55] Crosby, *Early Coins*, p. 235.
[56] Vice, *Wilkinson*.
[57] See Table 10; Newman, *Colonial Virginia*, p. 20.
[58] Craig, *Mint*, p. 221; Craig, *Newton*, pp. 100-101; Doty, *RCR 1961*, p. 36.
[59] *Schenkel*, lot #5478.

TABLE 22

Summary of the New York Legislature Report of March 5, 1787, Defining the Profits Accrued to the Minters of Copper Coins and the Loss to the Public When Accepting Token Copper Coinage (Crosby, *Early Coins*, pp. 291-92)

All entries are in N.Y. money of account, where all coppers were required to pass at 14 to the local shilling.

Coinage	*A*	*B*	*C*	*D*	*E*	*F*
English halfpence[a]	48	41d.	21d.	51%	36%	57%
weight corrected	46	39.4d.	19.4d.	49.2%	34%	51.5%
Birmingham halfpence	60	51d.	31d.	61%	49%	96%
New Jersey coppers[b]	46.4	40d.	20d.	50%	35%	54%
weight corrected	46.7	"	"	"	"	"

Column A: number of halfpence or coppers per pound avoirdupois of copper.
Column B: token value in N.Y. pence in commerce of one pound of coppers. Since A ÷ 14 = N.Y. shillings per lb. of coppers, then, 12(A ÷ 14) = B in N.Y. pence. The figures in Crosby are rounded off.
Column C: difference between token value (B) and intrinsic value of copper at 20d. per pound.
Column D: % difference between token and intrinsic values (C ÷ B).
Column E: % "perceived" loss in commerce between the token value (B) and the total cost of one pound of coins, 26d., i.e. copper (20d.) plus estimated mint costs (6d.), as estimated by committee. (B-26d.) ÷ B.
Column F: % "perceived" profit to minters = (B-26d.) ÷ 26d., as % of token value, B.

[a] The weight of the regal English halfpence was misstated in the report at 48 to the pound and corrected here to 46.
[b] The weight of the New Jersey coppers was very slightly in error but the calculations are not altered.

Some indication of the actual operating expense for a quality mint can be gleaned from the accounts published by the Massachusetts mint which is known to have incurred substantial losses.[60] A report by John Hancock made on June 19, 1788, to the General Court estimated the cost of minting coppers, exclusive of the metal, not to exceed 7.9d. per pound, Massachusetts currency.[61] The amount quoted by Hancock does not specify exactly what processes are included in the figure. The sum is equivalent to 5.9d. sterling and is within the same order of magnitude of the 7d. price from the Tower Mint. When the reported Massachusetts mint costs are converted to New York currency, the price for manufacturing a pound of quality coppers translates into 10.5d. Other information regarding contemporary mint cost was published in *The Pennsylvania Mercury, and Universal Advertiser* of July 30, 1789, regarding the Congressional contract for the Fugio cents. The news release placed the cost of minting one pound of copper at 12¢ (10.8d. Pennsylvania money) which converts to 11.5d. New York currency.[62] The three

[60] As of November 21, 1788, the Massachusetts mint had an accumulated loss of £519 14s. 4.5d. on the production of £939 ($3,130) in coppers, excluding the investment in land, buildings, and equipment (Crosby, *Early Coins*, p. 262).

[61] Crosby, *Early Coins*, p. 260. Hancock reported that the expense to mint $15,000 in coppers (exclusive of metal) would not exceed £1,200. See Appendix 1 for calculations. Recall that there were 108 cents per six shillings, lawful money (Crosby, *Early Coins*, p. 273). ($15,000 × 108) ÷ 44.4 coins/lb. = 36,486.49 lbs. £1200 ÷ 36,486.49 = 7.9d. (Mass.) = 5.9d. sterling = 10.5d. (New York) to mint one pound of 44.4 coppers.

[62] These values were from a treatise on copper coin submitted to the newspaper by John B. Bordley. The essay, revised and reprinted in booklet format, is a valued, contemporaneous commentary on copper currency and is found in Appendix 5. Bordley's estimates on the cost of Fugio coinage cannot reflect the actual amounts due to Jarvis's manipulations of Federal copper supplies. Continental money was usually quoted at the Pennsylvania rating of 90d. to the Spanish dollar (Schilke and Solomon, *Foreign Coins*, p. 13). See Williamson, *CNL 1986*, p. 936.

quotations from the Massachusetts mint, the Tower Mint, and the Congressional contract for the cost of turning one pound of copper into regal halfpence, Massachusetts cents and half cents, and the Fugio coppers are in good agreement with each other. These values are presented in Table 23. When converted into New York money, these sums are about double the 6d. supposed by the New York committee. If the mint costs in New Jersey were of the same order as those in Massachusetts, and there is little reason to suppose otherwise, the committee again made a significant understatement as it did with the Tower Mint and the regal English halfpence. In Massachusetts, the initial engraver Joseph Callender was dismissed because his dies were so expensive at £1 4s. each.[63] These charges were formidable for the struggling mints and were not properly appreciated by the New York Legislature.[64]

Although erring in one area of their report, the committee was quite accurate in estimating the price of a pound of copper at 20d., New York currency. The same material was purchased by the Massachusetts mint at 13.6d., Massachusetts currency (18.1d. New York money) and was quoted for the Fugio coinage in the same article of *The Pennsylvania Mercury* at 20¢, or 18d., Pennsylvania money.[65] Another newspaper account placed the European cost of sheet copper

[63] Crosby, *Early Coins*, p. 251.

[64] While we need to extrapolate to estimate mint costs during the Confederation period, the costs for minting coppers at the new Federal Mint in 1794 are readily available, although not directly comparable to this earlier period. David Rittenhouse, the Director of the Federal Mint, quoted the following expenses to mint 600 lbs. of copper into $202.00 (*A.S.P.F.*, vol. 1, p. 273).

To obtain 600 lbs. in blanks, one must start with 1,000 lbs of sheet copper, the clippings from which (i.e. 400 lbs.) need to be cast over. If one were to cut the sheet copper "to the best advantage," Rittenhouse stated that 700 lbs. would be available for planchets with only 300 lbs. wastage.

Cutting the 1,000 lbs. of sheets into slips [*sic*] cost	$2.00
Rolling the slips	4.00
Cutting the slips into 600 lbs. of planchets	2.00
Annealing 600 lbs. of planchets	1.00
Cleaning 600 lbs. of planchets	1.00
Milling 600 lbs. of planchets	2.00
Coining 600 lbs. of planchets	7.50
Quarter cord hickory wood	1.50
Four horses	1.50
Salt, sal enixum, &c. for boiling copper	1.00
Mint costs	23.50
600 lbs. of copper cost	160.00

At the rate of $23.50 in mint costs and $160 in copper, $202 in coin (or actually $201.92 for a 208 grain copper cent) could be manufactured which left a profit of $18.50, or a 10.1% gain. This figure agrees well with the profit quoted from the Tower Mint of 10.8%. Rittenhouse quoted his 600 lbs. of copper at $160 which would figure at 26.7¢ a pound but it is unclear what allowance was made for the salvage value of the wastage which could be recast into ingots. In 1794, the market price for copper in America was about 26¢ a pound (25d. New York money) as per Table 24. See note 170.

[65] 7,613.5 pounds of copper were required to produce £939 containing 338,040 Massachusetts cents. (72d. in Mass. currency = 108¢ at 18 coppers to the shilling). This metal was stated to have cost £431 19s., or 13.6d. per pound (Crosby, *Early Coins*, p. 262). The intrinsic value of the copper (103,668d.) equaled 46% of the monetary value of the coin (225,360d.) in keeping with other legal copper coinages.

£939 × 20s. × 12d. = 225,360d. monetary value
225,360d. ÷ 72d. = $3,130
$3,130 × 108 = 338,040 Mass. cents
338,040 ÷ 44.4 coppers to the lb. = 7,613.5 pounds at a cost of £431 19s. or 103,668d.
103,668d. ÷ 7,613.5 lbs. of copper expended = 13.6d. per lb, Mass. money.

In Massachusetts, James Swan had proposed a copper coinage scheme which was rejected by the General Court, in favor of the state-run mint. In his calculations Swan budgeted for "One pound weight of sheet Copper thinned to the size or thickness of Coppers ... 1s. 4d. sterling [16d.]" or 21.3d. Massachusetts money.

TABLE 23

Tabulated Costs Quoted for Minting Regal English (Tower Mint), Massachusetts and Fugio Coppers
(Data from text)

Costs Expressed in Sterling and Various Local Monies of Account.
The quote marked ♦ is the primary reference area, and equivalent values for other localities are calculated from this.
The 10.0d. cost for England excludes shipping charges which are implicit in the quotations for Massachusetts, New York and Philadelphia.
The costs for Philadelphia were those cited in that city for the Fugio cents, 20¢ per pound for the metal and 12¢ minting expenses (although they were minted in Connecticut).
These figures exclude whatever credit may be due from reprocessing the scissel.

A: Local Cost of Copper per Pound, avdp.

Local Cost in:	*England*	*Massachusetts*	*New York*	*Philadelphia*
Sterling	♦10.0d.	10.2d.	11.25d.	10.8d.
Mass. money	13.3d.	♦13.6d.	15.0d.	14.4d.
N.Y. money	17.8d.	18.1d.	♦20.0d.	19.2d.
Pa. money	16.7d.	17.0d.	18.75d.	18.0d.
(Continental money)				♦(20.0¢)

B: Local Minting Expenses: England for Tower Mint, Massachusetts for state coppers, and Philadelphia for Fugio cents, per pound of copper. The values in the N.Y. money line are about double those estimated by the legislative committee, see text.

Local Cost in:	*England*	*Massachusetts*	*New York*	*Philadelphia*
Sterling	♦7.0d.	5.9d.	N.A.	6.5d.
Mass. money	9.3d.	♦7.9d.		8.6d.
N.Y. money	12.4d.	10.5d.		11.5d.
Pa. money	11.7d.	9.9d.		10.8d.
(Continental money)				♦(12.0¢)

ready for manufacture at 10d. per pound (17.8d. New York) but excluded shipping costs to America, which the New York committee estimated at from 20 to 25%.[66] The same account claimed that in Pennsylvania cut pieces of scrap copper, "which are no good to the coppersmith," sold for 10d., local money. Other data from about 1782, already cited, places the cost of the highest quality copper plate available in Europe at 10½d. sterling per pound and when the value for the salvage of the 22% wastage was considered, then the cost of finished planchets, excluding labor, was nearly 11½d., sterling, or 1s. 9d. New York money.[67] Thus the price of copper during this period is corroborated by these various sources with similar quotations (see Table 24).

The revised data cited above permit a more accurate revision of the New York legislative report. The new appraisals, based on the information derived from the Tower Mint, Massachusetts mint, and Fugio quotations, allow for the recalculation of the cost of producing the

---

This estimate was inflated by about 20% to cover certain risks and to compensate for wastage of "clippings or Corner pieces" since he claimed that these scraps could not be reprocessed in America but would have to be returned to England (Crosby, *Early Coins*, p. 235).

[66] *Fed. Gaz.*, Aug. 1, 1789.

[67] *A.S.P.F.*, vol. 1, p. 101.

corrected number of New Jersey coppers per pound in New York funds and passing at 14 to the New York shilling, prior to August 1, 1787.[68] These following calculations are at best only estimates of possible profits (or losses) available under several enumerated circumstances.

Correct yield New Jersey coppers per pound at 150 grains	46.6 coppers
Cost of copper per pound:	18.1d. (Mass. mint data)
Revised minting costs per pound:	10.5d. (Mass. mint data)
Royalty of 10%:	4.0d.
Total cost:	32.6d.
Token value at 14 coins/shilling:	39.9d.
Profit per pound:	7.3d.
% profit = profit/cost:	22.4%

This recalculated 22.4% profit statement differs significantly from the 54% proposed by the committee and does not include other unknown costs such as cartage and distribution. A devaluation from 14 to 20 coppers per New York shilling would reduce the token value of a pound of New Jersey coppers to 28.0d. and thereby turn a profit into a 14.1% loss on those coins circulating in a New York jurisdiction. An exchange rate of 17¼ coppers to the shilling would have approached the break-even point where all costs and royalties would have equaled the token value. Above a rate of nearly 31 coppers to the New York shilling, the intrinsic value of the copper metal would have been at par with the monetary value of the coins and technically these copper coins would no longer be a token or fiduciary coinage.

If the franchise owners of a New Jersey mint recovered only a 22.4% profit exclusive of any other miscellaneous expenses such as interest payments, rents, bonds, insurance, distribution, loss on scissel, and cartage fees, it is understood why both the Rahway and Morristown operations had significant financial problems. Likewise, there was a distinct advantage for coiners to have engaged in producing illegal Connecticut coppers which were considerably lighter than the 144 grain Connecticut standard and from which no royalties were exacted. Table 21 (groups 12 and 13) lists the average weights of such counterfeit Connecticut coppers. If an average "mint weight" of 122 grains is supposed, then a recalculation of the known data in New York funds, omitting the royalties paid to the State of New Jersey, demonstrates the profit motive, 72.7% by these calculations, for minters to have entered into this illegal scheme. This figure for illegal production is not unlike the amount supposed by the New York legislative committee.

Yield per pound at 122 grains:	57.4 coppers
Cost of copper per pound:	18.1d. (Mass. mint data)
Revised minting costs per pound:	10.5d. (Mass. mint data)
Royalty:	none
Total cost per pound:	28.6d.
Token value at 14 coins/shilling:	49.1d.
Profit per pound:	20.5d.
% profit = profit/cost:	72.7%

The advantages of overstriking existing coins have already been described. It was common practice at the Elizabethtown mint after June 1789, at Machin's Mills, and by those responsible for the "camel head" varieties (Maris 56-n etc.). Some estimate of the benefits accrued from overstriking can be extrapolated from our current evidence. In New Jersey after July 20, 1787, only coppers of that state and United States coppers were allowed to circulate.[69] In New York

[68] Calculation of these data in New Jersey money of account derives the same 22.4% answer due to the relative values of both New York and New Jersey monies of account pegged to the Spanish milled dollar as noted in Appendix 1.

[69] Newman, *Studies*, pp. 153-54.

all coppers lighter than 48 to the pound, 145.8 grains, were demonetized after August 1, 1787. Effectively, only Massachusetts, New Jersey, and Fugio coppers met these stipulations, all Connecticut issues having been excluded. These monetary restrictions made an enormous number of non-negotiable coppers available whose true identities could be masked by a quick pass through the coining press to imprint them with acceptable New Jersey designs. Coins thus altered could be spent in New Jersey, where they were legal tender for taxes at 15 to the local shilling, or in neighboring New York at 20 to the shilling, the rate imposed after August 1, 1787. The cost to the minter for the unwanted coppers, to use as host coins, is hard to ascertain but in a report to the New Jersey Assembly of June 7, 1790, it was quoted that 45 Birmingham or Connecticut coppers, at an average of 120 grains each, could be bought for a New Jersey shilling. This would amount to 15.6d. per pound for ready-to-use planchets. Scrap copper sold for an equivalent of 10d. per pound in Philadelphia, about half the cost of rolled-planchet stock. The cost for stamping blank planchets amounted to about 12% of the total minting costs at the Tower Mint so there was a considerable saving to be realized when cheap coppers were overstruck.[70] The availability of ready-to-strike host coins eliminated the expense and labor associated with reworking the scissel. However, there was another incalculable cost for annealing the existing coins which prepared them for restamping with new labels. Groups 6b and 9 from Table 21 give the average weights of the Elizabethtown overstrikes and the "camel heads." From these data a "mint weight" for a hypothetical, overstruck copper of 128 grains is extrapolated to demonstrate the augmented profits of 180% available from using host coins rather than original planchets. The example selected is heavier than the 120 grain specimens quoted above by the New Jersey Assembly. It is assumed that these coppers were overstruck in New Jersey and passed there at the legal rate of 15 to the shilling.[71]

Hypothetical host coin:	128 grains
Yield per pound at 128 grains:	54.7 coppers
Estimated cost of coppers at 45 per shilling:	14.4d.
Stamping costs (12% costs):	1.2d.
Royalties:	none
Total costs per pound:	15.6d.
Token value at 15 coins/shilling:	43.8d.
Profit per pound:	28.2d.
% profit = profit/cost:	180%

Since many of the above numbers are only educated guesses and cannot be verified with certainty, the primary purpose of these computations is to show the order of magnitude of the potential profits when minting procedures were manipulated to decrease fixed costs. As the exchange rate of coppers per shilling increases, the token value of the coppers and the potential profits dwindle. Such happened in New York when the rate was advanced from 14 to 20 effective August 1, 1787. The particular overstruck issues cited above appeared after that date, perhaps by the summer of 1788, but at any rate prior to the Coppers Panic. New Jersey coppers overstruck on lesser coins elicited official attention in the New Jersey legislative report of June 7, 1790, which will be detailed later.

Primarily because of their unfamiliarity with production costs, the New York Legislature's *ad hoc* committee on copper coinage substantially exaggerated the profits earned by the legal mints in England and New Jersey on the manufacture of coppers, although they were correct to have concluded that counterfeit operations fared very well. Motivated perhaps by this inaccurate

[70] Craig, *Mint*, pp. 427-28.

[71] During the Confederation period, East New Jersey was probably still in the economic orbit of influence of New York where coppers were 14 to the shilling. See Williamson, *CNL 1986*, p. 941.

study, the legislature denied the petitions of Ephraim Brasher and John Bailey and subsequently that of Captain Thomas Machin to supply a quantity of contract coinage for the state. Rather than facilitate more alleged windfall profits for private minters, the legislature instead devalued the copper currency, thereby reducing the losses incurred to the public when they accepted this inflated token medium in commerce. The devaluation occurred in the midst of a significant economic depression suggesting that public pressure must have been considerable.

Effective August 1, 1787, only those coppers could pass in New York which met a standard of one-third ounce (145.8 grains), avoirdupois, pure copper or 48 to the pound. (The regulation was probably unenforceable since it was unlikely that the public would weigh its individual copper coins.) Such acceptable coppers would be current at 20 to the New York shilling instead of 14, a 43% reduction in value. The new law effectively demonetized all coppers in New York except those legal halfpence from the Tower Mint, which were few in numbers, Massachusetts and legal New Jersey coppers, and the new Fugio cents which were supposed to adhere to the new Federal standard. This regulation, while removing many lesser coppers from circulation, also encouraged mint operators to salvage their shrinking profit margins by overstriking acceptable designs on non-negotiable coppers by reducing planchet weight, and by decreasing the overall quality of their coinages. The fact that so many Connecticut coppers were used as host coins for New Jersey issues indicates that the Connecticut series were not well regarded in commerce in the New York and New Jersey area even though such money was only slightly less than the new weight requirement.

It appears that at both the state and federal levels, New York had adopted an official hard line policy to regulate better the token copper medium and refrained from minting their own. Their Congressional delegation had been instructed to alter the Federal standard so that the value of copper coins would equal the intrinsic value of the metal plus no more than the actual expense of minting.[72] The instruction was an additional attempt to close the gap between intrinsic and commercial values which would discourage counterfeiting and profiteering, increase public confidence in the medium, and drive inferior coinages out of circulation.

THE COPPERS PANIC OF 1789

Following the copper devaluation in New York of August 1, 1787, no further action regarding the small change medium is recorded until the summer of 1789 when the situation became more unstable. A meeting of the New York Common Council was convened on July 21, 1789, "on Account of some Difficulties which had arisen among the Inhabitants relative to the circulating Copper Coin and several of the principal Merchants, having attended at the Request of Mr. Recorder [Richard Varick], gave the Board their Information and Advice on the Subject ...."[73] The Common Council made the following "Determination" which was subsequently carried in newspapers from Massachusetts to Pennsylvania:

> Whereas great inconveniences have arisen to the inhabitants of this city by the depreciation of the present circulating copper coin, occasioned by the transportation thereof from neighboring states, in some of which this board is informed the same is estimated at a much less value than it has for some time passed at in this city, and this board conceiving it their duty to interpose their advice on this interesting occasion, do recommend to all the inhabitants of this city, to receive and pay the same coin at a rate of *forty-eight coppers* for *one shilling*.[74]

[72] Douglas, *CNL 1969*, pp. 285-86.
[73] *Common Council*, vol. 1, pp. 471-72.
[74] The account appeared originally in *The Daily Advertiser*, July 22, 1789, and was reprinted without comment in over a dozen other major newspapers.

A warning about the potential speculation in devalued coppers was delivered in an editorial in *The Connecticut Journal* of July 29, 1789:

> The sudden and merited death of *Coppers*, must be gratifying to the Commercial Interests of this State, which has long been burdened with that unwieldy medium. I wish that the farmers and industrious poor may have such timely notice of this event, as to prevent their being imposed upon by the pitiful rascality of those vermin called *Takers-in*. Coppers are now passing in New-York at sixty-four for a shilling lawful money, and very dull at that; and in this place [New Haven, Connecticut], at five and six for a penny [60 to 72 per shilling], and no larger quantity received (even at any rate) than is absolutely necessary for change. I am informed from substantial authority, that a considerable quantity of coppers have been purchased up in this town, since their depreciation, at a very low price, and carried into the country, with a view of inlisting [*sic*] the unsuspicious farmer with them, at a rate of twenty-seven to the shilling.

The financial chaos of late July and early August of 1789, caused by the collapse of circulating coppers is well described by another report datelined New York and reprinted in many localities.

> A correspondent believes that the confusion, and consequent distress occasioned by the sudden stoppage to the circulation of copper coins, are subjects that call for the immediate attention of authority: The poorer class of citizens are particularly affected by this circumstance, many of whom had their little *all* invested in this most uncertain of all human possessions—a fluctuating medium: Many of the retail shops are shut: The cries are suspended in the streets, and it is with difficulty the poor can purchase bread of the bakers,[75] or vegetables in the market: This evil has long been foreseen, and yet the base trumpery called coppers (greatly inferior to Wood's infamous brass money)[76] has been pouring in on us like a flood for many months past: Many of the merchants and shop-keepers, it is said, have large sums by them of this coin, by which they will be great sufferers.[77]

The preceding commentary describes an almost complete cessation of circulation of coppers and subsequent damage to many small businesses and the poor. The disaster occurred during an exceptionally hot spell of weather in August 1789, when the temperature was so oppressive that "several shop keepers have shut up their shops and retired to the country for a few days."[78] In Philadelphia, "the thermometer stood at 96 for several days," "deaths are numerous," and "all the meat in the market [was] carried away and thrown into the Delaware" because it "was in a state of putrifaction."[79] Whether the commercial holiday was caused by problems with copper

[75] The cost of a loaf of bread gives the modern reader some perspective as to the contemporaneous purchasing power of copper currency. Newspapers of the period published the "Assize of Bread," which was the regulated price fixed on the price of a barrel of flour. Before the Revolution in New York, a 1 lb. loaf sold for an equivalent of 2.1 coppers (*N.Y. Jour.*, June 3, 1766, and June 27, 1776). The price in Philadelphia quoted in June 1789, just before the coppers panic, was 3.33 coppers for a pound of white bread [1d. per 6 oz.] (*Penna. Merc.*, June 20, 1789). When the value of coppers plummeted and the rate advanced from 15 to 48 to the local shilling, the anticipated price would have increased to 10.66 coppers per pound, provided the baker would still elect to receive copper money. In Massachusetts, which did not suffer the effects of the coppers panic, the published price per 1 lb. loaf in September 1789, was 4 coppers [2d. per 11.75 oz.] (*Salem (MA) Merc.*, Sept. 8, 1789). In New York, by January 1790, the best white bread was 6.2 coppers per pound (*Common Council*, p. 520).

[76] Wood's coinage was also recalled in Philadelphia Common Council debate. " ... and any person that was acquainted with *ancient* history, might *remember* the kingdom of *Ireland* was nearly ruined by one Wood, who procured a patent from the *House of Commons* to coin 108,000 l. sterling in copper" (*Ind. Gaz.*, Aug. 1, 1789). There was never any indication in these references that "Wood's money" was used in this country.

[77] *Ind. Gaz.*, July 27, 1789, and repeated in other Massachusetts, Vermont, Rhode Island, Connecticut, and New York papers.

[78] *Penna. Merc.*, July 30, 1789.

[79] *N.Y. Pack.*, Aug. 18, 1789.

coinage or the intensity of the heat, or a combination, the result was that the poor and those merchants holding a large number of the "fluctuating medium" bore the brunt of the devaluation. Again it is emphasized that the coppers lost their acceptability during a postwar depression with a continued specie shortage. Although the price for bills of exchange remained stable during this same time,[80] there was an unexplained ripple effect which resulted in a 20% reduction in the value of certain fractional silver coins.

> It has been remarked that since the outcry was raised about Copper Coin, the Silver has depreciated in value, and, what is entirely unaccountable upon any just principles is quarters, eights and sixteenths of dollars of the old stamp, are depreciated by many into pistareens, half pistareens, &c.[81] The dollars and parts of dollars of this description, are really worth a premium upon the value of the new dollars, as is well known.[82]

It is of interest to recall the contemporary descriptions of the circulating coppers in which the public had lost confidence. Previous mention has made of the March 16, 1786 report from Massachusetts asserting that "nearly one half of the copper coin in this country for twenty or thirty years past" had been counterfeit English halfpence and that more recently "a large number of counterfeit Copper Coin manufactured in this and the Neighboring States, [had] ... been in circulation in this Commonwealth."[83] In March 1787, the New York legislative committee listed the principal coppers currently in circulation as "a few" regal halfpence of George II and earlier monarchs, "a number" of Irish halfpence, "a very great number" of counterfeit English halfpence presumably of George III, as well as "a very considerable number" of legal and counterfeit New Jersey coppers.[84] Another writer described the following coppers which he had encountered in circulation: 1727 French copper at 182 grains, 1698 French liard at 54 grains, 1773 Virginia halfpenny at 120 grains, 1783 Constellatio Nova at 145 grains, 1764 quarter stuber at 38 grains, and a smoothly worn English halfpenny at 156 grains.[85]

Another assertion appeared which stated that 95% of the coppers in New York were counterfeit

> ...about 19 parts in 20 of the copper coin now in circulation in America are counterfeit—some of them are made of copper tolerably fine, but about one third part of their proper weight deficient: others are about the proper weight, but so adulterated with a baser mixture as to be more than one third deficient in value: and others deficient both in weight and fineness.[86]

While the contention that 95% of the coppers were false was challenged by another writer as an exaggeration, it was agreed that the coins were lightweight.[87] The Philadelphia Common Council itself drew attention to the circulating copper medium and remarked that it is was so variable both in weight and fineness that it was impossible for them to offer an opinion about its

[80] *Fed. Gaz.*, Aug. 19, 1789.

[81] From Tables 3 and 5 it is recalled that the "old stamp" Spanish-American silver were the pillar dollars and their fractional parts at .9166 fine. The newer portrait silver dollars, after 1772, were .9038 fine. Except for worn or clipped coins, there is no legitimate explanation why an old quarter dollar, or two bit piece, at .9166 fine, worth 25¢, should have been depreciated to a pistareen, or two reales piece at .8333 fine, which passed for 20¢. There is no reference that other specie depreciated at this time. This depreciation for specific fractional coins suggests that either money speculators were at work using the excuse of the coppers panic, or the other simplistic explanation is that "during panics, people panic."

[82] *Newport Her.*, Sept. 10, 1789; *Va. Gaz.*, Sept. 17, 1789; *N.H. Spy*, Sept. 12, 1789.

[83] *Mass. Spy*, March 16, 1786. This statement implies there were several clandestine mints active in the region; however, without firsthand knowledge, it is unlikely that its author could have distinguished between locally manufactured and imported counterfeit English halfpence.

[84] Crosby, *Early Coins*, p. 291.

[85] *Penna. Merc.*, July 30, 1789. See p. 301, n. 15.

[86] *Fed. Gaz.*, Aug. 1, 1789.

[87] *Fed. Gaz.*, Aug. 8, 1789.

real value, hence that board would not commit itself to a recommended exchange rate as had their New York counterparts.[88] The decision regarding exchange rate was left to the discretion of the individual, but the Council did observe "that the copper contained in a pound weight avoirdupois of the best of them is not equal in value to one shilling Pennsylvania money, and that the far greater part of them are mixed with base metal, of which it will require from sixty to eighty to weigh a pound." One editorialist actually experimented with weighing twelve coppers "of [the] kind generally in circulation among us" and calculated the average at 116.6 grains. He further observed that, "For these coppers, the coppersmiths in this city will pay 9d. per lb. weight."[89] Although there was no further description of the actual copper coins weighed, their deficiency is obvious.

Despite this well publicized excess of inferior coppers, a news report from July 31, 1789, exposed the scheme of an unnamed Philadelphian, who, already an importer of counterfeits, was preparing to open a mint for the manufacture of spurious copper coins in order to increase his profits.[90] Other domestic counterfeiting operations were smashed during that summer and the public was warned through the press to beware of false 1781 and 1789 Spanish American milled dollars, 1770 French crowns, and doubloons which contained 16 to 20% alloy.[91]

The answer to the generic problem of an unstable copper medium and the current panic can be traced back to the comments of Sir Isaac Newton in 1713, when he was the Master of the Tower Mint (1699-1727). He advocated that the token value of copper coins should never exceed the actual cost of the metal plus the expense of manufacturing. No profit should be allowed. He urged that the supply of token coinage be limited to the needs of the economy and an excess supply be avoided.[92] All these tenets had been violated in both England and America where the Crown and minting patentees derived a profit. The potential gain encouraged illegal operators to engage in wholesale counterfeiting until soon false halfpence outnumbered the genuine and these false coins clogged commerce on both sides of the Atlantic. Not only were the legal coppers greatly outnumbered by the false, lightweight ones, but it was also recognized that "the quantity of this coin in circulation throughout America is ten times greater than necessary for change."[93] As could be predicted from Newton's admonitions regarding copper coinage, it was only a matter of time before public confidence in a surplus of mostly counterfeit token coinage would fail and the house of cards collapse.

Much editorial speculation regarding the cause of this coppers panic appeared, particularly in the Philadelphia papers. It was suggested that there should have been governmental intervention and it was "acknowledged that the power of regulating the value of coin or money is in the Congress, but this is a desperate case that requires immediate relief; and therefore something should be done until that body took it up."[94] Realizing that local governments were impotent to provide a final solution for copper devaluation, most municipal authorities anticipated that with the promised appearance of the new Fugio coins from Congress, the copper problem would be solved, but alas, that expectation was only wishful thinking.

> When this emission appears all foreign copper coin may be thrown out of circulation, and if Congress limit the quantity they issue within reasonable bounds, the evil will be wholly done away.[95]

[88] *Fed. Gaz.*, July 28, 1789.
[89] *Fed. Gaz.*, Aug. 3, 1789.
[90] *Ind. Gaz.*, July 31, 1789.
[91] *Bos. Gaz.*, Aug. 24, 1789; *N.H. Gaz.*, July 30, 1789, and Aug. 13, 1789; *Mass. Spy*, July 23, 1789; *Ind. Chron.*, Aug. 20, 1789; *Am. Merc.*, July 27, 1789; *Mid. Gaz.*, July 25, 1789; *Penna. Pack.*, Aug. 4, 1789, and Aug. 20, 1789; *U.S. Chron.*, July 16, 1789.
[92] Craig, *Mint*, p. 220. Recall the surplus of coppers authorized under William Wood's patents.
[93] *Fed. Gaz.*, Aug. 1, 1789.
[94] "Strictures on the Publication of the Common Council Respecting Coppers," *Fed. Gaz.*, July 30, 1789.
[95] *Fed. Gaz.*, Aug. 1, 1789.

One writer observed that the lack of small bills of paper money below five shillings was another factor responsible for the troubles with the copper medium.[96] He postulated that in the absence of a paper money alternative for small change, the public became dependent on copper which was then introduced in massive quantities until its confidence was abused. If small paper notes redeemable in specie had been available, then less reliance on copper would have developed, discouraging manufacturers, speculators, and importers of counterfeits.

In a letter to the editor of *The Independent Gazette*, one reader made an astute commentary further defining the cause of the copper problem and proposing a solution:

> The present confusion at New-York and Philadelphia about the coppers ... has altogether arisen from the currency given to base falsifications of the British half-pence. Had these counterfeits, easily discoverable ... been steadily refused at the time, (above a year ago) when the regulation of 24 [*sic*] coppers for a shilling took place, all had been well. But the alteration just mentioned, instead of relieving us, has only given new opening for speculation; then foretold, and since eagerly laid hold of. The true British copper coin, lowered under its value in England, has ever since been collecting and sending to London, as a profitable remittance; whilst the makers of the base imitation have still found their advantage in sending over their manufactures, which the Americans, though these raps for the most part have not even the colour of copper, are weak enough to receive. The direct remedy to the disorder is obvious and easy; restore the genuine British half-pence, such as bears the effigies and inscriptions, plainly and legibly, to the rate of 15 or 16 to the shilling, here and at New York; and inflexibly reject all raps, counterfeits, and worn coppers. This is the only, but the sure guard against a deluge of false copper coin in Europe. Thus the coppers which remain in circulation, would be nearly worth the price at which they pass, we shall be relieved of the counterfeits already here, and wholly prevent further importations of them. It is strange that the fathers of *New-York* and *Philadelphia* should not have advised to this course here pointed out, till Congress interpose, and supply a legal medium for change and small dealings.[97]

The quoted "regulation of 24 coppers for a shilling" appears inconsistent with the New York rate of 20 coppers per shilling even when considering that the author was from Philadelphia where the Spanish milled dollar was less inflated in value. Although the New York Legislature was able to establish exchange rates in 1787, the new Constitution came into effect March 4, 1789, granting this right only to Congress which took no positive role in alleviating the crisis. The writer of this letter observed that with the devaluation of the halfpence in 1787, it then became profitable to gather up all genuine and unworn halfpence in New York at a reduced cost and return them to England where they could be negotiated at full value of 24 to the shilling, thus gaining 48% in the transaction.[98] The flux of coppers into England, where they were more highly valued, was a reenactment of the Philadelphia situation of 1735 and New York 15 years later where coppers were attracted due to more favorable exchange rates. It, therefore, comes as no surprise that genuine George III halfpence, which were not even a common coin in New York in 1787, have not been reported in colonial American excavations or hoards since most which arrived here were likely returned to England by speculators, perhaps the same people who imported the counterfeits. The reference that "these raps ... are weak enough to receive" appears to suggest that they could still be purchased abroad in bulk at attractive discounts so as to return a profit to the investor. Thus the New York Act of April 20, 1787, designed to regulate

[96] *Ind. Gaz.*, July 31, 1789; *Gaz. of U.S.*, July 25, 1789.

[97] Aug. 4, 1789.

[98] The profit to the exporter of genuine regal halfpence sent back to England would vary according to the New York exchange rate. At 20 coppers to the shilling it is 48%, at 24 to the shilling it climbs to 78% and so on. See Appendix 1.

and improve the circulation of coppers actually encouraged the exportation of acceptable regal halfpence and increased the ratio of "Birminghams" to genuine coppers in circulation, up to 95% according to one account.

It had been anticipated that the Fugio coinage would terminate this problem, when actually the Congressional issue was due for its own disaster which will be recalled below. Following ratification of the new Constitution, only the national government was enpowered to regulate currency and the lack of Federal intervention was criticized. It was suggested that if the public were faced with "a large influx of ... base coins of gold and silver" that it would be a "dreadful situation ... without ... an immediate interposition by some authority."[99] But since copper was not a coin of intrinsic value as were gold and silver, it was "little regarded; hence in the last, the public are liable to great impositions."[100]

Numerous solutions were proposed in the press to end the Coppers Panic. One approach suggested that market forces would determine in the long run how many coppers the public would accept for a shilling.[101] A more immediate answer was for the Philadelphia Common Council to recommend a rate of 48 to the shilling as had happened in New York.[102] These rates would not be equivalent due to the inequality in the monies of account between the two cities, 48 coppers in New York being on par with 45 in Philadelphia, and 48 in the latter equal to 51 in the former. It was emphasized that such suggestions were but recommendations since only Congress could now regulate the currency. In addition to the devaluation, it was urged that all counterfeits be rejected, commenting that a child of three could soon learn to tell the difference between genuine and false coppers. A more radical proposal from Philadelphia advanced the recommendation of 96 coppers to the shilling,[103] and one New York distiller advertised that he would accept 60 to the shilling or 10d. per pound.[104] A Philadelphia merchant, Amos Wickersham, publicized that he had "use for a quantity of Coppers now in circulation, [and] will sell, either wholesale or retail, such goods as he has on hand ... at as reasonable rates for these as for any other species of money."[105]

Fig. 70: AD FROM *THE DAILY ADVERTISER* (NEW YORK), JULY 24, 1789. This advertisement, which ran for one week at the height of the "Coppers Panic," attested to the significant depreciation of coppers while attempting to maintain a "business as usual" posture. Courtesy American Antiquarian Society.

[99] *Fed. Gaz.*, July 30, 1789.
[100] *Fed. Gaz.*, Aug. 1, 1789.
[101] *Fed. Gaz.*, Aug. 1, 1789.
[102] *Fed. Gaz.*, Aug. 8, 1789. An interesting commentary written in 1838 by Dr. James Mease (1771-1846) of Philadelphia, recalled the Connecticut copper as "the old farthing of our boyhood," consistent with the exchange rate of 48 to the Pennsylvania shilling. The implication is that the inflated exchange rate for these particular state coppers was of longer duration than just the summer of 1789 (Mease, "Coins").
[103] *Fed. Gaz.*, Aug. 3, 1789.
[104] *Daily Adv.*, July 24 through 30, 1789. Sixty coppers per New York shilling equaled 50 per pound at 10d.
[105] *Penna. Pack.*, Aug. 1, 1789.

One published treatise on copper urged that copper never should acquire legal tender status nor should a creditor be obliged to receive even partial payment of a debt in copper.[106] The logic advanced for this pronouncement included the financial loss which would be incurred since copper passed at a rate greater than its intrinsic value. It was also argued that due to the weight and bulk of a large payment of copper, there would be significant transportation and storage problems. For example, if one were required to accept only 5% of a $10,000 debt in copper, the payment would weigh 1,180 pounds. The writer also emphasized the relatively greater expense to mint copper coins as compared to gold and silver, and that the final result would be a greater quantity of copper in circulation than would be necessary for small change. A compromise proposal would be a billon coinage of half copper and silver so that the coin would be physically large enough and yet have intrinsic value so that creditors would not suffer. Congress eventually heeded the ideas advanced in the treatise since copper coinage from the Federal mint did not become legal tender until 1864, and in fact, half cents were rejected as currency by the public in 1811.[107] The billon coinage, as well as a later idea to insert a silver plug in copper coins to augment intrinsic value never came to fruition.[108]

Some less serious ideas were tendered to cope with the surplus of coppers including their consumption in the manufacture of sleigh bells which were to be required of all horses in Philadelphia to prevent pedestrian accidents.[109] The Philadelphia Common Council interrupted their solemn discussion of the copper problem when some members proposed that the excess coppers could be exchanged for tea or used in the manufacture of frying pan bottoms, and copper buttons:

> Mr. E. ... then proposed, that the coppers be immediately sent to Botany Bay, and exchanged for the best Hyson and Tonkay teas.
>
> Mr. L. said, the proposal was a good one, ... whenever the first ship-load is gone, they [coppers] will immediately flow in upon us from the other states, and at that rate we may ship them [coppers] off to eternity.
>
> Mr. S., an able statesman and renowned politician ... moved that it be recommended to the good people of the United States, to convert into [buttons] the coppers now in circulation; thus ... computing the number of souls in North America at 2,000,000, and allowing each person twenty-four buttons, the whole will amount to 48,000,000, a number far exceeding the coppers in circulation; the importation of frying pan bottoms from Britain would then cease, our manufacturers would be encouraged, our wisdom and economy would astonish the world.[110]

The question was moved and defeated.

Satirical comments regarding the Coppers Panic were not limited to the Philadelphia Common Council chambers as recorded in the following poems:

The Complaint of a Copper[111]

Long have I been the slave of man;
I do to please him all I can.
From hand to hand I love to pass,
And none accuses me of *brass*.
A foreigner I am, 'tis true;
But what is that to him or you?

[106] *Penna. Merc.*, July 30, 1789. See Appendix 5 for the complete text of Bordley's treatise on copper coin.
[107] Taxay, *Catalogue*, p. 54.
[108] Yeoman, *Guide Book*, p. 10; Breen, *Encyclopedia*, pp. 156-57. 1369.
[109] *Fed. Gaz.*, Aug. 1, 1789.
[110] *Ind. Gaz.*, Aug. 1, 1789.
[111] *Fed. Gaz.*, Aug. 1, 1789.

A stranger, serving the community,
With natives ought to live in unity.
Perhaps, to serve some views of state,
I suffer scandal from the great;
Perhaps some mercenary knave
Against my worth pretend to rave.
Swindler, to gain their private ends,
Will sacrifice their worthy friends.
Because a few vile interlopers
Have got amongst us honest coppers,
Must fear to flame consign us all
In every shop, at every stall?
The villain truly was satanic,
Who first began this cruel panic.[112]
And should the horror widely spread,
The child shall cry in vain for bread.
Too often mad infatuations
Will run like wildfire, through a nation.
But, though this satire may be true,
What harm, alas! can Coppers do?
Trifles at most, we serve for change;
Then far and wide pray let us range.
If not imprison'd in the state,
We soon will ease you of our weight;
But since a bad name thus you give us,
No other land will e'er receive us.
Treat us no worse than we deserve,
If we must suffer, you may starve!

The Coppers Done Over[113]

Of all the late hubbubs urg'd on, by foot-cloven,
From shop board to office, from tap room to oven,
From college to brothel—could hell e'en discover,
More wicked a whim, than we Coppers done over?
Done over, o.

Our nominal value for ages pass'd muster,
With 'squire, brewer, baker, punk, bailiff and huckster;
But 80 a shilling, 'twixt butcher and drover,
Must prove, that poor Coppers are sadly done over, &c.

Kite-faced bills of credit,[114] altho' they did wonders,
Fell not half so fast into b-mf dd-r [*sic*] flounders;

[112] Of interest, this is the only contemporaneous reference found which calls the collapse of coppers a "panic."

[113] *Ind. Gaz.*, Aug. 5, 1789. Some words are unclear due to broken type in the original. The phrase "done over" has the connotation, "defeated or finished." Another poem in similar style, "The Farmer not Done Over," appeared (*Norwich Pack.*, July 31, 1789).

[114] "Kite-faced bills of credit" is a poetic reference to the Continental notes of January 14, 1779, printed in black and red with kite-like silhouettes appearing on the design in a contrasting color. See Newman, *Paper Money*, pp. 47-49 and color plate on p. 311; see above, p. 147, Fig. 47.

Perhaps they'll yet start from this vault into clover,
To ouster us Coppers, thus flatly done over, &c.

Were Swift sent from Styx, with political caution,
To sing wooden half-pence again, out of fashion:
'T would not cause such fuss, between London and Dover,
As here, in Columbia, poor Coppers done over, &c.[115]

Had we and slut Conty, who dropt long before us,
Still kept with the wealthy, they'd prize and adore us;
But catch'd in hands needy, we feel her false lover
Repeat his fell stab, on us Coppers done over, &c.

Beware gold and silver your fate seems precarious,
The mediums of trade, are so jadish and various;
Keep clear of the poor, or be sure under cover,
Some speck shall condemn you, like Coppers done over, &c.

Ye minting brass founders, now, now is your harvest,
For fresh speculations, lo! Satan, thou carvest,
"Till ev'ry oppressor, and spect-money rover,
Shall weigh'd be like Coppers, and smartly done over, &c.

Away, now, ye beggars, and small-ware retailers,
Go, all suck your paws, through our downfal and failures;
Else, lay siege to Heaven—your pray'rs may recover
The death of the D—l [*sic*], and Coppers done over,
Done over, o.

It is probable that those whom the devaluation of copper affected the most, namely the poor and the smaller merchants, did not see much levity in the situation or appreciate the jokes poked at their misfortune. Such is the tone of a letter written to the editor of *The Federal Gazette*.

Mr. Brown.
It is really laughable to hear the different opinions offered about the copper coin. But to be serious, I would advise the Corporation of the large trading cities to endeavor to come to some agreement about the rate at which coppers shall be received in payments as change, at least such of them as appear to be good copper.[116]

This was essentially the course that many cities adopted. The New York Common Council recommended a rate of 48 coppers to the shilling on July 21, 1789, an action also taken by Albany four days later where the following scenario was described:

The immense quantities of light coppers made of base metal, which have been teaming in upon us for near a twelve-month at different parts of the state, particularly New York [City], have at length occasioned a depreciation of near 3/4ths of their value. Many of the merchants and shop keepers of this city [Albany], must sustain considerable losses, by so sudden a depreciation, nor are they the only sufferers on this occasion, every class of citizen will experience it, in a greater or lesser degree, particularly the bakers and

[115] Another reference to Wood's coinages.
[116] *Fed. Gaz.*, Aug. 1, 1789.

butchers; there is an instance of one of the former receiving, in the course of one day last week, in trifling sums, upward of six pounds.[117]

Philadelphia refused to endorse a position but deferred to an exchange rate for coppers set by market forces since they recognized they had no right to act under the new Constitution. By September 5, 1789, the exchange rate for New Jersey coppers in New York had improved to 24 per shilling, which were the only coppers authorized to circulate in the state. This fact was noted in the press by the following news item with an admonishment: "Coppers with the Jersey stamp, are now current at two for a penny: It is hoped, that the mint masters [*sic*] will be so moderate as not to glut the market."[118] New Jersey coppers were preferentially received since they enjoyed a legal tender status in their home state for the payment of taxes.[119]

Not only were the municipalities struggling under this deluge of unwanted copper coin, but also the state governments of Connecticut and New Jersey were perplexed as to how to empty their respective treasuries of this rejected money. The constitutional prohibition against state coinages notwithstanding, the Connecticut Assembly directed the state treasurer in December 1790, to sell or dispose of the coppers remaining in the treasury in exchange for liquidated notes or state securities, provided that that "he can obtain two shillings in said Notes or Securities pr [*sic*] pound weight for said Coppers." This would imply an official "suggested" exchange rate for this fiscal paper of 24.3 coppers per shilling for regulation weight coins of 144 grains. It is to be recalled that Connecticut never published an exchange rate for coppers in that jurisdiction. Apparently the move did not rid the state coffers of coppers since a May 1791 instruction to the state treasurer authorized him "to dispose of the Coppers now in the Treasury and the property of this State to the best advantage ...."[120]

Massachusetts apparently had no problem with its coppers and did not alter the exchange rate of the residual cents and half cents remaining in the treasury as evidenced by a resolution passed on June 10, 1790. The document instructed the state treasurer to pay out copper cents for debts of the Commomwealth at the rate of 108 for six shillings, lawful money, and to receive such coppers into the treasury at the same rate, "any law or resolve to the contrary notwithstanding."[121] It certainly appears that Massachusetts coppers maintained their regulated value throughout this period.

An interesting comment made by Jeremy Belknap in relation to English coppers circulating in New Hampshire is worthy of examination.[122] The historian described various scenes of patriotism at the time of the Revolution where citizens of the state profaned in one way or another all images of the monarchy "and the half-pence, which bore the name of George III, were either refused in payment, or degraded to farthings." To conclude the passage written in 1791, Belknap added, "These last have not yet recovered their value." The implication of this statement is that English coppers in New Hampshire were depreciated in 1776 for an entirely different reason and never regained their former value. It is unlikely that this continued depression in that state in the value of English coppers, most of which were likely counterfeit, had anything to do with the Coppers Panic.

The legal tender status of legitimate New Jersey coppers was threatened by the presence of the overstruck Elizabethtown issues and "camel heads" previously described in detail, which it is believed, came on the scene after the summer of 1789. These lightweight coppers became

[117] *Penna. Pack.*, Aug. 6, 1789. Six pounds, or 120 shillings, in coppers at 48 to the shilling would yield 5760 coppers! Six pounds, avdp., at about 60 to the pound, approximates 360 coins.

[118] *Gaz. of U.S.*, Sept. 5, 1789; *Fed. Gaz.*, Sept. 8, 1789; *N.H. Spy*, Sept. 12, 1789; *Va. Gaz.*, Sept. 17, 1789.

[119] Although the authorization for New Jersey coppers did not grant a legal tender status *per se*, they were receivable for all debts owed to the state implying *de facto* legal tender recognition.

[120] Crosby, *Early Coins*, p.224.

[121] Crosby, *Early Coins*, p. 273.

[122] Belknap, *New-Hampshire*, vol. 2, p. 311.

such a concern to the New Jersey General Assembly that they were later the subject of a committee report submitted on June 7, 1790:

> That the depreciation of the Copper Coin appears to be entirely owing to the fraudulent practices of persons who have stamped Bermingham [*sic*] and Connecticut Coppers with the same impression as those of this state, and afterwards passed them to others : That the New-Jersey Coppers coined by law, are superior in weight to the British,[123] are of pure metal, and weigh six pennyweight six grains each, and that most of the counterfeits are of bass [*sic*] metal, and weigh less than five pennyweight each : That the New-Jersey Coppers lately passed at fifteen for a shilling, the rate directed by law, and the Bermingham and Connecticut Coppers could at the same time be procured for forty-five for a shilling, and that some persons have availed themselves of the difference, and have changed the impression of a considerable quantity of bass [*sic*] Coppers, converting one shilling's worth of those Coppers into three shillings worth of New Jersey Coppers, which practice has occasioned so great a dapreciation [*sic*] of the Coppers in this state, that in some places they do not circulate, and in other places they pass at an unequal and uncertain value, from forty-eight to thirty-six for a shilling, though they lately circulated at their full value, even in the neighbouring states [i.e. New York, ed.] where no other Coppers would pass.[124]

The committee further urged that the counterfeiters be discovered and prosecuted, although a suitable punishment could not be agreed upon. Since the overstruck coins were so numerous, it would be "extremely difficult and troublesome, and indeed almost impracticable to distinguish the real Jersey Coppers from the counterfeits." The state treasurer was in a quandary to decide at which rate to receive this potpourri of coppers in payment of taxes. If negotitated at 15 to the shilling, the state revenue would suffer financial loss from taking in the counterfeits, but if received at a depreciated rate of from 36 to 48 per shilling, an amount far below issue, then it would be a breach of faith on the part of the state. The treasurer was spared having to solve this dilemma when the assembly directed him, by a June 10, 1790 resolution, to accept no more coppers into the state coffers. The predicament of assigning an equitable exchange rate to New Jersey coppers was effectively circumvented, or postponed, by the legislature when they refused to accept more copper coin. The *de facto* legal tender status of New Jersey coppers was suspended since these coins were no longer receivable in payment of obligations to the state. Still the Assembly had to reckon with the large supply of coppers remaining in state custody and so in November 1792, directed that coppers in the treasury be paid out at the then customary rate of 24 to the shilling.[125]

The action which seemed the most decisive in curtailing the Coppers Panic was taken by the Bank of North America in Philadelphia when on August 6, 1789, it issued paper tickets in denominations of $ 3/90, or 3d. specie, Pennsylvania money, and $ 1/90, or 1d. specie, Pennsylvania money. The rationale expressed in support of this emission of paper money was "merely for the publick convenience at the juncture when the Circulation of Copper Coin is nearly suspended ...."[126] This initiative was well received as evidenced by a notice thanking the Bank for the "tickets" at this time "when the copper coin is in continual fluctuation."[127] On February

[123] This is a misstatement since the regal English halfpenny was 152.2 grains. The average weight of the overstruck pieces, groups 6b and 9 in Table 21 was 126.4 grains, but of course such values are highly subject to sampling error.

[124] *New-Jersey*, June 7 and 10, 1790.

[125] Hodder, *CNL 1990*, p. 1152.

[126] *Fed. Gaz.*, Aug. 11, 1789. The Bank of North America small change notes were printed "on thin and weak white paper furnished by Benjamin Franklin" for the $20 Continental Currency of May 10, 1775, and hence are very fragile (Newman, *Paper Money*, pp. 38, 314-15 (color plates), and 358).

[127] *Fed. Gaz.*, Aug. 12, 1789.

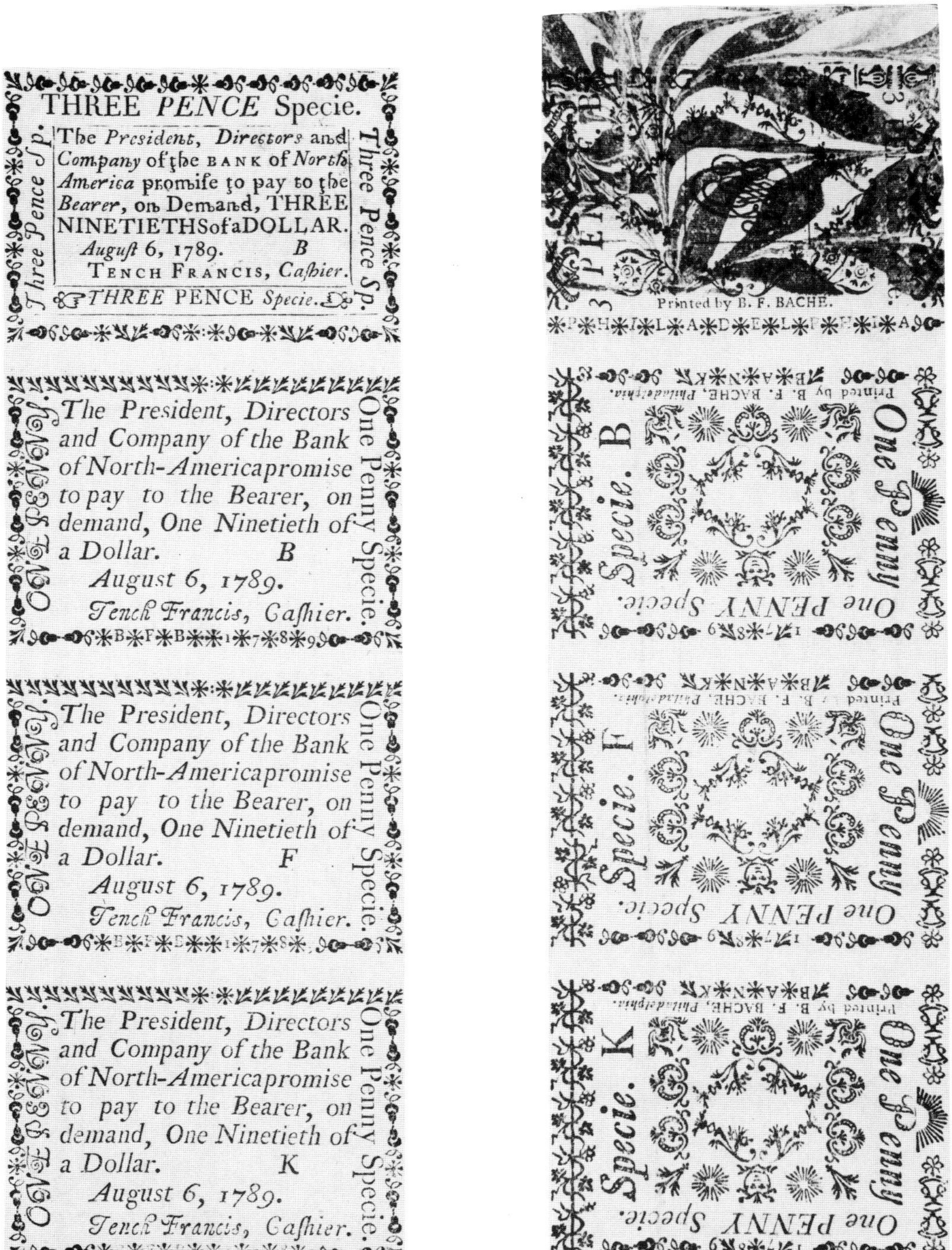

Fig. 71: Bank of North America. Issue of August 6, 1789; an uncut strip of four notes from a sheet of sixteen.

2, 1790, the Corporation of New York City followed this practice and issued small change notes of 1d., 2d., and 3d. This emission is of particular interest since these small change notes were counterfeited in England and the forger was later apprehended in London.[128] More small change notes were printed by the New York communities of Albany, Hudson, Kingston, and Poughkeepsie, and in New Jersey by Elizabeth, New Brunswick, and Perth Amboy. In New York

[128] *AnRep 1989*, pp. 28-29.

Fig. 72: Following the devaluation of copper money in the summer of 1789, there appeared in New York, New Jersey, Pennsylvania, and Connecticut low denominational paper currency to provide small change. These notes were issued by banks, municipalities, individuals, merchants, churches, and organizations. Included here are a few representative samples of these emissions.

(a) Corporation of New York City, 3d., February 20, 1790.

(b) Borough of Elizabeth, New Jersey, 4d., March 25, 1790.

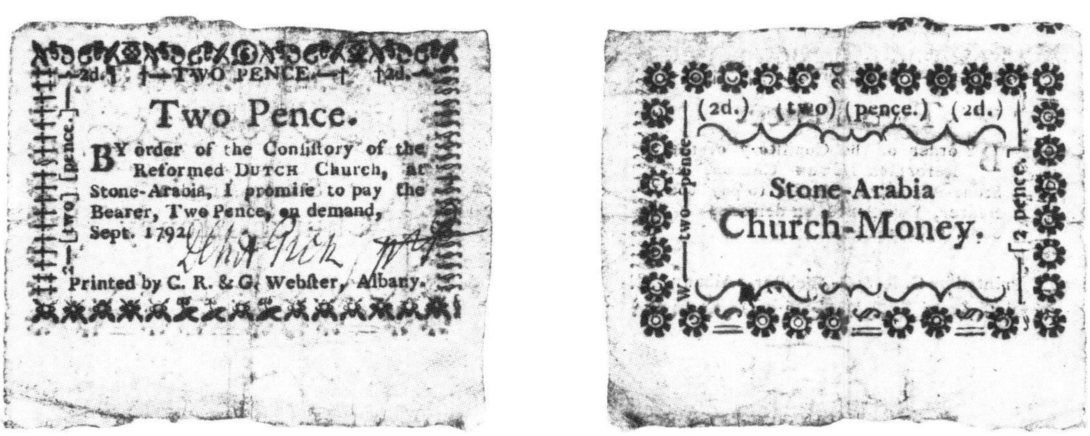

(c) Reformed Dutch Church of Stone-Arabia, New York, 2d., September 1792.

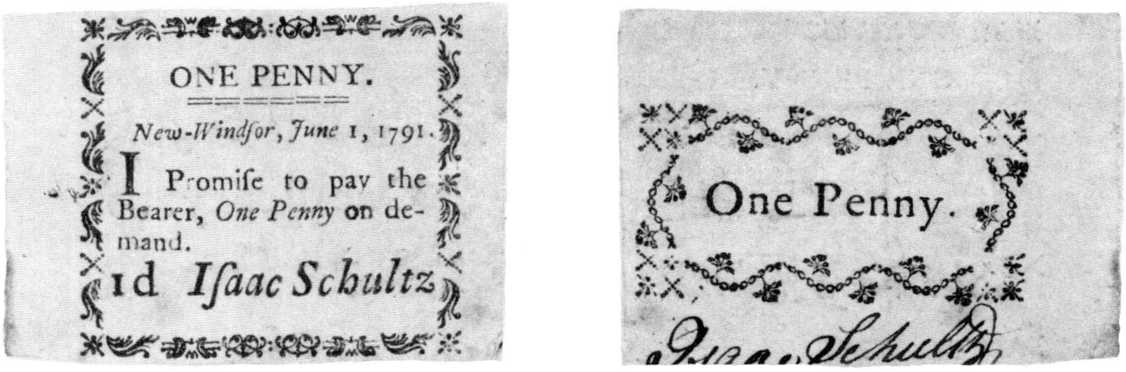

Fig. 72 (cont.): (d) Isaac Schultz, New Windsor, New York, 1d., June 1, 1791.

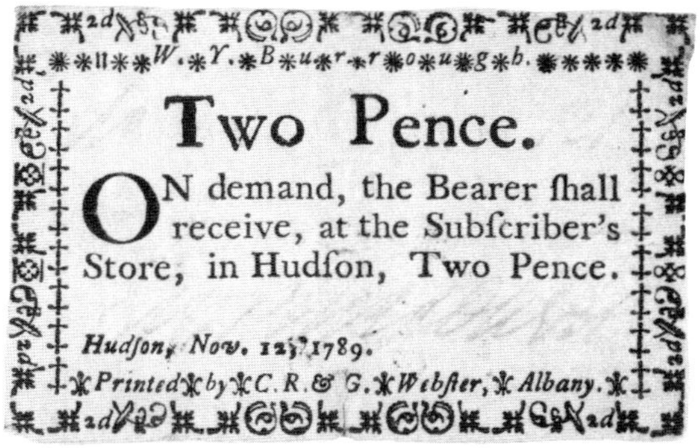

(e) W.Y. Burrough, Merchant, Hudson, New York, 2d. November 12, 1789.

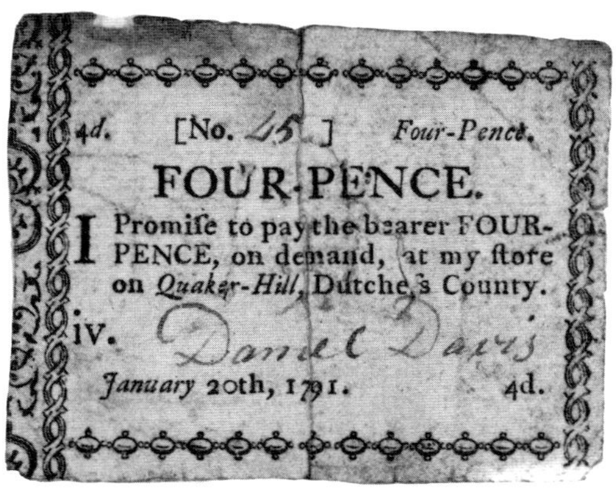

(f) Daniel Davis, Merchant, Quaker Hill, New York, 4d., January 20, 1791.

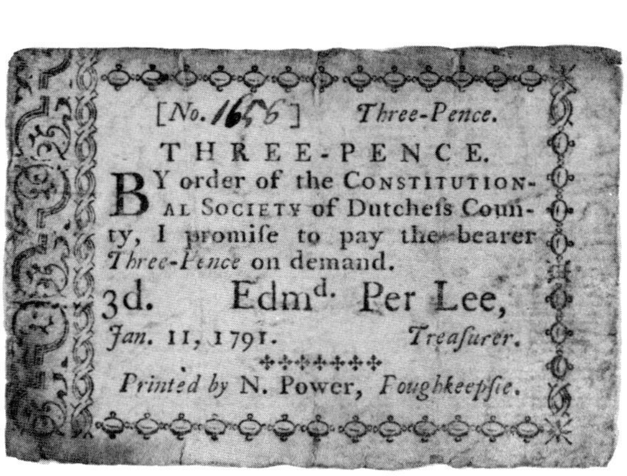

(g) Constitutional Society of Duchess County, New York, 3d., January 11, 1791.

State, alone, from the period 1789 to 1792, 54 different municipalities, individuals, businesses, churches, and other organizations printed small change paper money. This is evidence that New York was hardest hit by the demise of coppers and greatly needed this small denominational paper, since there were only eight known issuers from New Jersey, four from Pennsylvania,[129] including the Bank of North America, and two from Connecticut, there being no other New England state represented. Outside of the economic orbit of New York, the only other small change notes were those authorized by the City of Charleston, South Carolina, on October 9, 1793, in penny and twopence denominations.[130]

In this period, nine New York congregations chose to issue paper notes instead of receiving devaluated coppers in their collections. The notable exception to this practice was the First Presbyterian Church of Albany which uttered the famous Albany Church one penny token on January 4, 1790.[131] "One thousand coppers [were] stamped 'Church penny' and placed in the hands of the treasurer, for the purpose of exchanging with the congregation at the rate of twelve for one shilling, in order to add respect to the weekly collection." One such copper in the American Numismatic Society collection is struck over a counterfeit George III halfpenny.

All paper small change notes were not received with the same enthusiasm as that recorded for The Bank of North America initiative. On June 7, 1790, the New Jersey Assembly also heard from their select committee, in the report already cited, that due to:

> ... the depreciation of the Coppers, and the want of small change, a practice has almost universally prevailed throughout the state, of private persons issuing notes payable to the bearer for small sums; this practice the committee conceives to be improper, the same notes do not circulate throughout the state, and are therefore inconvenient to the holders; there is no security that they will be paid on demand, and indeed there are instances of persons issuing notes, and afterwards becoming insolvent, thereby defrauding the holders who are generally of the most ignorant class, and who ought therefore more particularly to be under the protection of the Legislature—Further, the notes increase the circulating paper medium, banish the small silver coins, and are a considerable profit to those who issue them, from the great number lost or destroyed in circulation, and which profit ought to be the emolument of the state and not of individuals.[132]

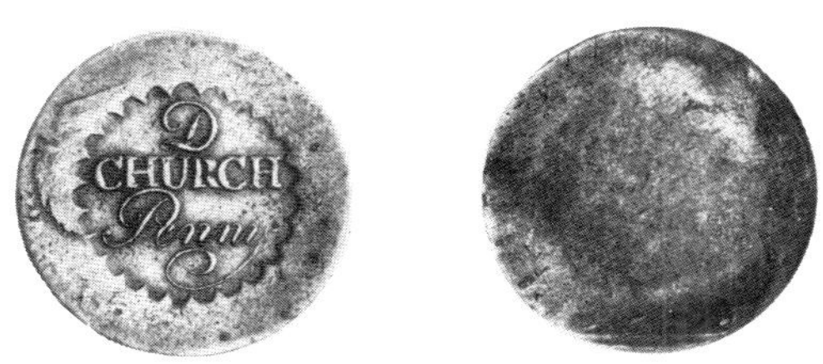

Fig. 73: Albany (N.Y.) Church Penny (uniface), overstruck on a counterfeit George III halfpenny whose details are noted on the "blank" side (101.1 grains).

The resolution was approved and a committee appointed to draft a bill "to remedy the Evil." Nothing could have come of this intention at a state level due to the restrictions of the new Constitution.

[129] The account of the small change issue of John Wray and James Lamberton from Carlisle, Pennsylvania, was carried in *Carlisle Gaz.*, Sept. 16, 1789. See Newman, *Paper Money*, p. 358.

[130] There were five other issuers of small change notes from New Jersey prior to 1789 (Newman, *Paper Money*, pp. 91-92, 239-42, 243, 271-85, and 427.

[131] Kurth, *NumSm 1944*, quote p. 284; Breen, *Encyclopedia*, p. 131.

[132] *New-Jersey*, June 7, 1790.

There is a subplot in the story of the Coppers Panic of 1789 involving the Fugio cents which had been authorized by Congress on April 21, 1787. The new coppers, passing at 100 to the Spanish milled dollar, conformed to the 157.5 grain standard recommended in the April 8, 1786 Report of the Board of Treasury to the Continental Congress, and passed by resolution four months later.[133] The attempt to replace the hodgepodge of circulating coppers by a Federal coinage was also sanctioned by the Ordinance of October 16, 1786, which confirmed that only these coppers, and none others, would be legal tender for United States taxes, that only coppers of the 157.5 grains standard could circulate, and that after September 1, 1787, no foreign coppers would be current in the Confederation.[134] The decree seems to have been so much rhetoric and achieved little respect since only the Massachusetts mint adopted the required standard, and there continued a plethora of foreign coppers. Moreover, in New York, the new exchange rate of 20 coppers to the local shilling, effective August 1, 1787, would have reduced the Fugio cents from the Federal standard of 100 per dollar to value of only 70¢ for coins circulating in that jurisdiction.[135] The unanswered question remains, if the Fugio coppers still retained the legal tender status intended by the Ordinance of October 16, 1786, why were the Federal standard and Fugio cents ignored in New York? Douglas suggested that "the subsequent decision not to establish a mint and to instead secure coppers by private contract evidently nullified this [legal tender] provision."[136] This must have been the situation since early documents are silent on the subject of legal tender status and redemption for the Fugio coppers.[137] Because of the unfavorable economic climate, the newly minted Fugios which were delivered to the Treasury by James Jarvis in May 1788, were held out of circulation. Massachusetts, the only area where the Fugios and the indigenous state coppers would have been at par on the same standard, would have been a logical place to have released the new Federal coins. An August 1, 1789 report from Boston suggests that this action may have been considered but the option was never pursued.[138] Instead the Fugio cents were sold in bulk in New York to a speculator, Royal Flint, in June 1789. If the Fugio cents had the legal tender status as originally proposed, it is inconceivable that the government would have dumped them in such a manner. Had they been receivable for taxes, this money would have enjoyed the same preference as the New Jersey coppers. Unfortunately for Flint, he could not dispose of his new purchases by the time the Coppers Panic struck later that summer. At the rate of 48 coppers per shilling recommended by the New York Common Council, the owner of 100 Fugios could expect to receive 29¢!

There was a strategy developed in May 1788, to increase the Federal standard to 210 grains, whereby the Fugio cent would have circulated as a three-quarters cent.[139] Nothing ever came of this proposal which would have brought the token value of the Fugios more into line with their intrinsic value and discouraged the currency of counterfeits. This positive action could have bolstered public confidence in coppers to the extent that the subsequent collapse might have been moderated or even averted. Congress, both under the Confederation and new Constitution, ignored the problem of an inadequate copper medium for many months and took no action despite indications of a developing crisis. Although the Federal government was occupied with more important issues, an interest on its part might have prevented the calamity which injured those dependent on small change, an opinion supported by many editorialists of the era.

[133] *Papers*; *Jour. Cong.*, Aug. 8, 1786.

[134] "An Ordinance for the Establishment of the Mint of the United States of America; and for Regulating the Value and Alloy of Coin." *Jour. Cont. Cong.*, vol. 31, p. 878.

[135] Douglas, *CNL 1969*, p. 289; Kessler, *Fugio*, p. 5. (There were 112 coppers to 96d., New York, at 14 per shilling.)

[136] Douglas, *Fugio*, (original ms.) note 182.

[137] Crosby, *Early Coins*, pp. 297-99.

[138] "... we are told, that attempts are making to palm on the inhabitants of this town [Boston], New York Coppers for cents ..." (Douglas, *CNL 1969*, p. 290).

[139] Douglas, *CNL 1969*, p. 285; Taxay, *U.S. Mint*, pp. 26-38.

The previously mentioned token, the Mott storecard, dated 1789, and issued by a New York City firm, has been attributed to this period or possibly antedated from the late 1830s. The coin arouses particular interest at this juncture since it comes in two distinct weights, a light one slightly over 100 grains and a heavier one from 164 to 233 grains. The heavier planchet is compatible with the proposed increase in the Federal standard to 210 grains which never survived the legislative process. If the token is actually of 1789 vintage, it can be speculated that the heavier coin was a purposeful attempt to provide a token of more acceptable intrinsic value and thereby assure popular approval at a time when the circulation of coppers was at a low ebb.

A contemporaneous account of life during the Coppers Panic is provided in the diary of Samuel Davis who recorded his trip from Plymouth, Massachusetts, to New York City and return during the autumn of 1789.[140] Stopping in New Haven on September 3, 1789, the diarist encountered difficulty in making change since all coppers including "AUCTORI CONN." passed at 72 to the shilling. Davis was "chagrined that old Massachusetts, with his bow and arrow, should be undervalued." The traveler commented,

> New York regulates their [Connecticut] trade ...[141] The crown passes there [New Haven], and here [Massachusetts] now at 6s. 9d. ...[142]
>
> September 17, 1789 (New York). Coppers pass at twenty-four the shilling. Only the Jersey coinage are current in the market, where are melons, peaches, and other fruits, superior, I think, to these of Boston....
>
> September 21, 1789 (Long Island Sound). Coppers seventy-two the shilling at the ferry....
>
> September 24, 1789 (Voluntown, Connecticut - on the Rhode Island border). Coppers pass at forty-eight the shilling, to those going east, as they pass thus at Providence [Rhode Island].

Davis's diary confirms that the Coppers Panic which hit New York hard in July began to slacken by early September and provides further evidence that after September 5, 1789, only New Jersey coppers were acceptable in New York at a rate of 24 to the shilling. In Connecticut, the circulation of coppers, including those of Connecticut and Massachusetts, still stagnated at a deflated rate of 72 to the shilling. Mr. Davis was appropriately "chagrined" that the exchange rate current in Connecticut would require 432 Massachusetts cents to the dollar, or about half their intrinsic value.[143] There must have been a complete lack of public faith in coppers to have sustained this ludicrous devaluation of superior quality coppers. The traveler does not comment on the exchange rate in Massachusetts but implies a rate of 48 to the shilling in Rhode Island. No contemporaneous evidence can be found which indicates that the rate for coppers was altered in Massachusetts under the influence of the Coppers Panic. On the contrary, there was an action of the General Court in June 1790, already cited, which instructed the state treasury to continue to receive and disburse cents at the legally established rate of 108 for six shillings, lawful money, or 18 to the Massachusetts shilling.

Another account of the events of the day is contained in a letter written from New York on August 1, 1789.[144] "There has been a mighty convulsion here lately on account of the coppers.

[140] Davis, *Journal*, pp. 9-12.

[141] Recall that Connecticut never set an official exchange rate for coppers.

[142] English and French crowns should have passed at 6s. 8d. in the local money of New England (and Virginia) and for 8s. 9d. in New York money of account (Schilke and Solomon, *Foreign Coins*, p. 16).

[143] The Connecticut shilling passed for six to the dollar, therefore, 432 Mass. ¢ ÷ 44.4 Mass. ¢ per pound copper = 9.7 lbs. 9.7 lbs × 13.6d. per pound = 132d. = $1.83.

This $1.83 was the intrinsic value of copper which was to pass at only $1.00 currency at that rate!

[144] Letter from Paine Wingate to Mrs. H. Wingate (*Coppers*, *Num 1928*).

We abound with them in this place and they are generally light and bad. On a sudden the merchants refused to take them at more than half, and some at more than one-third, that they had passed at. At Philadelphia I hear they have fared much in the same manner." This commentary suggests that the devaluation was initiated by the merchants who objected to the condition of the copper medium.

The extent and severity of the Coppers Panic along the northeastern seaboard cannot be determined with accuracy. "The real injury lay in the unrestricted volume [of coppers], which was aggravated by the concentration in certain cities."[145] Based on newspaper accounts, Philadelphia and New York City were hardest hit, and there the panic may have been fanned by city press hyperbole.[146] If the prevalence of small paper notes issued during the recovery is any indication, then the effect was broadened into New York State. There were significant problems throughout New Jersey. The Davis diary documents depreciated coppers in Connecticut, where the panic seemed to have lingered longer. Rhode Island was the only other New England State touched by the Coppers Panic, while Boston and more northern points either emerged unscathed or there was not sufficient impact to have warranted contemporary notation. "The panic was worst in degree in those areas [e.g. New York] having moneys of account most inflated to sterling."[147]

The initial notice of the action of the New York Common Council and subsequent news releases were repeated as far south as Pennsylvania, all through Connecticut, northward into Boston and Bennington, Vermont, but not into New Hampshire, which was still in the grips of a severe depression. The event was not mentioned by Felt in *An Historical Account of Massachusetts Currency*, a chronicle of all significant events in the Bay State's monetary history. This is not to say that Puritanical New Englanders were not interested in money. Another news story about money matters, datelined Providence, July 16, 1789, reporting the discovery of counterfeit 1781 dollars, was widely circulated within Connecticut, Massachusetts, and New Hampshire. This suggests that the devaluation of coppers was not a newsworthy item in areas away from the economic sphere of influence of metropolitan Philadelphia and New York, the center of the panic. Local newspaper accounts relate that Massachusetts also had a large proportion of counterfeit coppers in circulation,[148] as well as an assortment of European copper coins.[149] Nevertheless, it can be speculated that another difference between Boston and New York is that the Bay Staters had confidence in the quality of their well-regarded Massachusetts state coinage, which by then was in circulation and brought a stability to the small change medium, a notion which is confirmed by the legislature's June 1790 resolution to accept and disperse cents at their established rate. Thus the collapse did not spread into the Boston area, although there could have been some minor, local, fluctuation in the exchange rate for coppers which remained at 18 to the New England shilling.[150] Any significant devaluation in Massachusetts would certainly have attracted the attention of the local press, diarist Davis, or Felt. Rhode Island did have an increase in the exchange rate, as noted by Davis, which did not approach the degree seen in Connecticut. The conclusion that Massachusetts cents and half cents stabilized the copper medium locally is not unreasonable since in New York, in September 1789, when only New Jersey coppers were accepted, the exchange rate rapidly fell from 48 to 24

[145] Carothers, *Fractional Money*, pp. 44-45.

[146] In an extensive review of this manuscript, Raymond H. Williamson, commented in a personal communication, "I think the real reason for the panic was city press hype." Certainly the contemporary treatment in the Philadelphia papers was provocative.

[147] Raymond H. Williamson, personal communication.

[148] *Mass. Spy*, March 16, 1789.

[149] Newman, *Studies*, p. 148.

[150] Newman, *Coppers*, p. 107. Although there were 100 cents to the Federal dollar, there were 108 Massachusetts cents or coppers to 72d., or six shillings, lawful money, which was the rate for the Spanish milled dollar in Massachusetts.

and thus sustained the rate. The apparent reason is that the public had regained partial confidence in New Jersey coinage which had a legal tender basis and was more consistent in quality than the alternative counterfeits. Finally, after repeated urgings, the citizens of New York gathered sufficient courage and insight to reject all coppers, other than the New Jerseys, having been so recently injured by the lightweight Birminghams. Massachusetts throughout this period always had a reliable copper coinage of its own to depend upon and for that reason it can be postulated that no widespread devaluation occurred.

One outcome from the Coppers Panic of 1789 was sure; all previous governmental attempts to regulate the circulation of coppers failed and now the public looked to the Federal government for a permanent solution to the problem of an unstable copper medium under the authority of the new Constitution. The Coppers Panic should have come as no surprise to anyone since it had been brewing for years. Minor riots occurred in Philadelphia in 1741 and New York in 1753, but these isolated events triggered no definitive correction. While all classes could be hurt with the devaluation of copper currency, it appears that most, if not all, the agitation for a revaluation of the small change medium originated with the merchants. All the enabling legislation which had established the state mints spoke of the base coppers in circulation and the need for a better copper coinage. However, when such a proposal came to the New York Legislature to mint state coppers, it was rejected in favor of an action to devalue the existing medium. A legislative committee report was issued alleging the enormous profits made from minting copper token coinage, and their Congressional delegation lobbied for an increase in the Federal standard. The bubble finally broke in the summer of 1789, when the circulation of coppers from Connecticut to Pennsylvania virtually ceased.[151]

In Chapter One it was observed that the economic climate in British North America, no matter how local in scope it may have appeared from time to time, was in large measure a domestic manifestation of the more global situation. Whereas the Coppers Panic has been interpreted thus far in the regional context of an excessive, inflated, unsound copper medium whose token value would no longer be honored in commerce, this is a major oversimplification. In fact, the Coppers Panic was only a local symptom of an international condition, namely a major post-war depression during which many commodity prices, including copper, fell on the worldwide market. There is a parallel which can be drawn here with the collapse of the tin medium in Great Britain some 90 years earlier. The major difference between the Coppers Panic in 1789 and the late 1690s when the price of tin could not be maintained as it lost its commodity value on the world market, is that the patentees of the tin coinages were obliged to redeem their failing currency with copper coins. Hence, the unwanted tin money did not glut the marketplace but was removed and replaced by a more desirable copper currency. Any loss then was not borne by the public but rather by the tin speculators.

The condition of the world copper market was of particular importance to North America since the domestic copper industry here remained insignificant until the Lake Superior ore deposits were opened in 1844. Although copper was discovered in Massachusetts as early as 1632, in Connecticut in 1709, in New Jersey in 1719, and in Vermont where mines were operating from the eighteenth century,[152] there remained little incentive to develop local supplies since the refined metal and manufactured objects were so easily imported from England.[153] In fact the rich

[151] The term "ceased to circulate" was the actual language recorded in the minutes of the New York Common Council meeting of January 29, 1790 (*Common Council*, vol. 1, p. 520).

[152] Davis, *Copper*, p. 65.

[153] Whiteman, *Hendricks*, pp. 3, 48; Dennis, *Metallurgy*, p. 128. It is recalled that the Trade and Navigation Acts discouraged local American commerce and industry. At first copper was not an "enumerated commodity" meaning there was no regulation to prevent it from being landed in foreign ports without first passing through England. When it was learned in 1721 that the rich ore from the Schuyler mine was being shipped directly to Holland, copper was promptly added to the list of enumerated goods (Andrews, *Colonial Period*, p. 104, 104n).

output from the American mines, including the famous Schuyler mine in New Jersey and the Higley mine in Connecticut, was exported to England for processing, an industry stimulated there by the abundant supply of cheap coal; there was virtually no copper manufacturing in America.[154] The first rolling mill, established in 1801 by Paul Revere in Canton, Massachusetts, had to rely on brittle scrap copper for its production.[155] For domestic coinages, the metal for the 1737 and 1739 Higley issues was procured from the high grade Connecticut deposits whereas the copper for the Vermont series was from a poorer grade local ore.[156] The Massachusetts mint reprocessed scrap copper belonging to the state.[157] Similarly the Machin's Mills mint melted down "old brass cannon and mortars, the zinc from the copper being extracted by smelting in a furnace."[158] Since this country lacked the raw materials and technology necessary to produce quality fillets, the Federal Mint preferred to purchase already prepared copper planchets from England. In addition, the mintmaster was very protective of his rolling presses which were quite liable to damage from processing copper, thus the ready availability of imported blanks avoided the need to recycle scrap metal and risk damage to the new mint's vulnerable rolling equipment.[159] In 1791, Alexander Hamilton reported that to his knowledge there were no active copper mines in the United States, and by 1800, the only operational mine "of any consequence" was the old Schuyler works in New Jersey which had been rehabilitated by Nicholas J. Roosevelt.[160] In 1807, "there is not in the United States ... any copper mine, which at the present time, can furnish the raw material for the manufacture of copper; and that, consequently, the manufacturing of sheet copper, copper plates, and raised bottoms of copper, in this country, must at present, be confined to the scanty supply furnished from the collection of old copper, and the occasional importation of pigs from South America."[161] The entire country remained very reliant on foreign refined copper which was imported duty free although manufactured copper was rated at 7½%.[162]

Since the economies of all major American cities moved independently of each other and of the large European centers, recovery from the post-Revolutionary War depression was asynchronous. Prices in Amsterdam, a major international commercial center, had already started to climb by the spring of 1786 while America was still in the grips of a severe depression.[163] Postwar recovery, as measured by wholesale commodity prices, did not begin in Boston until after December 1788, when prices had reached a low point comparable to that of October 1767, following the end of the French and Indian Wars.[164] In New York, after some moderate advances during 1788 to 1790, prices of domestic commodities fell again to a low point in March 1791, before a sharp upward trend developed. The 186-commodity index for Philadelphia was the only one to include copper. In both Philadelphia and Charleston, South Carolina, the nadir of price decline occurred in April 1789, when an advance began which

[154] There was small scale copper manufacturing in America with a trivial 1,480 pounds of manufactured copper exported from Massachusetts in the fiscal year 1790-1791 destined for the Dutch West Indies and Africa (*A.S.P.C.*, vol. 1, pp. 107, 149).

[155] Whiteman, *Hendricks*, p. 49.

[156] Breen, *Encyclopedia*, pp. 39, 61; Crosby, *Early Coins*, p. 326. A comprehensive analysis of Confederation planchet fabric has not yet been undertaken. This is an excellent area for research employing energy dispersive X-ray flourescence spectrometry.

[157] Breen, *Encyclopedia*, p. 87; Crosby, *Early Coins*, pp. 243-45.

[158] Crosby, *Early Coins*, p. 191. As noted in Chapter Five, impurities in copper, such as zinc and tin, while making it easier to cast, rendered it more brittle when struck.

[159] Williamson, *Penny-Wise 1984*; Julian, *RCR 79*; Julian, *Seaby 1977*. Breen makes the apt observation (*Encyclopedia*, p. 146) that planchet preparation was responsible for "99% of the trouble facing any mintmaster of the time."

[160] *A.S.P.F.*, vol. 1, p. 39; Ewing, *Num 1987*, p. 1626; Whiteman, *Hendricks*, p. 49.

[161] *A.S.P.F.*, vol. 2, p. 258.

[162] *A.S.P.F.*, vol. 2, pp. 139, 653, 705.

[163] Bezanson, *Prices and Inflation*, p. 59.

[164] Cole, *Commodity Prices*, passim.

continued until 1796. Thus by using the wholesale commodity price index as an indicator, it appears that New York lagged behind the other centers in recovery from the depression.

The price of copper in New York in the summer of 1789 has previously been quoted at 20d., local money. Examination of wholesale world copper prices from the Amsterdam exchange during this period is most instructive.[165] These data, for the period 1775 to 1795, concerning refined Norwegian copper, originally quoted in Dutch guilders, are converted to New York currency and related to other events in our study.[166] In Amsterdam, the wholesale sterling price of copper was at its lowest point from December 1789 to May 1790 at 9.3d. per pound. In August 1789, when the circulation of coppers stagnated, the price was 9.6d., a value in excellent agreement with the previously quoted 10d., sterling, for copper in England.

Table 24

Wholesale Sterling Prices per Pound for Refined Copper on the Amsterdam Exchange, Converted also to New York Money of Account and Correlated with Other Significant World Events

(Data from Posthumus, *Prices*)

Year[a]	*Sterling Price*	*New York Price*[b]	*Significant Events of the Period*
1765	13.2d.	23.5d.	The previous high for copper.
1775	10.6d.	18.8d.	Outbreak of Revolution.
1776	11.2d.	19.9d.	Declaration of Independence.
1778	11.4d.	20.3d.	Wartime high for copper.
1781	11.3d.	20.0d.	End of Revolution.
1783	11.0d.	19.6d.	Peace of Paris.
1785	10.7d.	19.0d.	State coppers first minted.
1786	10.6d.	18.8d.	Prices begin recovery in Amsterdam.
1787	10.4d.	18.5d.	Coppers devalued to 20 per shilling, N.Y.
1788	10.2d.	18.1d.	Prices begin rise in Boston in December.
1789	9.7d.	17.2d.	Recovery starts in Philadelphia in April. COPPERS PANIC in August.
1790	9.7d.	17.2d.	Domestic commodity prices fall again in N.Y.
1791	9.8d.	17.4d.	Recovery starts N.Y. in March.
1792	not recorded		Federal standard reduced from 264 to 208 grains for copper cent.
1793	13.9d.	24.7d.	War in Europe.
1795	14.2d.	25.2d.	Federal standard reduced to 168 grains for copper cent.

[a] Based on the average price for the year. Prices for 1792 not listed.
[b] Derived from 96/54 of sterling price; excludes transportation to America of about 20%. The base 1789 value of 17.2d. would then become 20.6d., in excellent agreement with the quoted amount of 20d.

The recovery of world copper prices after 1790, was accompanied by a restoration of faith in the domestic copper medium. "The rise in the price of copper metal helped restore mercantile confidence in copper coins and their acceptance was reestablished in some parts of the Middle Atlantic and northeastern states."[167] As the world commodity price for copper climbed during

[165] This information is from Posthumus, *Prices*, p. 375, passim.

[166] In this period, the Dutch guilder contained 9.61 grams (148.30 grains) of pure silver, compared to the English shilling with 85.9 grains. Therefore, one guilder equaled 1.73 shillings, or 20.7d. In August 1789, 100 pounds of copper was quoted at 45.00 guilders × 20.7 = 9.3d. per pound.

[167] Newman, *Coppers*, p. 102. It was Mr. Newman who suggested to me the important role of world copper prices as the ultimate cause of the Coppers Panic.

the French Revolution, the Federal standard for copper coins from the Federal Mint required readjustment and was lowered to 208 grains for the cent on April 2, 1792. The world copper prices were watched carefully in this country as witnessed by a letter from Alexander Bilsland of Philadelphia to the Mint Director, Elias Boudinot,

> Sir: I have examined with attention the different prices of copper in the English Market for the last 4 years. In 1791 it was 10d pr lb. at which rate it had continued for a number of years. A Letter from the Manufacturer dated 3rd Dec '91 informs me that it had risen to 11d. In the summer of '92 it advanced to 12d. On the 10th October '92 it rose to 12½d at which price it continued till the 23rd Feb '93 when it rose to 14d. On the 4th Nov. of the Same Year it fell to 13½d and continued at that price until the 5th March '95 when it fell to 13d. at which price it still continues. The prices above stated are Money prices.
>
> I will engage to supply any quantity of the best manufactured copper that comes from England ...[168]

A communication from the Mint Office by Henry William De Saussure to President Washington on October 27, 1795, stated in part, "the price of copper having risen considerably, from causes which, it is said, will be operative for some length of time, if not permanently, it has been suggested that it would be useful to diminish the weight of the cent, as the copper would, thereby, be brought nearer to its proportionate value to silver, and might prevent its being worked up by the coppersmiths."[169] Heeding this suggestion, Washington subsequently reduced the copper cent to 168 grains on December 25, 1795. Had these downward adjustments in coin weight not occurred, then the market value of the copper in the Federal coinages would have soon exceeded their monetary value with the predictable consequence that the new United States cents and half cents would have rapidly disappeared into the melting pot and ended up as copper implements of one sort or another.[170] "The wheel is come full circle."

The question asked in the preface of this book can now be answered. Why did the state coinages endure only from 1785 to 1789? There are several reasons. The most obvious political answer is that under the Constitution, states could no longer mint coins, print paper money, or regulate currency. For years there had been an unwieldy expansion of copper currency, primarily because of the unrestricted volumes of lightweight counterfeit halfpence imported from England. State legislatures failed in their attempt to stabilize the copper medium since, in a large part, they only encouraged expansion of an already unwieldy currency pool which was greatly in excess of commercial requirements. The public did not actively discriminate which coins they would accept as copper currency as long as they received the prescribed value for their money. The abundant coppers accumulated in unspendable quantities, since they were receivable only in small, domestic transactions. When the merchants began to accept coppers only at reduced rates, their circulation could no longer be supported in the metropolitan areas of New York and Philadelphia and the bottom dropped out of the market. Then all coppers were viewed with suspicion, even "old Massachusetts, with his bow and arrow," as the entire medium collapsed. New Jersey coppers with legal tender status made an early recovery. The surplus of unwanted coppers did not even command a favorable price as a commodity since this Coppers

[168] ANS Mint Microfilm reel No. 4, p. 3, dated Dec. 12, 1795.

[169] *A.S.P.F.*, vol. 1, p. 357.

[170] The point at which the market value for copper would exceed its token monetary value is predictable. This is not unlike the calculations made by Sumner concerning the Pine Tree coinages, or the situation on July 8, 1963, when silver reached the "numismatic melting point" of $1.29 per Troy ounce when it became worth more as a commodity than money (*CW Almanac*, p. 204). On February 8, 1794, David Rittenhouse, Director of the Mint, communicated that the profit derived from 600 lbs. of copper struck into $202 of cents and half cents was only $18.50. If the price of this copper increased to $178.50, or to 29.75¢ per pound, this would then be the break-even point for minting cents at the 208 grains standard (*A.S.P.F.*, vol. 1, p. 273). See note 64.

Panic coincided with, or was spurred on by, a slump in copper prices on international exchanges; as worldwide copper prices recovered and the public became more discriminate as to what money they would accept, good quality coppers regained their usefulness as a small change medium.

From a purely numismatic viewpoint, it is both remarkable and surprising that such little attention has been paid to the most prevalent copper coin circulating in America during Colonial and Confederation times, namely the counterfeit English halfpence. Both the domestic counterfeit halfpence from Machin's Mills and the imported Birminghams are very important coins in our numismatic legacy and deserve equal consideration. Other coppers which deserve numismatic recognition as having circulated in America as a part of the small change medium include the genuine English halfpence and farthings, especially those dated 1749, and the regal and counterfeit Irish halfpence.

The Coppers Panic of 1789 was a multifactoral phenomenon. The determinants of the panic essentially involve a recapitulation of the prior history of North American currency as detailed in earlier chapters. To understand the factors leading up to this exigency when the copper medium collapsed during that scorching summer of 1789, requires an appreciation of our numismatic heritage from those earlier periods. The salient points can be briefly summarized:

1. British North America, lacked a uniform currency and relied on foreign silver and gold and English coppers.
2. Over the years there developed an absolute surplus of coppers, far more than commerce required. Since coppers could only be used as change and for small transactions, merchants encountered problems in disposing of excess numbers of coppers which would accumulate.
3. The majority of these coppers were counterfeit, as in England.
4. The coppers probably concentrated in seaport cities where they were imported by profiteers. "The real injury lay in the unrestricted volume, which was aggravated by the concentration in certain cities."[171]
5. State authorities considered that such cheap coppers defrauded the public.
6. States endeavored to mint true value coppers to correct this perception of a fraudulent copper medium.
7. State coppers failed in their task to provide a stable, just, copper medium. Due to counterfeits and lightweight overstrikes, many state issues became just as inferior as those they were intended to replace.
8. Good English coppers were exported back to England at a profit as the exchange rate here became favorable to do so.
9. All coppers were treated as equal and passed "without discrimination." For years the public did not care about the quality of their coppers as long as they received the established exchange.
10. Since only New Jersey coppers had any legal tender provisions, there was greater advantage to counterfeit them.
11. Low denominational silver coins had always been in short supply, but now the postwar depression aggravated this shortage. The scant supply of small silver was further drained, as predictable from Gresham's law, since the abundant, cheap, coppers would have encouraged hoarding of the more desirable currency. "The more valuable metals are daily giving place to base British half-pence, and no means are used to prevent this fraud. This disease, which is neglected in the beginning, because it appears trifling, may finally prove very destructive to commerce."[172]
12. There was no small denominational paper.

[171] Carothers, *Fractional Money*, pp. 44-45.
[172] *A.S.P.F.*, vol. 1, p. 101.

13. Because of a worldwide decline in the price of copper, copper tokens even lost their commodity value.
14. New York was slower to recover from the postwar depression.
15. New York's money of account was the most inflated in terms of sterling.
16. After two earlier skirmishes, the copper medium lost public confidence in July 1789. The situation was probably ignited by merchants who were being harmed by the accumulation of more coppers than they could spend.
17. The situation in New York and Philadelphia was probably aggravated by local newspaper accounts and mercantile interests.
18. Due to Constitutional restraints, the state and local governments could not deal effectively with the crisis, and for whatever reasons, the Federal Government would not tackle it.

Faith in the copper medium returned and the circulation of coppers resumed as:

1. Small denominational paper was made available.
2. People became more discriminating in what coins they would receive and recognized the superiority of New Jersey coppers.
3. The depression lifted and trade again flourished.
4. Copper became more valuable as a commodity as a result of market forces stimulated in part by war in Europe and its price advanced on international exchanges.
5. Federal coppers of greater and consistent weight appeared.

This numismatic history continues as the events leading up to the development of the new Constitution and subsequent founding of the Federal Mint are recounted.

CHAPTER NINE

Toward a More Perfect Union

As the end of the Confederation period approached, the new union still lacked uniform exchange rates between the states, the country depended on diverse foreign specie for currency, and both the state and Federal governments had the power to regulate and produce money. The country was just edging out of a disastrous postwar depression and lacked both direction and unanimity. This chapter examines how this challenge was addressed.

In an attempt to respond to some of these outstanding problems of the day, delegates from several states convened in Annapolis, Maryland, on September 11, 1786, to examine the trade regulations between their jurisdictions. It was all too evident that the Articles of Confederation were inadequate to cope with the current trade and economic crises and the need for their revision was obvious. "... Congress was doing little more than performing the function of a stately debating society."[1] A second meeting was planned for May 1787, to propose amendments to the Articles of Confederation to make them "adequate to the exigencies of the government, and the preservation of the Union" and report back to Congress.[2] The country was still in a deep depression, seven states had resorted to "rag money," a negative trade balance continued, hard money had all but disappeared, and experiments in copper coinage were destined for failure. Shays's Rebellion against taxation, which had occurred in western Massachusetts through the summer of 1786 and into the early months of 1787, was fresh in everyone's memory, and more than any single event since the Revolution, drove home the need for a stronger national government.[3] Although some historians suggest that too much emphasis has been placed on this "organized resistance to the collection of personal debts,"[4] others suggest that Shays's Rebellion was one of the major events catalyzing the Constitutional Convention of 1787, in addition to calming the paper money craze all over the nation.[5] Jensen postulated that Shays's Rebellion and its potential for civil unrest frightened George Washington out of retirement and into politics.[6]

The convention scheduled for May 1787, disregarded previous instructions. Rather than revise the existing Articles, it set to the task of framing an entirely new constitution. The new document significantly limited the powers of the individual states and vested additional authority within the Federal government. Congress was to become financially independent of the state legislatures since it was to be empowered to tax directly. Only the Federal government would have the power "to coin money, regulate the value thereof, and of foreign coin, and fix the standard of weights and measures."

On September 17, 1787, the entirely new Constitution was finished and approved by the Convention.[7] It now had to be ratified by the several state conventions. Felt writes of its

[1] McLaughlin, *Confederation*, p. 81.
[2] Stephens, *Popular History*, p. 277.
[3] Hawke, *Experience*, p. 667.
[4] Stephens, *Popular History*, p. 274.
[5] Nevins, *American States*, p. 537.
[6] Jensen, *New Nation*, p. 250.
[7] The credit for writing the Constitution is given to Gouverneur Morris of Constellatio Nova coppers fame. It was he who penned the "marvelous, felicitous" Preamble, "We the People of the United States, in order to form a more perfect Union ... do ordain and establish this Constitution for the United States of America." See Sparks, *Morris*, vol. 1, pp. 284-85; Morris, *Morris Diary*, vol. 1, p. 17; Swiggett, *Morris*, p. 129; Mintz, *Morris*, pp. 199-200; McDonald, *E Pluribus Unum*, p. 186.

reception in Massachusetts. "It is regarded by the friends of order and rational freedom, as essential to endow the National Administration with power sufficient to repair and regulate the system of the currency."[8]

Support for the new constitution was far from unanimous. Proponents urged its acceptance in a collection of essays titled *The Federalist* written by such advocates as Alexander Hamilton, John Jay, and James Madison. These commentaries stressed the need for the Federal government to be the only jurisdiction with the authority to coin money and regulate its value. In regard to state mints, an author of *The Federalist* continues, "... a right of coinage in the particular states could have no other effect than to multiply expensive mints and diversify the forms and weights of the circulating pieces."[9] This indeed had been the experience of the state mints under the Articles of Confederation. *The Federalist* concludes, "The extension of the prohibition to bills of credit must give pleasure to every citizen ... and that all currencies must be managed at the Federal level."[10]

The several state legislators who had supported paper money during 1785 and 1786 were the very ones who opposed the ratification of the new constitution when it was submitted to their respective assemblies.[11] In Maryland, voters were urged to send only those members to the ratifying convention who supported the new constitution since it was argued that those who favored paper money and the debtor bill "did not want an orderly government, but a chaotic one where they would be free to speculate."[12]

Less than ten months after the Constitution was reported out of the Convention, it was ratified by the ninth state, New Hampshire, on June 21, 1788 and became the new order of the land on March 4, 1789. It has been proposed

> ... that economic deprivation was the major issue in the campaign for ratification of the Constitution. Because of the depression and its unwanted effects of a collapsing economy, a shortage of money and burdensome debts and taxes, the people accepted the United States Constitution as a means that seemed to promise a way out of their troubles.[13]

In his book, *An Economic Interpretation of the Constitution of the United States*, Charles A. Beard developed the argument that the Constitution was written and directed by those leaders who were personally interested in, and derived economic advantages from this new system of government.[14] He concluded that there were large and important economic interests and factors which were adversely affected by the government under the Articles of Confederation, including the largely still unpaid obligations of the Revolutionary War. Beard stressed class differences as determining factors in the evolution of the new Constitution but this theory has not withstood the scrutiny of modern day historians since "state and local studies have shown that in many areas political divisions did not reflect a pattern of conflict between rich and poor, creditor and debtor, merchant and farmer."[15] Specifically from Virginia, Beard's thesis is refuted where it has been shown that the leaders of the factions, both supporting and opposing the new Constitution, were all from the same socio-economic group of the landed aristocracy.[16] But no matter what the motivation of the framers of the Constitution of 1787, this document has withstood the test of time.

[8] Felt, *Massachusetts*, p. 205.
[9] Lodge, *Federalist*, No. 42 (by James Madison), p. 264.
[10] Lodge, *Federalist*, No. 44 (by James Madison), p. 278.
[11] Bullock, *Essays*, pp. 76, 198-99, 273; Sumner, *American Currency*, pp. 52-53.
[12] Behrens, *Maryland*, pp. 86-87.
[13] Flannagan, *Trying Times*, pp. 3-4.
[14] Beard, *Economic Interpretation*.
[15] Daniell, *Experiment*, quote p. ix. See also McDonald, *Origins*, p. 357 and Lucy, *Revolution*, pp. 263-67.
[16] Thomas, *Virginia Convention*, pp. 63-72.

Fig. 74: WASHINGTON'S INAUGURATION, APRIL 30, 1789. This is the only contemporary representation of this historic event which took place on the balcony of Federal Hall in New York City, the seat of the national government from 1784 to 1790. (Stokes and Haskell, *Prints*, pp. 61-62.) Courtesy The New York Public Library.

The first Federal elections were held on January 7, 1789, and George Washington was inaugurated on April 30. Neither North Carolina nor Rhode Island had yet ratified the Constitution and remained outside the government, an action quite consistent with their paper money and inflationist policies. When Congressional action on the Bill of Rights was in progress, North Carolina approved the Constitution in November 1789, followed by Rhode Island in May of the next year.

Even though the country had initiated a strong central government, it would take many years to sort out the monetary problems of the past 180 years and before the currency would be in order. The major difference now was that prices and foreign exchange were quoted consistently in both Federal dollars and state currencies. Old habits die hard, and even today transactions on the New York Stock Exchange, established in 1792, are carried out in 1/8ths, a hold over from the New York shilling, when eight traded for a Spanish milled dollar. Table 25, dated July 25, 1789, printed in the *Virginia Gazette and Weekly Advertiser*,[17] was the contribution of one reader

TABLE 25

JULY 25, 1789

CENTS turned into shillings, pence, and farthings, with the decimal fractions of a farthing in the currency of the several States of the Union, where the dollar is rated at 4/8. 6/-. 7/6. or 8/-. (*Virginia Gazette*, August 6, 1789)

Cents.	*4/8.*	*6/-.*	*7/6.*	*8/-.*[a]
	s. d. qrs.	*s. d. qrs.*	*s. d. qrs.*	*s. d. qrs.*[b]
1	0- 0-2.24	0- 0-2.88	0- 0-3.60	0- 0-3.84
2	0- 1-0.48	0- 1-1.76	0- 1-3.20	0- 1-3.68
3	0- 1-2.72	0- 2-0.64	0- 2-2.80	0- 2-3.52
4	0- 2-0.96	0- 2-3.52	0- 3-2.40	0- 3-3.56
5	0- 2-3.20	0- 3-2.40	0- 4-2.00	0- 4-3.20
6	0- 3-1.44	0- 4-1.28	0- 5-1.60	0- 5-3.04
7	0- 3-3.68	0- 5-0.16	0- 6-1.20	0- 6-2.88
8	0- 4-1.92	0- 5-3.04	0- 7-0.80	0- 7-2.72
Dimes. 9	0- 5-0.16	0- 6-1.92	0- 8-0.40	0- 8-2.56
1 or 10	0- 5-2.40	0- 7-0.80	0- 9-0.00	0- 9-2.40
2 or 20	0-11-0.80	1- 2-1.60	1- 6-0.00	1- 7-0.80
3 or 30	1- 4-3.20	1- 9-2.40	2- 3-0.00	2- 4-3.20
4 or 40	1-10-1.60	2- 4-3.20	3- 0-0.00	3- 2-1.60
5 or 50	2- 4-0.00	3- 0-0.00	3- 9-0.00	4- 0-0.00
6 or 60	2- 9-2.40	3- 7-0.80	4- 6-0.00	4- 9-2.40
7 or 70	3- 3-0.80	4- 2-1.60	5- 3-0.00	5- 7-0.80
8 or 80	3- 8-3.20	4- 9-2.40	6- 0-0.00	6- 4-3.20
9 or 90	4- 2-1.60	5- 4-3.20	6- 9-0.00	7- 2-1.60
10 or 100	4- 8-0.00	6- 0-0.00	7- 6-0.00	8- 0-0.00

[a] The States with an exchange rate of 4/8 (56d.) in local money of account to the Spanish Milled dollar, or U.S. dollar were South Carolina and Georgia.
At 6/- (72d.) were New England and Virginia.
At 7/6 (90d.) were New Jersey, Pennsylvania, Maryland, and Delaware.
At 8/- (96d.) were New York and North Carolina.

[b] qrs. = quarter of a farthing. The chart gives the example that 6 Federal cents are worth 4d. 1 28/100 farthing in Virginia currency.
To find how many shillings, etc. Virginia money are in 47 cents:

	s.	*d.*	*qrs.*	
4 dimes (40 cents) are	2 :	4 :	3.20	
the 7 cents are	0 :	5 :	0.16	
the sum is	2 :	9 :	3.36	Virginia currency

[17] Aug. 6, 1789.

who wished to perform a public service. His desire was to reduce the "perplexity" of "the new money of account established by the late Congress" and familiarize "the good people of these United States" with the new Federal decimal system as expressed "in the currency of the several States of the Union." Local monies of account did not disappear overnight but remained in use for at least another 40 years.[18]

While it can be reasonably assumed that about every description of foreign money could have eventually found its way into North American commerce, some specific gold and silver issues were more commonly encountered. In conformity with the Federal decimal system, exchange rates for popular world specie coins of the period were established by the Act of July 31, 1789. These coins, many of which have not been previously mentioned during the colonial period, are listed in Table 26, where the value of gold to silver is maintained at a 16:1 ratio.

The new regulation, which actually set the rate at which foreign coin would be received for the payment of duties, did not meet with universal approval. It was calculated by opponents that gold was overvalued by nearly 3% and silver was undervalued by more than 3% thereby giving gold a 6% advantage.[19] It was argued that because of this exchange differential, the public would pay revenues in overvalued gold, speculation would develop, and "a very lucrative trade will commence of bartering our silver for gold whereby our country will be immediately drained of silver." Others claimed that the French crown was overvalued by 1.5% and that importers could make a substantial profit.[20] According to Table 8, it appears that French silver was overvalued in terms of English crowns by 5.8%, and so this assertion was an underestimation.

Table 26

Tabulation and Relative Rates of Foreign Coins Established by the Act of July 31, 1789. (*The Connecticut Journal*, July 22, 1789.)

Coin	*Dollars*	*Cents*
The pound sterling of Great Britain	4	44
The livre tournois of France		18½
The florin, or guilder of the United Netherlands		39
The mark banco of Hamburg		33½
The rix dollar of Denmark	1	
The rix dollar of Sweden	1	
The ruble of Russia	1	
Real plate of Spain		10
The millree of Portugal	1	24
The pound sterling of Ireland	4	10
The tale of China	1	48
The pagoda of India	1	94
The rupee of Bengal		55½
The Mexican dollar		100
The crown of France		111
The crown of England		111

All silver coins of equal fineness 111 cents per Troy oz.

The gold coins of France, Spain, England and Portugal, and all other gold coins of equal fineness, to be valued at 89 cents per dwt.

[18] Newman, *Coppers*, pp. 106-10. *The Scholar's Arithmetic; or, Federal Accountant*, by Daniel Adams, published in 1828, still contained rules for the conversion of local state currencies into Federal money. See Appendix 5 for Bordley's proposal for a new American dollar and his solution to facilitate conversion between decimal Federal currency and the traditional pounds, shillings, and pence used in England and in local monies of account.

[19] *Free. Jour.*, July 22, 1789.

[20] *N.H. Gaz.*, July 30, 1789.

Despite the apparent disagreement by some parties as to the wisdom of this new regulation, at least one editorialist was able to look on the light side of the situation with the following humorous ditty:

Collection Law[21]

To show that crowns are of small consequence
Republicans their value prize in cents;
One hundred and eleven cents laid down
Will buy the gallic or English crown.

In his first message to Congress, President Washington urged "uniformity in currency ...." It was not until April 2, 1792, that legislation finally was passed which established a Federal mint.[22] Under this new law, copper was still to remain a token coinage without legal tender status, while gold and silver were to be minted and circulated at a bimetallic standard ratio of fifteen to one. Foreign specie was to remain legal tender with Spanish silver retaining its position of eminence in the national currency until finally demonetized in 1857. The new Federal standard for copper was indeed increased to a significant 264 grains for cents and 132 grains for half cents, an action undoubtedly viewed with great favor by the New York legislature which had campaigned unsuccessfully for a change under the old Articles of Confederation.[23]

Copper prices rose abruptly after 1792, requiring a decrease in the standard weight for copper coins on January 26, 1793, even before any regular issues could be minted. A second reduction in standard, effective December 27, 1795, soon followed. It was anticipated that by the time $50,000 in new cents and half cents had been placed in circulation by the Federal Mint, the small change supply would be sufficient so that all other coppers could be demonetized following an additional six months. With this end in mind, Congress, on May 8, 1792, stipulated that this foreign and miscellaneous copper demonetization would follow a proclamation to that effect when the output of the mint reached that target level. Although the Director of the Mint, Elias Boudinot, communicated to President Adams on January 1, 1800, that the mintage of copper was then $50,111.42, this proclamation was ignored and never promulgated and no definitive action against the bulk of sundry coppers occurred until 1857.[24] A possible reason which may have prompted the President to disregard the demonetization of these other coppers was the fact that during its seven years of operation, the new Federal Mint had not supplied sufficient coppers for circulation needs. Responding to the expense of operating the mint, a Senate committee proposed that "perhaps a more economical, and the most effectual mode [to furnish and supply coppers] would be by contract."[25] Boudinot opposed any option to import United States coppers minted in England under contract since it "would hazzard the running of a flood of cents, lighter than allowed by law, into the United States, and the difficulty of preventing the evil would be great."[26] In 1789 and 1790 a similar idea had been submitted by John H. Mitchell of South Carolina, who proposed that he could produce in England pure copper coins at 14d. sterling per pound, ready for shipping. In a like manner, Jefferson opposed the concept of having our coins minted in a foreign country.[27] It was obvious that both Boudinot, the Mint Director, and Jefferson were mindful of the lessons learned during the Confederation

[21] *N.H. Gaz.*, July 30, 1789.
[22] Schilke and Solomon, *Foreign Coins*, p. 17, passim.
[23] Taxay, *Catalogue*, p. 54.
[24] *A.S.P.F.*, vol. 1, pp. 615, 731.
[25] *A.S.P.F.*, vol. 1, p. 632.
[26] *A.S.P.F.*, vol. 1, p. 744. At this time the U.S. Mint was importing finished copper planchets from Boultons in Birmingham, England. See Williamson, *Penny-Wise 1984*; Julian, *Seaby 1977*.
[27] *A.S.P.F.*, vol. 1, pp. 44-45; Julian, *Seaby 1977*, p. 51.

period and were wary of the potential for abuses within the copper medium. They wished to maintain tight controls over the currency and ensure that history not repeat itself.

By 1795, and probably earlier, the exchange rates for the Confederation coppers had returned to the values as reported in Table 11. At this time, however, the value of a "copper" was also expressed in terms of Federal currency at a value of 9.25 mills each, or 108 to the dollar.[28] State and Federal coppers continued to circulate together as confidence in the medium returned due in great part to the increased price of the metal. "The unauthorized copper pieces gradually disappeared without loss to the holders, since copper was much needed for industrial purposes."[29] This was certainly a reversal from the situation of 1789 when coppers could not be given away.

Newman, in his classic essay on the subject of early American coppers, has compiled many commentaries from various sources which attest to the fact that Confederation coppers, including state and Constellatio Nova issues, Virginia halfpence, 1749 English halfpence, Fugio coppers, and other miscellaneous "Bungtown and wretched coppers" "were still acceptable in trade in certain parts of the United States in 1856."[30] These pre-U.S. Mint coppers circulated concurrently with Federal issues, their value and acceptance greatly determined by the current price of copper and prevailing economic conditions. The average citizen, however, was primarily interested in being able to spend them at the same rate they were received. But when the price of copper increased, the old copper coins would then be more valuable as scrap metal for industrial purposes than as money, and so would disappear from circulation into the melting pot. As conditions reversed, the old coppers would reappear as money, again illustrative of the interdependence of economics and numismatics. Felt reminisced on this subject of the small change medium in 1839, while still anticipating a Federal sanction against the coppers of his youth:[31]

> ... thus the pennies, half-pennies, and farthings, dear to the early associations of many yet alive, and bearing the representation of Britannia and their Majesties, as well as other coins of several states, are placed under the ban of legislative authority. Now and then the remains of them have come forth and passed for a season, till driven back by new regulations ....

The copper coinage of the Confederation period had failed and the Federal mint, born of necessity to create a national coinage, was now a reality. "The halcyon days for coiners of copper were at an end and were never to return."[32] The struggle for a uniform national currency which had started in the early days of colonialism was now in its last phase, but America would not be independent of all foreign currency until all such money was finally demonetized. The Act of February 21, 1857, brought about the "termination of the long checkered history of the sanction of foreign coins as legal tender in this country." [33] At long last the American Colonies, now the United States, could finally boast their own coinage! A colorful, formative phase of numismatic history was now at an end, while another was just beginning.

[28] Chaplin, *Companion*, pp. 34, 35.

[29] Carothers, *Fractional Money*, pp. 71-72. See also Newman, *Colonial Virginia*, p. 36.

[30] Newman, *Coppers*, pp. 110-13. Some late 18th century British trade tokens, when no longer needed there to serve as small change, were shipped to this country in the early 1800s where they circulated as cent substitutes up until the Civil War in such places as Savannah, Georgia (Doty, *Coin*, p. 134). This is one possible explanation why other unwanted coins, such as the Hibernia coppers, have been reported to have circulated in this country.

[31] Felt *Massachusetts*, p. 210.

[32] Douglas, *CNL 1969*, p. 291.

[33] Schilke and Solomon, *Foreign Coins*, p. 59.

APPENDIX 1

Conversion into Various Monies of Account

Because of unequal exchange rates between the standard Spanish American milled dollar and local currencies, it was necessary for Americans of the Colonial and Confederation periods to consult printed tables to determine the value of specific specie coins in the various monies of account. Contemporary publications such as *The Philadelphia Directory*,[1] *The New York Directory*,[2] *Gaine's Universal Register*,[3] Nicolas Pike, *A New and Complete System of Arithmetic*,[4] and Joseph Chaplin, *The Trader's Best Companion*[5] aided the early merchant in these currency calculations. The par of exchange differed from place to place based on the relative strength of the local economies but were fairly stable with some episodic fluctuations. McCusker, in *Money and Exchange in Europe and America, 1600-1775, A Handbook*, has published an exhaustive list of commercial exchange rates for the major world markets for which records are extant.

Tabulated below are the exchange rates between the states and England published from 1785 to 1787, from data printed in the contemporary resources cited above.

Locality	*Value of Spanish American milled dollar in local monies of account*
England	54d. (sterling)
South Carolina, Georgia	56d.
New England, Virginia	72d.
New Jersey, Pennsylvania, Maryland, Delaware	90d.
New York, North Carolina	96d.

A simple proportion formula can convert one currency into another. So, if one needs to change a sum of money, stated in one local money of account, into another currency, the following formula is used:

(local money × other standard) ÷ local standard = other money.

For example: You wish to calculate how much £100, New Jersey money, would be worth in English currency. The sterling standard is 54d. to the Spanish milled dollar, whereas the New Jersey, or local standard is 90d.

(£100 New Jersey × 54) ÷ 90 = £60 sterling

If you now want to find how much the £100 in New Jersey money would fetch in Boston where the Spanish milled dollar is rated at 72d., then

(£100 New Jersey × 72) ÷ 90 = £80 New England money of account.

In New York, where the Spanish milled dollar costs 96d. in local currency, the calculation would now be,

(£100 New Jersey × 96) ÷ 90 = £106.66 New York money.

[1] *Philadelphia Directory.*
[2] *New York Directory.*
[3] Gaine, *Register.*
[4] Pike, *Complete System.*
[5] Chaplin, *Companion.*

These conversions were made easier for citizens of the period who had access to printed reference tables and mathematical methods such as those included in the text by Nicolas Pike, written in Newburyport, Massachusetts, in 1786, which is particularly complete in these details. The following excerpt from Pike demonstrates his interesting short-cut methods for converting the various monies of account into other currencies, the illustration being the changing of New England and Virginia monies of account passing at 72d. to the Spanish milled dollar, into English, Irish, Canadian, French, Spanish, Federal, and other state currencies:

RULES

For reducing the Federal Coin, and the Currencies of the several United States; also English, Irish, Canada, Nova-Scotia, Livres Tournais and Spanish milled Dollars, each to the *par* of all the others (Pike, *Complete System*, pp. 111-13).

I. To reduce New-Hampshire, Massachusetts, Rhode-Island, Connecticut, and Virginia currency.

1. To New-York and North-Carolina currency.
   Rule.—Add one third to the New-Hampshire, &c. sum, and the sum total will be the New-York, &c. currency.
   Reduce £ 100 New-Hampshire, &c. to New-York, &c.
   3)100
   \+ 33 6 8
   £ 133 6 8 Answer

2. To Pennsylvania, New-Jersey, Delaware & Maryland currency.
   Rule.—Add one fourth to the New-Hampshire, &c. sum.
   Reduce £ 100 New-Hampshire, &c. to Pennsylvania, &c.
   4)100
   \+ 25
   £ 125 Answer

3. To South-Carolina and Georgia currency.
   Rule.—Multiply the New-Hampshire, &c. sum by 7, and divide the product by 9, and the quotient is the answer.
   Reduce £ 100 New-Hampshire, &c. to South-Carolina, &c.
   100
   7
   9)700
   £ 77 15 6 2/3 Answer

4. To English Money.
   Rule.—Deduct one fourth from the New-Hampshire, &c. sum.
   Reduce £ 100 New-Hampshire, &c. to English money.
   4)100
   − 25
   £ 75 Answer

5. To Irish Money.
Rule.—Multiply the New-Hampshire, &c. sum by 13, and divide the product by 16.
Reduce £ 100 New-Hampshire, &c. to Irish Money.

```
          100
      ----------
            4×3  + the given Sum.
          400
            3
      ----------
         1200
         +100
      ----------
16=4×4)1300
       4) 325
      ----------
      £  81   5 Answer
```

6. To Canada and Nova Scotia currency.
Rule.—Multiply the New-Hampshire, &c. by 5 and divide the product by 6.
Reduce £ 100 New-Hampshire, &c. to Canada, &c.

```
  100
    5
---------------
6)500
---------------
£ 83   6   8 Answer
```

7. To Livres Tournais.
Rule.—Multiply the New-Hampshire, &c. pounds by 17½ and the the product will be Livres: - or multiply the sum in shillings by 7 : divide the product by 8 and the quotient will be livres, sous.
Reduce £ 100 New-Hampshire, &c. to Livres Tournais.

```
            100         Or,            100
            17½                         20
        --------                 ---------
            700                       2000
           1000                          7
             50                  ---------
        --------                   8)14000
                                 ---------
   Answer 1750 Liv.          Answer 1750 Liv.
```

1d. = 1 sou 5½ deniers [1.458 sou]; 1s. = 17½ sous.
1 £= 17½ livres [since 20 sous = 1 livre]

8. To Spanish Milled Dollars.
Rule 1.—When the sum consists of pounds only: annex a cipher to the pounds, and divide the whole by 3 : the quotient will be in dollars.
Reduce £ 100 New-Hampshire, &c. to dollars.

```
   3)1000
   ----------
Dol. 333 1/3 Answer
```

Rule 2.—When the sum consists of pounds and shillings, divide the pounds by 3, and the shillings by 6, not separating them in the quotient, and the quotient will be dollars.

Reduce £ 152 15s. 6d. to dollars.

	£.	s.	d.
£'s. by 3 & s. by 6.	152	15	6

509 dol. & 1/6 Answer

Note: This article may be applied to the Federal dollar, it being of the same value with a Spanish dollar.

[This is a very interesting computation. The £152 is divided by 3 and the whole number answer is "50" with a remainder of £2, or 40s. The 40s. is added to the 15s. for 55s. and then divided by 6. The nearest whole number is "9," which is added to the "50" and the answer is "509." The whole dollars are expressed as 509 dollars, but the remainder is 1 shilling 6 pence, 1/6, which remains in the old money of account. One shilling and six pence, or 18d., equals 25¢ when there are 6s., or 72d., to the dollar. The answer could have been expressed $509.25, but Pike chose this hybrid system, using both the old and new notations.]

Practical everyday problems involving currency conversion are also presented and solved by Pike. These unequal monies of account created very real problems in early America as demonstrated in these following examples:

Sold a cargo of flax-seed in Ireland, for £1795 10s. Irish money; what does that amount to, in Massachusetts currency, £81 5s. Irish being equal to £100 Massachusetts?

Irish		Mass.		Irish		Mass.
As £81¼	:	£100	::	£1795½	:	£2209 16s. 11d. (Answer)
Or £13	:	£1795½	::	£16	:	£2209 16s. 11d. as before, because £13 Irish are equal to £16 Massachusetts.

My correspondent in Maryland purchased a cargo of flour for me, for £437 that currency, how much Massachusetts money must I remit him, £125 Maryland being equal to £100 Massachusetts?

As £125	:	£100	::	£437	:	£349 12s. (Answer)

A Bill of Exchange was accepted at Newbury-port [Massachusetts] for the payment of £345 10s., for the like value delivered in New-York, at £133 1/3 New-York currency for £100 Massachusetts ditto; how much money was paid in New-York, £75 Massachusetts being to £100 of New-York?

£ Mass.		£ N.Y.		£ Mass.		£ N.Y.
As 75	:	100	::	345 10s.	:	460 13s. 4d. (Answer)

If I draw a bill of exchange for £537 10s. 6d., to be paid in Ireland, at £123 1/13 Massachusetts, per £100 Irish; for how much Irish money must I draw the bill?

Mass.		Irish		Mass.		Irish
As £ 123 1/13	:	£100	::	£537 10s. 6d.	:	£436 14s. 9¼d. (Answer)

Or, because £16 Massachusetts are = £13 Irish,

16	:	£537 10s. 6d.	::	13	:	£436 14s. 9¼d. (Answer)

Since Pike's book is primarily an arithmetic text, it also contains many other methods which would have been helpful in computing contemporary business math problems. Many of the commercial procedures addressed by Pike have been discussed elsewhere in this book, and so other interesting illustrations are included in this appendix. Pike instructed his readers how to calculate the most economical route by which to send specie abroad for payment of foreign debts by taking advantage of the prevailing exchange rates. The following exercise illustrates his method:

ARBITRATION OF EXCHANGES

By this term [arbitration of exchanges] is understood how to choose, or determine the best way of remitting money from abroad with advantage; which is performed by conjointed proportion : thus,

Suppose a Merchant has effects at Amsterdam to the amount of 3530 dollars, which he can remit by way of Lisbon at 840 Rees per dollar, and thence to Boston, at 8s. 1d. per Milree (or 1000 Rees): Or, by way of Nantz at 5 2/5 livres per dollar, and thence to Boston at 6s. 8d. per [French] crown : It is required to arbitrate these exchanges, that is, to choose that which is most advantageous?

1 Dollar at Amsterdam = 840 Rees at Lisbon.
1000 Rees at Lisbon = 97d. at Boston [8s. 1d.]
3530 Dollars at Amsterdam

(840 × 97 × 3530) ÷ 1000 × 1 = £ 1198 8s. 8.4d. by way of Lisbon
1 Dollar at Amsterdam = 5 2/5 livres at Nantz.
6 Livres [French crown] at Nantz = 80 pence at Boston [6s. 8d.]
3530 dollars at Amsterdam

(5 2/5 × 80 × 3530) ÷ 1 × 6 = £ 1059 by way of Nantz

Here it may be observed that the difference is £139 8s. 8.4d. in favor of remitting by way of Lisbon rather than by Nantz, which depends on the course of exchange, at that time; but the course may vary so, that, in a short time, by way of Nantz may be better; hence appears the necessity and advantage of an extensive correspondence, to acquire a thorough knowledge in the course of exchange, to make this kind of remittance.

Apparently in 1786, barter was still of sufficient importance in commerce for Pike to include instructions in his book of how to perform this without incurring loss. Typical problems he solves are: "How much Tea at 9s. 6d. per lb. must be given in barter for 156 gallons of wine, at 12s. 3½d. per gallon?" Following conversion of the value of the wine into 23,010 pence, the answer is given as 201 lb. 13 54/114 oz. of tea.

Barter could also be complicated when hard coin or "ready" money was also a factor in the transaction as illustrated in the following examples:

Two Merchants barter; A has 30 Cwt. of cheese at 23s. 6d. per Cwt. and B has 9 Pieces of Broadcloth, at £3 15s. per piece; which must receive money, and how much ? (Answer: B must pay A £1 10s.)

A has Ribbands [ribbons] at 2s. per yard ready money; but in barter he will have 2s. 3d. B has broadcloth at 32s. 6d. per yard ready money: - At what rate must B value his Cloth per yard, to be equivalent to A's bartering Price, and how many yards of Ribband, at 2s. 3d. per yard, must then be given by A for 488 yards of B's Broadcloth? (Answer, B values his broadcloth, at £1 16s. 6½d. per yard; A must give B 7930 yards of ribbon for 488 yards of cloth.)

Another important conversion used frequently is as follows: if copper halfpence passed in England at 24 to the shilling, how many such halfpence would pass for a local New York shilling so that the relative values would remain equal?

(English standard ÷ New York standard) × sterling amount = New York money
Thus: (54d. ÷ 96d.) × 24 halfpence = 13.5 halfpence

Hence at 14 halfpence to the New York shilling prior to August 1, 1787, these coppers were slightly undervalued in terms of sterling.

A second example converts state money to its sterling equivalent:
In New York after August 1, 1787, coppers were valued at 20 to the local shilling. If one received 20 genuine British halfpence at that rate, how much would that sum be worth if exported to England?

To convert from an American value to sterling, the formula would read

(New York standard ÷ English standard) × New York amount = Sterling value

(96d. ÷ 54d.) × 20 halfpence = 35.6 halfpence

Thus the 20 genuine British halfpence circulating in New York after the devaluation of coppers were highly undervalued. If one could buy 20 regal halfpence for a New York shilling, this sum would be equivalent to 35.6 halfpence when converted to the sterling shilling for a 48.3% increase in investment if exported to England.

or 35.6 halfpence - 24 halfpence to the English shilling = 11.6

11.6 ÷ 24 = 48.3% gain

Now if the New York rate increased to 24 coppers to the local shilling, then the calculation is as follows: (96d. ÷ 54d.) × 24 halfpence = 42.7 halfpence

and when exported to England

42.7 - 24 = 18.7, 18.7 ÷ 24 = 77.9% gain.

When the exchange rate for halfpence in New York was advanced to 48 to the local shilling in August 1789, the scenario was as follows:

(96d. ÷ 54d.) × 48 = 85.3.

At this rate if genuine English coppers were bought up and returned to England the profit to the exporter would be

85.3 - 24 = 61.3, 61.3 ÷ 24 = 255.6% profit!

These calculations demonstrate that the very process of devaluating the halfpence in New York, while designed to discourage the currency of lightweight counterfeits, actually drove the genuine issues of proper weight out of circulation and probably back to England for a handsome profit.

APPENDIX 2

Summary of Overstruck Coppers

Frequent mention has been made in this book of the economic advantage from overstriking existing coppers to give them a new identity. Appendix 2 catalogues all known state coppers overstruck on host coins in an attempt to understand better the pattern of this practice which was not as haphazard as it might appear at first glance. Table 27 lists the Vermont coppers overstruck on host coins. The Rupert mint used Constellatio Nova coppers as planchets for three of its four 1787 issues, the exception being Ryder-Richardson 34 (Bressett 10-J) for which only three specimens are known. It is easier to visualize this process of overstriking when the coins are studied according to their emission sequence from the mint as indicated by the new Bressett nomenclature.[1] Hence, there are none for 10-J, occasionally for 10-K, nearly always for 11-K and frequently for 12-K, and none thereafter for the 1788 dies. The Ryder-Richardson 3 over a Connecticut and the Ryder-Richardson 15 on the landscape Ryder-Richardson 4 seem to be interesting incidents without pattern or logic.

After mid-1787, Vermont coppers were simultaneously minted at Machin's Mills after the two mints entered into a business arrangement. The Newburgh operation used Irish halfpence, dated 1781 and 1782, as planchets for six of their products but weight analysis shows most of the host coins to be counterfeit. The only recorded exception to this practice is the presence of a single Bressett 19-X (Ryder-Richardson 18) appearing over a 1785 Constellatio Nova copper. There is a pattern to these emissions as described by Bressett.

After July 1787 until 1788, the Machin's Mills Vermont coppers were those muled with, or similar to the imitation halfpence, viz. Ryder-Richardson 13 and 27 (Bressett 17-V and 18-W). These two Vermonts and all the imitation halfpence appear on original planchets, with a solitary exception recorded in Table 30. Many 1788 and 1789 Vermont coppers may be found minted over Irish halfpence with the three exceptions of Ryder-Richardson 24 (Bressett 16-S), the final issues of Ryder-Richardson 25 (Bressett 16-U) and the last use of Ryder-Richardson 29 (Bressett 22-U). But why were no imitation halfpence struck on host coins? It is possible that those issues had ceased production by that time rather than for any aesthetic motives of the mintmaster. Hence the pattern is established that the overstriking at Machin's Mills on Irish halfpence occurred for a short period in 1788 and into 1789, usually with dies that failed early since there are so many rarities in this group. A practical reason why these dies failed early could have been due to the fact that the host coins were not annealed or softened prior to overstriking. Thus this copper was "too work-hardened to readily take the new image, and ... [it] would also have been especially hard on the dies, and might have contributed to early failure."[2] On the contrary, the New Jersey Maris 56-n coinage was so prolific and contained so many overstrikes that it suggests a different and more sophisticated process which preserved the longevity of the dies. The last overstruck copper must have been Bressett 16-U (Ryder-Richardson 25) since further use of the U reverse is not associated with Irish halfpence and the 16 obverse with the "horned bust" die break is then wedded to the old Rupert S reverse to produce the common Ryder-Richardson 24 or Bressett 16-S. The remainder of the Machin's Mills Vermont coinage consists of "muled, worn, or rejected dies," all on original but frequently defective planchets. In summary, it

[1] Bressett, *Studies*.
[2] James C. Spilman, personal communication, March 26, 1986.

appears that the Rupert mint in 1787, used Constellatio Nova undertypes, first occasionally, and then exclusively. The practice abruptly stopped for the 1788 issues. During parts of 1788 and 1789, the Machin's Mills Vermont coinages are extant on (probable) counterfeit Irish halfpence for six emissions and then this practice suddenly stops with Ryder-Richardson 24 (Bressett 16-S). It is not revived again despite the continuous deterioration in the quality of the coinages from Newburgh. This would suggest that the supply of Irish halfpence was exhausted. One consistent feature of these Vermont coppers is that each mint employed just one kind of host coin, the Rupert mint using the Constellatio Nova coppers and Machin's Mills, the Irish halfpence, for which many counterfeits were known to have existed.[3] This consistency will be addressed again.

Table 28 shows the occurrence of two reported 1787 Connecticut overstrikes which does not indicate a trend but probably just a extraordinary event at the Jarvis and Company mint. There are so many 1787 Miller 33 coppers that certainly more overstruck issues would have surfaced if overstriking had been a motive of that mint. The 1788 Connecticut coppers which appear overstruck on Constellatio Nova coppers are the first Mailed Bust Right coppers, which bear great resemblance to their Vermont and imitation halfpence cousins, and next the Triple Leaves busts by Buell. The 1788 Draped Bust Left Connecticut, Miller 16.3-N, may rarely be seen over a counterfeit Massachusetts cent. A review of Spilman's Die Analysis Chart places these coins in distinct groupings,[4] some of which are doubtlessly from Machin's Mills.[5]

Trudgen presents a chronology of the Machin's Mills output and notes that both the Vermont and Connecticut series were minted from mid-1788 into late 1789, a sequence which was followed by the New Jersey Maris 56 to 58-n "camel heads."[6] It seems curious that Captain Machin would have reserved the Constellatio Nova host coins for the Connecticut series, the counterfeit Irish halfpence exclusively for his Vermont coppers, while impressing the New Jersey coins over every type and description of lightweight coppers current in that period, including some of his own products. This was also accomplished without any apparent mixing of host coin "planchets." In addition, the Connecticut coinages would have been simultaneous with the terminal, inferior Vermont emissions which do not appear overstruck. How could all these various activities and styles of production have occurred within the same mint?

One sure fact is that the Vermont coppers came from Newburgh at that time. Since it seems unlikely that an illegal mint would have remained so fastidious in the way that "blanks" were fed into the presses there must be another explanation for the distinct host coin "personalities" of the 1788 Connecticuts and "camel head" New Jersey coppers if they were to have originated at Machin's Mills near the same time. An unlikely explanation would be an excellent quality control program at the mint which kept all the host coins isolated from each other. In modern times, batches of planchets may become mixed up and fed into the wrong presses. I find it difficult to conceive that the Vermont series on Irish halfpence, the "camel heads," and the 1788 Connecticuts overstruck on Constellatio Nova coppers came from the same manufacturing process. The most logical answer is that the three minting operations were separated from each other, either in time or place. Since the "camel head" series appears on host coins similar to the practice of the Elizabethtown mint, it is my opinion that Maris 56 to 58-n came either from that location or one with the technological capacity to harden dies and anneal host planchets.

The three series that used Constellatio Nova coppers were the 1787 Vermonts, the 1788 Mailed Bust Right Connecticuts, and the 1788 Triple Leaves Connecticuts. The Vermont issues were from Rupert while the last two were from Machin's Mills, but separated in time from the

[3] Batty, *Descriptive Catalogue*, pp. 1023-47.
[4] Spilman, *CNL 1977*, p. 577.
[5] *EAC 1975*, p. 44.
[6] Trudgen, *CNL 1984A*, p. 871.

Vermont coppers struck over Irish halfpence. The very rare 1788 Connecticut Draped Bust Left overstruck on the counterfeit Massachusetts cent, itself a possible Machin's Mills creation, bears similar features to other coppers which originated in Newburgh and stands within that grouping in Spilman's Die Analysis Chart. Since a genuine Massachusetts cent would have been heavier than the Connecticut standard, a minter would not have used a legitimate cent as host for a lighter coin.

The New Jersey overstrikes are an entirely different situation as compared to the relatively uniform host coins of Connecticut and Vermont. Table 29 reveals a disordered array of contemporary coppers with the notable exception of Massachusetts and Fugio cents, due to their greater intrinsic weight. Apparently anything lesser in value than the New Jersey standard was a potential candidate to become a host coin. The reason for striking the Maris 34-V over the 34-J and 35-J is illusive, the V reverse being inferior in execution to the J.

The overstruck New Jersey coppers fall into two major groups, the first being the Elizabethtown emissions from June 1789 into 1790. The dies used were remnants from the old Rahway operation and the planchets were anything lighter than the New Jersey standard which could be purchased, probably at significant discount since after July 20, 1787, nothing but New Jersey coppers were negotiable in that state.[7] It became profitable for the Elizabethtown minters to

Table 27

Vermont Overstruck Coins
(References follow Table 30)

Bressett Number	*Ryder-Richardson Attribution*	*Host Coin and (Reference)*
2-B	R.R. 3	1785 Conn. Miller 4.1-F.4 (24).
9-I	R.R. 15	1785 Vermont B.3-C/R.R. 4 (19 p. 6); George III halfpenny, 1775 George III halfpenny (39).
10-K	R.R. 14	Occasionally on Constellatio Nova coppers (27); 1785 Constellatio Nova (2, lot 564).
11-K	R.R. 12	Nearly always on Constellatio Nova coppers (27); 1785 Constellatio Nova 4-D (15, lot 663), 5-E (p).
12-K	R.R. 32	Of the few known, most are on Constellatio Nova (41, lot 2092), (33).
19-X	R.R. 18	Usually on Irish halfpence (27); 1781 Irish ½d. (7, lot 11); 1782 Irish ½d. ? counterfeit (15, lot 685); British halfpenny (22), (42, lot 327); counterfeit George III ½d. (4, lot 101); an exception is 1785 Constellatio Nova (43, lot 1284).
20-X	R.R. 35	On Irish halfpence (27), with one exception (33).
21-Y	R.R. 33	Nearly always on Irish halfpence (27); counterfeit George III English ½d. (3), (22).
21-U	R.R. 28	Nearly always on Irish halfpence (27); counterfeit 1781 and 1783 Irish ½d., counterfeit 1782 English ½d., Machin's Mills copper 178? (4 lot 111).
22-U	R.R. 29	Occasionally on Irish halfpence (27).
16-U	R.R. 25	All overstruck on Irish halfpence when dies removed to Newburgh, before dies shattered (27), (2, lot 570), (26); 1781 counterfeit Irish ½d. (8, lot 304), (12, lot 89); 1781 Irish ½d. (15, lot 677).

Note: Sources frequently list English or Irish halfpence undertypes without any opinion or comment as to whether they are considered genuine or counterfeit. Weight documentation would be helpful to assist in this determination.

[7] Newman, *Studies*, p. 154.

impress acceptable designs over any lighter coppers and pass them off on the unsuspecting. The second group of New Jersey overstrikes, Maris 56 to 58-n, has already been mentioned. Breen[8] attributes this group to Machin's Mills whereas Anton[9] regards them as an Elizabethtown product. Because the host coin characteristics of these coppers is so different from the practices of the Newburgh mint, I would support the Elizabethtown hypothesis. If the "camel heads" came from Machin's Mills at the time indicated by Trudgen, they would have coincided chronologically with the Vermont series overstruck on counterfeit Irish halfpence or the last Vermont issues from old, rejected dies which were on original planchets. The only way that these New Jersey coppers could have come from Newburgh is if they were the last product of that mint, issued when all other operations had ceased.

These conclusions as to the mint of origin for those coppers overstruck over other coins are only speculative but are supported by examination of the style in which the host coins were used and the characteristics of the mint in question. Not only are the identities of these mints still shrouded in doubt, but there is still mystery regarding the origin of many other coppers, even with normal planchets. An accurate assignment of mints is difficult, but perhaps with advanced techniques, such as energy dispersive X-ray fluorescence spectrometry, there will be more reliable methods to study these undertypes and planchets.[10] At any rate, speculation, controversy, and doubt serve us well if they spur us on to further research in this fascinating period of numismatic history!

TABLE 28

Connecticut Overstruck Coins
(References follow Table 30)

Miller Attribution	*Host Coin and (Reference)*
1787	
5-P	Counterfeit Irish 1781 halfpenny (44, 779).
33.38-gg.1	1783 Constellatio Nova 3-C (23).
33.20-Z.9	Scottish bawbee (23).
1788	
3-B.1	Always struck over Constellatio Novas (Breen [22]); C. 4-C (13, lot 109); C. 4-D (p). One exception (33).
3-B.2 and	
3.2-B.2	Usually on Constellatio Nova coppers (22); C. 4-C (14, lot 289); C. 5-E (23)(13, lot 110).
4.1-B.1	Frequently on Constellatio Nova (22); C. 5-E (23); C. 4-D (9, lot 34).
4.1-K	Occasionally on Constellatio Nova coppers; C. 5-E (23).
4.2-R	Always on Constellatio Nova (18, lot 717); C. 4-D (14, lot 293).
5-B.2	Usually on Constellatio Nova coppers; C. 5-E (14, lot 290).
10-C	Usually on Constellatio Nova coppers; C. 2-A (14, lot 387); C. 4-C (p).
11-G	Rarely on Constellatio Nova 5-E (p); one recorded.
12.2-C	Usually on Constellatio Nova; C. 5-E (13, lot 122); C. 2-A or C. 4-C (14, lot 299); Richard Picker records a 12.2-C over a 4.2-R over a Constellatio Nova 5-E (29).
16.3-N	Occasionally on counterfeit 1787 Massachusetts cent Crosby 1-B (22); (13, lot 131). Nine recorded.

[8] Breen, *CNL 1969*, p. 256.
[9] Anton, *CNL 1975*, pp. 499-501.
[10] Frey et al., *CNL 1980*.

Table 29

New Jersey Overstruck Coins
(References follow Table 30)

Maris Attribution	*Host Coin and (Reference)*
16-d	1723 French copper (45, p. 205).
17-J	Usually over Connecticut coppers; Conn. (21), (28).
17-K	Occasionally on Connecticut coppers; 1787 Conn. M. 32.3-X.4 (2, lot 1404); Machin's Mills 1772 6-72A (21).
17-b	About half are overstruck and usually on Connecticut coppers; 1782 Irish halfpenny (2, lot 1406); 1787 Conn. 24-FF (48); 1787 Conn. 33.2-X.2 (48); 1787 Conn. M. 33.2-ZZ.5 (2, lot 1407); 33.7-r.2 (57); 1788 Conn. 16.3-N (p); 1774 Louis XVI one sol (2, lot 1408); Nova Eborac (21); Vermont RR-9 (21); Vermont RR-20 (p); 1783 Constellatio Nova (38, lot 1347).
34-J	Nearly half are overstruck, usually on Connecticut coppers; Conn. (21); 1785 Conn. M. 4.1-F.4 (45, p. 212n); 1788 Conn. M. 15.2-P (p); Nova Eborac (21); 1772 English halfpenny (28).
34-V	Usually overstruck on Connecticut coppers; Conn. (21); over New Jersey M. 35-J (28); over New Jersey 34-J in turn over a possible Vermont RR-12 or RR-16 (36, lot 207); over a New Jersey M.35-J in turn over a Connecticut (56, lot 1356).
35-J	Occasionally overstruck; over New Jersey M. 35-W (21); counterfeit English halfpenny (36, lot 209); Constellatio Nova (41, lot 2209); 1787 Conn. (45, p. 215).
35-W	Georgius Triumpho copper (21).
40-b	Occasionally overstruck; Conn. coppers (21); Irish ½d. (21); 1780 French sou (25).
56-n	The 56 to 58-n series are almost always overstruck on every description of host coin, about a half of which are Connecticut coppers: Irish ½d. (28); 1782 Irish ½d. (11, lot 42); 1783 Irish (or English) ½d. (56, lot 1411). George II English ½d. (21); English ½d. (28); 1774 English ½d. (28); ? genuine 1772 English ½d. (55, lot 1323). Constellatio Nova (11, lot 44); 1783 Constellatio Nova C. 3-C (31, lot 595). Nova Eborac (21); Nova Eborac Crosby 1 B (46, lot 1416). Vermont (Ryder-Richardson attribution): 2 (4, lot 196); 25 (21); 13 (p); 16 or 17 (36, lot 231); 20 (p); 3 (51); bust right (2 lot 1455). George Clinton copper (21). ? Georgius Triumpho (34, lot 186). Machin's Mills imitation halfpence (Vlack attribution): 1772 6-72A (21); 1774 (11, lot 43); 1775 4-75A (21); 1787 17-87A (21); 1787 17-87B (21); 1787 18-87C (21); 1787 19-87C (p); 1788 23-88A (21). 1785 Connecticut coppers (Miller attribution): 2-A.4 (55, lot 1321) 1787 Connecticut coppers: 2-B (p); 4-L (21); 6.1-M (49, lot 170); 11.2-K (21); 25-m (54 lot 64); 30-hh.1 (21); 31.1-r.4 (48); 32.6-X.6 (14, lot 2100); 33.2-Z.5 (21); 33.2-Z.12 (21); 33.34-Z.11 (21); 33-Z family (4, lot 200); 37.4-k.1(57); 37.8-LL (52, lot 5479); 42-kk.2 (21); 43.1-Y (48); 52-G.1 (21); ? 53-FF (4, lot 199); 100-I (48). 1788 Connecticut coppers: 3-B.1 (47, lot 59); 2-D (p); ? 11-G (4, lot 201); 16.3-N (p); Parmelee Sale (30, lot 428) notes 1785 and 1788 Connecticut coppers.
57-n	1787 Conn. M. 31.2-r.3 (2, lot 1456); Machin's Mills imitation halfpenny or Vermont R.R.31 (50, lot 1633).
58-n	Conn. (2, lot 1458); 1787 Conn. M. 1.1-A (48); 1787 Conn. (4, lot 205); 1788 Conn. (4, lot 208); Vermont (?) (21); Vermont Bressett's obverse 16 (41, lot 2252); 1775 English ½d. (28); 1775 Machin's Mills ½d. V. 4-75A (11, lot 45).
70-x	Counterfeit ½d. ? English (21); 1786 Conn. M. 3-D.1 (5 p.15), (2, lot 1475); 1787 Conn. (56, lot 1436); Machin's Mills V. 6-76A (46, lot 1443).
71-y	Conn. (21); 1787 Conn. Draped Bust Left (41, lot 2276), 1787 Conn. 32.2-X.1 (50, lot 1651); 1788 Conn. M. 5-B.2 (48); 1788 Conn. M. 15.1-L.1 (56, lot 1438); 1787 Machin's Mills V. 19-87C (21); George II counterfeit English ½d. (2, lot 1476); counterfeit 1775 English ½d. (4, lot 228); Vermont RR-9 (4, lot 229).

Maris Attribution	*Host Coin and (Reference)*
72-z	1783 Constellatio Nova 1-A (2, lot 1478); Machin's Mills Vlack 13-88 CT (p); Conn. 1788 D reverse (50, lot 1652); counterfeit 1781 Irish ½d. (4, lot 230); George III ½d. (4, lot 231).
73-aa	Always overstruck on a wide variety of host coppers; Conn. (21); Spanish four maravedi (21); 1774 English ½d. (28); counterfeit 1774 English ½d. (p); counterfeit 1775 English ½d. (4, lot 234); counterfeit Irish ½d. (4, lot 233); 1787 Conn. M. 10-E (56, lot 1442); 1787 Conn. M. 33.17-r.1 (14, lot 2095); 1787 Conn. 33.29-gg.1 (48); Machin's Mills imitation ½d. (1, lot 34); Nova Eborac Crosby 1-B (p) and 1-A (50, lot 1653); Vermont (30, lot 440); Vermont RR-14 (34, lot 206); 1787 Conn. 33.17-r.1 (41, lot 2279); 1787 Conn. M. 33.9-s.2 (36, lot 245); 1788 Conn. (50, lot 1653), (33).

Note: Sources frequently list English or Irish halfpence undertypes without any opinion or comment as to whether they are considered genuine or counterfeit.

TABLE 30

Miscellaneous Overstruck Coins

Attribution	*Host Coin and (Reference)*
Immunis Columbia	1786 New Jersey (2, lot 605); New Jersey M. 26-S (32, lot 73).
George Clinton	Immunis Columbia (2, lot 603).
Machin's Mills imitation ½d.	
Vlack 6-76A	Counterfeit brass pistareen of Pretender Charles III (1701-1714), (35) (53).
Vlack 2-71A	Vlack 8-74A (40).
Nova Eborac	Irish halfpenny (44 specimen 986).
Albany Church Penny	Counterfeit George III halfpenny (101.1 grains) (53)

See "Numismatic Auction Catalogues and Price Lists" in *Bibliography and Key to Abbreviations.* The ( ) contains the reference number below and the accompanying lot number in the auction sale.

p. Private collections.
1. *MacFarland.*
2. *Garrett.*
3. Richardson, *Num. 1947*, p. 335.
4. *Frontenac.*
5. Maris, *New Jersey.*
6. Taxay, *Catalogue.*
7. *Allen.*
8. *Breen III.*
9. *Bryan.*
10. *Hall.*
11. *Branigan.*
12. *F.U.N. 1977.*
13. *51st Sale.*
14. *Weimer and Hirt.*
15. *Brown.*
16. *EAC 1975.*
17. *Morton.*
18. *Turoff.*
19. *B&R* 34.
20. *Park.*
21. Anton, *CNL 1975.* pp. 503-513.
22. Breen, *CNL 1963*, p. 72.

23. Barnsley, *CNL 1965*, p. 131.
24. Anton, *CNL 1979*, p. 701.
25. Barnsley, *CNL 1963*, pp. 61-62.
26. Partridge, *RHSQ 1979*.
27. Bressett, *Studies*, pp. 183-94.
28. Pullen, FPL.
29. Picker, *CNL 1973*, p. 395.
30. *Parmelee.*
31. *N.Y. Collection.*
32. *ANA 1976.*
33. Michael Hodder, personal communication.
34. *Bareford.*
35. Newman, *Studies*, p. 170.
36. *Picker.*
37. Barnsley, *CNL 1962*, p. 50.
38. *Mail Bid 1986.*
39. Bonjour, *CNL 1985*, p. 920.
40. Trudgen, *CNL 1987*, p. 967.
41. *Taylor.*
42. *Roper.*
43. *Norweb.*
44. Breen, *Encyclopedia.*
45. Hodder, *AJN 1989.*
46. *Foreman.*
47. *Romano.*
48. CNL Collection.
49. FPL Spring 1989, Rosa Americana.
50. *Saccone.*
51. Stoutjesdyk and Hoge, *ANA 1989.*
52. *Schenkel.*
53. ANS Collection.
54. FPL 4, Rosa Americana.
55. *Hessberg.*
56. *Quartette.*
57. FPL, Apr. 1992, Mike Ringo.

APPENDIX 3

Assay Calculations

The Proclamation of 1704 was an attempt to fix the exchange rates of European silver coins circulating in British North America based on their silver content priced at 5s. 2d. per troy ounce of sterling (.925 fine) silver. These assays were made at the Tower Mint under the able guidance of Sir Isaac Newton. Other of Newton's calculations have been used in the construction of Tables 3, 5, 7, 8, and 9. Since these assay results were so important in the establishment of foreign exchange, it is interesting to review the mathematical methods used in their derivations.

In regard to silver coin, the quality of its composition, or degree of purity, is expressed in millesimal fineness, 1000 fine being 100% silver. Sterling silver contains 925 parts of pure silver and is debased with 75 parts of alloy, usually copper. This can be expressed .925 fine, 925.0 millesimal fineness, or 92.5% silver. A typical assay report prepared by Newton at the Tower Mint would read as follows:

THE VALUE OF SEVERAL FOREIGN COYNS - SILVER COYNS UNWORN[1]

Dwt. = pennyweight, Gr. = grains, Mi. = mite or 1/20 grain.
"W" = weak, "S" = strong; see text for explanation.

Coin	*Assay*		*Coin Weight*		*Standard Weight*			*Value in Pence*
		Dwt.	*Dwt.*	*Gr.*	*Dwt.*	*Gr.*	*Mi.*	*D.*
The three-Guilder piece of Holland or piece of 60 Styvers [*sic*]	W	2	20	8	20	3	12	62.46
The Ducaton of Holland or piece of 63 Styvers	S	3	20	21	21	3	15	65.59
The Lyon Doller of Holland or 2/3 of the Ducaton [*sic*]	W	44	17	14	14	2	7	43.7

GOLD MONIES - UNWORN See text for explanation of Car. Gr., or Carat-grain.

Coin	*Assay*			*Coin Weight*		*Standard Weight*			*Value at 4£ per oz.*	
		Car.	*Gr.*	*Dwt.*	*Gr.*	*Dwt.*	*Gr.*	*Mi.*	*s.*	*d.*
The Spanish Pistole	W	0	0½	4	8	4	7	8	17	2.8
The Moeda of Portugal	W	0	0¼	6	21	6	20	11	27	5.1
The Ducat of Campen in Holland	S	1	2	2	5½	2	9	3	9	6.3

[1] "Sir Isaac Newton's Mint Reports," 7 July 1702, from Shaw, *Monetary History*, pp. 136-43.

EXPLANATION OF NEWTON'S ASSAYS

Unfortunately such tables as this appear without any explanations. In order to decipher these values, one can proceed as follows:
For the Dutch three guilders the given measurements are:

> Weight of actual coin, 20 Dwt. 8 gr. = 488.0 gr.
> Weight of standard, 20 Dwt. 3 gr. 12 mites = 483.6 grains; this is the assayed weight of the sterling silver (.925 fine) in the coin. A mite is 1/20 grain.
> Therefore, setting up a proportion,
> sterling silver weight : 0.925 :: weight of coin : coin's fineness, or
> (standard weight × 0.925) ÷ weight = fineness of the foreign coin, or
> (483.6 × 0.925) ÷ 488.0 = 0.91666 fine
> The Dutch three guilder piece is .91666 fine, that is, its composition is not quite as pure as sterling at .925 fine.

For the assay results as recorded by Newton in column one, one is looking for the difference between the actual silver content in a troy pound of the test coin, in this case at .91666 fine, and a troy pound of sterling silver.

> One troy pound of pure silver contains 5760 grains of silver.
> One troy pound of sterling silver contains (5760 × 0.925) = 5328 grains of pure silver.
> One troy pound of .91666 fine silver contains (5760 × 0.91666) = 5280 grains of pure silver.

Then each troy pound of three guilder pieces of 488.0 grains lacks 48 grains of being of sterling fineness (5328 - 5280 = 48). Therefore, the assay column has a " 'W' Dwt. 2" meaning that coin is "weak" by 2 Dwt., or 48 grains, of achieving the sterling standard per troy pound.

Since the three guilder piece has an equivalent of 483.6 grains of sterling, and one ounce (480 grains) of sterling was valued at 62.0d., the value in English money for the Dutch test coin is derived by a simple proportion:

> 480 : 483.6 :: 62.0 : × or,
> × = (483.6 × 62.0) ÷ 480 or, 62.46d, as in the last column.

So in summary, the Dutch three guilder piece, was slightly "weaker" than sterling fineness but its actual weight was so great that it contained slightly more than an equivalent ounce of sterling silver placing it over 62.0d.

These calculations can be carried out for the other coins represented in the chart. The actual weight of the ducaton (ducatoon) is 501.0 grains, and the weight of the equivalent amount of sterling silver is 507.75 grains. The fineness of the ducatoon is (507.75 × 0.925) ÷ 501 = 0.93746 fine.

One troy pound of pure silver from ducatoons weighs 5399.78 grains which is 71.78 grains heavier, or "stronger," "S," in silver content than one troy pound of sterling silver. This value of 71.78 grains, or 2.99 Dwt., is rounded up to 3 Dwt. At 62.0d. per ounce for sterling, this large coin with a standard weight of 507.75 grains would fetch 65.58d. which Newton reported as 65.59d.

The lion dollar is a coin of low silver content since the actual weight of a single specimen was 422 grains, and the equivalent in sterling weighed 338.35 grains. The fineness calculates out as .74164. A troy pound of such coins would have 4271.86 grains of pure silver which is 1056.13 grains (44 Dwt.) less, "weaker," than the pure silver in a pound of sterling. The assay column thus records " 'W' 44 Dwt." The 338.35 grains of silver equivalent to sterling would be worth 43.7d.

The gold assay, expressed in carats and carat-grains, is more complicated. The term carat represents the relative amount of gold in a mixture, or alloy, a carat being 1/24 of the total weight. Therefore, anything which is pure gold is 24 carat, or if 50% gold, it is 12 carat. Purity of gold can also be expressed in fineness as is silver. Twenty-two carat gold, or 22/24, would thus be .91666 fine.

The English standard for gold was 22 carats, or .91666 fine. The last column indicates that the value for gold of this purity was £4 per ounce.

> For the Spanish pistole,
> Gross weight per coin was 4 Dwt. 8 grains, or 104 grains.
> The equivalent weight of 22 carat gold standard in the coin was 4 Dwt. 7 grains, 8 mites, or 103.4 grains.
> The millesimal fineness of the gold in the pistole can be solved by the following proportion:
> weight of 22 carat gold : 0.91666 :: weight of coin : coin's fineness, or
> (standard weight × 0.91666) ÷ coin weight = fineness of foreign coin, or
> (103.4 × 0.91666) ÷ 104.0 = 0.91138 fine, or 21.87 carat gold.

Calculation of the assay in column one similarly is the difference in the weight of one troy pound of test coins and a pound of gold standard at a purity of 22 carat, or .91666 fine.

> A troy pound of 24 carat gold contains 5760 grains pure gold.
> A troy pound of 22 carat gold contains 5280 grains of pure gold.
> The pistole at .91138 fine contains 5249.5 grains of pure gold.
> The difference is 5280 - 5249.5 = 30.45 grains.

The interpretation of the gold assay is complex because of the use of the archaic unit of measurement, the carat-grain, but a key was provided to help with this conversion.[2]

24 Carats = a troy pound of gold (240 Dwt, 5760 grains)
1 Carat = is ½ an ounce, or 10 penny-weight, (240 grains)
1 Carat = 4 Carat-Grains (240 grains)
1 Carat-grain = 2½ penny-weight, 60 grains troy.

Decimals.

¼ Carat-grain	= 0.0625	Carat	=	15 grains
½ " "	= 0.125	"	=	30 "
1 " "	= 0.25	"	=	60 "
2 " "	= 0.5	"	=	120 "
3 " "	= 0.75	"	=	180 "
4 " "	= 1.0	"	=	240 "

The pistole fineness is 30.45 grains less, or "weaker" than the standard. From the conversion chart above, this is roughly equal to ½ Carat-Grain, 0.125 Carat, or 30 grains. This quantity is expressed in the assay column of the table by "W" and "0 ½ Carat-Grain."

The value of the gold in the pistole at the rate of £4 (80s.) per ounce (480 grains) .91666 standard is calculated by the proportion:

> weight of standard in coin : 480 grains :: value in s. : 80s.
> (103.4 × 80) ÷ 480 = 17.23s. = 17s. 2.8d.

Similarly the calculation for the very popular Portuguese coin, the moeda, or moidore, can be carried out. This coin weighs 165 grains and the equivalent weight of 22 carat gold in the coin is 164.55 grains. This coin falls short of standard purity at .914 fine or 21.94 carat. A troy pound

[2] Simon, *Essay*, pp. 177-80.

at this purity would contain 5264.6 grains of pure gold, or 15.36 grains less than standard. This value is, therefore, "weaker," "W," by "0 ¼ Carat-grain" as noted in the assay column.

For the gold ducat of Campen, the actual weight is 53.5 grains, but there is an equivalent of 57.15 grains of standard. For this to be the case, this coin is obviously purer than the 22 carat standard and figures out to .97919 fine, or practically pure gold at 23.5 carat. A troy pound of such ducats contains 360 grains more pure gold than the standard which according to the conversion scale "stronger" by "1 carat" (240 grains) and "2 carat-grains" (120 grains). The value of this coin relative to the standard is 9s. 6.3d.

APPENDIX 4

Weight Distribution Analyses of Confederation Coppers

The purpose for tabulating the weights of the 4,300 Confederation coppers in Table 21 was to determine whether these coins met the weight standard prescribed by the respective state legislatures. The major problem in interpreting the results is that no documentation from any Confederation mint exists which affirms if any weight variance from the standard was permitted under the contract. Based on the experience from the Tower Mint, it has been assumed that an average weight deviation less than 5% for any series of Confederation coppers is probably justifiable considering the imprecision of late eighteenth century domestic planchet technology. Such a variance should not necessarily raise the suspicion of dishonesty by the mintmaster. It is just as likely that overweight planchets were due to the inability to roll the copper fillets sufficiently thin, and hence there is a wide distribution of planchet weights as seen on the following curves. In general, weight for base coinages was calculated on the number of pieces per pound rather than on the basis of individual coins. For the most part, the average weights of coppers from authorized mints were very close to their required standards whereas those from illegal operations made no attempt to give fair measure. The other important benefit from Table 21 is that conformity in planchet weights can be studied; those coppers with a lower first standard deviation have more consistency in weight as a group indicating greater uniformity in planchet size. This regularity confirms greater consistency and better quality control in planchet manufacture typical of a more technologically sophisticated operation. If different populations of planchet weights become evident when plotting any weight distribution curve, it is suggestive that such coppers were minted from different stock and perhaps those varieties may not be as closely related as assumed. There are several examples of two or more planchet populations, corresponding to specific coin varieties in the following charts.

A typical distribution curve is seen for Massachusetts cents, in Chart 5. These 156 coppers are arranged in ascending order of weight, the lightest one weighing 134.6 grains and the heaviest, 185 grains. This is the range of weight. The middle, or median, coin in this arrangement, number 78, happens to weigh 154.3. The average of all 156 specimens is 153.9 grains; 34.13% of the specimens on either side of the average comprise the statistical expression for the first standard deviation, or 68.26% of the entire sample. In this instance, the value 34.13% below the mean is 144.8 grains, indicated by the left arrow, and for that 34.13% above the mean is 162.9, marked by the right arrow. This quantity is written 153.9 ± 9.1. This sample of Massachusetts coppers conforms very well to the bell-shaped curve of normal distribution and the mean is within 2.3% of the required 157.5 grains.

CHART 5

Weight Distribution for 156 Specimens of Massachusetts Cents. The two arrows indicate the range of the first standard deviation, or 68.26% of the entire sample.
Group 2 in Table 21. (M = mean; S = 157.5 standard). (See fig. 64a).

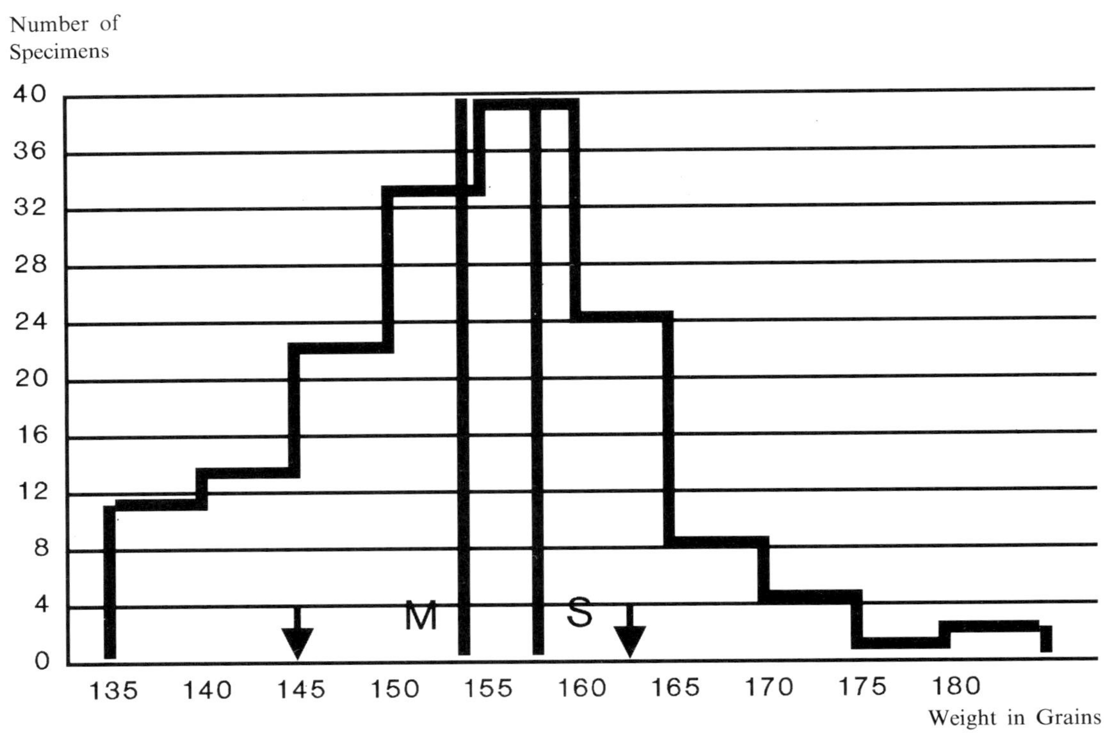

CHART 6

Weight Distribution for 68 Specimens of Massachusetts Half Cents. Group 3 in Table 21. (See fig. 64b).

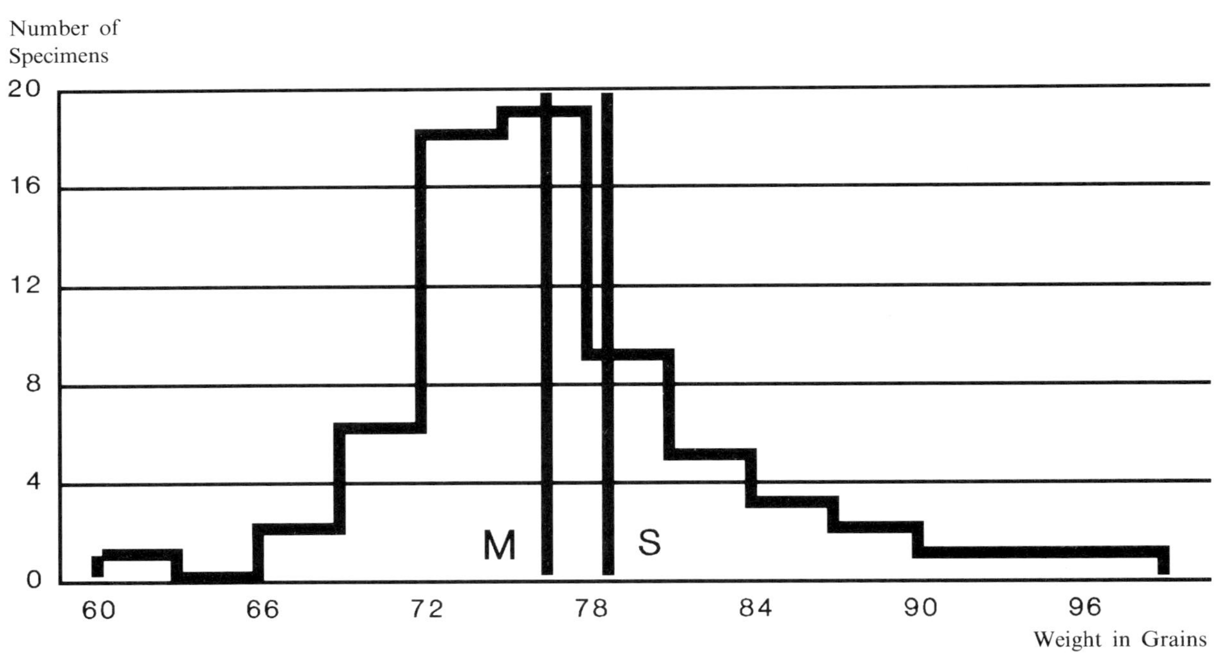

Massachusetts half cents (Chart 6), also made at the same state operated facility, while conforming to a normal distribution curve, fall about 2.9% below the standard. For comparison, Chart 7 indicates the weight distribution for 47 mostly uncirculated Virginia halfpence from the Tower Mint. It is known that while individual coppers in the Virginia series were allowed to vary by as much as 3.33% from the standard of 116.7 grains, it was expected that the entire output would conform to the authorized weight. In this sample the mean is slightly greater than the standard. In our analysis of Confederation coppers, we have been more liberal in our expectations and have suggested that a 5% deficiency in average weight of the entire sample was probably justifiable since planchet manufacture in America was not as advanced as in England.

The Fugio coppers have been well studied. The weight distribution curve for 675 Fine Rays specimens is presented in Chart 8. This symmetrical curve indicates a normal distribution pattern but the average weight falls 4.8% below the required standard. Since the Jarvis Mint was known to have employed some unethical practices in obtaining the patent, it remains a matter of speculation whether this deficiency in weight was intentional or due to mechanical imprecision of planchet preparation. The average values for the Round Club Rays in Chart 9 are the same but the sample is much smaller and the curve less reliable. Only 19 of the rare Concave Club Rays specimens are available for study in Chart 10. The shape of the curve may not be meaningful due to the small sample size but the average is significantly greater than in the two previous examples. Since these coppers do not appear to have the same planchet fabric as the other two Fugio types, it is safe to conclude they were minted under different auspices.

Chart 7

Weight Distribution for 47 Specimens of Virginia Halfpence from the Tower Mint.
These coppers were minted under more exacting conditions than any contemporaneous American issues.
Group 19a in Table 21. (See fig. 42b).

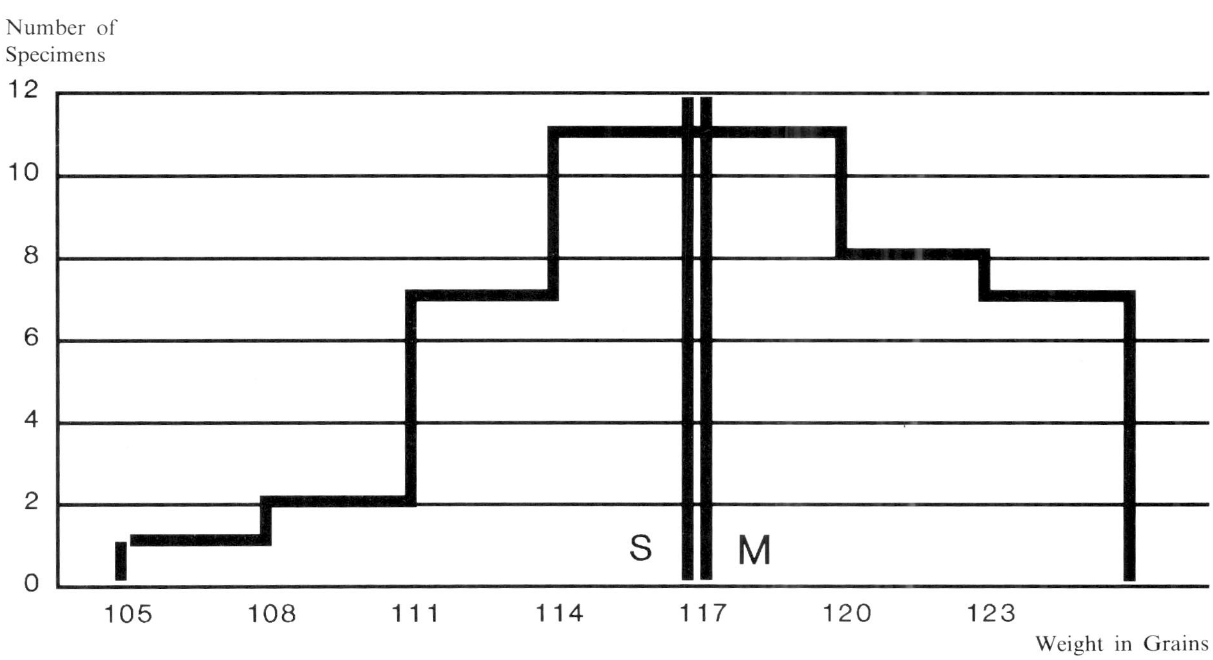

CHART 8

Weight Distribution for 675 Specimens of Fine Rays Fugio Coppers: Data courtesy of CNL. Group 1a in Table 21. (See fig. 67a).

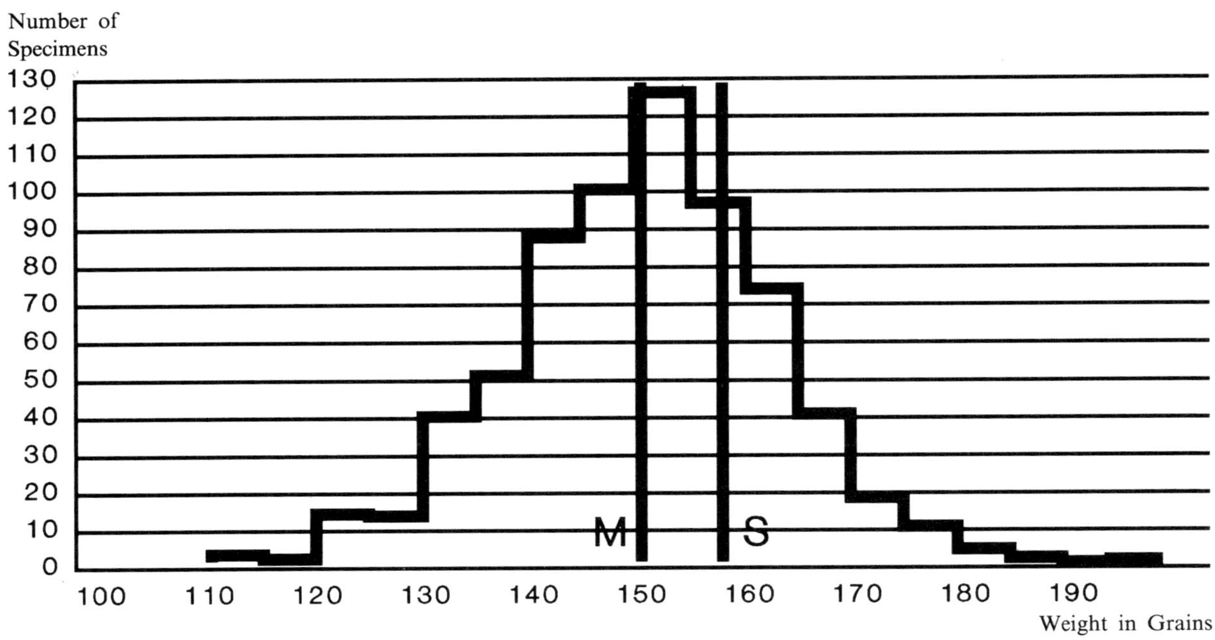

CHART 9

Weight Distribution for 65 Specimens of Round Club Rays Fugio Coppers: Data courtesy of CNL. Group 1b in Table 21. (See fig. 67b).

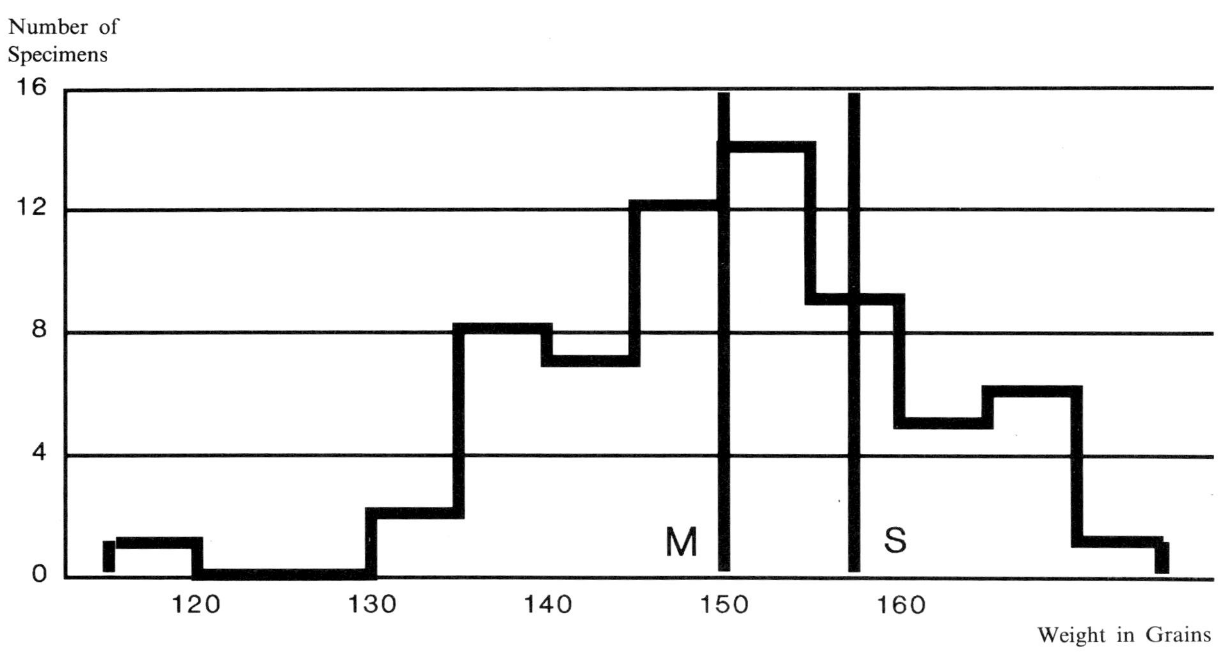

CHART 10

Weight Distribution for 19 Specimens of Concave Club Rays Fugio Coppers: Data courtesy of CNL. Group 1c in Table 21. (See fig. 67c).

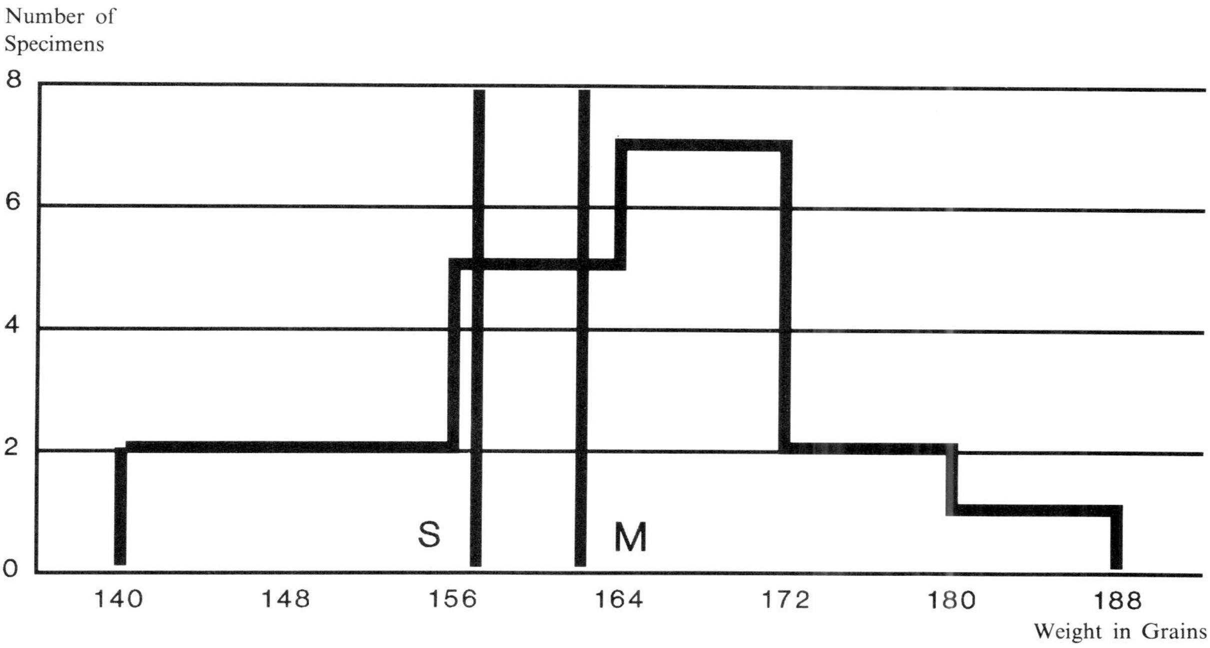

As noted in Chart 11, the Rahway coppers also conform to a normal distribution. Other issues attributed to that mint, the Heads Left group (Chart 12), and the Coulterless varieties (Chart 13) have fewer specimens and so the double peaks on their curves lack significance. Most late Elizabethtown coppers (1789 to 1791) were struck over lighter host coins, and thus no helpful information can be gained from planchet weight analysis since so few virgin flans were employed.

The coppers attributed to Brasher and Bailey were slightly (4.1%) below the standard as a group but certainly more hearty than the overstruck and counterfeit varieties. The fact that these issues had a reverse animal figure, either a horse or fox, believed by some to be a mintmark, indicated that their authors were willing to be traced. There is some evidence of collaboration with Walter Mould in the production of these coppers (Chart 14).

The 1787 and 1788 coppers attributed to the Morristown Mint have entirely different weight characteristics. Those from 1787 (Chart 15) show a normal distribution curve whereas the double peak from the next year (Chart 16) indicates a mixed population. Analysis of the right peak shows that it is comprised of 22 Maris 67-v coppers which are significantly heavier than the other 17 for that year. The immediate implication is that these two groups were not struck on the same planchet stock and possibly were not from the same mint. This is an area for additional research where energy dispersive X-ray fluorescence spectrometric analysis of the planchets would be very enlightening.

CHART 11

Weight Distribution for 471 Rahway Coppers.
Group 4 in Table 21. (See fig. 57a).

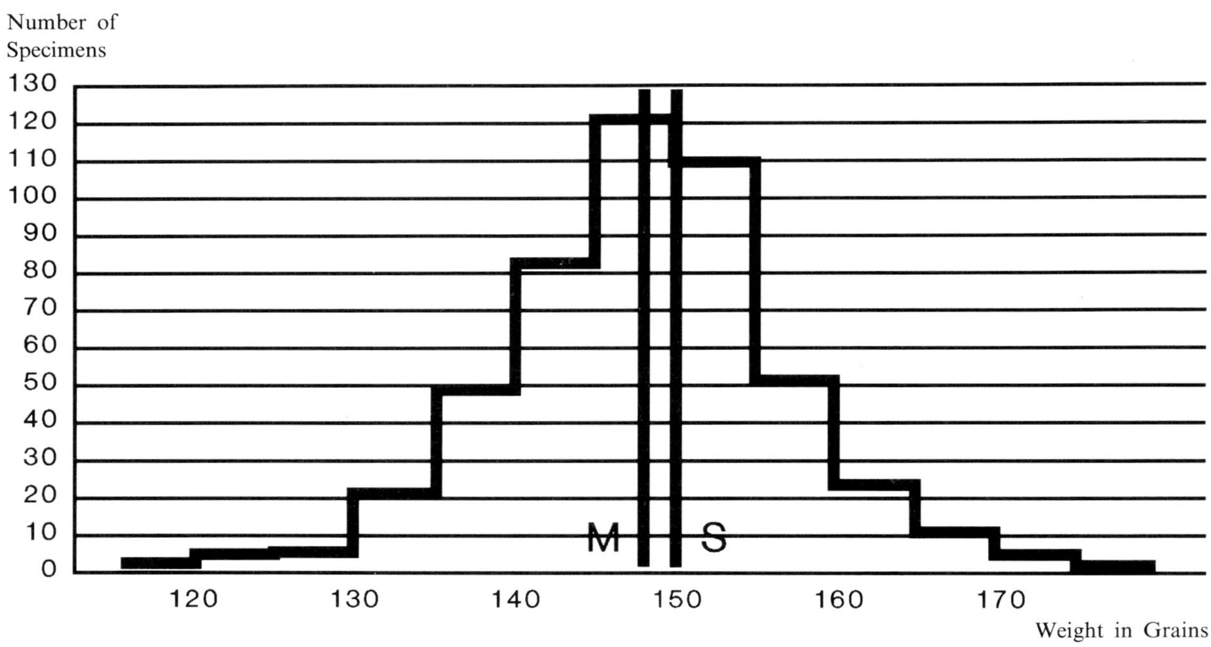

CHART 12

Weight Distribution for 26 Heads Left Rahway Coppers.
Group 4b in Table 21. (See fig. 57b).

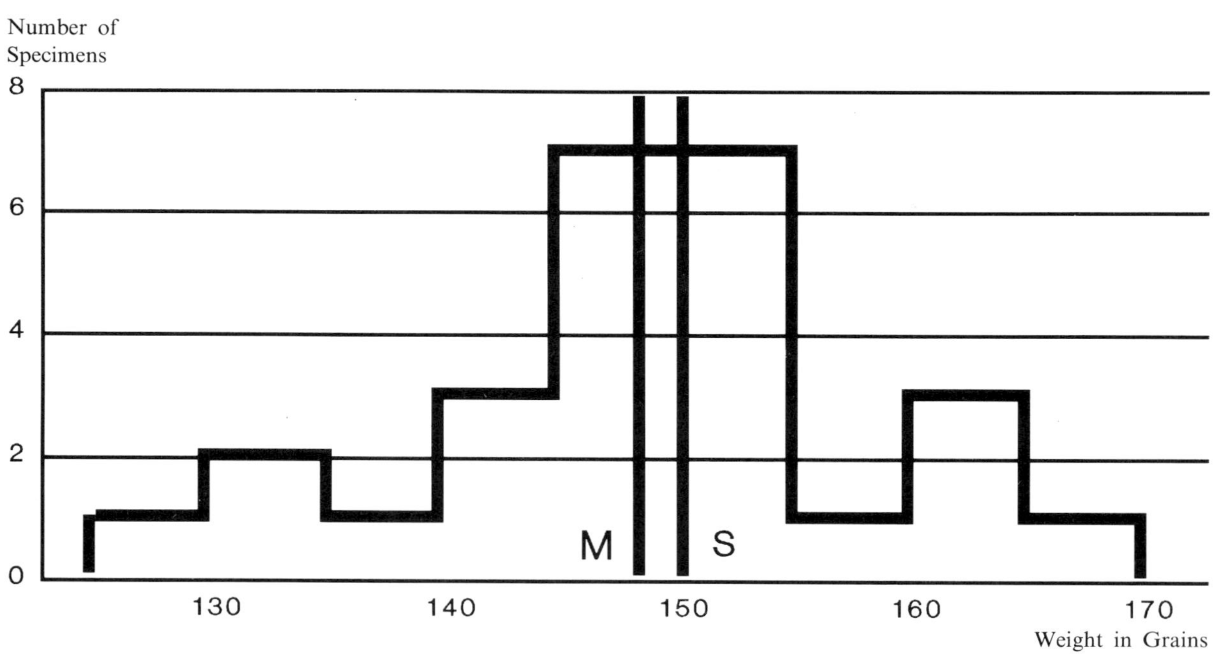

Chart 13

Weight Distribution for 48 Coulterless Rahway Coppers. (The plow depicted on these varieties lacked a coulter, or colter, which is a cutter to cleave the turf.) Group 4c in Table 21.

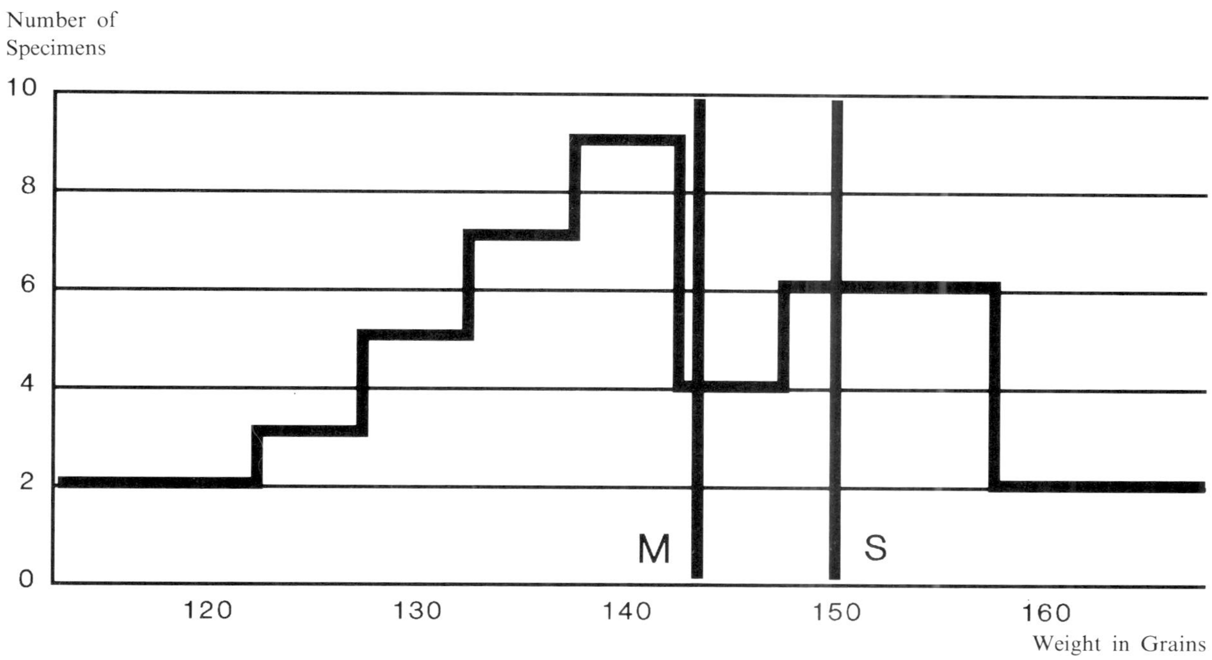

Chart 14

Weight Distribution for 53 New Jersey Coppers Attributed to the Mint of Brasher and Bailey. Group 7 in Table 21. (See fig. 57f).

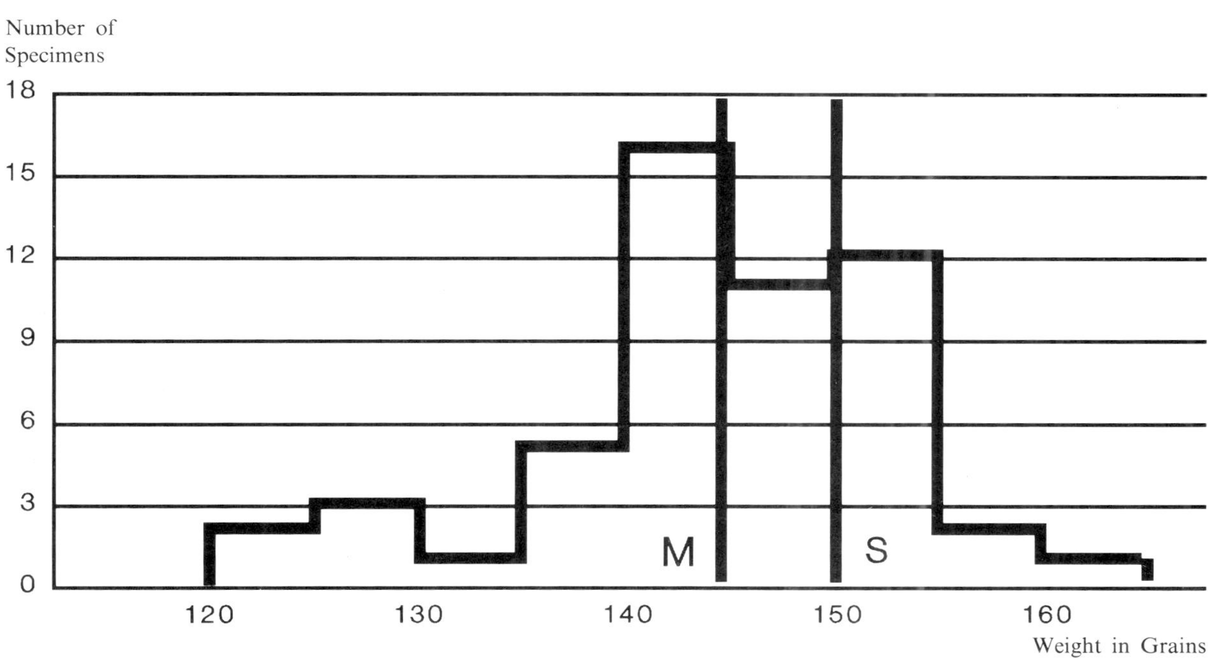

Chart 15

Weight Distribution for 132 Specimens of 1787 Morristown Coppers. Group 5c in Table 21. (See fig. 57c).

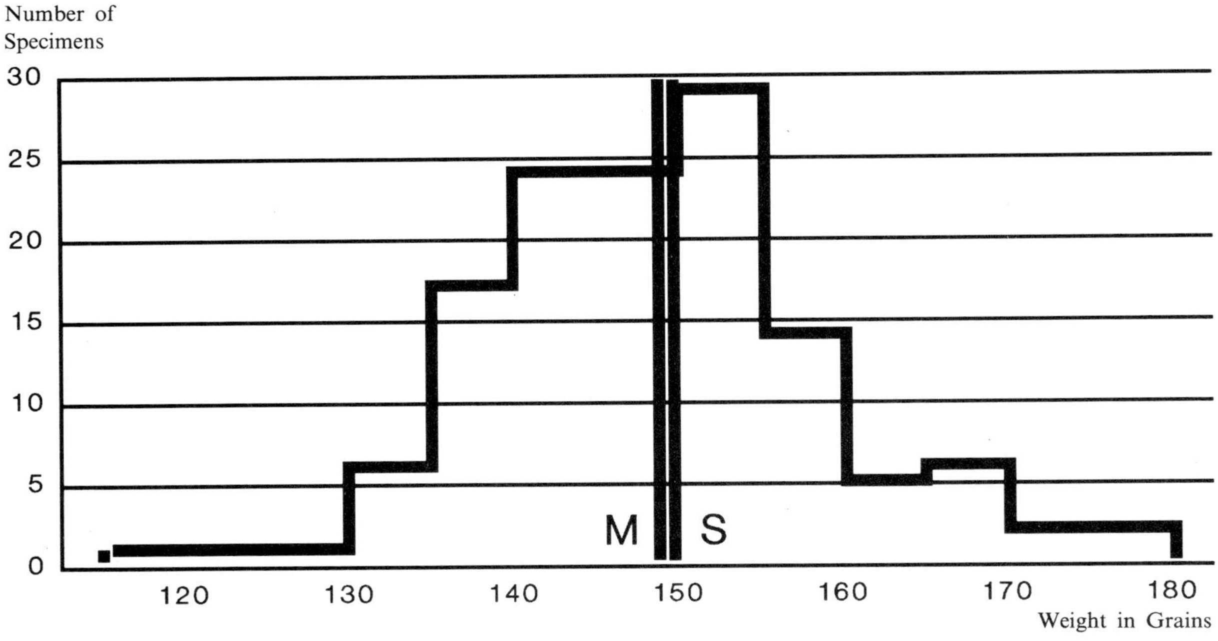

Chart 16

Weight Distribution for 39 Specimens of 1788 Morristown Coppers. The right peak comprises 22 Maris 67-v coppers which are significantly heavier than the other issues attributed to the Morristown Mint for that year. Group 5d in Table 21. (See fig. 57d).

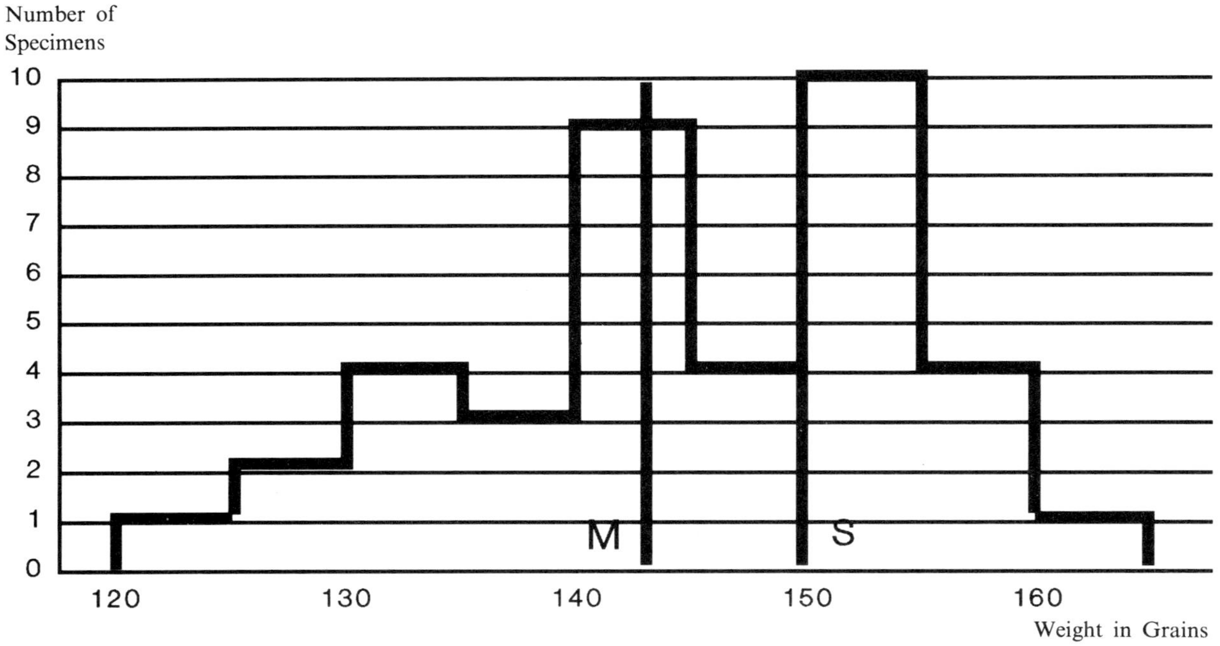

The Connecticut series is the largest and most varied of all the Confederation coppers. The 134 1785 Mailed Bust Right coppers and 160 1785/6 Mailed Bust Left coppers, all from the Company for Coining Coppers, are so similar in weight, they are combined as Group 10a in Table 21 and their respective curves are represented in Charts 17-18. These issues fall 6% below the standard, which is larger than the allowable 5%, but it has been postulated that this deficiency was due to technological problems in rolling planchet stock to the required dimension rather than a deliberate effort to deceive.

The 1787 Draped Bust Left issues are the most common Connecticut type coin. Although Abel Buell cut all the dies, the coins struck are not a homogeneous population in regard to weight and at least two mints were involved. In the previous two charts, it was observed that the Company for Coining Coppers used lightweight planchets in 1785 and into 1786. Starting with the rare 1786 Draped Bust Left coppers, it appears that the planchet weight exceeds the standard. This may have occurred during the time when the Company for Coining Coppers leased their equipment to another group of contractors. Then in 1787 (Chart 19) the Company for Coining Coppers resumed the Draped Bust Left design with essentially full weight coins. These issues are identified by the large lettering in the legends. The next Draped Bust Left coppers in order of emission are those with small lettering and crosses in the legends (Chart 20) but it is uncertain whether they are products of the Company for Coining Coppers or their successor in business, Jarvis and Company. These are full weight and in fact exhibit a double peak to the curve. The lower segment of the right peak, averaging 151.9 grains, is Miller 17-g.3 and then Miller 24-g.3 at 152.9 grains. The upper half of the right peak contains the Miller 24-FF specimens at 156.0 grains while in the uppermost limb rest the Miller 38-GG coppers at an average 156.1 grains. Although these varieties seem to have very definite weight characteristics, they are few in number and it will require the analysis of more specimens either to confirm or refute these observations.

CHART 17

Weight Distribution for 134 Specimens of 1785 Mailed Bust Right Connecticut Coppers from the Company for Coining Coppers. These data and Chart 18 are combined in Table 21 as the 294 Specimens of Group 10a. (See fig. 55a).

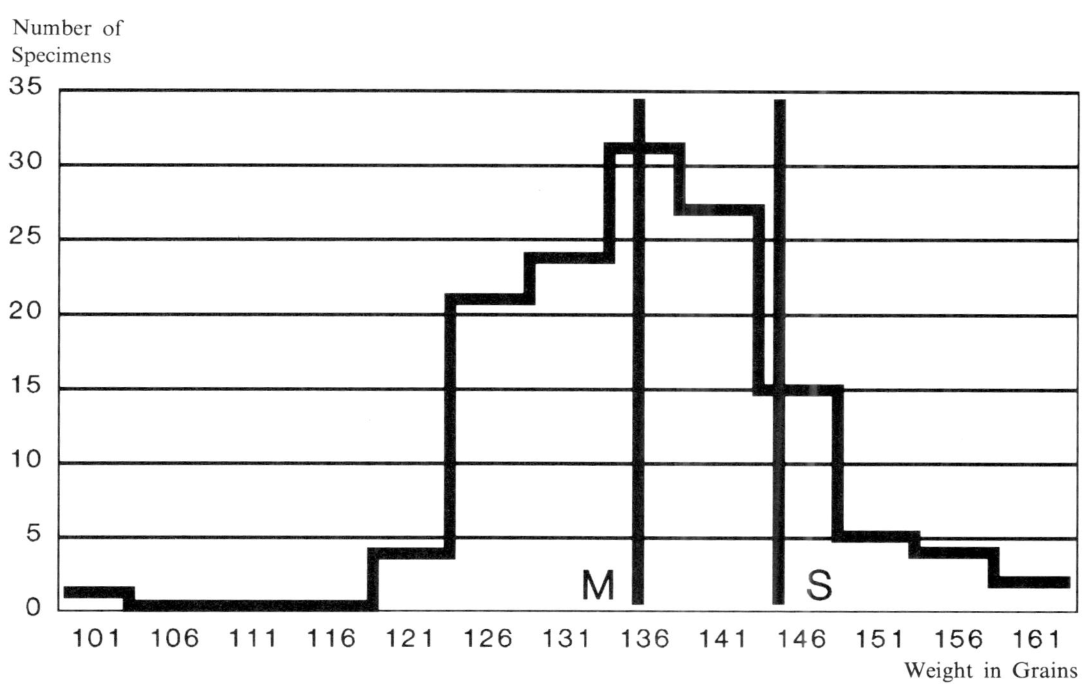

CHART 18

Weight Distribution for 160 Specimens of 1785/6 Mailed Bust Left Connecticut Coppers from the Company for Coining Coppers. These data and Chart 17 are combined in Table 21 as the 294 Specimens of Group 10a. (See figs. 55c and 55d).

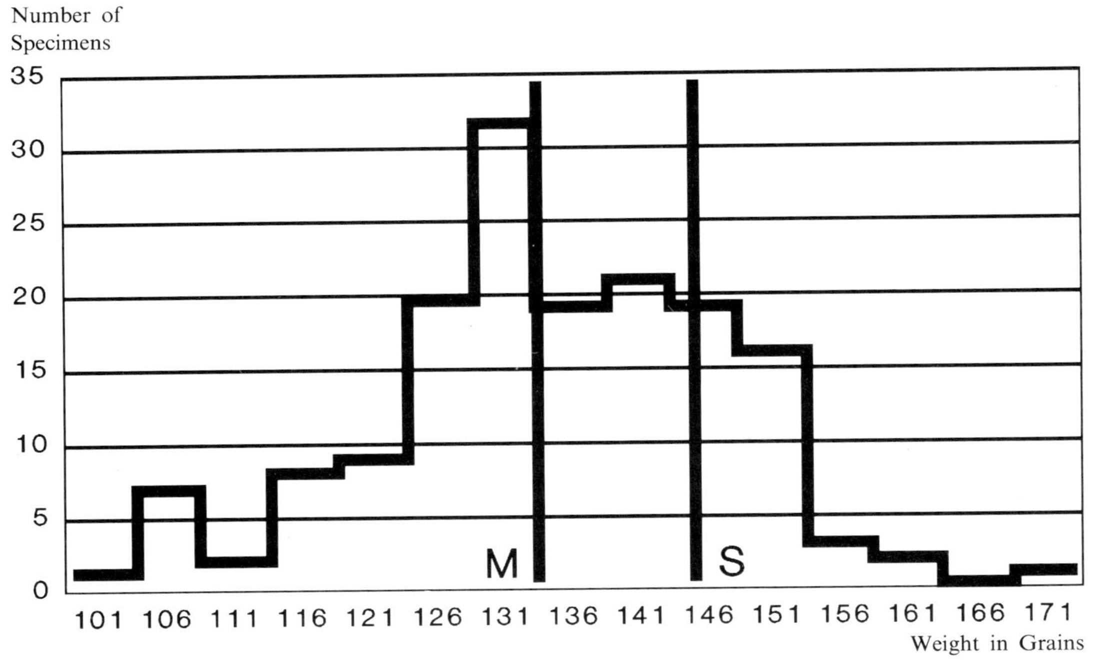

CHART 19

Weight Distribution for 109 Specimens of 1787 Draped Bust Left Connecticut Coppers from the Company for Coining Coppers. Group 10c in Table 21. (See fig. 55j).

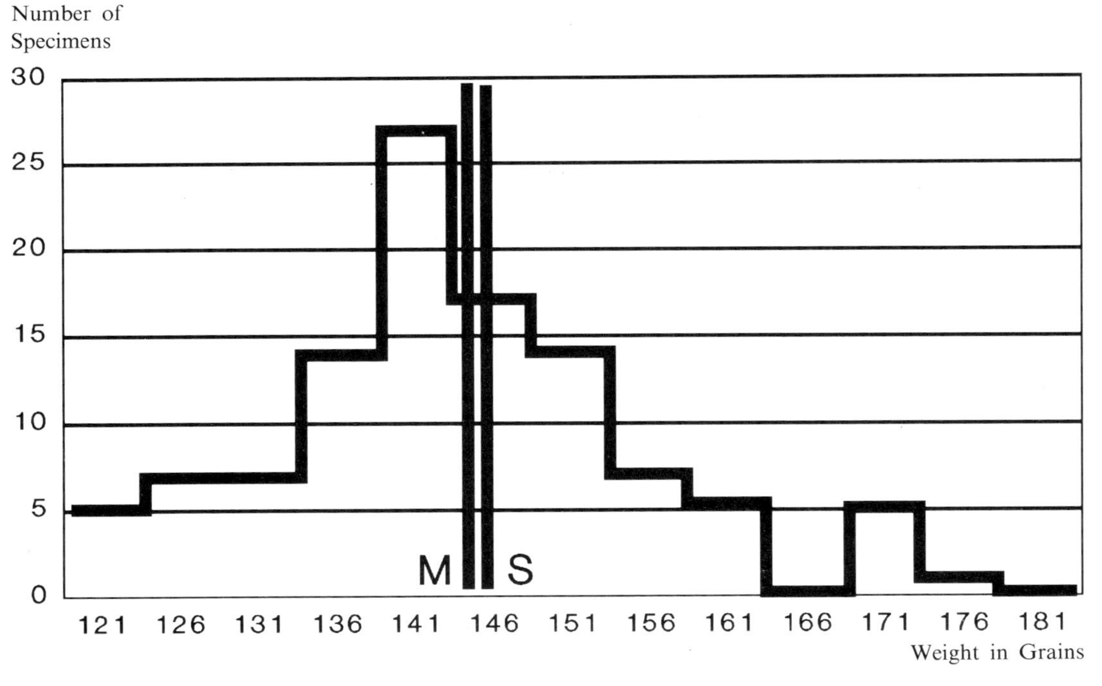

Chart 20

Weight Distribution for 73 Specimens of 1787 Draped Bust Left Connecticut Coppers with Crosses and Small Lettering in the Legends. The right peak is the heavier 17-g.3, 24-g.3, 24-FF and 38-GG varieties. Group 11b in Table 21. (See fig. 55k).

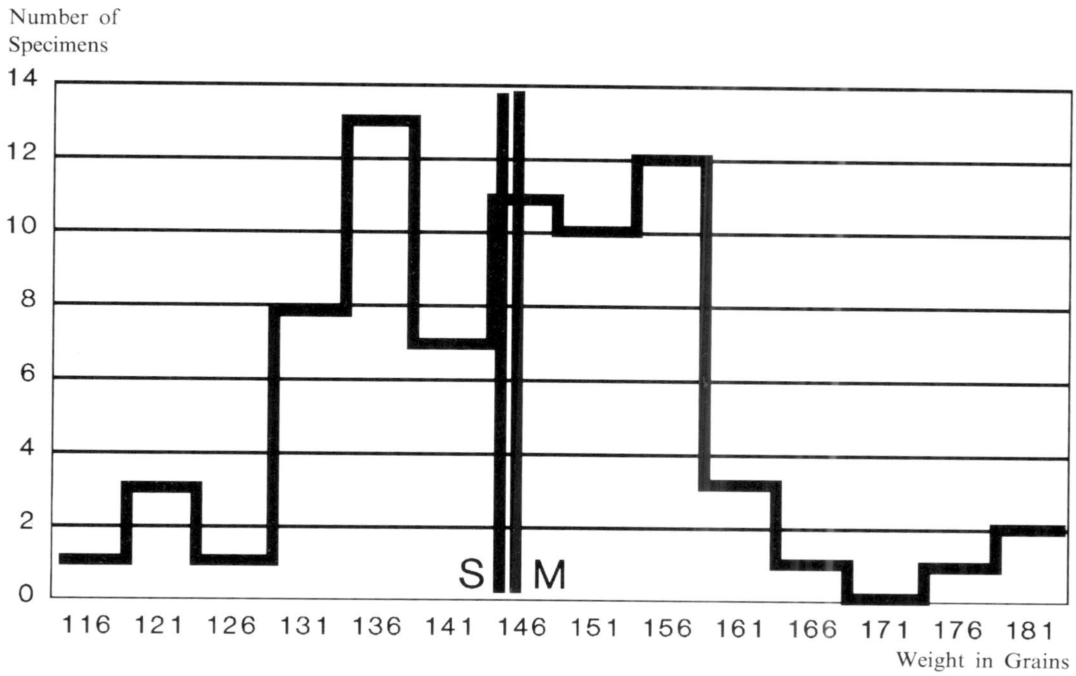

The second group of small lettering 1787 Draped Bust Left coppers to be issued were those with fleurons in the legends (Chart 21). These almost reach the standard but in any case are heavier than the last group with cinquefoils in Chart 22 from the Jarvis mint. This large collection of 610 specimens forms a normal distribution curve which is similar to Chart 8, the Fine Rays Fugios which were from the same mint. Since Jarvis could manufacture Fugio planchets at 150.0 grains, he should have been able to cut Connecticut planchets at 144.0 grains rather than at 134.6. It appears that the 6.5% reduction below the standard was purposeful. The Draped Bust Left motif was next used by the illegal Machin's Mills mint (Chart 23) for the 1788-dated varieties of that type. These coins were well below the standard and without doubt the reduction in weight was designed to deceive the public.

There were a large number of contemporaneous counterfeit Connecticut coppers minted by clandestine operations which not only skimped on the metal content of the coins but also ignored the 10% royalty required by the state from the authorized patentees. These spurious issues include the 1786 Mailed Bust Right coppers attributed to Atlee (group 12 Table 21), the Mutton-heads (group 14), all the 1788 Connecticut coppers, and the 1787 coppers which share common punches with Walter Mould's Morristown emissions, namely Miller 1787 1.3-L, 4-L, 6.1-M, and 6.2-M. Of the 64 such specimens in Chart 24, a distinct double peak is observed with the heavier 4-L on the right, although both are well below the authorized standard. This observation suggests that two populations of planchets were used and that the four varieties, although punch and die-linked together, were not minted simultaneously.

CHART 21

Weight Distribution for 134 Specimens of 1787 Draped Bust Left Connecticut Coppers with Fleurons and Small Lettering in the Legends. Group 11c in Table 21. (See fig. 55m).

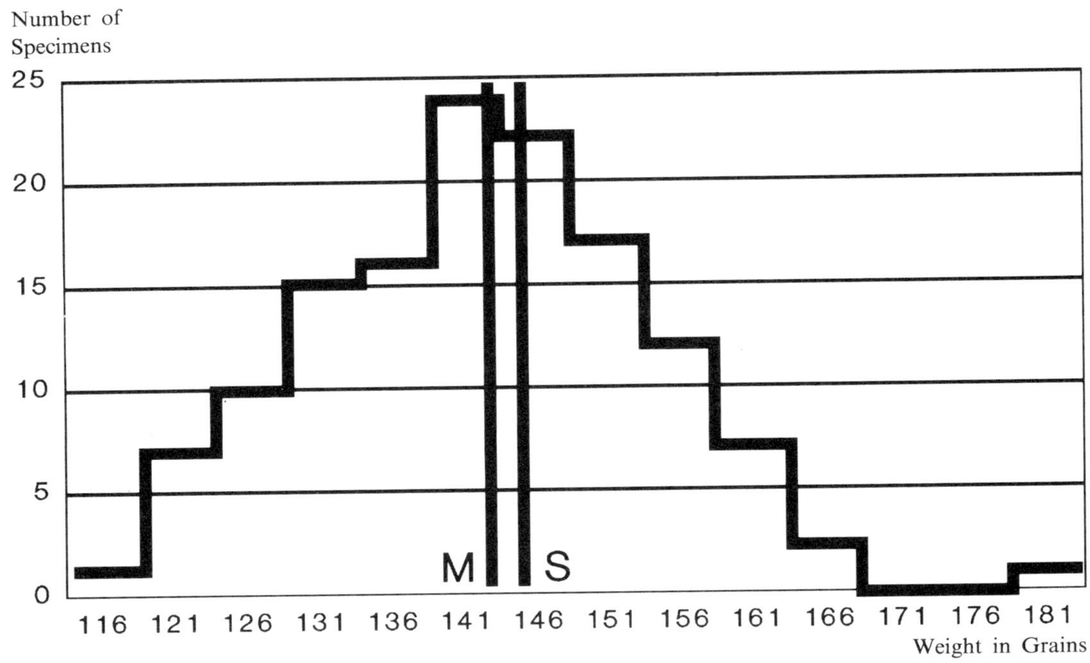

CHART 22

Weight Distribution for 610 Specimens of 1787 Draped Bust Left Connecticut Coppers with Cinquefoils and Small Lettering from the Jarvis Mint. Group 11a in Table 21. (See fig. 55n).

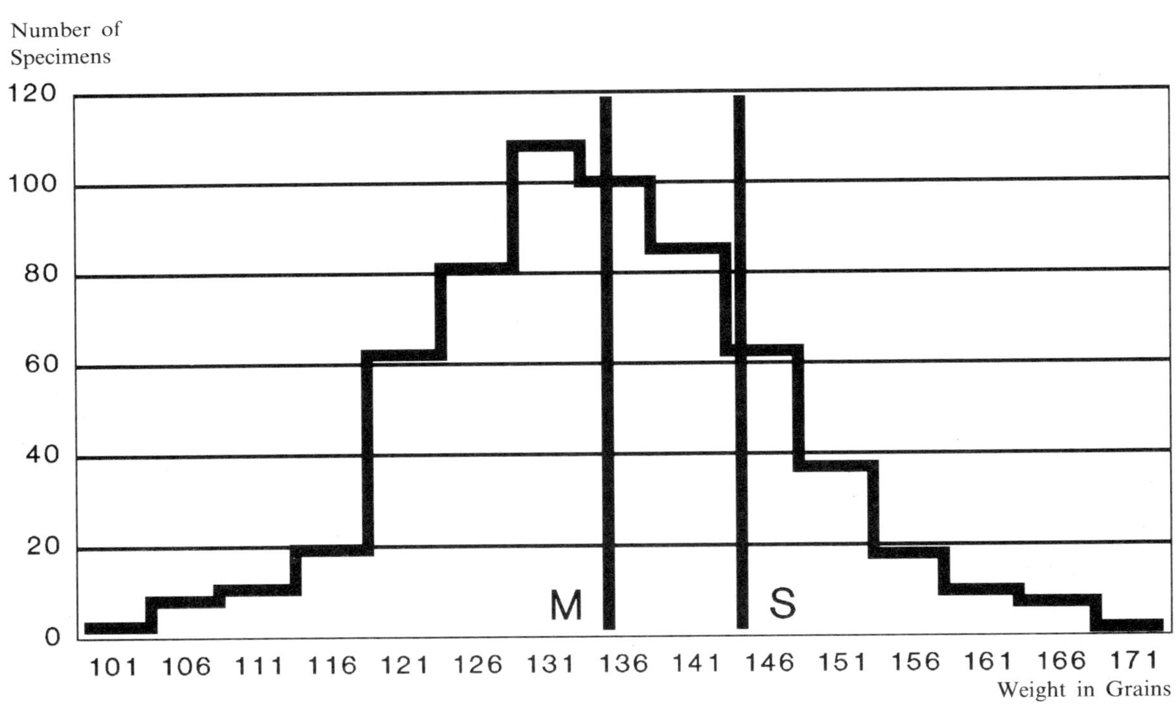

CHART 23

Weight Distribution for 79 Specimens of 1788 Draped Bust Left Connecticut Coppers probably from Machin's Mills Employing Old Equipment from the Jarvis Mint.
Group 17 in Table 21. (See fig. 55bb).

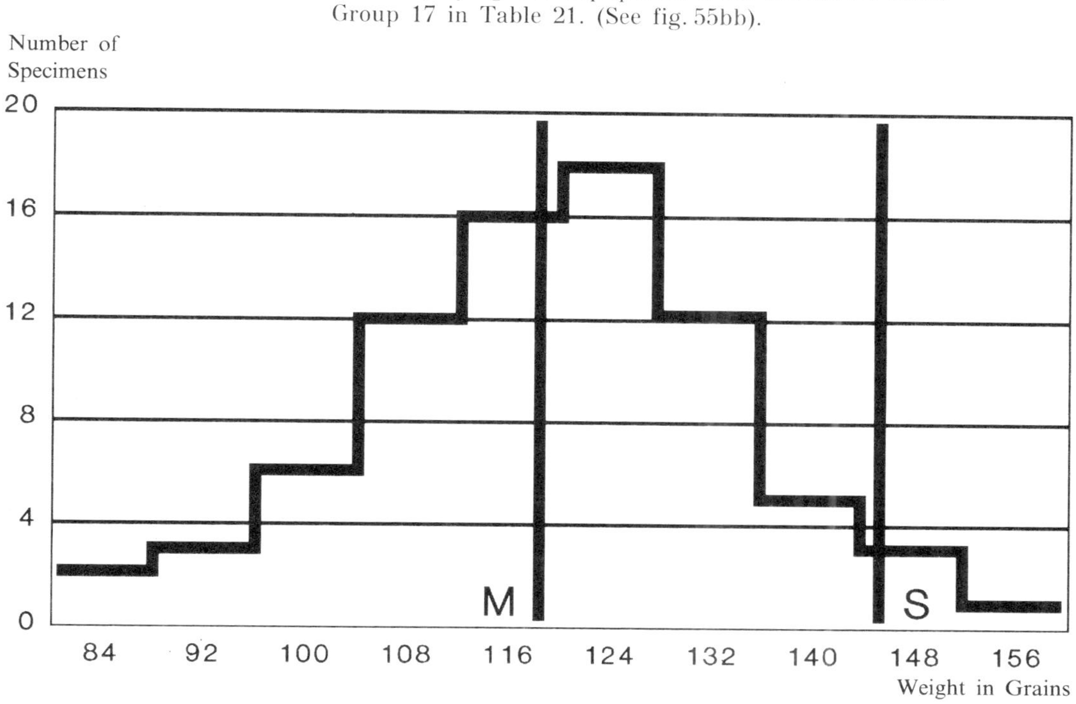

CHART 24

Weight Distribution for 64 Specimens 1787 Connecticut Coppers Which Have Been Connected with Walter Mould of the Morristown Mint. The heavier Miller 1787 4-L form the right peak of the curve.
Group 13 in Table 21. (See figs. 53, 55r, 55s, and 55t).

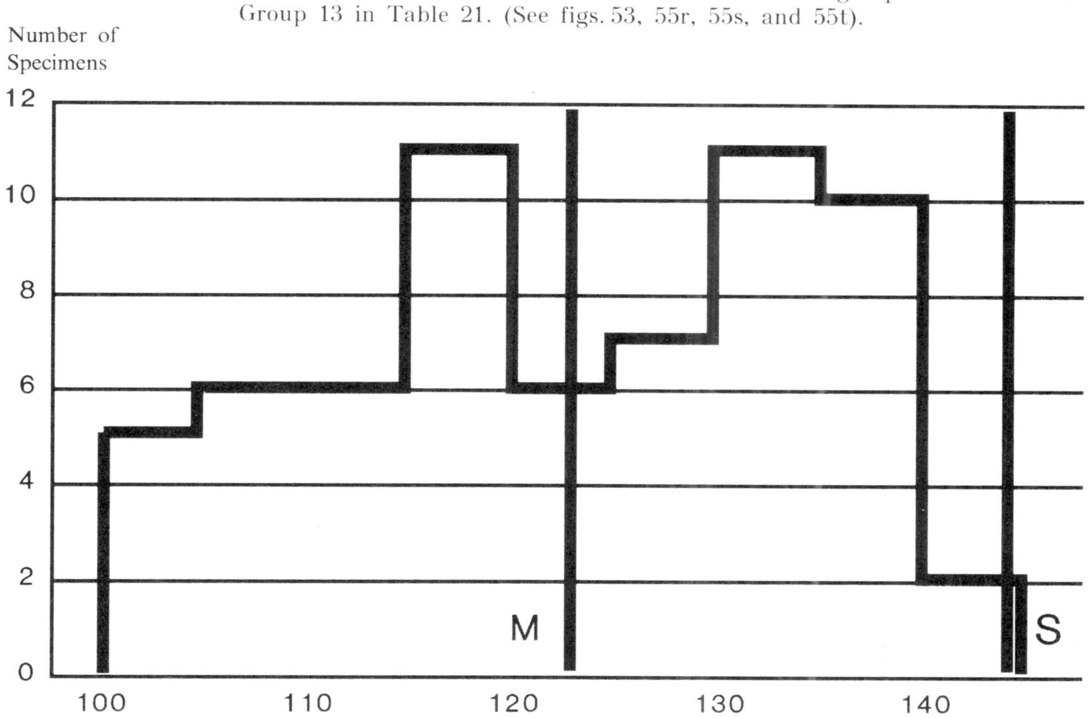

The Connecticut Triple Leaves dies were also engraved by Abel Buell but much less is certain as to where the coppers with these designs were minted. For those dated 1787 there are two distinct populations (Chart 25). Those designated Miller 2-B, 9-E, 10-E,[1] 11-E, and 11-K approach full weight and comprise the right segment of the curve while all others fall well below the standard and are similar to those 1788-dated issues (Chart 26). There are several possibilities to explain these observations. Perhaps the heavier 1787 coppers were from a yet unidentified legitimate operation, concerned for legal weight, and the lightweight 1787-dated varieties, likely from Machin's Mills, were back-dated since their planchet weight is similar to the 1788-dated varieties. In 1788, after Buell's residual equipment was relinquished to Machin's Mills, the light 1787 Triple Leaves, the 1788 Triple Leaves, and the 1788 Draped Bust Left coppers all could have been minted at that location. It is evident that this study has just scratched the surface of Confederation planchet analysis. It will require further investigation with die emission sequence and actual constituent metal examination to answer these questions.

Numismatists familiar with Confederation coppers are aware that poor quality and inconsistent planchets are typical within the Vermont series. Chart 27 shows a wide range in planchet weights for the 1785/6 landscape varieties with the mean weight well in excess of the authorized standard of 111.0 grains. The bust issues from the Rupert Mint (Chart 28), those from Machin's Mills (Chart 29) and the Machin's Mills halfpence (Chart 30) are very similar in weight characteristics.

CHART 25

Weight Distribution for 145 Specimens of 1787 Triple Leaves Connecticut Coppers from Unknown Mints. The heavier coppers on the right are Miller 1787 11-E, 11-K, 10-E, 9-E, and 2-B. Group 16a in Table 21. (See fig. 55p).

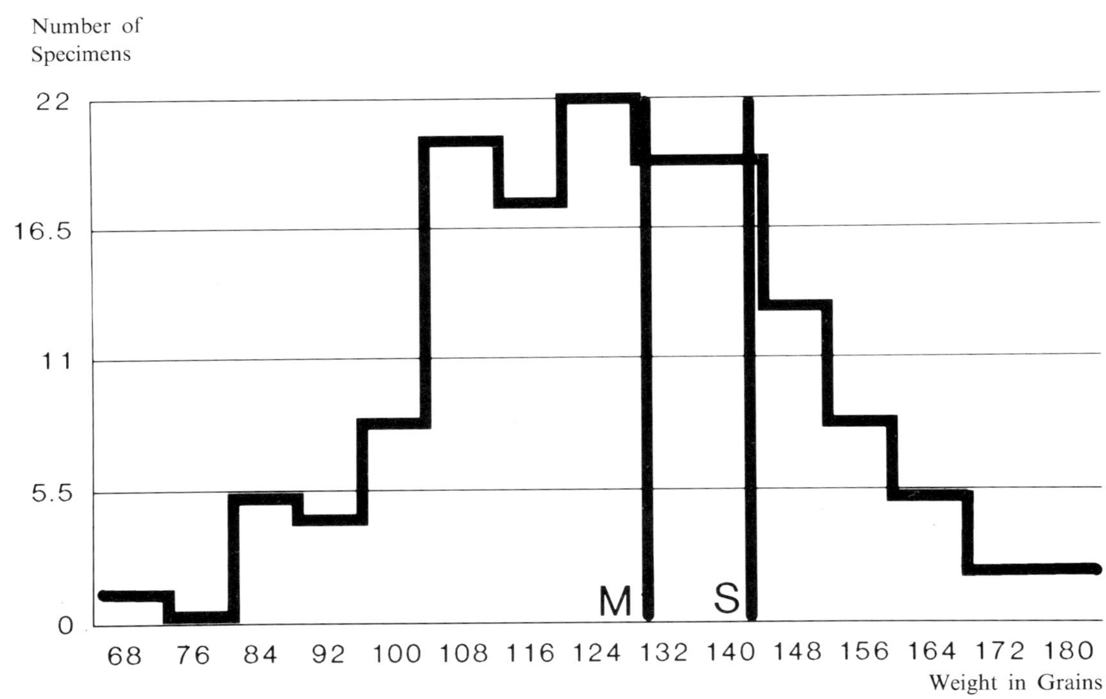

[1] Additional data is courtesy of Rob Retz whose research indicates that 1787 Miller 10-E is also a "heavy" variety of Triple leaves. While Miller 9-E is the heaviest of the group at 146.3 ± 26.2, there are too few specimens (7) to draw any conclusion. Its high first standard deviation indicates a great variation in planchet weight and the possibility of a sampling error.

CHART 26

Weight Distribution for 57 Specimens of 1788 Triple Leaves Connecticut Coppers probably from Machin's Mills Employing Old Equipment. This curve is similar to the left half of the curve in Chart 25. Group 16d in Table 21 (See fig. 55cc).

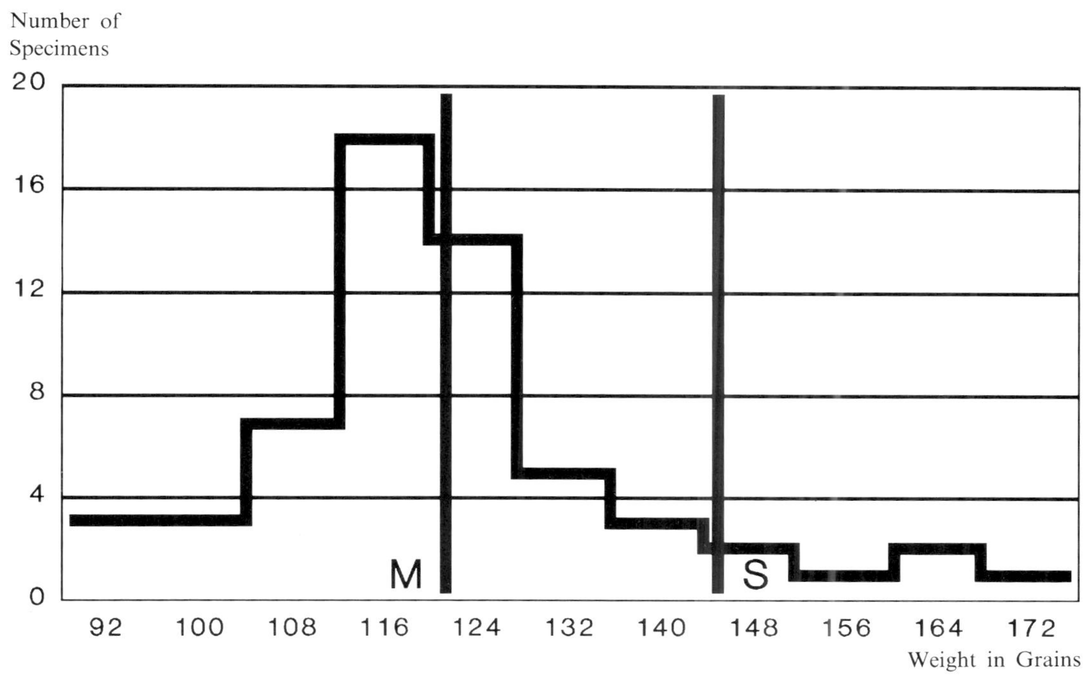

CHART 27

Weight Distribution for 58 Specimens of 1785/6 Vermont Landscape Varieties. Group 20a in Table 21. (See fig. 58).

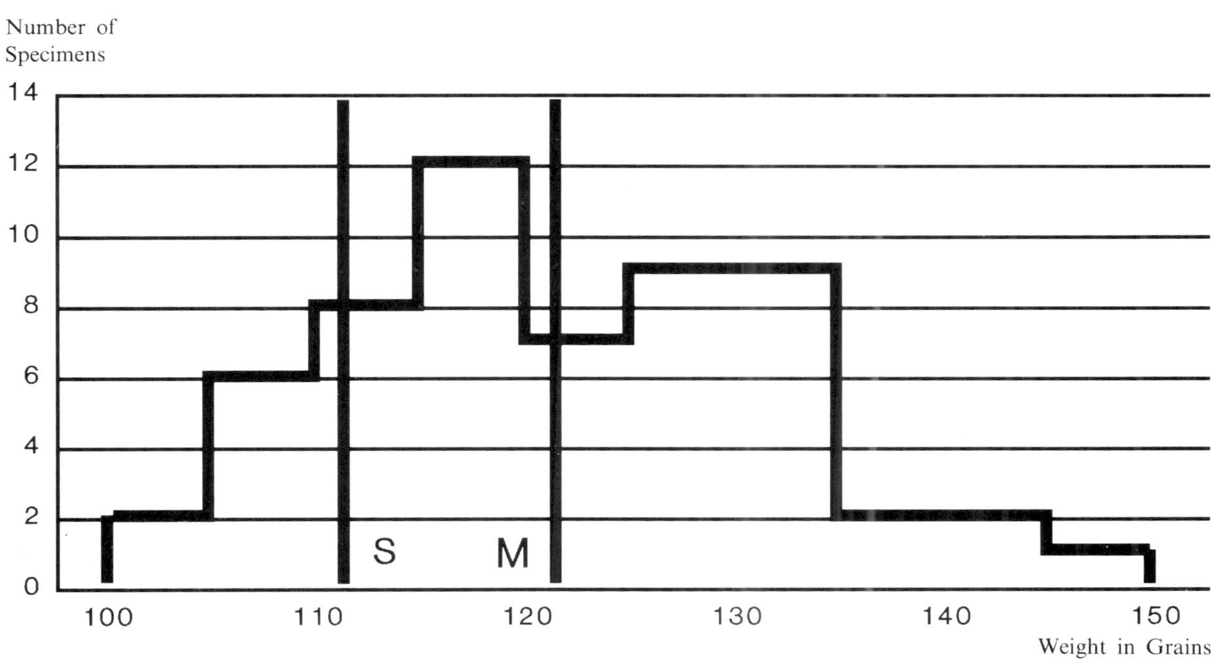

CHART 28

Weight Distribution for 79 Specimens of 1787/8 Vermont Bust Right Coppers from the Rupert Mint. Group 20c in Table 21. (See fig. 59c).

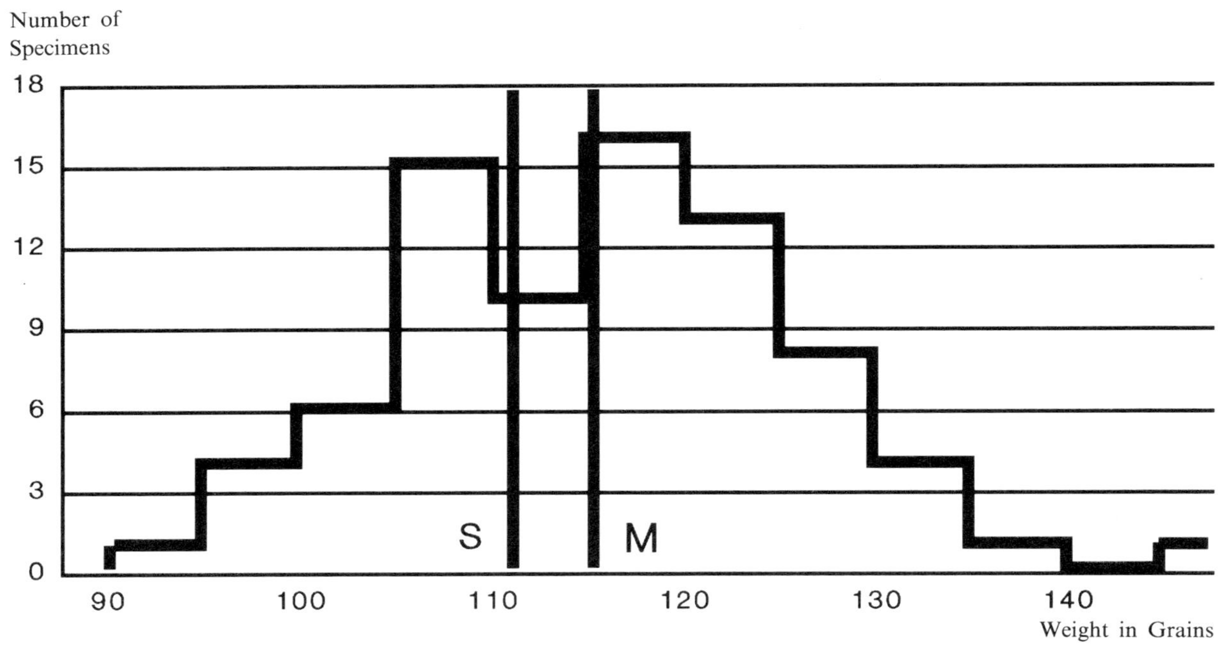

CHART 29

Weight Distribution for 57 Specimens of Vermont Bust Right Coppers Minted at the Machin's Mills mint at Newburgh, New York. Group 21a in Table 21. (See figs. 59d and 62b).

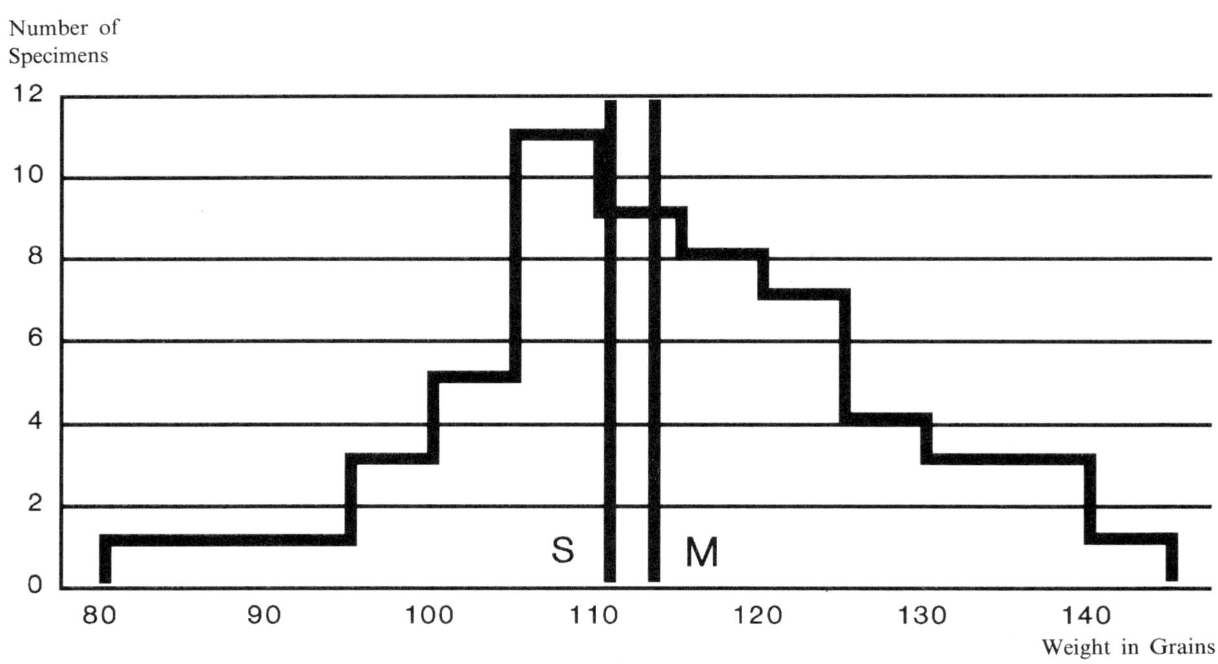

CHART 30

Weight Distribution for 46 Specimens of Imitation English Halfpence minted at Machin's Mills, Newburgh, New York. Group 22 in Table 21. (See figs. 61b and 62a).

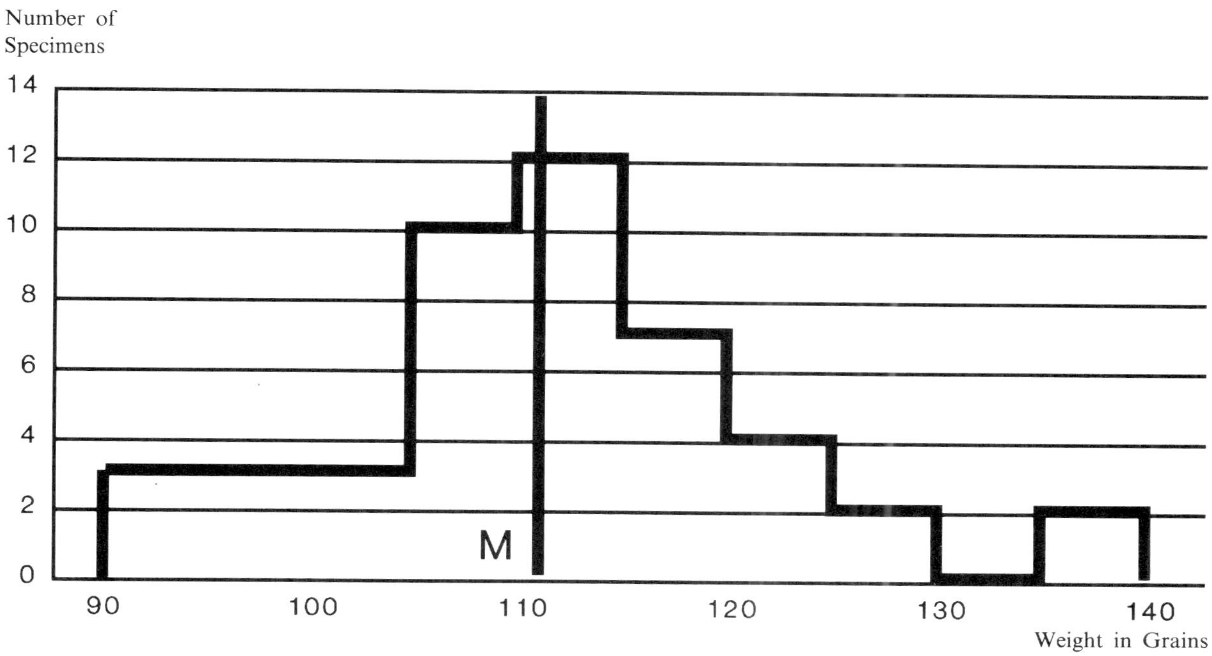

These distribution curves have been constructed from data in Table 21 for those groups with a sufficient sample size for meaningful information. For more important and rarer varieties, smaller sample sizes were used although the potential sampling error is recognized.

APPENDIX 5

"A Treatise on Copper Coin"

John Beale Bordley, a prominent Maryland lawyer, judge, and agriculturist, lived from 1727 to 1804.[1] His early education was very broad and he remained keenly interested in many diverse subjects, particularly those related to agricultural practices. He owned and operated what might be considered a large scale experimental farm where he introduced new and imported methods and technologies. From 1784 to 1799, he published three books describing his experiences, while in 1785, he was instrumental in the formation of the Philadelphia Society for Promoting Agriculture. In addition to his encouragement of agriculture, Bordley was also concerned about the coinage of the new nation. In 1789, he wrote a series of articles for *The Pennsylvania Mercury, and Universal Advertiser* on his proposals for a new coinage system for the United States and included as well his thoughts on standards for weights and measures.

The first of these articles, which appeared in the June 27, 1789 issue, dealt with his notions for simplifing the silver currency. In essence he proposed that the United States adopt the sterling standard of .925 fine silver which he called the "commercial standard" since it was equal to the standard of the commercial countries, Britain, France, Holland, and Spain, which were America's chief trading partners. His comments were based on the 1716 assays of Sir Isaac Newton of these foreign currencies.[2] The Spanish milled dollar, which remained the western world's silver standard, was pegged at 53.87d., sterling, an odd value which complicated computations.[3] Bordley opined that if the prospective American sterling dollar weighed 386 grains, then it would be worth 50d., sterling, a parity which would make the American cent equal to one English halfpenny. This equity would facilitate the conversion of English pounds, shillings, and pence into American currency through division by decimals. Bordley demonstrated his decimal method by converting a debt of £54 6s. 8d., sterling, into "Congress money." The sum contained 26080 English halfpence or 26080 American cents at the new proposed standard. When divided by tens, accomplished by moving a "series of dots," the 26080 cents became 260.8.0. or 260 dollars, 8 dimes, and no cents. The 260 dollars could be further reduced to 26 eagles, or 26.0.8.0. by further division by ten. Individual state monies of account would first require conversion into their English sterling equivalent before the resulting value could be reduced further into halfpence or cents and then expressed in the new "Congress dollars, dimes, and cents" by manipulation of the "dots." Being true to his vocation as a sheep farmer and ever mindful of the commodity value of wool in the economy, Bordley suggested that the device on the new coin be a "wooled sheep," implying a "fleece" which he suggested as a suitable name for the proposed silver coin.

In the July 30, 1789 edition of *The Pennsylvania Mercury, and Universal Advertiser*, Bordley's second installment regarding the national coinage was published. This essay, "treatise on copper coin," has been quoted in several instances in Chapter 8. Although the presentation is unsigned, its context shows it to be definitely the work of Bordley. Shortly afterward, the August 4, 1789 edition contained his next commentary on "weights," which was followed subsequently by the fourth sequel on "measures" on August 13.

[1] *Biography*, vol. 1, pt. 2, pp. 460-61.

[2] The authorized silver content for French, Spanish, and United Provinces coins was less than sterling alloy. See Tables 5, 7, and 8.

[3] This value is correct but is rounded up to 54d.

These four contributions on silver coins, coppers, weights, and measures were revised and combined in a pamphlet, *on Monies, Coins, Weights, and Measures, Proposed For the United States of America.* This booklet was printed by Daniel Humphreys, the publisher of the newspaper in which the original presentations appeared. Only the year 1789 is noted on the title page of the pamphlet, but the revised style of the text and the appearance of an erratum in the October 20, 1789 edition of the paper, suggests it was printed early in October 1789.

In an attempt to value more precisely foreign coins, Bordley updated his original monograph with *A Supplement to the Essay on Monies, &c.* which occurred in two installments in *The Pennsylvania Mercury* on February 25 and 27, 1790. In the same fashion as the previous work, these two updates also appeared in leaflet form, but this time without revision.

Other contributions by Bordley were printed during 1789 and 1790 in Humphreys' newspaper. On October 6, 1789, another letter on an agricultural subject discussed the relative merits of sheep production in America. Returning to coinage, a March 13, 1790 commentary was entitled "On the Moidore and the Par of Exchange with Portugal." On a different subject, Bordley submitted his thoughts on "National Credit and Character" which were printed in the April 1, 1790 edition.

While Bordley may be considered a visionary whose concepts on silver currency and the merits of decimalization never materialized, his comments on the copper medium, as presented in the "treatise on copper coin," have a very important place in the study of Confederation coinages. In this single, brief essay, he addressed many similar concerns which had been raised by other eighteenth century resources cited in this present book. His views on the base metal medium corroborate these collateral data and underscore the contemporaneous concerns regarding several aspects of copper currency such as low intrinsic value, the costs of manufacture, the consequences of oversupply, and the hazards of legal tender status. Because of the significance of Bordley's work, his revised essay, "Copper Coins," as it appeared in his pamphlet, *on Monies, Coins, Weights, and Measures, Proposed For the United States of America* is being reprinted in its entirety in Appendix 5 with annotations.[4]

COPPER COINS.

from "on MONIES, COINS, WEIGHTS, and MEASURES, proposed for the United States of America" by John Beale Bordley (pp. 12-16), Printed by Daniel Humphreys, Philadelphia, 1789

A Treatise on copper coin, as far as I know, is a new thing. There are reasons why these coins ought to be limited in their power. If they were to have the power to sink debts, as gold and silver have, they would be used vexatiously; and that would affect credits. Even if the forcing them in payments should be confined to 5 per cent. of debts, or be at all allowed of, it would have that tendency: and a creditor receiving a debt of 10,000 dollars, each cent thereof weighing 140 grains, at 5 per centum, would be burdened with 500 dollars worth, that is 50,000 pieces of copper of the weight of 1000 avoirdupois pounds; which selling as old copper, although it be at 20 cents a pound, would make a loss of 20,000 cents on his whole claim; and moreover would burden him

[4] Bordley's several articles quoted above, which appeared in *The Pennsylvania Mercury*, are photographically preserved and readily available for study, as are many other early newspapers. However, his revised pamphlet, *on Monies, Coins, Weights, and Measures, Proposed For the United States of America*, remained virtually unknown to numismatics until recently rediscovered by Eric P. Newman, who kindly made his copy of this exceedingly rare document available to the author. Because Bordley wrote two versions of his "treatise on copper coin," they must be distinguished in this Appendix. The first one appeared in the July 30 edition of *The Pennsylvania Mercury* and is referenced as "*Penna. Merc*, July 30, 1789." The second, a revision of the original essay, appeared about three months later in the pamphlet, *on Monies, Coins, Weights, and Measures, Proposed For the United States of America*, is repeated here unabridged.

with cartage, storage, and expenses of sales; so that near 3 per cent. of his debt would be lost: which would affect commerce, especially with foreigners.[5] An ordinance of the late Congress, enacts that the treasury; and if I rightly understand it, the proprietors of bullion carried to the mint, shall be paid 5 per cent. of their claims in copper cents. Ought those who carry bullion to the mint, to be burdened with inconvenience?

It is said, the late Congress contracted for copper, to be coined at their mint and issued as above;[6] and their ordinance seems to intend that the public mint shall have the coining of copper cents. It is proper it should be so, exclusively. Having found, from the report of a committee of the General Assembly of New-York, in 1787,[7] that the best red copper in *sheets* costs, at the factories in England, 11d. sterling a pound; on which they say the charges are 20 to 25 per cent. and that copper in mass, or old copper to be melted into ingots and drawn into sheets in the plating mills costs 9d. sterling—charges included, I thereon make an estimate of the cost of coining copper cents, of 50 to the pound of copper, for a dollar worth 50d. sterling, thus: for a pound of copper, 24 cents;[8] coining 12 cents;[9] together 36 cents, the cost. The pound of copper so coined passes for 50 cents.—The ordinance of the late Congress says, 2¼ lbs. of copper shall be coined into 100 cents, (for a dollar of the value of 52d. 46/100 sterling value) at which rate each cent weighs 157½ grains. The old English half-pennies, I suspect, weigh about 166 grains.[10] I have one which weighs 156 grains and appears to be true Tower coin, such as were not uncommon fifty years since; it is, however, so worn that the impressions are nearly lost: it therefore may be presumed that it weighed 8 or 10 grains more when new: the Britannia side is quite smooth—the other side faintly shews the impression of a head or heads in the manner of a William and Mary halfpence. The New-York committee further report, that 48 genuine British halfpence, when *new*, weigh 1 lb, avoirdupois, each piece 146 grains: 60 Birmingham coppers, are 1 lb. or 116½ grains each; and 46 $\frac{4}{10}$ genuine Jersey coppers are 1 lb. or 151 grains, each.*

The thought entertained by some of making the copper cent to be of intrinsic value, is alarming; as it threatens a design to enforce a base and cumbersome metal in discharge of debts. The copper coin in that case must be 2½ times as large as is proposed at present, or 350 grains.[11] Why encrease an odium, or overbusily [*sic*] adventure on a hazardous innovation in a delicate affair?

Copper coin, from the baseness of its metal, is not proper for a *money* to be forced on creditors.[12] It is to be considered merely as a convenient substitute in the closing a payment, for want of silver coin small enough for minute fractional purposes: as such it is *voluntarily* received. Hucksters choose to receive it, as do others, occasionally, in

[5] In *Penna. Merc*, July 30, 1789, Bordley quoted the weight of 50,000 coppers at 165.2 grains each (1180 avdp. lbs.). In the pamphlet version, he reduced the hypothetical weight of the coppers to his proposed copper standard of 140 grains. If the creditor in question only could have recovered the intrinsic value of 20¢ per pound of scrap copper for the $500 he was forced to receive, it would appear that his loss would have been 30,000 cents ($500 - [1000 lbs. × 20¢] = $300), rather the "loss of 20,000 cents on his whole claim." Indeed, it was a 3% loss on the debt as quoted ($300 ÷ $10,000 = 3%).

[6] An obvious reference to the Fugio coppers.

[7] Bordley added the New York General Assembly report to this revised version, having omitted it in *Penna. Merc.*, July 30, 1789.

[8] In *Penna. Merc.*, July 30, 1789, Bordley quoted copper at 20¢ per pound, while in this version published less than three months later, he cites 24¢, although world copper prices had not yet started to rise.

[9] Bordley quoted this 12¢ figure also in *Penna. Merc.*, July 30, 1789, a value which is discussed in Chapter 8 and found to be an accurate estimate of the cost of coining corroborated by other sources.

[10] From 1685 until 1701, the standard weight was 166.7 grains which was then reduced to 152.2. See Table 10.

[11] Without knowing the suggested exchange rates, this figure cannot be verified.

[12] See p. 109, n. 20.

small sums as is convenient to them. There would be no need of copper coins, were it not that cents and pence would be in too small pieces, for preservation, when in silver; wherefore the base and bulky metal was introduced, merely for small change. If, however, it shall be thought proper to give to copper any force,—which it is wished may be never attempted, it ought to be, if possible, without injury or alarm to creditors. Forced payments in copper may in that case be limited to 5 or at most 9 cents on the close of *full* payments, large or small: on the payment of 10,000 dollars, no more to be forced on the creditor than in a case of the least sum; because there is true and honest money in gold and silver of standard intrinsic value as low as ten or 5 cents, and the coppers are no further useful than for closing the fractional balance. [13] If the necessity of a copper coinage can be avoided, it may be considered how far it would answer to coin cents in pieces of silver, whose periphery is enlarged by forming them into a sort of rings with milled edges or coined surfaces: or rather the composition called billon may be coined, solid as are common copper halfpence: it is more valuable than copper alone, being of copper and silver, yet bulky enough to be easily preserved. A billon-cent of a 50d. dollar, half copper and half silver, which is the exact mint alloy for fine gold, would be near as large as a quarter of a Spanish dollar. But, copper cents, the size, very nearly, of an English halfpenny, with its division into half pieces of 5 mills, are preferable to billon-cents, and to small rings worth a cent each, as these would be too slender. The half cent in copper would be about the size of a farthing English.

On the whole of what I can collect concerning copper coins, it seems, they do not pass so much by virtue of their small intrinsic worth, as by common consent, induced by a degree of necessity, merely as they are tokens for fractional sums which cannot be well issued in real money of the precious metals.[14] This inference is countenanced by the considerable deviation in their weights, when issued even by the authority of nations tenacious of their character. English halfpennies of *pure* copper have been issued from the English mint of the contents of 156, if not 166, down to 146 grains, as they now are and have been for upwards of sixty years: and *base* copper issued by private coiners light as 116 grains, by consent, have passed currently as the best, to a vast amount, and great loss of the community. The quality of metal appointed by public authority to be contained in *copper* coins, being a good deal arbitrary, the American States may have their cent coin, of fine copper, that shall nearly have the weight of a British halfpenny: The British halfpenny weighs 146 grains of fine copper.

Two pounds of copper will give 100 cents, each weighing 140 grains. The cents, for a device, may have a man, on one side of them, erect, comfortably cloathed, and holding a spade in his hand: read,—Fro. Indust. Cents beco. Eag.—On the reverse, of this base coin—a coin that cannot well be deemed *money*, instead of the eagle let there be, on the margin of the cent, this reading:—"United States of America;"—and in the middle of the piece read—"Cent." There will be a fair blank between the readings; which may be lightly ornamented or left blank, or crowded in Gothic taste—if it be the taste.

[13] Bordley's comment here does not appear to reflect that there was a small silver change shortage at the time. See below, n. 17.

[14] This passage summarizes the fact that coppers passed "by consent" for so many years without regard to variations in weight or intrinsic value. Now, in 1789, there was concern expressed about the potential havoc that the unrestricted currency of coppers could raise with commerce.

*The undermentioned copper coins, weigh as follows:[15]

	A.D.		Grs.
Produit des mines de France	1727	—	182
Liard de France	1698	—	54
Virginia halfpenny	1773	—	120
U.S.	1783	—	145
¼ Stuber[16]	1764	—	38
+ Spanish milled piece	1774	—	174
English halfpenny, worn smooth		—	156
‡ Ditto, new and bright, never circulated	1729	—	146
‖ Eight Birmingham coppers, average,		—	116

+ Quere, whether this piece is of the composition called *Billon*?

‡ This is from a barrel of halfpence imported by the late Mr. Bennet of Wye, from England, above 40 years ago; and I am favoured with it by his executor.

‖ The fairest sort of Birmingham coppers that are now in circulation.—The coined impressions are good and plain. Two of them shew partial marks of sand:—therefore, I presume, they are first cast into blanks of the proper size, and then coined; which saves expence [*sic*] of rolling the copper into plates, cutting them, &c.

B.

(The following is part of a footnote from page 10 which deals with copper coins.)

...Small change is greatly wanted: for supplying this, and abolishing the trashy, light, and base coppers abounding in the states; if the mint shall issue a good quantity of cents, immediately so however as not to superabound, it will be of important service.[17]

[15] This table first appeared in *Penna. Merc.*, July 30, 1789 and was enlarged in the subsequent revision (see p. 231, n. 85). It specifically notes a 1783 Constellatio Nova copper and Virginia halfpenny plus various regal and counterfeit English halfpence.

[16] The "stuber" was a small copper or billon coin of varying value issued by several German states along the Rhine and North Sea. A quarter stuber bearing this particular date could have been from the Archbishopric of Cologne or the Principality of East Freisland (Craig, *World Coins*).

[17] Here he mentions a shortage of small change (copper?) which would be remedied by the controlled emission of good copper coin.

INDEX

Italicized pages contain pertinent illustrations.

G

H

I

N

O

P

R

S